S0-ADN-977

WORSHIP
AND
MISSION
FOR THE
GLOBAL CHURCH

The voices I treasure resonate in this book. The topics are compelling, from "Beauty in the Bible" to "Japanese Black Gospel Choirs" to "How to Disciple Worship Leaders" to "Composing at the Speed of Light." Chanting and memorization, trauma healing, how hymnbooks stimulate literacy, how to commission artistic works—with over 148 chapters the scope is mind blowing, yet the material remains highly accessible and applicable. This book would appear to be the definitive work. I can hardly wait to get my hands on a copy for my library.

Miriam Adeney, PhD
associate professor of World Christian Studies, Seattle Pacific University
teaching fellow, Regent College

Compiling the wisdom and experience of more than one hundred writers from around the globe, this volume serves as an invaluable resource for *the whole church* to take *the whole gospel* to *the whole world*. This compilation brings together the critical intersection of the arts, worship, the church, and mission on both the theoretical and "how-to" levels—challenging and equipping those engaged with the arts in a cross-cultural context. Mission leaders, students, field practitioners, and worship leaders around the globe will find this resource invaluable.

S. Douglas Birdsall
executive chairman, The Lausanne Movement

Wow! What a great gift to the global church! This book and the accompanying resources can only enhance the ministry of worship and evangelism for those who give time to studying and applying its lessons. Well researched, creative, stimulating, and biblically rooted, this is a highly significant resource for all those who have a vision to see the church planted and growing amongst all the peoples of the world.

Lindsay Brown, DD
international director, The Lausanne Movement

It is not that those who lead worship around the world are not connected; we share the deepest connection by way of the Spirit of Jesus. It is only that we hunger for integration with fellow sisters and brothers and long for a means to share with one another. James Krabill and his team of contributors have provided all we need to nurture that kind of integration, to share our stories, our creative seed with the family of faith around the world.

Michael Card
Bible teacher, songwriter

Understanding and embracing culturally appropriate worship and applying the accompanying sensibilities and resources is absolutely critical for every church leader, mission worker, and student preparing for ministry. This important, accessible, and thorough compendium is a much-needed and long-awaited resource for the global church. Drs. Krabill, Fortunato, Harris, and Schrag have responded to God's call, collecting and organizing essential materials that represent the very heart of God—his mission expressed through Christian worship around the world. And they have done it with excellence.

Dr. James R. Hart
president, Robert E. Webber Institute for Worship Studies

With over one hundred writers from more than twenty countries, this is a work that lives up to its name: *Worship and Mission for the Global Church.* Drawing on theological, historical, and contextual perspectives on worship and the arts, the handbook pursues new and significant territory for the life of the church. Holding worship and mission together is a much-needed emphasis for our times.

Dennis P. Hollinger, PhD
president and Colman M. Mockler Distinguished Professor of Christian Ethics,
Gordon-Conwell Theological Seminary

The world's leading ethnodoxologists have assembled an impressive array of contributions from every part of the world to present us with a snapshot of what global Christianity is all about. It is a picture of unity in diversity—Christians from a wide variety of cultural backgrounds worshiping the same Lord in innumerable tongues.

Todd M. Johnson, PhD
associate professor of Global Christianity, Gordon-Conwell Theological Seminary

As one who has spent long years pioneering in the trenches, it is a real joy and delight to endorse this handbook of ethnodoxology as it offers a much-needed, critical foundation for global ministry in the twenty-first century. The sheer breadth of the project speaks of the multitudes of peoples around the world longing to offer worship and witness drawing from their cultural wealth in ways that that bring glory to God. Especially significant is how the dual volumes, a textbook and a companion "make-it-happen" practical guide, offer opportunities for continued growth in the ministry of the church worldwide.

Roberta R. King, PhD
director, Global Christian Worship program, Fuller Theological Seminary

We are global people. Our lives are daily influenced by what happens to other global people all around the globe. People like us, with their own history, their own culture, their own ideals and struggles, their own way of calling God. This book makes us aware of this fact, and challenges us to approach it in positive terms. Leaving aside our fear and apprehension towards strange people, this unique, multifaceted multitude of authors, scholars, and amateurs invites us to see them as part of the great human family, made up of all of God's children, united in a marvelous polyphonic doxology.

Pablo Sosa
emeritus professor, Liturgy and Hymnology
church music composer, conductor, and scholar (Buenos Aires, Argentina)

If you are searching for a textbook on the arts in global worship, look no further. This thoughtfully arranged book written by over one hundred theorists and/or practitioners from more than twenty nations traverses the globe to define and describe missional ethnodoxology. True worship of the Triune God will never be the same; nor will the lost.

Tom Steffen, DMiss
professor of Intercultural Studies, Cook School of Intercultural Studies, Biola University

Some resources are simply unique. And this one fits that rare category. When and where in the history of the Christian church have evangelical Protestants produced something of the quality of this anthology? It is unique due to its depth and breadth—such a rich variety of themes and writers from so many nations and cultures; its creativity of composition and content; its reach, penetrating the same global and ethnic dimensions; its purpose and those who conceived and produced it; its teaching-reproductive purposes; and its timeliness—it arrives for such a chronos as ours. The role of art in mission is not simply mime acting on short-term mission—i.e., pragmatic arts. This William Carey Library gift flows out of a theology of vocation and calling as arts, and emerges as a vital and visible dimension of the full creativity of the creative Trinity. I could not praise any resource higher than this.

William D. Taylor, PhD
senior mentor, WEA Mission Commission

As a worship director and pastor I have longed for a resource that could help me train worship leaders. In the past I had to piecemeal various chapters from books or journal articles from different voices. Now, however, I have many of these very expert voices in one timely resource. The variety of theological, historical, and practical articles by both academics and practitioners in both global and domestic contexts make this handbook truly unique. I wish I had been given this either in seminary or in the church.

Sandra Van Opstal, MDiv
Worship Director of Urbana 12 Missions Conference, author of *The Mission of Worship*

God continues to use the arts as one of his mighty tools to build bridges to reach people. Here is a treasure—a big one—that will equip an army of artists to have a part in God's kingdom purposes for all peoples.

George Verwer
founder, Operation Mobilization

What a privilege it is to live in a time of artistic renewal and proliferation; a time of artistic expression in a host of genres, styles, registers, and cultures; a time that has not only witnessed the rise of a discipline like ethnomusicology, with all its resources for understanding the interplay of musical forms and cultural contexts, but also the rise of networks of "ethnodoxologists"—those called by God to learn from and encourage faithful artistic expression done in the name of Jesus Christ across the entire span of global cultures . . . Welcome, then, to a sanctifying feast. Whether you are a missionary, art-lover, artist, pastor, theologian, anthropologist, pilgrim, tourist, migrant, indigenous person—or any combination thereof—this project will introduce you to an astonishing range of geographical locations and to disciplines of thinking. [Excerpt taken from the Foreword to this *Handbook*]

John D. Witvliet, PhD
director of the Calvin Institute of Christian Worship
professor of Worship, Theology, and Music, Calvin College and Calvin Theological Seminary

WORSHIP
AND
MISSION
FOR THE
GLOBAL CHURCH

AN ETHNODOXOLOGY
HANDBOOK

James R. Krabill
GENERAL EDITOR

Frank Fortunato
Robin P. Harris
Brian Schrag
EDITORS

www.ethnodoxologyhandbook.com

WILLIAM CAREY
LIBRARY

Worship and Mission for the Global Church: An Ethnodoxology Handbook
Copyright © 2013 ICE (International Council of Ethnodoxologists)

All rights reserved. No part of this book may be reproduced, stored in a retrieval system, or transmitted in any form or by any means—electronic, mechanical, photocopy, recording, or otherwise—without prior written permission of the publisher, except brief quotations used in connection with reviews in magazines or newspapers.

All scripture quotations, unless otherwise indicated, are taken from the Holy Bible, New International Version®, NIV® copyright ©1973, 1978, 1984, 2011 by Biblica, Inc.™ Used by permission of Zondervan. All rights reserved worldwide. www.zondervan.com. The "NIV" and "New International Version" are trademarks registered in the United States Patent and Trademark Office by Biblica, Inc.™

Scriptures quotations marked "ESV" are taken from The English Standard Version® (ESV®) copyright © 2001 by Crossway, a publishing ministry of Good News Publishers. All rights reserved. ESV Text Edition: 2011.

Scripture quotations marked "NASB" are taken from the Amplified® Bible, copyright © 1954, 1958, 1962, 1964, 1965, 1987 by The Lockman Foundation. Used by permission. (www.Lockman.org)

Scripture quotations marked "NJB" are from The New Jerusalem Bible, copyright © 1985 by Darton, Longman & Todd, Ltd. and Doubleday, a division of Random House, Inc. Reprinted by Permission.

Scripture quotations marked "NLT" are taken from the Holy Bible, New Living Translation, copyright © 1996, 2004, 2007 by Tyndale House Foundation. Used by permission of Tyndale House Publishers, Inc., Carol Stream, IL 60188. All rights reserved.

Scripture quotations marked "NRSV" are from the New Revised Standard Version Bible, copyright © 1989 National Council of the Churches of Christ in the United States of America. Used by permission. All rights reserved.

Published by William Carey Library
1605 E. Elizabeth Street
Pasadena, CA 91104 | www.missionbooks.org

Melissa Hicks, production editor
James R. Krabill, general editor
Frank Fortunato, Robin P. Harris, and Brian Schrag, editors
Koe Pahlka, Carol Brinneman, Linda Neeley, and Brad Koenig, copyeditors
Cory Cummins, DVD editor and compiler, with Paul Neeley
Hugh Pindur, graphic design
Josie Leung, graphic assistant
Rose Lee-Norman, indexer

William Carey Library is a ministry of the
U.S. Center for World Mission
Pasadena, CA | www.uscwm.org

Printed in the United States of America

17 16 15 14 13   5 4 3 2 1 COU 2000

Front cover photos courtesy of The Lausanne Movement ©, Cape Town 2010; photos by James R. Krabill, used by permission.
Section divider photo, "The Dancing Feet," courtesy of Leo Vartanian
Nadëb NT Celebration, July 2012
Wycliffe Global Alliance ©
http://www.wycliffe.net

All other section divider photos courtesy of James R. Krabill.

Library of Congress Cataloging-in-Publication Data

Worship and mission for the global church : an ethnodoxology handbook / James R. Krabill, general editor ; Frank Fortunato, Robin P. Harris, and Brian Schrag, editors.

    p. cm.

Includes bibliographical references and index.

ISBN 978-0-87808-493-7 (alk. paper)

1. Worship. 2. Christianity and the arts. 3. Worship--Anecdotes. 4. Christianity and the arts--Anecdotes. 5. Worship--Handbooks, manuals, etc. 6. Christianity and the arts--Handbooks, manuals, etc. I. Krabill, James R. II. Fortunato, Frank. III. Harris, Robin P. IV. Schrag, Brian.

BV15.W655 2013

264--dc23

2012040682

CONTENTS

SECTION I: FOUNDATIONS

ENCOUNTERING GOD: WORSHIP AND BODY LIFE

BIBLICAL

CULTURAL

HISTORICAL

MISSIOLOGICAL

LITURGICAL

PERSONAL

ENGAGING GOD'S WORLD: WITNESS AND COMMUNITY–BASED MINISTRY

BIBLICAL

CULTURAL

SECTION 2: STORIES

AFRICA—SOUTHERN

AFRICA—WEST

ASIA—SOUTH

ASIA—SOUTHEAST

SECTION 3: TOOLS

ARTS ADVOCACY

HOW TO ADVOCATE FOR ARTS ON THE FIELD AND IN THE CHURCH

HOW TO ADDRESS OBJECTIONS IN THE WORK OF ARTS ADVOCACY

TEACHING

HOW TO DESIGN AND CONDUCT AN ARTS WORKSHOP

HOW TO CREATE AN ARTS CURRICULUM

HOW TO MENTOR AND LEARN FROM ARTISTS

WORSHIP

HOW TO DEVELOP CULTURALLY APPROPRIATE WORSHIP

HOW TO FOSTER MULTICULTURAL WORSHIP

HOW TO DISCIPLE WORSHIP LEADERSHIP

HOW TO INTEGRATE ARTS AND PREACHING

HOW TO INTEGRATE ARTS WITH SCRIPTURE PROCLAMATION

RESEARCH AND COCREATION

HOW TO PLAN FOR MORE LOCAL ARTS EFFECTIVENESS

HOW TO CREATE LOCAL ARTS TOGETHER

XXI

INTRODUCTION

SECTION 1: FOUNDATIONS

SECTION 2. STORIES

SECTION 3: TOOLS

CLOSING

FOREWORD

By Rev. Dr. John D. Witvliet

The vast sweep of biblical and Christian history features an astonishing display of fusion experiments no less dramatic than those developed by enterprising modern physicists—fusions not of subatomic particles, but of deeply ingrained cultural dynamics with the incarnate Word and the dynamic Spirit of God.

When a Spirit-inspired ancient writer discovered the gift of trust in God in the middle of grief and strife, having previously absorbed the current convention of poetic parallelisms, the result is a stunning piece of poetry that dares to imagine how a Lord could be a Shepherd, and how trust in God could be as effervescent as resting in lush pastures beside gurgling streams of water. Psalm 23 is the product of such a fusion.

When Martin Luther pondered Psalm 46, with ears shaped by a vigorous folk music culture and a heart shaped by a years of personal anxiety and theological study, the result was "A Mighty Fortress Is Our God"—a testimony that continues to fortify weary and discouraged peoples who have never tasted monastic formation or heard a German folk song. This hymn is one of thousands of fusion-produced Psalm-based riffs over the centuries, from the Dead Sea scrolls to hip-hop.

When contemporary Argentinian hymn writer Pablo Sosa pondered the majesty of the Christmas gospel, having absorbed the infectious dance rhythms of his indigenous culture, and faced the challenge of engaging a generation of children in intergenerational worship celebrations, the result is his much-loved eight-measure "Gloria," now sung the world over in Christmas pageants and worship services.

Whatever artworks would make your Top 10 list of "most life-sustaining, gospel-embodying, Christ-proclaiming artworks of all time"—whether music, drama, dance, painting, sculpture, architecture, graphic arts, or anything else—realize that they are the fruit of an astonishing combustion of elements, the juxtaposition of the enduring gospel of Jesus Christ with the altogether contingent dynamics of the multiple cultures that overlap in any given time and place. And realize what potential they have not only to strengthen your faith, but to advance God's reconciling and redemptive work all over the globe.

At the center of all that is faithful and righteous is the Word, Jesus Christ, as told by a Bible that masterfully unfolds God's grand narrative of creation and redemption. And precisely because of the way that God is revealed in Jesus—through a Messiah who lived in a particular culture, as told by a book written in a particular set of languages, all made possible by a Spirit who freely blows throughout God's good but fallen world to inspire those who wrote the Scriptures, to raise this Messiah from the dead, and to not only open the eyes of many to behold this Jesus as Lord, but also to help us when we struggle in prayer—the Christian faith is not static, timeless, or disembodied. Rather, the Christian faith opens up a dynamic, fusion-producing way of life in which the glory of the Triune God is contagiously proclaimed and evoked again and again—like a fireworks display that, to the delight of the young children who watch it, only grows in intensity.

What a privilege it is to live in a time period when more and more people have access to take in the brilliant fireworks of artists across six continents and thirty or more centuries—where we can hear and sing the songs and see the artworks generated by medieval peasants, embattled reformers, and zealous missionaries; by both indigenous artists and immigrant artists; by wordsmiths, painters, dancers, and songwriters; by those "who were near" and by those "who were far away" (Eph 2:11–17).

What a privilege it is to live in a time of artistic renewal and proliferation; a time of artistic expression in a host of genres, styles, registers, and cultures; a time that has not only witnessed the rise of a discipline like ethnomusicology, with all its resources for understanding the interplay of musical forms and cultural contexts, but also the rise of networks of "ethnodoxologists"—those called by God to learn from and encourage faithful artistic expression done in the name of Jesus Christ across the entire span of global cultures.

As this book unfolds, my first prayer is that it will awaken a sense of gratitude and wonder for the kind of God we worship through Jesus in the Holy Spirit—a God who both demonstrates and elicits creativity; a God whose love both embraces the whole world and comes to expression in such tangible, local, accessible ways; a God whose call to missionary service and faithful discipleship engages not only preachers, but every single one of us; a God who is calling people of every tribe, language, and culture into the peaceable kingdom of the Messiah, along with all their treasures and gifts (see Rev 21:24,26).

This perspective of wonder, delight, and grace is crucial, for the terrain is filled with challenges. Any one of these fusion experiments can become an idol instead of a witness. Any one of them can end up eroding rather than strengthening Christian discipleship. They can end up creating fission and schism rather than fusion and fellowship. Indeed artworks of all kinds done in Jesus' name have been used as forms of propaganda and coercion, to boost fragile egos and adore golden calves, to distort rather than clarify God's triune glory.

In light of this, how important it is to recognize that God's grace comes to us not only as forgiveness from past sin, but also in the Spirit-provided resources to grow in grace and in the knowledge of Christ, our Lord (2 Pet 3:18). That is what this is—a project designed to be a catalyst for learning and growing in the grace and knowledge of Christ, our Lord.

God's grace comes to us in the form of the host of biblical commands that undergird this material: "go into all the world," "sing to the Lord a new song," "love one another," "be transformed by the renewing of your mind," "pray continually," and many others. The resources you will find here came about as a way of practicing obedience to these biblical commands, and they in turn commend this kind of obedience to us.

God's grace comes to us in the form of mutual encouragement and interaction within the body of Christ, where we can learn from and be encouraged by:

- both insider and outsider perspectives on any given culture;
- both expert artists and experts in the arts;

- both people who travel freely among cultures and those who stay put in one culture;
- both those who create art and those who receive these creations;
- both the "prophets" among us, who challenge idolatries, and the "priests" who shape the prayers of God's people;
- both those from Christian traditions very much like our own, and those who represent traditions far different than those which formed us; and
- both those who are called to strengthen the institutional church and those called to ministry beyond the institutional church.

Notice how many gaps and divides this project bridges! This should remind us that poise in ministry comes, in part, by the communion of all parts of the body of Christ, in which complementary gifts and perspectives can challenge and enrich others.

Like all forms of God's grace, these graces come to us in ways that are utterly free, but not cheap. Studying these two volumes invites us to flex growing muscles in biblical interpretation, cultural discernment, historical understanding, and missiological visioning. These volumes lead us on a globetrotting travelogue unimaginable even a few generations ago. There are enough academic disciplines represented here to establish a university. While delightful, all these "both/and," interdisciplinary, ecumenical, boundary-crossing moves do challenge us to engage in a great deal of loving attention and study, all done in a spirit of self-awareness and humility.

We need not, however, look at this challenge as burden, but rather as gift. For exerting ourselves to study God's word, to learn from God's people across time and space, and to revel in the privilege of being catalysts for new fusion experiments in Christian witness is itself a gift. It is the gift of sanctification in action. We become like athletes who discover that their morning exercises are as life-giving to them as food and drink, like painters whose day is not complete until they have mixed a new hue, or poets whose days are parched were it not for a new metaphor to propose or savor.

Welcome, then, to a sanctifying feast. Whether you are a missionary, art lover, artist, pastor, theologian, anthropologist, pilgrim, tourist, migrant, indigenous person—or any combination thereof—this project will introduce you to an astonishing range of geographical locations and to disciplines of thinking. It may, like a guidebook, lead you to discover whole clusters of Christian thought and practice that can only be briefly touched upon here. It may lead you to continue in the path of ministry you have established or to an abrupt fork in the road that will demand that you choose a new route. It may lead to new fruitfulness in ministry almost immediately, and it may plant seeds for new ways of approaching faith and discipleship that will bear fruit in emerging paradigms or approaches that we can't even imagine in the near future. May God's Spirit grace every reader of this material with new insight, renewed vision, and many opportunities to put these lessons into practice.

Rev. Dr. John D. Witvliet
director of the Calvin Institute of Christian Worship
professor of Worship, Theology, and Music, Calvin College and Calvin Theological Seminary

PREFACE

By the ICE Editorial Team

Although the historical streams feeding the rise of ethnodoxology[1] stretch back decades—if not centuries—the impetus behind the creation of these two volumes can be traced to the year 2003. It was then that Robin Harris began working with Paul Neeley and a small group of colleagues who were serving cross-culturally in the arts to imagine and launch the International Council of Ethnodoxologists (ICE).

From the beginning, ICE associates shared a vision to see Christ-followers from every culture express their faith through their own arts. A sense of isolation in their ministries and distant locations drew these arts mission workers to the connections and community provided by the ICE network. They began to gather and post resources at http://www.worldofworship.org, a site that soon became the world's largest available source of information on culturally appropriate arts in mission. In its first decade ICE grew to over three hundred associates, some of whom launched their own national and regional networks in Latin America, the Philippines, India, and the Korean diaspora.

As networking capabilities grew with advances in technology, ICE national partners in the Global South, along with mission agencies, seminaries, and colleges in the Global North, began to clamor for academic and practical resources for training. By 2005 this burgeoning ethnodoxology network had a website and hundreds of people in over seventy countries, but no comprehensive textbook to use in its training programs.

Dr. Tom Avery, a pioneer in this field, challenged the ICE leadership in his closing address at the 2006 Global Consultation on Music and Missions to develop such a resource. By the time he unexpectedly stepped into heaven in 2008, conversations about how to plan this "reader" were moving forward. That year a team of ICE leaders began to teach an intensive one-week Ethnodoxology in Christian Mission course at seminaries and colleges, sharpening the already acute need for an academic text. Over the next five years, ICE leaders gathered several times each year to plan these volumes. James R. Krabill, a mission leader experienced in publishing, joined the ICE board and agreed to lead the writing team. By 2009 the *Handbook* aims and general outline were in place. In 2010 Frank Fortunato started gathering case studies and stories, drawing on an extensive international network and years of experience. In addition, Brian Schrag began to write the second volume—a manual—drawing on the methods and approaches he had developed for the graduate program in world arts at the Graduate Institute of Applied Linguistics (GIAL) in

---

1   For an essay exploring the term "ethnodoxology," see http://www.worldofworship.org/Ethnodoxology.php.

Dallas. In 2011 and 2012, he and Robin Harris field-tested the manual, using it at GIAL and as the curriculum for week-long training events on two continents with participants from over twenty countries.[2] In 2012 the DVD component was added, designed and coordinated by Cory Cummins with the assistance of Paul Neeley.

The range of voices in these two volumes—over one hundred contributors from more than twenty nations serving on every continent but Antarctica—illustrates an underlying value in the ICE network: global collaboration. We hope that as you read the "Foundations," "Stories," and "Tools" this international team of writers has contributed, you will rejoice at their kingdom-focused passion for fostering creativity in every community on earth.

---

2   The first of these training events was Arts in Mission (September 3–11, 2011) at All Nations Christian College in the UK. The second was Arts for a Better Future (June 18–22) at the International Linguistics Center in Dallas, Texas. For videos and descriptions, see http://www.worldofworship.org/events/index.php.

XXVI

INTRODUCTION

SECTION 1: FOUNDATIONS

SECTION 2: STORIES

SECTION 3: TOOLS

CLOSING

INTRODUCTION
By Dr. James R. Krabill

When I began my study of West African indigenous hymns in the early 1980s, the resources for such an endeavor were indeed few and far between. How helpful it would have been in those lonely days to bask in the wealth of knowledge and spiritual support that the contributors to these two companion volumes represent!

There is no reason, however, to lament the past. The time has come to celebrate the present and to anticipate an even richer future. For this will most certainly be our lot as increased efforts are made to bring to bear the best of what we are learning from ethnomusicology, linguistics, worship studies, missiology, and the arts on the holy task of creating and nurturing a healthy diet of culturally appropriate worship for the life and mission of the church.

Dr. John Witvliet, in his Foreword to these publications, calls this project a "sanctifying feast," and indeed it is. Invited to the table are more than one hundred guests from over twenty countries and dozens more cultural contexts. The menu spills out over hundreds of pages and on to a DVD, serving up a veritable banquet of delectable sights and sounds for our savoring and enjoyment.

The first volume, *Worship and Mission for the Global Church: An Ethnodoxology Handbook* offers biblical/theological reflection, case studies, practical tools, and a well-stocked pantry of bibliographical and audiovisual resources. The main courses of the *Handbook* feast are three: "Foundations," "Stories," and "Tools." The "Foundations" section is divided into two parts, "Encountering God" and "Engaging God's World," each featuring reflections from six points of view, "Biblical," "Cultural," "Historical," "Missiological," "Liturgical," and "Personal."

In the second section of the volume, called "Stories," an abundant smorgasbord of nearly eighty international case studies is offered up to the reader. These provide an overflowing cornucopia of illustrations on the many ways the arts manifest themselves in the life and witness of the church across the years and around the globe.

The third section then focuses on "Tools," the staple rice-and-beans fare for practitioners hungry for more details on how to apply these many insights and images to specific contexts of ministry. For those interested in second and third helpings, the companion volume to this handbook, entitled *Creating Local Arts Together* by author-editor Brian Schrag, is made to special order with a well-designed seven-step process for assisting a local community's efforts at integrating its arts with the values and purposes of God's kingdom.

The bountiful banquet set before the reader in the following pages can be accessed in a variety of ways—in bite-size portions (single sessions), appetizer samplers (weekend seminars), multicourse meals (Sunday school or small-group study series), weekly specials (one-week intensives), or full-menu buffets (semester-long courses with broad curricular focus). Ideas on how to design and implement shorter and longer sessions for making the best use of these two volumes can be found on the *Handbook's* website http://www.ethnodoxologyhandbook.com.

In the meantime, welcome to the feast! You're in the divine company of God's people. The table is set. Eat heartily. Drink deeply. And enjoy!

> *On this mountain the LORD Almighty will prepare*
> *a feast of rich food for all peoples,*
> *a banquet of aged wine—*
> *the best of meats and the finest of wines . . .*
> *In that day they will say,*
> > *"Surely this is our God;*
> > *we trusted in him, and he saved us.*
> > *This is the LORD, we trusted in him;*
> > *let us rejoice and be glad in his salvation." (Isa 25:6,9)*

> *For the wedding of the Lamb has come,*
> *and his bride has made herself ready . . .*

> *"Blessed are those who are invited*
> *to the wedding supper of the Lamb!" (Rev 19:7,9)*

Dr. James R. Krabill
Handbook and *Manual* general editor

INTRODUCTION

SECTION 1: FOUNDATIONS

SECTION 2: STORIES

SECTION 3: TOOLS

CLOSING

INTRODUCTION

SECTION 1: FOUNDATIONS

SECTION 2: STORIES

SECTION 3: TOOLS

CLOSING

SECTION 1
FOUNDATIONS

ENCOUNTERING GOD: WORSHIP AND BODY LIFE

1. BIBLICAL FOUNDATIONS OF CHRISTIAN WORSHIP

By Andrew E. Hill

WORSHIP IN THE OLD TESTAMENT

Definitions of biblical worship abound. For the purpose of our study, worship in the Bible may be defined briefly as "the expression of a relationship with the Triune God—always simple and always complex, both an event and a lifestyle." This relationship is God's initiative, established with humanity through a series of covenant enactments.

Although the term covenant is not specifically mentioned, the foundation for the biblical covenants is established at creation in God's special relationship with Adam and Eve (Gen 1–2). These covenants begin formally with Noah and his family (Gen 9), continue with Abraham (Gen 12; 15; 17), and are renewed with his descendants (Gen 26:2–5; 28:10–15). The covenants are extended to the Israelite nation through Moses at Mt. Sinai (Ex 19–24), and are expanded to include the kingship through the line of David (2 Sam 7). Finally, they are consolidated and universalized in the New Covenant proclaimed by Jeremiah (Jer 30–33), and fulfilled in the person of Jesus Christ (Luke 22). Covenants are initiated by God and regulated or maintained by stipulations or laws attached to the covenant agreements. In both the Old Testament (OT) and the New Testament (NT), the requisite response to God's covenant initiatives is one of absolute loyalty motivated by loving obedience (Deut 30:15,16; John 14:15; cf. Matt 22:36–40).

Who is the God of the biblical covenants? Why does this God declare himself worthy of the unequivocal worship of humanity? Above all, this God is a holy God (Ps 99:3–9; Rev 4:8). Indeed, a favorite epithet of the OT writers for God is the "Holy One of Israel" (2 Kgs 19:22; Ps 71:22; Isa 1:4). The holiness of God speaks of his otherness or transcendence, his inaccessibility and inapproachability, his mysterious and inscrutable nature. If this inscrutable transcendence alone were true of him, how could we worship such a terrifying and unknowable God?

Thankfully, not only is God holy and transcendent, he is also "the Holy One in your midst" (Hos 11:9, NJB). God is the one who dwells "in a high and holy place, but also with the one who is contrite and lowly in spirit" (Isa 57:15). God's autobiographical declaration to Moses reveals his basic nature and is a call to worship: "the LORD, the compassionate and gracious God, slow to anger, abounding in love and faithfulness, maintaining love to thousands, and forgiving wickedness, rebellion and sin. Yet he does not leave the guilty unpunished" (Ex 34:6,7). God merits worship because he is able to answer those who call on him in prayer and repentance and to forgive their wrongdoings (Ps 99:8). The presence of a holy God abiding with Israel made them a holy people and raised their consciousness of sin and their need for forgiveness (Isa 6:4,5). The intimate presence of a holy God also prompted heartfelt worship and praise (Ps 99:3) and a keen desire for holy living (Lev 19:2).

But such forgiveness, worship, and holy living would be impossible for us if God's holiness was not conjoined with his sovereignty. The sovereignty of God involves his absolute authority and power over all creation, which he uses to accomplish his redemptive will. God's sovereignty is basically the application of his attribute of omnipotence, his utter and unlimited power to providentially care for the created order, including the natural world and the progress of human history (Gen 50:20; Isa 14:24; 40:22–24; Dan 2:20–23). Israel's deliverance in the OT and humanity's redemption in the NT could only be accomplished by such a God.

The holiness of God, the immanence of God, and the sovereignty of God are aspects of his uniqueness. The prophet Isaiah understood this uniqueness of God as a call to worship the Lord as King and Redeemer of Israel. He quotes God as saying, "I am the first and I am the last; apart from me there is no God. Who then is like me? . . . Is there any God besides me? No, there is no other Rock; I know not one" (Isa 44:6–8). The only proper response to this unique God is to assemble before him, turn to him in repentance for salvation, and bow to worship in his presence (Isa 45:20–23).

Knowledge of God is central to biblical worship because covenant obedience, whether in the OT or the NT, is dependent upon an understanding of God's words and deeds (Deut 4:35; Ps 100:3; Eph 1:17). In the OT, the prophets attribute Israel's covenant failures to their lack of the knowledge of God (Hos 4:6; Mic 4:12), indicting both the political leaders and the Levitical priesthood for failing to lead and instruct the people in the knowledge of the Lord (Jer 5:4,5; Mal 2:7). The pervasive knowledge of the Lord is one of the features of God's work of restoration in the *eschaton* (Isa 11:9; Hab 2:14). Not surprisingly, this knowledge of God was meant to spread to the nations so they too will worship the Lord God of Israel (Isa 49:26; Zech 2:9–11). In the NT, the incarnation of Jesus the Messiah became the ultimate invitation to the knowledge of God, making known the Father to Israel and the world (John 1:18; cf. Heb 1:1,2).

Worship is a verb in the Bible. In the OT, the Hebrew people were called to an active and whole-person response to the God who initiated covenant relationship with their ancestors—Abraham, Isaac, and Jacob (Ex 3:15). This holistic worship response is grounded in the creedal affirmation of the *Shema*, which calls the Hebrews to love God fully with heart, soul, and strength (Deut 6:4). The multidimensional nature of OT worship is demonstrated in the various terms used to express the worship response. Although the NT employs fewer terms to describe the worship response to God, it also presents worship as an active expression of the whole person in the celebatory telling and enactment of the Christ-event.

The exodus from Egypt was the defining event in ancient Israel's redemptive history, and it was the basis for their worship of YHWH (Deut 4:32–40).[1] The Sinai covenant mediated by Moses is founded upon YHWH's deliverance of Israel from slavery in Egypt (Ex 20:2). As a result, the

---

1　The consonants YHWH represent the divine name of the God of the Hebrews, often rendered "Yahweh." Later Judaism chose not to pronounce this most sacred name for God. YHWH ("Yahweh") is the name by which God revealed himself to Moses at the beginning of the Hebrew exodus from Egypt and is usually translated "I AM" (cf. Ex 3:14).

expression "the God who brought you out of Egypt" becomes an identifying divine epithet in the OT (e.g., Deut 7:19; 8:14; 13:5; Ps 81:10). Israel's worship response to God is contained in the psalmist's lyric, "I will consider all your works and meditate on all your mighty deeds. Your ways, God, are holy. What god is as great as our God?" (Ps 77:12,13). When viewed through the lens of the NT, the exodus event foreshadows the life and ministry of Jesus the Messiah, the Lamb of God (John 1:29) and the ultimate Passover sacrifice (1 Cor 5:7).

Numerous other biblical themes undergird OT and NT worship. For example, the scores of names and titles for the Triune God in both testaments reveal his being, existence, character, personality, reputation, authority, and purposes for humanity. This revelation deepens our knowledge of God and consequently informs and enriches our worship of him. Along with God's redemptive work in the Passover and the Christ-event, God's handiwork as Creator is a core theme of biblical worship. The hymns, songs, prayers, and doxologies of the Bible extol God's power and wisdom as Creator and his sovereign grace in making all things new—creating new heavens and a new earth (Isa 65:17; Rev 21:1,5).

The theme of divine presence is central to the biblical story and is the goal of redemptive history. God's desire to live with his people is symbolized and represented in the tabernacle and in the temple of the OT (cf. Ex 25:8; 1 Kgs 8:10–13). This desire is realized in the NT through the incarnation of Jesus the Messiah (John 1:14) and the gift of the indwelling Holy Spirit at Pentecost (Acts 2:4; 1 Cor 3:16), and it culminates in the Triune God living with humanity in the new creation (Rev 21:3,4).

Hebrew worship centers of tabernacle and temple are pilgrimage destinations for Israelite worshipers, and they give rise to the place of the visual and musical arts in worship, especially with the Psalms—the hymnbook of ancient Israel. The church, too, developed pilgrimage as a form of worship, and as a result of the Incarnation, it has employed the visual, dramatic, and musical arts in worship. Historically, the Psalms play a pivotal role in the church's liturgy, music, and prayer life. Finally, the worship of the Triune God by the nations is a theme that unites the OT and NT, finding its roots in the Abrahamic covenant, through which God chooses one nation to bless all nations (Ps 86:9; Isa 66:23; Zech 14:16; Rev 5:9,10; cf. Gen 12:1–3).

TOWARD NEW TESTAMENT WORSHIP

A cursory reading of the New Testament reveals that early Christianity was essentially Jewish. Jesus the Messiah was a Jew from Nazareth in Galilee. The twelve apostles were all Jewish. The outpouring of the Holy Spirit at Pentecost was largely a Jewish event (Acts 2:5–11), and the initial missionary outreach of the church focused on the Jew first (Acts 6:7; 13:5; cf. Rom 1:16).

The hyphenated worship heritage of the church, Judeo-Christian worship, is rooted in the Mosaic covenant of Mt. Sinai. The basic structural elements of this treaty between God and his people Israel constitute the essence of corporate public worship in Judaism and Christianity, namely:

- God called his people to meet with him;
- the entire assembly of the people shared responsibility for the worship of God;
- God proclaimed his divine word and revealed his person, will, and purpose to Israel through his covenant law;

- the Hebrew community accepted God's covenant and was continually involved in the experience of covenant renewal;
- and lastly, God sealed his covenant with Israel by blood sacrifice.

There are numerous Jewish sources that shape NT understandings and patterns of worship, including: the Holy Scriptures of Judaism, the Hebrew Bible or Old Testament; the synagogue; and the development of Jewish worship practices in the Jewish diaspora during the intertestamental era.

> **Along with God's redemptive work in the Passover and the Christ-event, God's handiwork as Creator is a core theme of biblical worship.**

The continuity between Judaism and early Christianity in the first century AD is directly linked to the OT, since this was the Bible for the early church. Especially important was the first-century Jewish-Christian methodology of biblical interpretation known as typology. Biblical typology is a form of literary foreshadowing in which the redemptive events and other OT realities implicitly anticipate the Christ-event (cf. 2 Cor 1:20). More specifically, formal typology is a method of biblical exegesis which seeks to establish historical correspondence between OT events, persons, objects, or ideas and similar NT events, persons, objects, and ideas by way of analogy or prototype. The OT correspondent is usually identified as the "type," while the NT correspondent, which expresses the OT truth more fully, is regarded as the "antetype" (cf. Rom 5:14, where Paul identifies Adam as the type and Jesus Christ as the antetype). Therefore, although the Bible contains two covenants, the old and the new, it is one continuous record of God's redemptive activity in human history.

The NT book of Hebrews is a distinctive example of this interpretive approach. The writer considered the OT to be incomplete and imperfect (Heb 8:13; cf. Jer 31:31–37), and understood the OT from a decidedly Christo-centric perspective—recognizing Jesus Christ as the fulfillment of the redemptive promises in the OT (Heb 10:11–18; cf. Luke 24:44–48). Four specific typological interpretations of OT religious form and practice from Hebrews are realized in NT worship, including: the priesthood of Melchizedek (Heb 5–7), the Mosaic covenant (Heb 8), the tabernacle of the Mosaic covenant (Heb 9), and the sacrificial worship of the Mosaic covenant (Heb 9:23–10:18).

The origins of the Jewish religious institution known as the synagogue are obscure. The synagogue probably evolved from some kind of informal gathering or association of Hebrews during the Babylonian exile. Development continued and perhaps was even spurred by the Torah-based reforms of Ezra and Nehemiah during the mid-fifth century BC. The synagogue rose up as a parallel worship center to the Jerusalem temple during the Hellenistic period of the Second Temple era.[2] After the destruction of the Jerusalem temple by the Romans in AD 70, the synagogue became the primary religious center for Judaism. Wherever Jews settled in the Diaspora (the voluntary and/or involuntary scattering of the Jews from Palestine across the Gentile world), a synagogue was established. According to the first-century-AD Jewish historian, Josephus, it was difficult to find a place without a synagogue.[3]

---

2   The Second Temple era of Jewish history extends from the rebuilding of the Jerusalem temple under the leadership of Zerubbabel (completed ca. 515 BC; see Ezra 5:1,2; 6:15,16) to its destruction by the Romans in AD 70 (having been impressively renovated by Herod the Great from ca. 20 to 4 BC). The Hellenistic period of Jewish history roughly spans the years from 330 BC (Alexander the Great's conquests of the East) to 63 BC (the Roman conquest of Palestine).

3   Flavius Josephus, "Antiquities of the Jews," bk. 14, ch. 7. 2, in *The Complete Works*, trans. W. Whiston, reprint (Grand Rapids: Kregel, 1960), 295.

The synagogue was a place of prayer; of reading and teaching the Hebrew Scriptures; and of almsgiving, exhortation, and fellowship (cf. Acts 4:21; 13:15). The influence of the Jewish synagogue on Christian worship is seen in many ways. The house-church gatherings of the NT church emphasized instruction, fellowship, the eucharistic meal, and prayer (cf. Acts 2:42–47). The church, like the synagogue, was driven by lay leadership. The leaders and officers of the synagogue had similar counterparts in the NT church (e.g., bishop, elder, and deacon). Later, as Christian worship moved into public spaces, the influence of the synagogue was evident in the use of the *bema*—a raised platform and podium at which to stand for reading and teaching the Scriptures. The basic synagogue liturgy of prayer cycles, praise (rooted in the Psalms), and instruction in the Law of Moses (including creedal recitation of the *Shema*, and cycles of Scripture readings, and preaching and teaching) was infused with Christological content and became the staple of Christian liturgy.

Jewish literature of the intertestamental era highlights prayer, fasting, and almsgiving, among other worship practices, as essential features of individual worship expression and as marks of spirituality (e.g., Sir 3:10; 7:14; 28:2; 40:17, 24; Jdt 4:10–14; Tob 4:5–11; 12:8–15; 13:1). Jesus offered commentary on these three so-called "pillars of Judaism" in his Sermon on the Mount (Matt 6:1–18). He rebuked the abuse of these practices of religious piety by his contemporaries and taught the importance of an internal disposition of faith and humility so that a proper spiritual attitude would accompany the external acts of righteousness. The importance of prayer as a central feature of the Christianity inherited from Judaism is seen in the church's motto: *lex orandi, lex credendi*. That is, the law of prayer is the law of belief; or as we worship, so we live.

NEW TESTAMENT DISTINCTIVES OF CHRISTIAN WORSHIP

As discussed above, early Christian worship owes much to Jewish worship of the Second Temple era. Yet the NT identifies several important distinctives of Christian worship. Chief among these distinctives is the triune nature of God—a Godhead of Father, Son, and Holy Spirit (cf. Matt 3:16,17; 28:19; 2 Cor 11:14; 1 Pet 1:22; Jude 20,21). Christian worship praises God the Father for who he is, offers thanks to God the Son for his work of redemption, and invokes the presence of God the Holy Spirit as the enabler of Christian life, ministry, and worship.

Christian worship is also Christo-centric, in that it recognizes that God's redemptive work in Jesus the Messiah is heralded through the reading of Scripture, through preaching, and through the drama of the Lord's Table. Jesus Christ has the supremacy in everything, since he preexisted before all things, and in him all things are held together (Col 1:17,18). Thus true Christian worship is a narrative. It is a retelling, a rehearsal of God's story from creation to recreation—especially emphasizing the fall of humanity, the incarnation of Jesus the Messiah, and his redemptive work known as the Christ-event. The NT story of redemption centered on the person and work of Jesus Christ becomes in many churches the basis for the church calendar, which features two major cycles: Advent narrating the Incarnation of Jesus the Messiah, and Easter retelling[4] and reenacting the Christ-event—his passion, death, burial, resurrection from the dead, appearance to his disciples, and ascension to the Father.

---

4   For more, see James R. and Jeanette Krabill's chapter in this *Handbook*, "Holy Week Drama according to Matthew," chpt. 64.

The dynamic role of the Holy Spirit is another NT distinctive of Christian worship. Christians worship in spirit and in truth (John 4:24). Christian worship is spiritual, in keeping with the nature of God, and motivated by God's Holy Spirit—since no one can proclaim that Jesus is Lord except by the power of the Holy Spirit (1 Cor 12:3). Christian worship is based upon the truth that Jesus is both the Son of Man and the Son of God (cf. Matt 16:16,17; 2 Tim 2:8; Rev 22:16). The Holy Spirit guides the Christian and the Christian church in God's truth, speaks the things of Christ, and thus brings glory to God (John 16:12–14). By the agency of the Holy Spirit, Christ has equipped his church with spiritual gifts for church leadership, ministry to the church and the world, and worship—enabling the offering of one's very life to God as worship (Rom 12:1,2,3–8; 1 Cor 12:1–11; Eph 4:11–13; Heb 13:15,16).

The NT understands the events surrounding the OT Passover as the prototype of Jesus' sacrificial death by Roman crucifixion. John's Gospel identifies Jesus as the "Lamb of God" who will take away the sin of the world (John 1:29; cf. John 3:14,15). The Apostle Paul relates Jesus' death to the substitutionary and redemptive aspects of the sacrifice of the Passover lamb by the Hebrews at the time of the exodus from Egypt (1 Cor 5:7). This relationship leads to the development of the title "Lamb" for Jesus Christ and the worship of the Lamb described in the book of Revelation (Rev 5:6,12,13; 6:1; 15:4). The depiction of Jesus Christ as a Lamb with the banner of the cross, the *Agnus Dei,* becomes an important Christian symbol in later Christianity. The recitation or singing of the *Agnus Dei,* with lyrics based on John's declaration of Jesus as the Lamb of God (John 1:29) is a part of the liturgy of the Eucharist in many Christian worship traditions.

The defining worship ritual of the Christian church is the memorial meal established by Jesus for the perpetual retelling of his sacrificial life, death, and resurrection to redeem humanity and the created order (Luke 22:7–23; 1 Cor 11:17–33). The NT designations for the table-event invest the observance with rich theological meaning and set a range of emotional tones appropriate for the worship experience.

- The "breaking of bread" emphasizes the presence of the resurrected Christ and symbolizes joy and fellowship (Acts 2:42,46; cf. Luke 24:30–32).
- The expression "the Lord's Supper" combines the deliverance theme of the OT Passover with the call to remember Christ's death in a retrospective memorial meal (1 Cor 10:20).
- The term "Communion" calls attention to the fellowship between God and humanity and the fellowship within the church as the body of Christ made possible by the cross (1 Cor 10:16).
- The word "Eucharist" evokes the attitude of joy and the expression of great thanksgiving in the celebration of the Christ-event (Matt 26:26,27; Mark 14:23).

Historically, the rite of Christian baptism is the *entrée* to the Lord's Table and marks the individual as a member of the universal body of Jesus Christ, the church. In baptism, the Christian identifies with the death, burial, and resurrection of Jesus Christ and passes from death to life (Rom 6:1–4). This new life in Christ is the Spirit of God living in the Christian, a Spirit of adoption making us children of God who are welcome at his Table (cf. Rom 8:9,16). Baptism and the recitation of the historical Christian creeds are acts of worship that contribute to the church's telling of God's story.

The aged Simeon recognized Jesus as the Messiah at his dedication at the Jerusalem temple and proclaimed this child a light to the nations and the glory of Israel (Luke 2:32). Fittingly, the mission of the church is global, making disciples of Jesus Christ among all the nations (Matt 28:19,20). The NT closes with the church's mission realized, as the nations are seen and heard worshiping the Lamb as a kingdom of priests unto God in a new creation (Rev 5:9; 7:9,10). Let those who have ears, hear what the Spirit is saying to the churches.[5]

---

5   For more reading on biblical foundations of worship, consult the *Handbook* bibliography, especially Bartholomew and Goheen (2004), Borchert (2008), Dyrness (2009), A. E. Hill (1993), Peterson (2002), Ross (2006), and Webber (2008).

2. THE SIGNIFICANCE OF BEAUTY AND EXCELLENCE IN BIBLICAL WORSHIP

by Emily R. Brink

Two enduring and overarching biblical themes or norms set the direction for all the arts in public worship: beauty and excellence. Another word describes the aim of worship: glory—all our worship is to glorify God. God provided for us a beautiful creation, each aspect of which he declared "very good." We are called to offer back to God our very best of the good gifts he has given us.

Those themes are clearly stated in Psalm 29:2—we are called to worship God "in the beauty of holiness," ascribing to God "the glory due unto his name" (KJV). The Apostle Paul prays for the saints in Christ Jesus at Philippi, that they may "approve things that are excellent" (KJV) and "discern what is best . . . to the glory and praise of God" as they live out their calling to follow Christ in both daily life and communal worship (Phil 1:10,11).

The aesthetic norms of beauty and excellence will be the focus of this brief review of scriptures, especially from the Old Testament, that provide rich detail as they describe and inspire the worship of the people of God.

WHAT WE SEE: ARCHITECTURE, FURNISHINGS, DRESS, AND DECORUM

Before the temple was built, the Israelites worshiped in a portable tabernacle that moved with them through their wanderings in the wilderness. The final chapters of Exodus provide very specific instructions for the building of this center of the liturgical life of Israel, the place where God chose to dwell. The instructions were given directly from God through Moses to Bezalel from the tribe of Judah. God filled Bezalel "with the Spirit of God, with skill, ability and knowledge in all kinds of crafts." In addition, God gave him the gift of teaching others who were skilled craftsmen, designers, embroiderers, and weavers, all of them "master craftsmen and designers" (Ex 35:30–35, NIV 1984).

The result was an extravagant display of beauty in the tabernacle, using precious jewels, fabrics, metals, and woods for the furnishings, as well as for the vestments of the priests. The command at several points to include pomegranates in the designs is especially significant, because it instructs the artists to include details that go beyond what is seen in creation. Exodus 39:24–26 asks not just for red pomegranates (their natural color), but also for blue and purple ones, showing that creativity is not limited to functional purposes. It is also to hint at the limitless splendor of God's glory.

Eugene Peterson spoke gratefully of the architect that built a church he pastored, calling him another Bezalel.[6] All who work in church architecture and design—interior and exterior—are similarly called by God to develop their skill, ability, and knowledge, using the best and most excellent resources available to a given worshiping community.

A few words about decorum: Christians in some countries have adopted practices rooted in Scripture or their culture, such as removing shoes when entering a place of worship (in Nepal, for example). Dress for worship, including for leaders, changes over time, ranging from traditions of "Sunday best" for the people and vestments for the clergy to informality, with encouragement for the people as well as the worship leaders to "come as they are." This range reflects the different interpretive meanings behind the traditions of various cultures, extending even to the use of color. The colors white and red have the most diverse interpretations in cultures around the world. For some cultures, the themes of excellence and beauty are often considered to be internal, rather than externally visible matters.

WHAT WE HEAR: POETRY, SINGING, MUSIC, AND PROCLAMATION

The first biblical reference to the arts is in Genesis 4:21 (NIV 1984)—Jubal was "the father of all who play the harp and flute." Music and singing are found throughout history in Israelite culture, from trumpet blasts in battle to songs celebrating important events in the life of the community. Poetry, singing, and music were not completely separate arts but were combined in the long history of civilization.

Today we speak of recorded history, but before the written word and continuing to this day, stories have been passed down from one generation to the next. Storytelling still has a place in worship, from illustrations in sermons to testimonies by those who give grateful expression to what God has done for them or also by those who bring laments before God. The concepts of beauty and excellence apply here too; even pain and sorrow can be brought before God with craft and care. Beauty is not to be equated with something pretty so much as something honest, offered in trust to the God who loves this broken world.

King David, the "sweet" singer of Israel, stood in this long tradition of storytelling, poetry, song, and music (2 Sam 23:1, KJV). The literary devices he employed in the psalms give evidence not only of skill but also of training, both in the smaller details of concise parallel lines, assonance, alliteration, and word play as well as in the larger sectional designs. The details of the ways the psalmists sang and accompanied the texts is lost to us, but the instruments named to accompany singing were the softer ones, since in worship the text was primary, in contrast to the louder music and often orgiastic practices that some of the surrounding cultures used in their worship.[7]

Leading worship was a priestly task. In preparation for temple worship, David organized the Levites, who were set apart for training in impressive guilds or schools established even before the temple was built. Four thousand Levites were trained in music (1 Chr 23:5) and 288 set aside

---

6   Eugene Peterson, "The Pastor: How Artists Shape Pastoral Identity," in *For the Beauty of the Church*, ed. W. David O. Taylor (Grand Rapids: Baker Books, 2010), 89–97.

7   Calvin Stapert, "Singing Psalms from Bible Times," in *Psalter Hymnal Handbook*, eds. Emily R. Brink and Bert Polman (Grand Rapids: Faith Alive Christian Resources, 1998), 17.

SECTION 1: Foundations

11

INTRODUCTION

SECTION 1: FOUNDATIONS

SECTION 2: STORIES

SECTION 3: TOOLS

CLOSING

as singers—those who "prophesied, accompanied by harps, lyres, and cymbals" (1 Chr 25:1, NIV 1984), "all of them trained and skilled in music for the Lord" (1 Chr 25:7, NIV 1984). Among those singers were the sons of Asaph, credited with many of the psalms. But most of the psalms are attributed to David, who was not a Levite but from the tribe of Judah. The Psalter is therefore a collection of the most excellent Hebrew poetry arising from the entire assembly of the people of God, to be offered in worship by those who were best skilled, trained, and equipped to lead God's people in songs of many types, including wisdom, thanksgiving, praise, and lament.

> Singing the psalms is giving back to God the words inspired by the Holy Spirit.

The Psalter is God's own songbook. Singing the psalms is giving back to God the words inspired by the Holy Spirit. The psalms therefore deserve a primary place in the sung repertoire of the church and deserve to be led by worship leaders equipped to give God their most excellent offerings from their own cultures in terms of poetic and musical craft in composition and in performance.

In each part of worship we honor God by using words either directly from Scripture or crafted with care to be totally consonant with Scripture. In the sermon we listen to God's word proclaimed, explained, and applied. Sermon making and delivery have their own aspects of art; in fact, Protestant seminaries in particular concentrate much of their curriculum on preaching.

WHEN WE MOVE: PAGEANTRY, DRAMA, AND DANCE

Nehemiah 12 describes the dedication of the rebuilt wall of Jerusalem after the exiles had returned. All the Levite singers were brought to Jerusalem "to celebrate joyfully the dedication with songs of thanksgiving and with the music of cymbals, harps and lyres" (v. 27). A double choir was assigned to process on top of the wall, one choir in each direction until they met in the house of God. The same day, the Torah was read in the hearing of all the people. The worship on this special occasion merited an extravagant display, as do contemporary celebrations of dedication and renewal.

Pageantry is dramatic, though drama as understood today is not specifically mentioned in Scripture. What is mentioned is the need for proclamation of the word in a way that can be understood (cf. Rom 10:14). For centuries, dramatic presentations of Scripture stories, both in and out of worship, have been helpful in proclaiming the good news.

Two passages often mentioned in support of dance in worship are Exodus 15:29, when Miriam the prophetess led women in dancing after the crossing of the Red Sea, and 2 Samuel 6:14, when David danced with all his might before the Lord at the return of the ark to Israel. Neither of these took place in a liturgical context as we now might define it, but they were certainly acts of worship. Dancing was an important part of Jewish culture (Eccl 3:4; Matt 11:17), as it is for many cultures. For example, Christians combine song and dance in worship in sub-Saharan Africa, extreme Northeast India (the state of Mizoram), and in many South American churches influenced by the Pentecostal movement.

In each part of our worship we are not only called to offer our best to God in the beauty of holiness, we do so in the context of responding to God in the back-and-forth dialogue of a worship service. God calls us to worship; we respond in praise. God calls us to confession; we pray for mercy and God grants us forgiveness. We pray that we may hear, understand, and apply God's word proclaimed. We give thanks, and God sends us out with his blessing. In each of those movements in worship, we offer and respond to God, using the gifts of sight, movement, speech, and song.

The Spirit of God worked through Bezalel and David and countless other artisans—named and unnamed in the Bible—so that the people of God could bring their worship to God with the best and most excellent of what God had given them. The church today can be confident that the Spirit still moves, calling artists to shape the gifts of creation for worship and calling all the people to offer worship that is woven with beauty and excellence, to the glory of God.[8]

---

8   For additional reading and reflection, see the following in the *Handbook* bibliography: Begbie (2001), especially chapters by Aldrich, Begbie, Cray, Forest, Guite, Hart, Rumsey, and Savage; Dyrness (2001); Ross (2006); W. David O. Taylor (2010), especially chapters by Banner, Begbie, Crouch, Nicolosi, Peterson, Taylor, Winner, and Witvliet; Westermeyer (1998); and Wolterstorff (1980).

3. GOD'S CREATION AND HUMAN CREATIVITY: SEVEN AFFIRMATIONS
By Harold M. Best

The subject of God's creation and human creativity is considerably complex. In light of space constraints, I shall present a series of linked, integrative concepts that begin with the person and work of the Triune God and move theologically into a wealth of creational and creative particulars, especially related to the world(s) of artistic action. Terms such as "art," "the arts," "artistic," "artistry," and "beauty" will be used as open-ended handles with full realization of their limits.

Affirmation 1: The Triune God—I AM THAT I AM—is uniquely the Uncreated One. There is nothing prior, alongside of, or exteriorly supportive of this all-in-all mystery.

Affirmation 2: God's attributes are eternally inherent, coequal, inseparable yet individual, and harmoniously at work at once and always.

Affirmation 3: Among these attributes is God's creatorhood. God simply *is*. He is not Creator in order to create himself—this confuses an action taken to begin a beginning with eternal all-at-onceness.

Affirmation 4: With a plethora of actions and in complete freedom, Father, Son, and Spirit chose to create the heavens and the earth, *ex nihilo*—from *no-thing* into a staggering array of interconnected, interdependent, individually variegated *some-things*.

Affirmation 5: Everything created completely satisfies the Creator. He calls it good. Each entity has intrinsic worth, is infinitely loved, and is eminently useful, both interdependently and individually. Furthermore, the entire creation both "works" and has worth, following a principle deep within God's counsel that guides the work of humankind.

Affirmation 6: This interconnectedness can be broken down into two parts. The first articulates a unique relational hierarchy: *Creator, creation, creature, creativity.* The second forces a clear, inviolable distinction between the absolute and the relative in God's person and work, and therefore in ours.

INTRODUCTION

SECTION 1: FOUNDATIONS

SECTION 2: STORIES

SECTION 3: TOOLS

CLOSING

- Regarding the relational hierarchy:
  - The Creator is *not* his creation (otherwise pantheism), and the creation is not the Creator (otherwise idolatry). Everything made is contingent, material, and temporal.
  - This creation/cosmos, in the most generic sense, is called "creature" but, in a more particular sense there is creaturely *life* with which the creation swarms.
  - Within the plethora of living creatures, there is a magnificent uniqueness: human personhood, which, while participating fully in the bounty and materials of creation, rises in sovereign station as a steward above it. Created in the image of the Creator (*imago Dei*), humankind is finitely but variably capable of uniting with the person, ways, and works of the Triune God. While God alone is Creat-*or,* humankind is creat-*ive*—endowed with the ability to think up/imagine and make/craft some-thing(s) from other thing(s). "Artistic" creativity is but one aspect of this enormous gift.
  - The doctrine of *imago Dei* is theocentric. It necessarily subsumes and informs all anthropological and cultural considerations—diversity, multicultural(ism), ethnic(ity), etc.—and not the reverse. Otherwise, we would end up with anthropocentric pseudotheology. No anthropological work is complete, therefore, outside of a theocentric foundation. The following shows how this can be worked out.

    - *Imago Dei* guarantees the glory of *anybodyness*. Every human being, *imago Dei*, is simply and fully *anybody*.
    - *Anybodyness* is where the primal glory of *imago Dei* universally shows itself. No one is more "image of God" than another. This guarantees universal equality, personal worth, and steady dignity. Hence, prejudice, superiority/inferiority, domination, and the like are more than a direct affront to the moral laws of God. They attack God's very nature.
    - Within the richness of *anybodyness,* multiplied capabilities reside. They are interrelated and variegated. Among these, we must say this: to one degree or another *anybody* sings, *anybody* dances, *anybody* draws, *anybody* carves, *anybody* sculpts.
    - But *anybodyness* by itself would be a duplicable genericism. Thus, each *anybody* is at once *somebody,* uniquely individuated, with a distinct panpersonal "fingerprint." Within *somebodyness* certain capabilities rise above others: this *somebody* shows more skill(s) in certain areas than another, and no two *somebodies* are gifted exactly alike. These principles extend into all individual particulars of work and leisure.
    - Culture, simply stated, is a seamless interplay of what a community of *somebodies* thinks up, makes, and believes in. Here again, theocentrism informs cultural anthropology.

- Regarding the clear distinction between the absolute and the relative:
  - As to the absolute, God alone is such, as are all his attributes. All in all and once for all, the Triune God is Truth. God is word. God's word speaks Truth. Truth is final. There are no absolutes apart from God (cf. John 14:6).
  - As to the relative, it is a gift from God, therefore fully valid and fully to be celebrated. It pertains to God's physical handiwork in which there is no fixity, no center, no supremacy. All is freely relative to all else. It is in this sense that the creation cannot speak Truth; it is morally neutral. It cannot redeem, nor articulate any path to re-

demption. While the creation cannot declare Truth, it declares the glory of God and points to the Truth while continuing in fully ordained relativity.

- Humankind, being both creature and image of God, participates in and must distinguish between absolute and relative. That it fails to do so is not creational but self-imposed, as explained further on.

- As with Creator, so with *imago Dei.* If God's material handiwork is freely relative to itself, humankind's handiwork must accord similarly. There is no final center, no final absolute in the arts. A Quechuan dance is no more, no less "final" than a Taj Mahal or the Saint Matthew Passion, nor is there an aesthetic finality in any one cultural sector. Likewise, there is

> While the creation cannot declare Truth, it declares the glory of God and points to the Truth.

no absolute aesthetic to which the world of artifactual action submits. Someone in Philadelphia or Tekedan Papua New Guinea may prefer one drawing over another, but this is interiorly relative. If we use the word "aesthetics" in a global, unlabeled way, we can say that *anybody* is endowed with an innate sense by which qualitative choices are made. Hence it is shortsighted, even prejudicial, to say that while culture *x* is creatively or linguistically capable of action *y* and culture *q* is not, *y* holds an edge over *q*.

- It is eminently desirable, however, to laud what *each* individual or culture is capable of. This inv*ites both positive comparison and cross-cultural complementarity, even synthesis.* To state this more fully: no one, no language, no style, no culture is capable of everything, every meaning, every insight, every nuance. Hence no human action should be discouraged from inter- and intrapersonal/cultural exchanging or borrowing. And if undertaken in a neighborly way, indigeneity can both evolve and retain its uniqueness. It can be both challenged and protected. It need not and must not devolve into a neutered globalism.

- It is unfortunate that certain inherently contrasting forms and distinctive languages of human expression have been lumped together into "the arts" for at least two reasons that, in the broadest sense, allow us to distinguish between artistic *eisegesis* and *exegesis.*

- In the purely linguistic sense, as contrasted with language-istic sense, all art forms, large and small, are in some way syntactical. Linguist Noam Chomsky proposes that people are born with with the intrinsic ability to form sentences.[9] This sentence "sense" is creationally primal, irrespective of any specific language used in any given discursive medium. Thus, painting or music or dance cannot "mean" each other. This is probably the most unfortunate and misleading issue in lumping the arts together, as if they guaranteed discursive synonymity.

- However, the arts still "mean," by interiorly meaning themselves. Yet, there are two extremes within which exterior "meaning," with its inevitable shifts, nuances, and contexts, must be considered. On one extreme, object-specific art and most particularly texted art, including the textual component of song, cannot help but strongly allude to or directly transmit Truth and Truth-related meaning, even though this may reflect nothing of the actual worldview of the author/composer. As with God's material handiwork, the art points to or "declares" the artist, but the artist must speak

---

9　Noam Chomsky, *Language and Mind,* 2nd ed. (New York: Harcourt Brace Jovanovich, 1972).

for herself/himself. On the other extreme, music *qua* music is incapable of any Truth message whatsoever, even though the composer might intend it to (as, for example, the doctrine of *affekt* in eighteenth-century music where motivic ideas are used to represent different images/conditions).

- While texted art directly *informs* a context—hence preaching as the unique, informing Truth-sayer—nontexted art, and most especially music, does not inform context as much as *absorb* it, *gather* it up into some sort of affective reality, or *associate* with it, all of which easily changes if and as context changes. There may be affective power in the arts, but not causal power. A fully Christian perspective is both trans- and metacultural by insisting that there is no such thing as Christian art or pagan art or morally causal art, even though there are Christian or pagan contexts in which it can be made.

- This is so because, by creational principle, anything that is made—from a painting to a political system—is both relative to and less than its makers, who by virtue of *imago Dei* are *a priori* sovereign over it. In one of many respects, therefore, human handiwork—the "textless" arts among them—can never be used to "cause" behavior, be blamed or credited for it, to induce worship (idolatry), or bring God nearer (creaturely work over Creator).

Affirmation 7: There are two, all-important "howevers" that take in the wonders of fall and redemption:

- All of the opening concepts in all of their *primal* glory, have only suggested a reality that both surrounds and infuses everything in the creation. The whole of our primal glory was horribly distorted—glory gone, death in pursuit—when Adam and Eve exchanged gods and fell, turning from Creator to creature and invited the pantheon. Their in-created worship continued but became inverted. Absolute and relative were enclosed and confused in the darkness of fallenness. The things in God's and our handiwork which were and are still in themselves neutral—no god—became charged with false power and imbued with god-ness. The *imago Dei*, while not erased, was obscenely set against itself. Self took the throne and enslaved itself, and in a confusion of artifact, ego, power, and darkness, our every path since then has been marked by delusion and error.

- Only in and through God-in-Christ-through-the-Spirit can the inversion be righted, our sojourn cleansed, our pantheon slowly dissolved, our priorities set right, our worship redeemed, and the primal glories invited back. Creator and creature assume their rightful places. The absolute and the relative are reestablished and separated. There is no god but God; there is no such thing as an idol. Content and context are gradually separated and understood. The arts, in all of their God-given freedom and relativity, all of them in their pancreative glory, are no longer proxies for God and his presence; nor are they the lords of the liturgy. They are, in all walks of life, purely and simply offerings—variegated acts of continuing worship. Quality, however perceived, is no longer worshiped for its own sake, but sought as an aspect of "anybodyness-in-Christ," joining with the glossolalic "alleluias" of redeemed human action.

CULTURAL

4. "THE BRIDGE": WORSHIP BETWEEN BIBLE AND CULTURE[10]

By Ron Man

Every grounded and mature believer would maintain that the Scriptures must guide us as our supreme and final authority in understanding and shaping our worship. After all, worship is *about God*, and it is through the Scriptures that God has revealed to us his nature and ways. Worship is likewise *for God*, and it is the Scriptures that tell us what he expects of us creatures. The Bible is to be our guide in every area of life. So certainly in this crucial area of worship, we must look to it to guide us.

People change. Times change. Cultures change. Only in the pages of Scripture can we hope to find an unchanging standard for our worship. And with all the debates about worship forms, styles, and practices which continue to rage today, the church of Jesus Christ desperately needs a *unifying* understanding of the unchanging, nonnegotiable foundations of worship—and we must turn to the Scriptures for that purpose.

Yet even with this commitment to the Scriptures as our guide for worship, we immediately run into a problem when we go to the New Testament for models and guidelines for congregational worship. That problem has been summarized by John Piper as the "stunning indifference" of the New Testament writers to issues of form and practice in corporate worship.[11] We search the pages of the New Testament in vain for detailed instructions, much less structures or liturgies. Even in the Epistles, where we might reasonably expect Paul and the other writers to address these issues as they write to guide brand new churches, we find frustratingly few details.[12]

This presents us with a crucial question: just what is it in the Bible that is supposed to govern and determine our worship? It is a reasonable assumption that the virtual silence of the New Testament writers on the matters of form and style for worship means that the Lord intends for us to

---

10   Originally published in a slightly different form in Ron Man, "Worship Bridges," *Worship Leader* (September 2005): 18–21. Reprinted by permission of the author.

11   John Piper, *Gravity and Gladness on Sunday Morning: The Pursuit of God in Corporate Worship* (Minneapolis: Desiring God Ministries, 2000), 13.

12   Piper suggests that this lack of detail may arise from the need for the message of the gospel to go out into every nation and culture (we are to "go and tell"). Therefore, Christian worship must be flexible to allow for cultural differences—whereas in the Old Testament the worship of the one true God was rooted in one culture and place (Jerusalem), and the message to the world was one of "come and see." For more on this, see Piper's chapter in this *Handbook*, "The Missional Impulse Toward Incarnational Worship in the New Testament."

have considerable latitude and flexibility in these areas. Yet our worship services still need to look like *something*, so how are we to make choices? Is it just a case of "anything goes"?

A MODEL FOR BIBLICAL GUIDANCE AND FREEDOM: "THE SUSPENSION BRIDGE"

I would like to suggest a model that gives biblical guidance, yet at the same time allows for biblical freedom. By way of illustration, this model may be based on certain characteristics of a *suspension bridge*, similar to the Brooklyn Bridge in New York City or the Golden Gate Bridge in San Francisco.

> Like any art form, Christian worship allows for much creative expression, but within defined parameters. The Bible provides for those parameters, as well as that freedom.

In a suspension bridge, the weight is supported by both the towers and the suspension cable. The towers are sunk deep in the earth and are meant to be as stable and immovable as possible. The suspension cable or span, on the other hand, while sharing a significant portion of the load-bearing, nevertheless has by design a great deal of flexibility to expand and contract, thus allowing the bridge to withstand variations in temperature, wind, weight load, and other conditions. It should also be pointed out that, while both the stationary columns and the flexible span are important parts of the bridge's construction, it is ultimately the cable that transfers much of the weight of the road bed and its traffic to the towers, so that the towers are crucial to the bridge's integrity and durability.

What can we learn about our worship from this illustration? Our worship needs to be supported by firmly rooted biblical foundations—the two towers of the bridge. The flexible cable span suggests the liberty that the New Testament seems to allow for individual faith communities to constitute their corporate worship in ways that fit their situation. Like any art form, Christian worship allows for much creative expression, but within defined parameters. The Bible provides for those parameters, as well as that freedom.

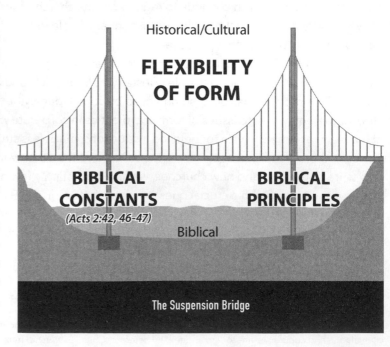

Historical/Cultural

FLEXIBILITY OF FORM

BIBLICAL CONSTANTS
(Acts 2:42, 46-47)

BIBLICAL PRINCIPLES

Biblical

The Suspension Bridge

THE FIRST TOWER: "BIBLICAL CONSTANTS"

The first tower suggests an immovable aspect of Christian worship that we could term "Biblical Constants." These are nonnegotiables, elements that simply *must* be present for our worship to be considered Christian.

What are these elements? One clue may be found in Acts 2. Luke has just recounted the events of the day of Pentecost: the coming of the Holy Spirit upon Jesus' followers, Peter's sermon, and the conversion and baptism of about three thousand people (2:41). In the very next verse, Luke tells us what these believers did when they gathered together: "And they devoted themselves to the *apostles' teaching* and to *fellowship,* to *the breaking of bread* and to *prayer . . . praising God* and enjoying the favor of all the people" (2:42,47; italics added).

The words in italics suggest a list of crucial activities for the people of God when they congregate:

1. The word of God
2. Fellowship
3. The Lord's Supper
4. Prayer
5. Praise

A number of commentators have assessed these verses as something more than simply a *description* of what the earliest church did, but rather as a *prescription* of normative practice for the church of all ages.[13] Indeed I have often given an assignment to students to list what activities are consistently found in *every* Christian worship service, in *every* denomination around the world, and down through history—and the results they come up with generally correspond very closely with the list found in Acts 2:42,47! These elements seem to be nonnegotiable constants which define and characterize truly Christian worship—elements that must therefore be represented in some form in every church's corporate gatherings.[14] These "Biblical Constants" serve as one foundational pillar for our worship.[15]

THE SECOND TOWER: "BIBLICAL PRINCIPLES"

Just because the New Testament does not provide many specifics about how to do worship in local congregations, this does not mean that "anything goes" and that we have no biblical guidance concerning worship. As with other areas or practices in our lives that are not specifically addressed by the Scriptures (e.g., movies, smoking, Internet use), there are most certainly biblical principles in God's word to be applied with wisdom and honesty to our situation.

---

13   For example, R. C. H. Lenski writes: "Here we have a brief description of the religious life of the first Christian congregation. All the essentials are present and are in proper order and harmony. The church has always felt that this is a model." See R. C. H. Lenski, *Interpretation of the Acts of the Apostles* (Minneapolis: Augsburg, 1961), 117.

14   Allowing, of course, for periodic rather than weekly celebrations of the Lord's Supper—though the practice of the early church was certainly weekly if not more often!

15   Some scholars who advocate drawing more guidance for Christian worship from the Old Testament might want to add more elements to these biblical constants.

The same is true with worship. There are a host of principles that can be drawn from the pages of Scripture to guide us and to guide the leadership of local churches in fashioning biblically appropriate yet culturally meaningful expressions of worship. These principles serve as the second tower in our illustration, giving further stability and strength to the worship structure as a whole.

Biblical principles are different from biblical constants because, as has already been mentioned above, principles must be *applied* and sometimes applied differently in different situations.

What follows then is a list of biblical principles that pertain to the practice of worship in the local church.[16] In each case, the principle is stated, followed by a supporting scripture verse (or verses) and an explanatory paragraph.

1. God's glory, and our joyful celebration of it in worship, should be the focus and goal of all life and ministry.

    "Whether, then, you eat or drink or whatever you do, do all to the glory of God." (1 Cor 10:31 NASB)

    Worship is an end in itself. By definition, other types of ministry necessarily have horizontal, human-focused aspects. But worship is vertically focused. It is the primary purpose for which God created us and therefore our highest endeavor and greatest fulfillment (Ps 16:11; Isa 43:6,7; Matt 22:35–38; 1 Pet 4:11).

2. Worship is first and foremost for God.

    "Worship God." (Rev 19:10; 22:9 NASB)

    God is the subject and object of worship. Worship is about God and for God. God is absolutely unique and therefore the only One worthy of our praise. As Creator, he alone deserves the worship of his creatures and of his creation (Ps 148:1–13; Rom 11:36).

3. Worship is a dialogue between God and his people, a rhythm of revelation and response.

    "Great is the LORD and greatly to be praised." (Ps 96:4 NASB)

> There are a host of principles that can be drawn from the pages of Scripture to guide us and to guide the leadership of local churches in fashioning biblically appropriate yet culturally meaningful expressions of worship.

In worship God speaks to us through his word, and we respond with our hearts, voices, and bodies. The impartation of theology is not complete until it is answered with appropriate doxology. This pattern is seen throughout Scripture: God always acts first to reveal himself and to reach out to us. All worship is a response to God's prior revealing and saving initiative. We should therefore allow for a healthy balance of the word proclaimed—through preaching, Scripture readings, and Scripture-based songs—and the people's response in song, prayer, confession, testimony, and the Lord's Supper (Ps 48:10; 150:2; 2 Cor 1:20).

---

16   These principles and their supporting material have emerged from the process of constructing a guiding philosophy of worship in a particular local church.

4. The word must be central in our worship.

"Praise Him according to His excellent greatness." (Ps 150:2 NASB)

Worship is our creaturely response to God's self-revelation. We are responsible to praise him as he really is, not as we would suppose or hope him to be. God has revealed himself and his glory through the inspired Scriptures. We should read the word, pray the word, preach the word, and sing the word in our corporate and private worship (Ps 56:4; 138:2).

5. Worship is the responsibility of all God's people.

"So we Your people and the sheep of Your pasture
Will give thanks to You forever." (Ps 79:13 NASB)

Worship is a verb. It is something we do, not something we watch. An important expression of the priesthood of all believers is that every individual has a vital role to play in the corporate worship of the church. We should encourage wholehearted participation in worship in every way possible (Ps 107:32; Rom 15:5,6).

6. Our worship is acceptable in and through Christ our High Priest.

"In the midst of the congregation I will sing your praise." (Heb 2:12, NASB)

Jesus Christ is the Leader of our worship. We come in him and by his worthiness into God's presence, and he gathers up our modest worship into his own perfect offering. We should strive for excellence in our worship, but not see technical expertise or artistic merit as ends in themselves, or as a means to gain God's favor or acceptance (Heb 8:1,2; 10:19–22).

7. Our response of worship is enabled, motivated, and empowered by the Holy Spirit.

"We are the *true* circumcision, who worship in the Spirit of God and glory in Christ Jesus and put no confidence in the flesh." (Phil 3:3 NASB)

As God, the Holy Spirit deserves our adoration and praise as much as the Father and the Son. Yet he chooses to glorify not himself but rather to point us to Christ (John 16:14) and thus lead us to the Father in worship. Jesus Christ is the Way into the Father's presence, and the Holy Spirit is our Guide. We can come to the Father in worship because of the work of Christ; we want to come into the Father's presence in worship because of the work of the Holy Spirit, assuring us of our standing by grace (Rom 8:14–17) and filling us for the work of praise (Eph 5:18,19). We should not focus unduly on the Holy Spirit in our worship, but seek to exalt Christ (1 Cor 12:3) as the Spirit himself desires to do.

INTRODUCTION

SECTION 1: FOUNDATIONS

SECTION 2: STORIES

SECTION 3: TOOLS

CLOSING

INTRODUCTION

SECTION 1: FOUNDATIONS

SECTION 2: STORIES

SECTION 3: TOOLS

CLOSING

8. Worship is the response of our entire lives to God.

    "Therefore I urge you, brethren, by the mercies of God, to present your bodies a living and holy sacrifice, acceptable to God, *which is* your spiritual service of worship." (Rom 12:1 NASB)

    Worship is not just a weekly event, but rather a way of living in dependence upon and gratitude toward our gracious Lord. While corporate worship is an important expression of that walk of worship, it must be fueled by lives of personal and private devotion and faithfulness (John 4:21–24; 1 Cor 10:31). Worship is the expression of the totality of our being—mind, emotions, will, actions: "all that we are responding to all that God is" (Ps 22:22; 98:4; 100:3,4; 135:5; Heb 13:15,16).

9. God is much more concerned with our heart than with the form of our worship.

    "I delight in loyalty rather than sacrifice." (Hos 6:6 NASB)

    The New Testament, in contrast to the Old Testament, is remarkably nonprescriptive when it comes to the shape and form of corporate worship services. We can only assume that God intended to allow considerable freedom in these areas. Both Testaments, on the other hand, are very clear about how seriously God takes the heart attitude and motivation of a person's worship (2 Chr 30:18–20; Mark 12:33).

10. Worship should promote the unity and edification of the body.

    "Now may the God who gives perseverance and encouragement grant you to be of the same mind with one another according to Christ Jesus, so that with one accord you may with one voice glorify the God and Father of our Lord Jesus Christ." (Rom 15:5,6 NASB)

    The body of Christ is not an affinity group, but rather a disparate band of saved sinners whom only the Spirit can unify. We must fight the rampant individualism of our age and of our natures and actively encourage the building up of the body. We should exult in our diversity and seek to learn from one another various expressions of worship (Eph 4:1–6,15,16; 5:19–21; Col 3:12–17; Heb 10:23–25).

11. Young and old need each other in the body of Christ.

    "Young men and maidens, old men and children: Let them praise the name of the Lord, for his name alone is exalted." (Ps 148:12,13, NIV 1984)

    The diversity of the body of Christ necessarily and significantly includes the mixing of generations. Young people are to honor and learn from the stability and heritage of their elders, while the young can add new energy and fresh expressions of worship (Ps 79:13; 149:1; Titus 2:2–8).

12. These things must be taught and retaught.

"Finally then, brethren, we request and exhort you in the Lord Jesus, that as you received from us *instruction* as to how you ought to walk and please God (just as you actually do walk), that you excel still more." (1 Thess 4:1 NASB)

The above truths are important elements of Christian understanding and discipleship, but must be consistently and persistently taught if they are to lodge in hearts and change attitudes and behaviors (2 Pet 1:12,13).

THE SPAN: "FLEXIBILITY AND FREEDOM"

The span, with its built-in elasticity and flexibility, represents the freedom that the New Testament seems to allow for wise, prudent, and biblically based application of culturally meaningful expressions. The "heart language of the people" is to be considered when making decisions about forms, styles, music, and other artistic expressions of faith.

> Recent developments in missions have given more weight to the importance of helping local faith communities develop their own indigenous forms of worship music, rather than simply borrowing and translating songs from the West.

We can certainly see the application of this principle, consciously or not, in the vast array of worship expressions that have developed throughout the history of the Christian church and in churches around the world today. There has been, and is, an enormous variety in terms of architecture, atmosphere, form, structure, style, dress, music, liturgy, and other expressions. God, who has created the world and humanity with such incredible diversity, must certainly rejoice in such worship variety from his people.[17] One would never use Bach organ fugues for worship in an African tribal village—a form that would have little or no meaning for this people. And conversely, some of the most natural cultural expressions of various African villages would be incomprehensible to most northern Europeans. In many contexts in Africa, drums are *the* primary instrument for worship—not a debated add-on! Recent developments in missions have given more weight to the importance of helping local faith communities develop their own indigenous forms of worship music, rather than simply borrowing and translating songs from the West—as was the practice for far too long in many church planting contexts.

The virtual silence of the New Testament as to the specifics of congregational worship practice seems to allow for local churches, as the fundamental unit of the body of Christ on earth, to have considerable autonomy and freedom in such specifics. Individual or clusters of congregations can work out the issues involving the balance of biblical constants and flexibility in the worship of their own churches. This does not mean that it is an easy task, however, as recent history has amply demonstrated. The so-called "worship wars" are symptomatic of the kind of danger into which freedom of this sort can cast us, and we might indeed be left wishing that Paul had simply

---

17   Reggie Kidd in his book *With One Voice* (Grand Rapids: Baker, 2005) explores various legitimate expressions of worship in the US today that use art music, folk music, and popular music.

prescribed a set liturgy for all time and left it at that! God obviously wants his people to apply biblical wisdom and discernment in this, as well as in many other areas where he has chosen not to spell everything out for us.

Several factors are particularly crucial for a local church in successfully navigating these treacherous worship waters. They include:

1. *Leadership.* The pastor and the elders, deacons, and church board must study worship in the Bible and study their own people as they seek to make prayerful conclusions.
2. *Communication.* Carefully soliciting input from members of the congregation is an important step for church leaders as they make worship decisions.
3. *Teaching.* The pastor and other leaders must promote a biblical understanding of worship in the public teaching ministry of the church. If any kind of change in worship is to be undertaken in the church, it is essential that the people are told the *why,* not just the *what,* of the change.
4. *Principle-based decisions.* The principles for making worship decisions relate to the second tower of our illustration above. Although the Bible does not offer much detailed instruction for worship services, the lack of specifics does not mean that we have no biblical guidance at all. Clear biblical principles can be discerned, and this gives hope for agreement on a foundational biblical level both within and among churches. But principles by definition must be applied, and that is where the leaders must pray seriously for wisdom and balance in making application of the principles to their particular local church situation. Also, as we have noted, principles may be applied *differently* by different people and in different situations. So we must learn to give grace to others in the church who would prefer a different application and to other churches choosing to apply principles differently to their situations.
5. *"Semper reformanda."* This Latin phrase, which comes to us from the Reformation, means "always reforming." It expresses the importance of regularly and repeatedly subjecting our worship and other practices to the scrutiny of the Scriptures. Culture and traditions change. The Scriptures do not. A church's traditions should not be ignored when considering worship issues in that church. But neither should they be allowed to assume the level of authority which is appropriate only to the Scriptures. As someone has said, "Tradition is a wonderful servant, but a terrible master."

CONCLUDING REFLECTIONS

"Man looks at the outward appearance; but the LORD looks at the heart" (1 Sam 16:7 NASB). We squabble about so many little things related to worship, but God is looking for people who will worship him in spirit and truth. The externals are not nearly as important to him as they are to us! God is not as worried about which songs you sing as he is about you "making melody with your heart to the Lord" (Eph 5:19 NASB).

In today's raging worship debates we desperately need to see that there are biblical constants and principles that we can really agree on. And then we need to have the grace and maturity to allow for the flexibility that God seems to allow for. There is far more that binds us as worshipers than divides us through our different expressions—"there is one body and one Spirit—just as you were called to the one hope that belongs to your call—one Lord, one faith, one baptism, one God and Father of all, who is over all and through all and in all" (Eph 4:4–6, NIV 1984). Let us obey Paul's command to "walk in a manner worthy of the calling to which you have been called, with all humility and gentleness, with patience, bearing with one another in love, eager to maintain the unity of the Spirit in the bond of peace" (Eph 4:1–3, ESV).

We must learn to give grace to other churches choosing to apply principles differently to their situations.

INTRODUCTION

SECTION 1: FOUNDATIONS

SECTION 2: STORIES

SECTION 3: TOOLS

CLOSING

INTRODUCTION

SECTION 1: FOUNDATIONS

SECTION 2: STORIES

SECTION 3: TOOLS

CLOSING

5. ARTISTIC EXPRESSION IN EARLY CHRISTIANITY

By Eleanor Kreider

In the early centuries Christians inculturated their faith by using symbols which deeply affected common life and worship. The following examples of historical, symbolic forms reach across cultures and enrich the transmission of the gospel. These examples pose questions for contemporary Christians seeking deep symbolic expressions in worship.

CATACOMB ART

Around the beginning of the third century, Christian communities began to produce and use visual art forms. Why so late? Injunctions against idolatry, resistance to the culture around them, insistence on an invisible God—these may have been reasons. We cannot know for sure. As we see in the Roman catacombs of the third century, Christians began borrowing and adapting a variety of contemporary symbols. Their theological reflection in written texts correlates with a visual language of sacred images. Visual art may have been illustrative or didactic, but it also could be richly exegetical and liturgical.

In catacomb paintings and as bas-relief sculpture on *sarcophagi* (tombs), heroes and stories of the Bible appear clad in the iconography of Greco-Roman culture. Jesus, as healer and wonder worker, sometimes carries a "magic" wand. Depicted as a clean-shaven youth, Jesus could as easily be taken for an adolescent Orpheus, who in Greek mythology charmed all living beings with his music and challenged the power of the underworld. Apostles sculpted as full-bearded men look remarkably like heroic Roman statues. Favorite Bible stories (Jonah, the fiery furnace, Lazarus) and depictions of Christ or saints are frequent subjects. Birds and flowers, trees and rivers evoked more than appreciation for nature—they could also be symbols of paradise, of life after death. It is often difficult to differentiate early Christian symbols from pagan prototypes. In the century after the emperor Constantine, when it became safe and advantageous to be a Christian, Christian symbolism became more explicit.

SIGNET RINGS

In Roman times men of substance wore signet rings, which they used to authenticate documents or to label goods for trade. In the late second century, Clement of Alexandria instructed Christian men to wear the signet ring at the base of the little finger. On no account could the ring's image be a lover, for we are a "chaste people," nor a sword or bow, "for we cultivate peace," nor a drinking cup, "for we practice temperance." The image on the ring could be of a dove, a fish, a ship in full sail, or an anchor, which could discretely evoke the cross.[18] In this way Christians used distinctive and potent symbols to reflect their faith, values, and life practices.

PEACE GREETING

In the mid-second century, Justin Martyr mentioned the peace greeting as a part of the eucharistic liturgy of the church in Rome. This gesture continued throughout early Christianity in weekly eucharistic services and also at the conclusion of believers' morning prayer following catechetical sessions. The kiss of peace is one of the oldest Christian liturgical practices, noted in several New Testament Epistles as the holy kiss or the kiss of peace (e.g., 1 Thess 5:26; 1 Pet 5:14). Kissing in public in Greco-Roman culture was reserved for relatives or social equals. The Christian liturgical kiss of peace was countercultural, even scandalous. Enemies of the Christians gossiped and slandered them because Christians exchanged the greeting across social and economic lines in their weekly eucharistic services, as they sought to be reconciled with each other following the teachings of Matthew 5:23,24.

> The Christian liturgical kiss of peace was countercultural, even scandalous.

At the appropriate time in the eucharistic service, a deacon announced the peace greeting, often asking if any member of the assembly had a grievance against another. This was the time to greet and be reconciled with the estranged person. Later, during the Christian centuries in Europe, this practice faded, becoming infrequent and in many places confined to the clergy. Since the twentieth century when the peace greeting was reintroduced into Christian liturgies, the physical gesture has varied according to culture—a bow, a hands gesture (*namaste*), an embrace, a kiss, a handshake.

EUCHARIST AS A FORM OF THE ROMAN BANQUET

In 1 Corinthians 11–14, the apostle Paul addresses the Christian community in Corinth about its worship practices. The church had adopted the familiar cultural form of Greco-Roman banquet (meal plus *symposium*—the after-dinner conversation) for their Lord's Supper. These chapters address a single worship event in a Corinthian house church. Chapter 11 relates to the meal. Chapter 14 deals with the *symposium* (conversation). Between these two chapters, chapter 12 presents

---

18   Clement of Alexandria, *The Paedagogus, The Instructor, book III*, chapter 11, "A Compendious View of the Christian Life," http://www.newadvent.org/fathers/02093.htm.

INTRODUCTION

SECTION 1: FOUNDATIONS

SECTION 2: STORIES

SECTION 3: TOOLS

CLOSING

Paul's vision for the multigifted church, and chapter 13 is a paean of praise to the virtue of love and a call to "table manners" of courtesy, deference, and honor. Paul, as a missionary theologian, accepted the inculturation of the church's worship within the forms of the banquet.

However, Paul as a pastoral theologian pointed to distortions in the church's practice of the meal and advised the church on how they should rectify these abuses and align their worship with the distinctive values of their Christian faith. For the meal, Paul admonishes the richer believers to stop showing contempt to the poorer believers and to share food equitably ("discerning the body"; 11:29). For the *symposium* (conversation), Paul rebukes the church's chaotic use of spiritual gifts, which prevented outsiders from participating in worship and which kept Christian worship from expressing the character of the God of peace (14:33). "Each" and "all" were to contribute according to the gifts of the Spirit (14:26,31). Multivoiced worship at table was what Paul considered to be "decently and in order" (14:40 NKJV). This inculturated form of liturgy included countercultural gestures and practices which created social bonding and radical equalization.

ARCHITECTURAL SPACE

New Testament churches were domestic gatherings. The host of the home often served as leader of the church. Worship on this domestic scale continued for several centuries, though in some instances the apartments or houses could be fairly large. In the fourth century, by imperial favor, churches in some cities were able to build large buildings to house growing congregations. But house churches continued into the fifth century, when in many places they were displaced by purpose-built church buildings. This new scale of worship necessitated an "amplification"— rhetorical sermons, glorious processions, and dramatic liturgy. Now churches were filled with standing crowds and kept in order by patrolling deacons. Imagine the change in how individuals experienced worship! No longer face to face in someone's home and courtyard, worshipers now stood in a grand public space, craning to see and straining to hear what was going on.

QUESTIONS THEN AND NOW

All of these symbols and gestures we have considered in early Christianity—in art, jewelry, meal practices, space—raise questions for today. How can Christians engage practices and create artifacts through which Christian truths become comprehensible yet challenge aspects of wider culture in the name of the gospel?

6. WAYS OF CONTEXTUALIZING CHURCH MUSIC: SOME ASIAN EXAMPLES

By I-to Loh

Since the time the term "contextualization" was coined by Dr. Shoki Coe, it has become an important concept in biblical interpretation and theological studies as well as in planning liturgies and composing hymns. Contextualization is an intimate and complicated double wrestling of the "text"—the word of God—with our present "context" (the *sitz im leben*). I believe that the ultimate goal of contextualization is, on the one hand, to seek for ways of interpreting the meaning of incarnation, and on the other, to utilize the *imago Dei* in human beings to fully develop our skills and art forms, using them to express our Christian faith and to participate in God's continuing creation.

Approaches to contextualization of church music involve both the contents of the texts and the styles of music. There are innumerable examples of Asian hymns that illustrate these two aspects of contextualization. Because of space constraints, we can mention only a few here, but further examples can be found in the Asian hymnbook *Sound the Bamboo* (STB).[19]

CONTEXTUALIZATION THROUGH *SITZ IM LEBEN* OR "LIFE SETTING"

Reinterpreting the Meaning of the Incarnation of Christ: "Sound a Mystic Bamboo Song." As we revisit various types of contextualization of church music, I would like to begin with an example called "Sound a Mystic Bamboo Song" (Global Praise 2 #103),[20] based on the poem by Bill Wallace for which I used a mixture of Kalinga (northern Philippines) and Taiwanese tribal music styles. In the song, a listener feels the vivid description of how Christ was incarnated as an Asian woman, living and suffering with the poor. This hymn does not stop merely with the *sitz im leben,* but urges singers to "free the Christ within the poor," and to give "cultures, creatures, plants, wholeness, stillness, growth and worth." In other words, the hymn seeks to motivate us to concrete actions to reach holistic salvation. The hymn below is self-explanatory and needs no further analysis. It is probably one of the most compact contextualized hymns in Asia that is in general use today.

---

19   I-to Loh, Francisco Feliciano, and James Minchin, eds., *Sound the Bamboo: CCA Hymnal 2000* (Tainan: CCA/ Taiwan Church Press, 2000).

20   Global Praise 2, (New York: GBGMusik, 2000).

Sound a Mystic Bamboo Song

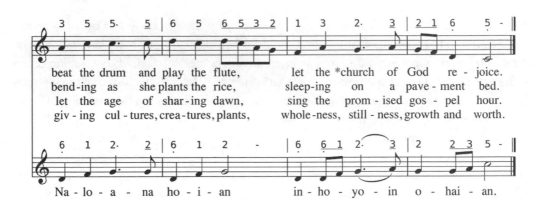

Performance suggestions:

Stanza 1 is non-lexical-syllables of the Kalinga (Philippines) and Amis (Taiwan).

Stz. 1, sing 2nd voice in non-lexical syllables; stz. 2, text with non-lexical syllables (2nd voice); stz. 3, all sing text without 2nd voice; stz. 4, both parts sing same text; stz. 5, sing text and non-lexical syllables.

*original for "church of God" = "Asian church."

Words: Bill Wallace, New Zealand
Music: I-to Loh, Taiwan

Sound a Mystic Bamboo Song (Global Praise 2 #103)

Naming God and Christ in Asian Contexts. In addition to some of the images of Christ mentioned above, Asians have contextualized their concepts and names of God and Christ with the following terms: Lover (STB #36, 71), Friend and Kindred (#26, 55, 220), Healer and Health (#55, 262), Noble One (#162), Spring Wind (#174), Morning Bird (#305), the Rice (#190) and the Water (#209), the Road and Map (#230), Big Dipper [Polar Star] (#52). The feminine character of God is especially expressed in the terms Mother Hen (#161), Mothering Bird (#222), Mother and Parent (#18, 23, 26, 84, 181, 220, 283). All these indicate that some Asian poets have contextualized their understanding of God and Christ through their daily experiences, no more a Western God or Caucasian Christ.[21]

Affirming the Love and Sovereignty of God through Agrarian Life. Although we have entered the space age with its digital world and high technologies, agrarian labor and produce are still the fundamental needs for the sustenance of human life. This is reflected through the hymn "Lord, Your Hands Have Formed This World" (Philippines, STB #178). Acknowledging the love and sovereignty of God in the world, the people affirm that all nature, natural resources, and everything that grows, including plants, animals, and human beings, are the signs that God is making all things new every day. In the song the people also apply the earthly realities to spiritual matters and ask God to uproot sins and provide "homes for Christ." The Ikalahan people of the northern Philippines are farmers living in a mountainous area. The contextualized expression of God's blessings to their agrarian community is unique, as shown below:

> Sweet potatoes fill our bags, when the garden yields its due.
> Chickens run, and pigs grow plump, children too:
> Your bounty's signs that you made all things new.

Identifying God's Salvation and Guidance through Natural Phenomena. In the hymn "Come, Smell the Scent of Sweet Wild Flowers" (Okinawa, STB #52), Seiei Yokota invites people to enjoy the beauty of God's creation, and at the same time to relate to Christ's sacrificial love in a symbolic way:

> With open arms on the cross outstretched,
> All earth touched by Christ's body . . . we trust such love.

Relating to the essential need that seagoing people have for a guide to help them find their way at night, he points to the Big Dipper (the Polar Star) as the shining Cross to guide us in our wandering life:

> In dead of night our boat's sailing, the Polar Star guides homeward.
> Seek when it's dark, the Cross shining, our Savior guides us home.

---

21   I-to Loh, *Hymnal Companion to Sound the Bamboo: Asian Hymns in Their Cultural and Liturgical Contexts* (Chicago: GIA Publishers, 2011), 18.

INTRODUCTION

SECTION 1: FOUNDATIONS

SECTION 2: STORIES

SECTION 3: TOOLS

CLOSING

This contextualized expression of Okinawan Christians, set to a lovely children's song *"Tinsagu* Flowers" in a typical six-tone scale (1 2 3 4 5 7), accompanied by a *jabisen* (plucked lute), has become very popular in their churches.[22]

CONTEXTUALIZATION THROUGH THE USE OF NONLEXICAL SYLLABLES

Words are sometimes insufficient to communicate certain ideas, feelings, and concepts. Hence some cultures have resorted to the use of nonlexical syllables (NLS); i.e., words or vocables that are without specific meanings, but they are by no means meaningless. NLS are frequently sung with their own typical musical phrases. The culture that sings them can understand their various built-in or hidden meanings. The use of NLS is widespread in Asia. The Ami tribe in Taiwan, who sing in NLS on all occasions, has one song that they sing on different occasions and in different places with different titles: "Old Song," "Song without a Title," "Drinking Song," and *"Amis no Kimigayo"* ("National Anthem of the Amis").

The Paiwan tribe of Taiwan begins a song with the NLS *alaiyoai,* which implies an invitation to people to participate in certain activities. Now Christians have added a new meaning to *alaiyoai*—"Hear now, God's own people"—to admonish them that "the law of the Lord is perfect, reviving our [the] soul" (STB #215, Ps 19:7–8, NRSV).

The Bunun tribe of Taiwan sing songs in which the congregation responds with NLS *u-i-hi-* (STB #224) in double thirds, which could mean "I support" or "I agree with what you sing." Thus the NLS gain meanings from the words sung before or after them.

The Kalinga people of the Philippines sing *dong dong ay* or *salidummay* songs to express joy, praise, and thanksgiving, or feelings of loneliness or sadness. In "Sing a Song to the Lord" (STB #92), the NLS *ayay salidummay* express the joyful praise of Psalm 96. In "Mary's *salidummay*" (STB #102), they reflect the Virgin Mary's humble obedience, recalling God's acts of lifting up the humble but bringing down the powerful. So the NLS sung in each stanza communicate the slightly different feelings of the text.

Therefore, understanding the meaning of NLS involves these four factors:

1. NLS have no specific meanings, but they are by no means meaningless.
2. NLS express what words cannot, but the meaning may be hidden or ambiguous.
3. NLS may gain meanings through the title, function, or purpose of the text.
4. NLS may gain meaning through their contexts (the words sung before or after them), thus having multiple meanings.

The phenomenon of singing in NLS could be comparable to the way Saint Paul describes the prayers of the Holy Spirit as "sighs too deep for words." He says, "that very Spirit intercedes with sighs too deep for words" (Rom 8:26, NRSV). This implies that the limitation of words makes it

---

22   For explanation of cipher notation see Loh: *Hymnal Companion to Sound the Bamboo,* introduction pp. xxxvi-vii, or read the following: Cipher notation (1 2 3 4 5 6 7 for *do re mi fa sol la ti*) is popular among Asians. The dot above the note means one octave higher, under means octave lower. Each underline below the note indicates half a beat; a hyphen [–] equals the same note extending one count; a dot increases the note value of one half; 0 marks rest. Two dots :ll at the end of a section calls for repetition of the whole section. 1 = D identifies the first note of the melody, i.e. 1 (*do*) is on pitch D. 4/4 time indicates quarter-note as one count and four counts per measure.

necessary to use something beyond one's comprehension, like "the untalkables through music" to communicate meanings or emotions which are "too deep for words." These vocables then become a vehicle for the Holy Spirit to work wonders. A Jewish cantor has stated that the Reformed Jews believe the best singing to be nonverbal—i.e., using nonlexical syllables to sing songs of praise, to communicate praise and thanksgiving beyond the limitation of words. Proper use of NLS may stimulate us to new thinking and new expressions of contextualizing our faith.[23]

We find a transformation of NLS in a Korean song, *Ohoradiya* (STB #101), which was originally associated with a farmers' dance during festivals. The syllables are shouts of joy and excitement. Geonyong Lee adapted this singing style and has transformed the nonlexical syllables *ohoradiya sangsa diya* into the meaning of "hallelujah" by simply adding a parenthetical "hallelujah" in the lyrics everywhere that *ohoradiya* appears. In the arrangement of Psalm 150, Korean instruments have replaced all the biblical instruments. The composer has contextualized and transformed the folk singing style into a hymn of highest praise.

CONTEXTUALIZATION THROUGH UTILIZATION OF NATIVE MUSICAL ELEMENTS

Direct Adaptation of Folk or Traditional Melodies. Adaptations of existing folk songs or traditional melodies for newly written Christian texts seem to have immediate appeal and are easily accepted by the general congregation. This type of adaptation is the same as the *contrafacta* practice during Martin Luther's Reformation, when he adapted secular melodies for Christian songs, substituting new Christian lyrics for the original texts. The melodies of such songs often reflect the "real" identity of the culture and may be easily identified by the people. We see this in Rev. Nobuaki Hanaoka's adaptation of a Japanese song, "*Sakura*," the Japanese national flower, to become "Praise the Lord" (STB #23) for the beauty of God's creation and for the glory of our Parent God's love. Singaporean pastor Samuel Liew also adapted a very popular Indonesian/Malaysian folk tune, "*Rasa Sayang*," for a song of praise, "Now Let Us Tell of Your Victory" (STB #22) to celebrate God's salvation, unity, and promise of justice and peace.

A noted Holy Communion hymn, "Far Beyond Our Mind's Grasp" (Philippines, STB #82) was adapted by Francisco Feliciano from a Bicol lullaby, "*Caturog na Nonoy.*" The melody reflects Spanish heritage, written in triple rhythm, with accents frequently falling on the second beat. The composer seems to have contextualized God's love as a mother's never-ending love for her own baby, even being willing to sacrifice her own life for her child. The music provides much room for imagination and theologizing.[24]

> Adaptations of existing folk songs or traditional melodies for newly written Christian texts seem to have immediate appeal.

One can also find the adaptation of a folk tune with added contextual harmony, as exemplified in "God, We Praise You for This Lord's Day" (STB #13). The music in a Chinese six-tone scale (1 2 3 5 6 7) is an adaptation of a Buddhist chant from Mt. Puto. In order to maintain its original Chinese character, Pen-li Chen provided a monotonous ostinato (0 3 6 56) to resemble the colotomic accompaniment of gongs in the temple chanting. Colotomic

---

23   Ibid., 25–26.
24   Ibid., 275.

INTRODUCTION

SECTION 1: FOUNDATIONS

SECTION 2: STORIES

SECTION 3: TOOLS

CLOSING

refers to the way in which different instruments play periodically in a certain order at different times, as in Indonesian *Gamelan*.[25]

Such *contrafacta* practices might cause some problems of association and may even in certain instances put contextualization on trial. Some cultures have no difficulty singing Christian texts set to secular folk melodies, while others may find the juxtaposition hard to digest. But the gospel principle is clear: the blood of Jesus Christ cleanses our sins and makes us acceptable to God. If we are sincere in adapting "secular" tunes of good quality to communicate Christian messages, Christ will sanctify our intention and effort and transform our fruits into sacred songs pleasing to God.[26]

Utilization of Typical Native Idioms and Elements in New Compositions. This approach does not adapt existing folk tunes per se. Rather, the elements, motives, and idioms that express the typical features or spirit of the culture are skillfully integrated into new compositions. Thus the melodic style is indigenous and has traditional accompaniment. The following hymns show strong evidences of such an approach to contextualization.

- "Come and Worship God with Songs of Praise" (Thailand, STB #2) uses a Thai traditional five-tone equidistant scale (1 2 3 5 6). The melody is constructed according to the natural intonation of the Thai language, with the accompaniment of concussion bells (ching, "o" open, weak beat, chap "+" closed, strong beat) and the thon (drum) in the following pattern: (1. 1 01 1).
- In "To the High and Kindly Hills" (Korea, STB #53), the composer utilized a typical Korean five-tone scale (1 2 3 5 6) with lively 6/8 time, shifting accents from the first note (3 3 2.) to the second note (3 3 2.) and vice versa, and the dotted note on the fourth note (1 1 1 6.5 6), all showing characteristics of *changdan* rhythmic contrast. The accompaniment by a *taegŭm* (long, transverse bamboo flute), a *kayagŭm* (board zither), and a *changgo* (hourglass drum) give further life and spirit to this contextual hymn.
- "Soft the Master's Love Song" (Indonesia, STB #203) is a paraphrase of Jesus' call, "Come to me, all you that are weary and are carrying heavy burdens, and I will give you rest" (Matt 11:28, NRSV). The music uses an Indonesian five-tone scale (6 7 1 3 4), accompanied by guitar, that imitates the Javanese *celempung* (plucked board zither) style, and repeats similar musical figures (6676 4676) with a haunting effect. Furthermore, a matchstick placed between the guitar strings near to the bridge produces a gonglike sound, adding a stronger contextualized feel.
- "In the Dawn of the Morn" (Japan, STB #158) is another good example that exhibits a Japanese farmer's daily routine. It describes three occasions for giving thanks daily:

    . . . with the sickle held in hand, I stand on the grass . . .
    . . . with my hands together clasped, I kneel on the earth . . .
    . . . with the loving family, humble meal we share . . .

---

25   Ibid., 61–62, 220–21.
26   See I-to Loh, "Revisiting Ways of Contextualization of Church Music in Asia," *Theology and the Church* 30, no. 2 (2005): 450–74. See also I-to Loh, *In Search for Asian Sounds and Symbols in Worship*, edited and introduced by Michael Nai-chiu Poon, (Singapore: Trinity Theological College in Singapore, 2012), 47.

All these phrases have repetitive notes on a series of eighth notes (3335656- / 77756-) in a typical Japanese six-tone scale (2 3 5 6 7 1) with final on the tone 2. The composer skillfully utilized Western classical harmonic language to support this typically contextualized Japanese hymn.

Creative Innovations. The ultimate goal of contextualization involves achieving a mature proficiency in technical skills in which lyrics exhibit sound theology infused with poetic beauty and reflect the needs and concerns of the culture. The composition, though infused with native elements and styles, is innovative in its melody, form, and any harmony involved. Thus the hymn expresses the highest level of creativity; unique and contemporary, its style is neither purely native nor Western, but incarnational, as illustrated by the following examples:

- A boy's prayer ("While I Am Asleep," STB #160) reflects tragedies and injustices in the Filipino society, where many a father's wages are insufficient to feed his family. Hence the boy prays for his parents and for himself that God would not let him go astray. The tune utilizes a five-tone scale (4 5 7 1 3) beginning with 4, derived from the Indonesian *pelog* scale (3 4 5 7 1). The very economical guitar accompaniment with opening and closing "chords" (D-B flat-E flat) conveys a sense of insecurity, uncertainty, and loneliness.
- Another example is "God of the Bible, God in the Gospel" (STB #255), the theme song for the Tenth General Assembly of Christian Conference of Asia in Colombo, Sri Lanka, 1996. The author, Shirley Murray, describes "how God abides with humankind through Christ, whose suffering empowers them to be fearless and faithful, even facing the cross. This is the only hope for the world to change."[27] The tune utilizes musical features to interpret this concept. Motif A uses D = 3 4 5 7b 1 (*mi fa sol tib do*) scale with an eight-count rhythmic pattern 3 + 2 +3 (reinforced by drum patterns), and motif B is in B flat = 1 3 4 5 7 (*do mi fa sol ti*) scale with 3 + 3+ 2 pattern. The time signature of 8/8 is intended to symbolize the faithfulness of God, which does not change through history. The two patterns of A and B exhibit changes in the scales, grouping of beats, figures of accompaniment with drones, intervals of fourths and fifths, and the formation of independent lines, all of which are my attempt to show the necessity of change on the part of human beings. Here is the way I contextualized it for the CCA Assembly: The musical elements are from India, but the accompaniment is neither Indian nor Western but my own. It is not Taiwanese but could perhaps be called pan-Asian. It is purposely scored to contextualize the faithfulness of God and the necessity for the world to change.[28]

---

27   Loh, *Hymnal Companion*, 367–68.
28   Loh, "Revisiting Ways of Contextualization," 10. See also Loh, *In Search for Asian Sounds*, 2012, 58.

free-dom or pri - son,   you are our home.
feed-ing, sus-tain - ing, from your own heart.
birth-ing new sys - tems, light-ing new lights.
small pa-per lan - terns, light-ing the way.
till our world chang - es, fac-ing the Cross.

God of the Bible, God in the Gospel (STB #255)

CONCLUSION

Contextualization of church music is not an easy task at this complex time, especially with the strong current of globalization sweeping most music cultures into the stream of rapid Westernization. In modern cities, we can generally identify at least four types of people; namely: (1) the younger generation, (2) the intelligentsia, (3) the preservers and protectors of native cultures and traditions, and (4) the general public. All of these types have different needs, views, and preferences in music, so the contents, methods, and styles of contextualization must vary accordingly. Therefore, we have to face the reality that no one approach will be satisfactory or appropriate for all. Hence theologians, pastors, poets, and musicians, all with *imago Dei*, ought to utilize their native poetic and musical styles and instruments[29] to enhance their creativity as they interpret their faith and formulate various forms of praising God and proclaiming the gospel, so that Christ's incarnation and the message of salvation may be embraced as meaningful and true for all people at all places in all times.

---

29   For further reading, see I-to Loh (2012).

HISTORICAL

7.   HOW SONG SUSTAINED THE CHURCH
By Frank Fortunato

In the Revelation of Jesus to John, God graciously allowed his banished servant to peer "behind the curtain" into the eternal realm. Among the revelations given to John was "a great multitude that no one could count, from every nation, tribe, people and language, standing before the throne and before the Lamb" (Rev 7:9–11). From the beginning of time, God has been preparing that multitude—a multitude of worshipers. The history of worship is the chronological story of the growth of the church to become a vast mosaic of redeemed peoples across the earth, in fulfillment of Jesus' words, "I will build my church" (Matt 16:18). As the church spread to the nations of the world, it adapted itself linguistically to new contexts, yet maintained such common traits as the practice of prayer, participation in the sacraments, and congregational singing. The church's songs have sustained God's people in all eras and in all regions. God's people have historically been a chanting and singing people.

THE ROLE OF SONG IN THE EARLY CENTURIES

The journey of the New Testament church begins in Jerusalem. The book of Acts describes how believers praised God with glad and sincere hearts, and "the Lord added to their number daily those who were being saved" (Acts 2:42–47). Paul wrote about the psalms, hymns, and spiritual songs of the emerging congregations. As the early church worshiped and grew, persecution did not stop the growth or stop the song. In Philippi, Paul and Silas, beaten and imprisoned, drew upon the growing hymnody of the early church and sang hymns at midnight.

During the early centuries the singing church spread across modern-day Turkey, Greece, Armenia, North Africa, and India, where the Apostle Thomas ministered. Late in the first century, Pliny the Younger reported that the Christians assembled before dawn to sing a song to Christ. The *Didache,* a document from the early second century, reveals that the church's fellowship included food, the celebration of the Eucharist, and the singing of Psalms. Wilson-Dickson indicates that early church growth included different musical and liturgical expressions that varied according to the geographical area and the language adopted.[30]

---

30   Andrew Wilson-Dickson, *The Story of Christian Music: From Gregorian Chant to Black Gospel* (Oxford: Lion, 1992), 26.

With the conversion of Constantine in the fourth century, the church entered a period of imperial favor. Missionary expansion and Bible translation led to the establishment of monasteries. Monastic writings discussed the singing of psalms and hymns,[31] and many monasteries established a cycle for chanting or singing through the entire Psalter every week.

THE BIRTH OF GREGORIAN, ORTHODOX, AND "PERFORMANCE" MUSIC TRADITIONS

As the church expanded, however, so did the problems. A diversity of beliefs led to various kinds of heresy. Late in the fourth century, Ambrose combated false ideas with hymns and boasted about their power to rescue people from heresy.[32] Singing was still primarily a matter of chanting in unison. As crude forms of music notation evolved, chants were collected. Many of these were associated with Pope Gregory and are remembered in history as "Gregorian chant."[33] Vocalizing or intoning the word provided a means to connect text with the power and emotion of melody, and in the early centuries the text dominated the music. Egeria, a Spanish nun living in the fourth century, kept a detailed journal of her visit to Jerusalem, and her account was saturated with references to music.[34] Singing continued to be the means of God's people living out their worship life.

> Vocalizing or intoning the word provided a means to connect text with the power and emotion of melody.

As a new millennium began, missionaries moved throughout Northern and Eastern Europe and the church kept expanding. The divide between the East and the West solidified and the Orthodox Church grew in importance. The Byzantium liturgy in the East and the Roman liturgy in the West developed musically in various ways. The Psalms continued to have a prominent place as Greek and Latin hymnody developed.[35] Other liturgies and hymn traditions also emerged as the Orthodox movement spread to include the West Syrian, Maronite, Syro-Indian, and Syro-Jacobite church movements.[36]

In the centuries leading up to the Reformation, the Roman rite in the West increased in complexity as many extrabiblical elements were added to the church's worship. *The Mass*, developed over previous centuries, continued to provide a rich resource for musical creativity, with settings for the *Kyrie Eleison, Gloria, Credo, Sanctus,* and *Agnus Dei.* Unlike the earlier centuries when text dominated, now music was taking on a more independent role in liturgical music compositions.[37]

---

31   Calvin R. Stapert, A *New Song for an Old World: Musical Thought in the Early Church* (Grand Rapids: Eerdmans, 2007), 84–86.

32   Ibid., 91.

33   The study of Gregorian chant has a central place in any overview of music history, since the development of music notation is directly linked to the collection of these chants. In turn, notated biblical chants became the major source of church music over several centuries.

34   Ibid., 46.

35   Richard C. Leonard, "Singing the Psalms: A Brief History of Psalmody," Laudemont Ministries, http://www.laudemont.org/a-stp.htm.

36   Peter E. Fink, "Worship in the Eastern Orthodox Tradition," in The *Complete Library of Christian Worship*, vol. 2, *Twenty Centuries of Christian Worship*, ed. Robert E. Webber (Nashville: StarSong, 1993), 44–48.

37   Similar to Gregorian chant, the musical development of the mass has an important place in music history. In fact, masses represent some of the finest musical compositions throughout the centuries.

Professional musicians were needed, however, to perform these masterpieces. Most of the congregation simply watched and listened.

CHANGES BROUGHT ABOUT BY SIXTEENTH-CENTURY PROTESTANT AND CATHOLIC REFORM

By the sixteenth century, the need for reform of corrupt practices in the church reached a critical peak, and Martin Luther protested, nailing his famous ninety-five theses to the Wittenberg Castle church door. As a practicing musician, Luther understood that music was one of God's greatest gifts. Before long, German congregations were again singing, but now in harmony.[38] However, John Calvin saw things differently. He allowed only nonharmonized and unaccompanied psalm singing. Metrical versions of the Psalter came into use to encourage congregational participation. The *Genevan Psalter* became the acme of psalm settings, greatly influencing future psalters.[39] As Roman Catholic masses added polyphony, music and singing became more complex. Elaborate musical settings left the texts largely obscured. The Council of Trent met over several years in the mid-sixteenth century and, among other reforms, called for a simplification of the church's music.

The centuries following reform in both Protestant and Catholic branches of the church resulted in the Christian faith becoming a worldwide reality. Missionaries circled the globe and music played a key role in this expansion.[40] In England various metrical versions of the Psalter came into use, patterned after the German models. Anglican chant soon became popular, allowing the Scriptures to be sung without alteration or paraphrase.[41] James White describes the phenomenal growth of singing that followed: "If the Reformation period saw an explosion in preaching, it was no more dramatic than the increase in music, particularly as regards congregational singing."[42] In the eighteenth century the Moravians published thousands of hymns and songs. Isaac Watts in England started adding New Testament interpretations to the Psalms, which launched the hymn movement in England. Wilson-Dickson mentions that more than 450 metrical psalters and at least 250 different hymnbooks were published in England during the eighteenth century.[43] In addition, a new interest in the Latin and Greek hymns of previous centuries led to the release of song collections in English and other languages.

Hymns were becoming a part of church life. Charles Wesley dominated a hymn explosion that propelled the Methodist movement forward. The Methodists stand out as a movement that was born singing. The avalanche of hymn texts from Wesley never diminished over his lifetime, resulting in a phenomenal 6,500 hymn settings. With his brother John, who served as editor and publisher of the many song collections, the two Wesley brothers shaped a movement through powerful preaching, teaching, publishing, and singing. They captured vibrant Methodist theology in rhyme, melody, and many new and varied meters, which added dynamism to early Methodist

---

38   Wilson-Dickson, *The Story*, 62.
39   Ibid., 66.
40   James F. White, *A Brief History of Christian Worship* (Nashville: Abingdon Press, 1993), 105.
41   Wilson-Dickson, *The Story*, 135.
42   White, *A Brief History*, 136.
43   Wilson-Dickson, *The Story*, 111.

singing. John Tyson estimates that there are still four hundred of Charles Wesley's hymns in use in contemporary hymnals, a remarkable record indeed in worship history.[44]

Meanwhile in Germany, Johann Sebastian Bach was writing his masterful church music, while his contemporary, George Frederic Handel, composed elaborate oratorios, including the *Messiah*. Some music historians consider Bach's *Mass in B Minor* and Handel's *Messiah* to be the greatest church music compositions of all time within the Western stream of the Christian story.

REVIVAL MEETINGS, THE CHARISMATIC MOVEMENT, AND VATICAN II

In the nineteenth century various denominations sprang up, and as they grew, songbooks also appeared as aids to preserve the denominational emphases. Typical of the denominational growth was the expansion of the Salvation Army, whose members provided loud, vigorous instrumental music both inside and outside the walls of their gatherings. Within a few decades the Army had became a worldwide movement. Revival movements sprang up in America with preachers like Dwight L. Moody and emotive singing that drew large crowds. In England, Bonar, Havergal, Montgomery, and others released a huge number of hymns. In America, Fanny Crosby dominated a hymn explosion with an output of lyrics that numbered in the thousands.

Early in the twentieth century the charismatic movement burst into existence, impacting North America, then South America, Africa, and Asia. Songs of first-person experience and fresh encounters with God propelled the new movement. By mid-century the Catholic Church realized that another global council was needed, and eventually the Vatican II reforms brought monumental changes, paving the way for cultural, linguistic, and liturgical adjustments across the Roman Catholic world. In many places this included the release of vernacular settings of masses and the Psalms.[45] Not long afterward the Jesus Movement burst onto the scene with a flood of new, vibrant songs, driven by the pulsating folk and rock rhythms of the time. This movement preceded yet another wave of new denominational and interdenominational hymnals and songbooks that further propelled movements of worship through song, including Scripture-based choruses and praise chorus genres.

SINGING WITH THE GLOBAL CHURCH

The 2010 edition of *Operation World* states: "Though small in number, all but concealed . . . there are now Christians living and fellowshiping in every country on earth."[46] In the various streams of church life, music continues to have a central role. Christian recordings have been released in almost every urban area of the world. Print and recorded music in North America has grown into a huge publishing industry, releasing a plethora of musical materials. But not everyone has ap-

44   John R. Tyson, *Assist Me to Proclaim: The Life and Hymns of Charles Wesley* (Grand Rapids: Eerdmans, 2007), viii.

45   Various authors speak of the three-thousand-year influence of the Psalms as a continuous resource for worship in Judeo-Christian history. Psalms were influential in building bridges to other religions as well. In parts of Islamic Africa, psalm settings have been used to introduce truths about the God of the Bible.

46   Jason Mandryk, *Operation World: The Definitive Prayer Guide to Every Nation*, 7th ed. (Colorado Springs, Biblica, 2010), 4–5.

plauded this musical growth. James White published "A Protestant Worship Manifesto," decrying the entertaining and bland quality of music in many Protestant churches.[47]

Despite White's rather stinging polemic, signs of maturity have surfaced in many parts of the global Christian family. A new wave of musicians from the United Kingdom has enriched the church with theologically sound hymns and choruses. In China, Xiao Min, a peasant woman has composed over 1,500 songs. Often referred to as "the Canaan Hymns," these folk songs have moved rapidly throughout the nation of China and across the Chinese Diaspora. [48] Christians can rejoice that Jesus truly has been building his church, a glorious church, comprised of a great multitude praising him in endless song.

Flowing like a subterranean stream throughout the church's worship history is the testimony of how God's people sang their way through trial and persecution. Stories abound across the continents. One recent example that I have personally witnessed comes from North Africa. Centuries ago Carthage, now modern Tunis, boasted a vibrant Christian community. Tunisia is now a severely restricted nation that hinders Christian activity. According to *Operation World,* only Turkey surpasses Tunisia as the nation with the smallest percentage of evangelical believers.[49] Into the midst of this challenging context, God was pleased to send a young music missionary named Irma (not her real name) from Sweden to work and stir up a small movement that rode on the wings of song.

> In the various streams of church life, music continues to have a central role.

In the mid-1980s Irma auditioned and was accepted to play cello in the Tunis Symphony Orchestra. Irma was the symphony's only Westerner at the time. Eventually she joined an ethnic music group, studied the local lute (*ud*), and learned to play microtonal Arabic scales, while mastering the Arabic language. At the time, no songs or hymns in Tunisian Arabic were available to the few believers. All Arabic songs were imported from Egypt or elsewhere. So Irma encouraged a young pastor who had an interest in poetry to write lyrics in Tunisian Arabic. Not finding any Tunisian Christian composer in the country, Irma composed the first compilation of authentic tunes for the newly written Tunisian lyrics.

When I met Irma, I asked if any plans were underway to record and distribute the songs to the few underground house fellowships scattered throughout the nation. Irma shared that there were no known Christian recording facilities in the country and that it was dangerous to go to a commercial studio. She sent me a demo tape that led to my visiting Tunisia with a team of four musicians and recording engineers. There we recorded what may have been the very first Christian worship CD in modern Tunisian history. We also set up a professional recording studio for ongoing recordings. Within a year, Irma and the pastor completed a second album's worth of songs, and a second team went to record them.

Tracking the results of those recordings and how they impacted scattered believers in Tunisia and beyond became a fascinating graduate research project. Resident missionaries worked with local believers to begin careful distribution of the recordings. A few thousand copies circulated throughout Tunisia, then secretly entered Algeria and Morocco, and eventually spread to Chris-

---

47   James F. White, "A Protestant Worship Manifesto," *Religion Online*, http://www.religion-online.org/showarticle. asp?title=1278.

48   See David Aikman, *Jesus in Beijing: How Christianity is Transforming China and Changing the Global Balance of Power* (Washington, DC: Regnery Publishing, 2003), 108–12. See also chapter 15 in this *Handbook* by Irene Ai-Ling Sun, "The Canaan Hymns: Songs of the House-church Christians in China."

49   Mandryk, *Operation World*, 962.

tian Arabic communities in Southern Europe. News was soon reported that house churches were learning and singing the songs.

Copies of notated music were compiled into songbook collections and aided the memorization of the songs. CDs were carefully distributed among women so they could listen to the recordings in the safety of their homes while their husbands were at work. The worship songs had an evangelistic thrust, since they expressed the joy of knowing Jesus as Lord and Savior. The recordings were sent to missionary radio stations and became part of broadcasts diffused back into Tunisia. Copies reached remote areas where isolated families of believers were unable to participate in house-church fellowships. Eventually the songs made their way to Arabic websites for broadcasting and downloading. In one report Irma mentioned that the songs had a way of uniting scattered believers, since they knew that they were singing the same worship songs as other fellow Christians throughout the region.

> God was pleased to send a musician from Sweden as a catalyst for the birth of indigenous worship.

The new recording studio enabled five agencies to release more indigenous worship recordings and audio materials. Musicians wrote new songs in hopes of getting them recorded. Christian workers rejoiced in how the new worship songs inspired an interest to learn about biblical worship, resulting in worship seminars. God was pleased to send a musician from Sweden as a catalyst for the birth of indigenous worship at a time when no Christian Tunisian composers existed in the nation. Though still a small part of the great multitude, one day Tunisian believers will add their voices to the singing that surrounds the throne.

PEERING INTO THE FUTURE

It seems likely that the global church will face increasing persecution as resistance to the gospel message grows in many quarters of our world. But it is also certain that God will continue to strengthen his people through song in the present as he did in the past. From David and the psalmists who sang through moments of trauma, to Paul and Silas singing at midnight following severe beatings, to the present-day North Koreans singing about their love for Jesus as their executioners mow them down, the church marches on with song.

Worship songs revive hope; rehearse God's greatness, love, grace, and mercy; celebrate the Redeemer and the work of salvation completed at the Cross; and anticipate the anthems of eternity that will praise the Lamb. Through song, the church on earth joins all redeemed humanity from every nation, tribe, and tongue, declaring the praises of "him who sits on the throne" (Rev 5:13).

8. GLOBAL SHIFT FROM NORTH TO SOUTH: IMPLICATIONS FOR LATIN AMERICAN WORSHIP
By David D. Ruiz

Worship has always been vital to the people of God. From the earliest Scriptures, worship and adoration are shown to be a central part of life in relationship with God. The first eight chapters of Leviticus describe sacrifices that are to be holy acts of adoration, specifying the ways in which these public sacrifices must be presented. But in chapter 10, an unexpected and terrible event is recorded: fire came from the altar and consumed Nadab and Abihu, Aaron's sons, who were anointed as priests. This reminds the Hebrew people that God looks beyond the horns of the altar to see the hearts of those who present the sacrifices.

Later, in the New Testament, Jesus defines worship by contrasting the nature of true worship with worshipers such as the Samaritan woman in John 4:21–24. He reveals that true adoration depends not on ethnic or national proximity, but on spiritual proximity. No longer is only one place acceptable for worship; now all places are acceptable. Worship is accepted by God not because of what we are offering or where we present the offering, but because our hearts adore him. Emilio Antonio Nuñez writes, "Praise and offering—or sacrifice—are a very important part of worship, but the culminating act, if we may so call it, is when the worshiper falls on his knees before Yahweh the King."[50]

THE COLONIAL HERITAGE

The Christian church is growing in the Global South. During the second half of the twentieth century, and continuing on into the twenty-first century, we have witnessed a southward shift within the Christian family. As Todd Johnson states it:

> Over the past 100 years Christianity has experienced a profound shift in its ethnical and linguistic composition. In 1910 over 80 percent of all Christians lived in Europe

---

50   Emilio Antonio Nuñez, *Hacia Una Misionología Evangélica Latinoamericana* (Miami: COMIBAM, 1997), 295: "La alabanza y la ofrenda (o sacrificio) son parte importantísima de la adoración, pero el acto culminante, si podemos así llamarle, es cuando el adorador cae de rodillas ante Yahvé el Rey."

and North America. By 2010 this has fallen to less than 40 percent, with the majority of Christians located in Africa, Asia, and Latin America.[51]

This paradigm shift has enormous consequences for the shape of Christianity, influencing particularly the ways in which worship is expressed. Christianity in Latin America has affected and transformed the social fabric of the continent. J. Andrew Kirk describes the first introduction of Christianity in our lands as "largely a disaster." He writes:

> Tragically, the Spanish and Portuguese *conquistadores* used religion as a weapon to control the subjugated people . . . For nearly 500 years the indigenous peoples were not allowed to bring any of their traditions into relation with the gospel.[52]

Of Protestant missions, he writes that those missionaries

> believed that the task of evangelism was to rescue the people from the darkness of their superstition . . . The challenge was to educate the people in the *Anglo-American traditions of freedom, democracy, work as vocation and sound economic practices.*[53]

At that time, worship in Latin America was a carbon copy of worship in the sending churches of the North; the instruments, the songbooks, and the way of singing were transplanted to our territories.

THE BEGINNING OF WORSHIP RENEWAL

In the beginning of the last century a renewal began in the Latin American church, involving not only theology but also worship in the church. Pentecostalism was described by Miguez Bonino in these poetic words: "The seed . . . was planted in Latin American soil, it was nourished by the vital juice of this land and the new popular masses verified that the new flavor corresponded to the demands of its palate."[54]

For the first time, many entered into an experience of Christianity that touched all aspects of life.[55] Christianity became for them the counterculture that shaped the way they were living, their relationships, and their understanding of the future; all those changes naturally resulted in contextualized worship. Federico Pagura captured this reality in his famous hymn "*Tenemos Esperanza*," written as a *tango*. This song expressed the engagement of the Christian church in Latin America with the social realities of the continent that precipitated the emerging of *misión integral* ("holistic mission"), one of the most important contributions of Latin America to the global church.

---

51   Todd M. Johnson and Kenneth R. Ross, eds., *Atlas of Global Christianity 1910–2010* (Edinburgh: Edinburgh University Press, 2009), 6.

52   J. Andrew Kirk, *Mission under Scrutiny* (Minneapolis: Fortress Press, 2006), 164.

53   Ibid., 166.

54   José Míguez Bonino, *Rostros del Protestantismo Latinoamericano* (Buenos Aires: Nueva Creación, 1995), 60: "La semilla. . . fue planteada en la tierra latinoamericana, se alimentó de los jugos vitales de esta tierra y las nuevas masas populares latinoamericana comprobaron que el sabor de los frutos correspondía a las demanadas de su paladar."

55   Philip Jenkins, *The New Faces of Christianity: Believing the Bible in the Global South* (New York: Oxford University Press, 2006), 180.

The effects of the emergence of a more contextualized worship were seen not only in its tunes but also in the instruments. In some churches, guitars replaced pianos but, in most churches, clapping hands were the only instruments available. The historical hymns with four stanzas and a chorus were replaced by *coritos* of one or two verses with strong rhythm accompanied by clapping of hands. Heavy songbooks with lyrics and musical scores were replaced by carbon-copy song sheets distributed at the outset of the worship service. The worship style took on a rich fullness that benefited all the believers.

PENTECOSTALS, EVANGELISTIC CAMPAIGNS, AND WORSHIP CONCERTS

Starting with the Pentecostal churches and moving to the more traditional denominations, the process that led to a new encounter with the word was moving the heart of the church in a dynamic direction. This process transported them to worship that called people to contrition, repentance, and confession of their sins. It started a transformation in the lives of the believers who, with their testimony and courageous evangelism, invited the lost to come to Christ by the thousands.

In the early 1960s, the emergence of evangelistic campaigns was a result of the evangelistic fervor of the church on our continent. Famous evangelists came to our lands and others emerged from the church, driving an evangelistic movement across the continent. This commitment was expressed in worship through songs like *"America Será para Cristo"*[56] that started movements, a battle cry that ignites the evangelistic passion of evangelicals in Latin America. Worship and singers were an important part of the evangelistic campaign—they led the process of transformation, from the traditional larger choirs to individual, but famous, performers who were, in some cases, the main attractive element.

> Sadly, in more recent times, the emergence of megachurches and the use of mass media, iPods, and iTunes are popularizing imported music, shaping the worship expression of the church.

When this process began to decline, the next step in the development of worship in Latin America emerged: the worship concert. Famous Latin American singers—great performers, but also prolific composers like Marcos Witt and Jesus Adrian Romero—started a worship movement in Latin America. This movement launched worship as the top expression of evangelical Christianity. It transformed and unified the forms of worship in the church, as well as providing the platform for the production of thousands of contextualized songs that expressed the reality of the Latin American church.

A WORD OF CAUTION

Sadly, in more recent times, the emergence of megachurches and the use of mass media, iPods, and iTunes are popularizing imported music from famous singers and groups from the North, which are, again, shaping the worship expression of the church. Deep reflection is needed to affirm our identity and to continue expressing through worship the discovery of our relationship with God that is taking place in Latin America.

---

56   By Alfredo Colom M. Guatemala (1904–71).

9. THE WHOLE WORLD HAS GONE "GLOCAL"

By Jaewoo Kim

GLOBALIZATION TO GLOCALIZATION

Over the past few decades, contemporary worship music from the West has been widely distributed and popularized in the non-Western world through the influence of mass media. Some of the top CCLI[57] songs have become familiar in non-Western churches around the world.

Singing worship songs from other parts of the world often brings spiritual benefits and a sense of unity with believers from those places. But when it does not happen mutually and on a complementary basis, dominant cultures may unintentionally communicate that one form of musical worship is superior to others. In a globalized world, churches with centralized power, capital, and mass media become major contributors to world worship while the rest become recipients.

But here is the good news: the world is now becoming more *glocalized*. No, that is not a misspelled word! The word *glocalization* refers to seamless integration between "local" and "global" matters.[58] In the present world, nothing is purely local or purely global. This increasing glocalization has resulted mainly from the effects of developments in communication and transportation on demographics and social media. In a glocalized world, Christian worship is becoming more decentralized and diverse than ever before.

BIBLICAL APPROACH FOR EMBRACING GLOCAL WORSHIP

Glocal worship lines up well with biblical worship. During the time of tabernacle and temple worship in the Old Testament, the place and form of worship were fixed by the Law. Everyone had to come to the same location and follow a prescribed sacrificial system.

But worship became radically decentralized in the New Testament. Jesus declared to the Samaritan woman:

---

57   Christian Copyright Licensing International.

58   Bob Roberts Jr., *Glocalization: How Followers of Jesus Engage a Flat World* (Grand Rapids: Zondervan, 2007), 14.

Woman, believe me, the hour is coming when neither on this mountain nor in Jerusalem will you worship the Father. You worship what you do not know; we worship what we know, for salvation is from the Jews. But the hour is coming, and is now here, when the true worshipers will worship the Father in spirit and truth, for the Father is seeking such people to worship him. God is spirit, and those who worship him must worship in spirit and truth. (John 4:21–24 ESV)

For the global churches that exist during the time between Christ's ascension and his return, Christ himself replaces the physical temple, and true worship happens anywhere and anytime his people gather to worship the Triune God in spirit and truth.

Glocal worship in the glocal world reveals the missional nature of God.[59] Until the day when the people of every tribe, nation, and tongue come to know Christ, our worship will fuel the work of missions. Wholehearted worship by the whole world is the goal of missions. Biblical worship in heaven will be like a global feast with a potluck dinner where every people group contributes its national dish and shares it with everyone.

> Wholehearted worship by the whole world is the goal of missions.

PRACTICAL IDEAS FOR DESIGNING GLOCAL WORSHIP

Times are increasingly challenging for churches, as more neighborhoods become global communities. Due to glocalization, Christian congregations throughout the world are more likely to embrace diverse cultures and people groups as part of their fellowships.

Some churches may react to the changes of glocalization as a threat. These churches will try to isolate themselves in order to preserve their ethnic and cultural identity. Others will welcome diverse groups of people into their church fellowships but only to grow in number with no expectation of sharing leadership roles. Other churches, however, will see glocalization as a God-given opportunity to advance the work of mission and will gladly share their leadership roles.

How can a congregation experience the missional nature of God in a typical church service? Glocal worship can be designed by a collaborative team of pastors, artists, musicians, and missionaries, using resources provided by specialists in ethnic worship arts.[60] There are many ways that congregations can use to encourage glocal worship:

- They can pray for the nations using updates on world news.
- They can pray for missionaries, national church leaders, and persecuted churches.
- They can learn and sing global worship songs.
- They can play video clips from missionaries and churches from other parts of the world in the church service. This creates the sense that your local congregation is part of the

59   "Throughout history, God has always been a sender. After all, he sent us His Son, who in turn sends us." Ed Stetzer, *Sent: Living the Missional Nature of the Church* (Nashville: LifeWay, 2008), 19.

60   For resources and suggestions, see International Council of Ethnodoxologists (http://www.worldofworship.org), Heart Sounds International (http://www.youtube.com/user/HSIOM), and Global Christian Worship (http://globalworship.tumblr.com).

larger Body. Video clips are often more effective, lively, and powerful than exchanging prayer and praise reports in text format.

It is true that congregations will not always feel comfortable when we bring worldwide music and practices into the worship services. However, many are open to such innovations when they are introduced gradually and when the purpose for them is stated clearly and often. The congregation also needs to have confidence that no syncretism is involved. It is not always easy to draw a clear line between contextualization and syncretism. In such cases, the planning team can consult with missiology experts and Christian leaders from various cultures who can help them practice "critical contextualization."

Glocalization has opened up many new possibilities, especially in the area of communications. In this glocal era the phrase "I think, therefore I am" can be replaced by "I connect, therefore I am." In a glocal world people can be connected without being in the same geographical location. Prayers, songs, and the use of media are only a few suggestions; there are many other creative approaches for worldwide Christian communities to use, according to their resources and context.

Jesus often intentionally crossed racial and social boundaries in order to meet and interact with people. Churches need to cross the same boundaries in order to share the gospel of the kingdom with everyone. If we persistently seek ways to interact with people from different racial, social, and cultural backgrounds, creative ideas will surface and flourish.

Glocal worship involves musical incarnation of the gospel in the musical styles of various people groups, both those near to us and those far away. It is a reciprocal sharing of the creative resources God has planted in various cultures. It is an invitation to enriching fellowship, and to singing and rejoicing with our brothers and sisters in Christ's far-flung Body.

CELEBRATING THE DECENTRALIZED PRESENCE OF JESUS IN DIVERSE CULTURES

Congregations that experience glocal worship on a regular basis will grow naturally and continuously in their understanding of the missional character of God. They will be learning about it throughout the year, not just at sporadic mission events. This understanding becomes a deeply embedded part of their identity and values, and naturally results in a dynamic move toward missions.

> Glocal worship involves musical incarnation of the gospel in the musical styles of various people groups, both those near to us and those far away.

Glocal worship is not merely a method to mobilize more people into missions but a direction of worship that reflects both the current era and the vision of a missional God. The goal of designing glocal worship is to help local congregations see the inseparable connection between Psalm 96:3; Matthew 24:14; and Revelation 7:9.

Through glocal worship, people will be able to celebrate the decentralized presence of Jesus in diverse cultures. Unity in diversity brings greater glory to God. When Christ is recognized and celebrated by worldwide communities, people will recognize that Christ is not a God who favors a specific region or culture but a global Savior and the Lord of all.[61]

---

61   Bob Sjogren, *Unveiled at Last* (Seattle: YWAM Publishing, 1988), 19.

MISSIOLOGICAL

10. ETHNOARTISTIC COCREATION IN THE KINGDOM OF GOD

By Brian Schrag

To act is to reveal what you believe to be good. Soon after I joined the *Ethnodoxology Handbook* and *Creating Local Arts Together* project, I realized that our team did not have a clear, common vocabulary for the good to which we hoped artistic action would lead. From our varied ecclesial, educational, and geographical histories, each of us brought different terminologies, which led us to a hodgepodge of goal categories, such as development, justice, worship, church planting, and evangelism. Such confusing variety gave birth to an urgent need for clarity.

My personal response was to immerse myself in a reflection on the kingdom of God—a reality that predates any church and by which Jesus defined his ministry. I explored the Bible (especially the Gospels), read theological literature,[62] dialogued with people who know different things than I do, and scoured hymns. I began to critique my prayers, interactions with my wife and coworkers, physical activities, daily ablutions—and in everything I did or thought, I asked, "How does this suppress or encourage expansion of the kingdom of God?" This process profoundly affected my soul and eventually led to the present organization of *Creating Local Arts Together*, the companion manual to this *Handbook*.

In this chapter, I explore how Christians who immerse themselves in the frustratingly incomplete, yet holistic and teleological nature of the kingdom of God can confidently join a community's artists in working toward a better future. Although I do not believe that the church and the kingdom of God are identical,[63] the church is the primary group of people through whom God embodies and proclaims his kingdom. In cross-cultural contexts, this foundation can guide the church's development of a vision, its stance toward a community's arts, its members' choice of friends, and its commitment to artists' spiritual formation.

---

62   Including, for example, Rick Brown, "A Brief History of Interpretations of 'The Kingdom of God' and Some Consequences for Translation," *Notes on Translation* 15, no. 1 (2001): 3–23; George Eldon Ladd, *A Theology of the New Testament* (Grand Rapids: Eerdmans, 1993); and *U.S. Catholic Church: Catechism of the Catholic Church*, 2nd ed. (New York: Doubleday Religion, 2003).

63   Cf. Ladd, *A Theology*, 103–17.

OUR VISION: THE KINGDOM OF GOD ON EARTH AND IN HEAVEN

Now and Not Yet. A common theological trope states that the kingdom of God exists both now and not yet. Many references surrounding Jesus' earthly ministry place the kingdom and Jesus as contemporaneous: "Jesus went throughout Galilee, teaching in their synagogues, proclaiming the good news of the kingdom, and healing every disease and sickness among the people (Matt 4:23); Heal the sick who are there and tell them, 'The kingdom of God has come near to you' (Luke 10:9); "The kingdom of heaven is like . . ." (Matt 13:24,31,33); "Blessed are you who are poor, for yours is the kingdom of God" (Luke 6:20).

But Jesus also spoke of the kingdom as having a future reality, referring to his reign, eternal life, salvation, and the final future judgment interchangeably. His conversations with the rich young ruler (Matt 19), the parable of the tares (Matt 13), and the story of the sheep and goats (Matt 25) all mention the kingdom in relation to future events.

So we can look at the kingdom of God as both an incomplete present reality and a future completed reality. Now and not yet. "Thy kingdom come, thy will be done in earth, as it is in heaven" (Matt 6:10 KJV). God's kingdom is complete now, just not on earth in its current form.[64]

All Encompassing. What does the kingdom look like? Jesus described it as centered on himself and his message (Mark 1:15; John 3:1–21). The kingdom grows mysteriously but to great size (Mark 4) and is marked by values contrary to human social systems (Mark 10; 12; Luke 6). It is realized by healing and spiritual warfare (Luke 9; 11). There is no death, crying, pain, or disharmony (Isa 11:6,7; Rev 21:4). There is unfiltered joy in and worship of God (1 Cor 13:12; Rev 7). Though it does not take a fixed social shape, it influences politics, laws, and morals, giving special preference to people on the margins, like the poor (Luke 6:20–26; Jas 2:5). The kingdom of God on earth mysteriously but concretely reflects every physical, emotional, social, intellectual, moral, and spiritual aspect of life in heaven.

Working toward a Goal. The kingdom of God is not a static reality, but something that God is nurturing and growing, in part through our actions. Scripture enjoins us to look for and value it above everything else (Matt 6:33; 13:44,45), to pray for it to expand on earth (Matt 6:10), to proclaim and bring it (Luke 10), and to fight spiritual battles for it (Matt 12:28). Our work as God's subjects is to do things with God that will result in his kingdom becoming more visible and extensive on earth, working toward its complete realization in heaven.

> The kingdom of God on earth mysteriously but concretely reflects every physical, emotional, social, intellectual, moral, and spiritual aspect of life in heaven.

Every Christian's role then is to fix what is broken and strengthen what already looks like the kingdom. We act to change contexts where Jesus is unknown, where there are no accessible Bibles, and where there is disease, human trafficking, and death. We also act to fortify contexts where there are signs of God's creative genius, where there is peace, beauty, health, and deep communion with God. We listen to God and garner every spiritual, intellectual, and physical resource we have to make things more like heaven, where Jesus is king and everybody knows it. In short, we act to increase the evidence of God on earth. The accompanying manual

---

64   Various writings by C. S. Lewis, Randy Alcorn, and Charles Spurgeon provide intriguing views on the relationship between earthly and heavenly kingdoms. Charles Spurgeon, *We Shall See God*, ed. Randy Alcorn (Carol Stream: Tyndale House, 2011) has been especially helpful to me.

to this volume, *Creating Local Arts Together*, describes this goal in terms of signs in the categories of culture, shalom, justice, Scripture, church life, and personal spiritual life.

OUR STANCE: THREE APPROACHES TO CREATIVITY

The arts—broadly defined here as any heightened form of communication—have characteristics that make them crucial for the kind of kingdom work we are talking about.[65] Artistic communication is embedded in culture and so touches many important aspects of a society:

- It marks messages as important and separate from everyday activities.
- It involves not only cognitive, but also experiential and emotional ways of knowing.
- It aids memory of messages.
- It increases the impact of messages through multiple media that often involve the whole body.
- It concentrates the information contained in messages.
- It instills solidarity in its performers.
- It provides socially acceptable frameworks for expressing difficult or new ideas.
- It inspires and moves people to action and can act as a strong sign of identity.
- Perhaps most importantly, artistic communication is generally created and owned locally. There is no need to translate foreign materials, and local artists are empowered to contribute to the expansion of the kingdom of God.

Throughout history, as Christians have recognized the impact that these characteristics of artistic communication produce, they have incorporated the arts into their lives. They have performed laments in response to trauma and danced in solidarity with those who are suffering. They have drawn and acted and told stories because they felt satisfaction in using their talents to the fullest. They have erupted into dance and song because they have come to know and experience God.

In the cross-cultural expansion of the kingdom, messengers of the good news have engaged in three broad roles in relationship to the arts:

- **"Bring It—Teach It."** First, some cross-cultural workers approach the arts in the "Bring It—Teach It" framework, in which they teach their own arts to people in another community. This has been a common practice throughout the history of the church. This approach can lead to unity among diverse Christian communities, but it excludes local arts and artists.
- **"Build New Bridges."** In a second framework, "Build New Bridges," artists from one community find ways to connect artistically with members of another community. This approach results in collaborative artistic efforts, often in response to traumatic events.
- **"Find It—Encourage It."** Third, arts advocates who take a "Find It—Encourage It" stance learn to know local artists and their arts in ways that spur these artists to create in the forms they know best. The advocate enters local creative processes, helping give

---

65   For more on the three approaches, see Brian Schrag's chapter in this *Handbook*, "Determining Your Role As an Arts Advocate and Facilitator," chpt. 118.

birth to new creations that flow organically from the community. This approach usually requires longer-term relationships with people, and above all, a commitment to learn.

Though none of these three categories is untainted by creation's groaning, we wrote the *Creating Local Arts Together* manual for people working primarily in the third approach. We did this for two reasons. First, we see Jesus as our primary missionary model. As king of the kingdom, he left his heavenly culture to become a human zygote, learning to walk, talk, sing, relieve, and dress himself in a minority society before entering his full ministry (Phil 2). Whenever possible, we should learn first. Second, we believe this approach is being neglected, with often tragic consequences.

OUR FRIENDS: CHOOSING ARTISTIC PARTNERS

Who will you choose to befriend? This is one of the fundamental questions for cross-cultural workers focusing on the arts, even if they decide to work primarily in the "Find It—Encourage It" mode. Monocultural societies exist in fewer and fewer numbers—if, in fact, they ever really did. Instead, most societies comprise *mélanges* of people with artists who practice local, regional, national, and international art forms. Which artists will you seek out and get to know? Will you concentrate on artists primarily skilled and interested in connecting with wider, multicultural audiences (e.g., using popular dance or music with national symbolism)? Or will you choose artists who focus primarily on communicating with their local community (e.g., sparking creativity in arts that have longer histories within the community)? I'll use these two simplified categories to provide some guidelines for working primarily toward multicultural goals, and then toward more local goals.

The discussions will help cross-cultural workers be deliberate in their choices of artistic partners: What are the partners' names? Who does their artistry connect with? Which artists and communities are being left out by choosing these? How can one encourage an artistic way forward that flows from deep connections with the past?

THE 1–2–3s OF ENCOURAGING MULTICULTURAL ARTISTRY

There are strong reasons to engage with people skilled in arts with regional and global reach: artistic repertoires and rituals in geographically and culturally diverse contexts (e.g., multicultural churches) engender invaluable bonds of unity. Such fusions of arts from different cultures are wonderful to experience and often result in new traditions. Here are three principles to help a multicultural community grow towards its kingdom goals:

1. Make sure you are hearing every voice. In a community like a church, it's easy for religious tradition and the strength of majority subgroups to diminish the voices of smaller groups. Survey the community and discover who has strong gifts and connections with every artistic tradition represented.
2. Design communal activities with kingdom characteristics. Not every event should include every art, but the warp and woof of the community's life should represent everyone. Meetings should be marked by peaceful freedom, challenge, and exuberance,

where everyone is building each other up. Together you will create a new community culture with creativity that connects near and far. Gatherings need not consist mostly of artistic lowest common denominators, but should celebrate the most penetrating expressions of everyone's arts for kingdom goals that you have identified.

3. Converse really well and often. A benefit of relying on long tradition for meetings like church services is that everyone knows what's going to happen. Creating a new culture that emerges from the people who happen to constitute the community at a point in time is very difficult. So plan regular times to pray and reflect together on the artistic life of the community, and expect to change things over time.

THE ABCS OF ENCOURAGING NEW HERITAGE ARTISTRY

During a songwriting workshop I led in Cameroon in 2005, I asked the six city-raised participants how many knew one of their traditional music styles well enough to compose in it. The number: zero. If losses continue at current levels, 50 percent of plant species and perhaps 90 percent of the world's approximately 6,900 languages will disappear by the end of the twenty-first century.[66] I'm not aware of parallel counts of artistic forms of communication like storytelling, singing, dancing, and carving. However, my experiences with composers like those above and many other

> Meetings should be marked by peaceful freedom, challenge, and exuberance, where everyone is building each other up.

stories I hear show that spoken and performed forms of communication are affected by many of the same social trends. The picture is grim: young people in ethnolinguistic communities are often not learning to sing their parents' songs, and the unique, God-marked systems that produce them are fading at a precipitous rate.

Forces arrayed against local art forms are formidable:

- urbanization that weakens ties between language speakers and their home cultures;
- globalized communication media that relegate local art forms to one choice among millions;
- media industries that relentlessly press their favored art forms into new markets;
- churches with long traditions of using foreign arts that create an unwelcoming environment for artists from their local communities;
- and short- and long-term Christian missionaries that promote the Euro-American "praise and worship" church music tradition all over the world.

Jesus consistently taught that his kingdom has a special place for the young, poor, humble, socially inferior people living in constant awareness of the "not yet." Many minority cultures are in this "least of these" category. Because artistic tradition is being lost at such a high rate of speed and there are so few trends supporting local artists, I here propose stark, unconventional guidelines for cross-cultural workers.

---

66   M. Krauss, "The World's Languages in Crisis," *Language* 68, no.1 (1992): 4–10; E. O. Wilson, *The Future of Life* (New York: Knopf, 2002).

In the late 1980s, Uganda's government responded to growing rates of HIV/AIDS with the effective and controversial ABC program. To avoid contracting AIDS, educators counseled Ugandans to **A**bstain from sex outside of marriage, **B**e faithful to their partners, and use **C**ondoms if necessary.

I believe we could propose an ABC approach to encouraging the kingdom's artistic forms of communication, and in so doing, attempt to convince as many people as possible to practice one or more of the principles. These principles aim particularly at preserving and encouraging artistic traditions that are part of the heritage of an ethnolinguistic community. These "heritage artistic traditions" are art forms that have been around longer, are more localized geographically, and with which the people identify more closely than with other traditions. Internalizing the ABC approach can be an important guideline for us as we move ahead in encouraging these heritage traditions:

> These are not merely ideas or systems, but human beings whose artistic voices are being silenced.

Abstain from promoting nonheritage traditions. Affirm and learn to enjoy all kinds of artistic performance, but graciously deflect invitations and activities that promote nonheritage traditions.

Be faithful to heritage traditions. Consistently communicate to all stakeholders your intention to invest in heritage artistic traditions, and intentionally plan cocreation activities with their artists.

Cocreate with contemporary performance traditions only when necessary. When a situation requires you to interact with popular, urban performance genres, do it with gusto, but then get back to your primary work with traditional artists.

Choosing which artistic traditions to encourage in complex social situations is not easy, so I have a few rules of thumb I follow. In short, I favor advocating for artists involved in traditions that are more

- rural, rather than urban
- old, rather than new
- geographically concentrated, rather than diffuse
- tied to ethnolinguistic identity, rather than to individual, regional, national, or global identities
- ripe for church use, rather than requiring force to "pick from the tree"
- fragile, rather than robust

I am not devaluing new, urban, or national art forms—these too reflect God's creativity. But I am trying to promote arts and artists with few champions. These are not merely ideas or systems, but human beings whose artistic voices are being silenced. Here are the names of a few such artists who are currently involved in redeeming their at-risk artistic traditions for God's kingdom:

- Punayima Kanyama (*kundi*-accompanied songs, Mono language, Democratic Republic of Congo)
- Ferdinand Doumtsop (dances and songs, Ngiemboon language, Cameroon)

Punayima in the late 1980s

- DeLaura Saunders (dance songs, Choctaw language, United States)
- Aidyn Kurmanov (epic song poems, Altai language, Central Asia)[67]
- Maria Kononova (poetry and song texts, Sakha language, Siberia)[68]
- Patrick Mang'esoy (*bukantiit*-accompanied songs, Sabaot language, Kenya)

These people are deepening their communities' worship of God and providing Scripture-inspired solutions to moral, social, and physical crises threatening their families. And they are doing it using some of the most outrageously penetrating and memorable forms of communication on earth. We want to encourage communities to look favorably on the artistic behaviors of their parents and grandparents, amidst a raucous, terribly attractive, and often financially persuasive group of artistic choices. Let's help local artists thrive.

OUR NECESSARY RISK: INTEGRATING ARTISTS INTO THE CHURCH

Harold Best defines worship as "the continuous outpouring of all that I am, all that I do and all that I can ever become in light of a chosen or choosing god."[69] He states that

> because God is the Continuous Outpourer, we bear his image as continuous outpourers. Being made in the image of God means that we were created to act the way God acts, having been given a nature within which such behavior is natural. The difference between God and humankind, merely and mysteriously, is one of singular infinitude and unique and multiplied finitude.[70]

The contrast between God's "singular infinitude" and human beings' "unique and multiplied finitude" underscores the difference between the way God creates and how we create. God creates *ex nihilo* (from nothing). Everything he makes is simultaneously malleable and stable, never before seen and existing eternally, outrageously unsettling and enormously reassuring.

We humans, on the other hand, make things *ex creatio*. When we sing, write, preach, tell stories, dramatize, dance, draw, and sculpt, we must rely on what God and others have already supplied. Even in this derivative capacity, however, there is power. That is why artists sometimes usurp God's authority. Why? Because when they sing or act or preach with great skill and passion, mastering not only their medium but the social context in which they deliver it, they are godlike. Their message penetrates, moves, motivates, and creates new ways of thinking and acting in the people who are experiencing their performance. There is great potential to influence and therefore great danger of hubris.

The solution to this danger is not to denude gifted communicators—restricting them from singing or preaching or acting—but to require them to imitate Christ. Christ emptied himself of his God status, and took on the form of a human being, mastering the gifts of communication

---

67   See a video clip of Aidyn Kurmanov's epic poem/song on the *Handbook* DVD.

68   See a video clip of Maria Kononova's poetry sung in an epic narrative style on the *Handbook* DVD.

69   Harold M. Best, *Unceasing Worship: Biblical Perspectives on Worship and the Arts* (Downers Grove, IL: InterVarsity Press, 2003), 18.

70   Ibid., 23.

that God gave him as fully human, fully God. Capable communicators must learn submission and humility, while never renouncing the skill, discipline, and passion of their calling.

Artists are not God. But if we are committed to the expansion of God's kingdom, we dare not neglect the people whom God has gifted to communicate this word with power.

CREATING INTO ETERNITY

Our approach in *Creating Local Arts Together* is to help Christians work with a community in deciding what aspects of the kingdom of God people want to see flourish, and then to explore that community's resources for artistic genres that should help in the accomplishment of those goals in lasting ways. This is cocreation, where we join in others' creativity, helping them use their existing arts for new purposes that will continue into the future.

The end of Revelation 21 and other biblical passages suggest that elements of every culture will last into heaven. When we get to heaven, there will be nothing left to fix. All will be right. But even in the new earth and new heaven, we will act and create. Even when Satan is fully defeated, we will create. God created when there was no sin to overcome, because it is his nature, and we reflect his image. And when we get to the completed kingdom of God, we will not be static. Our ultimate normal condition will include doing, making, exploring, reveling in the satisfaction of being fully who God created us to be. In our work now, the now and not yet are mixed, intertwined. But the future we work toward, only glimpsing on earth, will be continually new, forever unchanging, and always good. Hallelujah!

INTRODUCTION

SECTION 1: FOUNDATIONS

SECTION 2: STORIES

SECTION 3: TOOLS

CLOSING

11. DESIGNING MULTICULTURAL WORSHIP WITH THE *MISSIO DEI* IN MIND

By Josh Davis

"It's not about us." We say, and even sing, this all the time in our churches. Worship is not about us. But does the way we plan, discuss, and evaluate worship affirm or contradict what we claim to believe? We declare that we want to bless God's heart, but often we evaluate our worship services by whether or not our hearts were blessed. Ephesians 5:10 exhorts us to "try to discern what is pleasing to the Lord."[71] Instead of focusing on what is pleasing to us, let us find out what pleases God. As Hosea 6:3 says, "Let us press on to know the Lord." What is on God's heart? What does he value and desire? What is the *missio Dei* (mission of God)?

> Often we evaluate our worship services by whether or not our hearts were blessed.

Van Sanders has this to say about *missio Dei*:

> When kept in the context of the Scriptures, *missio Dei* correctly emphasizes that God is the initiator of his mission to redeem through the church a special people for himself from all of the peoples of the world. He sent his Son for this purpose and he sends the church into the world with the message of the gospel for the same purpose.[72]

How can we affirm the important truth that God's heart is for all peoples of the world in the way we plan and lead corporate times of worship?

GOD'S HEART IS FOR ALL PEOPLES

Scripture reverberates from beginning to end with the reality that God's heart is for all peoples. From Genesis 12:1–3 we understand that God's blessing of Abraham was not to stop with Abraham. God blessed Abraham in order for Abraham to be a blessing. In fact, God clearly states that

---

71   Scripture quotations in this chapter are from the ESV.

72   Van Sanders, "The Mission of God and the Local Church," in *Pursuing the Mission of God in Church Planting*, ed. John M. Bailey (Alpharetta, GA: North American Mission Board, 2006), 24.

his desire is that "all the families of the earth shall be blessed." From the beginning, God had in mind a mission to bless all the peoples of the earth through his Son Jesus and through his people. Similarly, the psalmist prays in Psalm 67:1–3: "May God be gracious to us and bless us and make his face to shine upon us, that your way may be known on earth, your saving power among all nations. Let the peoples praise you, O God; let all the peoples praise you!"

It is evident that God desires the nations to worship him, and that it will in fact happen as part of the *missio Dei*. Psalm 86:8,9 says, "There is none like you among the gods, O Lord, nor are there any works like yours. All the nations you have made shall come and worship before you, O Lord, and shall glorify your name." Notice that this text—among others, like Acts 17:26—clearly states that God created the nations. How should the realization that God created the nations affect our perspectives on cultures, ethnicities, languages, and diversity? How might it affect the way our local congregations worship?

Matthew 24:14 is further evidence of God's heart for all peoples. Jesus says simply, "And this gospel of the kingdom will be proclaimed throughout the whole world as a testimony to all nations, and then the end will come." God's mission, and therefore *ours*, will not be complete until all nations have received the testimony of the gospel. If God has the people of the world on his heart, should they not be on our hearts as well?

DEVELOPING A HEART FOR ALL PEOPLES

Practically speaking, there are a number of things we can do as leaders to position ourselves and our congregations for God to share more of his heart for people with us. Here are a few suggestions:

Look

1. Increase your awareness of the various ethnicities that are a part of your church's immediate neighborhood. If you don't know specifics, be general for now (e.g., "the Asian nail salon" or "the Hispanic mini-mart") and then find out more through encounters and dialogue.
2. Make a list of all the different ethnicities represented in your church body. Include the countries represented by mission workers or national partners with whom your church has a close relationship, as well as former missionaries who have returned from the field. If you don't know specifics, be general for now (e.g., "the man who sits on the pew in the back right-hand side") and then find out more through encounters and dialogue.
3. Is there a disparity between these lists? Why? Did you find it difficult or easy to complete this research project? Why?
4. Consider introducing your congregation to art and photography that represents the diverse people of the world. Such items can be displayed on videos, PowerPoint backgrounds, bulletins, and the walls of your church buildings. Never underestimate the power of what is seen.

Read Scripture

1. Study scriptures that give insight into God's heart for the nations. In addition to those already cited in this article, here are some others to consider:

Genesis 11:1–9	Psalm 45:17	Psalm 46:10	Psalm 57:9
Psalm 96:3,4	Psalm 117	Mark 11:17	Acts 2:1–11
Ephesians 2:14–16	Revelation 21:3		

2. Include Scripture on screens or in the bulletin in different languages.
3. Have Scripture read by different people in different languages and accents. Don't underestimate the power of what is heard.

Pray

1. Pray regularly and corporately for the peoples of the world. I know one congregation that has dedicated a time during their weekly services to pray for different churches in their area and in different countries of the world.
2. Have corporate prayer led in different languages.
3. Encourage your congregation to pray "Korean style," out loud all at once, in the members' various languages.

Sing

1. Invite believers from another culture into your home for a meal. Ask them to bring some of their favorite worship music to share with you. Listen. Ask questions. What do they like about these songs? What does their music express about God? To God? How does it express these things?
2. Invite a believer from a different country (someone within your congregation already? from another local congregation? a local missionary?) to come and teach your choir or congregation a simple worship song in his or her language and cultural style. Singing a song in a different language can be an opportunity to see God as bigger than our own language, our own cultural styles, and our own preferences. Diverse leadership gives us a powerful reminder of the reality that the body of Christ is multilingual and multicultural.

> How can we affirm the important truth that God's heart is for all peoples of the world in the way we plan and lead corporate times of worship?

3. Learn and sing a bilingual worship song or create a medley of songs in different languages that blend together. Be careful not to take the "separate but equal" approach to church and worship. It is clear from Scripture (Rev 5:9,10; 7:9,10) that we will be worshiping *together* in heaven forever. It is also clear that God's desire is for his kingdom to come "on earth as it is in heaven." Singing a bilingual song—something that cannot be sung in one language or the other, but must be sung in both—or linking a new global worship song to a familiar hymn is a great way to combat the "separate but equal" mindset.

INTRODUCTION

SECTION 1: FOUNDATIONS

SECTION 2: STORIES

SECTION 3: TOOLS

CLOSING

CONCLUDING WORD OF COUNSEL

Do not be afraid of being uncomfortable. You *will be* uncomfortable as God expands your heart. But God exists and must be worshiped outside our comfort zones.[73]

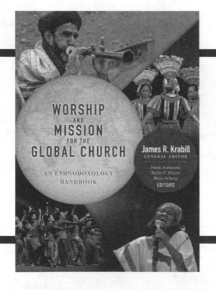

WORSHIP AND MISSION FOR THE GLOBAL CHURCH
AN ETHNODOXOLOGY HANDBOOK

James R. Krabill
GENERAL EDITOR

Frank Fortunato
Robin P. Harris
Brian Schrag
EDITORS

DON'T FORGET, THE HANDBOOK HAS ADDITIONAL RESOURCES AT THE SITE:

www.ethnodoxologyhandbook.com

---

73   For additional resources on this topic, see the *Handbook* bibliography: Roberta R. King (2006) and John Piper (2003); as well as *With One Heart*, a CD from Proskuneo Ministries featuring a collection of worship songs in a variety of languages and musical styles, including two fully bilingual songs as referenced above (available for purchase at http://proskuneo.info or on iTunes); and http://prayercast.com—a free website with short videos from different countries, including English-language prayers offered by local believers. This is very helpful for personal use, or for families, small groups, or congregations.

12. ETHNODRAMATOLOGY FOR COMMUNITY ENGAGEMENT

By Julisa Rowe

"We thought the Bible was a foreign book, but today I see the smells and sounds of my culture. Those who tell of *Bhagavata* (God) are *Bhagavatars*—storytellers of God." Those were the words of a Brahmin in Andhra Pradesh, India, after viewing a classical *kuchipudi* dance drama with a biblical message.[74] The play met with opposition from Christians but affirmation from Hindus. Prior to this, Dr. Suvisesamuthu, former director of the Christian Arts Centre in Chennai, was the first to use *bharata natyam*—the classical dance drama form of Tamil Nadu—to present the Gospel of Matthew. His attempt also met with great animosity from the church, but had wide acceptance and appeal to the general populace, resulting in many turning to Christ, including the dancers themselves. A government minister was the chief guest, and after the performance he said, "You Christians speak about God and heavenly glory somewhere, but I saw God and heavenly glory right here on stage." Dr. Suvisesamuthu's work inspired a large number of believers in India to pursue classical art forms to communicate Christ.

Kala Darshini, a Catholic arts training institute in Andhra Pradesh, has done some innovative works, including one piece on eight beatitudes of Jesus, done in eight different Indian styles of dance (*kuchipudi, bharata natyam, orissi, manipuri*, and others—one style for each beatitude). This piece was an attempt at showing to India the universality of the beatitudes. The institute also has done folk and classical pieces depicting the life and works of Jesus, such as shepherds dancing for joy at the birth of Jesus, and a *bharata natyam* on the miracles of Jesus. In the miracles piece, the dance master took the role of Jesus and other dancers took the roles of different people coming to him for healing, calming of the storm, and other miracles.

In Thailand the traditional Likay folk drama form has been used with great success for over thirty years by Christian Communications Institute (CCI), under the direction of Alan Eubanks, to tell numerous biblical stories and gospel messages. In Japan a Noh drama, "Wings of Love," was created as a dialogue between Buddhism and Christianity and as a means of beginning to bring out the message of the Cross.

---

74   The *kuchipudi* dance drama "What Is My Duty?" was created by Dr. Solomon Raj in the 1970s.

Kerala, India, has an interesting folk theater tradition called *Chavittunadakam*.[75] It is a Christian alternative to the usual folk theaters and was developed under the influence of Catholic priests and the Portuguese in the mid-sixteenth century. The scripts are from Christian European history, such as Charlemagne and the early Christian emperors. There are also saint stories and Bible stories. Although it originated as a Christian alternative to Kerala folk theater, it has become its own art form, just as traditional, and recognized by the Kerala government.

> Plays written out of the local worldview using indigenous styles are best able to resonate with contemporary audiences.

An immensely popular Christmas show in Nairobi, Kenya, was produced in 2000–2001. It was a fusion of traditional storytelling, song and dance, and modern theater. It brought together popular faces and comedy acts, such as TV game show presenters, comedy trios, DJs, radio announcers, and leading actors in a loosely woven retelling of the Christmas story, set in modern-day Dandora—a Kenyan housing estate. A jazz vocal group provided Christmas music between scenes, while a popular radio personality narrated the event and encouraged audience participation. While the acting style was along the lines of psychological realism, the mix of music, interaction, and story showed a more Kenyan structure and gave a model on which to base a contemporary fusion theater that speaks to today's urban audience. This model is called *sigana*, which

> seamlessly weaves together acting, narration, music and other expressive techniques, in the form of traditional call and response, chants, role-play, banter and communal dilemma resolution. *Sigana* performances take off from the traditional narrative form. But because it is performed in a more "contrived" environment, it also incorporates more entertaining forms like song, dance and music. These are organically woven into the shows.[76]

Active participation of the audience is encouraged, as the line between performers and audience is eradicated. This informs the "communal dilemma resolution" that is central to its teaching. Unlike traditional storytelling, *sigana* works in a multicultural setting, mixing music and movements from traditional and contemporary sources and challenging contemporary realities.

The above examples show how indigenous drama forms are being used to communicate Christ with great effect around the world. Plays written out of the local worldview using indigenous styles are best able to resonate with contemporary audiences and show them a reflection of themselves, while entertaining them at the same time.

Classical and folk theater forms are well worth considering as possibilities for incorporating the message of Christ, because their role is to affirm long-established social and religious beliefs. Development and health organizations have realized the potential that these forms have to reach the masses—particularly more rural-oriented groups—when a new message needs to be communicated. Such agencies have carried out a great deal of experimentation in this regard.

It is not a great stretch to understand how people can communicate the Christian message in folk forms that are already accepted and can be adapted for use with messages of various types. Given the lack of Christians trained in the traditional arts and the realities of economics, some

---

75   See http://www.chavittunadakam.com/.

76   Oby Obyerodhyambo, "Sigana: Re-engaging Contemporary Cultural Reality," The Swaraj Foundation, http://www.swaraj.org/shikshantar/ls3_oby.htm.

have suggested hiring a group of actors to perform Christian plays instead of giving money to a preacher. In many cases this has actually resulted in the conversion of the actors as they interact with the message of Christ.

As globalization continues in many countries, it is also important to look at developing theater styles that fuse contemporary realities with traditional, indigenous forms. Christian artists can blend the two worlds into an artistic heart language for today's urban audiences. Christian workers who truly desire to communicate Christ in a way that reaches to the heart of each culture, affecting change for the kingdom of God, should seek dramas that are indigenous to each country, whether historically indigenous or indigenous through fusion of contemporary culture and traditional cultural elements. In such indigenous drama, ideas and actions are communicated in a powerful language that is truly understood by the people.[77]

---

[77]   For additional reading, see the following resources in the *Handbook* bibliography: Byam (1999), Corbitt and Nix-Early (2003), Eubank (2004), Lapiz (2006), and Nicholls (1983).

13. SHALL WE DANCE?
REFLECTIONS ON THE *NAIROBI STATEMENT ON WORSHIP AND CULTURE*[78]

By Anne Zaki

"I need to quit my jogging class!" I said to my academic advisor on a cold winter afternoon during my first year of college. I explained that my Egyptian body had not adjusted well to Michigan's winter, and spending three hours of jogging weekly in subzero-degree weather might literally break my body, my mind, or possibly both. That's when she offered the most merciful alternative, "What about dance?"

And there it was, the genesis of my introduction to partner dances like jazz, swing, and ball-room, a wonderful hobby that I developed over the next four years of my college life—not to mention the added advantage of being practiced indoors! Partner dancing taught me to marvel at the beauty and fluency of the frame shared by the dancers, where each dancer has certain steps to perform, yet always remains conscious of a partner—now pulling together in a close embrace, now pushing away from each other, with the confidence the frame inspires.

THE DANCE OF WORSHIP AND CULTURE

Christianity, like every other religion, was born in a particular historical and cultural context, in a particular time and place. For Christianity, this context happened to be the ancient Middle East at the beginning of the first century. While the historical context of Christianity's birth is unchange-able and static, like the recorded time and place on one's birth certificate, its cultural context no longer exists. Culture by definition is dynamic and constantly changing, sometimes slowly and gradually, at other times rapidly and dramatically.

---

78   Lutheran World Federation (LWF) Department for Theology and Studies, *Nairobi Statement on Worship and Culture: Contemporary Challenges and Opportunities* (Nairobi: Lutheran World Federation Department for Theology and Studies, 1996). To view the full text, visit the Lift Up Your Hearts website at http://www.worship.ca /docs/lwf_ns.html. For Spanish and Korean translations of the *Nairobi Statement*, visit the Calvin Institute of Christian Worship website at http:// worship.calvin.edu.

Moreover, while every religion, including Christianity, has its solid, unshakable foundation, the form of a religion is flexible, based on the cultural mold in which it finds itself. From this paradoxical situation, a tension is born between preserving the orthodoxy of one's religion and trying to adapt to one's context with intelligence and versatility in order to stay relevant to contemporary cultures.

Christianity has always stood in tension with prevailing cultures, no matter where it existed. But as humans we hate tension. We are wired to resolve tension. We look for symmetry. We want a clean end to every mystery novel, an answer to every complex riddle.

But what happens when Christianity insists on maintaining its foundations *and* its original cultural forms, no matter what new culture it finds itself in? What happens when Christians see the tension as a chaotic mess, rejecting its constant demands to review one's priorities and revisit difficult questions? A crisis occurs.

A survey of various Christian traditions shows us that some churches try to resolve the tension by downplaying the differences between culture and faith. They try to blend in by matching their beliefs and practices—their entire religion, form and foundation—to those of the contemporary culture. History has proven over and over again that such faith communities lose their salty effectiveness (1 Sam 8; Matt 5) and give up their call to help reshape and reform culture (John 17). What *was* originally a dance of partners breaks down into an indistinct pair of copycats—a crisis.

Other Christian traditions have tried to resolve the tension by taking the opposite extreme, isolating themselves in opposition to the culture. This can take the passive shape of retreating to fundamentalist convictions, insisting that faith must be practiced in its original and purest forms, crediting the "good ole days" for bygone exuberance and growth. But it can also become aggressive, imposing itself on others, fighting about differences in worldview, faith, and practices—a crisis.

> What happens when Christians see the tension as a chaotic mess, rejecting its constant demands to review one's priorities and revisit difficult questions? A crisis occurs.

In their wisdom the writers of the *Nairobi Statement* foresaw the shadow of such crises hovering over the dance floor in our human tendency and temptation to resolve tension at all cost. In an attempt to navigate away from these checkmate crisis points between Christianity and culture, they produced this document to help churches view the tension as a beautiful dance to be protected, preserved, and even promoted. They have carefully designed an intricate four-step dance, where each dancer has certain steps to perform, yet always remains conscious of a partner—now pulling together, now pushing apart, ever moving, avoiding the checkmate crises.

They have chosen to focus on worship as "the heart and pulse of the Christian church,"[79] the most regular corporate event that is both expressive and formative of the beliefs and practices of a faith community.

INTRODUCTION

SECTION 1: FOUNDATIONS

SECTION 2: STORIES

SECTION 3: TOOLS

CLOSING

---

79   Lutheran World Federation, *Nairobi Statement*, section 1.1.

NAIROBI STATEMENT ON WORSHIP AND CULTURE

(www.worship.ca/docs)

"Christian worship relates dynamically
to culture in at least four ways.

First, it is **transcultural**, the same substance
for everyone everywhere, beyond culture.

Second, it is **contextual**, varying according
to the local situation (both nature and culture).

Third, it is **counter-cultural**, challenging what is
contrary to the Gospel in a given culture.

Fourth, it is **cross-cultural**, making possible
sharing between different local cultures."

> Nairobi Statement on Worship and Culture

FIRST: CHRISTIAN WORSHIP IS *TRANSCULTURAL*

Several years ago I attended a worship service in the Netherlands. Although my knowledge of the Dutch language paralleled that of a kindergartner's knowledge of Latin pharmaceutical terms, I was amazed by how much of the service I recognized. Certain elements, like the gathering of the people, the singing, the prayers, the preaching of the word, and the sharing of the bread and cup, though incomprehensible to the frontal lobe of my brain, were intimately familiar to the core of my soul. The anticipation of the mysterious was soon replaced by the comfort of the familiar, igniting in me afresh the hope that God is once again raising for himself a new generation in the European church.

Christian worship contains the same substance for everyone everywhere. In all its diverse expressions, it is beyond culture. This is true not only of the central actions mandated by Scripture, but also of the centrality of the person and work of Jesus Christ.[80]

This transcultural dimension is probably the single most important factor to the sensed unity of the worldwide church, visible and invisible, across time and space. We read the same letter to the Romans which was read long before us by Saint Augustine in Northern Africa and Luther in Western Europe. We remember and celebrate Christ's death and resurrection in the Lord's Supper, in parallel with believers in a megachurch in Korea, and in a reed-roofed hut in the Amazon, and together we all join the ongoing, never-ending hymn, "Holy, Holy, Holy."

Understanding these universal and ecumenical elements of Christian unity gives local churches the freedom to use disciplined creativity for authentic contextualization.

---

80   "The ways in which the shapes of the Sunday Eucharist and the church year are expressed vary by culture, but their meanings and fundamental structure are shared around the globe. There is one Lord, one faith, one Baptism, one Eucharist" (LWF, *Nairobi Statement*, section 2.2).

SECOND: CHRISTIAN WORSHIP IS *CONTEXTUAL*

As we walked around his home island of Sulawesi, my Indonesian friend remarked, "You've never seen anything like this." And he was right. I'd never seen architecture so unique and magnificent. The traditional homes of this particular people group are built on stilts of heavy logs, with open space under the house for animals and kitchen waste, an enclosed upper level where people live, and covering the whole structure is a saddle-shaped roof that rises at both ends like the fore and aft of a giant ship. The houses were covered with exquisitely carved wood panels painted in red, white, black, and yellow.

On Sunday we walked to church, and I don't know why I was subconsciously expecting a brick building on street level with a paved parking lot, wooden pews covered with red velvet, and organ pipes up front with wood trims to match the pulpit, table, and font. And I don't know why I felt shocked when instead my eyes were forced upward in the direction of the high stilts to a church building that looked like a larger version of everyone's homes, with a set of stairs to climb up to the sanctuary (a fitting image, I thought). Why was I surprised by the intricate wood carvings and paint adorning the pulpit and table (their font was the ocean), and an open floor with a notable absence of any pews or seats?

Worship reflects local patterns of speech, dress, architecture, gestures, and other cultural characteristics. Jesus' incarnation into a specific culture gives us both a model and a mandate. The gospel and the church were never intended to be exclusive to or confined to any one culture. Rather, the good news was to spread to the ends of the earth, rooting the church deeply into diverse local cultures. "Contextualization is a necessary task for the church's mission in the world."[81]

In his book on global worship, Charles Farhadian stresses how important it is to "appreciate the immense variety of expressions of Christian worship in order to take seriously the social and cultural context that plays such a significant part in worship . . . [with] emphasis on culture as the potential, not the problem of worship."[82]

The *Nairobi Statement* outlines two useful approaches to ensure adequate contextualization. First, *dynamic equivalence*—which involves reexpressing components of Christian worship with something from a local culture that has an equal meaning, value, and function. For example, the lordship of Jesus is taught among the Maasai tribe in Kenya by painting a black man dressed in a red robe, since red is the color of royalty and is always worn by the village chief. The second approach is *creative assimilation,* which involves enriching worship by adding pertinent components of local culture. For example, in Egypt the harmonic sound of an *oud* (lute) is used to add a fuller expression to psalms of lament.

Both of these tools go beyond mere translation and must be used with caution. Discernment is essential to decide how to equivocate and assimilate, while preserving the transcultural elements of unity and ecumenicity with the church universal. As the *Nairobi Statement* says, "The fundamental values and meanings of both Christianity and of local cultures must be respected."[83]

---

81   LWF, *Nairobi Statement*, section 3.1.

82   Charles E. Farhadian, *Christian Worship Worldwide: Expanding Horizons, Deepening Practices* (Grand Rapids: Eerdmans, 2007), x.

83   LWF, *Nairobi Statement*, section 3.5.

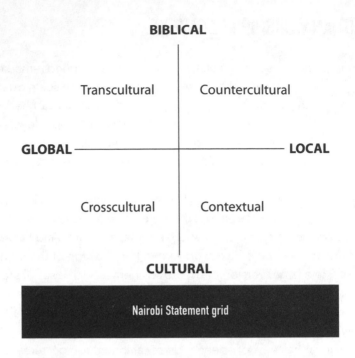

Nairobi Statement grid

THIRD: CHRISTIAN WORSHIP IS *COUNTERCULTURAL*

Christians in the Middle East take their call to be peacemakers very seriously, intentionally designing worship that breaks down barriers and promotes reconciliation through prayers like the following:

> Gracious God, you have promised through your prophets that Jerusalem will be home to many peoples, mother to many nations. Hear our prayers that Jerusalem, the city of your visitation, may be for all—Jews, Christians, and Muslims—a place to dwell with you and to encounter one another in peace. We make this prayer in Jesus' name. Amen.[84]

In a meeting with a delegation of Christian leaders, the president of a Middle Eastern country said that Christians have a vital presence in the region because they offer a moderate, mediating voice in the vicious conflict. This prayer demonstrates how worship goes decidedly against the surrounding cultures of intolerance and war, refusing to bow down to the false gods of greed, racism, and uncompromising self-righteousness, choosing instead to transform people and cultural patterns by acting justly, loving mercy, and walking humbly with our God, the Prince of Peace (Isa 9:6; Mic 6:8).

---

84   Churches for Middle East Peace, "Pray for the Peace of Jerusalem," Churches for Middle East Peace, 2006, http://www.cmep.org/sites/default/files/PrayforJerusalemLiturgy.pdf, 2.

Every culture contains some sinful, broken, dehumanizing elements that are contradictory to the gospel and present us with rival "secular liturgies that compete for our love."[85] Christian worship must resist the idolatries of a given culture. This doesn't mean that we become anticultural; rather, it challenges us to become careful readers of our culture in light of biblical truths. Reflect on these words that both affirm and resist culture:

> Wise is the church
> that seeks to be "in" but not "of" the world (John 15:19),
> resisting aspects of the culture
> that compromise the integrity of the gospel,
> and eagerly engaging its culture
> with the good news of the gospel of Jesus Christ,
> who comes to each culture, but is not bound by any culture.[86]

True worship challenges the oppression and injustice prevalent in local cultures (Rom 12:2). It makes room for grace to abound, freeing us to learn from another's perspective, and it gives us courage to work together for reconciliation so that justice may "roll on like a river, righteousness like a never-failing stream!" (Amos 5:24).

In commenting on Psalm 73, John Witvliet writes, "Public worship, then as now, is a superb way to practice not being the center of the universe and learn to see the world right side up. Worship is, by the Spirit's power, like spiritual cataract surgery that restores vision, clear and true."[87]

FOURTH: CHRISTIAN WORSHIP IS *CROSS-CULTURAL*

At a seminar in North America on using songs from other cultures in worship, a participant asked this question: "I am a pastor of a small rural congregation, and my entire congregation is Anglo-European descendants, so why would we sing African or Asian or Latin songs in worship?"

This question betrays a faulty assumption that when we worship with songs, prayers, instruments, and visual arts from other cultures, we do it for "them"—meaning people who come from those cultures. While it is a great act of hospitality to make "them" feel welcome and included (a most commendable practice in the growing context of immigration and refugee resettlement),

---

85   James K. A. Smith, professor of philosophy and adjunct professor of congregational and ministry studies at Calvin College in Grand Rapids, MI, explained in a lecture at the Worship Symposium 2011 that the heart is the fulcrum of our desire, and so if something can shape our love, then it has defined your identity, because we are what we love. "In the Fall, the capacity to love wasn't turned off, but it became misdirected . . . looking for love in all the wrong places with all forms of other false gods." Our culture experience is rife with worship, presenting us with secular liturgies that ultimately aim to shape our love by offering competing visions of what the good life is. When we respond to the call to worship, we are called out of competing secular liturgies into the true liturgy leading to the true love and vision of the kingdom.

86   World Communion of Reformed Churches, "*Worshiping the Triune God: Receiving and Sharing Christian Wisdom across Continents and Centuries,*" World Communion of Reformed Churches, 2010, http://wcrc.ch/sites/default/files/Worshiping_the_Triune_God.pdf, section 1.4. This document was developed by the worship planning team for the 2010 assembly in Grand Rapids, MI, of the World Communion of Reformed Churches in consultation with pastors, teachers, and other leaders throughout the world. It expresses the teaching of the Nairobi Statement in a poetic form, echoing the proverbial wisdom showcased in Scripture and common to many cultures around the world.

87   John D. Witvliet, "Worship in a Beatitude-Shaped World: Learning from Psalm 73," *Reformed Worship* 100 (June 2011): 5.

we must also realize that we do this for "us"—meaning people who feel at home in the commonly used language and musical style of "our" worship. Sharing worship resources cross-culturally expands our view of God and the church as transcending time and space, develops our repertoire of worship expressions, and crystalizes our understanding of the kingdom of heaven. Consider, for example, how this Brazilian rewriting of Psalm 137 confronts and enhances our view of community and justice:

> By the rivers in Fortaleza, we sat down and cried
> for the cholera victims;
> In those who lived there
> we saw sadness and we didn't know what to say.
> People who lived there
> did not have songs on their lips.
> They wanted joy
> But, with neither water nor health
> there was no way to be joyful.
> How could we sing praise to the Lord
> in the midst of such suffering?
> If we forget you
> If we don't bring back water, health and joy.
> Judge, Lord, our elites,
> for their neglect and greed
> have long mistreated us.
> But remember Fortaleza,
> your children in Ceara
> that suffer from thirst and cholera;
> Don't let the earth go dry.[88]

There are, of course, many issues to consider when engaging in cross-cultural worship—such as authenticity, instrumentation, language, race, and respect. To do this fourth step of the dance properly, we must faithfully practice the first three steps by asking questions like: What elements of transcultural faith are we celebrating? To what degree do these elements fit in our local context? What brokenness in my culture will these borrowed practices help redeem and reform? Asking such questions will help us avoid slipping into the danger of viewing our own cultural processes as superior to others.

As a statement produced in 2010 by the World Communion of Reformed Churches states:

> When the wisdom that is shared is a faithful echo and appropriation of scriptural
> wisdom, a faithful testimony to the Word and "Wisdom of God" (1 Cor 1:24), then this
> sharing of wisdom can be a sign of Pentecost, not Babel—a gift of the Holy Spirit, "The
> Spirit of wisdom." (Eph 1:17)[89]

---

88   Author unknown.
89   World Communion of Reformed Churches, "Worshiping the Triune God," Introduction.

One of the most common though often unspoken reasons for not engaging in global worship is our fear that somehow our own heritage will be lost. C. Michael Hawn responds to this fear most eloquently: "Liturgical plurality is not denying one's cultural heritage of faith in song, prayer, and ritual. It is a conscious effort to lay one's cultural heritage and perspective alongside another's, critique each, and learn from the experience."[90]

The *Nairobi Statement* reminds us of what is at stake when we plan Christian worship. It

> helps us to major in question asking. The topic of worship practices is important not just for cultural anthropologists, missionaries, and missiologists, but for all Christian leaders and believers. And those of us who are novices in this area must enter the conversation with more questions than assertions.[91]

My hope and prayer is that local Christian communities may be instructed and inspired by the *Nairobi Statement* to see a third way when viewing the tension between worship and culture. Though sometimes difficult and unsettling, it is not an evil that deserves rejection, but a dance that holds great potential to help us faithfully uphold the gospel's beauty and power while engaging culture, and in so doing we follow the example of Christ.

> True worship challenges the oppression and injustice prevalent in local cultures.

---

90   C. Michael Hawn, "Praying Globally: Pitfalls and Possibilities of Cross-Cultural Liturgical Appropriation," in *Christian Worship Worldwide: Expanding Horizons, Deepening Practices*, ed. Charles E. Farhadian (Grand Rapids: Eerdmans, 2007), 210.

91   John Witvliet, "Worship Worldwide" (seminar presented during a conference on World Christianity at Calvin College, Grand Rapids, MI, 2003).

14. WORSHIP CHALLENGES IN MULTICULTURAL CHURCHES: THE BETHLEHEM BAPTIST EXPERIENCE

By Chuck Steddom

For the last fifteen years I have gratefully served under the pastoral leadership of Pastor John Piper and other godly leaders at Bethlehem Baptist Church in Minneapolis. In 1995, not long before I arrived, Pastor Piper and the elders had led in a churchwide process of revisiting the congregation's core visions. God used this process to help the church identify and become unified around a set of specific values that they wanted to see reflected in corporate worship and other areas of ministry.

When I became a candidate for the position of worship pastor, Pastor Piper said, "Here is what we value in worship, but we have no idea how to 'flesh this out' in the normal week-to-week worship services. If you take this ministry position, your job will be to flesh out this worship vision." I joined the staff on June 1, 1997.

COMMITTED TO LIVING OUT OUR VISION

Our church has committed itself to the vision expressed in this statement: "We exist to spread a passion for the supremacy of God in all things for the joy of all peoples through Jesus Christ." Under the banner of this vision, our desire and gospel mandate, as God allows us, is to reflect here on earth the vision of the church that we see displayed in Revelation 5:9,10—a vision which depicts people from every tribe, language, people, and nation worshiping God together.

According to sociologists from the Brookings Institute and other similar organizations, our church's neighborhood on the south side of Minneapolis is one of the most ethnically diverse in the entire United States. Most of the pastors of our downtown campus also live there. God has called us to a ministry of reconciliation (2 Cor 5:17–20). But how are we going to fulfill it?

As we began the process of contextualizing the good news in light of the location to which God had led us, our new worship values became my "mantle of authority" and the driving force behind bringing our worship practices more in line with our newly embraced vision. There were three specific worship values that directly applied to our new efforts to reach out to our neighbors. These included our commitment to:

- being a singing people with growing appreciation for diverse expressions of love for God
- welcoming people different from ourselves for the sake of Christ
- becoming more indigenous in style and appreciating the diversity of our metropolitan cultural setting, both urban and suburban

Naturally, the cultural expressions of our Revelation 5 vision needed to be reflected in our weekly worship services. Two incidents that occurred during this period of transition stand out to me as humorous yet pointed indicators of our initial steps in broadening our local church's "heart languages."

FIRST INCIDENT: THE DRUMS

When I began worship ministry at Bethlehem we did not have a drum kit, nor had one ever been used in Sunday morning worship. It was understood by the congregation and staff that historic Reformed expository preaching should be reinforced with a traditional Reformed Baptist style of liturgical worship that focused on the praise of God through the theological truths of the hymnal. People came into corporate worship in reverent silence, longing to meet God. The defining sounds in this style of congregational worship came from the pipe organ, the piano, and the choir.

> The cultural expressions of our Revelation 5 vision needed to be reflected in our weekly worship services.

Drums were simply not part of the corporate worship experience. However, our newly approved vision, which expressed the desired ethos of our worship, was supposed to reflect the culture of our urban neighborhood where rhythm was king. Armed therefore with our congregationally approved "fresh new initiatives in worship," I went out within the first three months of my ministry and bought the congregation's first drum set for the church sanctuary.

The following Sunday I decided to simply leave the drum set sitting on the edge of the church platform without using it in the morning worship service. Needless to say, a number of people were quite concerned when they saw the drums occupying a corner of the platform. Comments from parishioners ranged from "I am deeply saddened that you have chosen to move our worship in this direction" to "It's about time, brother!"

Given the number of anxious comments I received that first week, I decided it would not be wise for me to use the drums the following week. Two weeks later was one of our Communion Sundays—which would have been the *least* appropriate service to introduce drums. So a full month passed and I had not once used the drums in corporate worship.

Finally, one of the more outspoken deacons in our church spoke to me about it. He was musically trained, with children who were classical music professionals and someone who was generally not excited about changing anything in the worship ethos of Bethlehem. He caught me in the hallway and said, "If you are going to have a drum set up there on the platform, for heaven's sake use it!" The very next Sunday I placed a drummer on the platform as a part of our worship team, playing innocuous accompaniments to Jack Hayford's "Majesty" and Rick Founds' "Lord, I Lift Your Name on High." This turned out to be the first step in a long process of worship reform.

SECOND INCIDENT: BLACK GOSPEL MUSIC

If one is going to be intentional about reaching out to a particular group of people, there must be some attempt at learning to speak their language. In the late 1990s we as a church became especially concerned about reaching our near neighborhood with the gospel. We were troubled by the well-published statement that the greatest display of segregation in our society occurs every Sunday at the eleven o'clock worship hour. The majority population in our neighborhood at that time was African-American, while our congregation was composed of white members who commuted to the church from other neighborhoods. Most were upper middle class, highly educated, and led by a pastor who used a lot of complicated theological words in his sermons. We did not reflect our neighborhood, either in the makeup of our congregation or in the language of our worship.

We had learned from our discussions with leaders of other ethnic groups that the language of a culture is often expressed in its music and that worship ministry is potentially a prime factor in bridging gaps between peoples. Personally, I was deeply challenged by our church's inability to engage our neighbors. I live within ten blocks of the church. We are talking about *my* neighbors.

One of our first attempts at speaking a different worship language for the sake of the gospel was for our choir to learn a black gospel song. The one I chose was "He Never Failed Me Yet" by Robert Ray. We worked hard as a choir on this piece. The instrumentalists, though all white, did a good job playing the piece in an authentic style. We worked on swaying appropriately to the style of the song. We asked an African immigrant who had come to the church through the influence of church missionaries to sing the stylized, traditional "testifying" solo. The Sunday came when we performed this piece. The choir was nervously excited and they really did sing their hearts out. They displayed a true work of transforming grace from within, in that they were willing to enthusiastically try something new in worship.

After the first service, a number of parishioners come up to me and expressed their concerns about the direction of worship in our church. Several made comments to the effect that this music "did not represent us as a congregation," that our singing that morning was disingenuous because "we aren't black" and, furthermore, that we "did not do a very good job stylistically on the piece." I thanked them for their thoughts and concerns. I was quick to remind them that this was an expression of the new worship values vision. My response to their critique did not seem to satisfy their concerns.

> Worship ministry is potentially a prime factor in bridging gaps between peoples.

At the end of our second service, two African-American families came to the platform. One family I was acquainted with and the other I was not. I braced myself for more criticism. But the first words out of their mouths were, "Thank you." I was shocked. They went on to explain that they had been at this church for over five years and, while they loved the preaching and teaching ministries, they had always felt like they had to "leave their culture at the door." They continued by saying, "For the first time, you led us in music that we understood and loved."

My first response to their comments was relief. And the second was to apologize. "I know that we did not do justice musically to this song," I told them. Their answer was quick. "We know!" they told me. "But you honored us by trying. We have been attending this church for a long time. Today is the first time we felt a part of this congregation."

"IT'S A MIGHTY LONG JOURNEY"

Since that time we as a church have been intentional about diversifying the membership of our worship teams and pastoral staff. We hold regular seminars and workshops on biblical diversity and racial harmony. The value of racial harmony permeates every one of our church documents. We converted our traditional sanctuary choir into one that was designed around the diverse ethnicities that God continues to bring to our congregation.

Many things have happened during the years since 1997. Pastor John has spent significant time and effort preaching and teaching the biblical foundation for a multiethnic church. There have been hundreds of transracial adoptions in our church. We are quick to acknowledge that there have been several big bumps in this process as well. Most certainly we have not yet arrived. But we join many other churches who pursue the vision of a multiethnic church in saying, "It's a mighty long journey," but one that we believe God is calling us to.

INTRODUCTION

SECTION 1: FOUNDATIONS

SECTION 2: STORIES

SECTION 3: TOOLS

CLOSING

15. "THE CANAAN HYMNS": SONGS OF THE HOUSE-CHURCH CHRISTIANS IN CHINA[92]

By Irene Ai-Ling Sun

ORIGINS AND SIGNIFICANCE OF THE HYMNS

The hymnody of the house churches in China is sometimes known as "the Canaan Hymns." They were written by Xiao Min, a peasant woman from Henan. She became a Christian in 1990 and began composing songs for the house church in her village. Since then she has written more than a thousand songs. Through oral transmission, her songs spread from one village to the next, and now they are known across one of the largest nations in the world.

The Canaan Hymns chronicle the footsteps of the missionary movement in China. These are the prayers and music of the persecuted church. They are the fruits harvested from fields soaked with the blood and tears of the faithful.

> We trod upon blood,
> Taking each step in tears to reach here.
> The geese have been flying North, flying South,
> Singing of God's love without end.
> China of today
> Is no longer desolated.
> One can see green buds sprouting everywhere.[93]

---

92   Originally published in a slightly different form in Irene Ai-Ling Sun, "Songs of Canaan: Hymnody of the House-Church Christians in China," *Studia Liturgica* 37 (2007): 98–116; republished in *EthnoDoxology* 4, no. 3 (2010): 1–10. Reprinted by permission of the author.

93   "The Dove Returned" (Canaan Hymn #546). All translations of hymns are by the author. For additional resources by Xiao Min, see *The Love of the Cross: Hymnal of 52 Selected Songs from the Canaan Hymns* (Petaluma, CA: China Soul for Christ, 2006); The *Love of the Cross*, CD (Petaluma, CA: China Soul for Christ, 2003), http://video.google.com/videopla y?docid=-6923892750736776389#; *Canaan Hymnal: 900 Hymns* (n.p., n.d.); and *Voice of the Soul* (Taiwan: Tien Ma Books).

The Canaan Hymns radically redefine the concept of religion for the Chinese mind. These songs paint a portrait of the Almighty God as a relational being, a friend, a beloved. Worshipers sing out of an intimate relationship with the divine. One song in particular is jarring to the nonbeliever:

> My Beloved leads me into his inner court.
> Words of understanding flow without end.
> Our love is as strong as death;
> Many waters cannot quench it.
> My Beloved is radiant—white beaming with red.
> His beauty surpasses ten thousands.
> My Beloved is mine and I am my Beloved's;
> For eternity, we shall not part . . .
> My Beloved and I shall walk together for all time.[94]

Translation obscures this hymn's debt to the Scriptures and to Chinese culture. Bible translators appropriated a term from ancient Chinese literature, *liang ren*, for the Hebrew term, the "beloved," in the Song of Songs. Xiao Min, steeped in Scripture, appropriated these verses and set them to a pentatonic melody. In the ears of Chinese listeners, this song destroys the prevailing stereotype that Christianity is a Western religion. For the educated Chinese, some find it unbelievable that this song was written by a peasant woman. For worshipers, this song reaches into the core of their beings, as they sing out of the depths of their souls.

> In the ears of Chinese listeners, this song destroys the prevailing stereotype that Christianity is a Western religion.

THE HYMNS EMBODY THE GOSPEL IN CHINESE

Echoing the flavor and rhythm of Chinese folk songs, the Canaan Hymns appeal to the aesthetic senses of the Chinese people. In ways inaccessible to foreign hymns, these songs make God comprehensible to the Chinese mind. For instance, the hymns draw heavily from images in nature.

> The small grasses never resent the barrenness of the soil.
> They are able to take deep root wherever they go.
> The stream never resents the height of many mountains,
> Flowing and bending, rushing to moisten the soil . . .
> We labor together,
> For one person cannot complete the Great Commission.[95]

The Canaan Hymns embody the gospel in Chinese. They transform symbols in culture to articulate an understanding of God. The Canaan Hymns resemble and effectively illuminate the Hebrew poetry of the Old Testament, because the two language systems share an affinity for

---

94   "Beloved and I" (Canaan Hymn #85).
95   "One Person Cannot Complete the Great Commission" (Canaan Hymn #270).

parallelism and natural imagery. Xiao Min composed a song while she was in prison, proclaiming the gospel to other prisoners:

> Why do leaves die and grow new buds?
> Why do spring, summer, fall, winter resurrect in cycles?
> Why cannot I see the wind and the air?
> Why do the sun, moon, and stars stay high in the sky? . . .
> I heard people say,
> Go, and seek after the true God.
> He will give you all the answers Because
> He created the heavens and the earth.
> Knowledge, wisdom, and everything is in Him.
> How I rejoiced when I found the mighty Most High,
> The One who answered my many, many riddles . . .
> Friends, do you also have these riddles?
> Please come and know the Most High!
> He is not far from you,
> Right next to you.
> He dwells in your heart of faith.[96]

MANY HYMNS FOCUS ON SUFFERING, LAMENT, AND "THE WAY OF THE CROSS"

The Canaan Hymns contain within them an anthology of lamentations of Christians in suffering. Loyalty is highly prized in Chinese culture. For many, loyalty to Jesus Christ means disloyalty to family and country; even homelessness and imprisonment. Their allegiance to God, their act of worship, is a costly thing. The Canaan Hymns record their laments.

> Although the *tao* road is hard to tread,
> There is not a word of resentment.
> Although tears cover the face,
> My heart is sweetly satisfied.
> Serving the Lord is not where,
> Not under the leafy shade . . .
> Not in the midst of a warm room.
> Must walk into the prison rooms.
> Walking by the valley of tears
> Must pass through Marah
> So we could reach Elim.[97]

---

96   "My Song" (Canaan Hymn #25).
97   "Because I Follow the Lord" (Canaan Hymn, number unknown).

> We've cried, we've laughed,
> We've sung, we've remained silent . . .
> We've trod in the lowest, lowest of all valleys,
> We've climbed the highest, highest of all mountains.
> Year and year again
> We've been through loss,
> A string of continuous bitterness.
> We've been through harvests.
> The great wave of time
> Passes by our sides.
> Tears of sorrow and joy
> Innumerably flowed.[98]

The faith of the believers is the cause of both their joy and sorrow. Like the Psalms, many of these lament hymns move from disorientation to reorientation, from lament to promise, pointing worshipers to God.

> Tears of gratitude for his grace,
> Flowing without end.
> The heartfelt words spoken
> Do not seem to suffice.
> One pair of hands marked by nails.
> The sound of knocking upon a door long sealed.
> One gentle voice
> Leading our hearts away,
> Knowing this road
> Is the path of the cross.
> The wind, the rain is strong,
> Extremely difficult and very bitter.
> The Lord's kind and loving hands
> Holding my hands at all times.
> I don't have any reason,
> Why I should not tread the path beneath my feet?[99]

Among Chinese believers, Christianity is often referred to as "the way of the cross." In their own broken bodies, Christians remember Christ's body that was broken for them; in their tears and pain they remember Christ's blood that was shed for them. They suffer "in remembrance of him."

THE HYMNS EXPRESS A DEEP LOVE FOR CHINA

Another distinction that sets the Canaan Hymns apart from other worship songs is their overtly patriotic sentiment. Though their allegiance is to God, Christians retain a love for China.

---

98   "We've Cried, We've Laughed" (Canaan Hymn #520).
99   "Tears of Gratitude for His Grace" (Canaan Hymn #303).

Even when I have only one drop of blood, one drop of sweat,
It would be shed upon China.
Even when I have only one breath, and one ounce of strength,
It would be offered to China.
China, ah!
How many of your children over the oceans
Are weeping in prayers for you,
Standing by the seashore
At all times holding you at heart?
Listen to the sound of a mother's calling across the ocean.
The people of China are sons and daughters of God.
China, ah! China!
Quickly come and find rest.
God has found you.
You are no longer lost while scaling mountains, crossing waters.
China belongs to the Most High![100]

Their faith and worship redefines even their ethnic identity. Chinese traditionally call them-selves "messengers of the dragon" or "children of the dragon," with the dragon representing the emperor. After conversion, however, Chinese rename themselves "sons and daughters of God."

The Canaan Hymns bear witness to the prayers of Christians for their nation. Prayer meetings begin at dawn in barns and houses. Extemporaneous prayers offered by men and women are punctuated with shouts of "Amen" from the congregation.

Five o'clock at dawn in China
The sound of prayers arises.
Prayers bring revival and peace
Bringing unity and triumph . . .
It soars over ten thousand waters and a thousand mountains
Dissolving the frost of cold hearts.[101]

Their ultimate hope for their country is for the gospel to be proclaimed and take root in their land.

Lord, ah! I earnestly beseech you:
Bestow grace to the church of China.
You hear the cries from far-off mountains:
Please open a way for China! . . .
Like the sky without boundary,
Gospel proclaimed upon the wide land.[102]

---

100   "China Belongs to the Most High" (Canaan Hymn #551).
101   "Five O'clock at Dawn in China" (Canaan Hymn #268).
102   "Sky without Boundary" (Canaan Hymn, number unknown).

SOME CRITICISMS HAVE BEEN RAISED

As the Canaan Hymns continue to spread and gain global recognition, they have drawn significant criticism. One frequent critique relates to a lack of theological depth and awareness in Xiao Min's hymns. Others react against the overt patriotic sentiment of the hymns and find this to be a barrier for authentic worship.

A faithful understanding of the Canaan Hymns takes into account the context from which they emerge. These hymns are most similar in genre to Chinese folk songs. Yet they are able to make the basic canonical teachings apprehensible. In many cases, Xiao Min directly quotes from Scripture. Although they may lack theological nuances and categories, the Canaan Hymns give a powerful testimony to how worship and theology must engage in an inseparable dialectic. The worship of the house-church Christians permeates all aspects of life. Their lives of worship lead them to the path of suffering in imitation of Christ. Under these circumstances, their knowledge and understanding of worship and of God reach a depth too difficult for many who profess the same faith to apprehend.

"MAY THE HOLY SPIRIT AWAKEN SOARING DESIRE!"

Through the Canaan Hymns, the Christian faith is made understandable to the Chinese people. The appropriated elements, such as natural imagery, loyalty, and patriotism, are significantly transformed and are subjected to scriptural truths. The Canaan Hymns redefine the understanding of religion and the God of Christianity. In remembrance of Christ, house-church Christians bear witness to lives of right worship, even to the point of suffering for the sake of the gospel.

China may be entering a new era; the message of the gospel, however, is not new. In one of the Canaan Hymns the gospel is allegorized as "beautiful fruits ripened by the sun" and "treasures nurtured and grown by the moon." The seeds were sown centuries ago by missionaries and other Christians who preceded this generation. Though the wait was long, the harvest is now ripe for the gathering.

> Revival kindles the flame of China.
> Lord, ah! We worship you.
> Chime once again the sound of the clock.
> Lord, ah! Ten thousand nations worship you . . .
> May they receive the beautiful fruits ripened by the sun,
> The treasures nurtured and grown by the moon.
> May they see the goodness of Jerusalem all of their lives.
> May the Holy Spirit awaken soaring desire, soaring desire.
> Once again kindle the flame of revival
> Blessing China![103]

---

103   "The Spark of Revival" (Canaan Hymn #284).

INTRODUCTION

SECTION 1: FOUNDATIONS

SECTION 2: STORIES

SECTION 3: TOOLS

CLOSING

PERSONAL

16. THE GREAT MISCONCEPTION: WHY MUSIC IS NOT A UNIVERSAL LANGUAGE

Robin P. Harris

—*"Ethno-what?" They always say that when they hear what I do.* I sigh, knowing the familiar script that will unfold.

—"I'm an ethnodoxologist." Eyebrows raised, the quizzical look ensues.

—"What in the world is *that?*"

—"Well, in ethnodoxology we study the ways people worship God in cultures around the world." The quick shake of the head and slow blink of the eyes demonstrate that it's the first time my conversation partners have thought about how other cultures worship.

—"Hmm," they respond. "What's the use of knowing that? Don't they just sing the songs we do?" *At least they're being honest.*

—"My job is to encourage and equip Christians in various cultures to express their faith through their own heart musics and other arts." Their eyes brighten.

—"Hey, heart music! Is that kind of like heart language? A missionary once told me that people should have access to the Bible in their heart language." *Now it's my turn to be surprised.*

—"Yep, that's right!" I respond, "Just like each person has at least one heart language, we all have our own heart music and arts; it's like a mother tongue for expressing your heart, and it affects how you worship."

—"Wow, that's, um . . . interesting. But isn't music, like . . . a universal language?"

A MUSICAL MISNOMER

"Music is the universal language." How often have we heard that statement? It's amazing the power of an oft-repeated, unexamined aphorism. This one about music sounds so romantic, so convincing. Yet this notion has had some significant ill effects on the worship practice of the North American church and the mission movement that grew out of it.

> A foundational principle of ethnodoxology is that music is not a universal language.

The statement, "Music is the universal language," first appeared in the writings of Henry Wadsworth Longfellow[104] in the early nineteenth century. Now, nearly two centuries later, it filters into our pop songs (e.g., "music is a universal language and love is the key"[105]) and permeates our collective consciousness— as one of those unexamined assumptions. For many, this additionally shapes their worship theology, their mission practices, and how they speak about music in everyday conversation.

What are the logical outcomes of thinking of music as a "universal language"?

- What it means to me, it probably means to you.
- There is only "good/bad" or "high/low" in this language of music, not *different* music languages.[106]
- Since I speak this universal language, I should know what qualifies as a "high" or "low" expression.
- Given a choice, people probably prefer to use Western music.

Unfortunately, the popularized "music is a universal language" paradigm has infected our weekly worship gatherings. One of the root causes of the so-called worship wars is that we fail to take into account some basic differences in "music languages." John Blacking, a well-known British ethnomusicologist, wrote, "The meaning of musical signs is ambiguous; culture-bound, rather than objectively self-evident: people are inclined to perceive and interpret them with reference to their experiences of different cultural systems, as well as according to variations in individual personality."[107] In other words, our ability to decode the sounds we hear is culturally conditioned. And it is quite possible for us to misinterpret musical and other artistic signs because they have attached meanings which we don't understand.

Some Western ears, for example, hear minor keys as carrying "sad" or "contemplative" meanings and connotations. But in many cultures, minor keys have a range of expression from impish and playful to majestic and triumphant, even exuberant and joyful. When I was in St. Petersburg, the American pastor of the church I attended forbade the Russian music director to choose songs in minor keys for the Sunday morning services. When I talked with him about the importance of minor keys as part of the heritage of the Russian church and a way of expressing a broad range of feelings for Russian people, he changed his mind. There are a host of *other* reasons why it is wrong for a foreign mission worker or pastor to have this kind of influence on the kind of music sung in a local church! But one of them is that he or she is likely to make the calls based on their own cultural bias and get it wrong.

A foundational principle of ethnodoxology is that music is not a universal language. This applies by extension to other arts as well. Blacking writes, "As public communication, musical

---

104   Henry Wadsworth Longfellow, *Outre-Mer: A Pilgrimage beyond the Sea* (1833; repr. Boston: Houghton, Mifflin, and Co., 1883), 197.

105   Statler Brothers, "I Believe in Music" (1973).

106   See my review of Kersten Bayt Priest's MA thesis in *EM News* 8, no. 3 (1999).

107   John Blacking, *Music, Culture, and Experience*, ed. Reginald Byron (Chicago: Chicago University Press, 1995), 229.

systems are more . . . culture-specific than any verbal language . . . we cannot make any sense of another person's speech without using an interpreter or spending considerable time and effort learning its grammar and lexicon."[108] Occasionally a perfectly normal word in one language can be a foul curse word in another. In addition, hearing foul words in an unfamiliar language does not have the same "gut impact" on you as it would in your mother tongue. Systems of music and arts are, according to Blacking, even more culture-specific than language, so true understanding requires a long process of learning the language, rather than relying on assumptions that may or may not be correct.

Confusion about the meanings of music and other artistic forms is not limited to cross-cultural misunderstandings. It happens even with different contextual microgroupings of a society or culture. Where can we go then to learn the meaning of a musical or other artistic form? Blacking provides a response:

> Not only can "the same" patterns of sound have different meanings in different societies; they can also have different meanings within the same society because of different social contexts. Thus . . . the emphasis must be on actors' *intentions to mean* something.[109]

The only way to know, therefore, what a musical or artistic form means is to *ask*—to do the hard work of research! This foundational aspect of ethnodoxology sets it apart from many other approaches to worship and arts in mission.[110]

You can begin the research process by asking a few simple questions in your local worshiping context, questions like:

- What is the state of the music debate in my church?
- What assumptions do people make about music in my faith community?
- How do these views affect the breadth of styles used in worship settings?

At the end of this chapter, we will address some of the implications of these questions for local churches in North America. But for now, let us take a look at what has been exported by the missionary community to ministry locations around the world.

WE WENT, WE SANG, WE CONQUERED

During the nineteenth and twentieth centuries, as European and other Western Christians traversed the globe, they took with them the prevalent philosophies of their home cultures—in particular, the idea of "cultural evolutionism." As late as 1962, Theodosius Dobzhansky, in *Mankind Evolving*, wrote that "biological and cultural evolutions are parts of the same natural process."[111] Due to ethnocentrism, Western culture was considered to be the most highly developed of cultures, further along on the evolutionary scale than other, more lowly, "tribal" societies and cultures.

---

108   Ibid., 239.
109   Ibid., 237.
110   See Brian Schrag's article "Ethnoartistic Cocreation in the Kingdom of God," chpt. 10.
111   Theodosius Dobzhansky, *Mankind Evolving* (New Haven: Yale University Press, 1962), 22.

SECTION 1: Foundations

85

INTRODUCTION

SECTION 1: FOUNDATIONS

SECTION 2: STORIES

SECTION 3: TOOLS

CLOSING

These ideas often resulted in the musical expressions of the newly encountered cultures being labeled as "primitive" and "heathen."[112] Some Western Christians even tried to "help" local music makers by encouraging the translation of Western Christian songs into indigenous languages and by teaching new converts to sing in four-part harmony or in unison. Stephen Feld, an ethnomusicologist who has studied the musical traditions of the Kaluli in Brazil, for example, has observed that

> one very significant generalization can be made about all Kaluli sound forms: no Kaluli sounds are performed in unison . . . missionaries have tried to get them to sing this way for twelve years [but] it is rare to hear anything approaching unison sung by Kaluli or emitted from any sound sources in their environment.[113]

Current practice no longer normally includes offensive labels such as "backward," "primitive," or "heathen," yet even today one can find cross-cultural workers who fail miserably at valuing the God-given musical and artistic resources of the host cultures in which they minister.

Because of the widely accepted view of music as a universal language, it never occurred to most early mission workers that, just as they needed to learn new, complex, and "strange-sounding" languages in order to communicate with local people, so also did they need to study and understand local music and other artistic systems like dance and drama as well as visual and verbal arts like proverbs, poetry, and storytelling. Instead many workers simply brought their Bible in one hand and their hymnbook in the other. The Bible was generally translated into vernacular languages, as were many of the song texts from the hymnbooks. But the musical language of those hymns remained unchanged in their original, Western form.

> Even today one can find cross-cultural workers who fail miserably at valuing the God-given musical and artistic resources of the host cultures in which they minister.

Concerned by the charges of "music colonialism," a number of mission workers have over the past few decades begun to resist this trend by incorporating into their thinking and practice the principles of ethnomusicology/ethnoarts (the study of music/arts and culture), mission-shaped anthropology (Scripture-grounded critical contextualization), and elements of the burgeoning field of global worship studies. At the nexus of these three disciplines, a new field of research is beginning to emerge, that of *ethnodoxology*.

ETHNO-*WHAT?*

Forty years ago Tozer wrote a book in which he described worship as "the missing jewel of the evangelical church."[114] In recent years there is a revival of interest in the topic of worship, with numerous courses and conferences specifically devoted to it.

---

112   For a treatment of this issue as it relates to Africa, see Roberta R. King, Jean Ngoya Kidula, James R. Krabill, and Thomas A. Oduro, *Music in the Life of the African Church* (Waco: Baylor University Press, 2008).

113   Stephen Feld, "Sound Structure as Social Structure," *Ethnomusicology* 28, no. 3 (1984): 391.

114   A. W. Tozer, *Worship: The Missing Jewel* (Camp Hill, PA: Christian Publications, 1992).

In the late 1990s worship leader and missionary Dave Hall coined the term "ethnodoxology" by combining three Greek terms—*ethne* (peoples), *doxa* (glory), and *logos* (word). The English word *doxology* combines "words" and "glory" into a concept signifying "words to glorify" or "worship" God. Hall defined ethnodoxology as "the study of the worship of God among diverse cultures." He stressed a broad understanding of worship beyond the Sunday morning corporate gathering to emphasize "first and foremost a life to be lived, and secondarily as an event in which to participate." The dual aspects of this definition are important, says Hall, because "scripture calls us to both."[115]

In more recent years the term "ethnodoxology" has gained increasingly wide usage. In 2000 the publication *EM News* was succeeded by a new review called *EthnoDoxology.* Sponsored by Artists in Christian Testimony, this new publication began offering articles "devoted to the multi-faceted music, arts and worship of every tribe, tongue and nation."[116] Contributors to the journal included a growing number of Christian ethnomusicologists and mission workers who were applying their training to diverse ministry contexts.

By 2003 when I, along with a few colleagues, launched a network for this global "tribe" of worship and mission-focused musicians and artists, the charter members expressed their desire to use the newly emerging term "ethnodoxology" as a part of the group's identity, thus giving birth to the network's name, the International Council of Ethnodoxologists—or ICE, as it is more commonly referred to. Growing rapidly within the first ten years to a group of over 280 associates in more than seventy countries, ICE has a website—a virtual library at http://www.worldofworship.org—dedicated solely to the issues and concerns of ethnodoxology. The site facilitates forums and conferences for training and networking on ethnodoxology-related matters. An online peer-reviewed journal, *Global Forum on Arts and Christian Faith,* was launched by ICE in 2012.

In addition to online resources, several seminaries and graduate schools have caught the vision as well and are collaborating with ICE to host intensive week-long courses on ethnodoxology. A growing number of other Christian educational institutions have also begun to offer both undergraduate and graduate degrees in world arts, ethnomusicology, and/or worship studies.[117]

Various seminars, tracks, and task forces on ethnodoxology—using the term in either title or approach—have been launched at mission conferences such as the Global Consultation on Music and Missions (GCoMM), the International Orality Network (ION), the Mission Commission of the World Evangelical Alliance (WEA), and a regional meeting of the Evangelical Missiological Society (EMS) held in 2012 at Trinity Evangelical Divinity School.

A 2011 "Arts in Mission" training event cosponsored by ICE, WEA, SIL International, and All Nations Christian College taught attendees how to put into practice basic ethnodoxological principles through a model called "Creating Local Arts Together"[118]—a process which involved working together with communities to:

---

115   International Council of Ethnodoxologists, "Ethnodoxology," ICE: A World of Worship, http://www.worldofworship.org/Ethnodoxology.php. His scriptural basis for making this claim is based on texts that he references, such as Psalm 95 and Romans 12:1. Hall has been significantly influenced in his thinking and writing by John Piper's reflections on the connection between worship and mission (see Piper publications in the *Handbook* bibliography).

116   See http://ethnodoxology.org/. The entire archives of this resource is available on the *Handbook* DVD.

117   Christian institutions offering training in world arts, ethnomusicology, and/or worship studies are listed at http://www.worldofworship.org/Training/index.php.

118   For a summary of what happened during this training, see the "Arts in Mission 2011" video on the *Handbook* DVD.

SECTION 1: Foundations

87

INTRODUCTION

SECTION 1: FOUNDATIONS

SECTION 2: STORIES

SECTION 3: TOOLS

CLOSING

- meet a community and its arts
- specify specific kingdom goals they hope to achieve
- select a particular arts genre along with the desired effects for its use
- analyze an event containing the chosen genre
- spark creativity by generating a new artistic work in the selected genre
- improve and celebrate both new and old artistic creations for integration into the community
- celebrate both old and new works as they become part of the community's life.[119]

These new streams of teaching, learning, thinking, writing, and ministry are being energized by the emerging ethnodoxology movement. Perhaps someday the conversation that we recorded at the outset of this chapter will be a rare one indeed, but how long it will take to arrive at that point is yet to be seen.

HOW DOES THIS APPLY TO CHURCHES IN THE NORTH AMERICAN CONTEXT?

The principles of ethnodoxology apply not only to international contexts of ministry, but also to churches located in North America. Ethnodoxologists are addressing the "worship wars" by emphasizing the importance of accepting diverse worship styles—especially those of marginalized groups—as a way of showing love to our fellow worshipers and to illustrate vital theological truths regarding the body of Christ. "Prioritizing the honor of Christ's name and the progress of his kingdom," writes Bryan Chapell, "can create harmony around a common mission that will enable us to unite in worship style choices even when personal preferences vary."[120]

Yet many Christian worshipers consider their different tastes to be more than "preferences," causing them to judge as "good" or "bad" another's music—and sometimes even the person themselves!—based on their own cultural values, tastes, or preferences.[121]

David Peterson elaborates on the "high" vs. "low" music debate with a challenge to examine carefully and prayerfully our response:

> We all know that music is a great encouragement to snobbery . . . We become so familiar with and comfortable with our particular styles of music that we end up saying, maybe overtly sometimes, "I am not willing to listen to your kind of music. I am not willing to sing one of your silly songs." We get even more intense than that. We say, "Your music is not true worship. Your music is not honoring to God."[122]

---

119   These seven points are unpacked in much more detail in Schrag's companion volume to this *Handbook*: *Creating Local Arts Together: A Manual to Help Communities Reach their Kingdom Goals*. For a highly condensed version of that manual, see Julisa Rowe's, "Creating Local Arts Together: The *Manual* Summary" in Section 3 of this *Handbook*, chpt. 148.

120   See Bryan Chapell, *Christ-centered Worship: Letting the Gospel Shape Our Practice* (Grand Rapids: Baker Academic, 2009), 297.

121   See Robin P. Harris, "Contextualization: Understanding the Intersections of Form and Meaning," *EthnoDoxology* 3, no. 4 (2007): 14–17.

122   David Peterson, "Psalms, Hymns, and Spiritual Songs: Does the Bible Direct Us in the Choice of Musical Styles?" (lecture, Institute for Christian Worship Lectures, Southern Baptist Theological Seminary, Louisville, KY, April 14, 2005).

Ron Man, one of the theological trainers in the ethnodoxology movement, writes that because the New Testament does not prescribe what worship expressions should look or sound like, we can be assured that God delights in a diversity of worship expressions that are grounded in culture yet faithful to biblical teaching:

> The bottom line is that God is much, much more concerned about the hearts of his worshipers than about the matters of form and style on which we expend so much energy. "Man looks on the outward appearance, but God looks on the heart" (1 Sam 16:7). To put it bluntly, God has no favorite songs or favorite style! Rather he rejoices in an infinite variety of worship expressions from his people (evident around the world, as well as down through the centuries), when lifted up with an attitude of thanksgiving and in dependence upon his Spirit. Let's not try to limit God or impose our own narrow tastes upon him.[123]

In the roiling free-for-all of the worship debates, ethnodoxologists are joining hands with the multiethnic worship movement to apply the principles of ethnodoxology to churches in the North American context. What is our goal? To see in churches expressions of heart worship which embrace not just the majority culture but also the various and multiple ethne in their communities. Applied in an even broader sense, the implications of these conversations affect far more than what happens in gatherings of worship. They also permeate the wide range of artistic expression which flows out of God's desired kingdom goals and values and impact every aspect of life within the rapidly growing multiethnic communities in our home settings and around the world.

> Music may be a universal phenomenon, found in virtually every culture around the world. But it is definitely not a universal language!

What then are some of the key ethnodoxology principles that apply to both home communities and ministries around the world? I propose that we start with these four:

1. Music, like other art forms, is *not* a universal language—our responses to music are learned, not intrinsic.
2. Just as in spoken language, music and other arts must be understood in their historical and cultural contexts to be interpreted correctly.
3. All peoples should have the opportunity to worship God in their own heart languages, heart musics, and other arts.
4. Churches that value and encourage heart music and arts in worship, reflecting the various and multiple cultures in their communities, are demonstrating the love of Christ to the world.

For an audio mp3, go to http://www.sbts.edu/resources/lectures/icw/psalms-hymns-and-spiritual-songs-does-the-bible-direct-us-in-the-choice-of-musical-styles.

123 Ron Man, "Global Worship: What in the World Can I Do about It?" *Worship Leader* (November–December 2009): 27–28, emphasis mine. For more on this matter, see two other chapters in this *Handbook*, one by Ron Man, "'The Bridge:' Worship between Bible and Culture," chpt. 4, and a second by John Piper, "The Missional Impluse toward Incarnational Worship in the New Testament," chpt. 19.

I realize that by calling myself an ethnodoxologist I will continue getting quizzical looks and responses. Moreover, the conversation that starts with "ethno-what?" will likely continue to be a regular part of my life. But what I love about this conversation is that I get to talk about the four important principles outlined above—principles that are slowly but surely infusing the minds and hearts of worship pastors, mission leaders, and laypeople around the world.

If you don't feel comfortable calling yourself an ethnodoxologist just yet, then at least help the rest of us out a bit. The next time you hear the comment, "Music is a universal language," do the world a favor and speak up! Point out that music systems, perhaps more than any other forms of verbal language, are culture specific and must be learned to be understood. Music may be a universal phenomenon, found in virtually every culture around the world. But it is definitely not a universal language!

INTRODUCTION

SECTION 1: FOUNDATIONS

SECTION 2: STORIES

SECTION 3: TOOLS

CLOSING

17. MENTORING ARTISTS

By Mary Elizabeth Saurman

"I pray that from his glorious, unlimited resources he will empower you with inner strength through his Spirit." (Eph 3:16 NLT)

The term "mentoring" is used in a variety of ways. We may each have different definitions. Here I will define mentoring as an opportunity:

1. for walking alongside others in their personal, spiritual, and ministry journeys;
2. for supporting and encouraging them in their development and discoveries.

A mentor is one who is invited into relationship and who invites relationship. Mentoring is a privileged position of helping and encouraging another individual. It is also a position of power and must always be carefully balanced by the humility and servanthood posture that Christ himself showed in his mentoring of others.

My own journey in mentoring came many years ago in working at a Christian mental health facility. Working as a music and dance therapist, I was mentored by solid, steady men and women of faith. They taught me much through their examples, care, and wisdom. And I, in turn, desired to pass that on to the music therapy interns I supervised in our therapeutic arts training program.

All of us were part of the team. Each person was treated as a valuable part of the total body. We worked together and learned from each other. We supported each others' uniqueness and desired for individual giftings to flourish.

Together we shared a growing overall vision in our work. We observed each other and worked together, based on our strengths and stretching us towards purposeful growth in many areas. And we celebrated each of our own gifts and creative skills in helping encourage the use of arts in moving through our own areas of healing and inviting others into their own healing.

Common themes in these mentoring approaches I have mentioned are the importance of:

- knowing each other well
- encouraging individual gifts
- integrating the gifts into the team so that all team members are working from their strengths.

These same approaches have worked well for mentoring artists throughout Asia.

WALKING ALONGSIDE

A primary foundational step in walking alongside others is seeking to know them well. Understanding their strengths and weaknesses and hearing their vision and passions is central in building a successful mentoring relationship. Praying with them and for them and seeking realistic growth areas for them is also vital.

Sarah arrived in her ministry location, and her supervisors quickly pushed her towards leading ethnoarts workshops. I received an email from her with a desperate cry for help, "I don't even know if I am capable of leading workshops. I've never even attended one."

Spending time dialoguing and praying with Sarah helped me learn what her areas of strength and gifting were. We developed a growth plan for her, thinking through the steps for helping her prosper in her passions and for strengthening her in areas of weakness over the years to come.

Sarah's first step in the plan was studying the national language so she could communicate well. As part of her language learning, she began building relationships with people in the community and researching the arts that were powerful communication tools. She also observed and participated in ethnoarts work with several experienced field-workers.

Through dialogue, I learned much from Sarah about how to walk alongside her—even from a distance—and best support her in her passions, strengths, and vision. Listening well, I heard some of the deeper cries of her heart and found ways of empowering her in her own growth process.

DEVELOPMENT AND DISCOVERIES

Individual gifts are like precious jewels for the mentor to help draw out and watch the Lord begin the buffing process. It is in the uniqueness of each individual shining in the place for which God has made them that we see more clearly the body of Christ.

As a mentor I must develop and continue allowing God to develop me. Some personal measures of development for me as a mentor include discoveries in

- listening well;
- understanding the gifts and passions of the individual;
- understanding how they relate to those around them;
- helping them relate better to those around them;
- speaking the truth in love;
- valuing my relationship with God and pointing them towards him;
- supporting them as they need it and letting them go as they find more solid footing and strength;
- stretching them in some areas regarding their vision and growth;
- praying for and with them;
- and being available to them as much as possible.

As for the mentee's development, how is that measured? For some it is in their own ability to work independently, proceed on the journey in confidence, and work from their strengths. For others, it is in knowing they can dialogue and talk through their needs, successes, and struggles in the process of growing. I often meet face to face, talk on the phone, or Skype with mentees. I try to listen to their hearts and learn what ways I can help support or encourage them for their next steps in personal, spiritual, and work growth.

As individuals are encouraged to work from their gifts, they are strengthened for work outside their areas of comfort as well. So when Sarah observed and stretched in coleading in a few workshops, she eventually decided to develop a workshop team of her own where all of the leaders would work from their own strengths.

In addition, she articulated a desire to encourage others in using their relevant art forms in worship and in mentoring others. We strategized together how she could more effectively come alongside the artists within the communities in which she works and mentor them.

Sarah has found her place. It is here that I am watching Sarah flourish. It is her spiritual journey, however, that grounds her. She has learned that her strengths and passions are from the "resources" mentioned in Eph 3:16. As she abides in him and her roots grow deep into his love (Eph 3:17), she continues to minister and mentor well. And, of course, her discovery of this on her mentoring journey is the most important piece of wisdom she will ever embrace and a model for those whom she mentors.

18. CULTURALLY APPROPRIATE WORSHIP: MY STORY AS A CAMEROONIAN PASTOR

By Roch Ntankeh

WAKE-UP CALL AT A SONGWRITING WORKSHOP

A few years ago I was in the Democratic Republic of Congo (DRC) for a songwriting workshop that brought together six different language groups. At the workshop a significant event happened that led me to realize more than ever before that it was time to do something for the restoration and development of our indigenous worship in a way that fits our culture.

At the end of the workshop we had a closing celebration. As usual for such occasions, we invited some church members and leaders to attend and hear about what was done at the workshop. Their presence is usually a great source of encouragement to the participants and a powerful way to promote the purposes and goals of the workshops. Among the guests was a third-generation pastor among African pastors of the DRC. He was in the first generation of those who held a BA in theology and was in addition, at the time, an important member of the federation of churches in his region.

According to the schedule for the celebration, the workshop participants were to present songs, and several guests had been invited to speak, but the pastor was not on the program. Toward the end of the celebration, however, he insisted on taking the floor. He was amazed, he said, that he had had an opportunity there to hear the Lord being praised, not only in his mother tongue, but also with rhythms and instruments from his village. He was so overwhelmed to have this wonderful experience during his lifetime that he burst into tears, unable to control his emotions.

> He was so overwhelmed to have this wonderful experience during his lifetime that he burst into tears, unable to control his emotions.

The pastor's reaction was a great shock to me because, according to my African education and training, a man, especially an elderly man, must not show his tears. The fact that this man was so overwhelmed by culturally appropriate worship that he could not control himself showed that the need for such worship in our society was critical and a serious cause for concern.

WHY IS CULTURALLY APPROPRIATE IMPORTANT?

One could ask: Why must we restore and develop culturally appropriate worship? Do we really need to invest in that domain? How will it benefit us? Moreover, is it possible for an African to achieve such a goal, considering the fact that he is sometimes hung up about many things?

The term "restoration" refers to putting something back into its normal state, making all necessary repairs or adjustments. It implies that something has been damaged in some way, either consciously or unconsciously. Culturally appropriate worship needs such restoration because of the actions and attitudes of some early missionaries during the colonial period. Some of their actions, whether right or wrong, resulted in tarnishing the image of culturally appropriate worship, degrading and diluting it so that it came to be considered as "non-Christian."

In this vein Paul Hiebert tells us that the early missionaries had a tendency to reject all that was not of their culture, even characterizing those values as pagan. This led many missionaries to replace local values with other values they did not consider pagan; most notably, Western values.[124] As Hiebert says, "Our drums, cymbals and other traditional instruments had to give way to keyboards and other pianos."[125]

USING OUR MUSIC AND METHODS TO WORSHIP IS PLEASING TO GOD

Today the question for us is, what is our responsibility with regard to this sad situation? We want to encourage the church and our people to understand that using our music, our instruments, and even our methods to worship the Lord is very pleasant to God. As the apostle Paul said to Timothy, all that the Lord created is good and nothing must be rejected (1 Tim 4:4). Moreover, the very first verses of the Bible tell us it was God, Elohim, who created all things from the beginning. It was not the devil, nor a people group, nor a culture that created these things (Gen 1:1). What the Lord expects from us is to receive his good creation with thanksgiving.

> We want to create an interest in traditional values without of course totally rejecting Western forms of worship.

The story about the pastor who was so moved by culturally appropriate worship shows us how important it is to work for the restoration of the kind of worship that takes into consideration local cultural values. It shows us, in fact, how urgent it is to develop such worship by helping us imagine the joy and freedom that can be unleashed in the hearts of local worshipers. It also enables local people to hear and receive the gospel. This is confirmed by Paul Keidel when he says that "music that speaks to the hearts of the Christians increases their desire to worship and stimulates them to talk to others about Christ, since it is in harmony with their faith."[126]

The joy and freedom that stem from culturally appropriate worship is, for us, the main reason to organize seminars and workshops on traditional music. Our objective is to make known and to promote the place of our cultural heritage in worshiping God. By so doing, we can help quench

---

124   Paul Hiebert, *Mission et Culture* (St-Legier: Editions Emmaüs, 2002), 206–7.
125   Ibid., 206.
126   Paul Keidel, *Les défis de la mission interculturelle* (Lyon: Edition Clé, 2008), 120.

the thirst of the people living in larger towns who are disconnected from their traditional realities and who do not master their mother tongue, but who love traditional music.

Besides, in most of our churches, services are generally conducted in the languages of the former colonizers and worship is always in the Western form. In such a context, we want to create an interest in traditional values without of course totally rejecting Western forms of worship. That is why we can say with Brian Schrag, "I am not devaluing new, urban, or national art forms . . . But I *am* trying to promote arts and artists with few champions."[127]

THE TIME HAS COME TO ASK SOME SERIOUS QUESTIONS

Conscious of the fact that we are better placed than most of our people to communicate through our traditional music, we work hard to help them grasp that vision, to understand its relevance and the challenges at stake. This hard work is needed, despite the fact that we are in a postcolonial context. It is true that we are at a peculiar moment in history where we witness revival among Africans and the development of Afrocentrism. It is still proper and urgent, nonetheless, that we ask ourselves some serious questions:

- Do we have the means to achieve our goal?
- How far are we ready to go?
- What price are we willing to pay for the fulfillment of our dream, knowing that we cannot correct one mistake by another mistake?
- Are our Western partners ready to trust us in the decision-making process?
- Are they ready to allow us to have our autonomy?[128]

---

127   Brian Schrag's article in this *Handbook*, "Ethnoartistic Cocreation in the Kingdom of God," chpt. 10.

128   For additional reading on this topic, see Delanyo Adadevoh, *Leading Transformation in Africa* (Orlando: ILF Publisher, 2007), and two other resources found in the *Handbook* bibliography: Kraft (1996) and Maire (2006).

ENGAGING GOD'S WORLD: WITNESS AND COMMUNITY-BASED MINISTRY

BIBLICAL

19. THE MISSIONAL IMPULSE TOWARD INCARNATIONAL WORSHIP IN THE NEW TESTAMENT[129]

By John Piper

THE CENTRALITY OF WORSHIP

Missions is not the ultimate goal of the church. Worship is. Missions exists because worship doesn't. Worship is ultimate, not missions, because God is ultimate, not man. When this age is over, and the countless millions of the redeemed fall on their faces before the throne of God, missions will be no more. It is a temporary necessity. But worship abides forever.

Worship, therefore, is the *goal* and *fuel* of missions:

- It is the *goal* of missions because in missions we simply aim to bring the nations into the white hot enjoyment of God's glory. The goal of missions is the gladness of the peoples in the greatness of God. "The LORD reigns; let the earth *rejoice*; let the many coastlands *be glad!*" (Ps 97:1 ESV, emphasis added). "Let the peoples praise thee, O God; let all the peoples praise thee! O Let the nations *be glad and sing for joy!*" (Ps 67:3,4 KJV Cambridge Ed.; emphasis added).

---

129   This chapter has been compiled by the *Handbook's* general editor, with permission of the author, from two sermons, one chapter, and one article by John Piper. The four sources are as follows: John Piper, "The Supremacy of God in Missions through Worship," *Mission Frontiers*, July–August 1996, http://www.missionfrontiers.org/issue/article/the-supremacy-of-god-in-missions-through-worship; John Piper, "The Inner Simplicity and Outer Freedom of Worldwide Worship," in *Let the Nations Be Glad! The Supremacy of God in Missions, 3rd ed.* (Grand Rapids: Baker Academic, 2010), 239–54; John Piper, "Our High Priest Is the Son of God Perfect Forever" (sermon, December 8, 1996), Desiring God Foundation, http://www.desiringgod.org/resource-library/sermons/our-high-priest-is-the-son-of-god-perfect-forever); and John Piper, "Gravity and Gladness on Sunday Morning, Part 1" (seminar for the Bethlehem Institute, September 12, 2008), Desiring God Foundation, http://www.desiringgod.org/resource-library/seminars/gravity-and-gladness-on-sunday-morning-part-1#InwardExperience.

- But worship is also the *fuel* of missions. Passion for God in worship precedes the offer of God in preaching. You can't commend what you don't cherish. We will never call out, "Let the nations *be glad!*" if we cannot say from the heart, "I rejoice in the Lord . . . I will be glad and exult in thee, I will sing praise to thy name, O Most High" (Ps 104:34 ESV; 9:2 KJV Cambridge Ed.). Missions begins and ends in worship.

I am not pleading for the diminishing of missions but for a magnifying of God. Where passion for God is weak, zeal for missions will be weak. Churches that are not centered on the exaltation of the majesty and beauty of God will scarcely kindle a fervent desire to "declare his glory among the nations" (Ps 96:3). But when the flame of worship burns with the heat of God's true worth, then the light of missions will shine to the most remote peoples on earth. Even outsiders feel the disparity between the boldness of our claims upon the nations and the blandness of our engagement with God.

The deepest reason why our passion for God should fuel missions is that God's passion for God fuels missions. Missions is the overflow of our delight in God because missions is the overflow of God's delight in being God. And the deepest reason why worship is the goal in missions is that worship is God's goal. We are confirmed in this goal by the biblical record of God's relentless pursuit of praise among the nations. "Praise the LORD, all nations! Extol him, all peoples!" (Ps 117:1 ESV). If it is God's goal it must be our goal.

Probably no text in the Bible reveals the passion of God for his own glory more clearly and bluntly than Isaiah 48:9–11 where God says:

> *For my name's sake* I defer my anger, *for the sake of my praise* I restrain it for you, that I may not cut you off. Behold, I have refined you, but not as silver; I have tried you in the furnace of affliction. *For my own sake, for my own sake,* I do it, *for how should my name be profaned? My glory I will not give to another.* (ESV, emphasis added)

I have found that for many people these words come like six hammer blows to a human-centered way of looking at the world:

> For *my* name's sake!
> For the sake of *my* praise!
> For *my* own sake!
> For *my* own sake!
> How should *my* name be profaned?
> *My* glory I will not give to another!

THE MODALITY OF WORSHIP

Having said this, we should note the startling fact that the New Testament contains remarkably little explicit teaching about corporate worship—what we call worship services. Not that there were no corporate gatherings for worship. First Corinthians 14:23 speaks of "the whole church" assembling together. Acts 2:46 speaks of the early church "attending the temple together and breaking bread in their homes" (ESV). And Hebrews 10:25 speaks of "not neglecting to meet together" (ESV). But this is not much, and the remarkable thing is that even when the gatherings are in view, the apostles do not speak of them explicitly as worship.

> The main word for worship in the Old Testament is virtually absent from the letters of the New Testament.

Let me illustrate this so we can feel its full force. In the Old Testament, the most common word for worship is the Hebrew word *hishtahavah* (or a related form of that word). Its basic meaning is "bow down," with the sense of reverence, respect, and honor. It occurs 171 times. In the Greek Old Testament, 164 of those instances of this Hebrew word are translated by the Greek *proskyneom*. In the Greek New Testament, this is the main word for worship.

But when we look at its use, we notice something astonishing.[130] It is common in the Gospels (twenty-six times)—people would often bow down worshipfully before Jesus. And it is common in the book of Revelation (twenty-one times) because the angels and elders in heaven often bow down before God. But in the Epistles of Paul, it occurs only once, namely, in 1 Corinthians 14:25, where the unbeliever falls down at the power of prophecy and confesses that God is in the assembly. And the word doesn't occur at all in the letters of Peter, James, or John.

This is remarkable. The main word for worship in the Old Testament is virtually absent from the letters of the New Testament.[131] Why is this? Why are the very Epistles that were written to help the church be what it ought to be in this age almost totally devoid of this word and of explicit teaching on the specifics of corporate worship?

THE LOCALITY OF WORSHIP

Jesus becomes the new "place" of worship

I think the reason is found in the way Jesus treated worship in his life and teaching. His main statement is found in John 4:20–24. But before we look at this text, consider a few other things he said. For example, his attitude toward the temple, the main place of Jewish worship, was not at all what the Jewish leaders thought it should be.

---

130   Heinrich Greeven, in Gerhard Friedrich, ed., *Theological Dictionary of the New Testament*, vol. 6, trans. Geoffrey Bromiley (Grand Rapids: Eerdmans, 1968), 765, observes the "astonishing fact" that while *proskyneom* is abundant in the Gospels (twenty-six times) and Acts (four times) and Revelation (twenty-one times), it is almost completely absent in the epistles (Heb. 1:6 and 11:21 are Old Testament quotations). Apart from Acts 24:11, where *proskynein* is a technical term for worship in the temple, the only instance of *proskynemsis* in the primitive Christian community is in 1 Corinthians 14:25, where there appears to be an actual falling down. Elsewhere there is reference to kneeling in prayer (Acts 9:40; 20:36) and lifting the hands (1 Tim 2:8), but the word *proskynein* is not used. Greeven concludes: "This is, however, a further proof of the concreteness of the term. *Proskynemsis* demands visible majesty before which the worshiper bows. The Son of God was visible to all on earth (the Gospels) and the exalted Lord will again be visible to His own when faith gives way to sight (Revelation)."

131   See the note above for the few apparent exceptions in the book of Hebrews.

When he wove a whip and drove out the moneychangers, he said he did so not for the sake of proper sacrifices but for the sake of prayer—in fact, prayer for *all the nations.* "My house shall be called a house of prayer for all the nations" (Mark 11:17 ESV). In other words, he focused attention away from the outward acts of Jewish sacrifices to the personal act of communion with God for all peoples.

Then he said two other things about the temple that pointed to a radically altered view of worship. He said, "Something greater than the temple is here," referring to himself (Matt 12:6 ESV), and "Destroy this temple, and in three days I will raise it up" (John 2:19 ESV). This attitude toward the temple got not only him killed (Mark 14:58; 15:29) but also Stephen (Acts 6:14). That's how important it was.

Jesus identified himself as the true temple. "Something greater than the temple is here." In himself he would fulfill everything the temple stood for, especially the "place" where believers meet God. He diverted attention away from worship as a localized activity with outward forms and pointed toward a personal, spiritual experience with himself at the center. Worship does not have to have a building, a priesthood, and a sacrificial system. It has to have the risen Jesus.

Jesus loosens worship from place and form

What Jesus did to worship in the way he related to the temple is made explicit in John 4:20–24. Here he uses the word *proskyneom*—the dominant Old Testament word for worship—and shows that it is laden with outward and localized meaning. Then he transforms it into a concept that is mainly inward rather than outward and mainly pervasive rather than localized.

The woman at the well said, "Our fathers worshiped on this mountain, but you say that in Jerusalem is the place where people ought to worship." [The word for "worship" used here is the common Old Testament word *proskyneom.* Note the localized emphasis in her mind.] Jesus said to her, "Woman, believe me, the hour is coming when neither on this mountain nor in Jerusalem will you worship the Father" (John 4:20,21 ESV).

Here Jesus loosens worship from its outward and localized connotations. Place is not the issue: "neither on this mountain nor in Jerusalem." He goes on: "But the hour is coming, and is now here, when the true worshipers will worship the Father in spirit and truth, for the Father is seeking such people to worship him. God is spirit, and those who worship him must worship in spirit and truth" (John 4:23,24 ESV).

Here is the key sentence: True worship, which was anticipated for the age to come, has arrived: "The hour *is coming* [in the age to come] and is *now* here [in me!]." What marks this true future worship, which has broken into the present from the glorious age to come, is that it is not bound by localized place or outward form. Instead of being on this mountain or in Jerusalem, it is "in spirit and truth."[132]

Jesus strips *proskyneom* of its last vestiges of localized and outward connotations.[133] It will not be wrong for worship to be in a place or to use outward forms, but he makes explicit and central

---

132   In line with what we saw in note 2, Heinrich Greeven remarks that "if instead of naming a place to which the pilgrims should go to worship, Jesus says that the true place of worship is in the spirit and in truth: this is an oxymoron. Undiluted *proskynein,* the act of worship which is concrete in place and gesture, is lifted up to a new dimension: 'spirit and truth.'" Friedrich, *Theological Dictionary,* 764.

133   I am aware that Jesus may not have spoken Greek with this woman at the well and so may not have actually used the word *proskyneom.* But I take it that John's rendering of Jesus' intention is accurate and that John's use of *proskyneom* faithfully captures what Jesus wanted to communicate about the meaning of worship carried by that word.

that this is *not* what makes worship worship. What makes worship worship is what happens "in spirit and truth"—with or without a place and with or without outward forms.

This is likely the best explanation as to why *proskyneom*—the central Old Testament word for worship—was virtually boycotted by Peter, James, John, and Paul in the letters they wrote to the churches[134]:

- The word did not make clear enough the inward, spiritual nature of true worship.
- The word carried significant connotations of place and form.
- The word was associated with bodily bowing down and with the actual presence of a visible manifestation to bow down before.

In the Gospels, Jesus was present in *visible* form to fall before, so the word *proskyneom* is used with some frequency. In the book of Revelation, the act of bowing down usually happens before God's manifestation in heaven or before false gods on the earth. Therefore the word *proskyneom* is widely used in Revelation as well.

But in the Epistles something very different is happening. Jesus is not present in visible glory to fall before. As a result, the tendency of the early church was to deal with worship as primarily inward and spiritual rather than outward and bodily, and primarily pervasive rather than localized.

THE TOTALITY OF WORSHIP

The next most frequent word for worship after *proskuneo* in the Old Testament is the word *latreuo* (over ninety times, almost always translating *'abad*). This is usually rendered "serve," as in "You shall not worship their gods nor *serve* them" (Ex 23:24 NASB).

When Paul uses it for Christian worship he goes out of his way to make sure that we know he means not a localized or outward form for worship practice, but a nonlocalized, spiritual experience. In fact, he takes it so far as to treat virtually all of life as worship when lived in the right spirit.

- "I serve (or *worship*) [God] in my spirit in the preaching of the gospel" (Rom 1:9 NASB; parenthesis added).
- True Christians "*worship* God in the Spirit of God . . . and put no confidence in the flesh" (Phil 3:3 NASB, emphasis added).
- "Present your bodies a living and holy sacrifice, acceptable to God, which is your spiritual service of *worship*" (Rom 12:1 NASB, emphasis added).

The praise and thanks of the lips is called a sacrifice to God (Heb 13:15). But so are good works in everyday life (Heb 13:16). Paul refers to his own ministry as a "priestly duties [of worship]" and he calls the converts themselves an "offering acceptable [in worship]" to God (Rom 15:16 NIV 1984; cf. Phil 2:17). The money that the churches sent Paul was described by him as "a fragrant aroma,

---

134   Another important word for worship, *sebomai*, is used twice in the Gospels ("In vain do they *worship* me" [Matt 15:9; Mark 7:7 ESV; emphasis added]) and eight times in Acts, always for God-fearing Gentiles except once for pagan worship (Acts 19:27). The absence of this word in the Epistles is again remarkable. It is as if the apostles, in their letters, avoided words that were current for synagogue worship, both *proskyneom* and *sebomai*.

an acceptable sacrifice, well-pleasing to God [in worship]" (Phil 4:18 NASB). And Paul's own death for Christ he calls a "drink offering [to God]" (2 Tim 4:6).

The same thrust is furthermore seen in the imagery of the people of God—the body of Christ—as the New Testament "temple" where spiritual sacrifices are offered (1 Pet 2:5 NLT), where God dwells by his Spirit (Eph 2:21,22) and where all the people are seen as the holy priesthood (1 Pet 2:5,9). Second Corinthians 6:16 shows that the new covenant hope of God's presence is being fulfilled even now in the church as a people, not in any particular service: "We are the temple of the living God; just as God said, 'I will dwell in them and walk among them; and I will be their God, and they shall be My people'" (NASB).

Worship, thus, in the New Testament is significantly deinstitutionalized, delocalized, and deexternalized. The whole thrust is gradually taken off of ceremony and seasons and places and forms and is shifted to what is happening in the heart—not just on Sunday, but every day and all the time in all of life.

THE RADICALITY OF WORSHIP

Worship in the New Testament, in short, moves toward something radically simple and inward, with manifold external expressions in life and liturgy. One of the reasons for this stunning indifference to outward form is a vision for missions that is usable across thousands of cultures and therefore not to be laden with externals.

All the focus of this worship is on the reality of the glory of Christ, not the shadow and copy of religious objects and forms. There is no authorization in the New Testament for worship buildings, or worship dress, or worship times, or worship music, or worship liturgy, or worship size, or thirty-five-minute sermons, or Advent poems, or choirs, or instruments, or candles. In fact,

> Worship is not trivialized in the New Testament, but intensified, deepened, and made the radical fuel and goal of all missions.

the act of getting together as Christians in the New Testament to sing or pray or hear the word of God is never even called worship. Do we distort the biblical meaning of "worship" by using the term almost entirely for an event for which the New Testament *never* does?

All of this makes us very free and, perhaps, very frightened—*free* to find place and time and dress and size and music and elements and objects that help us orient radically toward the supremacy of God in Christ. And *frightened* because almost every worship tradition we have is culturally shaped rather than biblically commanded. The command is a radical connection of love and trust and obedience to Jesus Christ in all of life.

There is a reason for this radical spirituality of worship in the New Testament. And the reason is this: the New Testament is a missionary document! The message found here is meant to be carried to every people on earth and incarnated in every culture in the world. And that is why our High Priest came and ended tabernacle and sacrifices and feasts and vestments and dietary laws and circumcision and priesthood.

The Old Testament was mainly a "come-and-see" religion. The New Testament is primarily a "go-and-tell" religion. And to make that possible, Jesus has not abolished worship, but made it the kind of radically spiritual engagement with God that can and must happen in every culture on the earth. Worship is not trivialized in the New Testament, but intensified, deepened, and made the radical fuel and goal of all missions.

The frightening freedom of worship in the New Testament is a *missionary* mandate. We must not lock this gospel treasure in any cultural straitjacket. Rather let us find the place, the time, the dress, the forms, and the music that kindle and carry a passion for the supremacy of God in all things. And may our communion with the living God be so real and the Spirit of God so powerfully present that the heart of what we do becomes the joy of all the peoples we are called to reach.

CONCLUSION

The New Testament is not a manual for worship services. Rather, it is a vision for missions in thousands of diverse people groups around the world. In such groups, outward forms of worship will vary drastically, but the inner reality of treasuring Christ in spirit and truth is common ground.

I believe that God intends to leave the matter of form and style and content to the judgment of our spiritual wisdom—not to our whim or our tradition, but to prayerful, thoughtful, culturally alert, self-critical, Bible-saturated, God-centered, Christ-exalting reflection driven by a passion to be filled with all the fullness of God. I assume this will be an ongoing process, not a one-time effort.

God is pursuing with omnipotent passion a worldwide purpose of gathering joyful worshipers for himself from every tribe and tongue and people and nation. He has an inexhaustible enthusiasm for the supremacy of his name among the nations. Let us bring then our affections into line with God's and, for the sake of his name, let us renounce the quest for worldly comforts and join his global purpose.

The Great Commission is first to delight yourself in the Lord (Ps 37:4). And then to declare, "Let the nations be glad and sing for joy" (Ps 67:4 ESV). In this way God will be glorified from beginning to end, and worship will empower the mission efforts of the church until the coming of the Lord.

103

INTRODUCTION

SECTION 1: FOUNDATIONS

SECTION 2: STORIES

SECTION 3: TOOLS

CLOSING

20. BIBLE STORYING WITH THE CREATIVE ARTS FOR CHURCH PLANTING

By Tom Ferguson

AYIZAN FESTIVAL: THE BEGINNING

August 1996: It was time for the festival celebrating the founding of Tsévié, the town where we were living in Togo. The stadium field was covered with traditional musical groups demonstrating their prowess, creating a veritable smorgasbord of sound for a new ethnodoxologist like myself. I went from group to group drinking in the amazing rhythms and phenomenal dancing. As the time for the official ceremony approached, the groups formed a parade around the field.

The central piece was a presentation of the story of the village's founding. *Atumpani,* the talking drums for the Ewé people, told the epic story that was translated into both Ewé and French languages for those uninitiated in the language of the drum. As the story unfolded, dancer-actors played it out for all to see. The crowd was thoroughly captivated. And then it occurred to me how powerful it would be if God's story could be told in this way. Thus began my journey into the realm of storying with music and other arts.

A TALE OF TWO PEOPLES

The first breakthrough happened among the Ifè people. After successful new song workshops in 1997 and 1998, I was asked to colead a music, storying, and church planting workshop in March of 2000.[135] I returned again in 2001 to do a miniworkshop focused on creating songs based on major events from the life of Christ and Pentecost. As things progressed, Pastor Odah Kodjo became the key champion for the use of the Ifè language and musical arts among the Ifè Baptist churches in Togo.

---

135   See Tom Ferguson, "Ifé Music in Evangelism and Church Planting Workshop," *EM News 9, no.1 (2000), 1–4;* or Tom Ferguson, "Music, Drama, and Storying: Exciting Foundations for Church Planting," in *All the World Is Singing: Glorifying God through the Worship Music of the Nations,* eds. Frank Fortunato with Carol Brinneman and Paul Neeley (Tyrone, GA: Authentic, 2006), 199–204.

Ten years later I spoke with Pastor Odah about the state of music in the *Jésus le Chemin* (Jesus the Way) Baptist Association, comprised primarily of Ifè-speaking churches. He shared that the arts and storying are still an integral part of evangelism and church planting. Associational leadership includes a *directeur de musique* (music director). There are annual music seminars and concerts in each zone of the association. Each seminar includes the composing of new songs, as well as topics for discussion. The 2010 topic focused on the role and appropriate use of Ifè traditional dance in the church. During their annual music week, churches are encouraged to take music out of the church and into the public spaces. Emphasis is placed on using indigenous Ifè performing arts. Daily performances include concerts, music-theater, and a picnic followed by traditional dancing.

At that same time I touched base on the work among the Waci-speaking community in Togo. In October 2003 I had proposed the creation of an evangelistic music-drama to the Glévé church. The music-drama would be used in conjunction with a chronological Bible storying pictorial evangelistic tract that was being produced. Over the next year church members created songs and dramatic sketches for each story. Their first presentation was at a conference on Bible storying as an example for the participants. Just as everything was coming together, my wife and I transferred to South Asia. Just before we left, the Glévé church presented some of the music and dramas as part of a church planting event in the village of Vo Kponou.

> As local believers around the world begin to craft and use stories for the first time in their heart language, some have naturally moved to creating songs based on the stories.

When I visited Togo in July 2011, I had the opportunity to speak with some Waci church leaders about how things had progressed. The church in Vo Kponou had an attendance of about forty people. The Glévé church had continued to perform the songs they created at various events but no new songs had been created. They discontinued using the dramas. The difference between the Ifè and the Waci is that among the Glévé church no "champion" arose. We are praying that God will raise up a local champion for the arts in our Waci churches.

LOCAL STORY CRAFTERS AND MUSIC

Since that first experience in Tsévié, storytelling has played an ever-increasing role in my work. It became necessary to improve my skills and knowledge of storytelling to the point that my role has evolved from "indigenous music catalyst" to "creative arts and orality consultant-coach." In this new role I have noted that as local believers around the world begin to craft and use stories for the first time in their heart language, some have naturally moved to creating songs based on the stories.

Among the Kotokoli people of Togo and the Bisa people of Burkina Faso, story-based songs have been used with radio broadcasts of Bible stories. These programs have become extremely popular within the predominately Muslim population. In Mali, a story crafter composed songs for every story in his language's story set. He also has begun creating music videos from these songs. Story crafters among a North Indian people composed a song in place of a story, finding that the story would be more easily told through song.

After being introduced to "Storying Training for Trainers" (ST4T),[136] a group of Malagasy musicians created a song on the creation account using a popular music style of the Masikoro. The traditional mandolin player is a popular Masikoro musician. The music group hopes to use the mandolin player's popularity to gather crowds to hear the gospel message. The group is participating in a story crafting project, and plans are underway to encourage and assist the creation of more story-songs in local styles.

VISUAL ARTS AND STORYTELLING

The visual arts are also being used in conjunction with stories. A small group of believers in North India created songs for a Christmas outreach party for family and friends. Two young artists in the group were commissioned to paint scenes from the nativity story on large canvases. These were hung around the venue and were used to tell the Christmas story. The following year the believers added drama to their presentation.

Believers in South Asia, the Middle East, and Africa combine Bible storytelling and henna art to share the gospel. Women use henna to draw beautiful designs on their hands and feet for special occasions. While drawing the henna designs, the women talk, build relationships, and share the Bible story they are drawing. When women are wearing henna, others admire the art on their hands, opening doors for the story to be shared again and again.[137]

EMPOWERING STORYTELLER CHURCH PLANTERS

The value of using the performing and visual arts with stories is growing among storying practitioners and trainers. Impromptu drama and storyboarding are tools regularly used to help teach a story. A new song creation module is included as part of the storying church formation training in South Asia. Participants are taught the *Handy Guide for Facilitating New Song Creation*[138] and given the assignment of creating a song for one of the stories from the book of Acts. When the story is told during "house church" time, they teach their song to the training "church."

Increasingly as church planters, storytellers, and creative artists are trained and empowered, creative arts paired with Bible stories become a powerful tool for communicating the message of Scripture.[139]

---

136   See Stephen Springer, ed., *Storying Training for Trainers (ST4T)* (n.p.: WigTake Resources, 2010).

137   See more about henna art in this *Handbook*, see Scott Rayl, "Contextualizing Visual Arts for Faith Sharing," chpt. 27.

138   See Brian Schrag and Paul Neeley, "Tool FF: Memory Aid Hand Motions," in *All the World Will Worship* (2005) on the *Handbook* DVD.

139   For additional reading on chanted narratives, see Kaushal (2001).

21. ART AND GOSPEL: THE NECESSITY OF ARTISTIC FULLNESS

By Steven C. Hawthorne

How shall we best think of the role of art in gospel communication? It is all too common to see art merely as a useful medium to help communicators transmit the gospel message more persuasively. In this view, art is utilized as a way of sparking attention, establishing rapport, gaining credibility, or evoking response. In our home cultures we may get by with such a utilitarian viewpoint, but in cross-cultural settings if we exploit local art forms merely to enhance our evangelism, we should not complain if we are suspected of peddling religious propaganda.

BEYOND UTILIZING ART

A much greater vision of the relationship of art to the gospel is found in the Bible. Despite our understandable fixation on our activity as cross-cultural evangelizers, the Bible clearly points beyond the task of cross-cultural evangelism to the movements of new believers that spring forth in response to the gospel. These movements evangelize within their own culture, usually with an effortless artistic splendor impossible for outsiders. The Bible is vividly clear about the ultimate purpose of the gospel: God will ultimately be worshiped in obedient love by some from every people. The love of the peoples will abound, expressed with offerings of the redeemed glory of their cultures.

There are three ways that art is important in gospel communication: First, art enhances communication for cross-cultural messengers. Second, art flows like a language of the soul for people to implant the gospel amidst their own people with life-giving clarity. Third, art enables a gathered people to offer worship to God with wholehearted devotion. Christ died to summon people from every culture to know and serve the living God with their utmost love. Such love always finds artistic form, involving all that our hearts can express, all that our minds can invent, and all that our skills can create.

My thesis is simple: Look beyond mere communication of the gospel to the fruition of the gospel. Envision and encourage the flourishing of art amidst the new and renewed movements of obedience to Christ. As these Christ-honoring movements mature in whole-life worship, they will increasingly and openly express their faith, hope, and love with art of every kind. The compelling beauty of their artistic celebration in worship becomes an eloquent communication of the gospel to their own people.

ART AND GOSPEL: A GREATER VISION

An example of this greater vision for the relationship of art and the gospel is found in Psalm 96. I admit that for years I ignored the opening lines of this Psalm. It was just something about singing, so I would hurry past those lines to put a spotlight on the mandate in verses two and three that calls for the evangelization of the nations.

> Proclaim good tidings of his salvation from day to day.
> Tell of his glory among the nations,
> his wonderful deeds among all the peoples. (vv. 2b–3)

This triplet of lines seems to sum up the world evangelism project: Crisply and constantly convey the good news of salvation. Clearly recount God's awesome deeds and outrageous excellence to every ethnic group. It is a solid mandate for world evangelization, only slightly obscured, in my former way of thinking, by the opening lines portraying an outlandish vision of the whole planet singing. But some years ago, as I became more involved with others in actually evangelizing the nations, I slowly began to "hear," as it were, the global song of the first lines of Psalm 96.

> Sing to the Lord a new song.
> Sing to the Lord, all the earth.
> Sing to the Lord, bless his name. (vv. 1–2a)

Hearing this song as a soon-coming promise has changed my vision of art and the gospel. The first few lines are not some kind of hymnic hyperbole. Neither do they merely call for music to play a part in the communication of the gospel. The global song is altogether necessary to fulfill the fullest purpose of the gospel. Notice four things in these opening lines:

1. **To "sing" implies art of every kind.** First, the psalmist calls for *singing* rather than telling or talking, explaining, or proclaiming. Singing is, of course, a form of speech, but people in most cultures elevate singing over speech as a more complex form of art. It is not bare-bones transmission of information. It is a profuse, almost excessive exclamation. This song symbolizes—and calls for—every way of doing art.
2. **To be "new" refers to continual creativity.** Second, the psalmist calls for the song to be something *new*. The newness suggests a constant creation of incessantly fresh music. To be ever-new, the song must actually be comprised of many songs. It is not too much of a stretch to see that such endless variegation will call forth the distinctive

beauties of particular cultures. Eventually, this call to worship will demand a contribution from every people.

3. **To be global means "all peoples."** Third, the song is a public affair, summoning singing from "*all* the earth," (v. 1) which becomes "*all* the peoples" (v. 3). This is as wide open as we can imagine. It is not private chamber music or tunes buried on one's iPod. The song is a community experience, involving and engaging many together. While there may be solo voices, the song is sung by a collective entity—a people. Art is the way that a people speaks to itself as a people—across generations or across town. Art is defined in many ways, but art is certainly the means by which a people affirms, reminds, or questions itself as a people. If you can imagine humanity without art, then you can imagine humanity as mere individuals without peoplehood, without a story, without a hope. The gospel is heard by persons, but God's call is addressed to entire peoples (*see vv. 7–10*). If the gospel ever comes to an entire people, it must be manifest as a work of art, resounding as a song, crafted with God's help by some who are of that people.

4. **To be directed "to the Lord" means the song really matters.** Fourth, and perhaps most profound, the singing is directed to God himself. This might seem a bit odd to a mind focused on sending messages efficiently. Why would anyone feel the need to communicate to the One who already knows everything? The rest of the psalm makes clear that this song is not merely a transfer of information. It is exclamatory praise, wide-open celebratory exuberance. God is not only deserving, he is desirous of this outpouring of love. Perhaps you've heard the expression about global worship—"A choir of millions for an audience of One." This psalm makes it clear that God himself is truly the ultimate audience.

ARTISTIC FULLNESS IS NECESSARY

If we sense the relational glory of the coming global song, we will urge those of every people to engage in every way of doing art to fulfill the purpose of the gospel. The fruition of the gospel is people living openly in worship together before their God, communicating and celebrating with every kind and way of art—an "artistic fullness." The all-encompassing greatness of the purpose of the gospel in Psalm 96 shows us the necessity of evangelizing with artistic fullness in at least three ways:[140]

1. **Truth encounter requires artistic depth.** To proclaim the gospel clearly, we must recount "his wonderful deeds" (v. 3) as a great story that intersects and completes all stories. Beliefs and assumptions lie embedded in underlying narratives, primordial myths, and legends that comprise the heart of all worldviews. Unless the gospel touches the minds of a people at a worldview level, nothing really changes. Multiple modes of art are needed to demonstrate in a profound way that God's deeds are truly marvelous events within the narrative framework of their people.

---

140   The three encounters framework (truth, power and allegiance) is the work of Charles Kraft, first published as, "What Kind of Encounters Do We Need?" *Evangelical Missions Quarterly* 27 (July 1991): 3, and developed in other writings by Kraft since then.

2. **Power encounter engages artistic wisdom.** A lively wisdom is needed to contend with evil powers and idols. "For great is the Lord and greatly to be praised; he is to be feared above all gods. For all the gods of the peoples are idols, but the Lord made the heavens" (vv. 4–5). Denouncing and renouncing evil powers often requires an actual showdown between the Creator God and lesser powers or idols. Such dramatic encounters may not involve art. But the story of such confrontations with powers must be retold to neighbors and children with persuasive authority that requires artistic excellence. Not only must false fears be exposed and shame confessed, a new aesthetic must be learned to replace the old ways. Power encounter means more than mere release from darkness. It means entering a life of praise in the light of Christ, a life in which there is a renewed imagination and new superlatives of virtue, beauty, and majesty. "Splendor and majesty are before him; strength and beauty are in his sanctuary" (v. 6).

3. **Allegiance encounter calls for art-formed corporate identity.** We are summoned to gather before God as a people, not merely as individuals. Artistic expression not only helps form our community, but mediates our communion with God. "Bring an offering and come into his courts. Worship the Lord in holy attire"—literally, "in the splendor of holiness" (vv. 8b–9a). People can meet God anywhere, but when we gather before him as a people, we delight in assembling in special spaces (architecture), finding diverse ways to come before him in special holy garb (clothing design), pacing ourselves with pageantry that is both solemn and joyous (dance and drama), interacting with images and symbols (visual and sculpted forms), prayers, songs, and stories (literature and music), and celebrating with meals both holy and common. The celebration of Christ's Lordship becomes an exclamation among the nations that "the Lord reigns" (v. 10).

CULTURAL

22. MUSICAL BRIDGES IN CHRISTIAN COMMUNICATION: LESSONS FOR THE CHURCH[141]

By Roberta R. King

As I stroll across the town square in Ferkessedougou, Côte d'Ivoire, the sounds of a traditional Senufo funeral hang in the evening air. Musicians are beating their wood-framed *balafons*[142] in counterpoint with a pair of *njembe* drums. A growing cacophony of sound surrounds me as two more *balafon* groups begin their songs to praise the deceased. Just one hundred yards from the funeral, goats bleat loudly in the town square, awaiting their sacrificial role at the Muslim celebration of *tabaski,* the big feast. The goats' cries intermingle with the droning buzz of motorcyclists on their way home from the fields and shops to their open courtyards near the center of town.

It is February 2002 and this is the season of all-night funerals and fasting for the Muslim period of Ramadan. This rich context with its interplay of music, life, and ritual is the perfect setting for the ten-day workshop that will bring together four Senufo language groups to compose new songs for the church. More than thirty-five Senufo believers from the Nyarafolo, Minyanka, Djimini, and Shenara ethnic groups gather in this multicultural West African town. They come saying, "We are here to learn how to sing in the language of our ethnic group. We are thirsty for it; we know that we have great richness there."[143]

---

141   Much of this chapter is adapted from Roberta R. King, "Toward a Discipline of Christian Ethnomusicology: A Missiological Paradigm," *Missiology: An International Review* 32, no. 3 (July 2004): 293–307. Reprinted by permission of Missiology.

142   A *balafon* is a 17- to 21-keyed xylophone set on a wood frame held with a strap over the shoulders of the player who is then free to walk and move while playing.

143   From the unpublished field notes of my colleague, Linnea Boese (2002), 1. The workshop was conducted in French with simultaneous translation into the four participating Senufo languages. The field notes are a compilation of these discussions by my colleague, Linnea Boese, who drew on her knowledge of both Nyarafolo and French, with eventual translation into English.

THREE SCENES FROM THE SENUFO MUSIC WORKSHOP

The goal of the workshop is to set the story of Abraham to song, to create an oral translation of Genesis 12–22 for use in the ministry of the local churches. While the traditional rituals of life and death surround us, the Senufo believers are drawing from their musical traditions to bring the Christian faith into the midst of their local context.

Let's listen in on contextualization in process as the Senufo consider a number of ethnodoxological issues in creating new songs for the church:

Scene 1:

The discussion centers on Genesis 12:1–3. The focus is on God's blessing in contrast to Senufo concepts of blessing. One participant explains, "Blessings come from family, older ones. It's a prayer to ask God to cover them with good(s)."

Yusuf, a Shenara from Mali, continues:

> To get the blessing, you have to satisfy the desires of your relatives. You have to respect the parents. Other gods—spirits—give blessings and curses. They can do good and bad. They also demand that you respect them, do as they say. We have more fear of God, because he can make you die . . . (we) don't want to get into a bad relationship with him.

Moise, a Nyarafolo, then takes it one step further:

> When we were born, we were told we had to follow our parents. Doing that was God's way, and no other way could replace it. But in the Word it shows that our parents' way and God's way are different. Worshiping the spirits, as our parents did, there is no blessing there, although our parents think that there is . . . We want to make it clear in our songs that God's blessing is not like that, to make life bad for us and take away our joy.[144]

Scene 2:

The discussion centers on how the Nyarafolo culture appears to surface in Scripture in the episode of Sarai sending Hagar to Abram (Gen 16). The group emphasizes that "Sarai did not stay proud, but did what she could to be helpful." They see it as a good thing, a selfless thing; one suggests that God even worked powerfully in her heart so that she had this attitude! After much discussion, they decide that "Sarai wanted to help arrange things for God, whereas God was able to take care of things himself!" Then Sikatchi, a Nyarafolo believer, reveals that

> the Nyarafolo custom is much like this. It's scandalous to see in the Bible. The custom is that if a woman gives another woman to her husband, usually the woman becomes the titular wife and the other is chased away. How did a Nyarafolo custom get into the Bible? Whose culture came first—the Israelites' or the Nyarafolos'?[145]

---

144   Boese, field notes, 3.
145   Ibid., 10.

Scene 3:

The discussion turns to "pagan"[146] versus "Christian" musical instruments. The Minyanka people share:

> We have many drums, but are not authorized to use them all in church . . . sometimes they are used for worshiping a certain fetish. They are also used for encouragement in agriculture (fields, millet harvest); so they are taken as "worldly," to be abandoned . . . There is a Christian dance that is approved called *samakabo (tirer-revenir)*. Other dances are not approved . . . What is a truly Christian dance? . . . Were some instruments used to praise God before they became worldly, or vice versa? What is the origin of instruments?[147]

Finally, Yusuf, helps to explain a major source of the confusion: "We (Christians) live before the pagans, not apart . . . We tend to think that Western instruments were all made for the church, so they are fine to use; no question involved."[148]

These three scenes reveal some of the dynamic interplay between culture, the Scriptures, and music making at the workshop. Though the most observable fruit of the workshop was forty-seven new songs based on the Abraham narrative, the composing process afforded opportunity to address critical issues for the church in Africa:

It brought the biblical message into the Senufo context. While Muslims in the town square were preparing to celebrate tabaski, the big feast, that teaches that Abraham was to sacrifice Ishmael, workshop participants were learning the biblical account and its redemptive significance.

Important insights into the cultural context were brought to the surface. Senufo believers were in this process growing in their understanding of God. An infant faith community was brought together, affirmed, and given freedom to develop their own indigenous heart songs to use in Christian witness, worship, spiritual formation, and leadership.

The Senufo workshop is representative of implementing ethnodoxology for the sake of the kingdom. Based on principles from ethnomusicology, it studies the intersection between music and culture in relation to communicating Christ in deeply meaningful ways. The goal is to impact and transform people's lives as they walk with Jesus Christ through the use of culturally appropriate musics and accompanying performing arts.

FOUR MUSICAL BRIDGES IN GOSPEL COMMUNICATION

The purpose of this chapter, therefore, is to identify key musical bridges critical to the effective communication of the gospel for the church in the twenty-first century. At the heart of mission is the imperative to make Jesus Christ known and worshiped. What then are these key musical bridges that can help to bridge the cultural gaps of understanding and worshiping Jesus Christ as Lord and Savior?

---

146   The word "pagan" as employed here is not my category, but rather is the *emic* term used by Senufo believers themselves. It is used in this context to be faithful to Senufo believers' religious worldview.

147   Boese, field notes.

148   Ibid., 7.

Musical Bridge #1: Recognize and respect the music of the receptor

Throughout much of mission history, when missionaries encountered musical sounds and music events such as the Nyarafolo funeral described above, they were often at a loss in knowing how to assess and interpret the proceedings. Indeed, the church in mission has regularly branded such events as heathen and worldly, something to be avoided. Certainly many elements in the funeral described above run contrary to Christian theology and practice. Yet it is unfortunate that rather than seeking to understand the music and related dynamics of cultural events, some missionaries have simply condemned them. The result has been that new believers are asked to withdraw from their social group, often their own families, and are not allowed to participate in showing appropriate grief and respect for the deceased.

> When the use of music is not limited to worship time on Sunday morning, it begins to foster dynamic vitality in churches.

The study of music and culture—ethnomusicology—speaks to the need to interpret such occasions. Drawing from its anthropological roots, ethnomusicology specializes in studying music in relation to the life events of a people. It offers insights for making sense of music and the significant roles it plays within societies. Thus it addresses questions that both local and global churches of the twenty-first century are asking. These include:

- How is it that the gospel message is still understood mostly at a surface level?
- How is it that an appalling lack of integration of the Christian faith into daily living continues to dominate the life of the church?
- How does music communicate in different cultures?
- How is the church singing its own faith?

When the use of music is not limited to worship time on Sunday morning, it begins to foster dynamic vitality in churches. As music and the arts enter the contexts of everyday life, they bring unexpected new understandings of how Christian faith affects various aspects of the worshipers' lives. It is the receptor who decides what is helpful or meaningful.

Understanding cultural musics is a crucial step toward understanding their significance for the life of the church. Employing ethnomusicology for the purposes of worship and witness requires both becoming intentional in learning about cultural musics and then strategizing to integrate music into the life of the church. In order to bridge cultural gaps in mission and ministry, an ethnomusicologist must identify with the musics of the culture.

Musical Bridge #2: Involvement in music-cultures fosters greater understanding among peoples

Effective communication requires involvement with people.[149] Music performance and participation provide opportunities to become involved with people and to learn about them. It is a way to show Christ's love by identifying with them. As Smith notes, communication is "a constantly broadening involvement that finds and builds more and more commonness, more areas of sharing."[150]

What we are seeking is more opportunities to come to know and appreciate one another. In my current research on "Songs of Peace and Reconciliation among Muslims and Christians,"

---

149 This conviction is developed more fully by Donald K. Smith (1992).
150 Ibid., 24.

for example, I have had the great privilege to learn Arabic musics by participating in the Kan Zaman Arab Classical and Folklore Ensemble that meets in the Southern California area. Two generations of immigrant peoples meet regularly just three blocks from where I teach at Fuller Seminary. If I had not looked for a group to perform with, I might not ever have known of such an opportunity for witness. One performer has now joined me in singing with my church choir, a broadening involvement that allows us to live out the gospel before and with her.

Becoming musically involved with differing people groups necessitates learning to exegete the cultural setting in which witness and worship take place.[151] Making sense of the music of the peoples of the world, both in terms of sound and behavior is critical. This will require moving beyond mere musical analysis to exegeting music-cultures through

- the study of people making music;
- the study of music *in* culture;
- the study of music *as* culture, as a way of organizing human activity; and
- the study of music in the context of human life.[152]

What was taking place in the midst of the Senufo workshop? What were the cultural dynamics that played into it? Several critical principles of ethnomusicology give us a foundation for beginning to understand music within the mission context:

1. *Music as a phenomenon is universal; its meaning is not.*[153] It is often said that "music is a universal language." Though well-meaning in intent, this adage assumes that any music is naturally understood and appreciated. If we listen to a genre of music for the first time, it might be natural to assume that we would perceive the music in a very similar way as a cultural insider does. However, we have learned that this is not generally true. In my early fieldwork among the Senufo, I unwittingly discovered this. I had decided to express gratitude to my Senufo hostess by offering a rendition of "How Great Thou Art" on the piano. My hostess left the room within five seconds. She had no idea that I was playing the music for her, nor did she recognize that it was a Christian hymn. It obviously did not rate as music, nor did it mean anything important to her.

    The ramifications of applying this principle are missionally significant. Before the development of Christian songs in Nyarafolo, the nonbelievers assumed that the Christian songs from the neighboring Cebaaras had no significance for them. Upon hearing the first Christian Nyarafolo songs, they exclaimed, "You mean that God is for us, the Nyarafolo? We thought he belonged to the Cebaara!" The Cebaara songs did not arise out of the Nyarafolo context and thus did not speak to them within their cultural setting. Although the musical sounds of both groups were similar, each musical style functioned like a musical language, sending the unintended message that God belonged only to the Cebaara. Identity through musical style was at stake. Thus we must

---

151   Roberta R. King, *A Time to Sing: A Manual for the African Church* (Nairobi: Evangel Publishing House, 1999), 327–28.

152   Titon (2009), xiii.

153   Ibid., 3. This issue is also addressed by Robin P. Harris in this *Handbook*, "The Great Misconception: Why Music Is Not a Universal Language," chpt. 16.

ask what is considered music within a particular society, and work within that society's definitions of and expectations for music.

2. *The study of a "music-culture" contributes to exegeting the mission context.*[154] The need to understand a people's music-in-context has led to the development of the concept of a *music-culture*.[155] The term is used to mean "a group's total involvement with music: ideas, actions, institutions, and material objects—everything that has to do with music."[156]

    Recognizing that music-*as*-sound cannot be studied "isolated from the human behavior that produced it,"[157] the music-culture model allows for the integration of the numerous and complex elements of music making by examining both the sociocultural and musicological dimensions of a people's music. We are always seeking to understand a music-culture in terms of the insiders' perspectives. We ask questions like, "How does one begin to make sense of the Senufo funeral in terms of their music-culture?" "What is the symbolic significance of both the music and its related behavior?"

3. *The uses and functions of music within a society point toward effective missional praxis.* One particularly significant aspect of the music-culture concept for witness and worship is the study of the uses and functions of music within society. Since "music is an everyday and all-pervading aspect of life," Merriam argues that "there is probably no other human cultural activity which is so all pervasive and which reaches into, shapes, and often controls so much of human behavior."[158] Thus music functions in many cultures as an essential integrator of life and a key means of communication and profound expression.

Musical Bridge #3: Music communication is a process

Music communication does not bring about change in one hearing or in the performance of one particular song. Rather, it plays dynamic, critical roles over an extended period of time in spiritual formation and emerging understandings of Jesus Christ and who he is. Two critical roles that music plays include:

1. *Music as life-processor.* Music takes up the strands of a people's way of life and weaves them together, revealing insights about deep levels of their thought life, their emotions, and their related behavior.[159] The process of setting Scripture to song provided a context for allowing cultural understandings about blessing and the role of women from the Senufo perspective to surface. In the midst of the discussion, biblical truth was taught and then processed for deeper understanding of the text within their particular

---

154   Alan Merriam's thinking on this topic developed from an initial investigation of music in culture, to music as culture, and finally culminated in his claiming that music is culture; see Alan P. Merriam, *The Anthropology of Music* (Evanston, IL: Northwestern University Press, 1964).

155   Titon's standard university text, *Worlds of Music*, centers its discussion on the "music culture," with exegeses of eight differing contexts for worlds of music.

156   Ibid., 3–32.

157   Merriam, *The Anthropology of Music*, 32–33.

158   Ibid., 211–18. Merriam identifies ten overarching functions that music plays in society (209–28). For the specific purposes of missiology, I am highlighting only three of the ten.

159   In discussing the "pathway of a song," research showed that Cebaara songs communicated in three dimensions: the affective, cognitive, and behavioral; see King, *A Time to Sing*, 165–92.

context. As Senufo believers wrestled with the biblical text, they developed song texts that told the Abraham narrative in a way that was appropriate for their cultural context. These texts were then transformed into song, where musical sound and movement added further meaning and significance in culturally appropriate ways.

2.   *Music as contextualizer.* All music making takes place within a cultural context. Senufo believers with their unique concepts and expectations for music were provided a platform for processing the Christian faith. When Sikatchi asked how the Nyarafolo culture found its way into the Bible (see Scene 2 above), he was processing biblical content into his own life world as he sought to think theologically about the God of Abraham. Working within the music-making process of the Senufo context created a natural means to doing contextualization of the biblical text.

Musical Bridge #4: Musical meaning lies within the receptor

Smith asserts that meaning cannot be transferred; it is internal and individual. Assuming automatic comprehension is just as dangerous as assuming that music is a universal language.[160] Without solid biblical foundations and theological underpinnings, our use of music in mission and worship is left to the mercy of ill-informed opinions. Careful interaction with the Scriptures is needed in order to question, shape, guide, and evaluate the role of music in communicating Christ. There are two arenas in which this evaluation must occur:

1.   *There is a critical need for a theology of music-in-context.*[161] The Senufo workshop participants came to a point where they could not proceed any further in composing new songs. They wanted to addresses theological issues related to music. Which drums, for example, could be used in the church setting? Were some instruments used to praise God before they became worldly? (The relationship between musical instruments and the associations developed through their use in a culture can cause tremendous controversy within the church.) Is God aware of the way in which music was used in the cultural contexts of the Scriptures?

A theology of music-in-context is required that addresses questions surrounding the origins of music and God's involvement with it. In the Old Testament, for example, statements like "he will exult over you with loud singing" (Zeph 3:17 NRSV), and that God's "heart laments for Moab like a harp (Isa 16:11)" reveal God as One who understands the dictates of the music-cultures of the people among whom he is interacting.[162] This is critical for working among peoples, such as the Senufo, who believe that the spirits are the source of their songs and instruments. Their pre-Christian worldviews regarding music require a theology of music-in-context that helps them understand God within their cultural context.

We must also identify biblical precedents for using music in mission and church ministry. What were the uses and functions of music throughout Scripture? What

---

160   Smith, *Creating Understanding,* 63-64.

161   Two helpful sources that address the music-culture of Israel are Sendrey (1969) and more recently Braun (2002); see Joachim Braun, *Music in Ancient Israel/Palestine: Archaeological, Written, and Comparative Sources* (Grand Rapids: W. B. Eerdmans, 2002). They bring helpful information to the theological conversation about music. The closest source of a theology of music-in-context is Corbitt (1998), where he identifies the theological roles of music in the kingdom.

162   In *Christianity in Culture,* Charles Kraft develops a model proposing a "God-*Above-but-Through-Culture*" position. See Kraft in *Handbook* bibliography (1979), 113–15.

about the use of musical instruments? Did God deem only a few instruments as sacred for his purposes? What about secular songs? How did biblical leaders integrate music into their ministry for God? The Song of Moses (Ex 15:1–21) shows Moses incorporating song into his leadership style. Song served as a means of theological reflection about God's deliverance and was ultimately incorporated into the worship tradition of the Israelites.

> Without solid biblical foundations and theological underpinnings, our use of music in mission and worship is left to the mercy of ill-informed opinions.

2. *Composing new songs fosters theologizing.* Recognizing the importance of a song's content, as we compose new Scripture-based songs, we seek to shape a song's message in ways that penetrate the thought processes of a people.[163] Significantly, songs communicate a complexity of experience that cannot be expressed through abstract language. Their ability to capture complex dimensions of life and relationships make them significant vehicles for interaction and communication with God.[164]

Moise, a Nyarafolo lay preacher, began processing the theological concept of "covenant" as he worked with the Abrahamic story. The concept was both new and not readily understood within the world of the Senufo.[165] Additionally, he introduced the startling truth that God talked with Abraham, a thought that runs counter to Senufo worldview that the creator God is distant and unapproachable. The song-composing process provided a means of interacting with the Scriptures within a nascent faith community and also launched theological formation of its people. Dynamic contextualization of the biblical text was taking place at the grassroots level.[166]

---

163   See my 1999 publication (cf. *Handbook* bibliography) for a full development of a method for composing new songs in fellowship groups. The method was developed in working with the Nyarafolos over a period of ten years.

164   Mark J. Hatcher, "Poetry, Singing, and Contextualization," in *Missiology: An International Review* 29, no. 4 (2001): 475. Hatcher argues, based on anthropological theories from Geertz and Turner, that the functional aspects of poetry and singing in relation to experience provide a means for "bringing the meaning of the gospel into inter-penetration with the cultural world of Christian believers" (ibid.). He adds that "worship facilitated the penetration of the word of Christ into the experience of Christian believers . . . Singing therefore functioned as a vehicle for the meaning of the gospel to be received in the inner self in such a way that it demanded an ongoing application of its meaning to the details of everyday social interaction" (ibid., 477).

165   Translators initially settled for the Nyarafolo word for "promise." However, having been challenged to probe deeper, they have begun using a term meaning "cut-mouth-give," which appears to be amazingly close to the Hebrew expression to "cut a covenant." The Nyarafolo term signifies an agreement that is extremely binding on both parties. Nyarafolo translators disagree about using the term due to its close association with the spirit world; cf. Linnea Boese, field notes (2003), 1.

166   See Lila W. Balisky, "Theology in Song: Ethiopia's Tesfaye Gabbiso," *Missiology: An International Review* 25, no. 4 (1997): 447–456. She has an excellent study of theology in the songs of Tesfaye Gabbiso, who has impacted Ethiopian Christianity through songs composed while in prison.

INTRODUCTION

SECTION 1: FOUNDATIONS

SECTION 2: STORIES

SECTION 3: TOOLS

CLOSING

MUSIC COMMUNICATION FOR THE GOSPEL'S SAKE

In conclusion, we have interacted with four musical bridges for closing the gap in communicating Christ. As we pursue fulfilling the Great Commission through discerning use of music and the performing arts, our purposes are to:

1. encourage dynamic and authentic expressions of Christian experience for each people and faith community;
2. facilitate the composing of culturally appropriate Christian songs that speak meaningfully into the lives of people;
3. foster the communication of the gospel in culturally appropriate ways that reveal Jesus Christ as the Lord of all nations; and
4. work toward contextualizing music for worship, witness, and spiritual formation.

May all nations come to worship before him!

119

INTRODUCTION

SECTION 1: FOUNDATIONS

SECTION 2: STORIES

SECTION 3: TOOLS

CLOSING

23. SPARE THEM WESTERN MUSIC![167]

By Vida Chenoweth

DEFINING "ETHNOMUSICOLOGY"

Before ethnomusicology has any relevance to missionaries, the term must not only be understood, but a particular theological point must be considered. Laymen often stumble over the pronunciation of "ethnomusicology" because the term is unfamiliar, but simply put, ethnomusicology is an expansion of musicology, the study of music. Because musicology has been devoted primarily to the study of music which is European in origin, a new term was needed to designate the study of music whose origin is not European, and in many cases, music that has never been written down. It was not until students of music began to examine music of non-European peoples that we became conscious of the fact that cultures of the world conceive of and structure music in ways very foreign to us. The variety is staggering, and while music types are not quite so diverse as languages, the comparison is parallel in many respects.

As for the theological point, unless we believe that individual cultures have a unique and valid contribution to make to Christian worship, the significance of ethnic music—along with all other means of expression—will escape us entirely. We must accept that the Holy Spirit can inspire and speak through vernacular music expression just as through vernacular prayer and Bible translation, or else we must deny the universality of God. God speaks through every language and every music system, regardless of whether the missionary has an aesthetic response to it. The Lord can bring any language or any music system into captivity. When he does, the rules of grammar will not change, but rather *what* is said.

We mentioned before that not all peoples structure their musical ideas in the same way. This means that across some cultural boundaries music is not intelligible. In such a case, we may be sure that we have come up against a different music system. That is, rhythm and melody are produced in ways entirely different from our metric or measured rhythm. In many cultures the rhythm of the words form a natural rhythm for the melody. In most other cultures, melodies are not composed to harmonize with certain chordal harmonies that underlie them.

---

167   This classic article was originally published in a slightly different form in Vida Chenoweth, "Spare Them Western Music!" *Evangelical Missions Quarterly* 20 (1984): 30–35. Reprinted by permission of EMQ.

MUSIC MAKING FOR PRAYER AND WORSHIP

Yet all these kinds of music making can and should be vehicles of prayer and praise. There is nothing in the New Testament to suggest that the evangelized need adopt the cultural ways of the evangelist. On the contrary, one of the prime controversies was the insistence by the Pharisees that all believers be circumcised, conforming to Jewish ways.

Indigenous worship does not need English, or singing in parts, or pipe organ, or a guitar in order to be valid worship. Observing European and American worship services often suggests to those who have been evangelized that this is the correct way to do things. This impression we must guard against.

During a recent tour through Africa, I found the enthusiastic response of missionaries and African Christians to be most heartening. In discussions that followed the lectures, several questions arose consistently. They were:

> Each culture should produce its own songs, pray its own prayers, and thus worship with true understanding.

1. Few missionaries are trained musicians, so what can they do toward fostering ethnic church music?
2. Do you give them a hymnal?
3. How do we missionaries have time to do all this?
4. Some music has strong association with what is antagonistic to Christianity, so how can we use it in church?

The reply to question 2 is the most direct. The answer is no. My students and I may compose a few Scripture songs to check our own grasp of the music system and to trigger the idea of creating vernacular songs for worship, but each culture should produce its own songs, pray its own prayers, and thus worship with true understanding.

In reply to question 1, it is true that few missionaries are trained musicians, and among them even fewer are trained ethnomusicologists, but we are making strides in that direction. Since my first efforts in 1963 in Mexico, interest has steadily increased. Musicians did not know there was a place for them on the mission field. By 1970 there was one more. Today we Christian ethnomusicologists are six, with four more in the pipeline.[168]

Combining questions 1 and 3, it would be unthinkable to expect missionaries to leave the field and begin the many years of training necessary to be an ethnomusicologist, unless he or she is already a well-trained musician who can transcribe music easily. However, there are valuable contributions the missionary alone can make toward building the foundation for ethnic music in worship.

He or she can from the beginning show an interest in the local music, all music, in order not to impede the flow of creativity that the church may need at a later date. This is not to say that one should participate yet in the local music, as it takes time and careful investigation for the outsider to understand either the music or the occasion for performing it. We must neither subscribe to nor reject what we do not fully understand.

---

168   [Ed.: These figures provided by Chenoweth in 1984 are truly remarkable given the veritable explosion of activity among Christian ethnomusicologists in recent years. The wide range of contributors to this *Handbook* is ample proof of how much progress has been made in this area over the past few decades.]

DANGERS RESULTING FROM REJECTING PEOPLE'S MUSIC

To reject music at an early stage of living with another culture may drive a practice underground. Last year a student and I visited an island in the Pacific, where it had been assumed for years that there was no indigenous music still remaining. After all, they had been Christians for nearly a century. It took several days of talking through an interpreter to convince the people that we wanted to record music that was truly traditional. Our being white and Christian, they were eager to show us what they assumed we wanted to hear, anthems sung in English. We listened but did not record. Finally they began to demonstrate their ancestral music, and it was astounding how much they had retained secretly, because early missionaries had condemned it.

There are several dangers resulting from rejection of a people's music:

- First, there is the danger of interrupting the transmission of all local singing so that the baby goes out with the bath water and the entire tradition faces extinction.
- Second, rejection may cause some rituals to be secretly retained, thus encouraging syncretism.
- Third, rejection alienates composers from the church and, as we are discovering in Africa, it also can alienate the mission from the people. Remember that not everyone composes songs. It is not like speech in that everyone talks. Let us be patient with composers and make every effort to introduce them to Christ.

It is therefore beneficial to keep alive the act of creating music in the local idiom. Later, after conversion, composers will spontaneously sing of the most important event of their life.

DANGERS RESULTING FROM ILL-DESIGNED MUSIC WORKSHOPS

We must not rush this phenomenon. Some of our number are trying to hurry this process by means of workshops during which time nationals are expected to produce Christian songs on demand.

However, a meeting with local composers and church leaders that explains and encourages the legitimacy of indigenous music for worship is beneficial. So is a course in writing down music, so long as it is in the music system of those people. Such a course can only be formulated by a trained ethnomusicologist who has an understanding by thorough analysis of just how a culture structures its music. A workshop—in the sense that a group meets in order to produce a repertoire on demand—can be superficial both spiritually and musically.

A couple of dangers inherent in the workshop method have been observed: the participant quickly adjusts some new text to a traditional melody (and is sometimes laughed down because of the lingering connotations of the melody) or, in some cases, the participant sweats with frustration and embarrassment, unable to fulfill the request.

In addition to simply appreciating the way in which people make music, the mission worker goes on about the task of bringing individuals into a personal relationship with Christ. At the same time, he or she develops a deep interest in the people and in their ways of dealing with life and the universe. One of the most profitable ways to learn of the culture is to investigate the kinds of songs sung and the reasons for singing them. A methodical collection of the kinds of music people make is valuable information for the outsider and a valuable repository for the insiders.

If a missionary wants to explore the actual elements of the music system and how they are put together, he consults an ethnomusicologist. To make a musical analysis, the ethnomusicologist needs a reproduction on tape of every style and kind of music in the culture and a translation of the text, if possible. This ought not to be collected haphazardly. Preceding each item there should be an explanation of what the song is about. For example, "This is a song of divination which has come down from the ancestors. It is sung only at full moon. The elders look into the fire and see visions of lost articles, impending disaster such as famine, and the like."

DANGERS RESULTING FROM INTRODUCING WESTERN INSTRUMENTS AND EQUIPMENT

When dealing with an oral tradition, one of the problems facing the ethnomusicologist is interference of other cultures. For example, the transistor radio and other electronic equipment such as amplifiers and public address systems may deprive the traditional composer of the silence he needs.

Other well-meaning teachers of Western music introduce Western instruments such as the guitar or a keyboard instrument. It is not out of personal bias that an ethnomusicologist raises objections to this. While this seems an innocuous and pleasurable act on the surface, it is inadvisable for several reasons. One, the immediate satisfaction may not be worth the ultimate consequences of thwarting the indigenous musical expression. Few realize the devastating effect that introducing the guitar can have on an oral tradition, but even the tuning of the instrument forces the newcomers into a chordal system that will influence the invention of melody along foreign, European-based harmony.

The newcomer learns the three basic chords (tonic, subdominant, and dominant) and thereafter is caught in a system that is not his own. Either he must copy the West or strum these Western chords nonsensically alongside indigenous melodies. Ultimately the player will lose the ability to think in the musical terms of his own people and, more often than not, will not be a master of the Western idiom either. The oral tradition will consequently be on the endangered list.

Any Western music introduces a mathematically contrived scale that is unnatural to oral traditions. It seems unfair to impose this on an oral system which, because it is not written down, has no defense against being swallowed up. Thus the well-intentioned missionary may, unawares, contribute to the obliteration of a culture's music system.

A second reason why the introduction of Western instruments and music seems unfair is that many ethnic groups that are just on the threshold of literacy do not have the historical perspective to anticipate the consequences of an immediate choice. It is not that we know their needs better than they, but that we know by case history what are the probable consequences of their choice. By and large, it is more productive to encourage local leadership in music rather than to assume the leadership in a culture not our own.

FOSTERING INDIGENOUS MUSICAL LEADERSHIP

The fruit of indigenous musical leadership in the church has resulted in a wealth of worship styles all over the world. In Papua New Guinea a student and I met a Komba tribesman who recorded for us their 368th hymn. In Irian Jaya another student and I visited a church service by Dani men who formed their own church. The singing was all from Scripture and composed by the Danis themselves in a vocal style unique to them.

In Nigeria I was privileged to attend a women's fellowship where each delegation was a choir. They listened to their own fiery preacher, a lady, then picked up their clay pots from the floor to serve as percussion instruments for accompanying their own songs to the Lord. Their joy was contagious as they sang without cultural confusion and without apology as to who they were.

> The well-intentioned missionary may, unawares, contribute to the obliteration of a culture's music system.

In Cameroon on Palm Sunday a choir of sixty or seventy adults stepped rhythmically, but with great dignity, into an open arena while waving their palm branches and singing mightily to the orchestral accompaniment of drums and xylophones. It was overwhelming in its complexity and fervor. It was their Christian expression.

Why would anyone want to capture all the birds of the forest, paint them gray, and give them all the same song? God made each one, and each has its song to sing for him.

24. MAKING A DIFFERENCE IN A WEEK: EIGHT PRINCIPLES FOR ART MAKING IN SHORT-TERM ENGAGEMENT

By J. Nathan Corbitt with Sarah Rohrer

AN OPENING STORY

Leah leaned across my dining room table and asked skeptically, "Can anyone make a difference in a week?" It was not really a question but a statement, and one I hear frequently from discerning people. I take it seriously. A professional muralist, Leah had spent a week working with gang members in prison, other weeks creating community murals with scores of kids in informal settlements in Kenya and Guatemala, and even a three-month stint restoring historic and community places in a hurricane-ravaged Caribbean island, all at her own expense. She was questioning the impact of a short-term artist's engagement in communities of poverty, crisis, and catastrophe. She has both a right and responsibility to ask.

What can an artist possibly do in a week that is effective, supports the local church in its mission, and leads toward the holistic transformation of both individuals and communities? The answer depends on a number of factors, including what skills the artist—in any art form—brings, the role the artist plays, the relationship the artist has with the local organization or community, and what the artist leaves behind.

Nearly eight thousand miles away in Kenya, Gideon, a Kenyan organizational leader, was asking a related question, "How do we motivate and assist local artists living in the poverty of our informal settlements to become active in the transformation of their own communities?" A highly educated and motivated leader, he was well aware of the resources needed to empower small, local community centers that work with children in poverty. An artist himself, he knew the power of the arts to assist in the process of instilling hope and providing healing from trauma. He was seeking resources to facilitate the growth and impact of local artists. He wanted to help them accept ownership of the programs and avoid depending on "foreign" resources that are often inconsistent. That was six years ago before Leah came to spend a week with them. How did someone like Leah assist Gideon's organization in only a week? What kinds of relationships were needed? Was the cost worth it? And did it work—are there results?

The truth is, community transformation—the journey to holistic well-being—is never short-term. Every short-term event is connected to other events that are, in turn, connected to personal and organizational relationships. These events happen in a context of the historical development of communities and the long-term transformation of people. Working together requires a strong relationship between organizations and people in leadership. In this relationship, people are intentionally engaged to seek the well-being of one another and their communities through experiences that transform their lives and communities.

EIGHT PRINCIPLES FOR SHORT-TERM ART MAKING

For the past ten years BuildaBridge International,[169] an organization I cofounded and now serve as president, has been struggling with issues of funding, relevance, and the impact of short-term engagement, much like a number of other arts organizations working in areas affected by poverty. We have concluded that short-term engagement is part of developing long-term organizational

> Our goal is to assist local communities to meet their own needs.

relationships that meet the needs of the local organization. Such short-term engagement involves the processes of networking, collaboration, and training. Our goal is to assist local communities to meet their own needs. In order to accomplish this, we have established the following principles:

Principle #1: Weigh the realistic cost of short-term mission

There are major practical issues to consider, primarily related to financial and cultural factors. Short-term missions are expensive, and the financial resources may be better used elsewhere. A trip to a Central American country for a ten-day short-term project can cost $2,400. That same amount covers the annual salary of two private school teachers in Haiti!

Local organizations certainly understand the money involved in hosting guests. Increasingly, as a result of globalization, leaders of these organizations come to the US and Canada to raise money for their projects and recruit interns and personnel. It is natural to ask whether it would be better to take the money needed for such interns' travel and instead give it directly to the projects. Recently we have begun creating an in-kind budget for short-term projects, including the contributed time of the artists/trainers, administration, and local contributions of food, transportation, and assistance. In one experience in Central America, the real cost for a weekend training with three trainers and a local supervisor was more than $15,000.

There are real cultural and class-related issues. Communicating in a second language and unfamiliarity with local customs—including art forms and the inevitable differences in cultural values—often lead to conflict or ineffectiveness.

Principle #2: Define your mission

When faced with cost and cultural issues, both the host and the guest artist should thoughtfully consider the goal and expected outcome of the project. They should communicate openly about

---

169   See the BuildaBridge International website at http://www.buildabridge.org.

them before the mission, giving preference to the needs of the host organization. BuildaBridge distinguishes two types of mission for the focus of our work abroad:

1. *Arts-based intervention and relief* (or psychosocial support). The term "arts-based intervention and relief" refers to the use of the creative arts as therapeutic healing in situations of catastrophe, violence, poverty, terrorist attacks, or homelessness. The goal is to help the survivors of such events through an arts-based process of healing. Working as second responders to a crisis, the artists assist to create environments that are physically and emotionally safe and to provide psychosocial support through training and therapeutic art making in the community context.
2. *Arts-based restorative development.* This type of mission is a long-term collaborative and restorative project. It assists both communities and individuals—primarily children—with the goal of restoring holistic wellness in the physical, psychological, emotional, social, and spiritual dimensions of life. These projects may include long-term training of local artists, strategic planning of community-based arts programs, and place-making projects to improve the environment.

Often the short-term intervention and relief type of mission leads to the long-term restorative development type, as an organizational alliance is built. In our opening story, Leah responded to a call for a muralist to work in an informal settlement that had been racked by political violence and a recent flood. The children were traumatized and the environment had been devastated. Leah was part of a BuildaBridge "artist on call" team of ten artists and creative art therapists, along with an equal number of local Kenyan artists. An Arts for Hope camp served over one hundred children. Training was a significant aspect of the intervention and relief. Now in our fifth year of collaboration, over twenty-five local artists are working with children in four informal settlements. They are assisted by an artist on call educator and administrator who has raised her own support for the past two years. Training and job creation have become the priorities.

> Intervention and relief missions may require training and expertise in emergency relief, arts-based psychological first aid, and therapeutic art making.

Principle #3: Match skills to the needs

Defining the type of mission helps delineate the type of artistic, educational, and therapeutic skills needed for a short-term project. Intervention and relief missions may require training and expertise in emergency relief, arts-based psychological first aid, and therapeutic art making. For longer term projects artists may need skills in arts-based community development, arts-assisted learning, and place making. It is for this reason that BuildaBridge began an annual institute to prepare creative people for such relief and development. An educational alliance was later formed with Eastern University near Philadelphia. Eastern offers an MA in Urban Studies with a concentration in Arts for Transformation.

Principle #4: Commit to long-term organizational alliances

A true alliance occurs when there are contributions and respect from both sides; each brings something that the other needs. An outside organization must look and listen to identify local leaders, rather than rush in with a program that does not take local gifts into account. As an outside specialist, you are going to a specific place and context, one that will remain after you leave. Ask questions to identify those who are already at work, what has already been tried, failed, or succeeded, and what strengths the community already possesses. Balanced partnerships make for sustainable development, since someone remains after you leave to continue the work. Indeed a true partnership builds the social capital of the local organization you work with, providing training and leadership experience to set up the local leaders for success. As we have learned, written letters of agreement are essential in setting expectations and sustaining good communication.

Principle #5: Focus on a motivation of service to others

The creative artist must be motivated by a sincere desire to meet the needs of a local community as the members define them, without the expectation of personal reward or benefit. This motivation and its positive results are often worked out and realized through personal sacrifice. Local organizations also have motivations. Mission statements and goals are often a first indicator of the organization's motivation. Artists should expect to make a sacrifice when they engage in short-term service. Service is not an opportunity for employment or a research project, though generally there will be much personal gain for the artist through the process.

Principle #6: Establish the role the artist will have

Here are three of the most common roles artists play[170]:

1. *Catalysts* have the largest role in short-term engagement. They lead by example among those with whom they work. They do what those around them had not yet imagined, and in the process give the community a new vision of what is possible. BuildaBridge International's Diaspora of Hope art camps strive to be such a catalyst through example. Established only a few years back, Diaspora of Hope was a November initiative that engaged artists to serve simultaneously in different parts of the world during the American Thanksgiving. The arts camps—based on the theme of hope—provided both training and experience for local artists to work with children through arts-assisted learning. This type of learning uses the BuildaBridge Classroom Model, which is trauma informed, hope infused, and child centered. Since then local organizations have taken the theme and continued the tradition in Guatemala, Haiti, Nicaragua, and Kenya. BuildaBridge has continued its support through training of local artists. Each organization involved has adapted the model to fit its own needs as they continue to determine the nature of the ongoing alliance.

2. The *consultant* comes on a contractual basis. He or she brings expert knowledge to do what no one else can do. For example, a consultant may facilitate a very specific project like a one-day arts-based psychological first aid training for NGO employees working with traumatized communities. While consultants' relationships remain limited, their influence is large.

3. Finally, *the connector* increases social capital by identifying organizations and individuals that could have beneficial partnerships, and by introducing them to one another. Connectors will often facilitate relationships between a small, local organization doing

---

170   For another approach to the role of the artist as outsider, see Schrag's chapter in Section 3 of this *Handbook*, "How to Determine Your Role as an Arts Advocate and Facilitator."

good work but going unnoticed and a larger organization with the ability to support and strengthen the programming it is already doing or planning. Connectors expand the influence of organizations outside of their original contexts.

Principle #7: Serve for the sustainability and capacity development of the local organization

When the needed skills have been determined, a final question must be asked: "What happens the day after we leave?" This question should guide all the planning and implementing of the engagement as it is key to the sustainability of the change the guest wishes to make. Such questioning is not meant to discourage the artist from going, but to encourage him or her to go for the right reasons and with the right mindset to have a partnership that is contextual, sustainable, and that builds capacity. This mindset and way of working will make the engagement more than just one short-term event, but rather one part in a series of relationships that transforms a community.

Principle #8: Stay connected and evaluate for impact

Creative artists are generally good at exploring, connecting, and building relationships across boundaries of difference. For nearly twenty years I have observed that those who have engaged in short-term mission often commit to long-term missions. In some cases, the artists who engaged in a short-term project return to help and sometimes become a part of the local organization. They return because they have experienced and see the impact of their efforts. From an organizational perspective, capturing this impact can be difficult, but it is essential in times when funders and supporters want to know if cross-cultural workers are making a difference. Organizations that partner for a mission are well served when they stay connected through formal and informal channels and when they plan for the formal evaluation of their joint efforts.

A CONCLUDING STORY

It was five years ago that Leah leaned over my table and asked me if anyone could make a difference in a week. Recently we met again over breakfast, in Chicago. "I've thought a lot about it since then," she told me. Over the years, as Leah has continued her work, she has come to believe that it *is* possible to make a change in a week. That is not all. She declared this: "If you can make a change in a week, then you can make a change in a day. And if you can make a change in a day, then you can make a change in a moment."

Every encounter has the potential to be a moment of transformation when you are engaged for good and are intentional about the process. A short-term arts-based engagement is just one part of a historical series of related events of transformation.[171]

---

171   For additional reading, see the following in the *Handbook* bibliography: Ausland (2011), Borrup (2006), Chambers (2005), Corbett and Fikkert (2005), and Corbitt and Nix-Early (2003). See also: Samuel Escobar, "Mission as Transforming Service," in *The New Global Mission: The Gospel from Everywhere to Everyone* (Downers Grove, IL: InterVarsity Press, 2003), 142–54; and J. P. Spradley, D. W. McCurdy, and S. B. Gmelch, "Why Tourism Matters," in *Conformity and Conflict: Readings in Cultural Anthropology* (Columbus: Pearson, 2009), 354–64.

129

INTRODUCTION

SECTION 1: FOUNDATIONS

SECTION 2: STORIES

SECTION 3: TOOLS

CLOSING

25. CROSS-CULTURAL COMMUNICATION THROUGH SYMBOL

By C. Michael Hawn and Swee Hong Lim

Second only to the translation of Scripture is the spread of the gospel through various symbols. Symbols provide modes of communication, establish identity, and engage the affective dimensions of personality. Many symbols communicate through nonverbal means. The imprecision of symbolic forms of communication allows for easier transmission across cultures and helps to establish Christian identity, especially in societies where Christianity exists in the midst of religious pluralism.

Historical symbols such as the cross may be adapted to any cultural context and still maintain their central shape and meaning. Musical forms and styles can also bridge cultures, often being creatively adapted in new environments.

Symbols are more complex than signs. Signs are arbitrary indicators that point to some aspect of reality; for example, a green light indicates that a car may go. A symbol embodies in some way the reality to which it points, and participates in its meaning. The Lord's Supper, for example, mirrors to some degree historical meals that Christ had with his followers and ritualizes the sayings of Christ as "the bread of life" and "the true vine." Through the symbolism of Communion we may participate in the reality of Christ's life and ministry on earth and the promise of eternal life in heaven.

The following are a sampling of historical and current symbolic forms that reach across cultures and enrich the transmission of the gospel.

VISUAL SYMBOLS

The cross

The cross, though not exclusively Christian, is central to the followers of Christ. The origins of the cross as a symbol are difficult to ascertain. However, from the Latin crux, the cross referred historically to an instrument of death by crucifixion during the Roman rule at the time of the life of Christ. Several meanings have been attributed to the crossbeams of the Christian cross, including the four quadrants of the earth and the intersection between heaven (vertical beam) and earth (horizontal beam).

INTRODUCTION

SECTION 1: FOUNDATIONS

SECTION 2: STORIES

SECTION 3: TOOLS

CLOSING

Numerous Christian traditions and cultures throughout history have designed variations on the simple crossbeams of this implement used for Christ's crucifixion. Thus one can distinguish the symbol used by Orthodox, Coptic, Celtic, and many other Christian groups throughout history. In the Roman Catholic tradition, the crucifix bears the body of the crucified Christ. Some Protestant traditions, such as the Reformed Church, have avoided any visual symbols in worship. Today, however, the cross as symbol appears in many worship spaces.

The cross functions as a part of Christian worship in several ways. In the Roman Catholic and Anglican traditions a crucifer bears the cross on a pole and leads processions into the worship space. Both Orthodox and Roman Catholic Churches, as well as some Anglicans and Lutherans, observe special feast days related to the cross. These include the Feast of Corpus Christi on the Thursday after Trinity Sunday, the Feast of the Glorious Cross celebrated in some form by Roman Catholics and Anglicans on September 14, and the Veneration of the Cross observed on Good Friday by the Roman Catholic, Orthodox, and some Anglican Churches.

The cross has also served as an object of personal devotion and adornment throughout Christian history. It has been, for example, attached to rosary beads, worn by men and women on a necklace, or embedded in a piece of jewelry. As adornment, it is used by Christians and non-Christians alike and may serve for some the role of an amulet.

Iconography

The use of icons has often been associated with the Eastern Orthodox Church. However, this sacred art form is broader and may originate in the first centuries after Christ's resurrection. Some scholars have indicated that the third-century Christian paintings found in the baptistery room of the house church in Dura-Europas, Syria, depicted biblical imageries and could have been the forerunner or catalyst to this sacred visual art form.

Suffice it to say that icons are not considered works of art, but rather artistic narrative about the kingdom of God. They serve as avenues for anamnesis—the actualization or active remembering of past saving acts of God—for those who choose to use them. Thus icons are venerated—shown great honor and respect—in stylized ways such as by being carried high in a procession or by physical acts of respect like bowing. They are not, however, worshiped. Sadly, some Christians have not understood this representational sacred art form and its worth in deepening Christian spirituality.

In the seventh and eighth centuries Christians clashed violently over the use of icons, the "iconoclastic controversies," at the end of which the Orthodox tradition affirmed the centrality of icons in their worship.

Today the use of icons is experiencing a revival. While the Orthodox and Coptic churches continue to lead in the use of icons as a part of liturgy, the Taizé Community in France also uses them in their worship space. They find that icons facilitate prayer in an ecumenical setting where too many words could encourage divisions. Likewise, congregations associated with the Emerging Church movement have also wholeheartedly embraced this liturgical practice. Interest in icons as a liturgical expression is also growing among mainline denominations as they seek a holistic approach in worship.

Icthus, the fish

The fish (icthus) symbol has long been a significant expression of Christian identity. Originating in the Greek word ιχους (fish), its individual letters serve as an acrostic for a Greek phrase that is generally translated as "Jesus Christ, God's Son, Savior."

This particular symbol was especially important to the early church, as members faced persecution from Roman authorities for their faith in Christ. It was used as a code for believers to recognize each other. Equally important is the fact that this symbol resonates strongly with the scriptural theme of fishing in relation to God's plan for people's salvation, as exemplified in verses such as, "And Jesus said to them, 'Follow me and I will make you fish for people'" (Mark 1:17 NRSV).

The fish symbol is typically used to mark catacombs, caves, or any places that denote the presence of Christians. This marking is said to have originated from Alexandria, Egypt, in the first or second century and to have subsequently spread to Europe. However, it is important to note that Christianity is not the only faith tradition that has used this symbol. Other faith traditions such as Egyptian mystery cults, Buddhism, and Hinduism have also done it. However, Christianity has been deliberate in fully developing the icthus as a distinctive symbolic faith expression.

Vestments

No special clothing set clergy apart from lay Christians before the fourth century. From that time onward, vestments became associated with Christian ritual and have served several functions in the subsequent history of Christian worship.

Vestments often indicate the role that a lay member or clergy holds in the church. For example, in various parts of Africa one may distinguish between Anglican, Methodist, or Presbyterian women by the uniform clothing that is distinct to each denomination. Various African initiated churches may be distinguished by their clothing. Choirs often wear special vestments, including various colors and styles of robes, depending on local and denominational tradition. Ministers or others who officiate often wear vestments to emphasize their vocational role and disguise or mute their individual identity. In some Protestant traditions, especially Presbyterians and some Methodists and Baptists, academic gowns, usually black, are worn as a vestment that indicates the authority of the minister to preside.

While primarily associated with worship leadership, some vestments may be worn in the broader community, especially the ministerial collar worn by Roman Catholic and Anglican priests, Lutheran pastors, and ministers in some other Protestant groups. This collar is a witness to their vocation in the broader community, especially in hospitals or at civic events. Members of Roman Catholic monastic orders often wear their robes and habits in public as a sign of their special commitment to Christ and the church. Rather than a symbol of distinction, the simple cassock is a sign of humility and shedding of as much individuality as possible, since those committed to monastic life are servants of the church.

In other traditions, especially in the West, the differences between clergy and laity are blurred, and no specific ecclesial vestments are worn. In these cases a business suit or more informal apparel is normative. The context distinguishes the leader, rather than any specific liturgical garb. Some worship teams wear uniform clothing and others choose clothing that might be worn by a secular band or that is similar to what is worn by the worshipers who attend. Though not historically thought of as vestments, intentional choices in clothing are made that reflect the witness, identity, and cultural context of those leading or presiding in worship.

INTRODUCTION

SECTION 1: FOUNDATIONS

SECTION 2: STORIES

SECTION 3: TOOLS

CLOSING

SYMBOLS

Congregational song

Singing is for Christians a biblical mandate. Psalm 96:1, 98:1, 104:33, and 149:1 are but a few passages that link singing with praising God's name. Furthermore, the biblical witness is replete with canticles (songs beyond the book of Psalms) that were sung by men and women within the context of specific narratives. Representative Old Testament examples include the songs of Moses (Ex 15:1–19) and Miriam (Ex 15:20,21), the song of Moses (Deut 32:1–43), the song of Hannah (1 Sam 2:1–10), the song of Habakkuk (Hab 3:1–19), the song of Isaiah (Isa 26:9–20), the song of Jonah (Jonah 2:2–9), and the song of the Three Holy Children (Dan 3:57–88).

The primary canticles in the New Testament are found in Luke 1 and 2: the song of Zacharias, or *Benedictus* (1:68–79); the song of Mary, or *Magnificat* (1:46–55); the song of the angels, *Gloria in excelsis* (2:14); and the song of Simeon, *Nunc dimittis* (2:29–32). In addition, the New Testament includes creedal hymns, the most famous of which is the *Kenosis* (self-emptying) hymn in Philippians 2:5–11. Finally, there are the great hymns of praise in Revelation; e.g., 5:12,13; 11:17,18; 15:3,4; and 19:1–8.

Ephesians 5:19 and Colossians 3:16 encourage variety in song—"psalms, hymns, and spiritual songs" (NRSV)—though scholars do not agree on the exact meaning of these terms. Acts 16:25 records an example of songs being a witness to the Lord when the prisoners Paul and Silas sang while in jail.

Though little is known about music in the worship of Christians in the first three centuries, some hymn texts have survived. What we do know is that music in worship meant *singing*—human voices. The purpose of this singing within the congregational setting is fivefold:

1. It is a point of identity for Christians throughout the ages. While there have been times when the people's voice was silent in worship, generally, congregational song has been a primary element in Christian worship across the years.
2. Congregational singing has been one of the ways that the church has connected with its heritage. The witness of those who have gone before is contained in the great hymns of the church.
3. Congregational singing bears theological insights; it articulates the way Christians in various traditions express their theology.
4. Congregational singing promotes unity of spirit among those gathered for worship. Unity may be experienced not only among those physically gathered for worship, but also with the "faithful of every time and place"—those Christians who have gone before and who are scattered throughout the world.
5. Congregational singing bears witness to those in the congregation who need the message of the song.

For many Protestant Christians who have either avoided or never explored visual symbols in worship, congregational singing bears an iconic quality. Many hymns indicate that the hosts of heaven begin the song and the earth responds with its own song. The idea of a cosmic song that is sung simultaneously in heaven and on earth represents the iconic quality of congregational singing.

Sacred music

Sacred music may be defined broadly as music with holy or religious themes. As such, this music extends beyond the church to the concert hall or other public venues and beyond the Christian context to any religious or cultic context where it is used for religious purposes.

In most Christian traditions sacred music generally adorns worship in some way. This sacred music, perhaps more appropriately called "church music," is most often vocal, including solo, choral, and congregational singing, but also includes instruments ranging from orchestra and organ to piano, guitar, electronic synthesizers, percussion, and various indigenous instruments, pitched and non-pitched, throughout the world. Related art forms such as dance often fall under the purview of the music director in local congregations.

Music is one of the primary forms of contextualization of Christian worship. Various denominations, ethnic traditions, and generational groups use music to establish their identity and promote the Christian message that represents their theological tenets and ecclesiological understandings. In Western church tradition, specific genres of musical composition developed to support the liturgy of the church. These genres included the mass, oratorio, passion, requiem, motet, anthem, and cantata. As Christianity has spread, many of these genres have been

> Generally, the text and the context of the music are better indicators of the sacred nature of the music than musical style.

embraced by cultures around the world in modified forms. More recently the term "ritual music" is used in some contexts to refer to music that supports the sacred ritual. This music may include the congregation's participation, as well as that of specialized choirs and instrumentalists.

Throughout church music history some styles have been identified almost exclusively with Christian worship, including plainsong and Protestant hymns. Other styles of sacred music have drawn from secular sources including opera, popular song styles of the day, gospel, rock, rap, and various ethnic styles around the world. Generally the text and the context of the music are better indicators of the sacred nature of the music than musical style.

Instrumental music

Instruments have often played a significant role in worship. The *shofar* (ram's horn) was very important for specific Jewish festivals. Psalm 81:3 (NLT) states, "Blow the ram's horn at new moon, and again at full moon to call a festival." Psalm 150 refers to a variety of instruments.

For both practical and ethical reasons, instruments were less common in the early church. A persecuted church could not risk the louder sounds of noisy instruments that might call attention to their worship. The young church was also distinguishing itself from its Jewish ancestry. And within the Greco-Roman context the church's resistance to the use of instruments—e.g., flutes and reeds—revealed concern about importing elements into the worship music that might evoke pagan rituals or entertainments.

The medieval Western church favored vocal music, preferably *a cappella,* even though instruments of various kinds may have been used locally in liturgy. Eventually the organ became the dominant instrument. Perhaps as a result of abuses of instruments in liturgy, the *motu proprio* (1903) of Pope Pius X on sacred music proposed a restricted role for instruments. The document echoes the principles set forth at the Council of Trent (1545–63), clearly favoring unaccompanied vocal music. The Reformers took various approaches to instruments, from banning them (Calvin and Zwingli) to incorporating the organ fully into liturgy (Luther).

> As Christian missions mature and ethnomusicologists have an increasing role in communicating the gospel, the use of indigenous instruments in worship is becoming more common.

During the 1960s in the United States the folk song revolution brought first acoustic and then electric guitars into the church, adding a sense of informality and accessibility to music making. Not only did the increased use of guitars and percussion identify more closely with the culture of the day, it also fostered music making that incorporated lay musicians and not just highly trained professionals. Today the use of instruments within Christian worship ranges from no instruments (Church of Christ) to primarily organ and/or piano to a fully electric ensemble with a percussion-based sound.

In missions, instruments continue to be a source of enrichment and controversy. In West Africa, for example, specific drums and drum patterns may communicate non-Christian associations with traditional deities or rituals. In Asia gongs and bells may be associated with indigenous temple worship and deemed, in some cases, inappropriate for Christian ritual.

As a result of these non-Christian associations and because of increased globalization, Western instruments became somewhat predominant in Christian worship around the world. However, as Christian missions mature and ethnomusicologists have an increasing role in communicating the gospel, the use of indigenous instruments in worship is becoming more common. A process of gradual "sanctification" is required, allowing the once "profane" instrument to assume a character appropriate for Christian worship.

Following the Second Vatican Council (1962–65), the Roman Catholic Church led the way in the use of indigenous instruments in the Mass. Protestants have more often incorporated Western instruments in worship. However, today indigenous instruments may be found in Protestant and Pentecostal worship around the globe.

MOVEMENT SYMBOLS

Lifting hands

Typically known as the *orans* position, lifting extended hands upwards is one of the earliest documented postures in worship. A popular practice particularly for charismatic Christians, lifting hands is commonly associated with petitionary prayer (Ps 28:2; 63:4; 1 Tim 2:8), though this symbolic gesture has other meanings as well. In Exodus 17:11–16 Moses lifted his hands, and as he did so, God gave the Israelites victory over the Amalekites. In Leviticus 9:22 this gesture conveys a blessing by Aaron on the Israelites. Like all other physical expressions, the practice of hand lifting is not exclusive to the Jewish or Christian worship tradition. Other faith traditions, such as Islam and Hinduism, also draw on this gesture in their times of worship.

This common expression of raising hands may sometimes be seen as an *instinctive* gesture rather than only as a liturgically prescribed *stylized* movement. Prior to the emergence of the charismatic renewal movement, this posture appears to have been used only in a limited way by the clergy of the Roman Catholic tradition. For example, it was used in the ritual act of narrating portions of the Eucharistic Prayer or in leading the recitation of the Lord's Prayer. However, with the onset of the charismatic renewal movement in the mid-twentieth century, this gesture has been significantly reclaimed by the laity and freely used by individuals to express their personal experience with God.

Tambourine and dance

Dancing with tambourine was first mentioned in Exodus 15:20 following the destruction of the Egyptian army by Yahweh (God) at the Red Sea. Aside from this biblical reference, dance activity has a long history and can be found in ancient civilizations such as Mesopotamia, Greece, and Rome.

Aside from its presence in festive functions, the tambourine also occupies a prominent place as an instrument in religious and cultural events. In the eighteenth century Mozart was known to have included its use in his musical compositions. Tchaikovsky in the nineteenth century was also known to have included the instrument in the "Arabian Dance" of the *Nutcracker Suite*.

At the present time tambourine dancing continues to be featured in Middle Eastern countries in both folk and religious settings. For some charismatic Christians the tambourine is primarily used as an instrument of praise and worship. Dancing with tambourines may be employed in spiritual warfare. Analysis of the use of tambourine with dance in Christian worship reveals that strict tambourine movement patterns often denote specific theological concepts such as covenant or grace. These patterns typically follow a sixteen-beat cycle. Tambourine dancers also tend to favor costume designs that bear specific colors associated with particular spiritual concepts. At the same time, such tambourine dancing may be used with the intention of establishing a link, albeit tenuous, to the Old Testament.

> The purpose of this liturgical act was to symbolically acknowledge the presence of God.

OLFACTORY SYMBOLS: INCENSE

From the earliest times, incense was frequently connected with religious ceremonies. Typically speaking, the use of incense seeks to acknowledge the presence of deities, to possibly appease benevolent spirits or to drive away evil spirits.

In the book of Exodus the offering of incense was a mandated ritual act in worship (Ex 40:27). The purpose of this liturgical act was to symbolically acknowledge the presence of God. At other times its use had the expressed purpose of placating the anger of God so that he would not destroy the Israelites (Num 16:47).

In our present time, there are two primary approaches to understanding and employing the use of incense. The evangelical segment of the church seems to focus on the symbolic equivalence of incense as prayer (Ps 141:2; Rev 5:8). Within more liturgical traditions, the use of incense in such rituals as censing the assembly or reverencing the altar or Communion table has several meanings. Such a ritual may symbolize the "setting apart" of people and things to experience God's holy presence, or it may serve as a tangible sign of God's blessing or to express the importance of the censed people or things in the worship experience. The response on the part of the assembly in such a ritual would either be the signing of the cross on oneself or bowing as the censing occurs. There is no liturgical significance in the manner of censing, though censing techniques are described in some present-day liturgical leadership books.

FILM

Just as stained-glass designs served as a tool in the early years of Christianity to educate generally illiterate believers, film has been harnessed in the twentieth century to convey the gospel, teach its principles, and do evangelism.

At the present time, Christian organizations involved in Web-based ministries such as Christianfilms.com, Outreach.com, and Christiancinema.com are providing another way for believers to nurture their spirituality or to view life's issues from a Christian perspective. Comparable to the Internet Movie Database (IMDb) organization, parallel organizations like the Christian Film Database (CFDb), and Christian Film News help believers nurture their faith through film media.

Christianity in the Southern hemisphere has harnessed media products such as films for the purpose of evangelism rather than entertainment. Campus Crusade for Christ has been in the forefront of this effort. Its most popular work, the *JESUS* film, is presently available in 1,100 languages. Unlike Western Christians, who show such films in homes or churches, Christian organizations in developing countries take advantage of the rural lack of technology and show films in open-air settings. These settings encourage the whole community to gather for this recreational and evangelistic activity.

With increased ambivalence among governing authorities regarding the presence of Christianity, it remains to be seen if this media will be viable in the long run, particularly if it is perceived as a tool of spreading Western ideals and values. In addressing this concern, indigenous Christian organizations like Sri Lanka-based Kithusevana Ministries and Hong Kong-based Media Evangelism Limited seek to contextualize Christianity with their own film productions rather than merely translating Western works. For the moment, film remains an effective way of communicating the gospel to a broad spectrum of people.[172]

---

172   For additional reading, see Dowley (2011), Mayer-Thurman (1975), Ramshaw (2009), and Routley and Richardson (2005) in the *Handbook* bibliography.

INTRODUCTION

SECTION 1: FOUNDATIONS

SECTION 2: STORIES

SECTION 3: TOOLS

CLOSING

137

INTRODUCTION

SECTION 1: FOUNDATIONS

SECTION 2: STORIES

SECTION 3: TOOLS

CLOSING

26. THE CHALLENGE OF INDIGENIZING CHRISTIAN WORSHIP: AN EXAMPLE FROM INDIA

By Jacob Joseph

One of the great challenges for the Indian Christian church is how to relate to its Western heritage. When missionaries first came to India, they translated the Bible and hymns in local languages for use in worship. Today most mainline denominations in India still follow a completely Western-ized liturgy and use Western music in worship. C. H. Dicran, an American musician professionally trained in Indian music, says about the present-day use of indigenous music in Indian churches:

> At best, on any given Sunday morning, one in three hymns is an indigenous song, and many of these, though composed by Indians, are reminiscent of Western hymns. If Christian songs are composed with the intention of sounding particularly Indian (songs that sound like those used by Hindus and Muslims), they are sung only in conventions, special performances at Christmas and Easter, or for evangelistic events in the villages. They have not been welcomed as a main staple and do not come close to replacing the Western hymn in the regular worship of the church.[173]

PROBLEMS FACED IN INDIAN CHRISTIAN WORSHIP

Because of the linguistic limitations of many missionaries, they were unable to make translations of hymns or liturgy that fit the patterns of the language in the way it was normally spoken. Most translations had numerous syllabic and structural problems, making it almost impossible for people to understand the texts of many of the songs, though they are still sung today by the Christian community.

---

173   Unpublished manuscript by C. H. Dicran, *Hindi Christian Bhajans: A Survey of Their Use by Christians and a Critique by Hindu Professionals in the Music World* (2000), 5. Full text available through library loan (OCLC number 173368036).

In spite of these problems, there have not been many attempts over the years to retranslate the *Book of Common Prayer* or the hymns or to create a relevant liturgy for the Indian context. Although many Indian Christians have written songs reflecting their theology in Indian terms, the church rarely took the initiative to use these songs in worship. Indigenized liturgies also had limited use, mostly within the walls of seminaries and *ashrams.* The primary musical instrument allowed in church was the organ,

> Christian churches neglected the culturally accepted form of sitting on the floor in respect to God.

and only a few of the Catholic, Pentecostal, and charismatic churches attempted to use some of the indigenous musical instruments for worship. During the Christmas season, churches in South India sing hymns that speak of winter and snow, though the temperature is eighty degrees Fahrenheit and the people have never seen snow in their lives.

Westernized posture

One significant loss that the Indian church experienced in adopting Western liturgical patterns was giving up their traditional postures in worship. In most Indian religious traditions, people sit cross-legged on a thick mattress spread on the floor for worship. People take this position as an expression of respect for God. In addition, during times of prayer, people kneel with their heads bowed to the ground.

The Christian churches, however, accepted the Western form of sitting on pews for worship and neglected the culturally accepted form of sitting on the floor in respect to God. According to the Hindu tradition, no one should enter a place of worship wearing sandals or being unclean, again out of respect for God. But Christian churches have not emphasized these aspects in their worship. In the minds of most Indians, failing to practice these symbolic gestures are signs of disrespect and a lack of devotion to God.

Westernized language

As has already been mentioned, many missionaries did not have the linguistic expertise to translate liturgies and hymns in a way that matched the natural patterns of the language. It is not unusual to hear Christians being mocked by the people of other religions for the strange form of language that is used in worship and other aspects of church life. Dayanand Bharati, a Hindu convert and leading Christian theologian, says this about the Westernized language employed in church:

> Where are the Christians who can speak in languages familiar to people? If a new believer ever goes to church service he cannot even understand the message, not to mention all the other activities of the church. If he wants to survive among them then he must become conformed to the images in all the areas of his life. But the church will remain Westernized and will not bother about either the new believer or the common people yet to be reached with the gospel.[174]

Westernized preaching

Preaching in Indian churches is also influenced by the Western heritage. Many Indian churches are characterized by an elevated pulpit or a preaching stand. In recent years due to the telecasting

---

174   Dayanand Bharati, *Living Water and Indian Bowl* (New Delhi: ISPCK, 1997), 44.

of charismatic preaching by international Christian TV channels, preachers tend to move around considerably behind the pulpit and preach very loud in their attempt to imitate the Christianity that has been seen on television. But in Indian tradition, teachers of the scriptures sat on the floor in a slightly elevated place with the scripture open in a small book holder. *Upanishads*, the name of Hindu scripture, describes the nature of teaching in the Indian context. *Upanishad* means "the inner or mystic teaching." The term is derived from *upa* (near), *ni* (down), and *s(h)ad* (to sit); i.e., "sitting down near."[175] Groups of pupils sit near the teacher to learn from him the secret doctrine. This does not match with today's Christian preaching.

> Preachers tend to move around considerably behind the pulpit and preach very loud in their attempt to imitate the Christianity that has been seen on television.

TEN SPECIFIC CHALLENGES FOR THE INDIGENIZATION OF INDIAN CHRISTIAN WORSHIP

Although indigenization of worship is desirable in the Indian context, it involves a number of specific challenges. Careless handling of these challenges has caused several theological issues over the years. Many times the struggle of dealing with these issues has prevented people from attempting the indigenization of worship. Here are ten such challenges:

1. The relationship between Indian culture and the Hindu religion is nearly inseparable.
2. The Indian church has strong roots in and attachment to the worship patterns of Western Christianity.
3. Few Christians are trained in Indian music and culture.
4. The linguistic and cultural situation in India is diverse and complex, with 4,635 ethnic groups speaking 1,652 different languages.
5. Indigenous Christian publishing and literature distribution is quite limited in scope.
6. The impact of global, mostly Western, media culture is strong.
7. There are few leaders with sufficient or sound training in biblical and theological subjects.
8. There is almost no use of Indian architectural styles and other indigenous art forms in Christian places of worship.
9. Indian musical forms, like *bhajans* and *keerthans*, are scarcely incorporated into Christian worship.[176]
10. There is a focus on time-bound Sunday morning worship, rather than worship for the whole of life.

---

175   The Hindu Universe, "Upanishads," HinduNet, http://www.hindunet.org/upanishads/index.htm.

176   This matter is discussed more fully in this *Handbook* by Christopher Dicran Hale in the chapter, "Where Hindu and Christian Worlds Meet through the Yeshu Bhakti Music of Aradhna."

THE IMPERATIVE OF FAITHFUL CONTEXTUALIZED WORSHIP

The indigenization of worship must be done with caution and integrity, and in faithfulness to the word of God. Lack of biblical and theological understanding can result in grave dangers. The goal is not to appear like other religions of the country nor to compromise with other religious faiths. In the words of Dayanand Bharati: "Contextualization is not compromise, not conforming to the image of the world, but rather allowing the gospel to become incarnate in the existing culture in faithfulness to the Bible."[177]

The words of Marva Dawn also offer good criteria for evaluating our attempts at indigenization. "We make use of the cultural forms, new and old," she writes, "but we dare never let up in the struggle to make sure they are consistent with the ultimate eternal world to which we belong."[178]

---

177   Bharati, *Living Water*, 48.
178   Marva J. Dawn, *Reaching Out without Dumbing Down: A Theology of Worship for This Urgent Time* (Grand Rapids: Eerdmans, 1995), 10.

141

INTRODUCTION

SECTION 1: FOUNDATIONS

SECTION 2: STORIES

SECTION 3: TOOLS

CLOSING

27. CONTEXTUALIZING VISUAL ARTS FOR FAITH SHARING

By Scott Rayl

TIBETAN CHRISTIAN *THANGKAS*

In 2001 as some expatriate workers in the Himalayas were puzzling over the persistent ineffectiveness of common approaches to connect with Tibetan Buddhists, they decided that a new approach was needed. They formed a group called the Tibetan Storytelling Project (TSP). Eventually they produced a DVD featuring traditional Tibetan art, songs, choreography, and rhythmic speech in presenting the gospel.

Two years later the TSP discovered the Hope DVD produced by Mars Hill Productions. Much of the DVD's content mirrored what the TSP had already decided to include in their own project, so they worked out an agreement with Mars Hill that would allow them to use the Hope DVD material and add fresh footage shot on the Tibetan Plateau with Tibetan extras. Some of these additional scenes portray a traveling Tibetan storyteller and his daughter who use traditional Tibetan paintings called *thangkas* to illustrate stories from the Bible. Other scenes have performances of Tibetan music and dance. The two-hour Tibetan Hope DVD was completed in 2007.[179]

A thangka is a traditional form of stylized Tibetan art. It is painted or embroidered on silk and is often mounted on a silk frame. The thangkas portrayed in the DVD demonstrate a style of story-based teaching that was traditionally used to teach Buddhist doctrine and moral truth. This style of thangka shows several scenes in a story, all in the same painting. The modern biblical thangkas produced by the TSP are printed posters designed for use either with the Hope DVD or by themselves with a trained presenter.

An excellent fourteen-page manual produced by the TSP explains the background of the biblical thangkas and how to use them correctly to explain the gospel. The manual not only explains

---

179   *The Hope DVD (Central Tibetan adaptation)*, (Nepal: Mars Hill Productions and Promise Productions Private Lmt of Kathmandu, 2007), http://www.rewahope.com/tibetanthangka. The video *The Hope* was produced by Mars Hill Productions of Houston, Texas USA in 2002. The Central Tibetan version, with additional scenes shot in Tibetan areas of various countries and traditional Tibetan songs and choreographed dances, was produced by Promise Productions Private Limited of Kathmandu (then called Rainbow Films Private Limited), Nepal in 2007. The Central Tibetan DVD and replications of the four paintings are distributed under the title "Rewa Namthar," by Central Asia Publishing, Thailand.

the meanings of thangkas but, along with the DVD, provides a powerful way to communicate the gospel. Free from the usual connections that create misconceptions for Tibetan Buddhists, these tools are effective in opening their eyes to the saving grace of Jesus.[180]

HENNA "STORYING"

Mina Rowland[181] has lived for the last few years in East Africa and South Asia. In her work she chose to explore the use of "henna storying." Henna is a plant that grows in certain regions of Africa, southern Asia, Australia, and Oceania. Among other things, it is used for body decoration in the form of temporary tattoos, which are popular for new brides and for special occasions including simple fellowship among women. Henna is even mentioned in the Bible in Song of Solomon (1:14; 4:13,14).

Rowland felt that God had gifted her in doing illustrations using henna, and she began to develop narrative designs based on the gospel story. Although traditional henna designs are mainly decorative and have no narrative content, she found that they lend themselves quite well to illustrating narratives. After developing a series of designs based on feedback from nationals, she began hosting henna parties as a form of outreach. She invited local women to attend the parties and shared the gospel with them while applying the designs to their hands. Some of the women, both believers and nonbelievers, had opportunities afterward to share the stories with others, because the designs typically remain visible for a few days or even up to a month. Since then, online resources for henna storying and henna parties have been well developed and are available for download.

Kimberly M. Stephens used a similar approach during her recent time in South Asia. She decided to create a public art exhibit entitled "A True Story." It was an exhibit of nineteen paintings, acrylic and *mehndi* (henna) on canvas.[182] Each painting depicts a *mehndi* design and tells a story from the Scriptures. Stephens intended her designs to give an overview of the biblical story from both the Old and New Testaments. Some of her paintings incorporate written scripture as a design element, though Stephens made sure that the scripture expressed God's character and narrated a part of the painting's story.

> After developing a series of designs based on feedback from nationals, Mina began hosting henna parties as a form of outreach.

Stephens reports that the art show was very well received. Most visitors had never seen anything like this before, and felt proud that a foreigner would take the time to learn their art forms and develop them in such a way. Like Rowland's henna designs, Stephens' paintings are very abstract and require explanation to understand their meanings.[183]

---

180   For more information and examples of thangkas, see http://www.wecnz.org/story/travelling-storyteller-takes-jesus-tibetans.

181   Name changed for security purposes.

182   Henna is known as *mehndi* in Hindi.

183   For more information and examples of henna evangelism, see http://www.go2southasia.org/resource/evangelism/henna.

SAFINA (FERGIE) STEWART, AN INDIGENOUS CHRISTIAN ARTIST

Safina (Fergie) Stewart is an indigenous Australian artist, educator, and follower of Jesus who lives in Melbourne, Australia, with her husband and two children. Born in Auckland, New Zealand, she was raised in the highlands of Papua New Guinea, where she learned to follow Jesus from her missionary parents and had many multicultural experiences. Her father is Australian with a Scottish heritage and her mother is a Torres Strait Islander and Queensland Aboriginal. At the age of thirteen Safina moved to live in mainland Australia.

In the last few years Safina has pursued an art career in painting, working in a style she calls "contemporary indigenous art." Her work is rich and vibrant, and her subjects range from sea creatures to topographic landscapes and traditional, indigenous totem animals. All of her work is infused with biblical meanings and a sense of joyful hopefulness. Through it she seeks in part to raise awareness of issues that hinder acceptance and mutual respect between indigenous and nonindigenous Australians.

Safina makes her living as an artist from the sale of her original works and reproductions at a local indigenous art market where she is able to informally share the meanings behind her artwork. Her indigenous heritage gives her the right in the eyes of Aboriginal Australians to use their traditional motifs and symbols which, when filled with gospel meaning, shine the love of God into the hearts of both indigenous and nonindigenous Australians.[184]

---

184 For more information and examples of Safina's artwork, see http://www.artbysafina.com.au/gallery.html.

MISSIOLOGICAL

28. WHAT HAPPENS TO MUSIC WHEN CULTURES MEET? SIX STAGES OF MUSIC DEVELOPMENT IN AFRICAN CHURCHES[185]

By James R. Krabill

"Africa's music," wrote Henry Weman more than a century ago, "is the mirror of the soul, an essential part of [the African's] inmost being; it has the power to liberate, and it is in the music and the dance that the African can best be himself."[186] If Weman's statement is true for music in Africa even before the arrival of Christianity, it should not be surprising that music would likewise emerge as an important ingredient in the life and identity of the newly formed Christian communities sprouting up across the continent. "*Ndiyanda kurinda!*" ("I want to sing!") is, in fact, the way many Zambians announce their desire to take on the Christian faith—a faith which for them could only be adequately expressed in the outpouring of song.[187]

For this reason it is indeed unfortunate that many Western missionaries, as Christianity's first messengers, failed to tap traditional African music sources and open the door "whereby at least some of this wealth might pass across into the worship of the young churches."[188] This constitutes for some observers a situation nothing short of "cultural genocide,"[189] one of the saddest chapters and most regrettable aspects of the entire story of Western missionary efforts. All too common have been experiences similar to the one reported of an elderly man in Chad who confessed with

---

185   Selected portions of this chapter have been adapted from James R. Krabill, "Encounters: What Happens to Music When People Meet," in *Music in the Life of the African Church*, eds. Roberta R. King, Jean Ngoya Kidula, James R. Krabill, and Thomas Oduro (Waco: Baylor University Press, 2008), 57–79. More emphasis is given in that study to the historical development of music in the life of the African church and the dynamics at work in the encounter between Western Christian and African traditional religious worldviews in the creation and usage of African Christian music.

186   Henry Weman, "*African Music and the Church in Africa*," Studia Missionalia Upsaliensia, vol. 3 (Uppsala, Sweden: Svenska Institutet för Missionsforkning,1960), 20.

187   Bengt Gustaf Malcolm Sundkler, *Bara Bukoba: Church and Community in Tanzania* (London: Hurst, 1980), 184.

188   Adrian Hastings, *African Christianity* (New York: Seabury Press, 1976), 48.

189   Bongaye Senza Masa, "The Future of African Music," in *African Challenge*, ed. Kenneth Y. Best (Nairobi: Transafrica Publishers, 1975), 157.

hesitation to the local American missionary, "I want to become a Christian, but . . . do I have to learn your music?"[190]

THE YEAR WAS 1914

Two contrasting case studies from mission work in Africa nearly a century ago illustrate the differing approaches used by gospel communicators at that time. One of them takes place on East Africa's Ruiki River in the then Belgian Congo and the British protectorate of Uganda. The other story unfolds in the newly established French West African colony of Côte d'Ivoire. The historical setting in both instances is September 1914—as European colonial expansion in sub-Saharan Africa was rising to a peak and World War I was beginning with all its devastating effects for both Europeans and their burgeoning empires in Africa and beyond.

A scene from *The African Queen*

The first story comes to us as a scene from John Huston's 1951 film drama, *The African Queen*, based on a 1935 novel of the same name by C. S. Forester. The backdrop for this Oscar-winning saga of adventure, humor, and romance is the missionary efforts of a stuffy and out-of-place British couple, Samuel and Rose Sayer, a brother and sister duo played masterfully by Robert Morley and Katharine Hepburn.

The stage is set already in the opening scene as the film credits come into view on a bright blue and billowy-clouded sky seen through palm branches of a tropical rain forest. The camera follows the treetops of the jungle before gradually descending upon a village cluster of thatch-roofed huts. On one of the buildings there is a cross perched atop a steeple as a title in bolded letters appears on the screen: "German East Africa, September, 1914." Focusing in more closely from the cross and slowly through the narrow doorway of the building, one catches a glimpse of a stone-carved plaque identifying the location: First Methodist Church, Kung Du.

We hear faint sounds of music as we enter the church building and find Rev. Sayer struggling valiantly, but with little success, to lead the congregation in a rousing rendition of the eighteenth-century hymn, "Guide Me, O Thou Great Jehovah." This faltering effort, we later learn, is not the only endeavor in Sayer's life which has turned out badly. His very decision, in fact, to volunteer as a missionary early in life came as a result of demonstrating low-level language facility by failing his Greek and Hebrew exams.

> "I want to become a Christian, but ... do I have to learn your music?"

Utterly devoted to her brother and adorned in a prim and proper high-collared Victorian Sunday go-to-meetin' dress, sister Rose works up a sweaty lather in the tropical heat as she fervently pounds and pedals a pump organ, almost as if to drown out the cacophony of atonal noises coming from the uncomprehending members of the village congregation. "Songs of praises, songs of praises, I will ever sing to thee," she bellows forth determinedly in a scene that leaves the movie viewer emotionally stranded somewhere between pain, pity, and pure hilarity.

We never find out what might have happened in the Sayers' unwavering effort to pass along to their East African congregants the "heart music" they had learned to love in their home country.

---

190 Laverne R. Morse, "Ethnomusicology: A New Frontier," in *Evangelical Missions Quarterly* 11 (January 1975): 35.

For soon after this worship scene German-led troops raid and destroy the missionaries' village, capturing and hauling off the indigenous population to become forced soldiers or slave laborers. Samuel protests the troops' violent and destructive actions and is dealt a blow to the head from a rifle butt. He subsequently becomes delirious with fever and soon dies, leaving behind a distraught and discouraged Rose, looking on helplessly as her world crumbles around her.

The "music ministry" of Prophet William Wadé Harris

On the other side of the continent during this same September 1914 period, William Wadé Harris, a fifty-four-year-old Liberian prophet-evangelist, was reaching the peak of his ministry popularity in southern Côte d'Ivoire. Equipped with little more than a passionate desire to share the good news of Jesus, Harris had left his native Liberia more than a year before and walked for hundreds of miles in an eastward direction along the coast, challenging people everywhere to lay aside their traditional objects of worship and turn instead to "the one, true God."

> "God has no personal favorite songs. It is sufficient for us to compose hymns of praise to him with our own music and in our own language for him to understand."

Harris' ministry lasted a mere eighteen months, but during that brief period an estimated 100,000 to 200,000 people from over a dozen different ethnic groups accepted the evangelist's call, received baptism, and took their first steps toward a new life in Christ.[191]

One of the questions new converts frequently asked Harris during their brief encounters with him concerned the type of music that they should sing when they arrived back home in their villages. "Teach us the songs of heaven," they pleaded, "so that we can truly bring glory to God."

Harris was himself a lover of Western hymns, which he had sung since early childhood—including, interestingly enough, "Guide Me, O Thou Great Jehovah!" Yet Harris refused the easy path of teaching his new converts the beloved Western church music of his youth. "I have never been to heaven," he wisely told the crowds, "so I cannot tell you what kind of music is sung in God's royal village. But know this," he continued, "God has no personal favorite songs. He hears all that we sing in whatever language. It is sufficient for us to compose hymns of praise to him with our own music and in our own language for him to understand."

Encouraged by these words of counsel, the new believers set to work, transforming their traditional music into songs for praising God. The repertoire of hymns sung by the Harrist Church today numbers in the thousands, all set to music by members of the church, for the church, and in a language that the church can well understand.[192]

---

191   A more detailed account of Harris' ministry and his approach to the creation of indigenous hymnody is told in section 2 of this *Handbook*; see James R. Krabill, "How a West African Evangelist Unleashed Musical Creativity among New Believers," chpt. 65.

192   Several hundred of these hymns have been transcribed in the Dida language (one of sixty languages in *Côte d'Ivoire*), translated into colloquial French, and analyzed for their historic and religious content in James R. Krabill, *The Hymnody of the Harrist Church among the Dida of South-Central Ivory Coast, 1913–1949* (Frankfurt: Peter Lang, 1995).

SIX STAGES OF MUSIC DEVELOPMENT IN MANY SUB-SAHARAN AFRICAN FAITH COMMUNITIES

Some churches and religious movements in Africa have from the very beginning sung their own locally composed music. In certain instances such as the Harrist movement described above, the use of imported music has for nearly a century not only been discouraged, but forbidden.

However, many if not most other churches—particularly those founded by Western mission societies or organizations, beginning with the chanting of the first Latin Mass on the west coast of Africa in 1482—have passed, or are currently passing, through a number of stages on their way to developing a music for worship they can call their own.

The six stages we will examine briefly are: importation, adaptation, alteration, imitation, indigenization, and internationalization. We do not mean to imply that all churches have passed through every one of these stages or have done so in this precise order. The stages occur frequently enough, however, to be helpful for ongoing reflection.

Stage 1: Importation—*where hymn tunes, texts, and rhythms all originate with the Western missionary*

For much of Africa's church history, the hymns of Watts and Wesley or portions of the Latin Mass were simply taken over from the West and reproduced as accurately as possible by new believers in African worship contexts. Interestingly, with time many African Christians came to genuinely cherish Euro-American music traditions and consider them as "their own." Asante Darkwa, speaking for many other Ghanaian Christians, has noted that

> the hymn tune is perhaps the most commonly understood form of Western music by literates and preliterate Africans. Christians sing their favorite hymns not only at church services but also at wakes and burials and in other situations in which they find solace and comfort in those ancient and modern hymns which have done a wealth of good spiritually to Christians all over the world.[193]

Catherine Gray reports a similar situation among the Baganda in Uganda where Western hymnody "is now so much a part of Christian worship and Baganda life that it could be called indigenous music."[194]

Not all Africans, however, have felt as "at home" with Western musical traditions as this might suggest. For many, there has persisted a lingering, underlying sense of alienation, of "spiritual unsuitability" with the Western music legacy introduced by the missionaries. Nigerian E. Bolaji Idowu stated it harshly when he wrote years ago:

> Again and again, as we have observed, choirs have been made to sing or screech out complicated anthems in English while they barely or do not at all appreciate what they

---

193   Asante Darkwa, "New Horizons in Music and Worship in Ghana," *African Urban Studies* 8 (Fall 1980): 69.

194   Katherine Morehouse, "The Western Hymn in Mission: Intrusion or Tradition?" in *Global Consultation on Music and Missions: The Proceedings*, eds. Paul Neeley, Linda Neeley, Paul McAndrew, and Cathy McAndrew, CD-ROM (Duncanville, TX: EthnoDoxology/ACT, 2006), 10.

are singing . . . We must not be deceived by the fact that people have borne their martyrdom to this infliction without complaint so far.[195]

And so we move to what often follows as the second stage of hymn development.

Stage 2: Adaptation—*where imported hymn tunes or texts are in some way "Africanized" by rendering them more suitable or intelligible to worshipers in a given setting*

At the adaptation stage of development, nothing is substantially changed with the imported hymn tune or text. But an effort might be made to adapt the *tune* to the context of a particular faith community by introducing the use of drums, rattles, or other locally produced instruments. The West African Cherubim and Seraphim Church frequently does this with well-known Western hymns such as "What a Friend We Have in Jesus," accompanied variously by harmonica, drums, electronic keyboards, or cow bells.[196]

Or again, the decision might be made to translate the *text* of a hymn from a Western language into a locally spoken one so it can be better understood. There would be no attempt or desire for the translation to change the actual text of the song, but simply to render it accessible in another language. Translating hymn texts has been a common practice throughout much of the missionary era and is generally as helpful to new converts as it is satisfying to the missionaries themselves. "You cannot appreciate what it means to hear 'Nothing but the Blood of Jesus' sung in a strange language away out in a bush town!" reported Christian and Missionary Alliance workers in 1930, one year after their arrival in Côte d'Ivoire.[197]

We must note here, however, that translated hymns—though perhaps more fully understood than those remaining in a "foreign" language—are often little more than "shortcuts," "temporary stopgaps," and in any case "from the point of view of their art, not the best."[198] One common predicament is that many African words, based on tonal patterns, have their tones (and meanings!) altered when they are sung to Euro-American tunes. One serious case is reported by Idowu where the English expression "miserable offender," translated into Yoruba and sung to a certain European tune, became "miserable one afflicted with tuberculosis of the glands."[199]

Stage 3: Alteration—*where some part of the missionary's hymn (tune, text, or rhythm) is replaced or otherwise significantly modified by an indigenous form*

What happens at the alteration stage is more than a simple "translation" of Western tunes (with rattles) or texts (with language) into an African idiom. There is rather a substantial alteration or total substitution of some part of the Western hymn by tunes, texts, or rhythms of indigenous composition or flavor. Examples of this type of modification might be: (1) where Western tunes are retained, but new, locally written texts replace the Western ones;[200] or (2) where Western texts

---

195   E. Bolaji Idowu, *Towards an Indigenous Church* (London: Oxford University Press, 1965), 30–31.

196   See video clip in James R. Krabill, "Theology of Song," in *Global Consultation on Music and Missions: The Proceedings*, eds. Paul Neeley, Linda Neeley, Paul McAndrew, and Cathy McAndrew, CD-ROM (Duncanville, TX: Ethno-Doxology/ACT, 2006).

197   Ruth Ellenberger, "Gossiping the Gospel in French West Africa," *The Alliance Weekly*, September 13, 1930: 598.

198   J. H. Nketia, "The Contribution of African Culture to Christian Worship," *International Review of Missions* 47 (1958): 274.

199   Idowu, *Towards an Indigenous Church*, 33.

200   For examples, see W. J. Wallace, "Hymns in Ethiopia," in *Practical Anthropology* 9 (November–December 1962): 271; and Mary Key, "Hymn Writing with Indigenous Tunes," *Practical Anthropology* 9 (November–December 1962): 258–59.

are retained and put to new, locally composed tunes. Vatican II's "Constitution on the Sacred Liturgy" ("*Sacrosanctum Concilium,*" no. 38) allows for variations and adaptations of the liturgy along these lines, engendering a lively debate in African Catholic circles about the need for "cultural enrootedness of the liturgy" and "incarnational Eucharistic celebrations."[201]

Stage 4: Imitation—*where tunes, texts, and rhythms are locally composed or performed, but in a style that is inspired by or replicates in some way a Western musical genre*

"Nearly all the well-known Ghanaian composers, as well as students, have tried to write hymn tunes," according to Asante Darkwa.[202] One of the most famous of these was Dr. Ephraim Amu, who as an expert in Ghanaian traditional music also studied at the Royal School of Music in London, 1937–40. He eventually composed and published a collection of forty-five choral works.[203]

> Indigenous, locally composed music does not need to be the only diet for the church. But a *healthy* church will make it a goal.

More recently, Catherine Gray has reported on songs from Uganda warning about the dangers of AIDS; these songs were composed in "hymnodic stanzaic structure."[204] Illustrations abound across the continent of African musicians who have composed songs for worship, for example, in the styles of nineteenth-century revivalist hymns, southern gospel, four-part male quartet arrangements, and increasingly on the contemporary music scene in the popular genres of "praise and worship" choruses, country and western, hip-hop, reggae, and rap.

Stage 5: Indigenization—*where tunes, texts, and rhythms are locally produced in indigenous musical forms and styles*

Many first-generation Christians in Africa have resisted using indigenous tunes, languages, and instruments in worship because of the emotional and spiritual associations these tend to conjure up from their former lives. It is generally held that the church with its music makers and worship leaders needs to take this matter very seriously and avoid any unnecessary temptations or "stumbling blocks" for new believers.

What is also true, however, is that nothing more inspires and brings to life the church in Africa than singing and dancing the indigenous "heart music" of the culture. Whenever such music is introduced into the African worship experience, something almost magical immediately sets in. "At once," writes Idowu, "every face lights up; there is an unmistakable feeling as of thirsty desert travelers who reach an oasis. Anyone watching . . . will know immediately that [the] worshipers are at home, singing heart and soul."[205]

Indigenous, locally composed music does not need to be the only diet for the church. But a healthy church will make it a goal, for "when a people develops its own hymns with both vernacular words and music, it is good evidence that Christianity has truly taken root."[206]

---

201 Krabill, *Hymnody*, 42, note 58.
202 Darkwa, "New Horizons," 69.
203 Ephraim Amu, *Amu Choral Works*, vol. 1 (Accra: Waterville Publishing House, 1993).
204 Morehouse, "The Western Hymn," 10.
205 Idowu, *Towards an Indigenous Church*, 34.
206 Vida Chenoweth and Darlene Bee, "On Ethnic Music," *Practical Anthropology* 15 (September–October 1968): 212.

Stage 6: Internationalization—*where tunes, texts, and rhythms from the global faith family beyond both the West and one's own local context become incorporated into the life and worship of the church*

This stage is the newest, almost unexplored frontier of worship music for the church. In contrast to "contextual" music, it is what the 1996 Nairobi Statement on Worship and Culture has called "cross-cultural" music.[207] This will be *the* encounter of the twenty-first century, vastly broader and richer than the bilateral relationships that have characterized so much of the colonial experience between Europe and Africa up until now. The internationalization of music today holds great promise for the church. For it moves us ever closer to the biblical vision of where all history is headed—the vision of a coming day described by the Evangelist John in Revelation 7:9,10 when all languages, tribes, and nations will *together* proclaim, "Salvation belongs to our God, who sits on the throne, and to the Lamb."

CONCLUSION

When one stops to consider the sheer volume of musical production being generated across the thousands of movements and denominations and the tens of thousands of local worshiping communities in Africa today, it simply boggles the mind beyond comprehension.

The dynamic encounter between African and Western music traditions will no doubt continue unabated in the years ahead. And perhaps the life and counsel of Ghanaian hymn composer and ethnomusicologist Ephraim Amu is the best we can do in imagining how the two will coexist as separate yet hybrid realities. Amu as a young student and professor during the peak of the colonial era of the 1930s and 1940s consciously chose to free himself from the cultural expectations of his day by refusing to dress in Western-style clothing and wearing instead traditional Ghanaian cloth made from locally spun cotton. Yet Amu clearly lived biculturally, operating with great ease in both Western and African worlds. He reportedly loved to serve soup to guests in earthen pots and water in calabashes on a table adorned with imported cutlery. "There is no harm in embracing the *good* things of other cultures that have *universal* values," Amu once said, "but by all means let us keep the best in our own."[208]

---

207   Lutheran World Federation, *Nairobi Statement*. See also chapter 13 by Anne Zaki in this *Handbook*, "Shall We Dance? Reflections on the *Nairobi Statement on Worship and Culture*."

208   J. H. Kwabena Nketia, introduction to Amu, *Amu Choral Works*, 8.

151

INTRODUCTION

SECTION 1: FOUNDATIONS

SECTION 2: STORIES

SECTION 3: TOOLS

CLOSING

29. A FRAMEWORK FOR INCORPORATING ARTS IN SHORT-TERM MISSIONS

By Ian Collinge

INTRODUCTION

As I jotted down Hausa lyrics and melodies on a four-week visit to church members in Nigeria, little did I realize that eight years later this focus on the arts of others would become central to my life's calling. In Nigeria I realized the power of local arts to move people as I saw believers struggling with English hymns, but becoming enthusiastic and animated when they sang indigenous praise songs accompanied by gourds.

On this trip, I had taken my violin to entertain a group of isolated foreigners. Artistic short-termers usually do demonstrate their own arts in the host culture, and for good reason: this is what they know! Such efforts can have powerful impact, but my reflections in this chapter emphasize that short-term workers can also make a significant impact through involvement with culturally appropriate arts. Potentially, short-termers can make an even greater impact in this area if they come humbly to learn from the culture and build friendships, with a desire to validate and encourage the arts of the local believers.

MISSIONAL QUESTIONS AND CONSIDERATIONS

Some practical and missiological questions, are crucial to ask at the outset: How can anyone learn enough about others' arts, culture, and language to play any useful role on a short-term trip? Will their efforts not actually result in importing arts from globally dominant cultures and unintentionally promoting models that undervalue local forms of creativity?

FOUR EXAMPLES OF MEANINGFUL SHORT-TERM ENCOUNTERS

The following accounts illustrate various ways that arts specialists can engage with local arts in short-term cross-cultural mission, with each type of engagement having the potential for life-changing effects.

1. In 2008 two music graduates went to Cambodia. Briefly trained in fieldwork methods, they visited a remote village. With their encouragement, local believers created a Christian song in their mother tongue—as far as they knew, it was the first Christian song in their language in that whole region. Not only did villagers, including a Buddhist monk, want to learn it, but the believers continued songwriting after the visit.

2. In 2010 a small team helped in a workshop for four language groups in Nepal. Each group created new songs, and the first Christian songs in a minority language and style were composed, inspiring a heavy metal musician to imagine a renaissance of his traditional culture. One team member has since returned long-term.

3. Working as short-term teams, visual artists have at times incorporated local imagery into their art or into their work with local artists. Then they have displayed the art in accessible spaces and set aside times for interaction with the public about the art. In one situation a painting on display depicted a lock, through which could be seen a light-filled opening.[209] An old man strolled past and then "stood stunned . . . someone had just painted his life." When he asked, "Can you please tell me, what is the key that will unlock the door of my life, and let me run into the light of God?" the artist was able to share about the light of Christ.[210]

4. In 2010 a professional harpist spent some months in Japan and started to learn the *koto* and *shamisen* and some Japanese melodies. The churches arranged harp recitals where she included traditional melodies, drawing many who otherwise excuse themselves from church events. Returning to her home country, she played outside for a wedding. A Japanese passerby stopped to talk, touched by the Japanese melody she was playing. This harpist has now returned full time to Japan, sometimes accompanying a Japanese Christian singer, ministering to many through music, including survivors of the 2011 quake and tsunami.[211]

---

209   See Bill Drake, "The Lock and the Door," OM Arts International, http://missions-trips-arts-billdrake.blogspot.com/2010/10/lock-and-door.html.

210   Also see Anonymous, "Peace Reflected Artistically in North Africa," OM Artslink, Summer 2007, http://www.omartslink.org/getInspired/inspiredNorthAfrica07.php; Anonymous, "Finding Riches Stored in Secret Places," OM Artslink, 2009, http://www.omartslink.org/news/news_NA_finding_riches.php; and similar stories on this website. For more on this type of artistic engagement, see chapter 30 by Geinene Carson in this *Handbook*, "Visual Arts as a Bridge to Engaging People of Other Cultures."

211   For more examples of artistic involvements in situations of trauma healing, see chapter 35 by Harriet Hill in this *Handbook*, "The Arts and Trauma Healing in Situations of Violence and Conflict."

HOW CAN SHORT-TERM MISSIONS TEAMS FACILITATE CULTURALLY APPROPRIATE ARTS?

Most disaster stories about short-term missions (STM) arise from inadequate preparation and self-centered attitudes of spiritual tourism. If the focus of a project is to encourage local arts creation, many of these hazards can be avoided, and the project can result in genuine benefits to all parties, since from initial recruitment to final debriefing the emphasis is on the needs of the receiving community. Particular attention needs to be paid to training, motivation, strategy, and relational intention.

1. *Training.* To prioritize culturally appropriate arts in STM requires specialized training that equips participants to focus on the people, culture, and arts of their host community. If ethnodoxology practice is new to these interns, their preparation will need to be longer than normal to equip them well for their roles as arts researchers and facilitators.

2. *Motivation.* During recruitment and training the expectations of all parties should be made clear. As learners and helpers, a short-termer's motivation should arise from a genuine desire to assist nationals. Demonstrating their own art may at times be desirable, but the main aim is to engage with the arts of that community and to encourage cultural insiders in their own creativity.

3. *Strategy.* A clear strategy needs to be agreed on so that guests truly serve the local church. Frequently the biggest service they do for the local church is to energize their creativity and provide special stimulus for them to arrange an event. The arts for the event are often produced in a workshop, and such an arts workshop should generally have an experienced facilitator—an "arts catalyst." This facilitator should guide the process, help if creativity dries up, mentor the short-term workers, and work with local leaders. Such a facilitator may be a leading member of the visiting team, a national, or a field worker.

4. *Relational intention.* If the guests' intention is to build authentic relationships, it is very helpful for the strategy of both senders and hosts to include plans for ongoing contact, often through successive visits. A long-term strategy of this nature is more likely to result in significantly greater benefits to the receiving community than can be achieved in a single visit. On a first visit, visitors build relationships as well as do research and encourage arts creation, as needed. On later visits this process can go to a deeper level. Eventually a worker may return for a more long-term stay or visit regularly, getting to know the people, language, and culture better. As this happens, the believing artistic community may also suggest continuing strategies.

CURRENT DEVELOPMENTS AND OPPORTUNITIES FOR SHORT-TERM ARTS ENGAGEMENT

How can arts students and practitioners get involved? Fortunately, since the rise of ethnodoxology from the mid-1990s, short-term programs with an explicit focus on culturally appropriate arts have been developing. Organizations with such programs include Heart Sounds International (OM Arts) and Resonance (WEC International).[212] In addition, since this field is developing so quickly, interested people can contact a range of agencies to consider where they can best offer their gifts to Christ's service.

---

212   See http://www.heart-sounds.org and http://www.wec-int.org.uk. Other agencies with cross-cultural arts training and/or ministry include ACT International (http://actinternational.org), GIAL (http://www.gial.edu), and OM Arts International (http://www.arts.om.org).

30. VISUAL ARTS AS A BRIDGE TO ENGAGING PEOPLE OF OTHER CULTURES

By Geinene Carson

The small town was full of abandoned houses. Old bricks, doors, and broken pots littered the sides of the streets. Upon arrival the artists began observing the people, spending time among them, and praying for an understanding of the culture. Every morning as they walked through town, they received invitations to enter homes and drink tea with locals. Over those cups, God began to teach these artists about the area and people he had brought them to.[213]

THE POSTURE OF A CONSCIENTIOUS ARTIST

The conscientious artist has great opportunities to build bridges with communities of different cultures. When an artist is willing to spend time prayerfully observing a culture and creating informed art, it is more likely that his or her art will attract and occupy people's attention. To go further, artists who invest in the lives of the local people and make themselves accessible along with their work will likely reap much favor. With favor comes the right to be heard.

> Artists who invest in the lives of the local people and make themselves accessible along with their work will likely reap much favor.

"There's a deeper meaning in this piece. I'm going to return tomorrow to sit and contemplate it," one young man proclaimed. And return he did, to sit silently for hours in front of a painting entitled "The Passage of Time"—an artist's response to the changes she saw in the local village over the course of two years. This North African man had read the Bible but had many questions. Standing in front of the painting, the artist shared her inspiration and the painting's deeper truth, centered on the gospel. This curious student returned for several

---

213   Anonymous, "Restoring Broken Jars," OM Artslink, 2009, http://omartslink.org/news/news_WAsia_09.php.

days to gaze at the painting that had captured his attention and to continue conversations with the visiting artists.[214]

As an expressionistic painting of a tree, there was nothing overtly Christian about the painting. The tree, however, resembled the locally common olive tree. And painted in prayerful response to the artist's perception of changes in the community, the artwork begged deeper engagement. Through the artist's availability, that engagement was made possible and meaningful conversation ensued.

However, particularly in the West, it seems that artists think their work should speak for itself, their only responsibility being to birth and release their work to the exposure received by hanging on a wall or sitting on a podium. What artists can learn in cross-cultural experience is the importance of their own presence to bring further depth and influence to their work.

THE ROLE OF THE ARTIST AS OBSERVER, LEARNER, AND RELATIONSHIP BUILDER

Artists who go into the community as learners not only create informed art, but also naturally initiate genuine relationships. Another opportunity for local interaction is through the artist staying visible during the art-making process by creating publicly or maintaining an open studio. With this approach, art exhibitions, for example, become less about viewing art and more about a celebration of shared experience.

Through being accessible at art events, the artist honors those viewing the artwork as well as the artwork itself. This accessibility places more importance on the actual message and expresses sensitivity to the people receiving it. In spite of the stereotype that art should speak for itself, the artist can show a motivation to communicate and build lasting relationships. Moreover, artwork created with a sense of shared ownership is better appreciated and its message more deeply received.

> **Artwork created with a sense of shared ownership is better appreciated and its message more deeply received.**

This practice of both working within culture and being accessible to it is not simply a pragmatic strategy. In so doing we follow in the footsteps of Christ, the incarnation of God, "full of grace and truth" (John 1:14). God in Christ gave grace through works of healing and provision, and through his death and resurrection. These works were in response to humanity's need and were a reflection of God's character. Through his accessibility, Christ also spoke the truth of God represented within his creative acts.

Artists who are believers should respond to this challenge by knowing what they are being called to communicate, standing confidently in their divine inspiration. If artists are never present with their work, then how can it be expected of those not of the kingdom, not of the same culture, to understand or interpret their artwork with the same insight? If there is no effort invested in building relationships with the viewers nor any level of citizenship with the community, people may not feel that questions and curiosities conjured up by a piece of art merit dialogue.

---

214   Anonymous, "Peace Reflected Artistically in North Africa," OM Artslink, Summer 2007, http://www.omartslink.org/getInspired/inspiredNorthAfrica07.php.

ARTISTS IN CONTEXTS WHERE MINISTRY IS CHALLENGING

Even though the exhibition was the goal they were working towards, it became quite apparent that much of their ministry would involve personal interaction with the artisans of the area. The group's prayer was that their creations would resonate with the very people they had built relationships with, speaking a message of restoration and redemption into their lives.[215]

In recent years God has opened unique doors for artists to minister in parts of the world that are typically closed to the gospel. We have been exploring ways artists can impact Muslim communities through murals, art workshops, exhibitions, encouraging creativity in public institutions, and establishing community art centers. This creative approach has allowed us to be less confrontational and yet more direct in communicating the good news of Jesus. People who would reject gospel tracts stop to ponder scripture that is associated with images that are familiar to them.

> Artists thoughtfully created art that displayed the familiar in a new light, creating a venue for deep spiritual conversation.

Some years ago a group of visual artists were invited onto a public university campus in one of these areas harder to reach. They had been warned that the town had the reputation of being one of the most hostile in the country. The artists did what came naturally, building relationships with local people by carefully observing the culture, prayerfully creating art, and producing an exhibition. The people were welcomed into the studio space to view the artistic process and, in some cases, to directly collaborate on a piece of art. This genuine encounter between the people, the artwork, and the artists helped to draw nearly one thousand visitors to the exhibition. The nonthreatening atmosphere created a perfect forum for reducing the distance between cultures. Locals were shocked to see an art exhibit focused on celebrating their own people. These artists thoughtfully created art that displayed the familiar in a new light, creating a venue for deep spiritual conversation.

Viewers gave each piece of artwork their undivided attention, seeking out each artist to ask in depth about the meaning behind every color, symbol, pattern, and title. Had the artists left their work to simply "speak for itself," they would have never encountered such keen interest. Through their availability, the depth of the artwork's inspiration and meaning was fleshed out, and opportunities for truth sharing and meaningful relationships were seized. The artists, thrilled by such an outcome, discovered that God has an exciting role for visual artists in his kingdom mission.[216]

---

215   Anonymous, "Restoring Broken Jars."
216   For an additional resource on this matter, see J. Scott McElroy, *Finding Divine Inspiration: Working with the Holy Spirit in Your Creativity* (Shippensburg, PA: Destiny Image, 2008).

INTRODUCTION

SECTION 1: FOUNDATIONS

SECTION 2: STORIES

SECTION 3: TOOLS

CLOSING

LITURGICAL

31. TRANSFORMATIVE WORSHIP IN A MALAYSIAN CONTEXT

By Sooi Ling Tan

A PERSONAL STORY OF WORSHIP AND MISSION

It was June 1985. About thirty of us sat on the floor of a small community hall at Sebako village in Lundu, Sarawak. In this simple setting we worshiped God, and that night those gathered testified that God's love was experienced in tangible ways. "There was something so bright, so beautiful. It was like a new hope that had dawned on the village," said Pastor B, as she recounted this event.[217]

As we continued to sing songs of worship, joy flowed. Many started clapping and jumping, and some even fainted. There were, of course, those who opposed this gathering, but even as they heckled and mocked, they also wondered, "Why are these people so happy? Why are they singing?" From this group, a church was born. Today the church has grown to over 150 members.

How did this happen? In hindsight I realized that there were no great preachers who ministered there, no "suitable, conducive" setting, no fancy music—songs were accompanied by an old guitar—and no elaborate church planting strategy. We simply *worshiped!*

This personal experience where worship played such an integral part in the planting of a church sparked my ongoing interest in worship and transformation. In the following pages I want to investigate the process and dynamics of transformation in worship and suggest a transformative cycle that occurs during worship. This cycle initiates spirituality, enhances vitality, and effects behavioral change. Data is drawn from an examination of psalmic worship as a biblical precedent and from interviews regarding Christian worship among the Salakos at Pueh and Sebako villages in Sarawak, Malaysia.

---

217   Pastor B, interview with the author, December 2006.

THE PSALMS AND TRANSFORMATIONAL WORSHIP

The Psalms, Israel's hymnbook of sung poetry[218]—and a powerful expression of their worship and thought life[219]—provides a biblical precedent for transformation during worship. Brueggemann asks astutely, "What is being done when the psalms are being done?" In answer, he proposes a useful sequence of orientation-disorientation-reorientation.[220] He further identifies two moves that take place in this scheme:

1. the move out of a settled orientation into a season of disorientation
2. the countermovement from disorientation to reorientation where Yahweh has intervened, creating a dramatic inversion of circumstances.[221]

This results in hymns of praise and thanksgiving and often in a new doxology. Psalm 73 is a good example of this three-part sequence of orientation-disorientation-reorientation.

Psalm 73 begins with a declaration of settled orientation, that "truly God is good to Israel, to those who are pure in heart" (v. 1 ESV). This is the premise and conclusion of the psalm. It is also the main issue that is being worked through in the psalm, so that at its end the psalmist has come full circle to this conclusion that God *is* good to Israel. In the second unit (vv. 2–16), the psalmist propels himself into a phase of disorientation by candidly articulating earthly realities (i.e., the wicked prosper, etc.) that do not match with the traditional beliefs that God blesses the upright. Verse 17 marks the turning point of the psalm, where a clear reorientation occurs. The psalmist enters the sanctuary and emerges with a new understanding that causes a refocusing based on a new reality. The last unit sees the psalmist adjudicating between the former values and these new assertions, and coming to a new faith in God and a new commitment (vv. 18–28).

TWO TRANSFORMATIONAL DYNAMICS ARE AT WORK— LAMENT/DISORIENTATION AND SANCTUARY/REORIENTATION

Let me highlight two transformational dynamics that occur in this scheme:

1. *Lament and disorientation.* The extreme experience of disorientation and the accompanying dissonance and dislocation experienced by the psalmist results in a deep lament. As Allender posits, lament forces a search, strips the heart of pretense, and

---

218 Westermann proposes that the Psalms were either "sung prayers" or "prayed singing," indicating a cohesive use of prayer, poetry, and song in the psalms. In differentiating the three components, he describes *prayers* as "words directed to God in supplication or rejoicing"; *poetry* as "poetical expressions of thought"; and *song* as going "beyond the mere speaking or even recital of a poem" to become music. See Claus Westermann, *Praise and Lament in the Psalms* (Atlanta: John Knox Press, 1981), 11.

219 Walter Brueggemann, *The Message of the Psalms: A Theological Commentary* (Minneapolis: Augsburg, 1995), 3.

220 Walter Brueggeman, *Psalms and the Life of Faith*, ed. Patrick D. Miller (Minneapolis: Fortress, 1995), 6.

221 Ibid., 9.

INTRODUCTION

SECTION 1: FOUNDATIONS

SECTION 2: STORIES

SECTION 3: TOOLS

CLOSING

enables a person to wrestle with God.[222] In the ensuing emotions of pain, anger, and confusion, the wrestler's arrogance and false piety are stripped away and he or she is brought a step nearer toward new insight.

Then following the stripping of pretenses, there is the inevitable wrestling with hard questions. The pertinent question in Psalm 73 is the nagging issue of theodicy, "Do the faithful or the wicked prosper?" Earthly realities reveal the aberration that God looks at the ways of the wicked and allows them to prosper. How is that so? This struggle leads to a string of more difficult questions: "What is God doing about it?" and "Does God really care about the faithful?" It is in pursuing answers to these questions that issues pertaining to who God is, who we are, and how we relate to God are clarified. To say it another way: one of the functions of lament is to formulate and rework our relationship with God.

2. *The sanctuary and reorientation.* Entering the sanctuary proved the turning point in the psalmist's quest for answers. Clearly a central concept in Old Testament worship, the notion of the sanctuary is tied strongly to the presence of God, the primary agent of transformation. Old Testament scholar Goldingay offers various words that are used in connection with the sanctuary:

    *   "dwelling" (*miskan*, tabernacle)[223]
    *   "sanctuary" (*miqdas*, a holy place)
    *   "meeting tent" (*ohel moed*)[224]

    These terms reveal the aspect of mediating the presence of God. Meeting with God is deemed by Goldingay to be "dangerous" and "frightening," involving "a deep transforming work that leaves nothing unchanged."[225] In the sanctuary the psalmist is confronted with the reality of God's sovereignty and goodness that subsumes every other reality that the psalmist is wrestling with.

A CYCLE OF TRANSFORMATIVE WORSHIP EMERGES IN THIS PSALM

At this point it is prudent to introduce a cycle of worship that suggests movements of transformation. Drawing from Westermann's concept of the cycle of worship, Goldingay points out that this cycle contains five elements of Israel's psalmody—address, lament, praise, petition, and vow—and it is a cycle that spirals.[226] As evidenced clearly in Psalm 73, after undergoing the cycle of lament (a devastating experience), pleading with Yahweh (to act decisively), and coming to a resolution, a person is renewed and transformed, as new convictions are forged and new meanings are ascribed to descriptive praise. The end result is doxology in its highest form.

222   Dan B. Allender, "The Hidden Hope in Lament," *Mars Hill Review* 1 (Winter–Spring 1995): 25–37.
223   In the English Standard Version.
224   John Goldingay, *Old Testament Theology*, vol. 1, *Israel's Gospel* (Downers Grove, IL: InterVarsity Press, 2002), 392.
225   Ibid., 389–91.
226   Ibid.

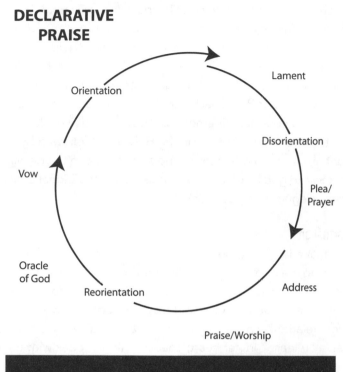

DESCRIPTIVE PRAISE

DECLARATIVE
PRAISE

Orientation

Lament

Disorientation

Vow

Plea/
Prayer

Oracle
of God

Reorientation

Address

Praise/Worship

Transformative cycle of worship in the Psalms[228]

THE SALAKO PEOPLE OF EAST MALAYSIA

We turn now to a particular context—the world of East Malaysia's Salako people—to test whether this transformative worship cycle is helpful in understanding worship patterns there.

There are approximately ten thousand Salako people living in the Lundu-Sematan district of Sarawak.[228] Of these, about 630 live in the village of Pueh and another 503 in Sebako, the two villages featured in the following pages. Prior to 1985 the vast majority of Salakos living in Pueh and Sebako adhered to a form of folk religion, symbolized by the Salako *adat*.[229] There were only a handful of Christians, with two Catholic churches, in the vicinity of these villages. By 2006 the religious demography had changed drastically. By then an estimated 50 percent of Salakos in Pueh were Christians, and in Sebako the majority of households were Christian.[230] The churches have not only experienced a steady growth numerically but have moved from being marginal communities to a position of influence in the social and political organization of the wider Salako community.

227   Adapted from John Goldingay, "Dynamic Cycle of Praise and Prayer in the Psalms," *Journal for the Study of the Old Testament* 6 (1981): 87.

228   Awang Hasmadi Awang Mois, *Selako Worldview and Rituals* (PhD diss., St. John's College, 1990), 1.

229   The *adat* is a one-foot-long talisman that is hung at the door of every house in the village. It symbolizes the notion of Salako identity, unity, and religious belief.

230   These are estimates given by TK2, the village chief of Sebako (December 2006).

Beginnings of the church

The inception of the church in both Pueh and Sebako villages began in December 1985 when Christian students, upon completion of their Ordinary level examinations, returned to their villages from the boarding school in the nearby town of Lundu. While in school, God had touched these students in a radical way. Many came to faith, were baptized in water and Spirit, and returned to their villages fired with zeal to share the gospel. Meetings were held in homes in both of these villages, and subsequently a big evangelistic rally took place in the school field of Pueh.

In Sebako, as the young people of the village gathered to worship and pray, God's Spirit moved in an unprecedented way. Pastor B recalled that some were "slain in the Spirit and others were touched." Some, unable to control their emotions, "began to cry very loudly."[231] During worship in Pueh, villagers testified to being baptized in the Holy Spirit, followed by speaking in tongues. As a result a substantial number of villagers, young and old, made the decision to abandon their allegiance to the folk Salako god by officially surrendering the traditional *adat* to the village elders and embracing a new allegiance to Jesus Christ.

Personal transformation

Research shows that a large number of Salako worshipers spoke of a transformative experience at some level during the worship event.[232] As one worshiper said, "During worship, there is an inspiration. It is as if something floods into my heart. We do feel at peace. I feel totally released." Another respondent added, "During worship, I experienced a freedom." Prior to that, she was experiencing a severe relational conflict. "It is not easy to forgive," she continued. It was during worship that she felt a "release" in her heart, enabling her to speak with the offender and seek reconciliation.[233]

---

231   Pastor B, interview with the author, December 2006.

232   See Sooi Ling Tan, *Transformative Worship among the Salako of Sarawak, Malaysia* (PhD diss., Fuller Theological Seminary, 2008).

233   Personal interviews with respondents (who because of security issues must remain anonymous), December 2006.

SECTION 1: Foundations

163

INTRODUCTION

SECTION 1: FOUNDATIONS

SECTION 2: STORIES

SECTION 3: TOOLS

CLOSING

THE THREE-PHASE SALAKO CYCLE: "COME–COMMUNE–RENEW"

Regarding Salako Christian worship, Salakos show that transformation occurs in a cycle consisting of three phases: (a) come, (b) commune, (c) renew:

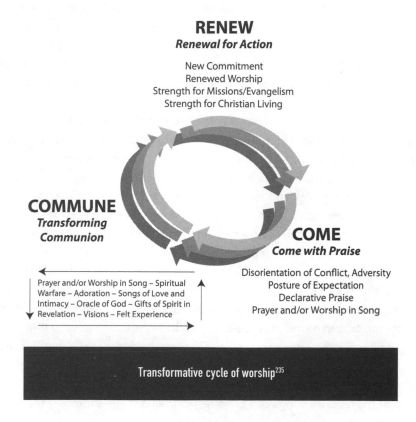

RENEW
Renewal for Action

New Commitment
Renewed Worship
Strength for Missions/Evangelism
Strength for Christian Living

COMMUNE
*Transforming
Communion*

COME
Come with Praise

Prayer and/or Worship in Song – Spiritual
Warfare – Adoration – Songs of Love and
Intimacy – Oracle of God – Gifts of Spirit in
Revelation – Visions – Felt Experience

Disorientation of Conflict, Adversity
Posture of Expectation
Declarative Praise
Prayer and/or Worship in Song

Transformative cycle of worship[235]

Come—the great impasse and the great expectation

The first phase—"Come"—is characterized by the tension between the opposing emotions of futility in conflict and hope in expectation. Those with conflict bring their appeal before God and submit their predicaments to him. A dominant characteristic is the acuteness of the adversity, the degree of which is so severe that it cannot be resolved by human means or by using human resources. When this severity is realized, a sense of total helplessness often descends on the worshiper. The only recourse is to seek divine intervention. One worshiper stated, "If I want to consider my debts . . . sometimes I count how much I owe and there is not enough money (to repay), once I go to church (and worship), my heart becomes at peace. My feelings smooth out . . . my heart is free from worry."

Worshipers in these two churches also strongly expect answers from God, which shows that this period of conflict is not a place of utter futility. As one worshiper stated, "Most of the time during worship, I *expect* God to move." In fact this place of impasse is the place where the Holy Spirit begins to work and the inner dynamic involves an exchange of sovereignty. In coming to God the worshiper relinquishes his or her control over the impasse and surrenders it to God. As

---

234 Tan, 2008, 238.

INTRODUCTION

SECTION 1: FOUNDATIONS

SECTION 2: STORIES

SECTION 3: TOOLS

CLOSING

Martin Luther aptly surmises, it is only when God is fully sovereign that he is truly free to work in a creative and redemptive way.[235]

Commune—encountering God in worship

In the stage of communing, the worshiper enters into a liminal time of encounter with God, which results in a type of knowledge that produces great assurance. During this time the worshiper in the Salako context alternates between components of worship such as prayer, song, spiritual warfare, and descriptive praise. The dynamics of worship and transformation associated with the gifts and work of the Holy Spirit are often manifested, for many Salako believers, in prophecy, a word of knowledge, visions, healing, and revelation. Let me highlight three characteristics of this stage:

1. *Song, worship, and prayer as pathways to God.* The striking question is, "How do we bridge this great impasse?" For the Salakos the bridge is composed of song, worship, and prayer. Worshipers come before God singing praise and worship songs. Other worshipers offer prayers to God. In still other instances, both prayer and worship songs are used, alternating back and forth between words and music. One Salako worshiper explained, "Sometimes when the situation or work at home is very difficult, I will quickly sing." Another says, "When I sing a worship song, the Lord is right in front of my eyes."[236]
2. *Spontaneous worship.* The liminal phase is also a time for spontaneous worship. During one worship service I attended in 2003 the drummer began hammering out a warlike drumbeat that signaled a change in the tone of the service. The church was subsequently led into a prolonged time of spiritual warfare, prayer, song, and intercession, during which church problems were laid before God. It is interesting to note that for the Salakos, there is a natural intertwining theologically between heavenly and earthly realities.
3. *Worship as world making.* A key feature of transformative worship is the use of texts that are true to the integrity of God's word and also to the interests of the Salakos. Text analysis of the favorite songs of Salako respondents reveals four key themes present in Salako worship:

   - the sovereignty, lordship, and worthiness of God
   - the expression of adoration, love, and surrender to God
   - the nature and work of Christ
   - community

As worship songs are sung, this reality of a world where God is sovereign, accessible, all-sufficient, and able to provide is enforced. Central to this reality is the abiding presence of Jesus and his constant availability that stands in opposition to the traditional Salako world where folk spirits rule and demand allegiance.

Renew—being renewed for action

For the Salako worshipers, affective experiences impact the behavioral dimension. My research would indicate that a major area here is the deepening of their relationship with God. In one survey I conducted, four Salako worshipers testified to making the life-altering decision to change alle-

---

235 Regin Prenter, *Spiritus Creator* (Philadelphia: Muhlenberg Press, 1953), 200.
236 Personal interviews with respondents, December 2006.

giances, to convert, and to begin a new relationship with God. Nine others decided to continue walking with the Lord as their relationship with God was strengthened. Seven others recommitted their lives to God. As this communion with God is deepened and enhanced, self-offering to God becomes an act of deepest worship. This in turn leads to the place where the person is renewed for action as energy and strength are released for missions.

EXPRESSING WORSHIP IN MUSIC MAKING FOR THE SALAKO COMMUNITY

What does it mean to be a Christian and a Salako? This questions hones in on an identity issue that is pertinent for the sustenance and future of the Salako church. Currently the Salakos live in the tension of being impacted by globalization as well as by their desire to uphold their local traditions and culture. For example, their musical world includes a mosaic of traditions, embracing both local and global characteristics. Within the wider Salako community, there is a current emphasis on reinforcing Salako identity and pride through music, dance, and ritual practices. Correspondingly, the church recognizes the need to incorporate more authentic Salako music expressions into their worship service. To this end, let me highlight three steps taken:

1. *Different genres, different occasions.* In Salako Christian and folk rituals, different genres are used for different occasions. For example, in the religious segment of the folk *gawai* (festival), traditional chants are employed. In the celebration segment of both the folk and Christian *gawai*, syncretic music[237] and social popular dances are used. During the Christian weekly worship services, the music used falls largely within the categories of social popular and contemporary popular music. Thus it is evident that certain genres of music are more suitable for some occasions than others.

2. *The use of participatory, storytelling musical styles.* During festivals the use of *pantun*, a syncretic form of sung poetry, is well received because of its highly participatory and celebratory elements. Pastor S has excitedly noted that in current church life new quatrains are being composed and discussions are being held regarding their incorporation into Christian worship.[238] In the traditional *gawai, pantun* is used in the *kadon-dong*[239] and functions as a storytelling device, as thanksgiving to gods, and as a cultural reinforcer. Similarly, in the church *gawai, pantun* is adapted and used to tell the story of the work of Christ, to declare the power and glory of God, and to do so in a cultural form that is identified as "Salako." For example, in the song "*Angin Batiup Agik*" ("The Wind Is Blowing Again"), God's love and work bringing freedom from sin are declared in the texts (see below, Salako Christian *pantun by Selian Jistar*).[240]

---

237   Syncretic or acculturated music is popular both in the rural and urban sectors of Malaysia. This music combines local elements from both classical and folk traditions with foreign elements from Arab, Persian, Indian, Chinese, and Western music, in addition to some theatrical sources. Cf. Patricia Matusky and Sooi Beng Tan, *The Music of Malaysia: The Classical, Folk and Syncretic Traditions* (Cornwall, UK: Ashgate, 2004), 7.

238   Pastor S, interview with the author, November 2007.

239   *Kadandong* uses *pantun* and is sung as a prayer of thanksgiving to the god of Padi (Jubata). It is accompanied by the *gendang* (frame drum) and *gong* instruments. The texts revolve around community, homecoming, and thanksgiving.

240   Selian Jistar, 2005. Verse lyrics, unpublished.

Angin Batiup Agik	**The Wind Is Blowing Again**
Oleh kerana darah, Mu Tuhan	Because of your blood, my Lord
Telah tebus semua dosaku	We have been redeemed from our sin
Kami di bebas dari belenggu	We have been set free from our chains
Saatu ku datang pada, Mu Tuhan	The day I came to you, my Lord
Chorus:	Chorus:
Angin batiup agik (2x)	The wind is blowing again (2x)
Aya ari Pentakosta	Just as the days of Pentecost
Angin batiup agik	The wind is blowing again

The strength of the song written in *pantun* verse style is twofold. On the one hand, the high text load of the verses enables a theme to be expressed or a story to be told, reinforcing the belief system. On the other hand, the simplicity and repetitive nature of the chorus allows the congregation or community to participate easily. Also, other verses can be added spontaneously, creating a format that stimulates interaction, creativity, engagement, and involvement.

3. *The effective use of instruments.* Traditional instruments such as the *dalu* (gong) and the *gendang* (frame drum) have been used effectively. Pastor S reported that during the 2002 gawai, when the gendang and the gong were used as a call for worship, three non-Christian families reported they felt a compulsion to walk up the hill to the church. "They could not help it. It was as if the sound was calling them to come," said Pastor S.

CONCLUSION: IN STEP AND IN TUNE

It is my contention that authentic biblical worship is in and of itself transformative in nature. Our role is to be in step with the transformative movements of God and to be in tune with the substance of worship as God has ordained. To this end, it is vital to understand the dynamics of transformation in the cycle of worship. This involves

- engaging with conflict;
- having a liminal encounter with God; and
- being renewed as a result.

Our other responsibility is to be in step with the times and seasons of the societies in which we are called to minister and to be contextually in tune with the sound of their musical cultures. For the Salako community, pursuing relevant expressions of Salako worship will contribute to the longevity and vitality of the Salako church and missions.

32. THE WORSHIP WHEEL

By Todd Saurman

We developed the "Worship Wheel" as a tool or set of modules for use in music workshops with Christ-followers from indigenous minority groups in Asia.[241] Many workshop participants have responded positively to this tool, and other workshop leaders throughout the world have reported on its usefulness in their specific contexts.

It is based on the idea that, depending on the culture, music can be used for a wide variety of purposes, as it is combined with beneficial texts. This music and its texts can be directed toward

1. us, the composers;
2. others;
3. God; or
4. various combinations of all three.

Although there were already beneficial uses of music in many communities prior to the coming of the gospel message, we had observed in our work that borrowed and translated songs were often being used for these purposes at the expense of the local music.

While the Worship Wheel can be used for liturgical development, it is also intended for use in the larger sense of "worship" as service to the Lord through transformed lives. This worship involves offering ourselves and our cultures as a living sacrifice of praise, where there is no need to conform to forms of worship imported from the rest of the world (Rom 12:1,2). The Worship Wheel has proved to be a useful tool, not only for contextualizing worship experiences at church gatherings, but also for engaging with communities outside of the church. It has often been used as a practical way to encourage believers who are cultural insiders to reflect on many possible ways to use the music and arts of their culture as acts of worship within their communities and throughout their lives.

> The Worship Wheel has proved to be a useful tool, not only for contextualizing worship experiences at church gatherings, but also for engaging with communities outside of the church.

---

241   See chapter 122, "Encouraging the Development of Relevant Arts in the Lives of Believers," describing these workshops in section 3 of this *Handbook*.

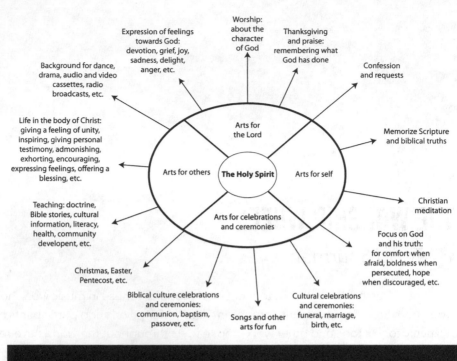

Expression of feelings towards God: devotion, grief, joy, sadness, delight, anger, etc.

Worship: about the character of God

Thanksgiving and praise: remembering what God has done

Background for dance, drama, audio and video cassettes, radio broadcasts, etc.

Confession and requests

Life in the body of Christ: giving a feeling of unity, inspiring, giving personal testimony, admonishing, exhorting, encouraging, expressing feelings, offering a blessing, etc.

Memorize Scripture and biblical truths

Arts for the Lord

Arts for others   The Holy Spirit   Arts for self

Christian meditation

Teaching: doctrine, Bible stories, cultural information, literacy, health, community development, etc.

Arts for celebrations and ceremonies

Focus on God and his truth: for comfort when afraid, boldness when persecuted, hope when discouraged, etc.

Christmas, Easter, Pentecost, etc.

Biblical culture celebrations and ceremonies: communion, baptism, passover, etc.

Songs and other arts for fun

Cultural celebrations and ceremonies: funeral, marriage, birth, etc.

The Worship Wheel[243]

The Worship Wheel is usually one of the last set of activities we lead during a music workshop. Sometimes we have even had to wait for follow-up workshops, especially if no local composers were present at the workshop. Together with the participants, we need to first deepen our understanding of how music and the arts are typically used within their communities. We also need to help them realize that we are not trying to impose forms used by other communities, nor are we trying to push people to create unnatural or inauthentic expressions of their faith. Usually we wait until people are already creating songs in natural and authentic ways. At that point, this tool helps them find a wider variety of culturally appropriate song genres, themes, and uses that may even incorporate other arts as well.

After various song genres and uses for songs have been explored, and at least some songs have been created, we reflect on how some of these song genres are used and how they might be adapted as expressions of a believer's life and faith. We begin by presenting only the inner four parts of the wheel, which consist of the following categories:

1. songs for when you are by yourself or songs for self
2. songs for others
3. songs to God
4. songs for special occasions—such as ceremonies, festivals, or celebrations

Often we present and explore just one of these categories at a time, depending on the genres and uses that the group has already explored. These four categories are not mutually exclusive. The advantage of the four categories is that they help participants think of types of songs not yet

242   Todd and Mary Saurman, 1999, adapted by Brian Schrag, 2011.

explored in the workshop. These new types include some that believers had not previously thought of using to express their faith.

The outer part of the diagram—at the ends of the arrows—is derived from previous workshops and is only a guide for the leaders to help them spark ideas, preferably from song types and contexts discussed previously by the group. Some of the uses listed on the outer part of the diagram may not be relevant or appropriate, and often groups will offer new ideas. The list is always expanding and changing, depending on the culture to which the activities are applied. Every group is different, and the participants will benefit most from the activity if the ideas come from them.

> The most important aspect of this workshop tool is the principle of exploring cultural song types and how believers could creatively use them to express and communicate their faith.

We added "the Holy Spirit" in the middle of the diagram at the wise suggestion of a seasoned missionary who no doubt saw that without the discernment and transformation that the Spirit brings, the activities could encourage conformity to the forms of a culture rather than an organic transformation of the culture.

The activity does not need to be presented as a circular "wheel" at all. One workshop leader has adapted it as a "tree." Others have just made lists under each of the four categories. The most important aspect of this workshop tool is the principle of exploring cultural song types and how believers could creatively use them to express and communicate their faith. The activity can be used to compare the types of songs sung in church and the types of songs typically used within their culture. For example, there may be no Christian songs that teach stories from the Bible, but there may be many songs from the culture that either tell stories or are part of traditional storytelling.

Ephesians 5:15–20 is a great devotional to introduce the four main sections of the wheel. There are various kinds of songs:

1. We "speak to one another"—*songs for others.*
2. Music we "make in our hearts"—*songs for when we are by ourselves.*
3. Music to the Lord, including giving thanks to God for everything—*songs to the Lord.*
4. Verses 15 and 16 talk about wisely making the most of every opportunity—which could easily include *songs for special occasions, such as ceremonies, celebrations, and festivals.*

The lists developed in a workshop can be a resource for church leaders and composers for years to come. About seven years after one workshop, we returned to that area. One of the participants showed me his notes around the Worship Wheel on the yellowed pages of his old weathered notebook. It soon became obvious that the exercise helped him do further research on his community's musical heritage and for contextualizing his faith.

33. LOCAL ARTS AND WORSHIP DEVELOPMENT IN CHURCH PLANTING

By William N. Harris

THE MOST UNDERAPPRECIATED KEY TO FRUITFUL MINISTRY

Having served as a church planting missionary in Siberia for ten years, I understand the effort that goes into language learning, training local leaders, Bible study, and just the practical logistics of living from day to day. So if I'm going to pour time and effort into supporting local arts and music, I really need to see that as important. The fact is that redeemed local arts and music is the most underappreciated key to fruitful ministry I know of. I have found that embracing appropriately contextualized arts and music in church planting has far greater results than the same amount of effort spent in other ways.

WEIGHING THE "MARGINAL" VS. "MAINSTREAM" IMPACT

Let's talk about the term "marginal innovator." This is a local person with a sweet tooth for the *new*. Everett Rogers proposed a "diffusion of innovation" theory, describing innovators as making up about 2.5 percent of a given population.[243] Such innovators in international contexts want to practice their English, are curious about the foreigner's lifestyle, strange clothes, and jazzy gadgets, and are often the ones who make themselves most available to help the newcomer settle in.

Marginal innovators don't want to settle for what is; they love to innovate. Anthropologists call them "marginal" because these people occupy the edge of society's mainstream psyche, not its center. Milroy and Milroy note, however, that "since innovators tend to be marginal individuals at the edges of networks who diffuse innovation via weak ties with others, the persons whom

---

243   Everett M. Rogers, *Diffusion of Innovations* (New York: Free Press of Glencoe, 1962), 13.

investigators actually identify as being strongly associated with a change are most probably the more socially central early adopters."[244]

In other words, marginals may be the first to be attracted to the *new*, but it is the more socially central slice of society that adopts change and integrates it into society. Applied to church planting, if the foreign-flavored church is attracting marginals but not drawing in more socially central societal members, the church won't really penetrate the surrounding culture. Therefore the church needs to be crafted not to the marginals' taste—styled after the alien culture the missionary embodies—but to the average society members surrounding the church.

REEXAMINING "HARD HEARTS" AND "STONY GROUND"

Realistically, most local people don't really care to learn the foreigner's language and aren't anxious to copy his or her ways. They prefer the comfortably familiar. The more pronounced the mission worker's foreignness, the more he or she is likely to attract marginal innovators while simultaneously repelling the mainstream. A handsome percentage of what gets attributed to "stony ground" and "hard hearts" is often just this dynamic.

To get free of this conundrum, local arts and music can powerfully come to the newcomer's aid. How does the foreigner stop looking so foreign? By donning local dress and learning how to behave, right? How do newcomers become free of their translator? By learning the local language! How does the fledgling church planter move his or her ministry past their own arts and music tastes and those of marginal innovators so that it appeals to the mainstream? By embracing the arts and music of the mainstream!

OUR EXPERIENCE IN SIBERIA

In Siberia the time came when our Sakha church services were intentionally made to feel comfortably familiar to the mainstream, and the effect was dramatic. As a rule of thumb, the less visible the foreign elements, the more at home guests from the mainstream culture will feel. In our work we encouraged local Sakha believers to pray and preach in the Sakha language and local musicians to play indigenous musical instruments, dance, and sing in Sakha styles that were appropriate to the sensibilities of the surrounding culture.

What happened? The church grew both in size and in quality. Sakha people were attracted to the warm, loving acceptance of God's welcoming grace. The Sakha made it no secret that they preferred hearing the gospel, not in the *Russian* language, but in the *Sakha* language. They tolerated Western hymns translated into Russian, and some even learned to enjoy Russian hymns translated into Sakha, but most people were far more passionate about hearing new songs written in Sakha using the Sakha song styles. Sakha artists even organized a huge festival of new Christian Sakha songs and packed an auditorium with non-Christians wanting to hear their message. Did I mention all the handmade national costumes they made for it? That cultural resonance made an unmistakable statement to their fellow Sakha that Jesus loves Sakha people.

---

244   James Milroy and Lesley Milroy, "Linguistic Change, Social Network and Speaker Innovation," *Journal of Linguistics* 21, no. 2 (1985): 381–82.

Of course the Russian missionaries I worked with were at first suspicious of Sakha Christians singing songs the Russians couldn't understand. That experience certainly helped me see from another viewpoint what we Westerners too often look like. I learned that church planters who can plant a church they don't feel at home in have done well. The more the new faith community can reflect the local context rather than the home culture of the mission worker, the better.

> The more the new faith community can reflect the local context rather than the home culture of the mission worker, the better.

I am obviously not suggesting that un-Christlike patterns in a society be carried over and reflected in the new church plant. But I believe it is possible to bring local people to spiritual maturity, teaching them to walk with God daily in a way that reflects an accurate understanding of the word of God and a vibrant communion with the indwelling Holy Spirit. If that is true, then we should work faithfully to those ends and trust mature believers to decide for themselves what songs they will write and how they should sing them in church.

New believers who have hearts right with God must be trusted to redeem their own culture, create biblically faithful worship patterns, and decorate their meeting places in appropriate ways that reflect local culture. Uncomfortable or not, mission workers can do their ministry a huge favor by stepping out of the gatekeeper role and encouraging local artists and musicians to get involved in redeeming their own culture under the leadership of mature local *mainstream culture* believers.

WHAT THEN IS THE TREND FOR ARTS AND MUSIC IN MISSIONS TODAY?

With increasing respect, mission leaders are discovering the effectiveness of church plants that complement the local culture through redeemed arts and music, without of course compromising the truth of God's word. This is indeed a powerful innovation in mission work today. And its time has come!

173

INTRODUCTION

SECTION 1: FOUNDATIONS

SECTION 2: STORIES

SECTION 3: TOOLS

CLOSING

PERSONAL

34. EACH PERSON'S PART NOURISHES THE WHOLE: MY STORY

By Jean Ngoya Kidula

EARLY MINISTRY OPPORTUNITIES IN KENYA

Nurtured by my family

As I grew up in a village in Kenya in a family of nine children, our parents were involved in Christian service in the local church, at the denominational level, and beyond—in missions. As a middle child caught between four older and four younger siblings, it would have been easy for my parents to neglect giving me any individual attention and simply let me "fall through the cracks." From early in life, however, I realized that my parents were aware of each child's individuality and that they nurtured each of us as appropriately as they could in their circumstances.

My parents worked in the local church as well as in the Pentecostal denomination, initially serving as leaders for the children and youth programs and eventually as top-level administrators. Both of my parents had been teachers by profession before my father became a full-time denominational administrator. Because of the prominent positions they held in both church and school, I was on stage rather early in my life, even singing about losing my teeth! I led my peers in song and dance, both in and out of church.

The Kidula Sisters

By the time I was thirteen, I became the principal guitarist for my older sisters' gospel singing group. Our repertoire consisted of hymns, gospel songs, and the contemporary Christian music of the time in English, Kiswahili, and Lulogooli, our first language. Our repertoire and language abilities expanded as we were exposed to new musics in the various boarding schools we attended away from the village.

Although I did not have the most powerful voice of my siblings, nor the most engaging stage presence—I was always too serious about the music and its intention!—my parents and my oldest sister nurtured my musical inclinations. They taught me composition and arrangement skills and challenged my instrumental ability through the diverse repertoire I learned in order to accompany our group, the Kidula Sisters. We sang not only at the local church, but also in national youth conventions and churches in different parts of the region. We adjusted our program not just to suit our audiences, but also to fulfill what we saw as our mission—teaching and encouraging Christian worship and witness. By the time I was fourteen, our group had made a recording that was aired on national radio in Christian music and devotional programs.

The Illuminators

While a member of the Kidula Sisters, I was also involved in the Illuminators, an eight-member Christian music group in my high school. In addition to singing and arranging vocal parts, I was the principal guitarist, one of the pianists, and the main percussionist. The mission of the group involved Christian witness and worship. Besides performances at our school, we were invited to other schools in Kenya's capital city of Nairobi. We also participated in youth conventions, were special guests at international meetings, and recorded for national television and radio programs.

This group was gifted in recognizing the strengths of the individual members, easily agreeing on who would take what role in which song. While we never made a commercial religious recording, we were featured on national radio and TV more often than the Kidula Sisters. Recently I was surprised by a former TV anchor who sent me a copy of one of the recordings we had made for television and radio at the Kenya Broadcasting Corporation (then VOK).

When I went on to college, the radio and television anchors—who were well acquainted with our group—followed up on us. Among the pieces aired were some of my compositions as well as collaborative work with other musicians that resulted in Easter and Christmas musicals. As had been the case in high school and in my village, I learned to maximize the different strengths of the groups' members—regardless of the ensemble—in order to be most effective.

I am amazed in retrospect at what happened. None of us was a media star, and our goal was not recognition in that sense. We had a mission—to encourage our generation toward Christian worship and witness. I was part of a collective reaching out to youth in the Kenyan nation—youth of various races, cultural groups, ethnicities, and nationalities. When our group eventually dispersed to take jobs in different parts of the country, most of us spread what we had learned in college to those new locations across Kenya.

Directing the Nairobi Pentecostal Church Choir

My college involvement in Christian arts expanded beyond national borders when I became the choir director of Nairobi Pentecostal Church. It was there that I learned the significance of having diverse individuals in the choir. Some members obviously had great voices and were capable of handling various musical and other stage tasks. For such members it was a critical place to develop musical skills.

But I also discovered a variety of giftings that one may not think of as being important in a choir. Some members looked to the choir as a primary place to serve the rest of the church and the larger community. The choir was a place to be discipled and built up in the Christian walk, or to be socialized to become profitable members of the larger secular society. Choir members were quite diverse. Besides Kenyans, there were Nigerians, Zimbabweans, Swedes, North Americans, and Ugandans. For some of our larger artistic projects, we invited a cross section of nationalities in the church to present special songs from their respective countries.

I found that my most effective years were those in which I drew on the outstanding gifts of different choir members. I discovered people in the group, for example, who were excellent prayer warriors. They organized others to pray, not just for the choir and our church, but also for the larger

Kenyan society. In the process we learned to pray beyond our individual concerns. There were other less "holy" tasks, such as organizing for retreats, advertising events, sewing costumes, visiting each other, and doing fund-raising for weddings, funerals, or for group members with special needs. I depended on different people to fulfill these tasks. While some considered it their Christian calling, they taught the rest of us to look beyond our own particular needs and see the wider world. We learned to pray in ways we had not thought of before, and we advertised our events in venues the church never imagined could be reached. So while most people think of a choir primarily as a place to sing, the individual members' input with their specific tasks expanded my outlook on that ministry. We also shared what we had learned with choir leaders from other churches.

CONGREGATIONAL OPPORTUNITIES IN THE UNITED STATES

Assisting with piano accompaniment

As I have moved from Kenya to international forums, I have been invited to sing, play, and teach in Bible schools and seminaries and have also been involved in local churches. One example is my current church situation in the United States. I moved back to the US after being in Kenya for two years following my doctoral studies. Prior to returning to Kenya, I had been involved in the church choir and occasionally played the piano during services. When I came back to the US, I contemplated moving to a different church closer to where I lived because of lack of transportation. It was a bit far to walk, especially on a Sunday morning. The performing arts pastor was a fantastic vocalist, but less good on instruments. In his search for a pianist, he was told about me.

I initially declined the invitation since, while I could possibly have considered the one-hour walk to church—the transportation system in the town was abysmally bad—I knew it would be difficult to attempt walking back home following Thursday night rehearsals. So I had a choice, either to miss rehearsals altogether—an idea that did not sit well with me, since I needed to learn new songs and become familiar with the style of the pastor—or simply decline the request.

The pastor decided to help me by picking me up very early on Sunday mornings and arranging for someone else to provide the transportation on Thursday evenings. While this town was not short on pianists in any way, I believe this was God's provision, because he knows of my love to play and sing in church and with other Christians. For some reason I feel a bonding there that happens in different ways than when I sing in other situations. The repertoire of music in our church was mainly contemporary American worship fare. But even after the original pastor left, the new leader still looked for me to help out. I am today still on the roster of pianists accompanying the congregation in song.

> While most people think of a choir primarily as a place to sing, the individual members' input with their specific tasks expanded my outlook on that ministry.

Organizing an international music ensemble

Beyond this avenue, God opened another door for me in music ministry. We have a number of African and international students in the church where I worship. Most of them hang around after the church service, much in the same way I remember doing in Kenya. I am not particularly good at hosting people and was too embarrassed to ask them to my house for a home-cooked African meal. Another church member and I decided to host an African lunch at church once a month.

INTRODUCTION

SECTION 1: FOUNDATIONS

SECTION 2: STORIES

SECTION 3: TOOLS

CLOSING

We asked several community members to cook an "African" dish for a potluck lunch. Always in these gatherings we played popular praise and worship songs, as well as gospel songs from different African countries. The church hosts an annual missions emphasis week. We were asked by the pastor in charge of the event to present something from "Africa." We therefore began to pay more attention to the songs people brought to the potluck, eventually selecting a few for learning as a group. It fell on my shoulders to organize the musical numbers.

I have through this process learned songs from various African countries, from India, and from Iran, arranging the songs for our gathering, and sharing them with people from the larger church and community that attend these events. We have even been invited to other churches to share. I cannot take credit for the success or satisfaction that is expressed by audience members or those participating in the singing. Each of us recognizes that it is the collective work of the body. Each does his or her part, and in the process we not only build up each other, but we are also able to bear witness to the world at large about who God is, what he has done, and what he intends for us.

MAKE YOURSELF AVAILABLE—FOR THE GLORY OF GOD!

I seriously believe the biblical message in Romans 12:4,5 that we have many members in one body, but all members do not have the same function. Each individual contributes to the well-being of the whole. We cannot just hope, however, that the gift will be self-evident. We cannot light a lamp and hide it from view, with the expectation that people will see the light or find their way.

I don't think that I aggressively seek out positions or try be noticed. I do, however, make myself available. Sometimes that creates a space for me. At other times I am sidelined in favor of others more competent—or lately younger!—than myself. I will not hide, however. I believe that I am called to continue doing what I know I should be doing. Whether or not I am noticed by the big brass and end up making my contribution by playing music for children's church, I will set a standard for those kids, and I will plant seed that will be nurtured by myself and others to eventually produce the fruit for which I yearn—filling the earth with the glory of God as the waters cover the sea.

35. THE ARTS AND TRAUMA HEALING IN SITUATIONS OF VIOLENCE AND CONFLICT

By Harriet Hill

SYMPTOMS OF TRAUMA

When people are overwhelmed with intense fear, helplessness, and horror in the face or threat of death, they are traumatized. Trauma manifests itself by symptoms such as

1. intrusive thoughts in which people reexperience the event;
2. avoidance of things associated with the event, along with detached, numb emotions; and
3. hyperarousal.

For traumatized people to find healing, they need to express their pain. They need a safe place to express it, where they will not be attacked physically or verbally. They need someone who will listen.

Both internal and external forces work against this expression of pain. Since pain hurts, denial can sometimes seem like a better option. The church is often complicit in this denial, teaching Christians that they should express praise and joy in all circumstances. Feelings of anger, doubt, and abandonment are not accepted as appropriate for Christians. As a Southern Sudanese priest said to me, "I saw my son get shot. I praised God. I need to be an example to the believers."

THE BIBLE HONORS VOICES OF PAIN

In fact, laments are sprinkled throughout the Bible. Christ lamented on the cross, "Why have you abandoned me?" A psalmist laments, "How long, oh Lord?" There are more lament psalms than any other category in the book of Psalms. One entire book of the Bible, the book of Lamentations, is a lament. Kathleen O'Connor writes, "*Lamentations* expresses human experiences of abandonment with full force. And because God never speaks, the book honors voices of pain. Lamentations is a house for sorrow because there is no speech for God."[245] She adds, "Any words from God would . . . undercut anger and despair, foreshorten protest, and give the audience only a passing glimpse of the real terror of their condition. Divine speaking would trump all speech."[246] Laments like the book of Lamentations show the way for those who are traumatized to express their pain to God honestly and forcefully.

THE USE OF ART FORMS IN HEALING PAIN

People can use their art forms as they seek healing of their pain. In Africa almost every culture has a lament tradition: certain melodies, certain kinds of poetry, certain dances and postures. Often these lament traditions have been condemned as heathen and off-limits for Christians. When African Christians understand the structure of lament Psalms in the Bible, it only takes a bit of encouragement for them to use their own lament traditions to express their pain to God. In thirty minutes of centering prayer and listening to the cry of their hearts, laments are expressed.

Sometimes these laments are expressed in prose, but more often words alone do not suffice; they must be sung and danced. Sometimes these laments are expressed by individuals, but more often they are performed by a group. The piercing cry of a Niaboua pastor grieving the death of his sister still rings in my ears.

Laments do not know age, color, or gender. Children can lament as well as adults, Westerners as well as Southerners. When pain is expressed, healing often follows. And the songs are shared and bring healing to others.

People can also learn new art forms. I lived in Africa for twenty years and never saw adults draw pictures; certainly not a church leader.

But when Africans were given some markers and paper and a bit of explanation at the workshop—"get quiet inside and let the pain come out through your fingers"—it seemed that drawing is a native language of Africa. As people draw their pain, they are able to express it in ways that words cannot. One Dan pastor from Côte d'Ivoire looked at his drawing and said, "That's it! That's how I feel! I didn't realize it was so bad." And as a small group we discussed the drawing, unpacking layer after layer of pain and loss.

BRINGING OUR PAIN TO THE CROSS

Getting the pain out is part of the healing process. As Christians, we can bring that pain—those drawings, those laments, those words—to the cross of Christ, because he died not only to forgive our sins but also to "carry our sorrows." At the cross of Christ those pains that we have been able to express are absorbed by his death, bringing healing to our wounded hearts.[247]

---

245   Kathleen O'Connor, *Lamentations and the Tears of the World* (Maryknoll, NY: Orbis Books, 2002), 15.

246   Ibid., 85.

247   For more on this topic, see Margaret Hill et al., *Healing the Wounds of Trauma: How the Church Can Help* (Nairobi: Paulines Publications Africa, 2004).

179

INTRODUCTION

SECTION 1: FOUNDATIONS

SECTION 2: STORIES

SECTION 3: TOOLS

CLOSING

36. THREE WORLDS CONVERGED: LIVING IN AN ORAL, LITERATE, AND DIGITAL CULTURE

By Samuel E. Chiang

Once upon a time, Sam made a Facebook posting, telling all his friends that he had eaten an extremely sweet pineapple grown on his apartment rooftop, and that there were nine more pineapples to harvest and eat. This entry fueled the imagination of his friends. They "liked" the posting and made comments. Then one friend who lived eight thousand miles away insisted on a picture of the pineapples. So Sam took a picture and uploaded the image. This satisfied that curiosity and fired the imagination.

In this simple true story, three diverse cultures—oral, literate, and digital—converge. We are also exposed to three complex interplays:

1. digital identity and narrative
2. living with the F-factor of friends, fans, and followers
3. recorded story and storytelling

From these interplays, there are far-reaching implications for community, worship, and gospel communication. Let's explore these further in the following few pages.

THE "GUTENBERG PARENTHESIS"

Communications from creation to the time of the Gutenberg press were primarily oral in nature, since writing systems took many centuries to develop[248] and technology for mass printing had

---

248   The earliest symbols and scripts were discovered around 3200 BC, and soon thereafter Egyptian papyrus captured and contained the scripts. In the Orient, the Chinese text developed differently with a picture-sound writing system. Later the Phoenician alphabet gave rise to both the Armenian and Greek text, from which the "Latins"—who became known as the Romans—adopted them in the fifth century BC. Two millennia later, the Gutenberg press popularized the Romanized script.

not yet arrived. In the fifteenth century, however, the Gutenberg press made possible printing *en masse*. This was coupled with the Reformation—when the church enthusiastically declared that all people should be able to read[249]—and fueled the trend towards reading, literacy, and privacy.[250] Social memory and community, which had been at the core of society, were outsourced to containers of paper and filing cabinets.

Oral cultures value face-to-face communication in context and living within the "story." The literate world communicates through textual means and often is not able to convey the whole context in a communiqué. The textual "story" is truncated or emptied of meaning. As we enter digital culture, one that is defined by collaborating with multimodal content and tasks,[251] we are strangely enough on a converging trajectory with oral culture.

In fact, academicians are labeling the period from the fifteenth century to the twentieth, "the Gutenberg Parenthesis,"[252]—a period where left-brain functions took over and gave birth to sciences, inventions, and philosophies, while silencing right-brain functions from whence creativity springs. As we proceed however into the twenty-first century, captured images, reality entertainment, and online video gaming[253] are actually drawing people closer to the pre-Gutenberg era, where the right side of the brain is increasingly more in concert with the left. The result today is a more holistic approach to society and tasks—an approach which is recapturing creativity, collaboration, and community.

KEY FEATURES OF THE DIGITAL REALITY

In oral cultures, information is local and always rooted in context and history so that the information has coherent meaning to the community. Digital culture, like the Facebook posting referenced earlier, is morphing the private and individual into open, specific, contextual, and communal experience, albeit at a distance.

---

249   We should note here that it takes, in general, about 120 years for a society to go from near 0 percent literacy to 30 percent. This is in accordance with Dr. Jim Slack's internal research materials at the International Mission Board of the Southern Baptists.

250   Interpretation of Scripture was no longer solely in the hands of the pope. Suddenly there were a mass of "paper popes" who could also read and interpret Scripture. This significantly redefined the authority of the church.

251   Educational research on learning has indicated that digital culture needs to pull together diverse disciplines and build coherent stories from images, sound, and text. These are skills with which "digital natives"—those born into the age of computers, gaming consoles, cell phones, and i-devices—are well acquainted.

252   Tom Pettitt, "Before the Gutenberg Parenthesis: Elizabethan-American Compatibilities," Massachusetts Institute of Technology, http://web.mit.edu/comm-forum/mit5/papers/pettitt_plenary_gutenberg.pdf; and others, including Jean-Francois Vallée, "Paradoxes of Orality and Literacy: The Curious Case of the Renaissance Dialogue," *Proceedings of the Media Ecology Association* 10 (2009), http://cmaisonneuve.academia.edu/jfvallee/Papers/314871/_Paradoxes_of_Orality_and_Literacy_The_Curious_Case_of_the_Renaissance_Dialogue_pdf_. See also Chris Lott, "Closing the Gutenberg Parenthesis," video, Ustream, October 22, 2009, http://www.ustream.tv/recorded/2403446.

253   All three domains mentioned herein have the elements of representational or presentational characteristics. Gaming, either by stand-alone consoles or online video gaming, veers toward the presentational mode where the gamer is a part of the narrative, lives in the story, and is a part of the community. Based on a 2011 report of the gaming community in the USA, the average age of a gamer is thirty-seven years old. While there are 58 percent who are males, there are now 42 percent who are females. In fact, women who are eighteen years and older outsized as a group the audience of boys who are seventeen years old and younger. Entertainment Software Association, "2011 Sales, Demographic and Usage Data: Essential Facts about the Computer and Video Game Industry," Entertainment Software Association, http://www.theesa.com/facts/pdfs/ESA_EF_2011.pdf.

This form of communal experience with a digital identity and narrative embedded into social networking is reinforced by the F-factor—fans, friends, and followers. So pervasive is this reality, that

- we often discover products and services by relying on our social networks;
- we are conscious of how our postings will be rated;
- we are constantly seeking feedback both to improve and validate decisions;
- our social networks often buy together;
- our digital communities are themselves becoming products and services[254]; and
- the F-factor is putting a hard closing parenthesis to the Gutenberg press period.

> What is needed is not more information but meaningful stories—a set of stories that inspire belief, renew hope, and recount a life in action.

The church can be described as a large social network, and Phyllis Tickle has suggested that it is experiencing what amounts to a large rummage sale, one that happens about every five hundred years.[255] In the midst of the convergence of oral, literate, and digital cultures, coupled with online digital identity and narrative, and further combined with the phenomena of the Gutenberg Parenthesis, what does the church have to say and how does it move forward in this very fluid situation?

DISCOURSES AND NARRATIVES INTO MEANINGFUL STORIES

With various projects underway to record oral history and digital storytelling, we have the ability for the very first time in history to record the full, living history of individuals and communities.256 Yet what is needed is not more information but meaningful stories—a set of stories that inspire belief, renew hope, and recount a life in action.

People want to know "who" we are. The Facebook posting on pineapples, augmented by a picture, established one part of the answer to the question, "Who am I?" The subsequent exchanges and comments became concrete and revealed a bit more of the answer. But ultimately there are broader and more fundamental questions we need to address as we are thrust into the digital age:

- Are we ready to communicate openly and transparently, both digitally and face-to-face, with "who am I" stories?
- Is our online digital identity and digital narrative the same as our in-person narrative?
- Is our narrative one that reveals to whom we belong and what inspires our belief?
- Do we also have "why" stories?
- As a part of a community, in church, at work, in a voluntary organization, or online, can we explain "why" we are here? "Why" we are collaborating with others?
- Do our stories inspire or renew hope for people?

---

254   See TrendWatching.com, http://trendwatching.com.

255   She talks about the five-hundred-year cycle, not only for Christianity, but also extended into both the Jewish and Islamic faiths. Cf. Phyllis Tickle, *The Great Emergence: How Christianity Is Changing and Why* (Grand Rapids: Baker Books, 2008).

256   Helen Klaebe and Jean Burgess, "Oral History and Digital Storytelling Review" (Brisbane: State Library of Queensland, 2008), http://www.slq.qld.gov.au/__data/assets/pdf_file/0006/126357/SLQ_Oral_History_and_DST_Review.pdf.

Finally, as we live our lives, orally, literately, and digitally, do these different "cultures" blend into one fine continuous fabric without any stitching pulls in the weave? Are they coherent, or segmented, compartmentalized, even ruptured? And most importantly, is the Master's message through us clear, convincing, and able to penetrate the multilayered, intersecting spheres of the oral-literate-digital world in which God has called us to live and serve?[257]

---

257   For additional reading on this topic, see Hipps (2005 and 2009) and Ong (1982) in the *Handbook* bibliography.

SECTION 2

STORIES

AFRICA—GENERAL

37. DO THEY HAVE SIN?

By Roberta R. King

In one church in Africa, worship is announced through drums, "speaking" to those who have not yet arrived: "Hurry, the service is about to begin!" As the drumming continues, rattles and bells enter in, and singing starts. Often in a call-and-response style, the singing includes vibrato and improvised harmony. The congregation rises and moves energetically in celebration of their new life in Christ.

One newly arrived missionary joined in the celebration of song and dance. Others sat motionless, uncomfortable with the non-Western form of worship and unaware of the statement they were making through their refusal to participate.

The service ended and the believers surrounded the dancing visitor with expressions of welcome and thanks for worshiping with them. Then they asked, "Why don't the others worship with us? Do they have sin in their lives?"

Apparently among these Africans only those who have sin in their lives find it difficult to enter into worship and dance.

38. A SABBATICAL YEAR IN AFRICA THAT CHANGED EVERYTHING

By Mary K. Oyer

In October 1972, at the beginning of a sabbatical in East Africa, I was invited to a three-day conference of Mennonite churches gathered at Shirati, western Tanzania. Each of the eighteen congregations in attendance brought a choir, and each choir sang at every session. Enthusiasm ran high and had to be subdued when one group made its way down the aisle so rhythmically that it felt like dance—an unacceptable worship expression in this church tradition. All singing was in parts and unaccompanied because the early missionary pioneers from the United States had represented Mennonites of the *a cappella*–singing variety.

In the midst of this worship experience, however, there emerged a young girl from the smallest choir, bringing to the front a soda bottle with molded rings at its neck. When the congregation heard the percussive rhythmic accompaniment she provided by rubbing a nail over the rings, they erupted with joy and pleasure. Women ululated in a way such as I had never heard with the singing of missionary hymns.

What an epiphany for me! I suddenly realized that East African Mennonites were worshiping with "foreign" materials, even though the English words of the songs had been translated into Swahili. The original style of the missionary music had simply not reached into their deepest sound pool, the kind of sound that flowed naturally from their cultural musical heritage.

MY WESTERN MUSICAL ORIGINS

I had been born into an American Mennonite culture in the 1920s when my group held to a long tradition of *a cappella* singing in worship. We learned to play instruments, but they belonged to the secular aspect of life.

During the 1950s I spent a sabbatical leave working on what was then the new doctor of musical arts degree, using cello as my instrument. In addition to serious cello playing, I had the excellent guidance of a cultural history professor in examining what Western Christian artists had experienced across the centuries in pursuing their craft.

Later, during the 1960s, my work on researching and editing a hymnal for Mennonites forced me to face problems of sources and styles of music for worship. I had been exclusively a classical music professor and performer up to that point. Not even folk songs were on my radar. But my colleagues and I agonized over those much-loved hymns we did not personally value. We had to come to grips with the reasons others liked them so well. The Moody-Sankey gospel songs, for example, we needed to learn to know on a different level. And our agreement to work by consensus as a committee forced us to find new ways of evaluating various musical styles and traditions.

This was the period in American hymnody when a few cross-cultural songs were beginning to appear in denominational hymn collections. The Catholics in the mid-60s the Vatican II Council lifted the ban on the exclusive use of Latin in worship and encouraged vernacular styles of music. In our new Mennonite hymnal we managed to include only six Asian hymns in the short time we had before publication. African hymns seemed either too difficult or too oversimplified for Western use.

A SABBATICAL IN AFRICA THAT CHANGED EVERYTHING

For this sabbatical leave (1972–73), I determined to study African music and arts, primarily to enrich the related music and visual arts course I taught throughout my career.

Most mission hymns that I had heard seemed so Western that I paid little attention to them. Only gradually did I realize that the changes Africans made to these songs—with additions, omissions, and various other alterations—actually revealed a great deal about what they loved in their own oral music traditions.

I set out to record on cassette tape African traditional songs and instruments but soon felt I was simply taking something away from the musicians who helped me. Kwabena Nketia, a fine musician, scholar, and professor at the University of Legon in Ghana, suggested that I study a few instruments, and he found teachers to help me do so. I learned immediately that I needed a printed page of music to study an instrument, that music comes to me first through the eyes and then the ears. I was introduced suddenly into the oral world—a reality vastly different from the literate one.

> I would have called the instruments "primitive" until I saw what my teachers did with them.

The instruments—especially the one-stringed fiddle and African thumb instrument, both known by many names across the continent—I would have called "primitive" until I saw what my teachers did with them. And my "perfect pitch" was quite useless in trying to capture the tonalities they produced.

The whole experience was both discouraging and enlightening for me. I have a distinct memory of practicing my one-stringed fiddle as I waited outside the locked door of my instructor's room. A Ghanaian woman on her way to market with a large gourd of peanuts on her head stopped to watch me. We could not speak, but after many minutes she reached for a handful of peanuts and handed them to me! It was another epiphany. The sounds I made certainly could not have interested her, but she must have been astonished that this person, both woman and white, would care to play a musical instrument from her culture.

INTRODUCTION

SECTION 1: FOUNDATIONS

SECTION 2: STORIES

SECTION 3: TOOLS

CLOSING

FOCUSING ON DIFFERENCES IS THE MOST FRUITFUL

As I studied African music, I gradually concluded that, rather than focusing on those similar qualities between African and Western musical forms and traditions, the differences were more fruitful for understanding and using music specifically in worship. In African hymns, for example, the frequent repetitions of both words and music contrast sharply with the "wordiness" of Western hymns, inviting improvised changes and encouraging dance. (It is noteworthy, for example, that *ngoma*—the word for music in the Swahili language—also means "drum" or "dance.") The persistent downward motion of a melodic line in Africa differs from a more arched shape in Western melody. Rhythmic vitality is far more important in Africa than harmonic richness and subsequent loss of rhythmic energy in the West. Musical form in Africa is often cyclical with no clear beginning, middle, and end; Western music, in contrast, tends to be structured around high and low points of intensity with clear parameters.

None of these ideas are absolute, I have learned, but recognizing the tendencies greatly enriches my musical life. We humans, created in God's image, are "fearfully and wonderfully made." And God opens ways for us of experiencing the worship music of other cultures and sharing our own, thus leading to justice, joy, and praise.

AFRICA—CENTRAL

39. ENGELBERT MVENG:
A THEOLOGY OF LIFE EXPRESSED IN ART
By Scott Rayl

Engelbert Mveng was born in 1930 near Yaoundé, Cameroon, to Presbyterian parents. He eventually became a Jesuit priest, as well as a historian, poet, artist, philosopher, and theologian. ArtWay, a website that seeks to open up the world of the visual arts to interested Christians, writes:

> Father Mveng studied the aesthetics of African arts and published his findings in numerous books and articles . . . His teaching was based on what he called the universal rules of African art. As a historian and theologian he made a great contribution to the study of African culture and history, especially in the realms of cultural and religious anthropology and iconology.[1]

Mveng vigorously promoted the inculturation of the African church, including its visual art forms. He strove to combine liturgy and traditional African arts as a way to illustrate a "theology of life," one which promotes the ultimate triumph of life over all forms of death. Mveng considered African liturgical art to be an expression of the cosmic celebration of life.

In order to enable the production of African liturgical art, Mveng founded a religious art studio where he trained artists. He himself also created several paintings and mosaics to adorn churches, chapels, and education centers in Africa and beyond, based on his own personal style.

One such example is the Ugandan Martyrs Altar at Libermann College in Douala, Cameroon. Mveng writes:

> The Christ in majesty standing above the altar recapitulates the offering of the whole world and all of humanity in the sacrifice of the cross.

> At the foot of Christ crucified stand the martyrs of Uganda: they are the image of all those people in Africa who have united the sacrifice of their lives to that of Christ crucified. The cross rises up out of a cosmic background of cruciform patterns (the four

---

1   ArtWay, "ArtWay Visual Meditation March 18, 2012," http://www.artway.eu/content.asp?id=1142&action=show&lang=en.

points of the compass), of sun and moon motifs (circles and crescents), and triangular and diamond shapes, symbols of fertility and life. The whole is in three fundamental colours: red the colour of life, black the colour of suffering, and white the colour of death.

Thus Africa, mankind, and the whole cosmos are evoked and comprised in the vast gesture of Christ on the cross: "Father into thy hands I commend my breath of life."

But the splendour and majesty of this cross sings the paschal triumph of the resurrection: "I am the resurrection and the life; he who believes in me, though he dies, yet shall he live, and whoever lives and believes in me shall never die."[2]

Sadly, after thirty years of teaching at the University of Yaoundé Department of History, Mveng was brutally murdered in his home by an unknown assailant in 1995. The incident was one of several murders of clergy in Cameroon at that time, and Mveng's murder remains unsolved to this day. Unfortunately, most of his books and writings (in French) have never been translated into English.

Ugandan Martyrs Altar[3]

---

2   Ibid.
3   See http://www.artway.eu. Copyright: World Council of Churches.

40. HYMNBOOKS AS A STIMULUS TO READING— AND MORE[4]

By Ken Hollingsworth

Many Bible translators and others involved with unreached people groups anticipate helping produce a hymnbook in the local language, should believers request it. Quite often it is an unarticulated goal or expectation. Even more often the rationale for doing a hymnbook is not based on any well-thought-out plan for using it as a means to a larger end. Unfortunately, hymnbooks are often produced solely on the premise that if there is a church, there should be a hymnbook.

When my wife and I began working with the Mofu-Gudur people of Cameroon in the late 1970s, the evangelical churches in the area asked us to help them prepare a hymnbook of locally composed songs. They were already using a book of translated hymns in the regional language, Fulfulde. The local Baptist church wanted their own book with their own songs in their own language.

We put the church off until we had done enough language analysis and testing to arrive at a stable, scientific alphabet that was acceptable to the larger population. Then we were ready to work with them. Not only were we creating a product so the church could remember Mofu Christian songs, but we could also further test the alphabet and encourage literacy through the use of the hymnbook.

In the process, we asked all the main evangelical churches whose people had produced Christian songs to collect and record songs. We accepted only Mofu songs, our excuse being that we did not know Fulfulde. We transcribed and checked the songs for biblical and theological correctness. We then produced the book and a recording of the songs, sung in order and announcing the number of the song in the hymnbook.

> The hymnbook contributed to familiarizing a large number of people with the alphabet and served to encourage the use of Mofu heart music to praise God.

Each church was given a recording. The books sold out in no time. Later, we helped the Catholics revise their hymnbook to reflect the accepted Mofu orthography.

I am convinced that the hymnbook contributed to needful prereading activities (how to hold a book, turn pages, and more), as well as familiarizing a large number of people with the alpha-

---

4   Reprinted with permission from Ken Hollingsworth, "Hymnbooks as a Stimulus to Reading—and More," *EM News* 8, no. 4 (1999): 5.

bet. The books and recordings also served to encourage the use of Mofu heart music to praise God. Today you can go to almost any church and find an individual or a group of people with a handwritten notebook full of locally composed hymns.

41.   THE LOVE MOTIVE[5]

By Brian Schrag

The truck's wheels were spaced further apart than the rotting logs of the bridge. No way would we ever reach the dirt road on the other side. So the sixty or so Congolese pastors and I got out of the truck and began to walk to the church conference, twelve miles up the road. We were in the Democratic Republic of the Congo (DRC), where my family and I had come a year earlier to help start a project to translate the Bible into the Mono language.

At each village we passed, mothers, fathers, and children I had never met yelled out the name our local pastor had given me, "Gyaregbo! Gyaregbo!" They ran up to shake my hand, laugh, and ask me to play and sing the one Mono song I had learned on the *kundi,* an eight-stringed harp. I felt like a rock star. The non-Mono pastors looked on in wonder: "They really love you a lot!"

When we reached the pastors' conference, I gave my report on our activities in the northwest region of DRC. As part of the report, I performed the same song, to great applause. Even people who didn't know Mono asked me to play it again. And again. And again.

Another pastor remarked, "They sure love you."

Mono music team 2006

---

5   Reprinted with permission. Original article was published under the title "Why Local Arts Are Central to Mission," in *International Journal of Frontier Missiology* 24, no. 4 (Winter 2007): 199–202.

Brian Schrag recording Congolese harpist

When it was time to elect a missionary counselor for the finance committee, two Congolese church leaders proffered my name. Fortunately, for the good of all, my nomination wasn't accepted. But a deaconess leaned over to me and said, "They sure do love you, Gyaregbo!"

But why? Why do they love me so much here? Then this thought struck me: "*They love you because they feel you love them.*" My interest and involvement in Mono music, along with Bible translation, served as a clear statement of respect and affection.

INTRODUCTION

SECTION 1: FOUNDATIONS

SECTION 2: STORIES

SECTION 3: TOOLS

CLOSING

AFRICA—EAST

42. HEAVENLY LITURGY
By Lila Balisky

"You have taken us to heaven and back!"

Enthusiastic comments such as this often followed the performance of *Heavenly Liturgy*,[6] a worship experience based on the New Testament's Revelation of Saint John. During the 1990s, this drama was performed in Amharic as part of a course called Worship and Music in the Church. Both the course and drama were enthusiastically received by various theological schools in Ethiopia, as well as the churches in their vicinities. The message and power of this drama left students, teachers, and congregations weeping in wonder, love, and praise.

Creating the costumes and props required little effort, as the national dress of Ethiopia is a traditional *gabi*. All the players wrapped themselves in this shining white fabric, while the angels were draped in the gauzy white *netele* worn by women. The elders wore handmade golden crowns, which they could "cast down," and carried palm branches. The four creatures fashioned their costumes by drawing big eyes on paper, cutting them out, and pinning them all over their clothes, front and back. The students excelled in replicating the biblical imagery and color.

We chose indigenous songs based on texts from Revelation.

The students were divided into four groups: four creatures, several angels, twenty-four elders (or a representational group), and a "great throng." Usually our classes comprised twenty-five students, so these divisions worked out well.

The drama proceeded as follows: Old John the Apostle, swathed in a coarsely woven, white cotton blanket and leaning on his walking stick, slowly hobbles onto the stage, calling out in a quavering voice, quoting from Revelation 4: "After this I looked, and there before me . . ."[7] Then after a brief introduction on guitar, the whole group breaks into a chantlike song, reflecting the Ethiopian Orthodox church liturgy: "Holy, holy, holy. *Qiddus, qiddus, qiddus.*"

John continues to read:

---

6   *Heavenly Liturgy* was created by Aurelia Keefer, who served with the American Presbyterian Mission and the Ethiopian Evangelical Church, Mekane Yesus. A skilled Ethiopian musician, Moges Berassa, traveled with Lila Balisky and Aurelia to provide cultural expertise and instrumental accompaniment on their ecumenical teaching expeditions. Since the original productions given over twenty years ago, the program has been replicated throughout Ethiopia and beyond.

7   Scripture quotations throughout this chapter are from the NIV 1984.

After this I looked, and there before me was a door standing open in heaven. And the voice I had first heard speaking to me like a trumpet said, "Come up here, and I will show you what must take place after this. At once I was in the Spirit, and there before me was a throne in heaven . . . A rainbow, resembling an emerald, encircled the throne. Surrounding the throne were twenty-four other thrones, and seated on them were twenty-four elders. They were dressed in white and had crowns of gold on their heads. (Rev 4:1–4)

Heavenly Liturgy being enacted at the Hosanna KMTC in Ethiopia
(Note the angels swooping up the steps)

Elders enter in procession and take seats. John continues:

From the throne came flashes of lightning, rumblings and peals of thunder. Before the throne, seven lamps were blazing . . . Also before the throne there was what looked like a sea of glass, clear as crystal. In the center, around the throne, were four living creatures, and they were covered with eyes, in front and in back. (Rev 4:5,6)

Four Living Creatures enter. John continues:

Then I saw a Lamb, looking as if it had been slain, standing in the center of the throne, encircled by the four living creatures and the elders . . . Then I looked and heard the voice of many angels, numbering thousands upon thousands, and ten thousand times ten thousand. They encircled the throne and the living creatures and the elders. (Rev 5:6,11)

Angels enter and encircle the others. John continues:

After this I looked and there before me was a great multitude that no one could count, from every nation, tribe, people and language, standing before the throne and in front of the Lamb. They were wearing white robes and were holding palm branches in their hands. (Rev 7:9)

The Great Multitude come in last and take their places. The Apostle John sits down.

This song is then sung: "When we enter the New Jerusalem, bearing the victor palms, earth's misery disappearing like chaff, we will sing as we enter . . ."

Then the Living Creatures chant: "Holy, holy, holy is the Lord God Almighty, who was, and is, and is to come" (Rev 4:8).

Elders then take off their crowns and place them on the floor, saying, "You are worthy, our Lord and God, to receive glory and honor and power, for you created all things, and by your will they were created and have their being" (Rev 4:11).

Next, the Living Creatures and Elders say:

> You are worthy to take the scroll and to open its seals, because you were slain, and with your blood you purchased men for God from every tribe and language and people and nation. You have made them to be a kingdom and priests to serve our God, and they will reign on the earth. (Rev 5:9,10)

The Elders put the crowns back on their heads.

Angels, in a swelling crescendo, say: "Worthy is the Lamb, who was slain, to receive power and wealth and wisdom and strength and honor and glory and praise!" (Rev 5:12).

All say: "To him who sits on the throne and to the Lamb be praise and honor and glory and power, for ever and ever!" (Rev 5:13).

The Living Creatures, bowing reverently, say: "Amen" in a modulating flow of voices, slowly dying away.

The Great Multitude, in all the different languages represented, say in turn: "Salvation belongs to our God, who sits on the throne, and to the Lamb" (Rev 7:10).

In one production, students spoke fourteen languages, each reciting this exclamation in their own mother tongues. There was not a dry eye in the audience.

This song is repeated: "Worthy is the Lamb, who was slain, to receive power and wealth and wisdom and strength and honor and glory and praise!" (Rev 5:12).

Then one of the Angels cries out, accompanied by waves of hallelujahs and ululations: "The kingdom of the world has become the kingdom of our Lord and of his Christ, and he will reign for ever and ever" (Rev 11:15).

Elders say: "We give thanks to you, Lord God Almighty, the One who is and who was, because you have taken your great power and have begun to reign" (Rev 11:17).

A loud voice quotes Revelation 12:10–12a, again accompanied by ululations and hallelujahs. The Great Multitude continues:

> Great and marvelous are your deeds, Lord God Almighty. Just and true are your ways, King of the ages. Who will not fear you, O Lord, and bring glory to your name? For you alone are holy. All nations will come and worship before you, for your righteous acts have been revealed. (Rev 15:3,4)

A loud voice responds with Revelation 19:5: "Praise our God, all you his servants, you who fear him, both small and great!"

All in unison declare: "Hallelujah! For the Lord God Almighty reigns. Let us rejoice and be glad and give him glory! For the wedding of the Lamb has come, and his bride has made herself ready" (Rev 19:6,7).

Saint John slowly rises again to speak in a tremulous but strong voice: "He who testifies to these things says, 'Yes, I am coming soon.' Amen. Come, Lord Jesus. The grace of the Lord Jesus be with God's people. Amen" (Rev 22:20,21).

WORSHIP

INTRODUCTION

SECTION 1: FOUNDATIONS

SECTION 2: STORIES

SECTION 3: TOOLS

CLOSING

43. DELIGHTFUL PANDEMONIUM: DANCE IN THE SUDAN[8]

By Frank Fortunato

The door was closed and fans switched off; the tiny room instantly became an oven. A large set of drums recently moved into the room now serving as a recording studio had drastically reduced available floor space. Undaunted, eighteen Sudanese Dinka choir members managed to squeeze in. Once the drumming and singing began, the choir became oblivious to their surroundings: the recording equipment; the four strangers from Heart Sounds International (HSI)[9] busy audiotaping, videotaping, and snapping photos. Hour after hour the Dinka sang medley after medley, and though drenching in perspiration, they sang with vigorous abandon, taking only short breaks to cool down, get a drink, or munch a sandwich. The choir knew their songs well, and most were recorded in one take. In all, thirty-three songs and almost eighty minutes of worship music were recorded in one day.

The African nation of Sudan has suffered unspeakably. Of all the people groups undergoing persecution, none has been more devastated than the Dinka. These were the very people whose children had been abducted and sold into slavery, whose women had been raped, houses burned, and crops and cattle destroyed. Through their worship, God had kept these people strong in times of difficulty and persecution. There was an abandonment and joy in the singing that the HSI team witnessed that day.

> Through their worship, God had kept these people strong in times of difficulty and persecution.

On the final medley, some of the teenage girls could not resist adding their local dance steps, and began moving about the cramped studio. Soon the older women joined in with their swaying. Before we knew what was happening, all the ladies joyously circled the tiny room, while the men jumped vigorously in place. A delightful pandemonium erupted as the choir praised, danced, and marched, oblivious to cables, stands, mics, whatever. One engineer quickly put down his digital

---

8   Originally published in a slightly different form in Frank Fortunato, "Dinka Worship: Keeping Strong in the Midst of Persecution," in Fortunato, *All the World*, 105. Reprinted by permission of the author.

9   Heart Sounds International is a fellowship of volunteer musicians and recording engineers who take ten-day mission trips to an area to teach on biblical worship and train believers in various music skills, as well as record indigenous worship songs. HSI exists to help ignite biblically appropriate and culturally relevant heart worship in places where Christ-followers are restricted, persecuted, or unknown.

camera and rushed through the circle to grab the microphone stands lest they fall over as the choir continued in their exuberant, abandoned worship. In the aftermath we videotaped the leader and, through translation, asked him the meanings of the songs. They spoke of their difficult situation in life but also expressed hope, faith, joy, and trust in the Lord.

We realized we had just vividly experienced the theme that drives all we do in Heart Sounds International: "Every people should worship our awesome God in an awesome way that reflects their own culture."

WORSHIP AN...

200

RODUCTION

SECTION 1: FOUNDATIONS

SECTION 2: STORIES

SECTION 3: TOOLS

CLOSING

44. ERITREA AND SUDAN: WORSHIP IN THE MIDST OF SUFFERING

By George Luke

ERITREA

In 2002 the government of the African nation of Eritrea banned all Christian denominations except the Eastern Orthodox, Roman Catholic, and Evangelical Lutheran, and all other religious practices apart from Sunni Islam. This signaled the start of severe persecution for members of every religious group the Eritrean government deemed illegal.

Helen Berhane
(Photo by permission of Release International)

One woman has become the face and indeed the voice of the three-thousand-plus Eritrean evangelicals imprisoned, without charge or trial, in detention centers where torture is routinely in use—the gospel singer Helen Berhane.

Helen was born in Asmara, Eritrea's capital city, in 1974. She grew up in the Orthodox Church, where she started singing as a little girl. But it was in her teens, when her family moved across town and she started attending a nearby Catholic church, that her musical gift really developed.

Helen later joined the Full Gospel Church and became friends with Yonas Hail, another Christian singer who was also a filmmaker. She appeared in an evangelistic film he made, titled *The Gospel is the Cure for the Land,* and in 2003 she recorded an album of her own, titled *T'kebaeku* (*I Am Anointed*). Shortly after *T'kebaeku* was released on May 13, 2004, secret police raided a Bible study meeting where Helen was singing. She was arrested and ordered to sign a statement saying she would no longer take part in any form of evangelism.

INTRODUCTION

SECTION 1: FOUNDATIONS

SECTION 2: STORIES

SECTION 3: TOOLS

CLOSING

When she refused to sign, Helen was detained at the Mai Serwa military camp, located north of Asmara. Here she spent two years, imprisoned in sweltering heat in a freight container. Beatings and humiliation became an everyday part of her life. But even while in captivity, Helen continued to write songs—songs that are still being sung by Eritrean Christians today.

Helen's plight caught the attention of several people outside her homeland. Amnesty International joined Christian groups such as Christian Solidarity Worldwide and Release International in campaigning for her release, with celebrities such as Angelina Jolie taking up her cause. Then in November 2006 came the news Christians all over the world had been waiting to hear: Helen had been released on health grounds and was now at home. The following year, Helen was granted asylum in Denmark, where she now lives with her daughter, Eva.

"I never dreamed I would leave my country, but most Eritrean Christians are forced to leave because of our faith," Helen writes in her autobiography. "My prayer is for all this to change and for God to bring the persecution in Eritrea to an end."[10]

SUDAN

Located about six hundred miles west of Eritrea, Sudan is another country where Christians have had to live with immense persecution. In 2005 the Sudanese government signed a peace agreement with the Sudan People's Liberation Movement, ending a decades-long civil war between the Muslim North and the Christian/animist South, a war that has claimed the lives of some 2 million people and rendered another 4 million homeless.

> I felt that God wanted me to take the Sudanese Christians' songs, which worshiped him in the midst of their suffering, and make them accessible to the West.

A bold joint venture between persecuted Sudanese churches and a worship leader from Louisiana has helped bring the vibrant worship songs of Sudanese Christians to the Western world. It all began in 1997 when Slater Armstrong,[11] a former Youth With A Mission music minister, attended an Episcopal missions conference and heard a preacher from Sudan's Dinka community speak about the situation there. (Throughout the war, many Dinka people were abducted into slavery.)

"In the midst of sobbing and weeping, I asked God why he wasn't doing something about it," Slater recalls. "To which I received the obvious answer: 'Why don't you do something about it?' I felt that God wanted me to take the Sudanese Christians' songs, which worshiped him in the midst of their suffering, and make them accessible to the West."

In summer 1999, Slater arrived in Sudan with a makeshift recording studio. He traveled the country and recorded several gospel choirs. Some of these choirs' instruments were so old that the subsequent recordings had to have their pitch altered to make them sound right. But Slater eventually returned to the US with the music that would form the nucleus of an album titled *Even in Sorrow: A Recorded Project for the Persecuted Church in Sudan*.

Slater has since become actively engaged with the advocacy community for Sudan, working alongside numerous antigenocide groups and organizations. At this writing, he was working on

---

10   Helen Berhane, with Emma Newrick, *Song of the Nightingale* (Tyrone, GA: Authentic Media, 2009).

11   Slater Armstrong's website is http://www.joiningourvoices.com and his YouTube channel is http://www.youtube.com/jasudanis18.

a personal music project inspired by his fourteen years of work with the church in Sudan, and on a jazz and blues–based project with indigenous music from the Nuba Mountains in the heart of the country.

"Back when I was first called to record *Even in Sorrow*, the level of media awareness in Sudan was pretty non-existent, especially here in the US," Slater says. "That's changed in the last few years."

INTRODUCTION

SECTION 1: FOUNDATIONS

SECTION 2: STORIES

SECTION 3: TOOLS

CLOSING

45. CHANTING THE SCRIPTURES
By Mae Alice Reggy

When a New Testament translation project for the Wolayta of Ethiopia began in the early 1970s, the government would not allow books to be printed in indigenous languages; only in Amharic, the official language. The solution, at least short-term, was to record the translation as it was being done, making it accessible immediately and especially to those who could not read—about 80 percent of the some 2 million Wolayta speakers.

The Wolayta may not have been book-oriented then, but they did have a rich oral tradition, which included their cultural chanting and singing styles. So chants and songs were added to the tapes to break up the reading. These also served as devices for memorizing the Scriptures. The word of God would become fixed in people's hearts and minds when reinforced by tunes and chants the Wolayta loved, and would spring to their lips throughout the day.

By the time the Wolayta New Testament was printed in 1981, many Christians already knew some parts of the text by heart.

To record each passage, a few verses were read, lasting about a minute. Different voices spoke for the various participants in Gospel narratives. Before the listeners could lose interest, the next few verses would be chanted in traditional Wolayta style, encouraging them to chant an antiphonal response along with the cassette. The chanter would sing only the words of the text, but the antiphonal response would provide an application of the passage to listeners' own lives or a reinforcement of the subject being taught. The antiphonal refrains emphasized major truths and stirred in the listeners a rhythm that prevented drowsiness, as they listened in the dark of night after a hard day's work in the fields.

After a minute or two of chanting had finished, another short reading followed. And then again the pace changed—the reading would be followed by a song composed from a key verse in the passage. The tune fixed the words in the listeners' minds, as the singer on the tape repeated the memory verse four times in a contemporary Wolayta song form. The listeners would again be encouraged to sing along with the cassette, to memorize the Scripture verse. And in this way they continued listening, chanting, and singing God's word.

46. "EVEN THE FROGS ARE SINGING!"
By Julie Taylor

When organising a song workshop, ethnomusicologists are interested in song styles, instruments, and performance practices, but what about singing frogs?

In September 2003 I climbed into a leaky boat and headed for Mfangano Island, an idyllic paradise on the eastern side of Lake Victoria. (Riding the "taxi" across the choppy waters reminded me of Mark 4:35–41 where Jesus calmed the storm.) On behalf of the Kenyan organisation Bible Translation and Literacy, I was to hold a five-day song workshop amongst the Suba people, and nineteen men and women of various ages were waiting when my boat crunched onto the shore. Together we lived in borrowed tents overlooking this vast lake—minus cars, phones, and electricity—enjoying the sounds of frogs, birds, fishermen, and their families.

My main objective was to encourage the composition of new worship songs based on elements of Suba cultural song styles, so I began the workshop by probing for examples of traditional genres.

"We can't remember them," the participants responded.

"Why?"

"Because the churches have encouraged us to sing other songs." This is a familiar response in Kenya so I waited, but holding my breath. Then an old man with a woolly hat and walking stick painstakingly got to his feet, cleared his throat, and started to sing. Broad smiles appeared on the faces of everyone as they responded in unison, the men now dancing in forward-shuffling steps and the women swinging their arms vigorously to and fro. At the end, excitement and laughter filled the air as they explained that this was a long-forgotten harvest song.

Yet it was incomplete without the *enkombi* horn, so the discussion swung to instruments. Without being asked, two middle-aged schoolteachers spent several hours drawing and writing descriptions for me of every instrument used by the Suba. These included the *ekimuga* (seed gourd), *ekitutu* (reed flute), *owukana* (eight-stringed lyre), *endigidi* (tube fiddle), and *eng'oma* (drum). The workshop had come alive; we were on our way!

The Suba were translating the New Testament into their language, so participants had draft versions of Mark, Luke, Acts, Romans, and the Minor Epistles from which to choose texts for new songs. The book of Jonah was also available and obviously very popular in this fishing community.

By the first evening the participants had broken into small groups of three or four, experimenting with several ways of using Scripture texts. Some could hear a melody emerging from the appropriate intonation and phrasing of a text, others took an existing melody and reshaped it to fit a story told in their own words, adding illustrations from their own lives. Eventually they all made at least two songs entirely on their own. As they sang and danced late into the nights, fishermen sat in their boats out on the lake and listened while songs overflowed on shore as abundantly as loaves and fishes. When finally the entire Suba translation and literacy team threatened to become full-time composers, I reluctantly had to dissuade them from leaving their already important roles.

Another aim of this workshop was to spend the last two days recording newly composed songs, and the word "recording" had already spread like wildfire across the island. Soon a church choir resplendent in robes and a youth group with homemade guitars appeared on the scene asking me to record them too. Not wanting to turn anyone away, I suggested they listen to everything going on around them and secretly hoped they would realise their songs were not the same "flavor." The next I saw them, they had replaced their robes with traditional flax skirts and were radically reshaping their songs.

> The priority was to help the Suba people realise that their own heart music could open the doorway to a deeper identification with God.

Meanwhile, a small translation room with a tin roof had become the recording studio, transformed with blankets and mattresses into an airless oven. A singer fainted as the temperatures rose, but still the groups continued to sing and dance with huge enthusiasm, waving leafy branches above their heads to symbolise the triumph of Christ. It was impossible to get them to stand still, much to my despair as the sound recordist, but we collected sufficient songs to make no less than three recordings. I edited these in Nairobi, and nine hundred copies have now been distributed amongst the Suba people, coordinated by the translation team and various churches.

With such a short visit, I could not attempt a definitive study of the traditional genres. Rather, the priority was to help the Suba people realise that their own heart music could open the doorway to a deeper identification with God, no matter how many other doorways beckoned in an increasingly multistranded culture. Even though this workshop was deemed a success, the true test comes long after the event is over. In the words of one participant, "We know the heart is very weak in introducing a new thing, and many of our people want us to remain as we are. But now we are *really* praising God, and even the frogs are singing!" Indeed, these singing frogs were an inspiration to the entire workshop, but hopefully God won't mind!

205

INTRODUCTION

SECTION 1: FOUNDATIONS

SECTION 2: STORIES

SECTION 3: TOOLS

CLOSING

47. "FROM NOW ON, GIVE US THIS BREAD"[12]
By Julie Taylor

"We had no idea the church could be like this!" said two elderly ladies from Tanzania, drawn to Christ through the music of their own culture.

They had come to an indigenous hymnody workshop among the Burunge people. Knowing older people are often the last guardians of local cultural practices, I had invited several to the church where the workshop was held.

Seven traditional ladies came, but they refused to speak Kiswahili, the national language of Tanzania, which is also used in churches. They were proud of their mother tongue, Burunge, and insisted on using it. These ladies had seldom crossed the threshold of a church, because the language and music used in the services was alien to them. Nevertheless, at the end of the song workshop, having spent a week combining Scripture texts in their own language with their own music styles, two of them gave their lives to the Lord.

Many people in eastern Africa worship God with music styles they cannot identify with, understand, or even enjoy. "This is the way it has always been," they say. "We sing these hymns because that is what we were taught."

Physical drought has existed so long in parts of eastern Africa that many children don't even know what bread is. Another kind of drought has hindered indigenous music from flourishing. In some areas, indigenous music styles have been almost completely abandoned in exchange for more modern, foreign, and/or "correct" styles. Younger generations no longer identify with or have any experience in singing songs from their own culture.

At the same time, hunger for better understanding of God's word persists, and one of the fastest ways to satisfy that craving is through music. We want to help meet that hunger through these indigenous hymnody workshops.

The ladies who attended the classes brought an instrument with them that I had never seen before—a friction trough (*khuu'usimoo*). Laid on the ground with a woman player sitting at either end, each simultaneously rubbed two large wooden "spoons" on the convex board to produce a series of pitched "grunts," not unlike a fire-making technique. I was so excited I could hardly speak. This highly revered instrument, traditionally reserved for secret female-only ceremonies, now was used—in the open—to praise God in a musical setting of Psalm 23.

12   Reprinted with permission from Julie Taylor, "'From Now On, Give Us This Bread,'" in Fortunato, *All the World*, 138.

INTRODUCTION

SECTION 1: FOUNDATIONS

SECTION 2: STORIES

SECTION 3: TOOLS

CLOSING

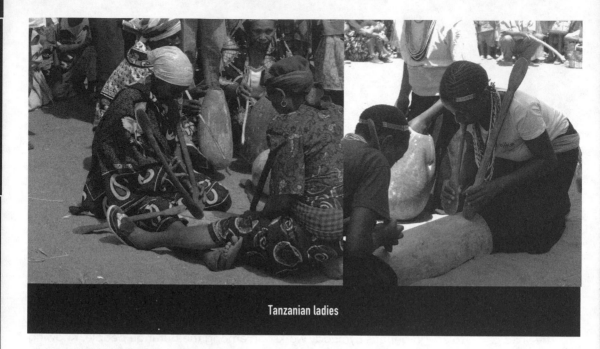

Tanzanian ladies

As the women began to play the instrument, and others began to sing and dance, men at the workshop fell respectfully silent, listening intently to the new words. No one was confused by the message or by the outward style—the "clothing"—of the song. It obviously felt entirely natural; the song belonged to the Burunge people, based on the culture God had given them.

In John 6:33–35, Jesus said, "For the bread of God is the bread that comes down from heaven and gives life to the world."

"Sir," they said, "always give us this bread."

Then Jesus declared, "I am the bread of life. Whoever comes to me will never go hungry, and whoever believes in me will never be thirsty."

The drought of culturally appropriate Christian music is ending for the Burunge people as the Bread of Life comes and satisfies them—body, soul, and spirit.

AFRICA—NORTH

48. GOD WILL MAKE A WAY

By Carol Brinneman

In a restrictive African country, three teams of nationals braved travel on bone-jolting roads to reach a remote area to show the *JESUS* film. A few Christians welcomed them, accompanying them from village to village. Using a portable 16 mm projection equipment set, each team showed the film every night for a month—a total of ninety presentations.

> He said, "I first taught the song to a few of my people—all eighteen pages. They learned it and then they taught it to others; it went from person to person and from heart to heart."

The team hoped to find local Christians they could train to follow up new believers and then start worship groups. However, suddenly a civil war broke out, forcing them to leave—extremely disappointed.

Six years passed without any word of the spiritual seeds they had sown. Their frustrations continued, as well as their prayers. Then one day a man who had accompanied the teams on the film showings visited the capital city and looked up a national staff person from the project.

Amazed to see the man again, the staff person invited him in. The visitor began, "You know, I was with you that month you and your team showed the *JESUS* film. I watched it every night. In fact, I memorized it."

Reaching into his pocket, he pulled out eighteen well-worn sheets of paper filled with words. They contained the story line of Jesus' life—set to music. He had written a song from the words of the film! It was all there: the Lord's birth, his teachings, his miracles, his death, his resurrection.

In an oral society, such as that of the composer, people have tremendous power of recall, and knowledge passes from generation to generation through stories and music. The man had created a most effective evangelistic tool for his culture. He revisited the areas where the teams had shown the film and began to teach his JESUS-film song to the people.

He said, "I first taught the song to a few of my people—all eighteen pages. They learned it and then they taught it to others; it went from person to person and from heart to heart."

Zephaniah 3:17 says, "The Lord your God is with you, the Mighty Warrior who saves. He will take great delight in you; in his love he will no longer rebuke you, but will rejoice over you with

INTRODUCTION

SECTION 1: FOUNDATIONS

SECTION 2: STORIES

SECTION 3: TOOLS

CLOSING

singing." God indeed, through his Holy Spirit, passed right through language and cultural barriers and the isolation of that remote region, singing his love and his story into thirsty hearts. The people could not get the captivating tune out of their minds.

The team's long years of disappointment and frustration soon exploded into praise. Seeds planted during their ministry and through one believer's song grew into forty-eight new churches!

In Psalm 2, God laughs at nations that reject his sovereignty. He must also laugh, even scoff, at barriers that threaten to stop the advance of his powerful word: man-made walls, confusing languages, cultural taboos, political isolation, and geographically remote places. His ways of breaching them astound us, and our hearts can only respond in songs of praise: "God will make a way where there seems to be no way . . ."[13]

---

13   "God Will Make a Way" by Don Moen.

209

INTRODUCTION

SECTION 1: FOUNDATIONS

SECTION 2: STORIES

SECTION 3: TOOLS

CLOSING

49. CHANTING THE GOSPEL OF JOHN: AN EXPERIMENTAL APPROACH[14]

By Sue Hall and Richard Shawyer

Sitting on mats under the shade of a tree, the group of men listened to the player while mint tea bubbled on the charcoal stove. All ears were bent on the chanted message coming from the speakers. Though children played nearby, no interruptions would be tolerated, because this was clearly a message of great importance. The melodic flow of the solo voice told of the Word of God entering into this world, bringing light into darkness and power from God that had never been seen before. *"Who is this Word?"* they wondered.

The missionary stopped the recording at the end of chapter 2 of John's Gospel and moved into the Bible lesson for the week, teaching through stories and questions.

The following week, however, he discovered that what really stuck in the minds of those listeners were the texts—chanted in the same form as those from their own religious book. Their preference for oral communication helped them retain the important, new messages and recall them a week later without prompting.

Chanting Scripture is one of many techniques used to encourage people to listen to and accept the Bible. The concept and planning of this trial project was done by a group of Christian workers reaching out to one large ethnic group in the interface between Arab North Africa and black West Africa. This group has resisted the Christian message for decades, especially since the gospel has often been presented in "foreign clothes" and seen as irrelevant to this self-confident and proud people group. As Scripture is translated into the local language, the challenge is to see it reach the ears of those who most need to hear its message.

Of the few local believers, one had been trained, as a student and during his pre-Christian years, to recite lengthy passages. He was asked to try reciting Scripture from the printed New Testament in the same way. The results were pleasing to other believers who heard his chanting of the Christmas story.

To share Scripture more widely and test out people's reactions, the media group decided to make a simple recording of this man's recitation. The recording, made in a local Christian studio, often captured a whole chapter or more in one take so not to disturb the flow of the text. In the

---

14   Reprinted with permission from Sue Hall and Richard Shawyer, "Chanting the Gospel of John: An Experimental Approach," in Fortunato, *All the World*, 27.

He discovered that what really stuck in the minds of those listeners were the texts—chanted in the same form as those from their own religious book.

final processing, some echo was added for aesthetic enhancement, which local people preferred. Most recordings of religious chanting sold in this area have a high degree of reverberation due to the size of the place of worship where they are recorded. Care was taken, though, not to add too much echo because the quality of most players used by local people is not good, and recorded sounds are easily distorted, which will, of course, affect what people hear and understand.

The final recording product is a set of three sixty-minute recordings. The cover format is simple but reflects designs used for religious literature in the region, with text presented in Roman and Arabic scripts in the local language to maximize comprehension. The chanting style demands serious attention—for a serious message.

50. SCRIPTURE MEMORIZATION: KEY TO PEACE

By Anne Zaki

In 1984 Islamic extremism had reached a frightening pitch in villages of southern Egypt, where many churches and Christian homes and businesses were being attacked. In that year, Islamist terrorists attacked a small church in the village of Gad Alseed, near Minya (about four hours south of Cairo), and killed one of their beloved Sunday school teachers. The church felt threatened and terrified, especially in light of the then-recent Islamic Revolution in Iran (1979), which banned printing Bibles. They feared Egypt was next on the Islamic extremism agenda.

To transform their fear into an act of restorative peace and justice, they committed themselves to memorize entire books of Scripture, to preserve the word of God in their hearts, come what may. Families would memorize significant portions, inviting every member, young and old, to participate. Years later, those who were present during those days can still remember what unity, peace, and joy the word of God brought them then and are thankful for the freedom of worship and access to the Bible they now have. Yes, even during these unsettled times, Jesus Christ, the Lord of the Church, is faithful!

AFRICA—SOUTHERN

51. NTSIKANA: THE FIRST GREAT XHOSA HYMN WRITER

By James R. Krabill

Ntsikana (c. 1780–1821) was one of the first converts to Christianity among the Xhosa-speaking people of southern Africa. Living at a time of growing conflict throughout the region, both among traditional chiefs as well as between the Xhosa and encroaching white settlers, Ntsikana served as a calming influence, a prophetic "servant of God," calling his people to prayer and peace and preparing the way for seeds of the gospel to be planted and take root.

Some believe Ntsikana's first encounter with Christianity may have been as an older teenager when Dr. J. T. van der Kemp of the London Missionary Society (LMS) lived for a year as an evangelist among the Xhosa in late 1799 to early 1801. Though van der Kemp's efforts were short-lived and largely unsuccessful, it was perhaps here that Ntsikana first heard the Christian message.

Another important development in Ntsikana's spiritual pilgrimage took place fifteen years later when LMS missionary Rev. Joseph Williams opened a mission station in his area. Though Ntsikana never chose to settle at the station, he did visit Williams regularly for a few years and, while on the grounds, received some biblical instruction and participated in worship services.

Despite these occasional contacts, however, Ntsikana's exposure to Western missionaries was for the most part limited. Many Xhosa Christians believe, in fact, that Ntsikana's spiritual insights came directly from God with no assistance whatsoever from missionary agents. One such story, widely acclaimed and recounted, tells of a turning point in Ntsikana's life when he reportedly saw a bright light strike his favorite ox. Later that same day, he was prevented from participating in a neighbor's festive party when a whirlwind blew up out of nowhere, requiring the guests to abandon their dancing. Sensing that the Holy Spirit had entered him, Ntsikana ordered his family away from the dance, quickly took them home, and declared, "People should pray [rather than dance]!"

On the following day, Ntsikana exhibited strange behavior and could be overheard humming a melody unknown to his listeners. This was the beginning of Ntsikana's experience as an indigenous hymn composer. With time, he added words to the chantlike melodies he was receiving and expressed his faith in a set of four hymns, all of which were quickly taken over by the mission community and became part of the core of Xhosa Christianity. In contrast to later Xhosa hymns, which were largely translations of English hymns based on European rhythms and melodies, Ntsikana's hymns were genuinely Xhosa—using language with its African idioms, rhythms, images, and figures of speech.

One of Ntsikana's hymns is known as his "great hymn": "*Ulo Tixo omkulu, ngosezulwini*" ("The Great God, He Is in the Heavens"). The song declares:

> The Great God, he is in the heavens.
> You are you, Shield of truth.
> You are you, Stronghold of truth.
> You are you, Thicket of truth.
> You are you, who dwells in the highest,
> Who created life (below) and created (life) above.
> The Creator who created, created heaven.
> This Maker of the stars and the Pleiades,
> A star flashed forth, telling us.
> The Maker of the blind, does he not make them on purpose?
> The trumpet sounded, it has called us.
> As for his hunting, he hunts for souls.
> Who draws together flocks opposed to each other.
> The Leader, he led us.
> Whose great mantle, we put it on.
> Those hands of yours, they are wounded.
> Those feet of yours, they are wounded.
> Your blood, why is it streaming?
> Your blood, it was shed for us.
> This great price, have we called for it?
> This home of yours, have we called for it?

Ntsikana's use of local imagery, language, and poetic style and his commitment to expressing his faith in his own words, rather than simply translating someone else's, has earned for him the title of "the first great Xhosa hymn writer."

52. A PENTECOST MOMENT

By Joyce Scott

I returned home to South Africa twelve years after the country's historic move from an apartheid regime to a democratically elected government. I had worked as a missionary in Kenya, assigned to encourage church musicians—in fourteen different cultures—to use their own indigenous music styles, languages, and instruments for heart-level worship, evangelism, and Bible teaching.

In 2006 I was in the process of moving house from one suburb to another in the South Peninsula of Cape Town. I "shopped" for a church where I could hopefully make some useful contribution.

My dream was to see long-held racial barriers in South Africa also come down in the churches. Surely Christians would welcome the freedom to celebrate our newfound unity by worshiping together. Admittedly, our music styles and languages were very different, but I had experienced this unity in diversity in Nairobi, Kenya, and looked forward to a paradigm shift, taking advantage of the freedom of our new political dispensation.

But as time went by, my dream faded. South Africans had been so effectively divided by apartheid that very few churches could cope with intercultural worship. Here and there some urban churches with racially diverse congregations tried to mix and match hymns and songs in different languages. They ended up sticking to a policy where the one dominant culture called the shots and occasionally included one or two songs in another language and music style. It was more a case of assimilation than accommodation, as if to say "Welcome! Come and join us. This is the way we do church here."

> South Africans had been so effectively divided by apartheid that very few churches could cope with intercultural worship.

Many expatriate Africans came to South Africa as political refugees from oppressive countries, or as students, or job seekers. These Christians tried to find somewhere to worship, but most African congregations, where the music style felt like home, worshiped in their own vernaculars—Xhosa, Zulu, and others. And white congregations used either English or Afrikaans and a very Western-oriented music style. A few of these homesick aliens, willing to be "assimilated" into the foreign Western style, stuck it out and stayed. But most ended up seeking out other expatriates from their own countries and forming their own congregations.

A few churches, however, practiced a beautiful unity in diversity of music styles. I knew this was possible. I believe this situation is an ideal platform for showing love and humility as our Lord intended it. Even where some people feared a takeover by a different style, it worked out to be enriching and led to a new understanding and joy. Surely this is what the Lord Jesus was praying for in John 17:20–23, "that all of them may be one."

One Sunday I attended a community church located at a theological college. This was one of five churches I was checking out to see where God wanted me to serve him. It was a delightful surprise!

Worship songs were led by a culturally mixed group. A young white man sat at the piano, black students played guitars and drums, and both black and white girls led the singing. They began with a few choruses in Xhosa and one in Tswana, with plenty of movement and the congregation singing and clapping to the rhythm. Then followed two songs in English and one lovely, old hymn. I watched carefully and noticed that everyone, both young and old, sang heartily with understanding (as English translation of the African languages was provided). The two pastors, one black and one white, shared the platform. It happened to be Pentecost Sunday.

When it came time for prayer, they asked those who had been invited to come up and lead in intercession. Nineteen people from nineteen different countries came forward and prayed for their homelands in nineteen different languages! I was blown away in wonder and worship—this was indeed a Pentecost moment! I was especially moved to hear the country of Zimbabwe prayed for by a young white woman, in Shona—the language of the majority of African people in her homeland. Of course, I was delighted to hear Kenya prayed for in Swahili, the language I had used for ministry there, so I could understand and say a fervent amen at the end.

After the service, when everyone gathered for coffee, the young man who had prayed in Swahili came running over. "Hey, Joyce!" he said, "Have you come to join us?" I had taught him at another evangelical seminary, and he was here now, doing a master's degree.

I sighed. "I wish! But no, Victor," I said, "The work God has called me to do in his Church has already been accomplished here. May your example of the grace of God in exhibiting this beautiful unity in diversity lead many other congregations to experience the joy of the Christlike fellowship I see here."

And so I moved on to a church where this kind of intercultural worship is not the pattern—yet! But I believe that one day we, too, will demonstrate to the world how Christ's prayer can be answered among us: "I have given them the glory that you gave me . . . so that they may be brought to complete unity. Then the world will know that you sent me and have loved them even as you have loved me" (John 17:22,23).

53. TURNING SERMON NOTES INTO SONG[15]
By Greg Kernaghan

So much of what Christians in the developed world consider mandatory—ostentatious church buildings, big-ticket conferences, "essential" tools and trappings—seems not only irrelevant but absurd in southeast Africa. There is no time or place in Mozambique for anything "extra." Yet God is here, as expected, in the unexpected. I counted it a rare privilege to spend a week in the heart of the country, far removed from concepts like roads, electricity, clocks, or world headlines.

One day we arrived in Nigula Ile for a pastors' conference. This "village" was nothing more than a handful of buildings where several

Mozambique—"teaching song" created by oral learners

footpaths converged, and on those paths some pastors walked for thirty kilometers or more in the African heat and sun to attend. Needless to say, they had expectations!

So what would you say to them? As we gathered under a huge mango tree—the best church structure I had ever seen—I sought words of encouragement and wisdom in the midst of my weakness; they were teaching me so much.

After forty minutes, it was time for lunch. As I sat down, one pastor stood up and immediately broke into that captivating African style where one person calls out and the others respond in harmony. Forget lunch; just keep singing, please!

I asked the translator what they were singing, and his answer was unexpected. "This is an oral culture; few if any of these men can read," he explained. "They will compare notes, so to speak, of what you have taught, and then 'pack' the teaching into a song that all will learn. Then they can sing this song as they walk the long journey home, after which they will unpack the teaching and give it to their people over the next weeks."

15   Reprinted with permission from Greg Kernaghan, "Turning Sermon Notes into Song," *Connections: The Journal of the WEA Mission Commission* 9, nos. 2 and 3 (2010): 60.

Mozambique—"teaching song" created by oral learners

Do we really think our seminaries and hermeneutics, our megaconferences, and an embarrassment of resources can hold a candle to this kind of purity and connectivity? God has given them music and verse—their own—and a passion to use them for his glory. We should be their humble students.

INTRODUCTION

SECTION 1: FOUNDATIONS

SECTION 2: STORIES

SECTION 3: TOOLS

CLOSING

54. CREATING PROCESSIONS AND PASSION PLAYS IN SOUTHERN AFRICA

By C. Michael Hawn and Swee Hong Lim

In Grahamstown, South Africa, the men's choir gathered on a rainy Easter Sunday morning and marched down the street toward the church arm-in-arm, singing songs—a witness to the black township to the power of the Resurrection. They entered the church and sang to the packed Sunday congregation. As they proceeded down the center aisle, the congregation rose and joined in the song. The three-hour service included nearly two hours of congregational and choral singing. The women's choir started the traditional Western hymns in Xhosa translation, and the men's choir, the African songs—a kind of African-Western hybrid, accompanied only by the thud of a hand slapping a leather pillow to keep the beat. As the congregation joined in the singing, people started to sway. Some contributed additional percussion by drumming on the back of the pews in front of them. Others improvised descants above the melody, enriching the sound and enhancing the vitality of worship.

In 1964 Robert Kauffman, a missionary and college professor at Kwanongoma College in Bulawayo, Zimbabwe, encouraged his former students to compose original songs for a passion play. He was counting, however, on using African-American spirituals to fill out the musical portions of the drama in case original compositions did not materialize.

With this need in mind, Kauffman suggested that Abraham Dumisani Maraire (1943–2000), a graduate, come to the Methodist mission station to write the music needed for Easter Sunday. Because of a misunderstanding, Maraire went ahead and composed over ten songs for the entire Holy Week story. He also recorded each of the parts of the songs and, using the recordings to prompt his memory, he taught them to the congregation by rote. His work resulted in a complete passion play, *Mazuva Ekupedzisa* (*The Last Days*), composed in 1965. One of its songs has become a staple of the Zimbabwean church, especially the "Alleluia" refrain with its cross-rhythms and three-part harmony.

AFRICA—WEST

55. TOUCHING THE HEART STRINGS[16]

By Tom Avery

"Do you mean I can't just jump off the plane in Yoruba country and give my new friends translated versions of worship songs that touch *my* heart deeply?"

Not if you want music to truly communicate God's love.

Thanks to the efforts of talented Christian composers and performers, urban Yoruba people, numbering in the millions, now have an opportunity to hear God's words in *juju*, the urban music style they grow up with—their true heart music. Though juju and Western praise music have guitars and keyboards in common, only one style will reach the heart of the Yoruba deeply and lead them into worship.

I am not talking about language differences or diverse ways the vocal lines interface, but about the significant differences in how the two music systems use the same instruments and tonal system. Both systems have guitar chords, but the way they are put together makes the music sound distinctively American or African. Each type of urban Christian music is potentially valuable for building the kingdom of God—each in its own setting. We want to help create an attitude conducive to true worship, not an emphasis on the novelty of the musical style.

> For cross-cultural Christian music communicators, the best approach is not to arrive in a foreign country saying, "Look at all the goodies I have brought."

For Yoruba who want to develop urban songs with Christian texts, *juju* is more appropriate—and sustainable locally!—than translating Western praise choruses. For cross-cultural Christian music communicators, the best approach is not to arrive in a foreign country saying, "Look at all the goodies I have brought," and start passing out copies of one's own favorite music. Rather, communicators need to research the local sociomusical situation and discover what the people are already doing—and could do—to create their own musical offerings to God and their society.

---

16   Originally published in a slightly different form in *EM News* 7(2–3) 1998:10–13 (from a letter intended for musicians interested in missions but with little orientation in cross-cultural communication). Reprinted by permission of Paul Neeley, editor, *EM News*. See the *Handbook* DVD for the *EM News* archives.

56. PHILIPPIANS AND JAMES, WITH A DASH OF MILLET BEER AND MADMEN

By Rob Baker

DAY 1

Amongst the crowd greeting us as we arrive in Baga village in northern Togo is a very old man. I assume he must be *le vieux du village* (the village elder) and quickly tell my friend Ken to hold his right upper arm with his left hand when shaking the man's hand, as a sign of respect. What I am yet to realize is that this guy is actually *le fou du village* (the village madman), who follows us into the church, mumbling all the way.

Yesterday I made the familiar journey north from Cotonou, Benin, to Kara, Togo, dodging goats, chickens, and dogs all the way, as usual. But this time Ken has come with me. He's a percussionist from the UK, with whom I made an album a few years back. He's keen to see what this ethnodoxology lark is all about and to become *au fait* with the local rhythms. We've traveled here to run a songwriting workshop, based on the books of Philippians and James, with the Nawdm people. They live in northern Togo and number around 150,000. There's also a significant number in Ghana.

After an overnight in Kara, we set off early for a forty-five-minute drive farther north. The road is well tarmacked with stunning scenery en route; less stunning than usual, though, because the *harmattan* (a dusty wind from the Sahara) is blowing strongly today. We turn off the main road into Baga, then just a few hundred yards down a winding dirt track to the large Catholic church. Those taking part in the workshop are from various churches, but this is an excellent location, as there's tons of space and two sizeable buildings.

The madman greets us, and throughout the first session of teaching he continues to interject incomprehensible comments at regular intervals, until someone finally ushers him out.

Rob explains the workshop to participants and asks them to list their song genres.
(Photo by Jon Assheton—used by permission)

As ever, we start by listing song genres that exist in the local traditional music. Here are some of them:

- *simpa,* used to express joy, including at funerals (but not for mourning in its truest sense)
- *balance*, as for *simpa*
- *santm*, for joy
- *kukpalɔa*, for joy
- *kamgu*, for joy
- *dagabina*, for joy, or after the death of an old man
- *fɔkabina*, sung following the death of an old woman
- *timbingu*, sung/played during a procession
- *kajaaga*, for joy
- *bagu*, for hunting
- *habara*, sung in the moonlight as exhortation and includes an interesting dance
- involving hitting your hip against your neighbor's

Following this, one of the Nawdm translation team gives an exegesis of Philippians, and then I split everyone into four groups—one for each chapter of Philippians. The participants' first task is to read through their chapter and

One of the groups composing their Bible-based new song.
(Photo by Jon Assheton—used by permission)

choose appropriate verses/themes for their songs. They go for Philippians 1:18–24; 2:3–8; 3:8,9; and 4:4–7. Following this, they need to choose which genre will fit best with the theme and meter of their words. We end up with four different genres, which is great news in terms of variety and the preservation of traditional music styles.

After a copious lunch on site, composition begins. Today is not only a baking hot day but also extremely dry due to the *harmattan,* with humidity levels down to as low as 10 percent. It's so dry, in fact, that between 8:00 a.m. and 5:00 p.m., I drink three whole litres of water! Before we close, each group sings its new song to the rest, and we share comments on how it could be improved, considering aspects such as clarity, content, instrumentation, and rhythm.

DAY 2

Today I do a bit more teaching, and they do loads more composing. We start by singing through yesterday's songs again, this time with percussion. Each group has written all its songs' words on blackboards, so those who are literate can follow as they sing along. I also encourage folk to bring along more instruments, so today there's a large clay drum, as well as a pair of *metal-bodied* (rather than wooden) congas and the ubiquitous *agogo* bells and shakers.

Having composed and perfected the Philippians songs, we move on to James. Following some biblical exegesis, we then divide into *five* groups to begin composing—again, one for each chapter. They choose the following verses as bases for their songs but refer to other verses too: James 1:12 and 2:14; James 3—a bit of everything; 4:6,11; and 5:11. The songs are finished by midafternoon, and we once again reunite to hear them and learn at least the refrains of each song.

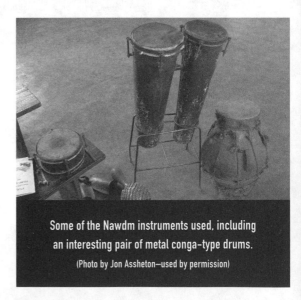

Some of the Nawdm instruments used, including an interesting pair of metal conga-type drums.
(Photo by Jon Assheton—used by permission)

DAY 3

Recording day is here! We meet up and go straight into groups to rehearse songs. The first thing to understand in this business is that there's always something that hinders your recording! Be it goats, motorbikes, ants, chainsaws, or parties, the sooner you realize there will be *something* to make life interesting, the better. This time it's the wind; the *harmattan* is stronger than ever this morning. In addition, many of the trees around our *paillote* (a round gazebo, often with straw roof) have dried pods hanging from them; these rattle loudly when the wind blows. No chance of recording over that din! I look around for alternative locations, but there's very little shade here apart from under the aforementioned trees. So we wait and keep rehearsing. By 10:30 a.m. the wind has died down sufficiently, and we set up and start recording.

The second thing to know when field recording is that there's likely to be some kind of technical, equipment-based problem. Today I accidentally set my phantom power to 12 volts instead of 48 for one of the songs, which means that some of the microphones do not work properly. Consequently, the choir is barely audible, giving a poor-quality, unbalanced recording. So, we have to re-record the whole song again, and some of the choir members are not pleased. Nevertheless, we soldier on, desperately hoping to get Philippians "in the can" before lunchtime, and conscious that the *paillote* is needed for a catechism class at 3:00 p.m. The singers and musicians are very tired, and I realize they probably haven't eaten a thing all day (especially as they now know how big the lunch portions are that we provide!).

To add to the drums, an elderly man from the village arrives with his three-holed flute, and some of the women put woven reed shakers round their legs for added percussion whilst dancing.

After lunch we crack on. The folks have been drinking millet beer over lunch. (I'm offered some but politely decline.) Predictably, they return for the afternoon session with an air of joviality and are much more relaxed than they were this morning. The rest of the recording runs more or less smoothly, apart from a mad *woman* who meanders in midrecording and is hastily escorted off. We finish just in time for the catechism class, then move out of the paillote to finish off and sign the copyright forms. We're all done and back on the road by 4:00 p.m. Phew!

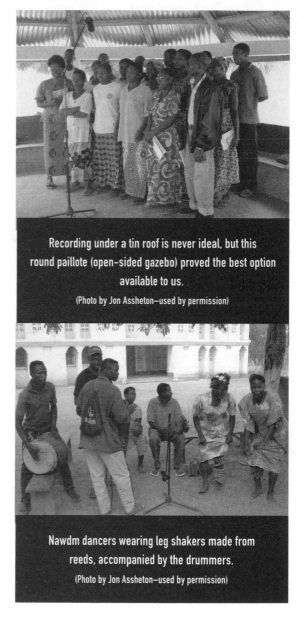

Recording under a tin roof is never ideal, but this round paillote (open-sided gazebo) proved the best option available to us.
(Photo by Jon Assheton—used by permission)

Nawdm dancers wearing leg shakers made from reeds, accompanied by the drummers.
(Photo by Jon Assheton—used by permission)

DAY 4

After a long drive home to Cotonou, I begin editing the music to make the recordings for distribution: one for Philippians and one for James. On a previous visit, I recorded readings of both books in Nawdm from start to finish. We had three or four readers, which made for a more interesting recording. So each of the two cassettes produced contains the reading of a chapter, followed by a song based on that chapter.

In the months following this work, the Nawdm team sold each cassette with a printed copy of the book, so that people could follow the text. This not only enhances Bible knowledge but also aids literacy amongst the Nawdm. Initially, I made a run of one hundred copies of each cassette—these all sold out in about two months, and a further one hundred of each was ordered, and they continued to sell well for some time.

INTRODUCTION

SECTION 1: FOUNDATIONS

SECTION 2: STORIES

SECTION 3: TOOLS

CLOSING

57. SKILLFUL MUSICIANS, COMPOSING AT THE SPEED OF LIGHT

By Rob Baker

After an early morning drive north over a steep and winding mountain pass, I make a right turn off the main road and travel down a bumpy dirt track toward the town of Gando. It takes so long to get there, I begin to doubt that I took the right road at all. I stop to ask a couple women carrying heavy stacks of wood on their heads. Neither speaks a word of French, the official language of the country, so I point forward and shout "Gando?" One of them nods and repeats "Gando," so I forge ahead on the washboard road, a cloud of reddish-brown dust in my wake.

The Gangam people live mainly in and around this small, remote town in northern Togo near the eastern border with Benin and number about forty-six thousand in the entire country. I am traveling there today to lead a songwriting workshop.

DAY 1

Around 9:00 a.m. I arrive at my destination: a small compound surrounded by dry fields, creepy-looking baobab trees, and a few wild-looking pigs. I park my Land Rover out the front and walk tentatively through the gate, surprised to find nobody there apart from the Bible translators who work there—two Gangam men. I've recently had problems trying to call Kandembe, my workshop contact here, but I presumed he'd at least remember the workshop was on. The translators agree to phone him for me, and he arrives a few minutes later. Apparently he thought the workshop was off as I had been unable to confirm. In addition, one of his children is ill, so he has to take him to the clinic immediately. That said, he promises to round up folk for me as soon as he can, and the first two participants roll in around 9:45 a.m. I greet them, then sit and wait . . . and wait. By 11:00 a.m. we have five people, which is clearly not enough for the workshop. I begin to wonder what to do. Should I just cut my losses, cancel the whole thing, and head home right away? That would be a shame, and I guess we could do *something* with this number. So I make a start, aware that lunchtime is fast approaching. By 11:30, we have *eleven* people, which is encouraging, and we end up with fifteen or so before the morning is out.

With introductions and a discussion of song genres out of the way, it's time to break for lunch. For some workshops, food is provided on-site, but in this case the participants all live locally. So they head off, and I tell them we'll reconvene at 2:00 p.m. The first few get back at 2:30 p.m. and everyone's there by 3:00 p.m.

> **Song composition tends to work better with a mixed group.**

In spite of the blistering heat, we soldier on with the exegesis of Bible verses and methods of composition. I ask them to divide up into three groups, each containing male and female, old and young. Song composition tends to work better with a mixed group because the older folk always know more about their traditional music. Having at least one literate person in each group ensures that the lyrics will be written down. The Gangam translation team is also on hand to help and have already translated all the readings from French into their language.

They asked me to choose verses from Psalms and Revelation, two very different books. However, I like to see a common thread going through the compositions, so we start off with a set of three references that praise the greatness of God. They are:

- "Glorify the LORD with me; let us exalt his name together," from Psalm 34:2–4.
- "All your works praise you," from Psalm 145:8–12.
- "Great and marvelous are your deeds," from Revelation 15:3,4.

I then teach them methods of composition and, once they have grasped these, it's time to start composing. This they seem to do at the speed of light. I'm amazed—it seems that composing and improvisation are almost synonymous to them. In fact, they start singing their creations almost before they've even sat down in their groups to compose!

Here are some of the main song genres used in Gangam music, as gathered at the workshop:
- *ijiguyuon*: sung when beating harvested millet
- *icɛncɛncieyuon*: sung when beating down the ground in preparation for building a new house
- *inɔpuogbenyuon*: a song of rejoicing, sung by women
- *ikɔnyuon*: sung during rites of passage to adulthood
- *ikunyuon*: sung during funerals / funeral celebrations
- *inɔnkpɔnyuon*: a song for hunting
- *ikɔkɔlyuon*: sung when planting, building up the earth around yams
- *ipɛñunyuon*: sung when ploughing fields
- *ibuyuon*: sung during fetish rituals (due to its pagan associations, it was decided that they would not use this genre in their compositions, as it could lead to misunderstandings)
- *ikɔnduunyuon*: sung at weddings
- *itelnyuon*: sung when telling a story

We finish at 5:00 p.m. with three songs composed. I remind the participants of the need to start promptly at 7:30 a.m. One of the Gangam team points out that this is the time schools start, so they need to leave home at the same time as the children.

DAY 2

I'm sitting having a typical Nescafé-and-bread breakfast at my hotel (the only one in Gando), when my cell phone rings. It's Kandembe. Apparently everyone's already there waiting for me! Admittedly, it is 7:45 a.m., but I figured I had plenty of time. Thankfully, it's only a three-minute drive to the compound, so I dive into the Land Rover and whiz off.

We start straight away with more teaching and biblical exegesis. It's getting hot already, and the sun seems ludicrously high for the time of day. The second set of verses we work with deals with the nature of God:

- Psalm 23:1–4: "The LORD is my shepherd."
- Acts 2:25–28: " I saw the Lord always before me."
- Revelation 7:12: "Praise and glory and wisdom and thanks and honor."

Finally, after lunch, we tackle a set of verses to do with the gospel of Christ and God's forgiveness:

- John 11:25,26: "I am the resurrection and the life."
- 1 Timothy 2:5,6: "There is one God and one mediator . . . Christ Jesus."
- 1 John 1:8–10: "If we confess our sins, he is faithful and just and will forgive us."

We manage to get these six songs composed by the end of the day. In fact, you could say seven—one of the groups has also composed a song which turns out to be identical in melody to one from yesterday! Thankfully, I've made short, low-quality recordings of each group's song as they composed, so it's easy to play yesterday's similar song to them on my MP3 recorder. They listen intently through the headphones and agree to alter their song, as it is indeed terribly similar to the other one.

Another obstacle we met today was the late arrival of one elderly woman. Because of this, the rest of her group—all very young—were unable to compose much, as only she knows the local music well. That's why it's always important to have some older folk attend courses such as this.

DAY 3

It's another early start, and I eat my breakfast with a tad more haste today to make sure I'm actually on time. We begin recording in the front yard of the compound as soon as I have set up my equipment. The teams now have nine new Bible-based songs, in nine different genres, four of which have never been previously used in church. This is very is exciting, and it will be interesting to see how other people react to them and how they are received in church. A highlight of this recording session

Two local musicians join in playing their traditional three-holed flues, enhancing the recordings.
(Photo by Marianne Harvey—used by permission)

was the arrival of a couple of elderly men from a nearby village, whom we drafted to play their traditional three-holed flutes for the recording. They're not Christians but are happy to join in with these songs. They do a great job, and their melodious interludes really enhance the recording.

In addition, some of the men are doing great drumming—often the case in Africa—and a woman is shaking a baobab pod filled with stones. She skillfully tosses it from one hand to the other, creating a driving 6/8 rhythm. At a previous workshop, it took me two days to figure out how to play it, and I ended up dropping the pod on the floor and cracking it. Oops! This time she won't let me even touch it.

Accompaniment provided by two traditional drummers and clapping singers.
(Photo by Marianne Harvey—used by permission)

At one point during the recording, my Edirol R-1 digital recorder starts behaving very strangely, making alien noises on playback. I reckon it's due to my being in direct sunlight. Although I am wearing a hat, the recording equipment is not. I move my table into the shade and wait a while before trying to listen back again. When I do, everything is crystal clear again—amazing. I really thought I was going to have to redo the recordings for the last few songs. However, I make a mental note for the future to always do my recordings in the shade.

Once the recording is finished, we sign the copyright form, which is important. Then the musicians say a warm "au revoir" and "merci" and are on their way.

I'm exhausted by now, but there's one final job left: to record readings of each Bible verse, which will then be interspersed with the songs once the recordings are distributed. We're finished by lunchtime and, after another plate of freshly slaughtered guinea fowl with couscous at my hotel, I head back south to nearby Kara for the night. The next day will be another long drive back to Cotonou, Benin, my base.

Several months after the workshop, I saw a member of the Gangam team and asked him whether the songs we composed had been used. He said some were sung in churches even before the recordings I made had arrived in Gando. I asked how many of the nine songs had been used; he said three or four. Could be worse. He couldn't remember which ones, but I wondered whether it was the newly used genres or those already well known in worship. I have a hunch it is more likely the latter.

58. STORY AND SONG IN KPELE-DAFO: AN INNOVATIVE CHURCH PLANTING MODEL AMONG AN ORAL CULTURE OF TOGO

By Jim and Carla Bowman

Harmattan winds have hovered over desert Africa for weeks, picking up Saharan sands and filling the sky of Kpele-Dafo village with a brown haze.

In this sand-gray dusk, the hushed, unnatural silence of the windswept, sub-Saharan village is spellbinding and disconcerting. Only a subtle breeze invades the soundless, palm-lined footpaths and the swept earth patios. But the silence of this southern Togolese village is about to end; the storyteller is coming!

And into the quiet hamlet the clear, resonant voice of his recitation will emerge, startling and powerful, heralded by drums. And when the departing flamingo sun finally sets, shirtless men leave their game of *adí* (mancala), the baguette sellers disburse, the tailors close up their makeshift stands, cranky bicycles are abandoned hastily, and yawning children resting on outdoor cots under coconut trees are wrestled from sleep. As the pulse of the drums intensifies and the storyteller takes his place on the low, carved bench, the village is mobilized and excitement permeates the air. The elders arrive in regal togas made of the wild, leaping colors of African cloth. Antoine, the animated storyteller–church planter exchanges ritual, formalized greetings with his audience. The fetish priestess, clothed in white and waving her horsehair amulet, acknowledges Antoine with penetrating eyes that speak of a past immersed in juju and prayer to the fetish. Night falls, the burning log crackles. They are ready for the story.

GOD THE CREATOR IN STORY, SONG, AND DANCE

The listeners are electrified as the biblical story of creation begins: "In the beginning God created the heavens and the earth." The poetic, melodious pattern of the story flows from Antoine's lips. When he reaches the repeating phrase "and God saw that it was good," he sings a song composed by Timothée Ayivi in call-and-response style. The song is designed to reinforce the story; the words of the song are: "In the beginning God created heaven and earth. It was empty,

INTRODUCTION

SECTION 1: FOUNDATIONS

SECTION 2: STORIES

SECTION 3: TOOLS

CLOSING

and darkness was over the surface of the deep." The call and response is choreographed by the composer in a traditional style that glorifies God the Creator. As the villagers quickly memorize the song response and join Antoine, their voices become a chorus of blissful harmony.

Then dancing intercepts the story. The headman dances as well, thus placing his approval on the story and the event. The drum language continues. Amidst the steaming equatorial heat sitting stiffly in the air, the pulsating rhythm of the drum reaches to the stars and sounds deep into the tropical night. The storytelling and singing continue in this way. As the fire dims, the story ends. There is not one villager who wishes to leave that place. The story in this setting has connected them to the Word and to their history. It has involved and inspired them as they interact with the story through song and dance.

GOD OF THE BIBLE IN STORY, SONG, AND DANCE

As the weeks unfold, story upon story is told. Antoine returns with narration after narration followed by dynamic and involving dialogue with the listeners. The foundations of God's story

Story and Song in Togo

are laid before the people. There are stories of Abraham and his sons, stories of the prophets, stories of Jesus, stories of God's community and the apostles, stories that address the felt needs of the community, and stories that change and reshape the listeners' worldview. Extended family conversions will take place. In surrender to Christ, a fetish priest will destroy by fire his protective amulets, talismans, and jujus. A house church will be established. The story will become a vehicle of the Holy Spirit for conversion, for worldview change, for surrender of strongholds, and for discipleship because it is the word of God brought to life in the African context.

TRANSFORMED COMMUNITIES IN AFRICA

We are witnessing a cycle taking place throughout countless villages in the Volta Region of Ghana, in Togo, and Benin, where a church planting movement has emerged under the leadership of Mr. Senyo Mawufemor Cudjoe. He has faithfully executed everything he has learned about communication bridges to oral cultures. These bridges include Scripture storytelling, recitation, oratory, drama, and song. Senyo is an oral Bible champion, because as he himself says, "It is the African way." The oral arts are relevant and compelling. Western-taught evangelism methods of campaigns, literature distribution, and door-to-door outreach were rejected long ago in the difficult Muslim and animist environments of this area. Not only has Senyo implemented everything he has learned about the oral Bible, he has also trained church planters throughout the area to do the same. He has taught them the integration of the oral arts, a strategy in which the story becomes a focal point, which then meets song in a rhythm of speech, harmony, and movement. The holistic, integrated approach to story—tell the story, sing the story, dance the story, drum the story, and dramatize the story—has allowed the story to be owned by the local people. It enters into the collective memory of an entire community; it becomes a permanent part of the lives of the people.

> The holistic, integrated approach to story—tell the story, sing the story, dance the story, drum the story, and dramatize the story— has allowed the story to be owned by the local people.

Senyo has taught the grassroots church planters to follow a God-given cycle of evangelism and discipleship, clearing the stones by establishing rapport and respect with elders, head-men, and chiefs through humility and an attitude of serving. He has established guidelines for sowing, through selecting the right story needed for each community. He has taught them that evangelism is a process, and harvest may come not necessarily when an individual is willing to be extracted from his community, but when the entire family or even community is ready for con-version. He has taught the church planters not to be negligent with discipleship but to use story, dialogue, and memorization to give the new believers their own foundation in the word of God—even though they cannot read and write. He has taught the church planters to establish leaders among those of oral cultures, empowering them with the stories of the apostles—each story of the book of Acts presenting a model of appropriate leadership behavior.

How can we help but rejoice to see such a church planting movement come to West Africa, a movement so in tune with the collective past of the culture and to the African way? In a place where the very rhythm of the earth lives inside villagers, where everything about them is art: from clothing to the very cadence of their walk. It is in this art of living—of rhythm, of sustaining joy amidst pain, this choreography of life—that creativity seems to emerge from deep within the very African soil. And when they rise to dance, the artist in every African emerges.

59. "NOW THERE'S SOMETHING INTERESTING IN CHURCH!"[17]

By Leticia Dzokotoe

An old woman, a church member, died. At the funeral, non-Christian relatives performed traditional funeral rites. Then they said, 'Now it's the Christians' turn.' Most of the townspeople started to leave, thinking nothing interesting would happen. As they walked away, church members started singing—not just any song, but new, indigenous Christian songs with traditional drumming. People turned on their heels and started running back from all directions. Some grabbed branches to wave as they danced, declaring, 'Now there's something interesting in church!'[18]

Not only did the indigenous hymns call people back to the funeral, they also drew more to church services in the weeks that followed. Previously, the church had used translated hymns and choruses from other languages that did not reflect the Bassari musical system. Now, church music is no longer considered boring, foreign, or irrelevant. The church uses Bassari music for Bassari people, and everyone wants to listen.

All this was the fruit of a hymn workshop in which participants had composed new Christian songs in a musical genre that was falling into disuse. This revitalized the genre and gave new life to traditional music at the same time that it effectively proclaimed the gift and excitement of new life in Christ.

---

17   Reprinted with permission from Leticia Dzokotoe, "Now There's Something Interesting in Church!," in Fortunato, *All the World*, 156

18   From a report by Pastor Emmanuel Nambou of Ghana, West Africa, on the power of new songs created at a Scripture Use Workshop for the Bassari people in the village of Kpandai.

233

INTRODUCTION

SECTION 1: FOUNDATIONS

SECTION 2: STORIES

SECTION 3: TOOLS

CLOSING

60. UNITY IN DIVERSITY THROUGH MUSIC AND LANGUAGE IN THE GAMBIA

By Sue Hall-Heimbecker

What a workshop—teaching in three languages with multiple translations for five Gambian ethnic groups and seven other nationalities. It's a wonder we understood each other at all!

This multicultural workshop focused on using the Bible in local languages in the urban church in The Gambia. The vision for this strategy was to reach Gambians more effectively with the gospel and draw them into a Christian community that reflects their cultures. We also wanted to help Gambians feel more at home in evangelical churches through using a diversity of music. Currently these churches are often dominated by English-speaking West Africans who have migrated to the country.

At the invitation of the Evangelical Church of The Gambia (ECG) and WEC International mission, a team of Gambians and expatriates held this two-day workshop. Participants came from several urban and rural churches.

We led discussion and teaching on the value of each culture in the eyes of God, of using multiple languages in church, and of communicating through culturally relevant media like music, dance, and liturgy. We talked about the challenge of accommodating the various ethnic groups, rather than assimilating them into the English-speaking majority.[19]

Day 2 was dedicated to song creation. It included teaching on worship and God's view of music, with language-by-language discussion of local music styles. The four ethnic groups that participated on this day had different levels of experience in making their own worship songs. The Jola team came with their *balafon* and matching outfits, ready to continue what they had begun at an earlier workshop (with Neil Barker of WEC International). The Mandinkas posed many questions at first but soon came up with some great Scripture songs rooted in traditional styles like *sewuruba* and *aarawuloo*—and with the funkiest dance of the lot! Wolofs and Manjaks added their diverse sounds, so that the final recording was a rich mix of languages and tunes, ready to be used in multicultural church settings.

---

19   *Accommodation* is allowing people to enjoy some part of the service (or other church activity) where they feel completely at home, using their language or kind of music. *Assimilation* forces everyone to use one language or kind of music for all meetings.

Six months later, feedback on song use indicates that some have been easily adopted for church, and that the workshop served as a catalyst for some groups, including the Wolof, to continue composing. However, one of the most traditional-style Mandinka songs created has been sidelined because "it sounds too much like a baby-naming ceremony song and not enough like a church song" (such ceremonies are connected to Islam or traditional African religion). Other songs are in styles that have been forgotten, so the expertise to perform them well no longer exists.

> We talked about the challenge of accommodating the various ethnic groups, rather than assimilating them into the English-speaking majority.

There is still a need to help church leaders and members become more aware of the value of using truly indigenous song styles for worship. This is a difficult discussion in the whole region, which has an established church with Western-influenced traditions. In order to continue this process, we left a minilibrary of resources with the ECG church leaders.[20] We also discussed how to begin a New Song Fellowship (an ongoing musical group for discipleship, creation, and performance) in their area.

A real benefit was having Gambian pastors and leaders share from their hearts (and with vivid song-and-dance illustrations!) about the necessity of using local music and language in the church. Their contribution made the workshop even more valuable. Using more of our limited time to discuss local song genres would have been beneficial. Some feedback suggests objections to some of the dance styles initially chosen for the Christian songs. We pray the gospel of Jesus will spread among the peoples of The Gambia, especially among those who have not yet heard his beautiful name in their language. A single two-day workshop can rarely change a mindset, but like a pebble dropped in a pond, we pray for ripples to spread over time.

---

20   Three resource books were left in the area for the use of church leaders: Roberta R. King, *A Time to Sing: A Manual for the African Church* (Nappanee, IN: Evangel Publishing House, 1999); Joyce Scott, *Tuning In to a Different Song: Using a Music Bridge to Cross Cultural Differences* (Pietermaritzburg, South Africa: Cluster Publications, 2007); and Margaret Hill, *Using Your Bible: A Manual in Scripture Use* (UK: Wycliffe Bible Translators, 1993).

235

INTRODUCTION

SECTION 1: FOUNDATIONS

SECTION 2: STORIES

SECTION 3: TOOLS

CLOSING

61. NEW CHOIR SONGS— ONES EVERYONE CAN UNDERSTAND

By Sue Hall-Heimbecker

How can a Protestant missionary stimulate the production of new songs for choirs in the Catholic Church? In Senegal the Catholic Church is very open to using the mother tongue and local musical styles, as sanctioned by the Second Vatican Council in 1967.[21] Nevertheless, minority language groups often end up singing songs written in more dominant languages, which they may not understand well.

By bringing together Noon community members—young student choir members (during their school holidays), elderly women who remember their traditional music, three choir leaders well-trained in choral music, and several professional musicians (guitarists and drummers)—we hoped to create a critical mass of talent and enthusiasm to overcome their perceived difficulties of composing new songs. Many of the group were well educated in French and music through the Catholic school system but felt that composing was outside their abilities.

The two-day weekend workshop was sponsored by the Project for Research and Translation in the Noon Language (PRTN), which also supports the translation of the Bible into Noon (population thirty thousand). Costs were covered by the PRTN, the visiting ethnomusicologist, and the local church choir. The local church leadership was very supportive and participated. The Catholic school offered their premises to host the workshop. By working through the local church structure (the Catholic church is the only church presence in Noon communities) and building on stated values within the system, such as those of Vatican II, we could ensure community ownership of the songs produced and acceptability in the church context.

Working from printed and hand-copied texts and making adaptations of Scripture verses into song lyrics on blackboards, the participants made eleven new songs based on texts from the

---

21 From Sacred Congregation of Rites, *Instruction on Music in the Liturgy* (Second Vatican Council, 1967), http://www.ewtn.com/library/curia/cdwmusic.htm, 47. Since "the use of the vernacular may frequently be of great advantage to the people it is for the competent territorial ecclesiastical authority to decide whether, and to what extent, the vernacular language is to be used," 61. "Adapting sacred music for those regions which possess a musical tradition of their own, especially mission areas, will require a very specialized preparation by the experts. It will be a question in fact of how to harmonize the sense of the sacred with the spirit, traditions and characteristic expressions proper to each of these peoples. Those who work in this field should have a sufficient knowledge both of the liturgy and musical tradition of the Church, and of the language, popular songs and other characteristic expressions of the people for whose benefit they are working."

INTRODUCTION

SECTION 1: FOUNDATIONS

SECTION 2: STORIES

SECTION 3: TOOLS

CLOSING

Gospel of Luke. These texts were carefully chosen from Catholic lectionary readings, published for use in church and at home, and were relevant to the Mass used most Sundays. (Some texts in the Mass were in the Noon language, but most were not.) The newly created songs were mostly harmonized, using all-Noon texts and traditional Noon drum accompaniments. Guitar accompaniment is widespread in the area and also appears on the recording of the new songs.

Previous visits I had made to the church and community helped to establish relationships and allowed me to conduct research on traditional and church music. This research provided background for the workshop. Most of the songs were composed in the *bilim* genre—the most popular genre, usually sung by women for about any occasion (weddings, parties, women's events, traditional funerals, newborns, youth events, and harvest). Another song genre used at the workshop was *digaal*, which is now remembered and sung by only a few old men in the community. It is a praise song genre, mostly used for distinguished visitors or at funerals.

> By working through the local church structure and building on stated values within the system, we could ensure community ownership of the songs produced.

The workshop was successful in producing songs and in demonstrating to the participants that they could actually compose good ones. Unfortunately the local church has not used these songs regularly in services. The professional artists involved perceived the workshop mainly as a recording project (desiring to make a more professional commercial recording later). Also, a change of local priest has affected the church's enthusiasm for using local music. The recordings, however, were very well received, so the songs are becoming known and enjoyed. We still hope these songs might be used in other settings and eventually find their way into church, increasing the *entire* congregation's understanding of what is being sung.

62. MINISTRY AND MUSIC IN SIERRA LEONE
By Kedra Larsen Kinney

I returned from a four-week trip to Sierra Leone, where I led Scripture song workshops for the Kono and Themne people. Both groups responded enthusiastically to the idea of composing songs straight from Scripture. Individuals in the churches had already begun to recognize weaknesses in some of the church songs they were using. One pastor said that the word "amen" was often tossed arbitrarily and sometimes inappropriately into the middle of a song. Many church choruses used elaborations on Scripture that could send inaccurate or mixed messages. For example, the words "Jesus is the light of the world" and "a light on a hill cannot be hidden" were woven together in one song without indicating that these verses were from two separate passages that taught two different truths.

KONO WORKSHOP IN KOIDU

The Kono workshop was held at the God Is Our Light church in the town of Koidu, an eight- to twelve-hour bus ride from Freetown, Sierra Leone's capital. The twenty-five participants comprised choir members and pastors from the area, including three churches: God Is Our Light, Lutheran, and Catholic. The focus for this four-day workshop was to compose songs to accompany a dramatic reading of the Gospel of Luke. The script was modeled after an abridged, audio Luke script by the United Bible Societies. For the Kono version, some parts, such as references to Isaiah and Handel's "Hallelujah" chorus, were omitted. Other sections, such as Jesus casting out evil spirits, were added. The readings in Kono, using a narrator and two readers, took over ninety minutes.

Toward the beginning of the workshop I asked, as I usually do, for the group to sing examples of traditional songs with traditional secular words, such as a song they would sing every day, a work song, or a song for a special occasion. I had found that this activity usually helps prepare people to think about composing in the context of their local indigenous music style(s) and gently guides them away from the desire to compose songs with Western melodies. Another benefit I expected was to get a glimpse of local music genres, their current use, and individuals' attitudes toward them.

The Kono participants, however, would not even consider singing traditional songs with secular words. Those from the host church stated that in their church building they sang only Christian songs. One well-respected soloist said that all his songs were dedicated to God and that he sang only Christian songs. They did, however, readily sing various Christian songs (both old and new) in Kono. They were able to distinguish between their Kono, regional, and Western categories.

The groups from all three churches came prepared with about five songs each. However, some of their songs came from passages that were not in the script (an abridgement of Luke). The four songs that did fit the script were used, and some of the others were included on the extra song recording. The songs composed before the workshop were loosely based on Luke passages but were not straight Scripture. During our time together we worked hard to compose songs that carefully followed the biblical text. Most of the songs done in the workshop were from passages that I recommended in order to space the songs at appropriate intervals throughout the readings.

> The national translators welcomed the opportunity to give CD copies to the Kono chiefs so they could hear the songs and be included in the results of the workshop.

Local pastors commented during the workshop that they felt it would have been helpful for the group to have access to the script well before the workshop. I am ambivalent about that approach, because only during the workshop can we work together composing Scripture songs that carefully follow the text and at the same time emphasize the importance of using traditional music styles. If people came with all the songs prepared to coincide with the script, it might be harder to put those songs aside in favor of more accurate ones in traditional styles.

During the workshop we repeatedly emphasized what makes for a good Kono song and how to stay true to the Scripture text. Participants were encouraged to compose songs using the words of Scripture, without adding anything to them and without changing them to reflect what seemed to them to be the main point of the passage. After first composing a few songs together, we divided into four groups. The participants responded well to working in small groups in a minicompetition format. When the groups were ready, they sang their songs for each other and decided which group came the closest to accurately using the entire text.

By the end of the four-day workshop, we had composed twenty-four new songs, more than I had originally anticipated. Sixteen were included on the Gospel of Luke recording. Three short drum interludes were used at various points to add further musical interest to the readings. An extra song recording was made that included all twenty-four songs without the readings.

> Many church choruses used elaborations on Scripture that could send inaccurate or mixed messages.

In addition to these, we also recorded two easy-reader gospel story books. These books will serve as a read-along aid for pastors and others who are educated and only need minimal help to learn how to read in Kono.

This workshop was the first time I had recorded such a large number of Scripture readings. It took the translators and me three whole days, working morning to night, to record the readers for both Luke and the easy-reader books. I was able to record straight to computer, which allowed us to listen to the recorded passage immediately after it was read and fix mistakes at that time.

Each participating church received two copies of the Luke set and one of the extra song recordings. The national translators welcomed the opportunity to give CD copies to the Kono chiefs so they could hear the songs and be included in the results of the workshop.

THEMNE WORKSHOP IN MAGBURAKA

The location for the Themne workshop was a Missionary Church of Africa in Magburaka, a four-to six-hour bus ride from Freetown. Usually other missionaries are involved in organizing these workshops but, in this case, the entire event was planned for and coordinated by two Themne translators. Participants were asked to register and pay a small fee to cover meals. The coordinators put a lot of effort into making the week-long workshop a success.

The participants composed sixteen songs on fifteen passages. Many of the songs used short verses, but there were also longer songs for Luke 6:43–45 (the good tree produces good fruit), John 14:1–3 ("Do not let your hearts be troubled"), and Matthew 8:23–27 (Jesus calming the storm). For the recording, the participants decided to arrange the songs in seven categories: songs of praise, testimony, teaching, evangelism, confession, courage, and hope. Readers introduced the song category and read the verses. For example, the category "songs of praise" was introduced, followed by the Revelation 7:12 reading, and then the song from the same verse.

The Themne participants said over and over how good it was to learn how to use straight Scripture in songs. They were eager to continue with what they had learned, and they invited me to come back the following year to do more workshops with them and other churches. But I also encouraged them to further the development of Scripture songs and related applications on their own. The workshop coordinators had already done much for this workshop, and so other workshops could also be self-run and self-taught. One striking evidence of their resourcefulness was that even before this workshop they had realized the need for recording the songs as they were composing and practicing them. Two of them had brought tape recorders to record and play back the songs as a memory aid for the group.

After our closing words of thanks to all, the participants stayed another hour or more to set up a committee to oversee the continuance of the work. This newly formed group is called the Themne Scripture Song Association. The members want to share the new songs and ideas with other churches and are determined to not forget anything they have learned. Every month they hold a meeting, from one church to another around the villages, to compose songs. They use these songs in church services, and many people enjoy them.

> The Themne participants said over and over how good it was to learn how to use straight Scripture in songs.

For the Themne Scripture song recording, we made a few for distribution to the media, including the Makeni (town) radio station. Each of the fourteen participants received one copy of the Scripture song recording. Initial reaction was good—the Themne speakers in the Freetown office were very excited to hear the new recording and wanted copies. Distribution was coordinated through the newly established Themne Scripture Song Association.

The recordings are used in women's annual meetings, in small groups, in homes, and also among non-Christians. My local contact reports, "The Themne songs are well known to many villages around Magburaka now."

CONCLUSION

While both the Kono and the Themne workshops were successful in producing new songs and encouraging regular Scripture song composition, a detailed plan for the use of such songs and recordings needs to be thought through in advance and encouraged. It is difficult for a traveling ethnomusicologist with limited time to make ongoing visits. In the case of the Kono and Themne peoples, the local translation/literacy teams are in charge of funding the recordings and their duplication. Perhaps in future workshops we can share more principles about the use of nonprint media that will help them make further plans to use media effectively.

63. YOUR WAYS ARE STRAIGHT: A SCRIPTURE SONG WORKSHOP IN SIERRA LEONE[22]

By Kedra Larsen Kinney

The Limba churches in northern Sierra Leone had many worship songs, but few came straight from Scripture. Local church leaders, literacy coordinators, and I held a workshop to help their musicians compose songs using the Limba New Testament as the text. Twenty participants came representing Wesleyan, New Apostolic, and Pentecostal churches, and together they composed songs reflecting on God's word and how his ways are indeed straight and true.

A main goal of the workshop was to compose songs based on Bible verses, which we chose and wrote on our chalkboard. Then Naphtali, a man particularly skilled at composing songs, along with the rest of the group would find a tune and poetically rework the words to make the best solo and chorus combination. The group used this method to compose a dozen songs on scriptural themes such as God's word, confession of sin, assurance of forgiveness, and dedication to the Lord.

One song the group composed was based on Revelation 15:3b.[23] Here are the Limba words and an English back translation:

Solo: Yindo Mariki wo.

Chorus: Masaala wo kathinthi won nthon nda fooma,
E yina wo wo maandin
Helen ko niya beinin ba bukuyuwe!
Gbonen ba kenda ban bathumbe.
Yina Mariki wo kentunwon Masaala won.

---

22   Reprinted with permission from Kedra Larsen Kinney, "Your Ways Are Straight: A Scripture Song Workshop in Sierra Leone," *EthnoDoxology* 4, no. 2 (2010): 20–21.

23   To hear an excerpt of this song, go to http://ethnodoxology.org/media.htm.

Solo: You are the Lord.

Chorus: God of all the heavens above,
You are so great
And you do wonderful things!
Your ways are straight.
You are our Lord God.

Workshop participants discussed how the new songs could be used in their churches as well as communities and decided to prepare a special launch for the recording. They wanted to feature the upcoming event by teaching local congregations only one new song, as a teaser. They were very enthusiastic about the recording, expressing confidence that they now have the ability to create more Scripture songs and continue on their own.

At the time, I hoped the Limba would follow in the footsteps of a neighboring language group, the Loko. The Loko had held a Scripture song workshop three years previous and a song and drama workshop just a year before the Limba workshop. This group has continued composing Scripture songs on their own—gathering musicians together for an extended weekend, pooling money and food for lunches, and recording their new compositions on a portable recorder. The songs are regularly sung in churches of all denominations throughout the Loko area.

It took over a year to get the Limba songs duplicated with good quality. Finally eighty quality copies were made, and the group sold these to individuals, which were well received.

VIDEO PRODUCTION

At about the same time as this distribution, the Limba literacy committee asked me to help them produce a Bible story video. Video is quickly becoming a popular medium in Africa—even in remote villages, which have only a generator or two for electricity. I made a return trip to the area to help with this project. Adapting what they had learned in the song workshop, the group chose two Bible stories and prepared dramas and songs. The stories chosen were taken from Acts 3:1–10 (Peter and John healing a lame man) and Matthew 25:14–30 (the parable of the talents). This was the first video in the Limba language with local actors, and the literacy committee was eager to show it in the Christian/Muslim community. They now have VCD and DVD copies, and the church youth have sponsored video showings in many area churches.

Our desire and goal for these activities was to help facilitate an engagement between God's word and the Limba people, leading them to trust in Jesus Christ, the one whose ways are straight and who can also make our paths straight.

64. HOLY WEEK DRAMA ACCORDING TO MATTHEW

By James R. and Jeanette Krabill

Our two oldest children, Matthew and Elisabeth Anne, spent their early years living among the Dida people of southern Côte d'Ivoire, Africa, and worshiping with us in the Harrist Church, an indigenous movement with some 200,000 members.

Here are the events of Holy Week 1985, when Matthew was five years old, as recorded in our diary:

MARCH 18

Today, just two weeks before the beginning of Holy Week festivities, death hit the village when one of our neighbors, Pita, left this world to join the next.

MARCH 19

As Dida tradition prescribes, on the night before burial the body is placed outside on a spacious double bed in the courtyard of the deceased, and the entire community gathers around to pass the night in singing. In order to attend the death watch, Mama and Papa put Matthew and Elisabeth Anne to bed a bit early tonight and left them for several hours in the care of Lassina, a Muslim friend from Mali who sometimes helps with work around the place.

MARCH 20

This morning was Pita's funeral service and burial, and Matthew accompanied his mama and papa throughout the entire affair, even walking the long distance in the scorching midday sun to the cemetery and back again.

Most people came dressed in black or dark blue and, before the service, assembled quietly around Pita's bed to pay last respects. Pita's sister sat beside her brother on the bed, wiping his brow and chasing away a growing number of flies also drawn to the occasion. "Fight, fight the war for me!" sang the choir in muted voices and without the usual musical instruments. "It is you, my God, who can fight for me!"

When Pita's body had been washed and placed in the casket, the mourners proceeded to the church in two long lines—men on the right, women on the left—on either side of Pita. "Women of honor," dressed in black uniforms, led the way, carrying bouquets of freshly cut flowers to be spread about Pita's grave.

We paused for several brief moments at the church to offer final prayers. The middle row of benches had been removed to make way for the casket. Everywhere one looked were signs of sadness: the sanctuary candles remained flameless, the flowerpots flowerless, and the floor unswept. Across the altar was draped a large black cloth in place of the usual white one. Preacher Alphonse's comments were short and barely audible; from where we stood only snatches reached us.

Matthew, normally bubbling with questions, was caught up in the solemnity of the occasion. He remained silent and, like the rest of us, simply moved along with the flow of things until Pita had been lowered into the ground and we had headed for home.

APRIL 1—GOOD FRIDAY

The practice here on Good Friday is to reenact a funeral—the funeral of Jesus. And so today we did it all over again. Black dress, muted singing, the symbolic removal of the benches and freshly cut flowers, this time deposited at the foot of the altar.

We explained the rerun to Matthew by telling him Jesus had died and on this day all other activity ceased in order to think about his passing. "You mean Jesus is like Pita?" Matthew wanted to know. "He's like Pita lying there on the bed?"

"Yes," we said, "Jesus is like Pita lying there on the bed."

APRIL 3—EASTER SUNDAY

Easter morning! We got up and began preparing for church. This day, we knew, would be one of great joy! There would be singing. Dancing. Bright flowers and palm branches decorating the sanctuary. And the musical instruments would be back in full force!

We dressed the children in their little white outfits prescribed for the day. "Hey, why aren't we wearing dark clothing?" asked Matthew, confused by his revolving wardrobe.

"Because Jesus isn't dead any longer," we replied. "He's come back to life!"

Matthew stopped, reflected for a moment, and then with a burst of inspiration added, "Jesus isn't on the bed anymore!"

"No," we said, "Jesus isn't on the bed anymore!"

65. HOW A WEST AFRICAN EVANGELIST UNLEASHED MUSICAL CREATIVITY AMONG NEW BELIEVERS[24]

By James R. Krabill

WILLIAM WADÉ HARRIS: THE PROPHET-EVANGELIST AND "ETHNOHYMNOLOGIST"

When late in 1913 Prophet William Wadé Harris left his native Liberia to begin his now well-known evangelistic campaign through southern Côte d'Ivoire, he found himself confronted with a population having had little, if any, previous exposure to Christianity. French Catholic missionaries had for almost twenty years been working tirelessly at establishing a credible and lasting presence in the area but had met with limited success. And the only Protestant presence was found in small and scattered groups of English-speaking African clerks from Sierra Leone, the Gold Coast (now Ghana), Liberia, and The Gambia, who had come to Ivory Coast, not as missionaries but as agents of British trading companies doing business with coastal peoples.

The evangelist's preaching, fetish burning, and baptizing ministry lasted a mere eighteen months until his expulsion from the colony in January 1915. The impact of that brief ministry, however, was most remarkable indeed, resulting in

- an estimated 100,000–200,000 persons turning from traditional religious beliefs and practices toward a new reality structured around certain rudimentary tenets of the Christian faith as prescribed by Harris;
- worship of the "one, true God";
- weekly gathering on the seventh day for preaching, prayer, and singing;

---

24   Originally published in a slightly different form in James R. Krabill, "'Teach Us the Songs of Heaven!': An African Evangelist Encourages Indigenous Hymnody," in Fortunato, *All the World*, 51–57. The reflections are based on several sections from my published dissertation: James R. Krabill, *The Hymnody of the Harrist Church among the Dida of South-central Ivory Coast (1913–1949): An Historico-Religious Study*, Studies in the Intercultural History of Christianity, vol. 74 (Frankfurt: Peter Lang, 1995).

- initial exposure to God's law in the Ten Commandments and to the Lord's Prayer;
- and choosing new "religious specialists" (preachers and twelve apostles) responsible in each village for watching over the general well-being of the church.

In general, Prophet Harris was a man on the move, never lingering long in any one location. In some instances, villagers would travel long distances to see the prophet, receive baptism from his hand, then return home all in the same day, never to see him again.

One of the questions frequently asked of Harris by new converts during those brief encounters concerned the type of music they were expected to sing once they arrived back home in their villages. "Teach us the songs of heaven," they pleaded with him, "so we can truly bring glory to God."

It is important to understand Harris' background in order to appreciate his response to the thousands of new believers who crowded around him, clinging almost desperately to every word of counsel he could give them. Born of a Methodist mother, probably in 1860, William Wadé Harris had spent over thirty-five years—nearly all of his preprophetic adult life (1873–1910)—attending and actively serving the "civilized" Methodist and Episcopal churches of eastern Liberia. Quite understandably, the Western hymn traditions that filled the liturgies of these churches had come to be the sacred music dearly loved and cherished by Harris as well. When asked in 1978 whether Harris had any favorite hymns, the prophet's grandchildren recalled without hesitation, "Lo, He Comes with Clouds Descending" (his favorite hymn, which he sang repeatedly), "Guide Me, O Thou Great Jehovah," "Jesus, Lover of My Soul," "How Firm a Foundation, Ye Saints of the Lord," and "What a Friend We Have in Jesus."

> "God has no personal favorite songs."

Yet faced with the crowd seeking his advice on this most important matter, the prophet refused easy answers. "I have never been to heaven," he wisely told them, "so I cannot tell you what kind of music is sung in God's royal village. But know this," he continued, "that God has no personal favorite songs. He hears all that we say in whatever language. It is sufficient for us to offer hymns of praise to him with our own music and in our own language for him to understand."

When asked further how exactly they were to proceed in composing these new "songs of God," Harris told the people to begin by using the music and dance forms with which they were already acquainted. For the Dida people—one of the first and largest ethnic groups to feel the impact of the evangelist's ministry—this represented a remarkable repertoire of at least thirty distinct classifications of traditional musical genres, ranging from love ballads and funeral dirges to songs composed for hunting, rice planting, and rendering homage to wealthy community leaders.

Not all musical genres, however, were suitable, according to Harris, for use in praising God. In one village, a female musician stepped forward and began singing for Harris a *zlanje* tune, a kind of traditional "love song" with suggestive lyrics aimed at seducing potential partners into sexual activity. "That song does not honor God!" Harris said. "Sing something else!"

So another singer offered a *dogbro* tune, a type of "praise song" that literally "hurls forth" or "shouts out the name" of a nature spirit, a wealthy family head, and a clan leader, deserving special attention or recognition. "That's it!" exclaimed Harris. "That is the music you must work with! Though now you must refrain from using these songs for earthly rulers and lesser spirits and begin transforming the words bit by bit in order to bring glory to God!"[25]

---

25   In another instance, Harris reportedly counseled composers to make much use of "forgiveness language"—language ordinarily employed by an individual who "wishes to reestablish with some other person a relationship that has

SETTING THE NEW FAITH TO MUSIC

Encouraged by these words of counsel, new believers set to work immediately, transforming various traditional genres of music into praise songs to God. One such early hymn proclaims:

> We, too, we have at last found our Father.
> We did not know that we were going to find our Father.
> But we have found our Father;
> Our Father is the King of Glory.

Another song celebrates:

> It was the Lord who first gave birth to us and placed us here.
> How were we to know
> That the Lord would give birth to us a second time?

> Thanks to him, we can live in peace on this earth!

In the years following Harris' swift passage, and continuing right up to the present day, composers within the Harrist movement have written thousands of hymns, exploring new themes and developing additional musical styles as they learned to read the Scriptures and grew in Christian understanding. Some of these hymns tell Bible stories or relate events from Harrist history. Other texts function as prayers, minisermons, and confessions of faith.

One song dating from the 1920s defends their practice of composing their own hymns when facing criticism from Protestant missionaries and catechists ("the Bible people") who had recently arrived on the scene:

> We have your name, yes indeed!
> Yet the Bible people tell us
> That with the work we are doing here,
> We cannot come near to the Lord.
> Why can't we come near to the Father?
> [...]
> Let us take our own wisdom and pray to the Lord.
> [...]
> Each village has its own language;
> Take this then to pray to the Father!

---

been broken or in some significant way greatly marred." This theme subsequently became important in many of the early hymns. For a fuller account of Harris' advice to new converts, see James R. Krabill, "Dida Harrist Hymnody (1913–1990)," *Journal of Religion in Africa* 20, no. 2 (June 1990), 119–20. A more recent rendition of the story is available in James R. Krabill, "Gospel Meets Culture," in *Is It Insensitive to Share Your Faith?* (Intercourse, PA: Good Books, 2005), 88–102.

INTRODUCTION

SECTION 1: FOUNDATIONS

SECTION 2: STORIES

SECTION 3: TOOLS

CLOSING

A MODEL FOR TODAY

The Prophet Harris never claimed to be a theologian, much less a cultural anthropologist or an ethnomusicologist. But today's ethnohymnologists, trained as they are in these disciplines, would do well to choose him as their patron saint. "God has no personal favorite songs," Harris told new believers. "He hears all that we say in whatever language. It is sufficient for us to praise him in our own language for him to understand."

66. FEEBLE KNEES AND A NEW PUGULI VOICE[26]

By Kember Lillo

I was glad that my long wrap skirt hid my shaky knees. After two summers of SIL[27] training as an arts specialist, six months of developing my partnership team, and one year of French study, I was finally here in Africa, ready to begin the research phase of my ethnomusicology internship. It was hard to believe I was walking down a hot, sandy trail to my first musician interview with the Puguli, a small people group in southern Burkina Faso. I knew that 97 percent of the Puguli still held to their traditional beliefs, and very few musicians had come to know Christ. I was nervous. *What if I said something that offended the musicians?*

> Swallowing hard, I took a deep breath and plunged in, stumbling over my first few questions in French.

It was rainy season and two days of downpours had hindered me from venturing into the village for interviews. Finally, one morning the skies cleared, and my hosts asked if I was prepared for my long-anticipated exploration into Puguli music. Adama, my young translator, guided me to the courtyard of a professional female singer named Dééba Gnenio. We sat down on a low wooden bench to wait for our interviewee. A sturdy woman in her midfifties approached us, wiping her soiled hands on the corner of her wrap skirt. Adama explained that I wanted to learn about Puguli music and help the church develop songs of praise to God with their own Puguli music styles.

Swallowing hard, I took a deep breath and plunged in, stumbling over my first few questions in French. "How did you learn to sing? For what occasions do you sing?"

Dééba observed me carefully, answering each question with a calculated, brief response. By the end of the interview, however, I detected a smile tugging at the corners of her mouth. I was surprised when she quickly rose and disappeared into her mud-brick dwelling, returning with a little bundle in her arms, which she laid right in my lap. Her baby granddaughter! I grinned, feeling a rush of delight to have ended my first interview with a baby instead of a boot.

From that day on, I involved Dééba in my research. Perhaps I was attracted to this woman because I'm a singer myself. Her low, husky voice reminded me of my love for gospel soloists who swoop down to unthinkable notes for females. In the village of Bonzan-Puguli, she is often invited

---

26   Originally published in a slightly different form in Kember Lillo, "Dééba's Story," *EthnoDoxology* 4, no. 2 (2010): 22–23. Reprinted by permission of Kember Lillo and Paul Neeley, editor, *EthnoDoxology*.

27   SIL International serves language communities worldwide, building their capacity for sustainable language development by means of research, translation, training, and materials development.

to sing at marriages and funerals. Her talent for fusing music and poetry provokes both tears and laughter. I was convinced she was a key to understanding Puguli song, so, in addition to further interviews, I encouraged her to sing examples of various musical styles, which I captured on my digital recorder. Every once in a while I would stop by her home just to greet her, as is the custom, and practice my freshly learned Puguli phrases.

A few months later, my internship advisor, Mary Hendershott, joined me in Bonzan-Puguli for a three-day Scripture song workshop with the Puguli. I felt like I was welcoming her to my own home! Around 1:00 a.m. that night, the wind began to pick up, cooling down the stifling hot room. I heard a pattering noise on the tin roof. *I must be dreaming. Is that rain? Silly me, it couldn't rain in February!*

I untucked the mosquito net from under my foam mattress and slipped out. Tiptoeing to the windows, I stretched out my hands in the dark to feel for moisture. Nothing! Maybe I was just imagining the wet drop-drop on the stick-dry bushes outside. I crawled back onto my floor mat and reinserted the ends of the net around me. It had been roasting hot over the last week, temperatures soaring above 40 degrees C (104 F). Perhaps the heat had warped my senses. Then the pattering grew to a tapping rumble. "It's *not* raining!" I blurted out.

"Yes, it is!" a sleepy voice affirmed from the cot next to me.

I laid my head back on my pillow, sighing in awe. Prayers began to silently rise upward as the blessed rain poured over the valley. *Is this God's physical way of showing his hand over this workshop?* At 6:30 a.m. the rain had become just a soft sprinkle. *Will people actually gather for the workshop this morning?* I wondered. Just before 9:00 a.m., one of the Bible translators greeted us, as Mary and I sipped our morning coffee.

"I think the people will be ready for you by 9:15."

"Really?" I set my cup down, eager to go but nervous again. So this was it. I had been praying seriously for this day for over a year. I couldn't help but wonder how the Lord would work among the Puguli musicians in the next few days. Around 10:00 a.m. Mary and I greeted the twenty-five or so assembled musicians. Only three women were present. How could we compose with less than the full complement of Puguli musical knowledge represented? We discussed the need for more women with one of the church elders, and he agreed to invite a couple more women from the community.

The next day, as we gathered for morning devotions in the church, a shadow at the entrance suddenly caught my attention. Dééba! I couldn't believe it. I watched her glance from one side to another, unsure of where to sit or how to act. This was probably the first time she had ever entered a church building. She was assigned to a composition group that was working on verses from John 1. I listened in as she began to hum and then slowly chant a few lines relating to the Light who has entered the world.

On Sunday morning, after an exhausting but fruitful week facilitating and recording new compositions from the Gospels of Mark and John, Mary and I walked across the fields of dry cornstalks to the church. We had witnessed Puguli musicians eagerly studying Scripture in order to form solid refrains and verses. We had watched the excitement build as they performed their songs for each other. The night before the recording, we were still searching for a professional *balafon* (xylophone) player, and by the next morning I was amazed at how God had provided a team of instrumentalists. I wasn't sure, however, what to expect on Sunday morning. Would the Puguli believers want to sing their new songs in church?

The service began with a few translated Western choruses, and my eyes strayed to the nearest window. I was watching a group of women outside when I caught sight of a familiar figure crossing the field. I couldn't stop myself from twisting around to check the doorway. A few moments later, Dééba appeared at the entrance. This time, instead of hesitating in the doorway, she marched right up the aisle to one of the front benches and sat down. The pastor's jaw dropped before he smiled widely and welcomed her to the service.

The worship in song continued, and Dééba was invited to lead her composition from John 1:1–5. As she began to sing in her clear, strong voice, dancing broke loose. I have never seen so many join in dance during a church service in Bonzan-Puguli. On an average Sunday, only three of the older woman dance in a circle near the front. Today more than a dozen joined the circle.

At the end of the service, Dééba stood to speak. I understood only a few words in Puguli, but as I listened to the translation, I was stunned. Tears filled my eyes. "I want to be a Christian," she declared. "I began thinking about it when Kember first came to the village."

How could I have known that the Holy Spirit began working Dééba's heart six months earlier during my first nerve-racking research interview with a Puguli musician? *Kember*, the Lord whispered to me, *at just the right time, I led you, feeble knees included, to this woman and her beautiful, strong voice.*

67. INDIGENOUS PROVERBS: OPENING DOORS TO THE HEART[28]

By W. Jay Moon

As the heavy metal gate to his home slowly creaks open, "Ali" approaches and peeks through a small crack between the gate and the compound wall to see who's entering. Suddenly he bursts through the gate like a broken dam spilling out pent-up water.

"You have come back! I knew you would not forget me," Ali exclaims with a loud voice, his eyes as wide as the newly opened gate. Rushing over to give me a big hug, the tall, lean African man then puts his arm around my waist and accompanies me to the house.

"Forget you? How could I do that? I have sent messages to you, but it's always better to come see you in person. The elders say, '*Tuntoming a yok ka nansa; ka kan yok suiya*' ('To send a message by someone cools the legs; it does not cool the heart')."

Ali's smile broadens as the proverb quickly sinks into his soul. This is the "sweet talk" that Ali enjoys since it's entertaining, memorable, and promotes quick understanding.[29] Amid the laughter, his grip around my waist tightens as he launches into the traditional greetings—asking about families, health, and more.

"We have a proverb in Hausa that says, 'What the heart loves, there the legs will go,'" Ali offers. I smile and then ponder the meaning.

Seeing the puzzled look on my face, Ali helps. "Think about it. What the heart wants to do and where it wants to go, it tells the feet to move, and the feet obey." Ali knows that much of the joy of proverbs lies in discovering the meaning. So he shouldn't explain it too quickly and spoil the challenge for me.

"Yes, I see. The heart leads the way, and the body then follows," I respond, as the fog slowly clears away.

---

28 Originally published in a slightly different form in W. Jay Moon, *African Proverbs Reveal Christianity in Culture: A Narrative Portrayal of Builsa Proverbs Contextualizing Christianity in Ghana*, American Society of Missiology Monograph Series 5 (Eugene, OR: Pickwick Publications, 2009). Reprinted by permission of W. Jay Moon. This book describes the use of African proverbs to create oral art that promotes contextual expressions of Christianity. For more information, see also two articles on gathering and using proverbs by Pete Unseth on the *Handbook* DVD.

29 To learn how indigenous proverbs can open ears to hear the gospel, rooting it in African soil, and clearing foggy communication, see Moon (2004), 162–69.

"Have you ever seen the heart go somewhere it did not want to go, but it had to listen to the feet?"

Wagging my head back and forth satisfies Ali. We are connecting at his cultural level, opening doors of understanding.

Ali concludes with his widest smile yet. "You see. What the heart loves, there the legs will go!"

Enjoying this bantering and negotiating meaning between two people from two different worlds, I respond, "Now I understand. The feelings of the heart are so strong that they pull the feet to where they may not otherwise want to go."

Ali now has a look of total satisfaction, like a school teacher who delights in the facial expression of a student who finally learns an important point.

"It is interesting how the heart pulls so strongly that it forces people to go to far away places," I continue. "I think God's heart is like that, as well."

Ali's curiosity is now aroused. We have had plenty of spiritual conversations before, but our cultural backgrounds are so far apart that the doors of understanding are often closed or, at best, slightly cracked open. Now, though, Ali's own proverb has opened a door for spiritual understanding.

"God loves people because he is the one who created them. He made them expressly to be with him. His heart pulled so strong that his feet had to come to earth and be with them."

"You mean he wanted to move among them?"

His choice of words surprise and delight me, as Jesus is perhaps best described as Immanuel, meaning "God among us."

"Yes," I affirm, "that is why Jesus came to earth. God's heart pulled so strongly that his feet had to come among us. Jesus was the feet of God!"

Ali listens intently. Now the door of his heart is opening widely, and meaning flows through like a river. While Ali's proverb is enjoyable and memorable, it also communicates spiritual meaning in a way that feels right in his own culture. I and other missionaries had spoken to him before about Jesus' life, death, and resurrection, and about putting faith in him. As a Muslim, Ali agrees that Jesus was a good person, but he does not understand the role Jesus plays in God's plan of salvation. Why would God want to come to earth anyway? Ali believes God created everything but now is far removed from daily events. He understands God as the ultimate judge but until now has not considered how God's heart may be moved by the people he created. And for Ali, it makes sense.

While all of Ali's questions are not answered this day, he's beginning to understand the ways and purposes of God through proverbs and concepts he appreciates. This explanation of Jesus' coming to earth is congruent with some of his own deeply held core values and affirms his own worldview. It describes Jesus in uniquely African and also fully Christian terms and metaphors. In the past, Christianity was presented to Ali in foreign terms and practices. Proverbs are now opening the door for Jesus to be at home in Ali's own culture.

"There is a God whose heart pulls so strong that his feet must come to be with us," Ali says. "Hmm, that is good news. I would like to know more about this."

The crack in the gate is widening for further learning—for him and for me. One day, will it burst open?

68. CREATING A FARM BLESSING CHURCH SERVICE

By Paul Neeley

The area where I live is under the domain of a powerful and famous shrine of African traditional religion. Many pilgrims travel to this shrine to seek spiritual help, as many as ten a day. Besides serving the local inhabitants, the shrine and its attendant priesthood aid pilgrims coming from far away, even from other countries. Buses have even been chartered in Ghana's capital city, a day's travel from the area, to transport pilgrims to the shrine.

One day while walking the ten miles to the village near the shrine, I fell in step with one of these pilgrims. It was the beginning of farm season, and he had brought some representative food stuffs to be blessed at the shrine. He put a lot of faith in the power of the local god to help his farm and had come in previous years as well.

Our conversation caused me to think about the felt need of farmers for spiritual help with their crops. Everyone in the area farmed, including the schoolteachers, schoolchildren, government officials, and even chiefs. A number of these farmers had sought spiritual help for their farms each year from the shrine. Now a tiny percentage of them were Christians. Did they still have the same felt need?

The answer was yes. My wife and I began searching the Scriptures for references that demonstrate God's concern for farmers, as well as biblical illustrations about farming. We found many such references and began to compile, translate, and arrange them into a "Farm Blessing Church Service." We also, with the church leaders, developed some public vows based on the passages. Here is the order of service we used:

Read Psalm 147:7–9,14
Read Genesis 1:11–13,29–31
Prayer
Read Psalm 145:13b–16
Prayer to ask God's blessing for the farms
Read Deuteronomy 11:13–17
Take Vows 1 and 2 (see below)
Read Deuteronomy 28:1–8,11–14
Take Vows 3 and 4
Read 2 Corinthians 9:6–1

INTRODUCTION

SECTION 1: FOUNDATIONS

SECTION 2: STORIES

SECTION 3: TOOLS

CLOSING

Take Vow 5
Read Malachi 3:10–12
Take Vows 6 and 7
Read a Jewish prayer for farms
Offering
Read Psalm 65:9–13
Blessing of the representative farm items
Read Isaiah 61:11
Read Mark 4:26–29
Prayer
Sharing of the peace
Communion

VOWS

"Today we want to bind ourselves to serve the Lord our God with all our hearts and to look in faith to him alone for blessings on our farms."

Vow 1: Do you promise to love the Lord your God?

Vow 2: Do you promise to pray faithfully to God?

Vow 3: Do you promise to serve God alone without going to other gods or powers?

Vow 4: Do you look to God in faith for the blessing he will provide?

Vow 5: Do you promise to share generously with people in need?

Vow 6: Do you promise to give God a tenth of what he gives to you?

Vow 7: Do you promise to try to keep God's Sabbath by worshiping God and coming together with other Christians for praise and prayer to him?

Each participant brought representative farm items, and church leaders asked for the Lord's blessing. Also, a variety of items were brought to be blessed by the church leaders, such as cassava sticks, yam seedlings, seeds, and tools.

The people were very responsive to this Farm Blessing Church Service, and it has spread to other churches in the area and has been repeated for two years now. Our hope is that it will become a firmly established tradition in the local Christian community.

We consider this service a successful example of Scripture use. The people hear a lot of Scripture in their own language (more than on most Sundays). They realize the Bible has relevant things to say to them as rural African farmers. And they more fully realize the responsibility that God requires from them in exchange for his blessing. Seeking a farm blessing from God is different from seeking the same from the local shrine; God expects you to live in a certain way and actually change your behavior to establish the kind of relationship in which he can pour out blessings. The local shrine doesn't require any relationship or obedience, only a token gift. This Farm Blessing Church Service can be a step toward helping farmers come closer to the heart of God.

69. USER-FRIENDLY HYMNS FOR THE AKYODE
By Paul Neeley

"How did Jesus walk on the water?"

"What is this heavenly town of Jerusalem like?"

"How did these Bible stories get turned into our kind of songs?"

Akyode (pronounced "ah-cho-day") people ask us such questions as these when they hear the good news presented on cassette—in their heart language and heart music. For many of them, this is the first time they have ever heard Scripture.

The fifteen thousand Akyode people of eastern Ghana, Africa, practice a traditional religion based, in part, around a famous and powerful shrine and its priesthood. The women's cult (Oku–Oku), built around the python snake, also thrives. Although churches and schools have been in the area more than fifty years, the impact of Christianity and education is still insignificant—about 3 percent of the people attend church on a semiregular basis. A mother-tongue literacy program has been ongoing for more than ten years.

In January 1994, a series of Scripture Use workshops in the Volta Region of Ghana helped five language groups, including the Akyode. We recorded an hour-long cassette of Bible readings and associated Scripture songs, composed, for the most part, in Akyode musical styles.

When we played the tape at a central meeting place in the village, about a dozen shrine priests listened with great interest and asked questions raised by the Scripture readings. "What did the dove at Jesus' baptism symbolize?" "Where is the Jordan River?"

"It is very good to hear our language and music on cassette," they concluded. "If you buy us a drink, we can dance to the songs in the afternoon!"

Shrine priests have strong taboos against anything to do with church and literacy in any language. So they will probably never *read* any Scripture portion. Yet a number of them purchased their own cassettes and played them for their peers. Give it to them in a user-friendly form—with their own singing and drumming—and they are ready to listen and discuss.

Co-wives stay up late in the night to hear the cassette. This stimulates new interest in Bible stories and gives rise to questions such as, "Are these stories true?" "Where did these stories take place?" "Where is Jesus now?"

At other villages, as soon as a tape player started singing its songs, old women and children began dancing, and middle-aged women learned the response chorus after a few repetitions and joined in. Men gladly paid for the tapes. The songs spread like wildfire, even among groups heavily resistant to the gospel when presented in other media. Women in the Oku-Oku cult, forbidden to hear church preaching or become literate, learned these songs with Christian lyrics.

During moonlit nights, children sing the songs with gusto to accompany their jumping and clapping games. Everyone already expects some of the songs will be sung at the next big village dance.

Previously, Jesus was completely irrelevant to their lives. Now they want to know more. The form of the message was so attractive and easy to use that they were drawn into its content.

The first duplication order of one hundred tapes sold out within a month (the time it took to arrive in all the Akyode villages), and more are being prepared.[30] Each tape costs more than a day's minimum wage.

Compare these exciting results to the long-standing Akyode literacy program: it takes two years to sell one hundred books, even when they are subsidized at one-tenth the cost of the cassette. Today among the Akyode, "buying" Scripture—through literacy—is as unappetizing as strange-tasting foreign foods. But offer Scripture songs and readings on cassette and they line up like we do at a pizza buffet. Make it good and hot, and they will pay for it, digest it, and come back for more.[31]

The Bible says, "Blessed . . . are those who hear the word of God and obey it" (Luke 11:28). We cannot yet tell how many people have been persuaded to *obey* the word of God by these indigenous hymn cassettes. But we know that in only one month's time, the majority of Akyode people have *heard* some of the word of God—without being literate or sitting in church. It's a great first step.

---

30   In partnership with Akyode musicians, composers, and singers, Paul and Linda Neeley eventually completed five different tapes. This story was written after producing the first tape.

31   Since the publication of the New Testament in the language, about seven years after this story was written, people became much more interested in obtaining the word of God through literacy. Approximately 10 percent of the people are now literate—a huge increase. Although it is still true that the majority of people may prefer to learn God's Word through oral means, the success of the literacy program has exceeded our expectations.

AMERICA—LATIN

70. WORSHIPING GOD WOUNAAN-STYLE

By Ron Binder

When my wife, Kathy, and I first went to live in a Wounaan (woe-NAHN) village in Panama in 1970 as Bible translators, we began documenting and recording not only the language but also the many vocal, instrumental, and dance styles we observed in ceremonies and celebrations. But one ceremony we did not observe until a strong earthquake shook the rainforest in that area near the Colombian border. The villagers' houses and ours, being built on stilts eight feet off the ground, swayed back and forth even as trees in the surrounding forest were toppling. But no one was hurt, so we didn't think much about it . . . until the next morning.

The sun had barely shed rays of light on our secluded village when everyone began filing into one of the large round houses. We wondered what was going on and soon began to hear a deep rhythm coming from the house, a virtual orchestra of flutes and women's voices. It went on for four hours. Finally, when all was done, I asked Toño, my language helper, what it was all about.

"That is the way we pray to Hẽwandam, Creator God," he replied.

The next day they repeated the ceremony again, and I was given permission to record the chants. With Toño's help, the prayers were later transcribed and translated, and soon it was obvious that this ceremony was at the heart of Wounaan culture.

Flash forward to the mid-1990s. I was teaching a series of three-week workshops designed to train Christian writers from four of Panama's minority languages. I had taught language awareness, creative writing, and was in the middle of teaching a poetry workshop. One of the students asked, "Could we study how to write hymns?" That was a sore spot for me. I recalled years before when the Wounaan began to form churches. I had asked them what they were going to do about singing. They knew that God's people always sing in their church services. They replied, "We'll just translate what the Latinos sing, then we'll have the right kind of hymns."

That didn't seem right at all to me, so I suggested they put Scripture and Christian lyrics to some of their own music. The silence was awkward. Finally, someone said, "We can't use our music in church. Our music is bad!"

Oops, what do you do if the music is bad?! I had never studied ethnomusicology and had no answer. By default, I did what many missionaries have done: I brought in Western and Latino hymns, which were then translated. All the years while Bible translation was going on, people sang these in church. They seemed to enjoy them, but I felt there must be a better way for the Wounaan to worship in a culturally appropriate way. And yet I still had no answers.

> They really have little use for the hymnbooks now. They've memorized all the hymns!

The next Christian authors workshop changed all that. Tom Avery, a PhD in ethnomusicology, agreed to come to Panama and teach our next workshop. As the Wounaan and others were exposed to the principles of ethnomusicology and how they applied to developing a culturally appropriate hymnody, Wounaan agreed to follow this up with several hymn writing workshops. This resulted in a constantly growing hymnbook. The latest one, published in 2010, contains 287 hymns. About 25 percent of the hymns are based on traditional Wounaan styles. The hymns were also recorded, and sets of CDs were produced so the people could also listen to them.

The Wounaan are internationally known for their beautiful woven baskets. In many of the basket-weaving circles, the women listen to the hymns all day long as they weave. They really have little use for the hymnbooks now. They've memorized all the hymns! An interesting hymn is posted on YouTube from the recording sessions (search for "Wounaan Hymn"). It's from the traditional prayer style, the heart of the Wounaan culture. The music for their prayers to Creator God is sung to the rhythm produced by pounding on the *k'ugwiu,* a large canoe-shaped instrument, plus a variety of flutes. Since the songs of the hymnbook were recorded in the city, there was no *k'ugwiu* available. But no problem. They just beat on a pulpit for the rhythm. And disassembled mic stands served well as long flutes! A keyboard imitated the panpipe flutes used in the ceremony. If you could catch a Wounaan congregation singing their own styles today, you might notice some very teary-eyed worshipers.

INTRODUCTION

SECTION 1: FOUNDATIONS

SECTION 2: STORIES

SECTION 3: TOOLS

CLOSING

71. BELIEVING IS SINGING[32]

By Robert Campbell

Bob and Barbara Campbell worked among the Jamamadi Indians of northwestern Brazil for over twenty-five years. The Jamamadi were at first indifferent to the Campbells' message about Christ. But then some of the leaders believed, creating a spiritual breakthrough—and everyone wanted to sing about it!

When Bob had tried to teach the people songs in the past, they had sat with their heads bowed, stubbornly not participating, and even scolding their children if they joined in. But when they believed, they composed their own songs with Jamamadi music. These Jamamadi songs were sung with even more vigor than the others.

Men came home from hunting, singing, "We've started on the Jesus trail. You come along too!"

Now when a child died, the people cried, even the teenage boys. They all prayed with feeling for the parents. A few years before, when another infant had died, they had said, "Oh well, a baby can't feel anything anyway."

On Christmas Eve, crowds gathered to sing a spontaneous version of the Christmas story and other Bible stories and choruses all night long. For a whole week they sang—the women in the daytime, the men at night. In this way they told neighboring people the news of what Christ had done for them.

The Jamamadi celebrate the coming of age of teenage girls. In the past, they would whip the girls or sing to the spirits. Now they sing praises to God and commit each girl to his care. The Jamamadi truly began singing a new song to the Lord!

---

32   Reprinted with permission from Robert Campbell, "Believing Is Singing," *EM News* 3, no. 1 (1994).

261

INTRODUCTION

SECTION 1: FOUNDATIONS

SECTION 2: STORIES

SECTION 3: TOOLS

CLOSING

72.   AT NIGHT HIS SONG IS WITH ME[33]

By Héber Negrão

The Parakanã of northern Brazil are a friendly, cheerful people who love to sing, play their flutes, and dance. The way they create their music is perhaps unique: they receive it through dreams and then teach the community.

I visited the Parakanã village on a trip to research their music and motivate them to use it for God, aiding the process of the translation of the Scriptures in their language. I was invited by Gino and Tati Ferreira, who are Bible translators there, now working on the book of Acts. In the village I met Xaperia and Kaworé, two Indians who have already composed several songs for God in their own style.

I held workshops about the biblical bases for making music for God, conducted interviews with local singers, and recorded the music they had composed.

Knowing that the Parakanã receive their music through dreams, I decided to emphasize this characteristic in the workshops and in conversations I had with them. I observed that the book of Revelation tells about the visions of John, including several mentions of music. I explained to the Indians that these visions were similar to dreams, that there were also people in the Bible who dreamed about music and whose music appeared in a book. When they heard that, they got very excited about creating their own biblical songs.

Psalm 42:8 says: "By day the LORD directs his love, at night his song is with me—a prayer to the God of my life." I was really excited when I read that text. The Bible tells us that God actually gives us a song at night. For the Parakanã, that made perfect sense and encouraged them.

After telling them about this psalm, I read some others that speak of nature praising the Lord. Then we began to imagine how trees could sing of happiness to the Lord (Ps 96:12) or rivers could clap hands (Ps 98:8). I asked how the Xingu River could clap its hands for God. One participant imagined this praise as when waves brake resoundingly on the stones, forming a white foam. That amazed me. They were interacting with the word of God, as the Holy Spirit communicated to them how all created things sang for God.

Before my departure, they said they now knew it was important to sing music for God because the Bible said so. They were very interested in creating new songs based on Scripture texts, beginning with the book of Acts.

---

33   This article first appeared in Portuguese as "De Noite Está Comigo a Sua Canção" in *Connections: The Journal of the WEA Mission Commission*, vol. 9, nos. 1 and 2 (2010), 70. Translated by the author with Carol Brinneman.

73. NOW WE CAN SPEAK TO GOD—IN SONG[34]

By Jack Popjes

We were stumped. The musical system of the Canela people of Brazil's Amazon jungle had us completely baffled. Not because my wife Jo and I were tone deaf or didn't appreciate music—we sang for years in many musical groups. Not because we never heard Canela music. We were constantly surrounded by it while in the village. Every night the Canela sang us to sleep with their massive sing-songs at the village's central plaza.

We tried to learn to sing Canela, but we just couldn't. We could not make heads or tails either of the rhythm or the tone system. Whenever we joined their singing and dancing, Jo didn't know what to sing, and I didn't know when to stomp my feet. How could we ever promote the composition of native Canela hymns when even after nearly twenty years of praying and trying, we just couldn't get the hang of their music?

Enter Tom Avery, an SIL ethnomusicology consultant. Tom taped Canela music for several weeks. He took the music to his study and analyzed it, using a computer. The next year we got together, and he introduced me to the rudiments of Canela music—at last.

DIFFERENCES

Now we knew why we had never been able to learn it. Instead of a musical system of eight notes with some half notes, the Canela system has many more notes. Although Canela music can be sung or played on an instrument, such as a violin or a slide flute, it is impossible to play on a keyboard.

Another difference was the words. So many additional syllables and fillers are put on the basic words, it was almost impossible to understand the lyrics. I guess we do something a bit like that with some of our songs. Think of a drawn-out "Gloria"/ "Glo-o-o-o-o-ria" in the Christmas carol with each "o" on a different note and beat, or "fa la la la" fillers in another carol.

The Canela system was not simple. Just as a symphony has distinct parts like the overture, etc., so the Canela music system has three main types. At every major or minor songfest, they always start with the slow, walking-style *ihkenpoc* songs. Then they move to the faster jogging-style *kyjkyj* music, and end up with a full cry, racing *ihkenpej* music. Tom discovered all this and more. Then

---

34   Reprinted with permission from Jack Popjes, "Now We Can Speak to God—in Song," in Fortunato, *All the World*, 147.

he came back to us. As I provided Scripture-based lyrics, Tom composed original Canela music for more than twenty hymns.

GREAT ACCEPTANCE

We traveled to the Canela village to introduce the songs to the people. It was almost like pouring gasoline on a campfire! Within a few nights, hundreds of Canelas crowded around wanting to listen and to learn the new songs. The main song and dance leader was deeply moved. He wanted a hymnbook for himself and sat for hours listening to a tape we had prepared. He eventually learned all the songs and made improvements on them. Other Canelas started adding verses to some of the hymns.

Every night during our evening Bible classes with the Canela, more than half of the time was taken up singing the new songs. One Canela, with tears in his eyes, said, "You gave us the book in which God speaks to us, but your friend Tom gave us songs in which we speak to him."

After the dedication of the Scriptures in 1990, all the Canela men and women who had received their copy of God's translated word crowded around the main song leader in the center of the plaza. They sang several of the Canela songs, such as "God's word is sweeter than honey to me" and "Let us hold onto and obey God's word."

Tom's culturally sensitive work sped up not only the acceptance of the newly translated Scriptures but the whole gospel message among the Canela.

INTRODUCTION

SECTION 1: FOUNDATIONS

SECTION 2: STORIES

SECTION 3: TOOLS

CLOSING

AMERICA—NORTH

74. CULTIVATING AND CONTEXTUALIZING ARTS IN WORSHIP FOR MINORITY GROUPS

By David M. Bailey

In America, we have a proverb: "The grass is always greener on the other side of the fence." Our neighbor's yard seems to look better because we don't see its deficiencies. The reality of the matter is, the grass is greener wherever it's cultivated best. In some cases, our neighbor's grass truly is greener because he's had time and resources to invest in it.

The ministry of ethnodoxology focuses on supporting and encouraging the development of relevant, cultural worship for people groups around the world as well as in our own backyard. My story of how I got involved in ethnodoxology reflects my desire to see greener pastures in my own cultural context and learn how to cultivate that grass in my own yard.

MY STORY

I grew up in the southeast United States, in Richmond, Virginia. Richmond is city with a lot of racial history. It had the largest number of slavery exports in America. It was the capital of the Confederacy during the Civil War. Richmond was one of the leading American cities in creatively using the rule of law to keep black people and other minorities legally isolated from resources and economic progress.

Growing up in this context, I saw that my family's grass was not as green as my suburban neighbors' grass. I also noted that my inner-city neighbors didn't even have any grass!

Because of my history, I can't help but see inequalities between people groups. As a musician, I've become keenly aware of the disparity in the cultivation of appropriate worship music for minority groups. One of the most formative events that propelled me into this ethnodoxology-related need was meeting Bob Kauflin, the author of *Worship Matters*.

I attended a conference where Bob led worship, and I noticed that the songs he used were rich in theology, with a contemporary style. During a break, I told him how much I enjoyed the music. Then I asked him, "Do you know of any music like this for black people?" Bob laughed and said, "They didn't have this kind of music for white people, so we had to make our own music."

Bob encouraged me to get a book on systematic theology and start writing songs from my own people's collective cultural experience.

That conference was the start of a significant journey in my life. I began to write songs for my context. After a while, I started to get work as a musician, leading worship in cross-cultural and/or multiethnic contexts. I soon discovered that no matter what the dividing factors may have been, the minority group inevitably experienced the least amount of consideration for their cultural viewpoints.

Over the past decade I've been engaged in applying principles of ethnodoxology to my own environment and have discovered three benefits that accrue when diverse Christian communities are intentional in making worship relevant for all:

1. Meaningful worship experiences are a great equalizer.

    When a Christian community decides to value the heart desires of the various cultures, they honor everyone and therefore avoid a struggle for power. Minority groups truly feel a part of the community.

2. Varying worship expressions is a great bridge-building tool.

    The more people understand one another, the closer they become in relationship with one another. In many cases, over time, people begin to appreciate, enjoy, and look forward to the variety of worship expressions.

3. Culturally appropriate worship engages the heart and mind with truth like nothing else does.

    Culturally appropriate expressions in worship speak to people's hearts best because there's no need for translation. Even when someone is "fluent" in a dominant cultural language, speaking his heart language communicates best.

ENCOURAGEMENT FOR MINORITY GROUPS

For those in a minority group, I encourage you to discover and learn to appreciate the beauty of your own cultural yard. Learn the history and artistic traditions of your people. Learn where your people come from and how you got to where you are today. Discover how they told their story through the arts.

Be a student of culture—your culture and that of others. Contextualize your discoveries.

ENCOURAGEMENT FOR MAJORITY GROUPS

For those of you who are a part of the majority culture, understand that you do indeed have a culture and an ethnicity. Realize that your culture is only one of many; there is no objective standard, no "normal."

Be aware of how you do your liturgy, preaching, music, and other artistic expressions of worship. Ask yourself and others how you can be a better cross-cultural missionary. Learn the culture of the minority groups in your community. Join in the creation and expression of culturally appropriate expressions of worship.

Encourage minority groups to cultivate their own cultural expressions of worship. Be Bob Kauflin to someone; you'll never know how that seed might grow and the grass become greener on the other side of the fence!

75.   A LAUGHING PARTY AND CONTEXTUALIZED WORSHIP

By Mark Charles

"Has your baby laughed?"

On the Navajo reservation, that's a common question posed to parents who have infants around the age of three months. The first laugh of a Navajo child is a very significant event. It marks the child's final passing from the spirit world to the physical world, meaning he or she is now fully human and present with us. This milestone warrants a party, and what a party it is!

The honor of throwing this party, including covering the expenses, falls to the person who made the child laugh first—a parent or someone else. That person takes charge of butchering sheep, preparing food, gathering rock salt, putting candy and gifts into bags, and inviting friends from near and far.

Once a baby has laughed, training in generosity begins immediately—a value held in high regard among our people. At the party, where the baby is considered the host, the parents or person responsible for the first laugh help hold the baby's hand as he or she ceremonially gives the rock salt, food, and gifts to each guest. The rock salt is eaten immediately, and then the plate is received. There are also bags of candy, money, and other presents that the child "gives" along with the food.

When our daughter, Shandiin, was a baby, my niece came for a visit and made her laugh for the first time. It wasn't a burp or a coo; it was a definite laugh. My niece was both proud and horrified. Proud, because she was the one who initiated this significant step for our daughter. And horrified, because as a teenager, she knew she did not have enough money to pay for the entire party herself. My wife and I quickly assured her we would help cover the expenses.

So the planning began. A menu was prepared, a guest list written, and a date set. We had just moved into a small house in Fort Defiance, but for the previous three years we had been living in a traditional Navajo hogan in a remote section of our reservation. (Traditionally, the hogan is not only the center of family life but also of religious life. Even today when many Navajo families live in modern houses, they keep a hogan where important family celebrations and traditional ceremonies are held.) So we knew where we would hold the laughing party—at our hogan. It was farther away and, depending on the weather, could be difficult to reach, but it was by far the most appropriate place.

Creating the guest list was a challenge. For the past ten years I have been involved in seeking ways to contextualize Christian faith and worship for the Navajo culture. Unfortunately, when the first Christian missionaries came to our people, they brought not only the good news of Jesus Christ, but also Western culture, and taught it as the most appropriate context in which to worship. I typically refer to this experience as being "colonized by the gospel." And many other indigenous tribes in our country and around the world have endured similar experiences.

Because of this influence, many Navajo Christians are strongly opposed to using many aspects of traditional Navajo culture in Christian worship. Some Navajos also argue that the traditional religion is deeply intertwined with cultural practices, making distinctions difficult. But I also have many Christian partners from our tribe who also question those views. When we get together, we like to share practices we have discovered that contextualize worship for our culture. Ninety-nine percent of the time, such sharing takes place in our homes or hogans, not in church.

Now, I wanted to invite people from both camps to Shandiin's laughing party. If we were only going to enjoy a dinner, give out gifts, sing hymns, and pray, there prob-

A "laughing party" contextualized for Navajo Christians.

ably wouldn't be any chance for controversy. We might even be able to get away with holding the party in a church, because among churchgoing Navajo Christians this is one of the traditional celebrations most widely practiced.

But we wanted to contextualize this celebration as much as possible. We had asked one of my elders to sing worship songs that he wrote, which drew on our cultural traditions. He likes to take passages from the Navajo Bible and simply sing the words, allowing the natural intonation of the Navajo language to dictate the tune instead of the Western music. The result is that his songs sound like those sung by traditional medicine men, and many Navajo Christians believe that sound is inappropriate when worshiping the God of the Bible. He would argue that the primary difference is that the medicine man knows how to sing the Navajo language, while the missionary does not. Navajo is a tonal language, so intonation affects the meaning of words, while the opposite is true of English. English intonation can easily conform to the melody of a song and not lose meaning. Most Navajo churches sing songs from the *Navajo Hymnal,* which contains English hymns translated into Navajo. Unfortunately, the melody was not translated along with the words. The result: many Navajo words in the hymns are no longer pronounced correctly, making them nonsensical or even take on different meanings.

In the end, we decided to invite people with strong opinions from both sides of this issue. I have to admit that on that morning I was questioning our judgment and felt nervous. I did not want a passionate, divisive theological debate dominating my daughter's laughing party.

As soon as our guests began to arrive, we put meat on the grill, and the celebration began. Our group was diverse: culturally, theologically, and even socioeconomically. Navajos, Americans, and Canadians came. Indigenous people, as well as first-generation immigrants from the Netherlands. People fluent in English, Navajo, and Dutch. We had shepherds, pastors, political leaders, computer programmers, teachers, missionaries, and rug weavers. There were Christians and those who practiced the traditional Navajo religion. But we were all there to celebrate one thing: my daughter's first laugh.

Shandiin learned her lessons in generosity by giving food, gifts, and even blessings to everyone in attendance. She honored her elders and paid respect to her relatives. Then I invited my friend to share some of his contextualized worship songs. He took out his drum, tightened his headband, and led us in worship. His words were from the Scriptures, but the tune and melody of his songs came from the Navajo culture.

I waited for people to walk out, but no one left. I watched for expressions of disapproval or discomfort but saw none. So we continued. After a time of singing, I invited people to pray for Shandiin—that she would grow up to be a generous and loving person and that she would know the joy that comes from the Lord. Beautiful prayers were offered in Navajo, English, and even Dutch.

As conversations concluded and people began leaving, I once again listened for voices of disapproval. Instead I received comments such as, "This was one of the best worship times I have ever experienced!"

True worship, like true love, can be elusive. It cannot be demanded, concocted, or coerced. Instead it must flow out naturally from a heart uninhibited in enjoying the presence of the Creator.

Our worship that afternoon did not take place in a church; it was not led by a theologically trained member of the clergy. I cannot even know for sure that everyone present was worshiping in the name of Jesus. But I do know the Creator was there, and I trust he was pleased. We experienced a small taste of heaven that afternoon, all because we chose to contextualize our worship, so it made sense for our surroundings:

- We met in a hogan.
- We heard the name of Jesus proclaimed in three different languages.
- We worshiped with songs reflecting traditional Navajo ceremonial singing.
- And we celebrated a gift that the Creator had given—the gift of laughter.

76. MOSAIC CHURCH OF NORTH CAROLINA: FROM THE GROUND UP

By Kenneth L. Wallace, Jr.

As I sat in Pastor Wes Ward's office, I was taken back when he told me about two men, church planters who shared my passion for Revelation 7:9: "After this I looked, and there before me was a great multitude that no one could count, from every nation, tribe, people and language, standing before the throne and before the Lamb."

I did not think such diversity could actually exist in one church. After all, didn't Dr. Martin Luther King, Jr. say "the most segregated hour of Christian America is eleven o'clock on Sunday morning?"[35]

Not long after, I met Mark Maltby and Peter Kim. Mark was a white man in his midforties with a ponytail and a silver hoop earring. Peter, a Korean man, sported a bald head and trendy, narrow frame glasses. I, a black man with locks and in my midtwenties, sat across from them in La Azteca, a local Mexican restaurant. They leaned forward as I talked—from a global perspective—about my experiences leading worship.

"I feel like God is calling people to worship together and to eat at his banqueting table. What's more, we all have a dish to share." As I finished my statement, Peter said bluntly, "You must come help us plant this church. We need you."

Mark quickly added, "Take some time to pray about it, but *know* that we have been praying for an African-American worship leader."

After talking it over with Achlaï, my Haitian-Canadian wife, we joined these two men and their families in embarking on a journey that would become Mosaic Church of North Carolina.

Both Mark and Peter, among others, are called to a movement that God is initiating in his church today. Both were independently given a vision of starting a multiethnic, multicultural, and multigenerational church. God called them both out of homogeneous church settings to attempt something that, up until this point, was barely heard of in North Carolina. So when I joined them, we became a "three legged stool," as we put it. We began the hard work of crossing the many barriers that exist when you bring African-Americans, Euro-Americans, French Canadians,

---

35   "Unfortunately, most of the major denominations still practice segregation in local churches, hospitals, schools, and other church institutions. It is appalling that the most segregated hour of Christian America is eleven o'clock on Sunday morning, the same hour when many are standing to sing "In Christ There Is No East or West."Martin Luther King, Jr., *Stride toward Freedom: The Montgomery Story* (New York: Harper & Row, 1958), 207.

Canadians, Haitians, Koreans, Nigerians, Argentineans, Colombians, Bahamians, Mexicans, and Chinese together.

One of the most encouraging things for me was that from the very beginning they asked me to establish a worship culture that reflected the mosaic we believed God's kingdom to be. This freedom allowed me to draw on varied traditions of worship to shape our weekly services. If I introduced a song in Swahili one week, and another in Hindi the next, no one was disturbed. In fact, the diversity of worship became one of the distinguishing marks of our community. I worried, though, that if it was just about the music, we would fall into the trap of multiethnic worship tourism. As we developed a worship team, however, the hearts of the people were open. The church was ready to be shaken up. The ruling sentiment was: there must be more out there than contemporary Christian music.

> They asked me to establish a worship culture that reflected the mosaic we believed God's kingdom to be.

The worship team and their heart orientation turned out to be a microcosm of the church at large. With people coming from diverse backgrounds, each person brought a cultural gift to the musical table. Some brought traditional gospel music. Others had worked with Burmese refugees and brought Karin songs. Haitian Creole flowed from our rehearsal space, followed by twangs of an old Gaither tune. The heart language of each member mingled, creating a musical worship Pentecost. We were many voices with one message: Christ came to draw us into relationship with God the Father, and then with each other. And what a witness it was.

And yet, singing the vision into reality was not always easy. We all spent many a long rehearsal trying to sing or play rhythms that were not our own. Brows furrowed as we tried desperately to pronounce languages foreign to us. And sometimes we relented and sang only songs that were easy for us. But the team pushed through because we believed the vision of a church that reflected God's kingdom, on earth as it is in heaven, was worth the effort to learn words that might bless a brother or sister.

One of the most touching memories for me was when our team, along with Peter's sister and niece, sang a blessing song called "Dang Shin Neun" over him on his birthday. This song says each of us was made to be loved and we are all beautiful. To hear such a blessing in his own language truly touched Peter. For me, to give that blessing was a meaningful gift.

Another moment of special joy was when an older, Euro-American woman, someone we would not have expected to enjoy diverse worship, told the church body that now when she doesn't hear music of various cultures juxtaposed, it just doesn't feel like home.

As I watched many young children grow up at Mosaic Church, I couldn't help but wonder how their generation would impact the church. I don't imagine they will all follow this particular multiethnic expression of the kingdom, but I can't imagine them not carrying this experience with them. As they become the future's worship leaders, pastors, counselors, and teachers, I am deeply hopeful they will choose multiethnic worship and ministry.

Can Revelation 7:9 be fulfilled in today's church? Yes, and more and more this mosaic of God's elect will become the new norm, to the glory of God and for the sake of his kingdom.

77. MULTIETHNIC WORSHIP IN THE CRUCIBLE OF THE CAMPUS:
THE STORY OF INTERVARSITY AT VIRGINIA COMMONWEALTH UNIVERSITY

By Kenneth L. Wallace, Jr.

When I sat down at InterVarsity Christian Fellowship's weekly worship meeting at Virginia Commonwealth University (VCU) in 2000, I was not sure what I was getting into. Little did I know that I was being placed into a crucible of Christian community that would forever change the path of my life. I was a young African-American man, and this fellowship seemed to attract predominately Euro-American females. However, I was hungry for connection and growth in my faith.

As the music started, a tall, skinny white man sat down next to me and introduced himself as Alex Kirk. He looked like an older student, so I was confused when he told me he was a "staff worker."

"What is a staff worker?" I thought.

As it turned out, he was the campus minister for the fellowship, and from that moment we began a wonderful journey together.

As the band started playing worship music at the front of the auditorium, I quickly realized this meeting was going to be a cross-cultural experience. Although I had experienced a variety of churches while I was growing up, my heart music remained African-American gospel. The music I was now listening to was not. The three acoustic guitars, the clapping on the first and fourth beat, and the occasional "yee haw" made me wonder how I would ever connect to this new style of worship.

At our weekly discipleship meeting, Alex told me it was called contemporary Christian music (CCM), one of the primary worship styles of contemporary white churches. I decided to give it a chance. Soon several songs touched me deeply, and I saw the value in this "strange" music.

Not long after, I was asked to join the worship team to bring some "differentness." What the team leaders meant was, they desired diversity on the team. I accepted and played the saxophone with the band. Once again, this was a completely new experience for me! *How could I mesh a jazz sound with a country worship song? Would a pop tune work with a sax solo?* My attempts were well received. The student community loved it! This mixture began to mark our fellowship's worship style.

That year I was invited by our InterVarsity chapter to attend Urbana 2000, a triennial global mission conference. As I entered the auditorium at the University of Illinois at Urbana-Champaign, it looked like a glimpse of heaven. Twenty thousand students my age were worshiping God passionately, and the music was distinctly different from what our team was playing at VCU. This music came from all over the world. We sang in Spanish, Haitian Creole, and gospel styles, as well as CCM.

One scene in particular remains etched in my mind to this day. A First Nations group called Broken Walls came onto the stage and sang a song that resonated with my soul. As they sang, the lights darkened and black lights came on as a dance troupe came out in traditional garb, dancing to the song. Their feathers glowed as the dancers twirled and stepped in worship to the Great Creator. These people were worshiping God with their own culture, and it blessed me immensely.

When I returned to our campus, I could no longer be satisfied with the status quo. As I discussed this with Alex, he encouraged me to share this passion with the worship team—instead of complaining about our lacks. Our worship team began to incorporate several of the songs we had learned at Urbana, which quickly became favorites in our fellowship. These songs connected us with the life-changing experience we had had at that conference.

A few years later I was invited to become the worship leader of this team. Alex encouraged me to bring all of who I was to the position. So I brought the gospel songs I grew up with, the First Nations Broken Walls songs that I had fallen in love with, and many other songs that various other culturally different Christians introduced me to. But many of these students, who had experienced only CCM, pushed back and complained that this new music was not connecting with them.

Alex, though happy to see more diversity in our worship, encouraged me to find ways to engage the fellowship slowly and effectively in this movement toward multiethnic worship. We did not want to alienate students or stress the worship team. He compared the transition to a rubber band. You can

Kenny Wallace at the Drum Circle

stretch it, and you should. However, you have to know how far to stretch it before letting it go, so it won't snap. This good advice helped me reevaluate how much new material to introduce. I pondered which songs to push through and which to jettison. We moved forward, gently pushing in some areas and pulling back in others. Just as the addition of the saxophone marked a change in our InterVarsity chapter, so did these songs.

As this diversity in music took root in our community, it significantly affected our ministry and outreach. As we sang gospel songs, we began to look for ways to partner with the African-American community. When we sang in Spanish, we began to pray for the Hispanic community. Asian songs led us to fellowship with a Korean group on campus. Multiethnic worship led us to pursue racial reconciliation. The songs served as a tool, leading us to press into relationships reflecting the kingdom of God on earth as it is in heaven.

The students from my time at VCU have since moved from the crucible of college, carrying those experiences with them into the varied ministries they are involved with today.

INTRODUCTION

SECTION 1: FOUNDATIONS

SECTION 2: STORIES

SECTION 3: TOOLS

CLOSING

ASIA—EAST

78. JAPANESE BLACK GOSPEL CHOIRS: A COUNTERINTUITIVE APPROACH TO CONTEXTUALIZATION

By Gary Fujino

It was a musical phenomenon; that was indisputable. But when I heard the statement, "Black gospel choirs are indigenous to Japan," it gave me pause. As a missionary to Japan, what immediately jumped to mind was this question: What is "indigenous"? Can something foreign become genuinely a part of its host culture?

THE BLACK GOSPEL CHOIR MOVEMENT IN JAPAN

The 1992 release of *Sister Act*, the hit movie starring Whoopi Goldberg, spawned the Black gospel choir movement in Japan. The vitality of black gospel singing portrayed in the film, with energetic choruses of "church music," somehow wonderfully and mysteriously appealed to Japanese sensibilities—in a country where less than 1 percent of its population are professing Christians. Within months of the film's release in Japan, black gospel choirs began to spring up by the hundreds, and then by the thousands. Non-Christian Japanese music directors began to lead choirs of unsaved Japanese who joyously sang, "O happy day, when Jesus washed my sins away!" without a clue as to its meaning. "How to Sing Black Gospel Music" workshops proliferated on television and in local community centers throughout the land. Ironically, though the black gospel choir (BGC) movement swept Japan at a time when karaoke music parlors, which were formerly prolific, had begun to lose their appeal, most churches in Japan avoided, even resisted, participation in this movement. In other words, few Japanese Christians were involved in the wave of singing black gospel that was sweeping most ordinary Japanese off their feet.

What precipitated this rage of singing Christian music by nonreligious Japanese? Why has it persisted? What can be learned for Christian witness and community building by the church in Japan? One Christian-led BGC excelled in answering these questions—Hallelujah Gospel Family.

THE HALLELUJAH GOSPEL FAMILY NETWORK IN JAPAN

The story of the black gospel choir network known as Hallelujah Gospel Family (HGF) has been chronicled elsewhere.[36] What bears repeating here is that it began with a single choir in the year 2000, when the popularity of BGCs was declining. Yet out of these modest beginnings, HGF has grown (by 2012) into a nationwide movement of fifty-five choirs, where it remains one of Japan's largest networks, with an explicitly evangelical and evangelistic focus on building up Japanese-led communities of faith. There are a number of reasons why HGF has grown despite the national waning of interest in the past decade. To understand them, it is necessary to know HGF's basic infrastructure, as well as its core values.

HALLELUJAH GOSPEL FAMILY INFRASTRUCTURE AND CORE VALUES

Hallelujah Gospel Family's organization is very simple yet promotes a strong lay-led core and facile reproducibility. Every HGF group is formed on the premise that it will be an extension of the local church, so the pastor is required to sing in the choir, even as he is responsible for its strategy and vision. The director is focused solely on music and leading the choir. Finally, a coordinator is in charge of administrative tasks such as communications, logistics, and planning. This triumvirate of leaders, who rarely double up on roles, is one of HGF's key components.

Another unique component of HGF is its core values[37]:

1. The overarching goal of the ministry is not to start a choir but to start *a new community*. The choir does not revolve around the director but is run by and for its members, which promotes growth! This community is "faith-based."
2. *Relationships are emphasized* over the event itself. People who join the choir come to faith when otherwise shy believers share their lives and the gospel in a natural way and in a nonthreatening environment. Attendees are in regular contact with both the gospel and believers in a way and frequency not possible in a church, yet "seed-sowing" and "discipleship" begin to take place organically within Japanese who are not yet saved.
3. Competition is discouraged; rather, *celebration is the motive*. Pastors are involved at a lay level, not as clergy.

Each of HGF's three values goes against the typical bent of a Japanese gospel choir group. Because most BGCs in Japan are business- or community-related activities, the choir is its own end. Therefore, HGF's way of creating community by building into a local church setting is both visionary and strategic. Secondly, HGF's emphasis on relationship building as its methodology—rather than building toward an event, such as a concert—bears out in its repeater trend

---

36   Paul Nethercott, "Japanese Flock to Join Black Gospel Choirs: Churches Harness New Outreach Strategy," *World Pulse*, June 4, 2004, http://www.jbfjapan.com/creative/images/WordPulseInterview.pdf; and Dan Wooding, "How *Sister Act* has Inspired the Formation of 30 Japanese Gospel Choirs Run by a Filipino Former Night Club Entertainer Who Found Christ," ASSIST News Service, July 8, 2009, http://www.assistnews.net/Stories/2009/s09070045.htm.

37   With slight changes from Gary Fujino, "O Happy Day! Using Gospel Choirs to Multiply Congregations," *Japan Harvest* 62, no. 2 (Fall 2010): 14.

(see below), as well as in its longevity and reproducibility. Finally, in contrast to many musical and artistic endeavors, HGF focuses on encouraging "the least of these" and teamwork rather than on competition or lone-ranger virtuosos. This celebrative aspect is a draw that brings non-Christian family and friends to the twice yearly semester-end concerts and even sometimes to rehearsals and informal HGF gatherings.

CULTURAL CONCEPTS THAT DRAW JAPANESE TO HALLELUJAH GOSPEL FAMILY

This infrastructure is what causes the Hallelujah Gospel Family and its network to flourish and expand. But there are also three key concepts to HGF that appeal to the Japanese psyche and draw people to join HGF choirs, even though they appear counterintuitive from a Western worldview.

> After twenty years of existence in the country, BGCs have become thoroughly Japanese.

The first two concepts seem to contradict one another. One is the foreignness, even the apparent antithetical nature, of black gospel music to both Japanese cultural norms and musical forms. The other is the incredibly well-inculturated and indigenized organizational structure of HGF, which makes it distinctively Japanese and reproducible by the Japanese themselves. First, let's look at foreignness.

Wakon yosai is a phrase that can be translated as "Japanese spirit, Western technology (knowledge)," meaning that regardless of the *outward* form, the *inside* is still Japanese. "Boom mentality" works in tandem with *wakon yosai*, where something foreign enters Japan and takes it by storm, as did *Sister Act* and black gospel music. Japanese history is replete with instances of these foreign booms, from the writing system imported from China, to the adoption of Portuguese, Dutch, and German words into common usage, to wearing Western clothing, to changing to the Western calendar, and now to eating Korean food and watching Korean dramas *in the Korean language*. Frequent cross-cultural shifts like this—from new foreign movement to societal norm—have been so pervasive in Japan that it is difficult at times to tell where "foreign" ends and "Japanese" begins.[38] The same may be said of black gospel music. After twenty years of existence in the country, BGCs—of which HGF is a part—have become thoroughly Japanese. This brings us to our second concept: organizational structure.

HGF's infrastructure has been appropriately contextualized and administrated well in a way that fits Japanese culture organizationally, which has been borne out by both the test of time and of context. Also, the well-constructed and easily reproduced HGF infrastructure described above has allowed for rapid multiplication from one to fifty-five choirs in just twelve years.[39]

Methodologically, HGF does its choral training by working from cultural pedagogical norms, which makes it easier for Japanese to learn black gospel music, despite all its foreignness, including

---

38   "In one sense . . . none of the generalities of Asia apply to Japan. It is ancient, medieval, and modern; it is Eastern and Western. And all these characteristics exist in dynamic interrelationship." William A. Dyrness, *Learning about Theology from the Third World* (Grand Rapids: Zondervan, 1990), 141.

39   Seeing these same possibilities, HGF's methodology and strategy have been adopted wholesale as a part of the evangelistic strategy of one of the largest evangelical denominations in Japan.

singing in English about Christian ideals! The pedagogy of group learning, rote memory, repetitious practice, and the ethic of "one for all, all for one" resonates powerfully with the sociological group-drivenness of the Japanese, as well as being a biblical concept (see 1 Cor 12).

On a practical level, the workshops are inexpensive, schedule-friendly, and fun. Inviting friends and family to join the choir is common practice. Often 80 percent or more of participants in any given BGC are not yet Christian. The low-cost, reasonable time commitment of weekly rehearsals and semiannual concert performances, as well as an enjoyable learning atmosphere, has engendered a string of "repeaters," non-Christian and Christian alike, who keep coming back to HGF's choirs each new semester, often bringing new recruits along with them.

The final concept that draws people to BGCs generally and to HGF in particular is the life-invigorating, experiential, uplifting sense of empowerment that comes from singing gospel music itself. Outside of the music, positive emotional expression is not only urged but expected as part of the regimen. This is important in a society where one's feelings are not openly or readily shared. Rarely are venues provided for people to release their feelings. So participation in a gospel choir allows for the manifestation

> It is not uncommon for participants to come to faith and even pursue baptism as a result of BGC involvement.

of "another self,"[40] which is concomitant to emotional expression, as gospel music permits the performer to be free and creative. Thus, even if only in the studio or onstage, BGC participants can live their lives differently from their workaday world, which gives them fuller meaning and purpose as human beings. This concept also enhances the sense of belonging and community that naturally and powerfully occurs as choir groups bond. Connections are formed at individual, small group, and large group levels, which invigorates and encourages all participants.

The *spiritual* force of BGC cannot be ignored. A sense of belonging and community is created, in large part, through the strong Christian emphasis of the genre itself. It is both *implicit*—the music itself is Christian, and lyrics speak of Jesus, the gospel, deliverance, heaven, and more—and *explicit*—in explaining the meanings of the lyrics to the choir, the gospel is often shared directly in both rehearsal settings and on the public (secular) concert stage. In Japan, a strict separation of religion and the state exists, yet because BGC is seen as a cultural phenomenon, few have problems with hearing explanations even though truly born-again pastors are often used to share these "explanations" (sermons). And as a result, it is not uncommon for participants to come to faith and even pursue baptism as a result of BGC involvement.

FACTORS MAKING BLACK GOSPEL CHOIRS INDIGENOUS IN TODAY'S JAPAN

In summary, a number of factors have led to the creation of black gospel choirs and their music becoming contextualized (indigenous) to Japan. *Historically,* BGCs' rise came on the heels of the bursting of Japan's economic "bubble," as well as with the decline in popularity of karaoke music; that is, at a time when people were seeking a release from their troubles. Culturally, Hallelujah

---

40   Japanese perception of self-identity is multifaceted, with the idea that one can become "another me (self)" and therefore live multiple, different lives *simultaneously* where "multiple and interdependent identities exist in the same person, with much of the shift between identities being intentional and specific to context and relationships." Gary Fujino, "'Glocal' Japanese Self-identity: A Missiological Perspective on Paradigmatic Shifts in Urban Tokyo," *International Journal of Frontier Missiology* 27, no. 4 (Winter 2010): 173.

Gospel Family yielded a strong match to existing Japanese cultural patterns, with *wakon yosai,* the boom mentality, pedagogy, and "another self." It was also definitively Japanese-centered and had very little expatriate or missionary involvement from the start. The pastor-coordinator-director combination has almost always been comprised of Japanese only. On a *ministry* level, meeting human needs through the creation of community and a sense of belonging were also key factors that have made Hallelujah Gospel Family enduringly popular with those Japanese who have participated.

In Christian mission in Japan, few efforts have flourished and expanded at the rate of what has been seen in the Hallelujah Gospel Family network of black gospel choirs.[41] Its emphasis on working both within and as an extension of the local church to build communities of faith is an innovative and creative new way to reach the lost with the gospel of our Lord Jesus Christ.

---

41   The ministry and work of Ken and Bola Taylor with Hallelujah Gospel Family was recognized by the Mission Exchange (now Missio Nexus), which awarded its eXcelerate Award for innovation in mission to the Taylors and HGF in 2010. See Byron Spradlin, "Ken & Bola Taylor: Innovators on the Frontier of Artists in Mission," *eXcelerate* 2 (2010): 12–13, http://www.themissionexchange.org/downloads/eXcelerate2010.pdf.

279

INTRODUCTION

SECTION 1: FOUNDATIONS

SECTION 2: STORIES

SECTION 3: TOOLS

CLOSING

79. PRAISE DANCE:
AN EXERCISE IN RELATIONSHIP BUILDING[42]

By Wil LaVeist

Daily in a park near Macau Mennonite Church, a group of mainly women move in unison, offering rhythmic praise in a form unlike that of typical Sunday morning worship.

To the left they sway, gracefully swirling their arms to the worship music, then toward the sky, and then to the right. Forward they step, arms pumping, like synchronized swimmers on land. They smile as sweat beads cool their foreheads.

Explaining this praise dance, Tobia Veith says, "I think it's beautiful to see people moving together. It's a picture of unity and joy in working together." Veith works with both the Mennonite Church Canada and Mission Network and is one of the founders of the Macau church, located on the southeastern edge of China's mainland.

Originating on the nearby island of Taiwan, praise dance at first glance might appear like *tai chi*, a Chinese meditative exercise rooted in the martial arts. "Dancing in groups in parks already has a long tradition in Chinese culture and society, so praise dance is an appropriate cultural form of outreach," Veith said.

Treasure and Bailey Chow

The music is composed by Wu Mei Yun, a Christian and a retired music teacher in Taiwan. She also choreographed the dances using a range of styles from Chinese traditional to aboriginal, Spanish, Hawaiian, ballet, pop, and hip hop. The lyrics are Scripture passages.

Praise dance offers health benefits such as reduced stress, weight loss, and the joy of connecting with others.

That joy is why church copastors Treasure Chow and her husband, Bailey Chow, began the praise dance group in the park in 2011 as outreach. Treasure Chow leads the group, having taken a ten-week instructor training course in 2010. Since the group formed, women who were not members of the church but who had been exercising regularly in the park have joined, bringing the total to ten.

---

42   Originally published as a news story by Mennonite Mission Network, August 25, 2011. Reprinted by permission.

Veith, who dances with the group occasionally, noted that "when Pastor Bailey was ordained, the ladies [non-church members] were really eager to help. For some of them, it was their first time in church."

"What's happening is that as the women get to know each other, they start to share their challenges," she said. "So they [church members] begin to pray with them and share more about Jesus."

Dancers at a citywide praise dance gathering in Macau

Veith regularly attends a different morning praise dance group of about forty members near her home in Taipa. She has had similar experiences, sharing with women who were otherwise disconnected from church. There are two men in that group.

Bailey Chow, the only man in the Macau Mennonite Church praise dance group, said he enjoys participating as a regular member rather than as a leader. Learning the movements along with the other beginners has strengthened his bond with members of his congregation.

"First, I wasn't used to being the only man, but it's healthy for anyone of any age, man or woman," he said. "I'm happy to go every day and soak in God's word. It's a whole person activity. I'm just hoping that in more and more other countries there will be an opportunity for praise dance to help people get to know God, and help their bodies."

"There are praise dance groups in Macau in two other parks, in four other churches, and at a senior citizen center," Veith said.

"As mission workers, we do hope for the day to come that they [participants who aren't church members] will embrace Jesus and become disciples," said Treasure Chow. "We seek to authentically share life with them and believe that God's Spirit will work through that with members of his congregation and others in the praise dance group."

80. THE AROMA OF BEAUTY: MUSIC IN DISASTER RELIEF

By Roger W. Lowther

It was hard not to stare at the devastation surrounding us or shrink at the stench of decaying fish and squid washed in by the tsunami that struck Japan on March 11, 2011. Our group of twenty-two volunteers—pastors, missionaries, church members, and others—drove two trucks and two vans into a gravel lot, recently cleared of debris, and started unloading supplies. Others started making meat and veggie stew on large propane burners. A little over a month after the earthquake, we were doing our best to help the survivors of a community in Ishinomaki.

The pleasant aromas of the cooking soup drifted through the air, a smell almost forgotten by those who began to line up. It awakened a hunger, an appetite, not only for delicious, hot food, but also for life. Hope itself was wafting through the air.

Bruce Huebner, graduate of Tokyo University of the Arts, walked up and down the lines of waiting people, playing his *shakuhachi* (bamboo flute). The traditional melodies gently carried familiar stories of both pain and peace, awakening a joy for life that had been forgotten. Bruce played, not to distract people from the boredom of waiting in line, not as mere entertainment. His music brought a delicious aroma of a different kind, one just as real and meaningful, pointing to something that will always satisfy and can never be lost. Workers and survivors alike heard it and remembered.

What part does music play in disaster relief? was not a question on my mind at the time, as I and everyone else were overwhelmed by the earthquake, tsunami, and nuclear disasters. But at the very first shelter I brought supplies to, I spied an old electronic keyboard in the corner. When I mentioned to the shelter manager that I was a musician, everyone started to set up chairs and gather around. Once I started playing, they didn't want me to stop.

Hundreds of thousands of people resided in shelters after the earthquake, grief-stricken and unable to move forward with their lives. People need love, and music opened doors for us to remain in the shelters and share that love long after the need for material supplies had ended. In the scores of relief concerts that first year after the disaster, building relationships was paramount. After hearing us play, people willingly opened their lives to us and shared their stories.

We have witnessed dramatic changes in the mood of a shelter during a concert. "Bravo!" and "Wonderful!" ring through the air in a festive way. Children come up to play with us. People repeatedly break down in tears as some deal with their grief for the very first time. As a thank-you to us, one energetic eighty-four-year-old gentleman sang songs from his youth, bringing cheers from everyone in the shelter. One damaged community center was transformed for a little while into an elegant concert hall as the music transcended the surroundings.

The most dramatic response occurred at Onagawa Nuclear Power Plant's shelter following a moment of silence for the two-month anniversary of the tsunami. The mood was incredibly somber, and we realized the usual upbeat opening to a concert was far from appropriate. Bruce came up with the brilliant idea to call out a melody on his *shakuhachi* from one side of the gymnasium. Steve Sacks echoed a varied response from the other side of the room on his flute. Calls and responses of comforting melodies crisscrossed the room, mesmerizing us with their healing power. As we were leaving, one of the junior high girls got up the courage to play her flute. Bruce and Steve quickly joined in, and before long a whole group of adults were joyfully dancing in their celebration of life!

I have played with other Tokyo-based professionals in schools, hotels, sports complexes, community centers, and even outdoors. Setting up my portable digital organ never fails to draw crowds and comments, but nothing compares to the reactions when I start to play. "Wow! You've turned our gymnasium into a beautiful cathedral," one shelter manager told me. People always send us away with "Please come back, and play longer next time!"

Ten Christians from The Juilliard School came with me to the Watanoha Elementary School shelter to help in musical relief work (one of fourteen concerts they gave in twelve days) three months after the tsunami struck. As the afternoon light began to wane, refugees pulled out their flashlights and lanterns so we could all see the music. The howling winds of a typhoon raging outside had knocked out the power and created an eerie atmosphere inside the gymnasium full of people. Torrential downpours created lakes of standing water surrounding the building. Yet the music allowed us all to relax and feel like everything was going to be okay.

At an International Arts Movement conference in New York City years ago, Jeremy Begbie encapsulated the importance of music in disaster relief. He said:

> In a world that is so obviously not as it ought to be, it is the calling of artists to be agents of a new world, a redeemed world. Whenever we start to believe that nothing can ever be different, that our homes, relationships, careers are basically stuck in a groove and can never change and never will change, whenever we start to believe that the horrors of the world just have to be, the emaciated child compelled to beg at a road side, or the prostitute forced to the streets to feed her drug addiction, whenever we start to believe that there can never be anything new under the sun, *it's the artist's calling to make us believe things can be different, that life can be new, that a new world is possible,* a world that ought to be.[43]

Neither my training in conservatory nor my job as church musician could have prepared me for that first year after the earthquake. However, my role as an artist in disaster relief fit as clearly and naturally as if we had planned for it all along. The aroma of beauty plays a powerful part in the healing of individuals and community reformation.

---

43   International Arts Movement Conference, "Redemptive Culture: Creating the World that Ought To Be," February 23, 2007. New York City.

81.   NAMSEOUL GRACE CHURCH:
GLORIFYING GOD THROUGH THE ARTS[44]
By Steve S. C. Moon

Visual art is an important medium for mission at NamSeoul[45] Grace Church, in Seoul, Korea. Its pastor, Rev. Hong, and church leaders have sponsored art exhibitions for talented local painters in different parts of the world. They also collect art works to exhibit in the Miral[46] Gallery, which is located in the church and is open to church and community members.

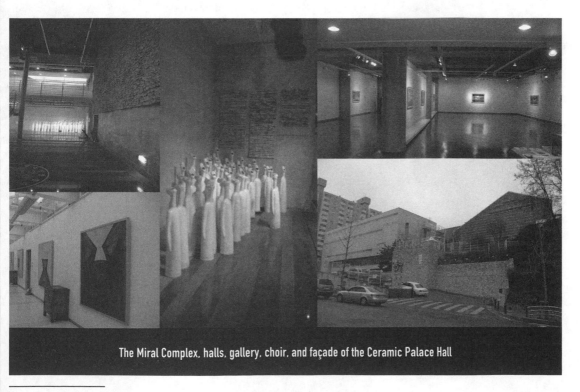

The Miral Complex, halls, gallery, choir, and façade of the Ceramic Palace Hall

---

44   Originally published with some changes from Steve S. C. Moon, "NamSeoul Grace Church: Glorifying God through the Arts," *Connections: The Journal of the WEA Mission Commission, vol. 9,* nos. 2 and 3 (September 2010); 40. Reprinted by permission.

45   *NamSeoul* means "South Seoul" in Korean.

46   *Miral* means "grain of wheat" in Korean.

Over the last thirty years, Rev. Hong has regularly visited art museums and galleries whenever he travels to foreign lands. He has befriended local artists and through these friendships sometimes leads artists to Christian faith. Some of them even begin to express what they have found in Christ through their art works.

NamSeoul Grace Church also runs an art class for people who want to learn to paint. Participants are rediscovering themselves through artistic activities and finding ways to create points of contact with neighbors.

Church services are held at the gymnasium of Miral School, a special education school that Rev. Hong and church members established. The Miral complex includes a gallery, a concert hall, a bakery shop, and two coffee shops. The Miral Gallery has collected nearly 1,400 art works from different parts of the world.

The church also has plans to build a separate mission center on the outskirts of metropolitan Seoul. The sanctuary will be surrounded by Christian art works collected worldwide. The whole purpose and concept of the space will be to come "before the throne of God" (Rev 7:15) with prayer, singing, and artistic expressions, according to Rev. Hong, who firmly believes that all genres of art exist only to glorify God.

With the God-given talents we possess, we are called to praise him. Arts cross not only cultures but also generations, as demonstrated through Rembrandt's works. More often than not, artistic expressions of faith will radiate God's glory beautifully even as time passes.

INTRODUCTION

SECTION 1: FOUNDATIONS

SECTION 2: STORIES

SECTION 3: TOOLS

CLOSING

82. GIFT RAP

By Chieko Larrimore

While a student at the Graduate Institute of Applied Linguistics in 2010, I took Applied Arts, a course for which we needed to commission an artist to create a new work of art. As part of the assignment, the students and artists would present their works in a special chapel service scheduled for December 8—Pearl Harbor Day on the Japanese calendar.

As a Japanese living in the US, I am often reminded of the bombings of Pearl Harbor, Hiroshima, and Nagasaki. Although I have dealt with my feelings concerning that history, it still stings my heart when I think of it.

For my commissioning project, I wanted two different songs about forgiveness and reconciliation in Christ—one from a Japanese perspective and the other from an American perspective. I chose the second chapter of Ephesians as the theme.

Of the two artists I chose, I was able to spend more time with my American friend, who lived in my neighborhood. She wrote a rap for me. Working with her brought me significant inner healing.

First, I wrote her an email including a brief personal history, something like this:

> I used to have latent, bitter feelings toward the US because of the atomic bombs
> dropped on Hiroshima and Nagasaki during WWII. At the same time, I was ashamed
> of my own country because of its actions during the war. The Lord helped me realize
> that I was binding both Americans and Japanese in spirit by my resentment, and he led
> me to forgive the US, Japan, and myself.

After I wrote her this general introduction, my friend asked me to talk more about it in person. She asked me questions in order to understand my emotions and how I was changed through this experience. As I talked, I was surprised to see her start writing a verse about me.

As she was writing, I felt unexpectedly warmed inside, touched by what I was beginning to recognize at that moment as a deeply kind gesture. I felt alive. I thought, "*Somebody is listening to me. Somebody cares about what happened to me and what I feel and think about it. And my story is becoming art.*"

It was a great honor. In my experience, forgiveness and healing have involved a long process, as well as definite points of decision. I often need to face the feelings that keep coming up and keep forgiving and receiving healing.

My friend listened to me, wrote a rap about my story, performed it publicly, and played a crucial role in my ongoing inner reconciliation process.

ASIA—SOUTH

83. ONLY GOD CAN WASH AWAY SIN
By Anonymous

Kola sat at his fruit stand with his eyes fixed ahead while farm workers quietly passed along the dusty road in Andhra Pradesh at dusk. Suddenly he heard traditional Indian music over a loudspeaker. His eyes brightened—a performance of *kolata* (a traditional dance song with sticks)!

Kola quickly shut down his shop and rushed to catch up with others. As the song continued, Kola found its message shocking: no one could achieve salvation through *dharma* (works of caste duties). When the music ended, he blurted out, "No! We must do good works!"

Just then a baby crawled up to Sampson, one of the Christian men performing the kolata. He gently picked up the child, who was soiled, and asked, "Can this child wash himself?"

"Of course not," snapped Kola.

Sampson continued, "Just as this child cannot come clean without his mother's care, you cannot wash away sin. God must do that."

84. THE HALLELUJAH *PERAHERA*: RELIGIOUS PROCESSIONS IN SRI LANKA[47]

By Michael T. Balonek

Perahera, the religious procession, is of great importance to devotees of Buddhist and Hindu faith in Sri Lanka. Every month at least one *perahera* commemorating an event or honoring a god takes place. Processions are a common sight, and people of all religions generally come to the street to see the sights and hear the sounds, regardless of their individual beliefs.

The largest and most famous Buddhist *perahera* of the year takes place in the city of Kandy every August. During this multiday festival, the tooth relic, said to be one of Buddha's teeth, is taken out of its temple and paraded around the town in celebration and to bless the people who come.

Major Hindu processions include those dedicated to the god Kataragama. Devotees pledge themselves to this god in exchange for assistance in some troubling matter. This devotion is shown through self-mutilation rituals, often during the procession. Men and boys dance with large hooks attached to their backs or sometimes swing suspended from hooks attached to wooden frames on the backs of trucks.

Smaller processions are also held each year, starting from local temples, some in honor of Buddha, Kataragama, or whichever god the temple honors.

When a Buddhist dies, friends and relatives procede to the cemetery to the beat of a *thammattama* (drum), a *daula* (drum), and a *horenava* (quadruple-reed oboe). Similarly, Hindu devotees celebrate on the way to the cemetery with loud, excited dancing, also accompanied by an ensemble, usually a *tovil* (drum) and a large reed instrument at the least.

The church and service organization The Salvation Army has carried out evangelization using brass bands as they march through cities' streets since its inception. Upon the Army's arrival in the mostly Buddhist and Hindu Sri Lanka, they continued holding these processions but adapted them to the local culture. In holding these parades they were not only using a Western symbol but also a truly Sri Lankan cultural form of celebration, which eased the transition.

The Salvation Army has created a hymnal for use in their churches in Sri Lanka, which contains hymns translated into Sinhala, the official language of the country, as well as newer, Sri Lankan–

---

47   Originally published in a slightly different form in Michael T. Balonek, "'You Can Use That in the Church?': Musical Contextualization and the Sinhala Church" (master's thesis, Bethel University, 2009), 52–58. Reprinted by permission of Michael Balonek.

composed (but still very Western-sounding) songs, which are used during the Army's processions. The main event is held in Moratuwa, a town just south of the capital Colombo, which is heavily populated with Anglicans and Catholics, as well as significant numbers of Hindus and Buddhists. The procession takes place on the most important day for the Christian church—the celebration of Christ's resurrection.

At 3:30 in the morning on Easter Sunday, a group of about fifty leaves the meeting point, a small church on a back road in Moratuwa. The group is led by a pickup truck topped with two speakers, each about two feet in diameter, playing Christian music in the Sinhala language with a variety of synthesized Eastern and Western instruments on the recording. The truck is immediately followed by the classic Salvation Army bass drum, complete with logo. Behind this drummer, people march, walk, or dance in the procession, many singing and clapping along with the recording, others holding lanterns with brightly colored tissue paper around the edges, though with the full moon people can see well without them. In the very back of the line marches a group of youths, ranging in age from seventeen to twenty-eight. They carry a snare drum and a conga drum and are also singing but not with the recording. They sing at the top of their lungs any Christian songs that come to mind. They jump, dance, and laugh as they process through the town.

> Processions are a common sight, and people of all religions generally come to the street to see the sights and hear the sounds, regardless of their individual beliefs.

People eagerly wait for the parade at the side of the road, and some come running out of their homes upon hearing the commotion. Many wait expectantly with fireworks and/or firecrackers on their front lawn and set them off as the *perahera* passes. Parishioners ring church bells anytime a church is reached, and they continue to ring until about thirty seconds after the procession has passed. This happens frequently, as Moratuwa is one of the most Christian communities near Colombo. About every twenty minutes or so a house is reached that has prepared coffee and sweets for everyone, ensuring the participants have energy to go on. Some of these stops are prearranged, and others seem to be pleasant surprises. After each stop, the head of the procession prays over the loudspeaker before they continue on their way.

Occasionally they pass members of other churches also in procession, such as ones led by Methodists and Anglicans. The Methodist procession does not have a truck playing music and, though they sing and drum, they seem more quiet and somber. Leading the way is the clergyman, carrying a large cross. The Anglican Church groups are quietest of all, carrying a large cross in front of the procession as they march and sing. At about 6:00 a.m., the processions reach their respective churches for sunrise services.

Similarities as well as differences exist between the church processions called the "Hallelujah *Perahera*" and the *Kataragama Perahera*. My wife and I have witnessed both in the town of Moratuwa on different occasions. Both occur at night, the Christian one at 3:30 a.m. and the Hindu one at about 9:30 p.m. Both have similar ranges of audience participation, all observers set off firecrackers. At the Christian festival people give sweets to the participants, whereas at the Kataragama festival they throw/offer sweets to the shrine. Both processions invited my wife and me to join in (we politely refused for the Hindu procession). In both kinds of events musical instruments were used, and processions led to places of worship—the church or the *kovil*.

Pictures of the god Ganesh lead Hindu processions, followed by a cardboard cutout of Buddha, and a shrine to Kataragama bringing up the rear. The Salvation Army procession, in contrast, followed no religious symbols, while the Methodist and Anglican processions followed a cross held aloft on a pole. The Hindu procession included organized dancing with costumes and props. The Christian procession had no choreography or costumes but did have informal dancing based on the song being played at the moment. Some people did dance among the Salvation Army group—a spontaneous and random occurrence. Included in the Hindu procession was a group of young boys under the age of ten holding clay pots and asking for donations of money. No such appeals occurred in the Christian processions. Very old and very young alike danced and marched in the Hindu procession. The Salvation Army procession involved mostly youth under the age of thirty accompanied by older, full-time Salvation Army workers, who seemed to act more as organizers and chaperones.

Processions could be a wonderful way for Christians to reach out to more of the island.

The Hallelujah *Perahera* is a common yearly occurrence only in Moratuwa. From my many interviews, I have heard of only one other such *perahera* among Protestant Christians in Sri Lanka: in the southern city of Matara, led by the Dutch Reformed Church, now the Christian Reformed Church.

Rev. C. N. Jansz says that though their Matara perahera occurred only once, it was "very well received by the community, and especially by the congregation, who were very excited to partake" of the festivities. "There were no adverse reactions," he told me, "but if it were done today we would absolutely need permission from the police and from the town, as the climate has changed somewhat [in Matara toward Christians], and there would be more of a chance of trouble."

It seems that processions could be a wonderful way for Christians to reach out to more of the island, provided they are done prayerfully and with the foreknowledge of the community and authorities. Processions are such a natural part of Sri Lankans' lives. They show the joy and celebration of people's lives. They are well attended and are usually not only tolerated but embraced by people of other faiths. Buddhists look on with excitement as Hindu processions pass and vice versa. Christians have much reason to display their joy as well!

As it stands right now, however, even people living in the next few towns over from Moratuwa have never heard of *Christian* processions. One way to encourage such an event in more areas of the island may be for one person or group to take the initiative and organize them. Perhaps if the event were covered by Christian/church periodicals, people would long to replicate the procession—a powerful way for Christians to express their love and devotion to God in a culturally relevant and acceptable way in Sri Lanka.

85. THE STORYTELLERS OF DULUMPUR

By Carla Bowman

At nightfall in Dulumpur, a hamlet in Jharkhand in eastern India, thousands of stars cling randomly onto an ebony sky. The welcome foot washing and artful, ritually paced meal served on giant leaves take place as if in slow motion. Below the star-encrusted sky this place seems suspended in time. Shrouded women dance in a millennia-old line. To the silken movement of saris they rock faintly back and forth on bare feet to an irrepressible, soft, high-pitched, repetitive chant of a biblical song.

The perceived sluggishness of the dance, of the foot washing, the ritual meal, and the hypnotic sounds of the music-chant are illusory because evidence of hard work is all around us: rice and lentils cooked for hours on dry, dung fires; swept dirt streets; immaculate, smooth, plastered, mud-brown walls adorned with white geometric designs and painted with whimsical gazelles floating in a line under tiny windowsills.

Abruptly, a loud beating of the *dolak* assaults the night silence. It is a drumbeat contradicting the slow rhythm of swaying hammocks that creak as the rope ends make contact with the trunks of *kikar* trees. Contrasting

Storytelling in Dulumpur

with the slow motion of village ritual, the drum heralds an arrival. A team of community church planters has arrived at the house of peace—a place for night fellowship, consisting of a ceremony of Scripture story, song, drama, dance, and prayer.

On this night the community church planters tell and enact the story of Adam and Eve. It is part of the Old Testament series, a set of stories being presented in Dulumpur and other villages. A pervasive silence hangs in the air as the drum stops and actors playing Adam and Eve stroll forward. The subtle chant-song of the narrator begins. Her voice penetrates the night as she begins to sing the enthralling tale from Genesis 3: "Now the serpent was more crafty than any of the wild animals the LORD God had made."

At this instant a large serpent slithers across the dirt, weaving and gliding toward Adam and Eve. The observers, enraptured and speechless, are gathered under the thatched roof veranda. One can hear a simultaneous, forceful gasp from the audience as the serpent moves across the ground. It is in reality a small woman wrapped in a silk-striped sari, slinking realistically in curved, slow motion toward Eve. As the serpent lets out a hissing sound, the narration in the form of song continues: "The serpent said to the woman, 'Did God really say, "You must not eat from any tree in the garden"?'" Eve is startled. Her face shows incredulity. The narrator continues in song, changing nothing from the Scripture, not adding to or deleting from the word of God. The story moves on to its conclusion as the villagers of Dulumpur have watched electrified, spellbound.

Storytelling in Dulumpur

The success of these talented and creative performer–church planters is due in no small part to flawless training by master trainers from Engage India, an Indian church planting agency based in Madhupur, located in the geographical center of the large state of Jharkhand. Engage India focuses on training church planters in an orality-centered curriculum called Communication Bridges to Oral Cultures, developed by Scriptures In Use (SIU, http://www.siutraining.org). The Engage India trainers have insightfully identified the communication style of the Santali people group and have used, to huge advantage, tribal skills in dramatic arts, music, and dance. Their repertoire of stories, complete with drama, song, and dance, reaches upward of thirty. The stories are sung to one of twelve traditional tunes with total fidelity to the biblical text.

Other stories have been memorized but are not yet developed in drama and song. The church planters have been taught to revisit these same stories with dialogue, as villagers sit in a circle around the storyteller. Trainers have taught the church planters to help listeners discover the meaning of the story through dialogue. Semiliterate storytellers use the printed Santali Bible as an aid to memorization. They are the ideal practitioners of this orality-based method of evangelism and church planting that has gained popularity and momentum in the past decade.

The SIU ministry ethos/vision is that a systematic church planting curriculum designed specifically for oral cultures is a powerful tool when in the hands of national churches, agencies, and trainers. We have seen evidence of the effectiveness and innovation of Indian trainers through the results in Dulumpur and in scores of other villages dotted around Jharkhand where many Scripture stories have been adapted to drama.

We have seen results north of Dulumpur several hundred miles away in the country of Nepal, where teams of master trainers travel by foot, boat, bus, train, jeep, donkey, and yak to reach their venues. For years now, these teams have faithfully multiplied Bridges training all across Nepal and on the borders with Tibet and Bhutan.

INTRODUCTION

SECTION 1: FOUNDATIONS

SECTION 2: STORIES

SECTION 3: TOOLS

CLOSING

We have seen the effectiveness of national trainers multiplying this training among dozens of non-Western churches and agencies of South Asia. Their ownership of the method and material has inspired the translation of manuals and video supplements into many languages of the Indian subcontinent alone. We have observed the leaders of training hubs develop their reproducible innovations: The House Church Bridges Model, Bridges in a Nutshell, Bridges for Women on-site demonstrations, integrated children's ministry, the Esther Institute, story Bible schools, Bible story training during tailor classes, story memorization after prayer meetings, and multiplying the Bridges for Women training in small groups.

Other innovations to multiply training and encourage self-sustainability have emerged. Some believers bring goats and rice so food may be shared with participants. Trainers meet with church planters once a month for coaching and mentoring. It is no mystery why oral communication methods have been so successful in South Asia. For people groups like the Santali of Dulumpur or the Banjara of South India, the creative arts are their heart and soul. But the success national trainers have had is not limited to that region of the world.

In Vietnam, storytellers journey with their "traveling Bibles," the word of God safely stored in their minds and hearts, as they go from village to village. In Sumatra, storytelling teams drama-

Cultural adaptations of Scripture stories in song and dance at Oral Arts Festival in Orissa, India

tize Old Testament stories of the prophets and chant corresponding Psalms. In Latin America we have seen innovative nationals create urban *barrio* story groups in Peru as well as rainforest story groups in Brazil.

Across the Atlantic to the continent of Africa, innovation and multiplication abound: among the Pygmies, an oral Bible school, which is in reality a simple grass-roofed veranda in the heart of the rainforest; long storytelling afternoons under the acacia trees among the Turkana of northern Kenya; storytelling among the nomadic Mbororo of Niger; story and dance by firelight among the Tuareg who have come to the Lord by family group conversion. In Ethiopia, hardworking trainers travel long distances to be greeted by church planters who welcome them eagerly and embrace their teaching. In Khartoum, nonreading oral-culture believers internalize stories from God's word after effective training by a Kenyan. In Chad, classes on oral culture communication are filled to capacity, sometimes exceeding seventy students. In Mauritania, stories are encouraged as sweet mint tea is passed.

All across the globe national training teams are presenting what we consider the essential elements of effective oral communication of the Scriptures. They instruct new storytellers to memorize the biblical story exactly as it is written. They teach that printed Scriptures are an aid to memorization and that stories must be told with complete biblical accuracy and fidelity to the text. At the same time, storytellers learn how to create introductions and develop dialogue. They are taught how to differentiate wisely between dialogue for "stone clearing" (preevangelism) and dialogue for discipleship. They are instructed to follow chronological order in their storytelling, as well as to select from worldview story collections. They are encouraged to have command of fifty to 225 stories. Although Scripture tapes, media, and radio presentations are useful tools, participants learn that face-to-face interaction and community relationships developed through storytelling and dialogue are crucially important. They have also learned that literacy is not dispensable. Literate mentors are essential to teach stories to nonreading believers and are a key to maintaining fidelity to the Word.

In addition to the quality of instruction in the essential elements of oral communication presented in hundreds of events yearly by national training teams, it has been a significant joy to the Scriptures In Use team to see innovative adaptations made by nationally led training hubs. It is a credit to mission leaders and practitioners in the non-Western world that they have so quickly become staunch advocates and champions of oral communication of the Scriptures. They have demonstrated vision, adaptability, and willingness to venture forward in a new paradigm for missions, utilizing ancient communication methods of the oral arts.

INTRODUCTION

SECTION 1: FOUNDATIONS

SECTION 2: STORIES

SECTION 3: TOOLS

CLOSING

86. LOCAL CULTURE COMMUNICATES BEST

By Frank Fortunato

In his book *Tribal Challenge and the Church's Response*, S. D. Ponraj includes a delightful chapter of his experience in North India among various people groups.[48] Of his ten years there, he mentions how the first two years' efforts in evangelism were a total failure. Paraphrasing his story, here's what he said: "We went in the daytime; they asked us to come at night. We went with literature; they told us to hold public gatherings. We went with Gospels and tracts; they asked for songbooks and stories. We went to preach; they asked us to sing and tell stories. We went to teach the Bible; they asked us to show films about Jesus and show pictures. We went to sing the English choruses we had learned; they asked us to sing their native tribal songs and tribal tunes. We went with guitar; they asked us to bring local instruments—the *dolak* and harmonium."

After repeated failures to reach the people, Ponraj and his wife then determined to prepare themselves with local needs in mind. He recounts (paraphrased): "We purchased lights for nighttime meetings. We purchased local instruments. We found local Christians to teach us how to hold meetings. We started collecting local stories. We learned local songs and printed songbooks. We ordered the *JESUS* film and arranged film showings."

Concerning singing, Ponraj shares the following: "We learned that the tribals in our target areas loved to sing. Their songs provided a living, lyrical theology. The tribal Christians helped us learn the local songs and apply Christian content to local tunes, which was accepted because the music and tunes were their own, and they obviously enjoyed it. We printed the songs and gave them to children in the schools, and soon the songs were sung everywhere."

---

48   S. Devasagayam Ponraj, *Tribal Challenge and the Church's Response: A Study of the Problems of the Tribals in India and the Possible Response from the Church in Terms of Holistic Mission* (Madhupur, India: Mission Educational Books, 1996), 199–218.

87. WHERE HINDU AND CHRISTIAN WORLDS MEET: THROUGH THE *YESHU BHAKTI* MUSIC OF ARADHNA

By Christopher Dicran Hale

It is not every day that a Caucasian music group, whose lyrics focus on the worship of Jesus, has the opportunity to lead a Hindu temple service. In 2007 my band, Aradhna,[49] was invited to lead the music and give a message at one of the monthly Sunday services at a temple in Virginia.

The invitation came about because a Caucasian Christian family, who loved Hindu culture and enjoyed celebrating major festivals with local Hindus, introduced Aradhna's music to the temple leader. Before the leader allowed us to come, he asked me a few questions related to his congregation's concerns about the Christian nature of the group. Would we sing only to Jesus or include songs to some of the Hindu deities?

I answered that our group had a deep love and respect for Hindu culture and that we expressed our love for Christ through *bhakti* (loving devotion and surrender). I further said that *Yeshu* was our *Ishta Devata* (God of choice)—where worshiping only one God and none other is an acceptable practice within Hindu devotional thought and practice. The temple leader was satisfied by my answer and welcomed us to lead the service.

Yeshu bhakti is the path of devotion to Jesus for Hindus who, when they become disciples of Jesus Christ, feel no obligation to leave the Hindu community. Some Hindus in the late nineteenth century realized and regretted that their conversions to Christianity carried much unnecessary baggage related to British cultural and communal loyalties. Therefore they began to reidentify themselves with the Hindu community, while maintaining an exclusive devotion to Jesus Christ. Examples include Narayan Vaman Tilak who, toward the end of his life, resigned from the American Marathi Mission and, along with his wife, became a *sannyasin* (renouncer), which Tilak would have defined as one who renounces worldly things in order to pursue a life dedicated to God and others. He established

> Some Hindus in the late nineteenth century realized and regretted that their conversions to Christianity carried much unnecessary baggage related to British cultural and communal loyalties.

---

49 See http://www.aradhnamusic.com.

what he described as "a brotherhood of the baptized and un-
baptized disciples of Christ."[50] Tilak died a short time later, but
his ideas remained. Some Hindus, particularly toward the close
of the twentieth century, began to form communities of faith in
India that embraced being followers of Jesus while retaining
Hindu communal identity. It was through these followers that I
encountered *Yeshu bhakti* in India and began associating it with
Aradhna's music when I formed the band in 1999 with my colleague Pete Hicks.

> Christians might gain
> much by discovering
> cultures and
> philosophical systems
> outside the Western world
> that can bring out new
> and life-giving insights
> regarding the nature of
> God and what it means to
> be a follower of Christ.

The first song we played at the Hindu temple was *"Ga Ga
More Manwa Yeshu Bhajan"* ("Sing, My Soul, the Song of Jesus"),
an arrangement by Aradhna of a *bhajan* (devotional song). For the
next hour and a half the congregation sang and clapped along
to simple antiphonal songs. Using the traditional format of the
satsang, I intertwined music with spoken word—recounting stories about Jesus and sometimes
explaining them in the light of poetry, not from the Bible but from well-known Indian poet-saints
such as Kabir, whose lyrics we sometimes use in our songs. *Satsang* means "gathering of truth,"
which describes Hindu spiritual gatherings where a message is preached, often with devotional
singing. As we concluded our final song, the leader stood and thanked the band for coming with a
spirit of humility and heartfelt devotion and for bringing such joy to the congregation. The temple
embraced an ecumenical approach to faith, he said, by welcoming the worship of God by many
different names, including the name of Jesus.

In earlier years I might have felt as though his concluding comments undid my efforts to present Jesus as unique. But within an essentially Hindu *Yeshu bhakti* framework, I could be satisfied
that by coming in the spirit of Jesus' name and telling the stories of his life, Aradhna had fulfilled
its purpose.

Clearly the Hindus at the temple in Virginia had taken a step of trust by inviting us to worship Christ and share his teachings with them. In doing so, they were no doubt enriched. It made
me wonder if Christians, in turn, could not stand to learn something from this Hindu community.
Surely Indian *Yeshu bhaktas* (devotees of Jesus), who do not view a close relationship with the
Hindu world and culture as compromising their exclusive faith in Christ, have valuable insights to
share. Because Hindu temples now dot the landscape of the United States, learning directly from
Hindus about what they believe may become increasingly important for Caucasians as well as for
Indians in what Diana Eck, professor of comparative religion and Indian studies at Harvard Divinity
School, calls "the new religious America."[51]

Could this loving approach to get to know and understand Hindus not be a healthy alternative to the sometimes unfortunate teachings about the Hindu world from Christian pulpits, often
given by people who have not lived among them or understood the complexity of their civilization? The Hindu temple that invited Aradhna set an example. They were enriched by the music
and message *without* compromising their deepest values.

For many Christians, their deepest value is an undivided devotion to Jesus Christ. Perhaps
exploring various Hindu philosophies and paths—with Hindus, face-to-face—would not threaten

---

50   H. L. Richard, *Christ-Bhakti: Narayan Vaman Tilak and Christian Work among Hindus* (Delhi: ISPCK, 1991), 110.

51   Diana L. Eck, *A New Religious America: How a "Christian Country" Has Become the World's Most Religiously
Diverse Nation* (New York: HarperCollins, 2001).

that exclusive devotion to Christ but rather deepen it. Christians might gain much by discovering cultures and philosophical systems outside the Western world that can bring out new and life-giving insights regarding the nature of God and what it means to be a follower of Christ. Greek culture and philosophy did just that for Jewish Christianity in the first century through the introduction of terms such as logos, which explained the nature of God as "the Word." The essential message of the resurrected Jesus did not change as Christianity took on Greek language and culture and moved away from its Jewish roots. Likewise, *Yeshu bhaktas* may be able to bring new beauty to the Christian faith by preserving the same message of the resurrected Christ, but sharing it, not from a Greek worldview, as the New Testament writers Paul and John did, but rather from a Hindu one.[52]

---

52   For additional reading, see Dicran (2009) ; Duerksen (2011); Duncan (1992); Hale (2007), 147–50; Richard L. Hivner, "The Christian Society for the Study of Hinduism, 1940–1956: Interreligious Engagement in Mid-twentieth Century India" (PhD diss., University of South Africa, 2011); Julius J. Lipner, *BrahmabandhabUpadhyay: The Life and Thought of a Revolutionary* (New Delhi: Oxford University Press, 1999); and Julius J. Lipner, *Hindus: Their Religious Beliefs and Practices*, 2nd ed. (Oxford: Routledge, 2010).

88. *BEL CANTO* IN INDIA'S NORTHEAST: YOUNG NAGA ARTISTS FUSE OPERA, ROCKABILLY, AND THEIR FAITH

By Michael T. Heneise

Kekhrie rushed into my study and popped in a CD. "Tell me what you think," he said, clicking the mouse and adjusting the speakers. The first track opened with beautifully recorded keyboard *arpeggios*, followed by a warm *bel canto* soprano:

> *Tei peso gei keba u N zabu keviu chiilie.*
> *N kedi chii pezhi vor teigei kemhie kijii nurei. N medo chiilie.*
> God of heaven, may your name be glorified.
> May your kingdom reign on earth as it is in heaven. Let your will be done.

Ledi's voice glided effortlessly through *A Kecha* (*The Prayer*) in her native Angami. A classical baritone voice soon appeared, harmonizing Ledi's voice to the end of the first verse. Suddenly, the rhythm changed to a 1950s rockabilly beat, with a two-pop snare, electric guitar, and synthesized brass section.

"Brilliant!" I shouted, as the chorus filled the room with sound. Kekhrie Yhome and Ledi Sekhose had composed and recorded one of the most original pieces of music I had ever heard anywhere. Even more surprising, my perhaps neurotic sensibilities as an ethnomusicologist were perfectly at peace with the creative mix of Western and non-Western styles.

Nestled in a corner of India's remote northeast, Nagaland is one of the epic stories in the history of Christian mission. Subdued by the British for their relentless raids on Assam's rapidly expanding tea plantations in the nineteenth century, the Nagas had long been feared across the region for their warfare and prolific head-taking practices. Late in that century, American Baptist missionaries braved the unfriendly landscape and inhabitants and, with some help from Assamese Baptists workers, managed to establish churches, schools, and medical clinics. By the 1920s, there were over five thousand Christians among the Ao Nagas alone, and thousands more among the Angami Nagas, Lotha Nagas, and Sema Nagas. Today, Nagaland is considered by many to be a Christian state, with most of its 2 million inhabitants claiming the Christian faith as their own.

Despite its great successes as a mission field, however, Nagaland has also been the staging ground for one of Asia's most protracted civil wars—the six-decades-long Indo-Naga War. Though a cease-fire has been in effect since 1987, small arms fire between competing underground rebel groups is commonplace, and security in the region is still a problem. Severely underdeveloped, basic services such as running water are nearly nonexistent, and roads are often impassable due to landslides and erosion, particularly in the monsoon season.

This makes the accomplishments of Naga Christian artists such as Kekhrie and Ledi all the more remarkable. Studio recordings with sophisticated equipment and seasoned instrumentalists for hire are now more and more commonplace in Kohima and neighboring Dimapur. Young Naga singers now appear as contestants in their own "Naga Idol" shows, and do well in India-wide, televised talent programs. Alobo Naga, a young Sema Naga singer and songwriter, along with his group Alobo Naga and The Band have toured major cities in India and filmed numerous music videos available on YouTube. His music video for the song "Painted Dreams" ranked forty-eighth in the VH1 International top fifty music videos of 2011.

Nise Meruno, one of Nagaland's most successful classically trained singers and pianists, has also composed choral works that are now widely performed. His 2008 composition "Echoes of Alleluia" combines a polyphonic melodic layering with a modern rhythm section accompaniment. Meruno often incorporates traditional Angami Naga pentatonic *ostinatos* into his compositions, effectively fusing distinct traditions, without significantly altering their unique qualities.

Much of this artistic "explosion" in Nagaland can be attributed to a few Christian visionaries who have promoted young artists relentlessly over the past decade. As the cease-fire has paved the way for greater exchange with the outside world, young leaders such as Theja Meru have capitalized on this opportunity to create spaces for young Christian artists to grow. I met Theja during my first trip to the region back in 2001 and recall his excitement as he shared about a new café he was opening in Kohima with the help of his church. Now a decade later, Dream Café has provided a powerful venue for dozens of young artists—painters, photographers, musicians, and others—seeking to showcase their creations. Theja's vision of fusing contemporary and traditional artistic forms is evident upon entering the café. Rothkoesque abstract oil paintings infused with unmistakable symbols of Naga traditional culture adorn the walls. Theja's own music often fuses rock with traditional Naga music, a feature that is common in most new compositions and artistic forms of expression.

> Much of this artistic "explosion" in Nagaland can be attributed to a few Christian visionaries who have promoted young artists relentlessly over the past decade.

Much of the excitement and success felt by the Christian youth and their newfound creative outlets is well-deserved. Though the traditional churches where many of them were raised continue to play an important role in nurturing young leaders, they have shown little willingness to incorporate the new ideas and music currently circulating the shops and playing on everyone's MP3 players. Traditional hymns translated from American Baptist hymnals a century ago are the mainstay and are as revered as the Bible itself. Off the beaten path, however, one finds the story a little different. Baptist revivalist and youth-led contemporary offshoots of the Baptist churches have been more open to incorporating the creative energies of young Naga Christian artists. One finds that many of the worship bands in these churches also meet and perform in other arenas, often playing original music.

When I entered this region to teach ethnodoxology among young Christian artists in Assam a decade ago, there was a great deal of excitement about what could be done to revitalize worship in churches throughout the region. Several years of conferences and workshops sponsored by church associations and conventions led many to believe that there was a general willingness among church leaders to incorporate the new compositions and ideas that had been developed. What transpired, however, was a more mixed picture. Many young people have remained as choir directors and youth leaders in the traditional churches wherein they grew up. However, more and more young people are gravitating towards those worship environments that are fluid and improvisational, where they are welcome to express themselves and participate in shaping the worship experience.

> *N kemhie puorei jii, N kevi kekhrie la, thie rei lhou a nei tuozo,*
> *No a zesituoiiyi, A nvie zeru, A kelhou se n medo chiicie.*
> There is no one like you, your goodness and love, [still] I find joy in living today, [since]
> you are always with me, I belong to you. Use me as you wish.

Unlike their parents and grandparents, Ledi and Kekhrie dress differently, wear their hair differently, talk differently, and have Facebook pages and sport iPhones. Yet their faith commitment, as expressed in the songs of their hearts, is unmistakable.

89. THE POWER OF MUSIC IN THE LHOMI CHURCH

By James Lhomi

The upper Arun Valley in the Sankhuwasava district of eastern Nepal is perhaps one of the most rugged regions of the country's entire northern border. It is here the Lhomi people (population ten to sixteen thousand) live in eighteen scattered villages. Others live in Tibet, and Darjeeling, India. They are adherents to the Bon and Buddhist religions. Agriculturalists and pastoralists, the Lhomis' culture is mainly an oral one, where reading is not a popular activity. And yet the word of God came alive to the people once they realized God can and does speak to them through their own language and culture.

The gospel came to the Lhomi through Finnish Bible translators. In 1972 a young missionary, Olavi Vesalainen, was sent by the Free Church of Finland to Nepal, and a young female missionary, Marja, was sent by the Finnish Evangelical Lutheran Mission. In 1973 Olavi learned the Lhomi language in a village setting. Later Olavi and Marja married in Nepal and moved to a Lhomi village.

Olavi and Marja had a vision of bringing the seed, the word of God, to the Lhomi. Even though they struggled to learn the difficult language and underwent many kinds of problems over the years, they hoped for some fruit from their lives and Bible translation work. The people in their village, Chepuwa, recommended Jyabu Lhomi as language assistant for the Vesalainens. Jyabu proved very capable and later, in January 1978, he became the first Lhomi believer. The Vesalainens said, "Jyabu is like a father to Lhomi Christians and to the Lhomi Church. He served as the church planter, and we can praise the Lord for all the miraculous work he has done in the lives of the Lhomi people." The Lhomi New Testament was completed in 1995.

The Lhomi church began to grow.

I became a Christian in June 1991 and attended the Lhomi church in the village, but I could not sing and follow the Christian songs in Nepali. At that time the Vesalainens and Jyabu were praying about the need for songs and a songwriter in Lhomi.

As I and other Lhomi became believers, some of us began writing music in our own traditional styles. We had tried to sing and worship in Nepali, the country's official language, but it just didn't feel authentic. Furthermore, when we practiced singing Nepali songs, many struggled with the melody, sometimes missing it entirely or distorting it.

But when we sang songs in our own style—using the pentatonic scale—and culture, believers started crying in church, finding God's message in their own melodies.

The Lhomi people love to worship—an expression of gratitude to God for the freedom they now have from nightmares and demons, a freedom they've found in Christ. Their worship paints a picture of the rich cultural heritage of their people group.

The Lhomi culture and language are very different from that of the surrounding Nepalese. Because of this prevailing influence, we had forgotten over time how to play our own musical instruments. But when Christianity came to the Lhomi, it affected their society's social norms, values, and belief system. It gave birth to Christian music.

The Lord gave me an interest and vision to reform Lhomi songs and music. Later I learned to play Tibetan instruments in order to develop Lhomi Christian songs and music.

Since 1995 the Tibetan lute is now played in church, and since 2003, the Tibetan dulcimer. Our motivated musicians were all self-taught.

Through the Word preached in Lhomi, the Christian community is growing in numbers. Today some three hundred Lhomi believers are exploring their faith, using their own language and culture.

Because tunes are emerging from their own Lhomi culture and language, non-Christians enjoy the Christian music, too. The audience knows and appreciates that these are "our own" songs.

Lhomi worship gathering

INTRODUCTION · SECTION 1: FOUNDATIONS   SECTION 2: STORIES   SECTION 3: TOOLS   CLOSING

90. THE GOSPEL AND LOCAL ART FORMS

By B. E. Bharathi Nuthalapati

In the late nineteenth and early twentieth centuries, women in the villages of Andhra Pradesh, India, were reached with the gospel through "Bible women." These local Indian workers taught the Bible to seekers, generally to women only, in *zenanas* (women's quarters of a home). They also provided them with general education. They served either voluntarily or as paid workers of Christian missions.

When Bible women entered a village, they would first sing songs, standing at the street corners to attract the attention of local women. In the Indian church, and especially in Andhra Pradesh, songs provided a significant and common way to preach the gospel. Especially for Hindu women, songs and storytelling that matched their culture served as the two main entry points for the gospel.

One Bible woman related that for six months she stood in the street in front of a Hindu house and sang gospel songs until finally the family invited her to come sit on the veranda to listen to her message.

Because Bible women came from an oral culture, they could easily learn and teach the gospel through song. They adapted some of the native forms of folk singing to teach the Bible. One missionary mentioned that "women with their *ekonadam* (one-stringed drone) and their inexhaustible store of songs can sing the whole Bible into their listeners' hearts."[53]

Bible women also formed into troupes and performed before villagers to preach the gospel. Both men and women would assemble in the evening after their meals. For such gatherings, Bible women adapted traditional forms of ballads, such as the *harikatha*, *suddulu*, *burrakatha*, and others. Here follows an explanation of these forms.

Harikatha means "the story of the Lord." Usually used for religious teaching, it is a popular form of entertainment in rural areas. It is also known as *kalakshepam* in Tamil Nadu and Kerala. In *harikatha* the narrator, accompanied by music and using gestures and comments, assumes the role of all characters and recites dialogues and songs in a dramatic style. A female narrator is called a *bagavatarini*. The themes of the *katha* (story) are drawn from the Old Testament and the birth and death narratives of Jesus.

Suddulu is a type of folk song, a narration plus song. The narrator sings certain portions of the story and switches to narration.

---

53   M. L. Dolbeer, "The Caste Mass Movements in the Telugu Area," *National Christian Council Review* 52, no. 8 (August 1933): 425.

Burrakatha is a popular art form, especially in Andhra Pradesh. This ballad singing is named after the *burra* (tambour), a stringed instrument played by the main storyteller, a male or female. She plays the instrument moving forward and backward, dancing sometimes, and tells the story using songs and speech. Standing between two other performers, she holds the *tambour* on the right shoulder and wears *andelu* (brass rings with iron balls inside) on the thumb and index finger of the left hand, along with a handkerchief.

The two assistants, called *vantalu,* play earthen drums. They interrupt the storyteller with questions and sometimes add emphasis to the story by repeating parts of the song or by voicing short words or comments similar to "Wow," "Aha," or "That's it." They then catch up to the main singer, joining her on the last line or uttering the rhythmic phrase, "*Tandana tana.*"

Although today this kind of singing is a dying art, it was considered a powerful means of communication in the past. Such performances and songs were striking features of the ministry of the Bible women, and provided one of the main mediums of communication, especially at large gatherings. Whole villages opened up to the gospel through this singing ministry. By using the local folk music genre, Bible women localized the "alien" message of the Christian gospel.

305

INTRODUCTION

SECTION 1: FOUNDATIONS

SECTION 2: STORIES

SECTION 3: TOOLS

CLOSING

91. FILM AND ART OPEN TIBETAN HEARTS TO THE GOSPEL

By John Oswald

The best of storytellers so fire the imaginations of their audiences that their enrapt listeners remember and enthusiastically retell the story to others. Surely it should be no different with the gospel of Jesus. But how can this "greatest story ever told" be communicated so it becomes relevant to people whose understanding of life is very different from that of the people of the Bible?

In the following arts-rich story, I relate how one group of people responded to that challenge by drawing on a variety of vivid indigenous arts to share the biblical story in modern video form with Tibetan people.[54]

Two couples in Nepal dreamed of creating a storytelling tool that would help Tibetans understand the gospel and, specifically, overcome two typical reactions: (1) "Jesus is for Westerners," and (2) "This is just like Buddhism." Unfortunately, many Christian media unwittingly reinforce these misconceptions. The couples drew up plans for this production using artistic media that match both the culture and the subject matter. Then they assigned a year to research.

In 2002 the team met a dedicated and gifted film producer and also discovered a new movie called *The HOPE*. Created by Mars Hill Productions, this is a masterful eighty-minute dramatic motion picture of God's redemptive story, from creation to the return of Christ. This movie has already been translated into many languages[55] and addresses many of the Tibetan project's biblical needs. Mars Hill gave the team permission for the existing movie to become the foundation for an extended one about a Tibetan man searching for truth, discovering answers through the Bible, and eventually becoming a storyteller of God's promised deliverer, Jesus. Using Tibetan song, dance, art, and poetic narration, the Tibetan movie tells the Bible's story of hope for all humanity.[56]

---

54   The resulting production is known as the Tibetan *HOPE* DVD. This project is sometimes referred to as *REWA HOPE*, to mark it as the Tibetan version, after the Tibetan word for "hope" (*rewa*) and its title *Rewa'i Namthar (The Story of Hope)*.

55   For an up-to-date list of *The HOPE* in different languages, see http://www.mars-hill.org/media/the_hope_main/chart.html

56   The entire movie and all its songs and artwork can be accessed on the project website http://www.rewahope.com by clicking the video, music, or art icons.

This adaptation currently exists in Central Tibetan, with options for English and Tibetan subtitles. Subtitles will be added in other languages. New dubbed versions of the movie will be produced in various languages for people groups who share Tibetan culture.

MUSIC, DANCE, AND DRAMA

Five lyrical songs reinforce the film's storyline and provide time for reflection. Two use an indigenous question-and-answer format and, in keeping with Tibetans' love of music videos, four are choreographed with Tibetan regional dances. The final song is a call to all nations to join the dance of faith in Christ, illustrated (in the revised version) by Thai, Nepalese, Indian, Mongolian, Filipino, and Western dance, as well as diverse Tibetan styles.

Most of these songs are also dramatised, including one where demonic beings are portrayed[57] with masks that draw on cultural imagery. The third song is a poignant lament in soaring nomadic style. In all five songs, the videography features the striking landscape of the high-altitude plateau.

Since animal blood sacrifice in the Old Testament elicits profound disgust in Buddhists, an additional dramatic scene uses an analogy from Tibetan life, graphically demonstrating how nomads build pits to catch wolves, which prey on their flocks. They lure the wolf into the pit with a lone sheep, sacrificed to save the rest of the flock. This illustrates both the concept of a substitutionary death and the meaning of the death of Christ, making it clear that now no more animal sacrifice is needed.

ARTWORK

The project team commissioned four exquisite and intricate paintings (*thangkas*) of the type traditionally used by traveling religious storytellers in teaching Buddhist stories. Two canvases depict Old Testament stories and two show New Testament scenes.

RESPONSES

This contextualized production has been used in two main ways: showing the DVD or telling the Bible's central storyline in person, using posters of the paintings. Responses to both have been extremely warm. Tibetan audiences love the songs, dances, and artwork. Some even join in the dances while watching the DVD!

One Buddhist monk read parts of the Bible and concluded that Christianity was just like Buddhism. Then he heard the story twice more, once told by a visitor using the paintings and again by watching the DVD. By the next day he had a radically revised conclusion—"This is not the same"—and what's more, he was hardly recognizable. He was dressed in layman's clothes, a sure sign of his new allegiance to Jesus!

---

57   In a revised version. Two dances were refilmed in 2011.

A woman believer was thrilled that she was now able to grasp how the Old Testament relates to the New and said she wanted to show this DVD to her husband and other villagers.

The *thangka* paintings have also been well received. The following four reports illustrate the way the posters have been used separately from the DVD in a wide variety of geographical contexts.[58]

In southwest China a believer shared the paintings with a group of Tibetans in a village for a couple of hours. A man at the back was talking, smoking, and not paying much attention. Later he started to listen to the stories more and became very interested. In the end, he believed and later learned to tell the stories himself using the *thangkas*.

In India a cross-cultural worker used the *thangkas* in teaching. He said, "People are very responsive." He reports that they enjoy listening to the Bible story in conjunction with the *thangkas* and, although they are initially surprised at their own conclusions, they readily accept the posters as both Tibetan and Christian.

In a remote, high-altitude town in China, a lady used the *thangka* posters at a Christmas celebration, preceded by much prayer and fasting. To her delight, a local teacher opened his family home to her. She said, "When I started telling the story, while showing the *thangkas* (Genesis to Revelation), the teacher stood up and helped translate. We really felt Father's presence!" The *thangkas* were passed around because people wanted to look at them again and again.

From Thailand, a missionary reported: "We are actually going to a village tonight where we have shared the gospel now two times using these posters. They are very useful, and the pastor who is sharing the story said that these can be used both to proclaim the gospel and also to teach believers."

CONCLUSION

The overwhelming feedback to the DVD and artwork shows that it is not simply the story but the way it is presented that helps hearers respond in new ways. It is the use of familiar forms of music, dance, and art, and culturally evocative scenes, that engenders this positive reaction. Presented in this way, Christ not only comes as deliverer for other people, but he addresses this audience much more directly—through film and the arts—as Tibetans.

---

58   For a fuller account, please see a blog by artist Scott Rayl, "Tibetan Christian Thangka Ministry," *Indigenous Jesus*, November 22, 2011, http://indigenousjesus.blogspot.com/2011/11/tibetan-christian-thangka-ministry.html.

92. GEOMETRIC DESIGNS AND SYMBOLIC COLORS: VISUAL GOSPEL CONTEXTUALIZATION AMONG HINDU IMMIGRANTS

By Scott Rayl

Cody C. Lorance has a heart for Hindu peoples living in diaspora and a special, deep love for Nepalis. His personal, day-to-day fieldwork is among immigrant peoples in the Chicago metro area, where he serves as the senior pastor and church planting leader for Trinity International Baptist Mission.

Because life-cycle events are very important to Nepalis, Cody is in the process of designing ceremonies that point people to Christ—ones for use at births, marriages, deaths, and more. He recently performed his first Christocentric Naam Karan—a baby-naming ceremony. He began the ceremony by creating a type of *rangoli* or *yantra*—a geometric design made with rice flour—on the floor where the ceremony was to take place. Dropping flour from his hand in intersecting lines, he created a large image pointing out in every direction: north, south, east, west, and directions in between. At the end of each line, another design is created, either a full waterpot (*purna kalash*) or a flower. Actual waterpots and plates of rice are then placed on the end of each line.

Lorance contextualizes a baby-naming ceremony by creating a *rangoli* and explaining its meaning

As he creates the design, he explains to the attendees that God is omnipresent, that the Bible teaches we cannot go anywhere he is not. He adds that the waterpots, flowers, and rice remind us that God desires to bless those who trust in him. This message is especially powerful to diasporic peoples, who are scattered and feel alone.

In addition, Cody seeks to provide a worshipful atmosphere by creating a visual display in the room where the Nepali church services are conducted. For example, he places crosses, candles, and incense in groups of three on the altar at the front of the room to suggest the Trinity. Also, a variety of colors are used throughout the room to symbolize specific ideas. The room's walls are painted yellow, a color associated with sacredness in Nepal and with heaven among Nepalese Christians. Greens, browns, and earth tones signify the earthly life of Christ, while purple is used during Lent to suggest mourning and repentance. Gold is added after the Resurrection, and orange is included as the Hindu holiday of Diwali approaches—to symbolize the victory of holiness over evil, and light over darkness. Red, an auspicious color for Nepalis, is also used throughout the Christmas season. Contextualized music and participatory worship round out the engagement of the senses.

93. RHYTHM AND RHYMES
By Eric Sarwar

On a hot, soporific day in May 2005, I was teaching music classes in the Habib Girls School, the largest Shiite girls school in Karachi, Pakistan. I had been working at this school as a music teacher for nine years and considered it my mission field. We were practicing a mode of classical Indian music, just waiting for the bell to ring, when a message from the head mistress of the nursery section called me into her office. She showed me a letter from the Aga Khan Education Board announcing a one-day seminar on "The Role of Music in a Montessori Curriculum." She had decided to send me, along with two other teachers and herself.

Arriving at the seminar we found more than thirty heads of various nursery schools, with their staff. We were surprised to see that the leader was a Muslim woman, trained in the UK in the Montessori teaching method, and that some Islamic scholars and clerics were present and sitting separately from the other attendees.

The leader began the seminar by questioning the Islamic scholars about the authenticity and use of music in education and for the betterment of society, according to Islamic theology and jurisprudence. All through the seminar my mind revolved around this question: *Why are they struggling to justify the use of music in education in the face of orthodox Islam's condemnation of music (which they called an abomination)?*

While sitting in the seminar, I felt a burden in my spirit for Christian children in Pakistan. *"In their schools and circles of friends,"* I wondered, *"how can they ever face such questions and arguments regarding their own faith? As a church, what*

Singing practice before recording

help have we given them? How are we using the power of music in our own Christian education?" The Bible tells us to sing songs in our worship, which we have been doing for centuries. Music has also played a key role in every movement of revival in church history.

This seminar motivated me to produce an album of worship songs for children. But the problem was, how to do it. What kind of songs would I need to write and compose? Which subjects should I choose from the Bible? Who would sing them? Where would I record the album, and who would arrange the music? Where would the necessary funding come from? I had a burden and vision but not a single penny to complete the task.

After praying, I researched what albums had already been produced. I was shocked to discover that not a single one had been created for children by any church or Christian music producer during the last twenty years in Pakistan.

For Christians, life today in Pakistan is not easy. Children face hostile questions from Muslims, such as, "Why do you have three gods? Why did you change the Bible? Why do you call Jesus 'Son of God'?" And comments such as, "Jesus was not crucified."

With the urgent need to provide Christian workers with resources to strengthen children in this Islamic context, we produced two CDs of children's songs. The first uses folk tunes to teach the story of Creation, the Ten Commandments, some Psalms, the Beatitudes, the Lord's Prayer, and various New Testament stories. The second album contains festival songs for Christmas, the New Year, Easter, and Palm Sunday, together with a few action songs. Both albums were launched at Pakistan's largest Christian convention, held in Sialkot since 1905. Additional launches were held in 2005 and 2006 in Karachi, Lahore, Faisalabad, and Quetta.

Setting up the studio for a recording session

God has blessed these two albums as a worship resource for churches throughout Pakistan. According to the Pakistan Sunday School Ministry's 2010 report, more than 2 million children all over the country are using these albums. Urdu/Hindi speaking congregations around the world are also using these albums to nourish the future church. Meanwhile, a third album, *Miracles and Parables of Christ,* is being prepared for distribution to Asian congregations.

I was also impressed with the need for similar resources for the youth of Pakistan. I wanted to write and compose songs that addressed the issues they were facing, especially during recent waves of persecution. And I desired to engage the churches as much as possible. I invited writers to compose songs.

Because it is very hard in Pakistan to find vocalists within our Christian community, producing our worship resources usually involve non-Christian singers. We have tried our level best to take musicians from the Christian community, and in an effort to develop Christian artists we tried out singers from our annual Psalm Festival. But it didn't work out. However, praise the Lord, two Christian *tabla* and *dholak* players were found in Karachi. Incredibly, a rhythm recording session of a song based on Ecclesiastes 12 led a dholak player to confess his sins. There is rejoicing in heaven over one sinner that repents (Luke 15:7)! During this album's compilation we added two new vocalists to our team. Praise God, they are still with us.

Recording with choir group

For the launch of our album entitled *Awake!* in Karachi in 2009, a Christian group of professional dancers was invited to perform live to the tracks, with youth groups, church leaders, and congregations from various churches attending. This was the first attempt to use music and dance together for a Christian worship album, engaging Christian artists for the glory of God.

Since then our CDs and video DVDs have been distributed to all the main churches and Christian bookstores in cities across Pakistan and also abroad in the US and Europe.

INTRODUCTION

SECTION 1: FOUNDATIONS

SECTION 2: STORIES

SECTION 3: TOOLS

CLOSING

ASIA—SOUTHEAST

94. BORN ACROSS BORDERS, RAISED IN A REFUGEE CAMP: THE HISTORY OF THE CAMBODIAN HYMNAL

By Alice Compain

Alice Compain, the veteran OMF International missionary to Cambodia and Laos, died in Pembury, Kent, UK, on September 4, 2008, at the age of 74. Alice was prepared by God to be a missionary to Laos and Cambodia. Born into a multilingual Christian family in London, English, French, and German were the languages of the home. At the age of six she began to play the violin, which would prove the key to much of her subsequent service.

She was converted as a teenager and called to missionary service while at the Royal College of Music. Bible college in France further equipped her for service in French-speaking Indochina. As a member of the Overseas Missionary Fellowship, she went to Laos in 1959. It is due mainly to Alice that the Lao and Cambodian churches can sing the praises of God not only in their own languages but also in their own cultural music forms.

We include this article written several years ago by Alice Compain as a tribute to this dedicated ethnodoxologist.

God created man in his image and blessed man with creative and artistic gifts. (Is that because God delights to create wonderful things himself?) I have discovered these diverse gifts in the cultures of Southeast Asia where I have been living the last forty years. My own music training for orchestral playing and teaching did not touch on ethnomusicology, yet I have always been fascinated by the different folk music styles of Europe. Why did God send me to the end of the earth, namely the little-known, land-locked country of Laos? He had an important item on his agenda for me.

Early missionaries had translated and put together a hymnbook of Western tunes. The one exception was the "New Jerusalem" hymn sung to the national anthem's melody. While I stayed in a Lao home to facilitate my language learning, I soon picked up some local songs from the young people. I notated them to help me remember the unusual melodies. Later, when put with new words, the best of these stirring songs were incorporated into an enlarged hymnbook, which is now being used by the Lao church the world over.

In 1974 I moved to Cambodia to teach at the Takhmau Bible Institute. The Khmer Rouge had not yet taken over, but they reminded us of their stranglehold on the city of Phnom Penh through daily rocket attacks. I soon found that Cambodians are very artistic. On the bas-reliefs of their twelfth-century temples in Angkor Thom we see a variety of instruments, most of which are still played today.

As in Laos, we found Christians writing their own hymns to traditional tunes—all in the public domain—used alongside the existing hymnbook of Western tunes. A famous musician, Mao Vinna, well-known for his youth songs, became a Christian in 1974 and had the vision to encourage indigenous hymn writers. Sadly, during the Khmer Rouge's reign of terror, he and many other Christians lost their lives. Only one student survived from a class of twenty I had taught for a year; I was able to meet up with that student in 1980 in a Thai refugee camp.

It was in such an unlikely place that the writing of Christian songs started up again. An Overseas Missionary Fellowship (now OMF International) colleague suggested that the refugee camp Christians translate some indigenous hymns produced in central Thailand. They recognized some of the tunes as actually being Khmer (the official language of Cambodia) in origin. (Seven centuries of cross-cultural exchange have affected Thai and Cambodian so that they share 30 percent vocabulary, though pronunciation varies.) These hymns translated from Thai were a great success, so some of the new believers started applying their newfound faith in writing poetry. They adapted traditional tunes so as to match various meters of their new songs. Some wrote paraphrases of the Psalms and other Scripture passages that could be chanted, rather like Scottish and French Psalms of the Reformation. Bible stories were put into verse, enabling them to be enacted in their theater forms, which always include dance and music. A rich heritage was being preserved and used in a fulfilling way for worship and evangelism in the Christian context.

> As in Laos, we found Christians writing their own hymns to traditional tunes.

I gathered all the songs I could and tried to jot down the tunes from tapes, but did not compile them in a book until a missionary colleague (Don Cormack, author of *Killing Fields, Living Fields*) challenged me to get on with it. My initial prayer was to find a Khmer Christian musician and poet who could edit and check all the material. God answered and put me in touch with Sarin Sam (pronounced "Som") in 1982. He started writing hymns himself, sometimes taking lyrics of Western hymns like "O for a Thousand Tongues to Sing" and rewriting them in Khmer.

The first edition of this book, called *Holy Khmer Songs*, came out in 1985. It proved to be extremely popular among Cambodians living abroad, for obvious reasons. Each following edition was expanded and included songs from another gifted writer, Barnabas Mam (pronounced "Mom"). Sarin emigrated to Australia and was soon resetting the hymnbook on the computer, a great improvement over the Khmer typewriter! The latest Kymer edition (1993) has over three hundred indigenous hymns—surely a feat for a small country with only a few believers.

Christians in Cambodia gather every Sunday in over one thousand groups, mostly in village homes. They sing in the language of their hearts, using their own music and poetry. The adults find Western songs difficult and foreign sounding, and often adapt the time and rhythm to make them more comfortable to sing.

Young people learn Western praise songs, but rarely sing them "correctly." Some of them were trained by Pastor David Bin to compose and arrange their own Cambodian songs. David was trained in Berlin and is indeed God's gift to the Khmer church for developing their music and worship. Another professionally trained musician is Naomi Sharp from England who teaches at the Music School attached to the University of Fine Arts. She encouraged the budding musicians to praise God in a meaningful Khmer style.

There are some minority groups in Cambodia, primarily in the east, who do not find singing Khmer songs easy because they are so different from their own indigenous musical styles. Though some of the instruments are similar in design, the minority musical systems differ from that used by the Khmer people. These minority groups are just beginning to create their own indigenous hymnodies. But for the Khmer people, God has already done a mighty work in raising up composers and musicians who have had a great impact.

Indeed God created Cambodians in his own image, and he has delighted to give them creative and artistic gifts. *Soli Deo gloria.*

95. FAITH AND THE ARTS IN BALI'S DIVERSE, CREATIVE CULTURE[59]

By John D. Pierce

Bali, Indonesia, is a haven for international artists. Since 1996, Jonathan and Tina Bailey have been living and serving within this diverse, vibrant, and talented community of artists, where they encourage Christians to be true to their culture, craft, and calling.

Tina, a native of Springfield, Georgia, is a dancer, visual artist, and graduate of the Savannah College of Art and Design. Jonathan, from Simpsonville, South Carolina, specializes in music and literature. They serve through the Cooperative Baptist Fellowship global missions program. "We walked through the doors that opened," said Tina. "[The larger art community] knows that we are Christians and artists and involved in the International Christian Church . . . We are artist-ministers working as coordinators for the Arts and Community Engagement. Our hope is that our work will open up doors of dialogue across religious and cultural lines that will enable an authentic experience of Christ."

Tina and Jonathan encourage Christian artists to use their gifts of music, dance, and visual arts to express faith in a way that is true to their own culture. In doing so, the Baileys believe, relationships are built across cultural barriers and authentic expressions of faith get heard.

Bali, Indonesia is a haven for international artists

Tina is a dancer, a visual artist, and a graduate of the Savannah College of Art

---

59   Originally published in a slightly different form in John Pierce, "Faith and the Arts: Baileys Share in Bali's Diverse, Creative Culture," *Baptists Today News Journal* 29, no. 8 (August 2011): 4–5, http://issuu.com/baptiststoday/docs/btaugust11_071611final?mode=a_p&wmode=0. Reprinted by permission of John Pierce.

Tina and Jonathan Bailey

Dance is one point where faith and art connect.

Sanur, Bali

"We don't see the arts as a tool," said Tina. "It's not a means to an end; it's an authentic way to be."

"Christian artist" can be a tough tag to wear in Bali, as well as in other cultures. If the artists' works are not solely focused on overtly Christian symbols and themes, fellow Christians will often criticize them for straying from or compromising their faith commitments. On the other hand, the larger arts community can see Christian artists as being one-dimensional, with less commitment to artistic expression than to getting across a religious message.

So Jonathan and Tina offer encouragement and support to Christian artists and help create opportunities for engagement with the larger arts community. From art exhibits to music and dance classes, to enhancing the use of arts in worship, the Baileys are finding many points where faith and art connect.

In every creative form of art—music, painting, dance—the Baileys see a connection to the Creator. "We see it as a gift from God," said Jonathan. He and Tina are helping artists grow in their own creativity and see themselves as gifts from God, as well. They offer spiritual formation retreats, cross-cultural art projects, creativity/body awareness workshops, interfaith music collaborations, art and spiritual formation, dance, visual art exhibits, *gamelan* lessons and performance, and care for international students.

"It's not a new idea," said Jonathan. "It is what the Church did for a millennium or more," noting its role in music, architecture, and other forms of art.

The Baileys feel not everyone understands how art can be an intrinsic part of life and faith for people in many cultures. For those who don't appreciate art or can't grasp how this could be a means of Christian service, Tina and Jonathan speak of a more common basis for their work: relationship building. "Our work is about as traditional as it gets," said Tina. "It's about relationships."

Jonathan added, "We live in a community where the arts are a way to relate; in fact, a primary way."

Growing, trusting relationships provide opportunities for the Baileys to host an artist-in-residence program, teach summer art classes in Hungary, and communicate faith in ways that are understood and appreciated in a pluralistic and artistic culture.

The Baileys often have artists and other guests come to participate in their classes and worship, and they invite collaboration and partnership. One visiting pastor told them that churches in US could learn some important things from their ways of engaging the arts community.

96. BALINESE CHRISTIAN PAINTER NYOMAN DARSANE: "BALI IS MY BODY. CHRIST IS MY LIFE."

By Scott Rayl

Nyoman Darsane is a Balinese Christian painter (batik and canvas), musician, dancer, and shadow puppeteer. He was born in 1939 to rice farmers, and his father played in the Indonesian orchestra (*gamelan*) of the local king. Due to his family's close contact with this ruler, Darsane was raised and educated in the king's palace along with one of the princes. Through this royal education he learned Balinese culture and religion (Hinduism), along with the cultural art forms he is known for today.

When Darsane later studied art at Universitas Diponegoro in Java, he met a Christian woman there named Deze, who introduced him to faith in Jesus. After finishing art school and returning to Bali, he eventually became a professional artist and teacher.

Nyoman Darsane's *He Came Down* (1978)[60]

As Darsane sought ways to combine Balinese arts with the message of the gospel, his motto became "Bali is my body. Christ is my life." Initially he was rejected by his family and community after becoming a Christian, but over the years Darsane has recaptured much of his family's respect because of his commitment to remain Balinese in his Christian art and life.

While attending art school, Darsane was exposed to a variety of Western art forms, which he incorporates into his evolving painting style, one that portrays biblical elements and simultaneously maintains a strong Balinese identity. He frequently features biblical characters in Balinese dance positions.

This earlier painting by Darsane, *He Came Down*, portrays the humility of Christ coming into human experience and sharing the life of the people. The worshiper prays with a lotus blossom

---

60 See https://picasaweb.google.com/lh/photo/SN-2CLe_SKv5uNv7X1ZYoA.

between her fingers in an attitude common to the people of Bali. Images of demons are pushed to the edges of the frame by the light that Jesus brings.

The demons in this painting are derived from carved, wooden masks representing the mythical creature known in Bali as Banaspati Raja (King of the Forest), also called the Barong Ket.

Every Balinese village has a Barong whom it considers its guardian. The Barong mask is a means of both giving the spirit tangible form and harnessing its energy. Stored in the village temple, the mask is brought out on special occasions and asked to bestow blessings on the community or restore the balance of cosmic forces. At these times, the Barong might be placed on an altar or worn, along with a full body costume, in ceremonial processions or theatrical events. During sacred performances, two members of the community dance the Barong mask and costume, which together can weigh as much as one hundred pounds. When a dancer, another performer, or an audience member falls into a trance, it is believed that the spirit of the Barong has been successfully invoked.

Nyoman Darsane's *The Angel's Whisper* (2002)[61]

Dancing is a form of worship in Bali. The Balinese believe that the dancer performs before the gods, delighting them. The gods take possession of them while they dance.

In *The Angel's Whisper* we see Mary, the mother of Jesus, dressed in a white blouse dappled with gold designs. Her colorful Balinese *sarong* is covered by a golden wrap that reaches to her knees. She wears a crown topped with white flowers. Mary's virginity is underscored by the fact that only premenstrual virgin girls are allowed to dance before the gods. She uses hand gestures called *mudras* as she dances.

Looking over her right shoulder, Mary sees a figure who resembles an angel. The appearance of the angel is based on a shadow puppet, or *wayang*, figure. He appears out of the abstract background to blow/whisper into Mary's ear through a lotus blossom that he holds between his hands. His message of the birth of a savior sets Mary into motion.

Darsane's paintings represent a fusing of form and content, where the gospel infuses the culture and can't be peeled away. Many of the concepts and images in his work would be familiar and recognizable to a Balinese but probably not to a Western Christian.

---

61   See http://www.omsc.org/art-at-omsc/darsane/angels-whisper-slide.html, Copyright: OMSC.

INTRODUCTION

SECTION 1: FOUNDATIONS

SECTION 2: STORIES

SECTION 3: TOOLS

CLOSING

INTRODUCTION

SECTION 1: FOUNDATIONS

SECTION 2: STORIES

SECTION 3: TOOLS

CLOSING

97. SAWAI CHINNAWONG: THE GOSPEL IN TRADITIONAL THAI ART

By Scott Rayl

Sawai Chinnawong is a member of the faculty of Payap University in Chiang Mai, Thailand, and also a minister of Thailand's United Church of Christ. He is an ethnic Mon who was born in Burma and moved to Thailand with his family as a young man. Formerly Buddhist, at age twenty-three he became a Christian while studying art in a vocational school in Bangkok.

Sawai's love for art began at an early age when he witnessed some elderly men painting a wall mural in a Buddhist temple; he would watch them paint for hours each day. Sawai's artistic interests continued into adulthood, and after his conversion he entered seminary at Payap University. While there he began creating liturgical art, and since then his paintings have been exhibited in Asia, Europe, and the United States. He was one of five artists chosen for the summer 2007 exhibition The Christian Story: Five Asian Artists Today, held at the Museum of Biblical Art in New York City, and from 2003 to 2004 he was the Paul T. Lauby Artist in Residence at the Overseas Ministries Study Center.

More recently he completed a book of contextualized New Testament illustrations called *That Man Who Came to Us*, cowritten with Paul DeNeui of North Park University. The book

> Christians in Thailand have generally been adverse to accepting an art style with such a "Buddhist" appearance. However, Sawai was able to sway many of them with a more abstract style that he developed.

tells the story of the life of Jesus Christ through traditional Thai art. Featuring black and white line drawings inspired by an art form born in northern and central Thailand, *That Man* tells the story of Christ as fully God, yet fully human. Artist Sawai Chinnawong employs the regions' popular distinctive artistic style originally used to depict Buddhist moral principles and other religious themes.

The text of the book avoids "Christian lingo" so that it might be distributed among Buddhists in Thailand, though it is still too early to tell how they will respond to it.

Christians in Thailand have generally been adverse to accepting an art style with such a "Buddhist" appearance. However, Sawai was able to sway many of them with a more abstract style that he developed for the stained glass windows of the Hamlin Chapel at McGilvary College of Divinity, Payap University. His designs for the windows (and accompanying wall paintings) utilize symbols rather than figures. Along with their vibrant colors, these window designs have resonated deeply with Thai churches and have been accepted as a legitimate form of Thai-inspired church design.

Sawai continues to create art inspired by his Christian faith and Thai identity as the artist in residence at Payap University. In so doing he strives to show how the beauty of Thailand's art history can be refocused to affirm the unique message of the gospel in Jesus Christ.

98. INDONESIAN SHADOW PUPPETRY ILLUMINATES BIBLE STORIES

By Scott Rayl

The Indonesian art form of *wayang* (shadow puppetry), has been used for centuries to tell the sacred stories of Hinduism. *Wayang* puppetry probably began after the arrival of Hinduism in Indonesia during the first century AD, though there may have been a form of oral drama present before that. The Museum of International Folk Art states that "most likely, the Hindu stories were applied to indigenous beliefs and local shadow puppet traditions, melding into a uniquely Javanese custom."

As time went on, wandering puppeteers (*dalang*) traveled from village to village to give performances and tell of news from the outside world. The *dalangs* were (and still are) held in high esteem by Indonesians. Most performances are spoken in classical Javanese and last a whole night or longer! Today, *wayang* performances are less frequent but are still an integral part of many Indonesian weddings and other traditional functions. They can also be seen at cultural centers, festivals, and special performances for tourists.

With the arrival of Islam into the islands of Indonesia, Muslim leaders prohibited the representation of God or human figures in art. In response, Islamic religious leaders made puppets from leather in a flat, two-dimensional style, so that only the shadows of the puppets could be seen on a screen. This style of puppetry (*wayang kulit*) is the most prevalent form still used today, by both Muslims and Hindus, and is most popular in Java and Bali. *Kulit* means "skin" and refers to the leather from which the puppets are constructed.

As mentioned above, the *wayang* stories last for several hours and are performed at night from behind a sheet illuminated by a light. The shadows of the puppets are projected onto the sheet, and the audience watches from the other side. The puppeteer

> plays the most important role in the performance as he operates all the puppets, performs all the narration and dialogue, sings the songs, and directs the musicians. He must be highly skilled to manipulate, direct, sing, and story-tell; for example, if he is using both hands to hold puppets, he would use his foot to cue the signals to the musicians.[62]

---

62   Gandhi Muljadi and Angeline Muljadi, "Wayang," Batik 'n Craft, http://www.batikncraft.com/art-in-indonesia/wayang.

The performances are accompanied by a live Indonesian orchestra called a *gamelan,* which accompanies dance and puppet performances, rituals, or ceremonies.

In 1960 a Catholic version of shadow theater called *wayang wahyu* was created in central Java by Brother Timotheus L. Wignyosoebroto as a way to communicate the stories and ideas in the Bible. Much of the following information came from Marzanna Poplawska.[63]

Wignyosoebroto's idea for creating *wayang wahyu* came after he saw "a performance of shadow theatre by M. M. Atmowijoyo, who presented a story taken from the Old Testament ("*Dawud Mendapat Wahyu Kraton*" [David Receives Divine Revelation]), using ordinary wayang puppets." Wignyosoebroto's use of wayang for the purpose of communicating stories and information fits into the historical tradition of the art form because it had been used for centuries,

> first by sultans and later by the Indonesian government to spread their policies. Traditional wayang was also meant to provide ethical and moral education based on different religions and philosophies. However, this was always done in a nondogmatic, nontheoretic, and often humorous way, that is, calling for an individual meditative approach, making choices for oneself, and looking for the best way of living life. The Christian Church adapted this philosophical and spiritual approach quite successfully. In this light, the special role undertaken by wayang wahyu to strengthen and broaden Catholic spirituality is quite understandable.

Wayang wahyu performances tend to emphasize Old Testament stories because they often involve more action than New Testament stories, though there are performances that portray the life, death, and resurrection of Jesus.

The *wayang wahyu* performances are usually reserved for special occasions, such as Christmas, Easter, and Pentecost, or anniversaries of particular churches, Catholic schools, or universities. The local Catholic church and/or individual Catholics sponsor the performances. Poplawska writes that "the performances of wayang wahyu are on the whole quite expensive, [and] therefore [are] not very often held. Their rarity is also caused by difficulty in gathering performers. There are only a few wayang wahyu dhalang [dalang], who are often busy with other activities."

> **Use of wayang for the purpose of communicating stories and information fits into the historical tradition of the art form.**

Apparently the golden period of *wayang wahyu* was from 1970 to 1990. After 1990, support for the art form began to decline among Catholics and today "is known only in rather small Christian circles." But in the last few years the practitioners of wayang wahyu have redoubled their efforts to revive it from its decline. Their current organization is a foundation called Paguyuban Wayang Wahyu.

Regarding *wayang wahyu's* future, Poplawska writes that it

> seems to depend on the efforts of particular individuals: priests who are interested in traditional arts, artists who are Christian, and those interested in experimenting in diverse areas. It unquestionably constitutes one of the domains of creativity for Javanese artists of Christian and also non-Christian background. Wayang wahyu . . . is an

example of the vitality of the traditional arts in Java, which unceasingly find new forms to manifest themselves. They are still developing, perhaps in directions unexpected and unforeseen by some of the early twentieth-century anthropologists, who lamented the annihilation of traditional cultures that was inevitable with the entry of Western religions and missionaries.

Lastly, Poplawska mentions a Protestant form of *wayang* called *wayang prajanjian,* which was invented in the 1970s. She writes that "wayang prajanjian takes its name from the word *prajanjian,* referring in Javanese to the Bible and its Old and New Testament." Unfortunately, there is little information available about *wayang prajanjian* on the Internet.

99. SINGING FROM THE HILLS[64]

By Janet Seever

Ben and Erna Thiessen had the opportunity to watch a woman in the southern Philippines sing the Scriptures from her mother-tongue translation of the Bible. A makeshift recording studio had been set up in a home for the singer and her helpers to record the book of Genesis in song.

"It was a very moving experience," writes Ben, "to see this young woman read a chapter of Genesis, make a few marks on the paper and then flawlessly sing the whole chapter in a beautiful, clear voice. During a break she shared how in their culture they stand on top of the hills and sing to the neighboring villages—now a way of singing Scriptures to and with their neighbors.

"While the words were in another language, the singing sounded to us 'like an angel singing,' and the Spirit of God reminded us, 'These are my children; this is my Word.' What a glorious gathering it will be when 'every nation, tribe, people, and language' will gather before the throne of God to sing, speak, and dance the eternal words of God Almighty!"

---

64   Originally published in a slightly different form in Janet Seever, "Singing from the Hills," *Prayer Alive* (Wycliffe Canada newsletter, Fall 2007): 11. Used by permission of Janet Seever.

CARIBBEAN AND AUSTRALIA

100. "I DON'T THINK IN ENGLISH!"

By Jo-Ann Faith Richards

In an inner-city, evangelical church in Kingston, Jamaica, about twenty people of various ages sat in a semicircle in the small sanctuary as we prepared to study the story of the Prodigal Son. We were using Scriptures in Jamaican Creole for the first time.

First, we all read the story together in English from the New International Version, which was projected on a screen. I then read it aloud again in Jamaican Creole, or Patois/Patwa as it is commonly called.

During the reading in Creole, the atmosphere in the room changed markedly. The listeners became deeply involved in the story and the session became highly interactive. When I finished reading, one bright-faced teenage boy declared, "That was so much clearer!" In itself that remark was significant, but the comments of an older woman took the veil off my eyes. She said, "When we were reading the English, it was just words on a page. But when you read it in Patwa, I could see pictures." She then made the comment that was life-changing for me: "The thing is, I don't think in English; I think in Patwa. Whenever I hear anything in English, I have to stop and process it. That means I am missing a lot of what's going on!"

As a world traveler who has participated in worship conducted in languages other than English—the language in which I think most of the time—I suddenly got it! Now I see clearly that we absolutely must move toward bilingual worship in Jamaica, including culturally relevant expressions of worship in the language in which most Jamaicans think!

101. MEET KEVIN "NANA MOSES" CALVERT

By Jo-Ann Faith Richards

Long twisted hair flying, bright eyes flashing, brilliant and perfectly aligned teeth on full display, head swinging from side to side as he flies through the air and bounces around, he leads his audience in singing along with him to the captivating strains of one of his own compositions, "*In Evriting Wi Du Wi Hafi Priez Im!*" ("In Everything We Do We Have to Praise Him!"). No, he is *not* a madman, as he emphatically declares in one of his poems. This is Kevin Calvert ministering live and in living color.

Born and raised in the lush, green parish of Portland on the eastern side of Jamaica, storyteller, poet, and songwriter Kevin Calvert has an ever-increasing passion for communicating the good news of Jesus Christ to his native Jamaican people, using the language and artistic expressions that connect with them at the deepest level. Because of his desire to blend theology with culture, he has done studies in both disciplines at the University of the West Indies at Mona, in Jamaica.

> Just talking to people will likely deliver the message only to the head. Translating it skillfully into visual art, poetry, storytelling, dance, drama, and music ensures that it will go straight to the heart.

Kevin's most recent project brings into sharp focus an issue affecting communities on a global scale—human trafficking. Utilizing all the major art forms, Kevin, or "Nana Moses" as he is commonly called, weaves a tale of intrigue based in a fictitious rural community called Buck Up. The production *Where Is Melissa?* is designed to not only entertain but to highlight the role that each member of society must play in protecting our children and other fellow citizens from the horrors of human trafficking, and to mobilize the members of the audience to action. Kevin understands very well that just talking to people will likely deliver the message only to the head. Translating it skillfully into visual art, poetry, storytelling, dance, drama, and music ensures that it will go straight to the heart.

The idea for Where Is Melissa? came from a study done by Rev. Dr. Margaret Fowler, a minister with the United Church in Jamaica and the Cayman Islands. So often academic works are created that address issues confronting the average man in the street but do not offer opportunities to interact. One of Kevin's passions is to use his work to create a circle wide enough to include both the intellectual and the nonintellectual in "reasonings" on issues that concern us all.

Kevin Calvert is founder and CEO of Kairos Creations, a Jamaican company committed to developing and promoting new artistes, and to producing culturally relevant artistic expressions. Under this umbrella he has also created a presentation called *Artical Worship,* which utilizes a wide range of arts to draw his audience into worship. Kevin's publications under the Kairos Creations label include *Fire in the Ashes,* a rich compilation of poetry and music covering a wide range of themes, and a Christmas album entitled *Love at Christmas.* His ministry is fully endorsed by the United Church in Jamaica and has spread outside of Jamaica to include countries in Europe and other territories in the English-speaking Caribbean.

102. REHAB IN JAMAICA: CREOLE SONGS AND SCRIPTURE

By Jo-Ann Faith Richards

The boys, some already hardened criminals, sat staring at me, sullen. Not there by choice, these thirteen- to eighteen-year-olds wanted to make sure my three colleagues and I knew this. We were conducting devotions in a facility for juvenile delinquents in Kingston, Jamaica.

We started by singing Scripture-based songs in Creole. Some of the boys began to loosen up. We then read the story of Zacchaeus in English. Stony faces returned. I then read the same story in Creole. What a transformation! The boys came alive, some even laughing as the story unfolded. At the end of the reading, they applauded enthusiastically.

On the spur of the moment, the leader of our outreach group asked me to "bring the Word." I, who had never delivered a message in Creole before, recognized it would be a huge mistake to speak to those boys in English. In fact, I thought it would have conveyed disrespect to them. I breathed a silent prayer for the Holy Spirit's assistance and continued in Creole. They listened keenly, appearing to hang on each word.

The leader then sang a song that tied everything together. At the conclusion of the meeting, when the boys were invited to give their lives over to Jesus Christ, almost every one was on his feet!

After that encounter, the director of the facility asked us to conduct a series of creative workshops. As both inmates and wardens together composed songs, skits, and poems, and even insisted on being given Scripture verses to memorize, they were powerfully impacted by the word of God in their heart language. Now, through engaging these art forms—in a language they truly understand—the word of God has been deeply embedded in their minds and hearts.

103. HAITI'S UNENDING SONG[65]

By Laurie Williams

Haiti's vibrant art, the voice for the unsung soul of its people, seemed to have been abruptly silenced on January 12, 2010, in the wake of a devastating earthquake. In sharp contrast to the images and reports that often paint a bleak picture of Haiti, art has provided a redeeming force in the world's perception of this Caribbean nation. The explosion of color, rhythmic sounds, and expressive movements found in Haitian art is unmatched and celebrated internationally. Among its many losses, Haiti's artistic community also suffered this year: the destruction of historic art, the sudden passing of talented artists, and the amputation of numerous musicians' limbs, to name a few.

Yet as heavy dust filled the air that day, a familiar sound in Port-au-Prince also took over: music. "I walked into the street and every person walking was singing a different song, some type of hymn," explains Nathalie "Talie" Cerin, a young Haitian musician who, like several artists in the city, was scheduled to record that fateful afternoon. Even in her state of shock, the Kreyol Soul singer was amazed at the reaction of the people around her. "It speaks to the faith of the Haitian people, but it also speaks to the power of music itself," she remarked.

As was documented by the media, outdoor concerts and worship services, which began in the aftermath of the earthquake, continued through Carnival season and beyond. Music seems to provide a much-needed therapeutic outlet, which Haitians have always relied on in the past. For this reason, Cerin strongly believes Haiti needs its art and its artists, more than ever before, to facilitate the extensive healing journey ahead. And although many may question if Haiti's artistic voice will ever regain its strength, Cerin is unwavering in her assurance: "No earthquake can break that."

---

65   Reprinted with permission from Laurie Williams, "Haiti's Unending Song," *Connections: The Journal of the WEA Mission Commission* 9, nos. 2 and 3 (September 2010): 175.

331

INTRODUCTION

SECTION 1: FOUNDATIONS

SECTION 2: STORIES

SECTION 3: TOOLS

CLOSING

104. AN AUSTRALIAN WORSHIP LEADER'S JOURNEY FROM HILLSONG TO "SINGING UP COUNTRY"

By Tanya Riches

I grew up in Sydney, Australia, attending an Anglican church and school, happily singing hymns in full harmony. Joining an Australian children's choir, I performed a wide repertoire, from Broadway to African American spirituals.

When my parents experienced baptism in the Spirit, they were forever changed, their charismatic prayers breaking outside the liturgy into spontaneous, joyful expression. Leaving the pipe organ behind, they sought a church accepting of tongues and choruses. After trying a number of local congregations, my family trekked out to the Hills District, attending Hills Christian Life Centre, better known now as Hillsong Church (http://hillsong.com).

On our first visit, hundreds of worshipers gathered in a warehouse, joyfully praising God. This church now boasts over twenty-five thousand adherents, with campuses on five continents. The music is a large part of the Hillsong experience. Each year an annual congregational album is recorded and released, as well as a youth and children's album. The songs of Hillsong, including "Shout to the Lord,"[66] are sung by millions of people worldwide in church each Sunday. Initially, American gospel heavily influenced Hillsong music forms with call and response, frenetic clapping, and the odd rap thrown in.

While attending Hillsong, over time I became more and more involved in the music ministry. At the church youth camp at age fifteen, I wrote what eventually became my best-known chorus composition, "Jesus, What a Beautiful Name," inspired by Mariah Carey's gospel Christmas album but in good Anglican strophic form. I joined the Hillsong choir and youth band that year and never looked back, finding a fresh expression toward God I so deeply desired.

The following summer at camp, our youth pastor Phil Dooley requested us to play songs from an album by the UK band Delirious?. Reminiscent of U2 performances, *Live & in the Can* (the band's first live album, released in 1996 and packaged in a tin can) contained spontaneous, Pentecostal-style rock worship. I remember photocopying chord charts for its numbers: "What a Friend I've Found," "Did You Hear the Mountains Tremble?," "History Maker," and "Oh Lead Me." Words can't describe the impact these songs had upon us as teenagers. They became anthems for the high school and university groups—and eventually the church congregation.

---

66   Darlene Zschech, "Shout to the Lord," *Shout to the Lord*, CD (Sydney: Hillsong Music Australia, 1993).

INTRODUCTION

SECTION 1: FOUNDATIONS

SECTION 2: STORIES

SECTION 3: TOOLS

CLOSING

The 1998 summer camp brought a crisis. We had learned the Delirious? tracks, dancing to the music until laughing and exhausted every Friday night. Weekly we had lifted our arms high in the air and sung in passionate refrain. And now, like overworn clothes, the songs and lyrics felt routine, far from the passionate spontaneity that marked their introduction. We knew something else was to occur.

The air was thick with God's presence and anticipation that morning. In a prayer meeting we petitioned God for something new, and Reuben Morgan, the youth band leader and a songwriter at Hillsong, retreated into his room. Hours later he called us to an urgent rehearsal, holding a chord chart entitled "My Redeemer Lives." He told me later he'd stood in his room jumping up and down until he found the "right" tempo. We introduced the song that night, which brought a new, iconic style of dancing into the church. Later that year it was included in the first recording of the youth band, dubbed "United," to represent the mixture of high school and university musicians. These first recordings were revolutionary. But it's all pretty hazy now, and the nature of Pentecostalism's mainly oral culture complicates history telling.

While completing my university degree from 1998 to 2003, I administrated much of the day-to-day running of United—now a worship band with massive worldwide influence, which had grown out of these early CD recordings. Additionally, in 2001 I moved to the newly acquired Hillsong "City Campus" to administrate and conduct the choir.

There, I lived on the edge of Redfern, an inner-city suburb known for its Indigenous population . . . and crime. Its layers of Australian national identity were as visible as a cultural archaeological dig. I sat in cafés, observing different communities interacting with each other. Meeting some local Indigenous Australian high school girls through Hillsong Church's urban ministry, I grew to love their cheekiness and resilience despite their relative economic poverty.

In 2003 our United leadership team handed the band over to a new leader, Joel Houston, and it has since grown considerably in influence. I decided to pursue further education, first in theology. Then, enrolling in a second research master's degree program in music in 2007, I was convinced by my supervisor to write about my ministry experience with Hillsong. My 2010 dissertation was entitled "Shout to the Lord: Music and Change at Hillsong, 1996–2007." To be honest, examining my past precipitated an identity crisis. (Perhaps I am still in it.) Of particular concern to me was Hillsong's marketing practices as related to its musical success. While musicians' names were initially kept anonymous, soon "star" performers were selected and promoted.[67] I wondered what this, a normal industry practice, communicated to other churches about what God had done in the midst of our community. And while early album covers proudly displayed Sydney's Harbour Bridge and Opera House, the music's origins are now largely irrelevant for those who consume it internationally. Perhaps Hillsong has outgrown its Australian roots and become a global brand—only time can tell.

> Will ignoring the rhythms and beats of our country's first peoples not put me in danger of a new imperialism?

But for me, this land holds a unique significance. There's something important about my native soil that still draws me. Sitting under the fig trees so characteristic of Sydney Harbour, I've long contemplated the emergence of this little settler colony on the edge of the world. Reading literature on the Anglo-Celtic diaspora has helped explain to me our deep Australian longings

---

67   Mark Evans, *Open Up the Doors: Music in the Modern Church* (London: Equinox, 2006), 87.

for rest and for acceptance—for a home.[68] I have felt for some time now that to truly engage music mission *as an Australian* means facing our history and all it entails: the colonisation of the Indigenous population, as well as the experiences of the original immigrants and their ensuing generations. Will ignoring the rhythms and beats of our country's first peoples not put me in danger of a new imperialism, one that threatens the realm of worship and which would be so far from the true spirituality God desires?

As I explored theology in Redfern, the Incarnation spoke to me of how God himself accultur-ated to this world (Phil 2:6–8). I realised Jesus was not a God of the center, but of the periphery, as African theologian Kwame Bediako describes.[69] If Australia is on the periphery of the world, its rural towns are perhaps the very ends of the world. And in those communities God himself is found.

I am still passionate about creating musical worship. Yet in this endeavour, justice is essential to the worship God requires. In showing Israel what is most important, God says, "Away with the noise of your songs! I will not listen to the music of your harps. But let justice roll on like a river, righteousness like a never-failing stream!" (Amos 5:23,24). The many atrocities that have been covered over in history books require a spiritual response of repentance in order for justice to "roll on." Australia again yearns for *new* songs—songs of reconciliation, songs of people restored to each other, to the land, and to God. I now am seeking to listen carefully to what remains of the ancient "songlines" of the land,[70] sung by the voices that stewarded them for so long.[71]

Ironically, this search for truth and a genuine Australian worship expression has led me to "emigrate" to another part of the world, to Fuller Theological Seminary in Los Angeles, California. I long for home as any pilgrim does. But my "listening" is being done with deep hope that the first Australians in Redfern and other urban centres may find the realities of Christ's reconciling love for them inside the walls of all Australian churches, and that we may together join Indigenous worship leaders encouraging us to "sing up country"[72] in new songs of praise to our King.

---

68   Ian Lilley, "Archaeology, Diaspora and Decolonization," *Journal of Social Archaeology* 6, no. 1 (2006): 28–47.

69   Kwame Bediako, *Jesus and the Gospel in Africa: History and Experience* (Maryknoll, NY: Orbis Books, 2004), 116.

70   Songlines are ceremonial songs and dances that also act as maps and traveling tracks across the land or sky. They hold knowledge about the Australian land and are important to the creation stories known as "The Dreamtime," and to indigenous law..

71   Fiona Magowan, *Melodies of Mourning: Music and Emotion in Northern Australia*, World Anthropology (Oxford: James Currey, 2007), 81.

72   To "sing up country" is a term synonymous to "perform ceremony" in some Indigenous cultures; this music is integrally connected to the land and its features, as well as to ancestral law and Indigenous Australian spirituality, which is often referred to as "The Dreaming "

INTRODUCTION

SECTION 1: FOUNDATIONS

SECTION 2: STORIES

SECTION 3: TOOLS

CLOSING

EUROPE—EURASIA

105. JUST AS IT SHOULD BE

By Mark Charles

As I sat in a small church in the outskirts of Ulan Ude, listening with fascination to "throat singing," I found myself feeling simultaneously excited, uncomfortable, confused, and at peace. To me, this call to worship sounded like a cross between an oboe playing and the singer clearing his throat.

I was excited because in this Russian city in Siberia, just north of Mongolia, I was attending a consultation on contextualized worship for the indigenous peoples of the region. God had already pulled a few strings just to get me there, and it was a privilege to be with this group of Christians from the Buryat, Altai, Tuvan, and Sakha peoples, as well as with missionaries from Russia, the US, and Europe, who had been working in this region for years.

I was excited to be a part of this groundbreaking gathering and to share what God had been doing in my own life and among our Navajo people as we ask the question, "What does it mean to be Navajo and Christian?" I did not come to teach but to tell stories. For that is how it's done within our indigenous communities. Our youth did not traditionally attend school. They did not earn degrees or pass written examinations. Instead they spent time with their elders. They listened to their stories and were mentored by their experiences. And that is exactly what we had come together to do.

This consultation did not begin with a flashy program or elaborate presentations. Instead it started very traditionally—with introductions. We simply went around the room and introduced ourselves. We heard where people were from, who they represented, and why they came. None of it was scripted or choreographed or pressured by strict time schedules, and yet I found it very exciting.

But I also felt uncomfortable and even confused. I had never heard throat singing before and did not know what to make of the sounds emitting from this man's throat. I did not recognize the tune of his song either. It was all very new and somewhat strange. Maybe if we had been touring a museum, or attending an academic lecture—in a "sterile" environment—then I might have felt more at ease. But we were not students studying a different culture, trying to get a good grade and earn a degree. We were Christians, coming together from different parts of the world, trying to work out our salvation and understand better how to share the gospel message with our peoples.

The throat singer was an Altai. He had grown up surrounded by the shamanistic culture of his people. He was raised in an environment where this type of song was often used to tell stories, as well as to honor and worship the gods and spirits of his people. But after he became a Christian, he had a desire to communicate God's love directly and plainly to their hearts, more so than he was able with translated songs taught by missionaries. So God gave him the ability to sing from his throat. And now he was using this gift to call our consultation together and lead us into worship.

You can learn about a culture as an observer or even as an outsider. But you cannot worship that way. Worship is personal and intimate. Having traveled extensively and worshiped among many peoples, with their particular cultures and languages, I would love to say that I no longer feel awkward when I encounter new experiences. But that is not true, and if I am completely honest, I have to say, "I felt uncomfortable."

Nevertheless, in the midst of this discomfort, I found peace. I remembered feeling this range of emotions sweeping over me before and had hoped I would feel them again—of being in the presence of God, initiated by experiencing the diversity of his body.

> No single language, culture, or people have a monopoly on understanding the vastness of his character … it is only when we come together, with each one bringing unique gifts, that we get a more complete picture of who he is.

I have felt God's presence in other situations as well: when I am in prayer, convicted by Scripture, watching the sun rise, or worshiping within my Navajo or American culture. Those experiences are familiar, wonderful, and frequently bring me to tears. But experiencing the presence of God through his diverse body is much different. On the surface it feels more physical and human than spiritual. Feeling God's presence in this way often tempts me to either flee or take control. It is exciting, uncomfortable, confusing, and at times even a bit irritating.

But in reflection, it brings peace. And I might even dare say it is a peace that passes understanding. This peace comes from remembering that sitting in God's presence should feel this way. We should want to sit there and soak it in for eternity. But we should also want to flee, to cover our nakedness and hide our sin.

God is wonderful. He is simultaneously powerful, holy, perfect, terrible, and good. And for me, the most authentic way I have found to experience him is to commune with my Christian brothers and sisters, embracing and sharing the diverse cultures, languages, and worldviews that he gave each of us.

God is bigger than any one person, tribe, or nation. No single language, culture, or people have a monopoly on understanding the vastness of his character. And it is only when we come together, with each one bringing unique gifts, that we get a more complete picture of who he is.

And so I was thrilled to attend this consultation. I loved coming together, introducing ourselves, and sharing our stories. And I was blessed that we were not alone. I knew that Jesus was in our midst and that the God of creation had graced us with his presence. I knew this because of his promise that where two or three are gathered in his name, he is there.

But I also knew this because I felt excited, uncomfortable, confused, and at peace, all at the same time. Just as it should be.

INTRODUCTION

SECTION 1: FOUNDATIONS

SECTION 2: STORIES

SECTION 3: TOOLS

CLOSING

106. THE JUBILATE FOUNDATION IN ROMANIA
By Richard S. Mauney

Jubilate, the Latin word meaning "make music or shout joyfully," is the name chosen for a worship and church music ministry in Romania, founded in 2001 by five Romanian and American musicians. The Jubilate team has worked together since 1996, first as music teachers in a Bible college and then as members of a Romanian nonprofit organization when God opened up the opportunity. Each member of the team has musical training and experiences in different facets of music ministry, as well as unique gifts and interests, all of which serve to meet the various needs of the Romanian church.

The purpose of the Jubilate Foundation is to encourage and equip music and worship leaders and to strengthen the worship life of the church throughout Romania. To fulfill this purpose, Jubilate is involved in church-based teaching and discipling ministries, publishing materials, and organizing concerts as cultural events that provide evangelistic opportunities. Our teaching and equipping focuses on a biblical understanding of worship and music, as well as on musical skill development through workshops, seminars, conferences, and concerts. In addition to working with adults, the foundation encourages the involvement of youth and children in meaningful service through music.

PROVIDING RESOURCES FOR THE CHURCH

Resources provided by the Jubilate Publishing House include scores and educational materials for music and worship ministries of the church. As a publisher, Jubilate is committed to finding and encouraging appropriate expressions for corporate worship that reflect the beauty and uniqueness of the Romanian culture. In compiling the Jubilate hymnal (published in 2003), a priority was to include a number of songs written by Romanian writers and composers. Included also are excellent translations of both new worship songs and traditional hymns from England, France, and America, as well as songs written by Romanian-speaking missionaries who have lived in Romania for a number of years. The hymnal is used among Protestant churches throughout Romania, primarily as a supplementary collection.

Other publications provided by our house include: choral collections for adult, youth, and children's choirs; a collection of original Scripture songs for children, with accompanying CDs; a music theory manual with auditory exercises included on CDs; a manual for those working with preschoolers in musical activities; a translation of a book by David Peterson, *Engaging with God: A Biblical Theology of Worship*; and audio CDs.

DEVELOPING DISCIPLES FROM MUSICIANS

Out of a burden to see disciples of Christ formed among the community of musicians, Jubilate members are involved in ongoing discipleship groups with conservatory students. For the same reason, in 2009 and 2010 the Jubilate Foundation sponsored an outreach to professional musicians throughout Romania–the Oratorium Project. A seven-day master course for orchestra and choir, it provides a Christ-centered model of excellence in music making for young Romanian professional musicians. The project grew out of the rich experiences of two Jubilate team members who in their ministries have intersected with musicians in conservatories and in various performance settings.

The Oratorium Project consists of rehearsals and performances led by international Christian professionals, providing a positive and creative musical environment that encourages participants to learn how to bridge the divide between their Christian faith and their careers. The project meets the need of Christian professional musicians by modeling how to live out their faith in their work, as well as for non-Christian musicians to meet Christ for the first time. In the summer of 2009 Haydn's oratorio *Creation* was presented in three concerts in Romania, and in 2010 the program consisted of works by J. S. Bach: *Magnificat*, two of his motets, and his *Orchestral Suite No. 3 in D Major*.

One violinist who participated in both of the oratorium projects is still a seeker in terms of faith in Christ. Whereas in his first year of participating in the project he would come late to the morning worship times and listen from a safe distance, the second year he sat front and center every morning. One day he told a team member, "It seems I'm supposed to be here more and more." As a result of the projects, the musician has met with a Jubilate team member in order to read together through the Gospel of John.

DEVELOPING MUSICIANS FROM DISCIPLES

As each one of the members of the Jubilate team is directly involved in music ministry in a local church, there is a deep commitment to discipling music and worship leaders, as well as helping disciples grow in their service and in their musicianship. Two particular types of projects that fulfill this purpose are periodic weekend choir workshops and an annual week-long summer course for Romanian worship leaders who come from all over the country, as well as from abroad.

The weekend choir workshops take place in strategic areas in the country and bring together choirs from area churches for times of singing, learning, worshiping, and ministry in the local host church. As many as one thousand choristers from about forty churches have come together for one such workshop. The annual week-long summer course includes rich times of learning, fellowship, and worship, as well as ministry in local churches. Along with plenary sessions on worship, optional courses offered throughout the week include conducting, voice, keyboard, string ensemble, guitar, recorder, principles of songwriting, music theory, serving on worship teams, and working with children.

Testimonies by some of the participants in such projects reflect the many ways God has worked:

> Many times I have wondered what I could do to get the guys in my brass band to play in tune, to phrase well, to love one another in such a way as to give one another preference. In this workshop I understood what I needed to do—simply help them discover the musicians the Lord has already made them to be. I understand again that *we find true worth in a musician not only in his skills, but in his humility—in what is given totally in service to the Great Maestro.*

> This week I've learned correct singing posture, how to work with children better, and how to teach others music theory. I've been encouraged for my work in the church, and the conference has opened my eyes to true, biblical worship. I'm glad that I could learn new songs, songs full of grace. I've learned what real music is and will try from now on to bring to God all my very best.

Our prayer at the Jubilate Foundation is that every believer who serves his church in Romania will be an example of joy in servanthood, purity, submission, and giving, so that together in our spiritual service of worship we will all "make music joyfully."

INTRODUCTION

SECTION 1: FOUNDATIONS

SECTION 2: STORIES

SECTION 3: TOOLS

CLOSING

339

INTRODUCTION

SECTION 1: FOUNDATIONS

SECTION 2: STORIES

SECTION 3: TOOLS

CLOSING

107. KONSTANTIN ZHIGULIN INTERVIEW

By Robin P. Harris

Konstantin Zhigulin's reputation as a Russian composer for church music stretches across six time zones in Russia and beyond. His music has also been performed extensively in America and Germany. I first met Konstantin at the home of mutual friends in the Siberian city of Novosibirsk. This interview was conducted by telephone on May 23, 2005. Konstantin speaks English, but our interview was conducted in his native Russian language; this is a translation, edited for clarity and brevity.[73]

When did you first learn about Christianity?

What initially got me to thinking about the Lord was a painting by the famous Dutch painter Hieronymus Bosch called "Christ Carrying the Cross." When I saw it, something happened in my soul. Christ is carrying his cross, surrounded by people who hardly even look human. The image of Christ in that painting affected me so strongly. The Lord shows himself to people in different ways: some find him through art, some through music or nature. I don't know why it happened to me through a painting, as I had never especially been struck by a painting before. What is interesting is that this picture kept appearing in my life at significant moments. I'd see it reproduced in journals, or somewhere on the street, or other places. It was so amazing to me.

Hieronymus Bosch, "Christ Carrying the Cross"

How has music helped or hindered evangelical Christianity in Russia?

This is a very difficult question to answer, but I know that for myself, when I first began to attend an evangelical church and listened to the music they sang, I was horrified. It was awful—it did not resemble any model I was familiar with. It was not at all related to anything in Russian culture, to say nothing of "high" Russian culture. There was no attention given to the Russian understanding of how to use words, no use of the literary use of words. These were American songs that had been

73   Read more about the ministry of Konstantin Zhigulin at http://www.psalom.org.

translated. Unfortunately the translations were not that good and the way they were sung was not very musical; it was unattractive to Russian culture. They grated on my Russian ears.

You know, our ideas of God and religion in general are developed in the context of the cultural mix in which we are raised. In Russia, the Russian Orthodox Church has an incredibly strong influence on our thinking. It influences our ideas of what spiritual music should sound like. Regardless of the textual content of the music, the form modeled by the Russian Orthodox Church music is what sticks in our minds as being connected with worship. This translated music struck me as strange because at times it was too off-the-chart fun or, on the contrary, too much like a march, rather than being associated with spiritual themes. For the Russian ear, it was a culture shock.

But then I began to understand that there was simply a lack of understanding on the part of the people who brought us the gospel. They were sharing what they had with us, out of good hearts. And those who heard and received the gospel were, naturally, very grateful for it. That's why I accept these missionaries; the work they did was a great work.

I should add that a large number of American and European songs do work just fine for the Russian ear. For example, songs like "Silent Night," "As the Deer Pants for the Water," and "O Sacred Head" are wonderful songs that resemble Russian music and are beloved by Russian people everywhere.

How do you see your role in church music in Russia?

In Russian society, people have a very strong mental image of what it sounds like when God is being worshiped. When these people began to listen to my songs being sung, this mental image worked in our favor, and they thought we were Russian Orthodox, even though we were singing my songs, not in Old Russian (as the Russian Orthodox do), but in my own poetic translations. When they talked to us afterward, there was an incredible level of respect and a positive response to the songs, not so much because they thought we were Russian Orthodox, but because they heard in the songs that special something that their spiritual, cultural, soul-level subconscious tells them is the Russian way to worship God.

And what makes you unique among other Russian Christian composers?

The kind of songs that I write are different in their basic approach from the translated songs in the Russian evangelical hymnbook. Those songs, by and large, talk *about* God, who he is, what he's done, and more. It's the third-person approach, rather than addressing God himself. This is a very important difference, because you can sing *about* God all the time—about his love and his mercy—and never sing *to* him.

In the Russian Orthodox Church music and in my music, the text is normally directed to God himself, and this is why I use Psalm texts and some gospel texts. I believe this is an important aspect of what should be happening in the church service. In other words, I'm talking about "sung prayers." I think it is important that we have these sung prayers in our services, and this is why I write songs like I do.

If you take Western music, American songs for example, often everything is understandable and clear, but there is something lacking in the soul of it—it misses something for the Russian's heart. I'm not saying all Western songs are like that, but many of them are. The kind of music I feel God laid on my heart is the kind that finds a middle road. I want to write music that is understandable and clear, music that challenges and exhorts, but at the same time that touches the heart and soul of Russian people. I think this is what we need in Russia today.

MIDDLE EAST

108. GLORIFYING GOD THROUGH ELOCUTION
By Pam Wilson

Turkish culture appreciates the art of what I call "beautiful reading." Turks are in love with their language, and well-spoken, articulate people are greatly admired. Radio and television programs often present people reading meditations or poetry, usually with an instrumental background.

The Turkish church had never taken advantage of this art form, so I decided to experiment with it at a workshop. I first played a familiar secular example and then divided people into groups of four and gave them a psalm to use for practice, as well as a poem written by a recently martyred believer.

Two people, volunteered by their groups as outstanding, then performed each of these readings over a musical track that I had chosen. The atmosphere was electrifying, with tears shed. So simple. So beautiful. I've now seen churches use this art form during worship, opening up a way for believers with this gift of elocution to use it for the glory of God.

INTRODUCTION

SECTION 1: FOUNDATIONS

SECTION 2: STORIES

SECTION 3: TOOLS

CLOSING

109. PARABLES THROUGH DANCE

By Pam Wilson

Coming to Turkey as a young missionary, I attended a folk dance exhibition and was particularly intrigued by one regional style. The dancers told a story about farming through their expressive motions: sowing, watering, and reaping. I was transfixed, imagining how the style could be used to tell Jesus' parables. But I was living in a city with almost no believers at the time and so, like Mary, I treasured that creative presentation in my heart.

As church planters we also sowed, watered, and reaped, and God allowed us to see a Turkish church emerge over the years. As a worship leader I would sometimes suggest using folk dance but rarely found anyone interested. We began camps to train worship leaders, but the one Turkish believer who attended as a dance teacher was more interested in modern and jazz styles.

I was thrilled when a dancer eventually joined our team. Later, prior to a worship event in December 2011, I suggested telling Bible stories through folk dance. He was excited about the idea and discovered a shepherd dance from the Bursa region. We decided on the story of the lost sheep, and at the event God provided a Turkish believer who had done undergraduate work in folklore. She picked out a number of girls to be "sheep" and, using a classic style, organized them in a line, with the lone "lost sheep" doing a solo. Put together with the musical track, the climax of the shepherd finding the lost sheep was powerful. The believers got so excited about the presentation that the group was asked to perform it for everyone at the morning meeting the next day. After twenty-eight years, the dream of seeing folk dance used in worship was finally realized.

110. ARTISTIC ADAPTATIONS OF SCRIPTURE STORY AMONG WOMEN OF ORAL CULTURES

By Carla Bowman

The narrative of Naaman the leper is dramatized on this stifling hot November night in the old Islamic Moghul city of Hyderabad in Andhra Pradesh. On a high rooftop, I hear, see, and experience the story of Naaman healed of his leprosy. In this story from 2 Kings 5, a perceptive, wise slave girl of Israel recommends to Naaman, a Syrian military commander, that he seek help from Elisha the prophet. The story is full of images of the East: kings, bearded religious men, slavery, silver, gold, palaces, horses, and chariots.

As the drama unfolds, a slight breeze sweeps across the terrace, and loud tropical birds squeal noisily. Their sound mingles with the high-pitched Eastern melody of the song composed for the story. It is a song both sung and danced in a centuries-old choreography. As the Banjara women dance the story, ankle and foot bangles click-clack to the rhythm of bare feet pounding the packed-dirt floor. The song is hauntingly beautiful.

I will never forget this story performance in my lifetime, I think to myself. If this is true for me, a Westerner, how much more so for a Banjara villager, for this is the heart and soul of his culture. It is a poignant and powerful way to present the word of God, one that has seen amazing reception among the Banjara people group, not only of Andhra but of Maharastra, Karnataka, and other states of India.

The night on the rooftop is to become still more unforgettable. The story of the woman at the well is sung, as an elegant sister leads the dance team with a large clay jar on her shoulder. Another woman gathers sticks and brush near a prop of a village gate as she represents the widow of Zarephath during the musical rendition of the story from Kings. Eleven other stories of biblical women are enacted, sung, and danced by teams from all over the state who have been implementing the Bridges for Women curriculum for some time now. Once again I am amazed at the creativity of our partners around the globe and

Scripture song in Cambodia

INTRODUCTION

SECTION 1: FOUNDATIONS

SECTION 2: STORIES

SECTION 3: TOOLS

CLOSING

their effective use of the oral arts to communicate the Scriptures among oral cultures. How fortunate I am, as a lead trainer of Bridges for Women, to witness the impact all over the world of lesson five: Integrated Oral Arts.

On a recent occasion, I find myself in the scorching desert of Alexandria, too far from the Nile to be cooled by tall papyrus or green fields. Here I am to experience the story of the ten virgins sung and acted in creative, new ways that I have seen nowhere else in the world. The team creates an Arabic song, surely inspired by God. It is very Middle Eastern in tune, and the words provide an evocative, lasting cultural metaphor for the oil, lamps, and preparedness for the Lord's coming. During the drama the women attending the wedding use the traditional, shrill Arab yodel to represent celebration, and the foolish women who cannot attend the wedding fall to the floor mourning and howling in an equally traditional mode. The storyteller then spontaneously rises to her feet, pauses, and repeats the last line of the story. "Watch therefore, for you know neither the day nor the hour wherein the Son of man comes" (Matt 25:13 AKJV). It is a powerful ending. The enthralled audience breaks into applause.

This Egyptian desert experience is worlds away from Bhutan in the Himalayas where one cold December afternoon the women dressed in traditional, handwoven, striped jackets to dance to the song of the ten virgins in a circle with slow-motion steps. They move to the tribal tune they have created to retell the story through music. This is slightly reminiscent of northern Cambodia where the dance of the widow's oil resembles the Apsaras of the ancient Khmer kingdom, with their graceful hand movements and slow-motion shifting from foot to foot.

In nearby Sumatra it is the story from John of the woman caught in adultery that captures the attention of women for its multifaceted messages and powerful impact. This story is enacted, sung, and danced in the fashion of the Aceh people group. It is one of the most beautiful adaptations of Scripture I have ever watched. But I have said the same of the song and line dance of Kathmandu and of the story of Ruth and Naomi, powerfully and emotionally

Drama of the Ten Virgins

Cambodia–A drama–dance of the Widow's Oil

Drama of the Ten Virgins in Bhutan

chanted and danced in Addis Ababa. I have thought at times that there is no rival for the Turkish believers—wearing headscarves and *shalwar* pants—singing and dancing the widows' stories of the Old Testament.

I am moved to tears when the women of Peru sing the story of the widow's offering from Luke in the fashion of the Quechua highlands, with bamboo flutes. Still more powerful is the dance of the ten virgins in Tamacheq, performed in Timbuktu, Mali. During the wedding circle dance, a man is recruited to be the groom. He enters the circle moving gracefully to the new song, twirling his black turban and wielding his silver sword.

On the Tana River in Kenya the women enact the Wisdom of Solomon: Two Women and a Baby with such emotion, volume, and confidence, it is hard to believe these are not the real mothers. In Vietnam the women surprise themselves with their first composition in the Asian style.

The creativity I have seen in women around the world is exceptional, as they are encouraged to develop Scripture use through the oral arts—drama that is engaging and contextual; song and dance forms lovely in sound and indigenous to the region; and biblical, poetic recitation that is also based on cultural practices—all done with great attention to accuracy of the Scripture story.

INTRODUCTION

SECTION 1: FOUNDATIONS

SECTION 2. STORIES

SECTION 3. TOOLS

CLOSING

WORLDWIDE

111. VICTORIOUS FAITH IN THE MIDST OF PERSECUTION[74]

By Nik Ripken

Interviews carried out from 1998 through 2011 in seventy-two countries with approximately six hundred believers undergoing persecution show common life experiences and practices among those who are victorious through it:

- Indigenous hymns, choruses, and songs are central to their daily life and worship.
- After prayer, the greatest comfort for persecuted Christians seems to come from having memorized large portions of the Bible and many indigenous songs.
- What a believer takes into persecution is all he has to build upon during persecution.
- Without songs of faith that are indigenous to the host culture, there was little evidence of victorious faith. Songs or choruses translated from another culture seldom, if ever, appeared.

---

74   Used with permission from Nik Ripken, "Victorious Faith in the Midst of Persecution" (manuscript, n.d.).

112. FLESHING OUT THE GOSPEL WORLDWIDE THROUGH THE ARTS

By Roger W. Lowther

Monica Ghali, a young missionary in Lima, Peru, wanted to tell street children that God loved them, so she started collecting used bus tickets. Littering the streets of Lima, the tickets are an eyesore—stepped on, run over, and water stained.

She asked neighbors and friends to help collect them. When asked why, she replied, "I want to take what has no value in the eyes of the world and give it value. I want to take what is ugly and make it beautiful."

Using her artistic training, Monica arranged the tickets into a collage of great beauty and worth in the eyes of all who saw it. In a similar way, she continued to work with the children, building relationships and fleshing out the beauty and value they have before God.

Art is essential to the way Joel Klepac, missionary with Word Made Flesh, builds the church in Bucharest, Romania. Using sand, clay, paint, and a myriad of other materials, Joel develops community among street children and children at risk and gives them hope in life. Together with the children, Joel made a movie about two apple seeds that were thrown away but eventually grew into a full, vibrant tree that produced fruit of its own. It had tremendous impact on the kids as they realized God saw them as those apple seeds, redeemed from a broken world and given the ability to flourish. This project brought the kids into Christian community and into nearby churches.

Sarah Lance works through the arts to build the church in Calcutta, India. Women who were involved in the sex trade are now given wages, retirement benefits, and medical care in order to make art. They are also given the word of God through worship services and Bible studies. As an artist, Sarah saw the value of scraps of sari, considered worthless as clothes. She taught the women how to cut and sew the pieces into beautiful wall hangings, bags, and other goods, to be sold abroad. The art of making these articles, along with her friendship, speaks the gospel to these women. Just as they were cut off in their sin, they have been redeemed and made into beautiful creations in the hands of the great Artist, who came to cleanse them from their sins. Through every stitch and knot, these women gradually came to see their beauty in the eyes of God.

After the earthquake, tsunami, and nuclear disasters of March 11, 2011, many in Japan became involved with local churches in the relief effort. Mr. and Mrs. "K" were so attracted by the freedom-filled fellowship that they joined one of our church's gospel choirs. Singing the gospel message every week in rehearsals led them to start reading the Bible together as a couple. The choir director herself had become a Christian by being part of a choir.

Not far away, Mr. "I" gathered musicians, including me, to perform J. S. Bach's *St. Matthew Passion* to help raise money for the relief effort. In the process of rehearsing and performing the work, the message became so real that it changed him. He became a Christian and was baptized the following Christmas morning. Historically, it has been hard for the gospel to take root in people's lives in Japan, and yet through the arts we are seeing more and more people become part of grace-filled Christian communities.

In Peru, Romania, India, and Japan, the arts help flesh out and express "the Word." Because of this, the gospel is being heard, seen, and felt there and in many other places of the world today.

Sarah saw the value of scraps of sari, considered worthless as clothes. She taught the women how to cut and sew the pieces into beautiful wall hangings, bags, and other goods, to be sold abroad.

113. FROM TRICKLING TRIBUTARIES TO RUSHING RIVERS: FIFTY YEARS OF MUSIC MISSIONS[75]

By Frank Fortunato

The Jordanian woman approached the visiting music team from several nations who had included an Arabic song in their music presentation. "Thanks for singing one of our favorite Arabic melodies. Now tell me, in what language were you singing?"

Like this team in Amman, Jordan, music missionaries decades ago were well-meaning in their efforts. In this instance, the team had added the token local song, yet were oblivious to their deplorable pronunciation. Other teams never even bothered learning a local melody.

Lacking in global music training, missionaries compared foreign music systems to their own and often naively found the local music traditions underdeveloped. So they did what seemed right to them. They translated their Western songs, taught Western notation, imported pianos and organs, and much more. Though not always appropriate, their early efforts were nevertheless sincere.

By the early 1960s Western pop started to blanket the airwaves. Groups like Youth for Christ (YFC) sought to capture the moment and cloak the gospel, in the nations where they worked, through Western song. Those YFC efforts then spawned a wave of music missions. Groups like the Continental Singers sent out hundreds of talented singers and instrumentalists, circling the world on short-term global music outreaches. People never tired of the ever-attractive sounds of Western pop, and through it unknown numbers came to Christ.

As music missionaries began to study the uniqueness and intricacies of non-Western music, a different wave of music missions emerged—encouraging and promoting indigenous music expressions. Vida Chenoweth, a linguist and professional musician with the then Summer Institute of Linguistics (SIL) in Papua New Guinea, released a landmark study in 1972, along with tools to help missionary musicians analyze local music. She helped launch the first worship songs created among the Usarufa people. Following in her footsteps, SIL music missionary Tom Avery encouraged similar activities with the Canela people of Brazil. Soon missionaries from various agencies were facilitating songwriting events and empowering locals to use their own melodies, rhythms,

---

75   This article first appeared (with some changes) as "From Streams to Gushing Rivers: Fifty Years of Music Missions," *Connections: The Journal of the WEA Mission Commission*, vol. 9, nos. 1 and 2 (2010), 20.

and instruments for Christian worship. Along with the surging tide of Western pop, streams of indigenous music began to flow.

Another wave emerged in the sixties and seventies with Catholic and Anglican missionaries encouraging the use of local music to accompany the timeless texts of the Mass. The firstfruits of these efforts took place in parts of Africa, Latin America, and Asia. But not everyone was on board. Some asserted that incorporating musical elements of the surrounding culture into their worship was "conforming to the world." In places like Brazil, people frowned on the use of *samba* among believers.

In the eighties various international agencies like Youth With A Mission (YWAM) and Operation Mobilization (OM) began to incorporate ethnic songs not only in their outreaches but also in their international gatherings. The second Lausanne Congress in 1989 prepared an international songbook to enable thousands of delegates to celebrate together the global growth of the body of Christ. David Peacock followed suit, compiling World Praise song collections for the global gatherings of the Baptist Alliance. The gigantic Intervarsity Christian Fellowship "Urbana" mission conferences began to add African, Asian, and Latin songs to their convention worship times. A trickle of global song was turning into a coursing stream.

Also in the eighties, Christian institutions such as Wheaton College started offering degrees in ethnomusicology. Several graduates went out from Wheaton to join mission organizations, armed with the tools to help local people develop their own ethnic worship music. John Benham began a graduate course to further train the growing army of music missionaries.[76] Soon courses sprouted in various institutions. At one time almost one hundred music missionaries went out with the International Mission Board of the Southern Baptist Convention. Graduate theses and dissertations devoted careful research into various global music activities. While far from a tidal wave, the music missions movement was growing.

Into the nineties the AD2000 Movement started the Worship and Arts Network, the first of its kind among global movements. SIL International developed a journal devoted mostly to ethnic music. Others developed ethnic worship email newsletters. Music missionary Dave Hall created the term "ethnodoxology" to define ethnic and global worship. Brian Schrag and Paul Neeley published a set of tools and techniques to do music missions. Across the body of Christ, people were discovering how indigenous heart music, not borrowed music, best ignites worship. A report, which reflected the widespread excitement, told how an indigenous worship recording in Ghana spread like wildfire, even among those heavily resistant to the gospel.

In 1996 the U.S. Center for World Mission released a landmark issue of their magazine, *Mission Frontiers*, which dealt with worship and mission.[77] Among the articles was one that captured the insights of John Piper, showing how mission leads to worship, and worship leads to mission. Several new ministries traced their roots to that one issue, including Heart Sounds International, a ministry devoted to releasing indigenous worship recordings, particularly in restricted parts of the world.

Into the new century, another wave of mission effort began with an increased focus on oral approaches. Indigenous music, chants, rhythms, drama, and dance could carry timeless biblical stories straight to the hearts of people everywhere. The riveting accounts—when accompanied by local music and rhythms—made them sound familiar, not foreign. This did not go unnoticed by the leaders of the International Orality Network and the World Evangelical Alliance Mission

---

76   Center for Worship, "Master of Arts in Ethnomusicology," Liberty University, http://www.liberty.edu/academics/religion/centerforworship/index.cfm?PID=17234.

77   *Mission Frontiers*, July 2, 1996, http://www.missionfrontiers.org/issue/archive/worship-and-missions.

Commission, who called for the creation of task forces to devote efforts to ethnic music and arts in mission. Also, the Lausanne Movement released "Redeeming the Arts,"[78] one of the most comprehensive documents ever on the arts. The river was gushing with more and more energy.

The time was ripe for global consultations on music and missions. Three such events emerged. These Global Consultations on Music and Missions (http://www.gcommhome.org) brought together practitioners who shared insights through a dizzying array of seminars. At the first consultation, Paul Neeley and Robin Harris launched the International Council of Ethnodoxologists (http://www.worldofworship.org), a network that within a few years grew rapidly into a global fellowship of associates serving in dozens of nations and through one hundred agencies, developing a huge online resource for ethnic and global worship.

Into the present, two new streams define the latest stirrings. The first stream sets music missions into the larger milieu of the arts. This is in keeping with the growing awareness that many of the world's cultures don't isolate music from other artistic expressions. In parts of Africa and Asia few expressions of music making exist apart from movement, whether improvised or stylized. SIL has been at the forefront of this development, working through this new reality. They have retooled many music-focused staff in multiarts approaches who now see their role as arts consultants across the nations.[79] Also, Colin Harbinson started Stoneworks (http://stoneworks-arts.org), a growing movement to provide tools and training for the artist, encouraging the arts in the marketplace, the church, and in mission.

The second new stream connects music missions to social justice. Caedmon's Call, a contemporary Christian band, was overwhelmed by the oppression of the Dalit people, which they observed on tour in India. They later wrote songs about the mistreatment and recruited two OM Dalit musicians, featuring them in their tour back in the States, raising awareness and funding for efforts to bring justice to Dalits. Other singing groups, such as Switchfoot, Third Day, and Jars of Clay took up the baton also in their music and concerts for social causes.

> While the river seems to be rushing and rising, it's more likely that its true current remains subterranean.

Christian musicians from the UK and the US now regularly address poverty, HIV/AIDS, and disease during their concerts. But beyond just talking about the needs, they go the extra mile, visiting poor sections of cities and participating in short-term missions that are part of sponsor programs by various aid ministries. Scott Moreau, professor of missions at Wheaton College, applauds these new efforts of the musicians but cautions them not to get so caught up in social justice that their work becomes "holism with a hole," reminding them not to forget to share the good news.

Borrowing from the writer of Hebrews, "What more shall [we] say? [We] do not have time to tell about" the Nepali and Tibetan songbooks; the thousands of songs birthed in China by three untrained Chinese women; Marcos Witt's stunning recordings, which have touched the far reaches of the Latin world; ethnic groups deep in the Himalayas who developed incredibly beautiful songs and dance, relatively untouched and influenced by the outside world; the two thousand women and children in South Africa who spent six weeks in continual singing before the police finally gave

---

78   Issue Group on Redeeming the Arts, "Redeeming the Arts: The Restoration of the Arts to God's Creational Intention," Lausanne Occasional Paper No. 46 (Forum for World Evangelization, Pattaya, Thailand, September 29 to October 5, 2004), http://www.lausanne.org/docs/2004forum/LOP46_IG17.pdf.

79   The Ethnomusicology and Arts Group, *Arts Consultant: Understanding* (SIL International, 2007) 4 min., 58 sec.; video; from "Master of Arts in World Arts," Graduate Institute of Applied Linguistics, http://www.gial.edu/academics/world-arts.

in and reversed the decision to send their husbands and fathers to starvation and death working in Transkei. We do not have time to tell about the rich, ancient melodies that sustained Orthodox believers to endure persecution and hardship; of Tuvan people weeping as they heard Christians using their traditional throat singing; of North Korean believers holding hands and singing hymns at the moment of their martyrdom.

While the river seems to be rushing and rising, it's more likely that its true current remains subterranean, as music in many nations, prompted by the Holy Spirit, goes mostly unheralded and unreported, awaiting eternity to unfold.

353

INTRODUCTION

SECTION 1: FOUNDATIONS

SECTION 2: STORIES

SECTION 3: TOOLS

CLOSING

114. EQUIPMENT

By Frank Fortunato

"What's all this equipment?"

The suspicious customs guard in a restricted Middle Eastern nation almost shouted the question when he saw mic stands strapped to our bulging suitcases. As he was about to look inside one of the cases—stuffed with all kinds of electronic equipment—we four team members panicked. To divert his attention, one of us blurted out, "We're a music team here to record the beautiful music of your nation. We want to make it famous everywhere."

The guard, now obviously pleased, smiled and waved us and all the equipment through customs. Fortunately he did not ask what *kind* of music would be recorded—some of the very first local-language *Christian* worship songs in the nation's history.

INTRODUCTION

SECTION 1: FOUNDATIONS

SECTION 2: STORIES

SECTION 3: TOOLS

CLOSING

115. ARTISTS HOLD KEYS TO UNREACHED PEOPLE GROUPS[80]

By John Oswald

Where are the tellers of parables, proverbs, and well-crafted stories?

Where are the singers of songs, ballads, and epics?

Where are the visual artists who, by a few strokes of a pen or brush, can sum up a thousand words?

Dedicated Christian artists have far more to offer than they realize when it comes to breaking through barriers that block communication of the gospel. In many cultures, three-point sermons often don't fit! Artists have the keys to thousands of unreached ethnic groups, each with an amazing and distinct culture.

Some years ago I participated in a local amateur song and dance group in a small Asian city. Learning to play their most distinctive folk instrument, a long-necked lute with six strings, I rehearsed with them, drank tea with them, sat in on their group discussions, and eventually participated in performances with them.

My interest in their lute gave me entry to this circle. Among other things, I discovered that music—for them—is only *one* facet of their performing arts. They do not see a dichotomy between music and dance, drama and song. Each part contributes to the whole, and what results is a highly colorful, energetic, and exhilarating all-round performance.

I also learned what my musical interest in their culture meant to them. A complete stranger's comment summed it up: "You have come from a foreign land and have learned our language and culture. That touches my heart."

My personal involvement in their music equipped me to fill a hole in this small Christian community's worship life—but the scope is unlimited. Christian artists prepared to learn the arts of such unreached peoples will discover new horizons for communication. This work calls for people with varied skills, including music, dance, and the dramatic arts. It does not necessarily require training in research, though such skills can be extremely helpful.

It especially takes a willingness to learn a new way of thinking, culturally and artistically, and most of all, a desire to communicate the love of Christ to a fallen world. If we lay aside our cultural pride and, like our Savior, associate with people in the ways that are meaningful to them, it will touch their hearts—not just for a performance but also for their eternal destiny.

---

80   Originally published in a slightly different form in John Oswald, "Artists Hold Keys to Unreached People Groups," in Fortunato, *All the World*, 205. Reprinted by permission of the author.

116. WORSHIP IN MY LANGUAGE

By Brian Schrag

By that Sunday morning, the circumstances of my life had conspired to emaciate my soul. Our life's work—translation of the Bible into the Mono language of the Democratic Republic of the Congo—was in jeopardy. Our Congolese friends were in the middle of a war that the rest of the world thought had ended. I was still jet-lagged from my flight from France to Dallas. Physically, emotionally, and spiritually weakened, I trudged into Southwest Harvest Church.

But at the first sounds of the choir and worship band, my deadened soul quickened within me. They were singing songs I knew. In English. They were standing, clapping, and swaying the way the congregation in my home church in Chicago does. After over a year of learning to worship God in new ways in France, and before that, three years in Zaire, here was something familiar. Tears streamed down my face. My broken voice reflected perfectly the broken spirit beneath it as I joined my brothers and sisters in worship. We stood and prayed together for each other. I sang and worshiped God with my heart, surrounded by people with skins and voices and clothes and words and gestures and improvisations that I knew and that had accompanied some of my life's most profound communication with God.

And God began to rebuild me.

Oh, I believe that anyone can learn to worship God in unfamiliar musical, linguistic, and cultural contexts; every missionary has to. And God can and does speak through and around all sorts of barriers. But there's something profound about being home. About the peculiarities and particularities of a culture that is somehow mine. My heart language. Heart worship. Heart music. And it is this depth and fullness of communion with God that I want all people in the world to be able to experience.

INTRODUCTION

SECTION 1: FOUNDATIONS

SECTION 2: STORIES

SECTION 3: TOOLS

CLOSING

SECTION 3

TOOLS

ARTS ADVOCACY

HOW TO ADVOCATE FOR ARTS ON THE FIELD AND IN THE CHURCH

117. PROMOTING ARTS AWARENESS AND EDUCATION IN THE CHURCH

By Dianne B. Collard

THE ABSENCE OF ART CREATES THE NEED

The subject of arts awareness and education is not one that is normally associated with the task and purpose of the church. The church exists for many things, but promotion of the arts is not often mentioned. This is because in the Protestant and evangelical expressions of the church, beginning in the sixteenth century, the arts—especially visual and dance—were systematically eliminated. For instance, Ulrich Zwingli of Zurich preached against all practices in the church that appealed to the senses, whether it be visual, musical, ritual, or olfactory (incense), and limited the parameters of worship to the verbal and those addressing the human mind.[1] The result is an artistic anorexia that we are just now beginning to reverse.

The result of this pervasive movement in the church has not only caused the elimination of artistic expression within the church, but an alienation of the artist. In my research done in Europe in 2001–2004, I consistently discovered either a feeling of frustration among artists trying to use their creative gifts within a "free church" context[2] or a feeling of rejection and abandonment. For instance, only 23 percent of the visual artists interviewed in Germany remained actively involved in such organized churches. In contrast, the artists-of-faith in Spain had remained connected to a local church, but had bifurcated his or her creative gift and any church or worship expression.

---

1   John Dillenberger, *Images and Relics: Theological Perceptions and Visual Images in Sixteenth Century Europe* (New York: Oxford University Press. 1999), 177.

2   "Free churches," in contrast to "state churches," generally refers to churches in Europe which have little reliance on municipal, regional, or national governments for leadership training, polity formation, theological monitoring, or financial support.

THE NEW RENAISSANCE

According to Sandra Bowden, artist and past president of Christians in Visual Arts, "There is a quiet Renaissance stirring in the Western church."[3] Books abound on the subject of the church and art. Church art exhibitions and galleries flourish. Conferences, such as *Transforming Culture*, held in 2008 in Austin, Texas, brought together eight hundred artists, church leaders, and arts advocates. Yet there remains a crying need for better understanding and ways to embrace the arts and the artist.

FOUNDATIONAL REASONS FOR THE ABSENCE

In my research, the reasons for the current disengagement of the "free church" tradition and the arts were clear:

1. The first was a *theological* issue. Clearly there is a need for additional theological reflection and dissemination of the teachings on the biblical role for *all* artistic expressions. This has been spoken to in other chapters of this volume. Such a theological discussion should be broad, according to Paul Tillich:

    Theology of art is possible when theology means, not talk of God as one object alongside other objects, but as it must mean, talk of the manifestation of the divine in all beings and through all beings . . . Art can be religious whether it is the kind of art usually called religious or the kind usually called profane, or secular. It is religious to the extent that in it the experience of ultimate meaning and being is given expression.[4]

2. The second reason given most often for not embracing the arts was *tradition*, which may have been rooted in the theological overreaction centuries ago, but remains today simply because of inertia. This can be challenged by the theological and practical teachings on the role of art. Books, such as *For the Beauty of the Church*, edited by David Taylor, and *Culture Making: Recovering Our Creative Calling*, by Andy Crouch, can assist in breaking the syndrome of "we've never done it before."[5]

    Interestingly, the reason behind the lack of art in the church as expressed by many of the pastors in my research was that they simply didn't know how to use the arts—even if they were convinced that it should be done. Very practical books are needed to assist churches in caring for the artists in their community of faith and in expressing the arts in a cogent, meaningful fashion.

---

3   Sandra Bowden and Dianne B. Collard, eds. *Helps in Planning and Developing Church Related Galleries*. (Wenham, MA: CIVA, 2009), xii.

4   Paul Tillich, *The Courage to Be* (New Haven, CT: Yale University Press, 1952), 205.

5   See the *Handbook* bibliography for full references to these sources.

3. The final element to the lack of art in the church is the perception by pastors that "artists are problematic people." Most artists first laugh when hearing this statement, and then many become very irate. This chapter isn't the venue for discussing this issue, but it does need to be considered and addressed.

CHURCH LEADERS MUST INITIATE ARTS AWARENESS

The first focus of arts education within the church needs to be a reasoned commitment of the leaders to such an effort. This would require attending seminars, reading, and researching on the theology of the arts and/or aesthetics. Many Christian leaders are expressing this need and also contributing to its fulfillment.[6]

The exclusion of the arts, especially the visual arts, was not a mere accident of history or practice. It was a developed, systematized, and well-taught part of the foundation of the Protestant church. Therefore, I call for a public process of forgiveness and reconciliation within the church. Church leaders should declare their rejection of such harmful teachings and practice, while asking forgiveness of any artists that might feel alienated from the church because of their creative gift. Forgiveness should then be offered by the artists and true reconciliation pursued. Every time I speak on this subject, I express my sorrow, as a member of the church, for how artists have been historically treated, and ask their forgiveness. The healing between the artist and the church often begins at that juncture.

> A public blessing of the arts and artists in a church service will contribute to the healing of the chasm between the artists and the Christian community.

A public blessing of the arts and artists in a church service will contribute to the healing of the chasm between the artists and the Christian community. This will underscore the commitment of the church towards the role of the arts in all aspects of the church ministry. Having an organized community of artists within the church—along with either pastoral or lay leadership—will enable spiritual care of the artists, as discussed in other chapters.[7] Upon these foundations the awareness and education of the arts for the laity can flourish.

THINGS TO CONSIDER

As already mentioned, the place to begin is with a clear theological understanding of the purpose and power of the arts. Once the church leadership has grasped this and is able to articulate it, then the education program will be natural for the church. This *Handbook* will certainly contribute to this process.

---

6   See, for example, the following in the *Handbook* bibliography: Begbie (2000), Dyrness (2001), and Wolterstorff (1980).

7   See in particular: Mary Elizabeth Saurman, "Mentoring Artists," ch. 17; Sue Hall-Heimbecker, "How to Mentor Artists," ch. 128; Byron Spradlin, "G-A-T-H-E-R: Six Principles for Discipling Worship Leaders," ch. 135; and Jaewoo and Joy Kim, "Seven Recommendations for Mentoring Worship Leaders," *Handbook*, chpt. 138.

Consideration about the scope of such arts education for the congregation is necessary. It is essential to first determine congregational goals and purposes. One church, Zion Lutheran Church in Schenectady, New York, has a clear purpose statement:

1. to provide the congregation with a visual expression of faith that will add to the community's spiritual growth;
2. to provide an education opportunity within Zion that will expand the congregation's visual literacy;
3. to provide an opportunity for Zion parishioners to share their creative expressions; and
4. to provide a variety of art events throughout the year from a wide range of techniques, subjects, and themes. There will be a representation from amateur to very professional levels.[8]

It is clear from this statement that the purpose of the arts in this church encompasses spiritual growth and education, as well as inviting artists with a full range of abilities and levels of expertise. These issues must be decided before beginning art education in the church.

Another church, Grantham Church in Grantham, Pennsylvania, has precisely stated goals, especially related to its visual arts ministry, striving to

*   learn to better appreciate the artists as members of the Christian community;
*   support the artist—and the art lover—by providing space to show and enjoy art;
*   begin to dialogue on a more meaningful level on the issues surrounding faith and art in our culture; and
*   incorporate more artistic expressions into the life of the church, its worship services, and the lives of the community.[9]

The Grantham Church includes yet another purpose of arts awareness and education in the church in that the arts encourage reaching out into their community. A quality art emphasis in a church will both contribute to the cultural transformation of the community around it and will build relationships that could have eternal implications.

EFFECTIVELY USING ART IN THE CHURCH

Simply having a sermon preached or a class taught on the biblical role of the arts will not produce effective art awareness or education. It is a beginning, but it must be followed up by the integration of the arts in every church program. Such activities must, of course, be age appropriate. Activities such as a song, a drama, or a visual art contest will engage people of all ages. It is in the producing of art that people take personal ownership and gain the most value from it.

It is beneficial to be clear whether the encouragement of creative expression is to be focused on the amateur or the professional. It requires great sensitivity to engage both levels simultaneously, at least in the same event. Again, the church must be clear in its purpose for the overall

---

8   Bowden and Collard, 2009, 3.
9   Ibid., 10.

inclusion of the arts and for a particular event. There is clearly a place for amateur craft fairs, open to everyone in the church, as well as juried professional art exhibits.

Another key component in an effective arts ministry is how integrated the arts are in the church's overall program. The churches that have gained the most benefit from an intentional inclusion of the arts have approached it in a systematic and thematic manner. Frequently such themes are religious or related to the liturgical year. During this time, all forms of the arts—performance, music, and visual—are drawn upon in the children's Bible classes, the adult Bible studies, the Sunday morning worship services, and special programs. Paintings are hung in the narthex or sanctuary of the church; musical pieces are played and sung; liturgical dances and dramas are performed—all on the theme for the day or season. The value of the arts is clearly underscored as people learn and express their relationship to God, while being led by the artists and other spiritual leaders. Advent, Christmas, Lent, and Easter are clearly key times in the year to begin this integration of art into the program of the church.

> Be clear whether the encouragement of creative expression is to be focused on the amateur or the professional. It requires great sensitivity to engage both levels simultaneously, at least in the same event.

Supportive education programs are also beneficial. Courses in art history will enable the congregants to understand the richness of diversity and artistic expression throughout the broader Christian church. Workshops may be offered that teach a particular artistic style or increase artistic ability. These can be offered in all art forms by qualified artists and will be of interest to the members of the church, but may also expand the church's influence in the community.

ADULTS LEARNING FROM ART

Children will learn through observation and repetition. Adults do not learn in the same way. David Kolb clearly demonstrates that adults learn best in an *experiential* context. His Experiential Learning Model posits that the best entry point for learning for an adult is having or recalling a concrete experience, even a simulation.[10] The next necessary component is reflection on the experience and consideration of its significance. This can be done in either a group setting or a personal reflection, such as a journal entry. Only then is abstract teaching optimal, as the person has a "grid" on which the philosophical or theological teaching can be "hung." Next, a new experience would be sought in which to use both what was introduced through personal reflection and abstract teaching. It is in the application of both subjective and objective truth that true learning occurs.

I would suggest that the most effective teaching strategy would be to offer a variety of artistic experiences—musical, visual, and creative expressions of all kinds. Then schedule intentional reflection on the power of this experience in both private and group settings. Follow this time with a series of sermons, workshops, and lectures offered to optimize the learning experience. Only then can a congregation develop further creative outreach and ministry opportunities. Robert Henri wrote, "Art after all is but an extension of language to the expression of sensations too subtle for

---

10   David Kolb, *Experiential Learning: Experience as the Source of Learning and Development* (Upper Saddle River, NJ: Pearson Education, 1983).

words."[11] That "language" would be a powerful learning experience about God and his creation through the combination of art experiences, reflection, and teaching.

CONCLUSION

The possibilities for raising art awareness and education in the church are as varied and vast as the number of churches in any given area. There will not be a "one size fits all" education program. The essential elements are clear:

- biblical and theological comprehension;
- church leaders who preach and demonstrate an appreciation for the arts;
- well-conceived goals and vision for the arts, particularized to each congregation;
- age- and ability-appropriate events and education;
- thematic and integrated approach that includes all genres of artistic expression, as well as verbal teaching and/or preaching and special events;
- reconciliation with and blessing of the artists in the congregation and general community, which may include spiritual formation and care as well.

Such a program will enhance the learning and spiritual formation of all who participate, as well as influence the community around it. May we proclaim, with Saint Augustine, "My God and my glory, for this reason I say a hymn of praise to you and offer praise for him who offered sacrifice for me. For the beautiful objects designed by artists' souls and realized by skilled hands come from the beauty which is higher than souls; after that beauty my soul sighs day and night."[12]

---

11   Robert Henri, *The Art Spirit* (Cambridge, MA: Basic Books, 2007), 86.
12   Saint Augustine, *St. Augustine Confessions*, trans. Henry Chadwick (New York: Oxford University Press, 1992), 210.

118. DETERMINING YOUR ROLE AS AN ARTS ADVOCATE AND FACILITATOR

By Brian Schrag

The arts—broadly defined here as any heightened form of communication—have characteristics that make them crucial for work in the kingdom of God. Artistic communication is embedded in culture and so touches many important aspects of a society.

- Art marks messages as important, separate from everyday activities.
- Art involves not only cognitive but also experiential and emotional ways of knowing.
- Art aids memory of messages.
- Art increases the impact of messages through multiple media that often include the whole body.
- Art concentrates the information contained in messages.
- Art instills solidarity in its performers.
- Art provides socially acceptable frameworks for expressing difficult or new ideas.
- Art inspires and moves people to action.
- Art often acts as a strong sign of identity.

Perhaps most importantly, local artistic communication exists and is owned locally. There is no need to translate foreign materials, and local artists are empowered to contribute to the expansion of the kingdom of God.

Christians throughout history have recognized the impact that these features produce and have incorporated the arts into their lives. We have erupted in dance and song because of the unlikely fact that we can know God. We have drawn and acted and told stories because we feel satisfaction in using our talents to the fullest. We have also performed laments in response to trauma and danced in solidarity with those who are suffering.

In cross-cultural mission, there are three historical roles that people have played in relationship to mission and the arts:

- "Bring It—Teach It"
- "Build New Bridges"
- "Find It—Encourage It"[13]

As you will see, these are more like three points on a multifaceted continuum, and they parallel common approaches to mission in general.

BRING IT—TEACH IT

People working cross-culturally in this framework teach their own arts to people in another community. This has been a common practice throughout the history of the church, and it is still going on. It is why I could sing *"Ekangeneli Na Yesu"* with a church in rural Democratic Republic of Congo a week after arriving. Previous missionaries produced the song by putting lyrics in the Lingala language to the tune of "Auld Lang Syne."

The "Bring It—Teach It" approach may ultimately result in a common artistic language that unifies people around the world. It also sometimes contributes to satisfying and pleasurable fusions and newness. However, this approach also has frequent downsides. It may result in miscommunication of emotions and messages, communities that see God as foreign to them, local artists who feel excluded or demoralized, a sense among local communities that Christianity is irrelevant, and a weakening of kingdom diversity.

BUILD NEW BRIDGES

Someone reaching out in the "Build New Bridges" approach will learn enough about another community's arts to influence how they use their own arts in ministry. Art therapists, for example, have used local materials or songs to guide children through a healing process from suffering (see http://www.buildabridge.org). This approach could also include collaborations between artists of different cultures for common purposes, where what is produced has characteristics of more than one tradition.

The "Build New Bridges" model often requires a relatively short time before making initial progress, and it can work in communities who are going through trauma and so don't have energy or resources to create their own arts completely. It may also promote healthy interdependent relationships where everyone equally shares their arts.

Problems can arise when there is a significant power differential between the missionary and the artists in the community. The higher global social capital of an outsider can dampen the resolve and courage of local artists. This approach may also produce unsustainable results; new collaborative artistic production that is not deeply rooted in local traditions and social systems will likely fade away.

---

13   Credit goes here to Robin Harris for first suggesting these three approaches.

FIND IT—ENCOURAGE IT

The "Find It—Encourage It" arts advocate learns to know local artists and their arts in ways that spur these artists to create in the forms they know best. You can think of this person as a catalyst for someone else's creativity, helping give birth to new creations that flow organically from the community. The approach usually requires longer-term relationships with people and a commitment to learn above all else.

The most important benefit of encouraging local artistic communication is that the art already exists and is owned locally. There is no need to translate foreign materials, and local artists are empowered to contribute to the expansion of the kingdom of God. This approach also avoids many communication problems common in translation and feeds into richer worship for all of God's people now and into eternity (see Rev 7). Problems may arise if communities allow their strengthening identity to lead to pride or their local creativity to guide God's truth into syncretism.

The "Find It—Encourage It" method is not new: Patrick and other missionaries to the Celts were engaging local arts already in the fifth century.[14] But the last couple of decades have seen bourgeoning interest, new training programs, affirmation by mission leaders, and publications that mark something new and solid. Much of this activity is centered around the idea of ethnodoxology—a theological and anthropological framework guiding all cultures to worship God using their unique artistic expressions.

Though none of these three categories is untainted by creation's groaning, we wrote the accompanying volume of this publication, *Creating Local Arts Together: A Manual to Help Communities Reach Their Kingdom Goals*, for people working primarily in the third approach. We did this for two reasons. First, we see Jesus as our primary missionary model. As king of the kingdom, he left his heavenly culture to become a human zygote, learning to walk, talk, sing, relieve, and dress himself in a minority society before entering his full ministry (Phil 2). Whenever possible, we should learn first. Second, we believe this approach is being neglected, often with tragic consequences.

---

14   George Hunter, *The Celtic Way of Evangelism: How Christianity Can Reach the West . . . Again* (Nashville: Abingdon Press, 2000).

HOW TO ADDRESS OBJECTIONS IN THE WORK OF ARTS ADVOCACY

119. DEALING EFFECTIVELY WITH OPPONENTS ON THE FIELD[15]

By Robin P. Harris

OPPOSITION AND ISOLATION

Early in my ministry, after receiving some initial ethnomusicology training, I began to get significant opposition from some coworkers to my use of ethnomusicological principles.[16]

They tried to discredit what I was attempting to do. It got to the point where I thought I might need to change field locations or give up my dreams for this kind of ministry. My mission agency at the time did not know how to deal with the problem, nor were they sure whether they should support me as I applied these "new ideas." Those were the most discouraging days I have ever experienced in ministry.

The situation was eventually resolved. God used that anguishing time in my life to stretch my faith in him and to teach me to be grateful even for antagonism. In that fire of opposition, he gave me something that has defined my life ever since—a vision for creating a network to support and encourage arts workers in mission contexts who struggle with opposition and isolation. Out of that vision came the founding of the International Council of Ethnodoxologists (ICE) in 2003, an organization which has grown to hundreds of people who use the network for connections, encouragement, and insightful help from one another. In 2004 I used an ICE forum to get ideas and stories from a variety of people, collaboratively writing with a number of people to address the question, "What do you do with ethnomusicology opponents on the field?"[17] The result of that collaboration was an early form of this article.

---

15   Originally published in a slightly different form in Robin P. Harris, "Tool Q," in *All the World Will Worship: Helps for Developing Indigenous Hymns*, 3rd ed., eds. Brian Schrag and Paul Neeley (Duncanville, TX: EthnoDoxology Publications, 2005), 130–36. Reprinted by permission of Schrag and Neeley.

16   In this chapter, the terms "ethnodoxology," "ethnoarts," and "ethnomusicology" will be used to indicate research-based approaches to the arts. Where "ethnomusicology" is used, it still implies an application to other arts, such as dance, drama, visual art, and oral/verbal arts.

17   Many thanks to Tom Avery, Darla Earnest, Sue Hall, William N. Harris, Katherine Morehouse, Paul Neeley, Todd and Mary Beth Saurman, Brian Schrag, Joyce Scott, Glenn Stallsmith, Julie Taylor, and Roger Thomassen for their invaluable contributions to this article.

CURRENT SITUATION

Due to the fact that ethnodoxology-related training for missionaries is still not prioritized by many mission agencies, churches, and training institutions, the vast majority of missionaries who go to the field are unaware of cross-cultural principles for the arts. So those with training for arts in mission—in approaches such as applied ethnomusicology, world arts, ethnoarts, or ethnodoxology—sometimes find themselves serving on a field with others who are either unaware of these principles or who resist them. The stress that results from a disagreement in approaches between coworkers can cause tension and discouragement, and can be a serious challenge to one's tact, wisdom, and patience. A lack of resolution to the resulting problems can often result in an arts worker experiencing distress in ministry, and in extreme cases may result in such discouragement that the worker requests a change of assignment or leaves the field. So what can we do to work effectively with, and influence the thinking of, people who oppose the contextualization of arts on the field?

VARIOUS APPROACHES TO OPPOSITION

The following approaches have been used successfully. Clearly, discernment must be used to know which approaches are the most appropriate for each context.

1. Pray often—on a regular basis—*for* and *with*, if possible, the people with whom you have the disagreement. Ask them to pray for *you* that the Lord will give you wisdom as you serve and show you where you can improve.
2. Keep an attitude of humility, valuing the other missionaries for their successes, gifts, sacrifices, and contribution to the work. Work hard to develop warm relationships with them by focusing on common ground, such as biblical principles of worship, Bible translation, or other related issues which are not quite as divisive in your context.
3. Meet with opponents and listen empathetically, drawing out their opinions and fears about local music and arts so that you can understand them better. Agree with them as much as you truthfully can. If you know of a case where their fears are legitimate, indicate that these are real concerns that need to be addressed. Don't simply dismiss concerns as baseless.
4. After listening to their views, if you have the kind of relationship that will allow for it, try to discuss with them in a tactful, nonthreatening way.
    a. Tell real-life stories of the positive effects of heart music and arts in ministry.[18]
    b. Loan, or even give, them a copy of this *Handbook* and discuss it with them later.
    c. Tell about or show them the ICE website and ask them what they think about the statement of values on this page: http://www.worldofworship.org/heartmusic.php.
5. Invite a respected, credible missionary ethnodoxologist or arts worker familiar with the arts of your area to offer a short fellowship or learning event—a retreat, "tea," team

---

18   See Frank Fortunato, ed., with Paul Neeley and Carol Brinneman, *All the World Is Singing: Glorifying God through the Worship Music of the Nations* (Tyrone, GA: Authentic, 2006).

meeting, etc.—where the expert can talk about local music and arts styles with the missionaries in the area. Make it nonthreatening and practical to local missionaries. One topic that has been used successfully on several fields is "Local Music and Arts Aesthetics"; i.e., how aesthetic criteria vary from one culture to another. Include a question-and-answer time for "doubters" to process their questions and objections.

6. In working with the leadership of a mission agency or church, it is important to help them see how culturally appropriate Christian music and arts are directly relevant to reaching the goals of their mission. In talking with a mission director, remember that Westerners, including leaders of mission agencies, are usually results oriented. To catch their attention and keep the presentation short, don't start with ethnomusicology theory or a theology of global worship, but instead highlight positive results from indigenous Christian music and arts elsewhere, possibly using the stories from this *Handbook*.

7. Work not just with mission leaders, but also with national, regional, and local church leaders to share with them the effective uses of heart music and arts, as well as other principles of ethnodoxology. If they do not accept these ideas, remember that as a general principle you should be willing to work under the authority of the local host church leadership. Remember that local leaders will take into account the maturity level of new believers, avoiding some styles to help young believers "make a break from their background."

8. Don't be in a hurry! The unity of the body of Christ matters more than having great songs. True worship can happen in any case, and although it will certainly be helped by suitable kinds of music, this is not the determinant for what makes for heart worship. In general, things will move towards greater musical freedom, given time.

9. In many cases, talking about the benefits of ethnodoxology is not nearly as profitable as simply letting the result of good arts work speak for itself. Do a pilot project quietly with the resources you have and see if the results are appealing to your opponents.

10. Find ways to involve your opponents in an arts project in a way that uses their strengths and at the same time gives them an opportunity to get a closer look at what you do. For example, in the area where I served, the local minority people were struggling with one particular obstructionist gatekeeper who kept shutting down the arts projects of others—if she couldn't run it, she didn't want it to happen. When our local arts fellowship planned a festival of new Christian songs in local ethnic song styles, her response was to forbid her church to participate or even to pray for the event. At the very last week before the event, they decided to take a risk and invite her to be one of the judges for the festival. She accepted—it was an important position, after all!—and even brought some participants. Her involvement resulted in the development of some warm, supportive relationships with the organizers of the event which continue to this day.

TAKE OPPORTUNITIES FOR LEARNING—EVEN LEARNING TOGETHER!

Consider the option of doing a short course of study with a national partner or coworker. When I was first beginning to learn about ethnomusicology principles, I took a week-long course offered by SIL in Dallas. Rather than take the training by myself, I brought a colleague with me—a majority-language national from the country in which I was serving—partially paying her way and rooming with her during the course. Although her English level made the course difficult for her, she enjoyed herself very much and understood enough to become one of my most helpful allies in my ethnomusicology work. She set an example for other missionaries by being among the first of the majority-language speakers to learn to sing indigenous songs—in a language she didn't understand—when she returned. Her credibility as an experienced national missionary has done much for the progress of ethnomusicology principles in that country, as she provided a local model that others could emulate.

MAINTAINING BALANCE

In the end, humility and an empathetic understanding of others' point of view will go far to maintain a Christ-like relationship with mission colleagues with whom you disagree on ethnodoxology issues. One ethnodoxology leader, Brian Schrag, urges us to remember that, in some cases, music and arts that a person didn't grow up with can still play a significant role in that person's life. He reports that he remembers seeing old men in a village in northwestern Democratic Republic of Congo meet in the late afternoon to sing songs from the *Nzembo na Nzambe (Songs of God)*. This songbook contained hymns translated from English, German, and other European languages into Lingala, maintaining in large part the melodies that missionaries had taught decades earlier. No heart language, no heart music, but these men were born and grew up in a portion of Christ's body with these songs, and they loved to sing the "Songs of God." Brian goes on to talk about two of the reasons why music in foreign styles can serve a purpose:

> First, music foreign to me reminds me that I am not the only person—or part of the only people group—in the universe. Others have gone before me, and others go beside me today. God's family is huge, spanning vast expanses of time and geography. This guards against loneliness, selfishness, and an inappropriate sense of self-importance.

> Second, *profoundly unfamiliar music helps me relate to God in physical, emotional, and intellectual ways that I would never have known plumbing the depths of only one musical culture.* Worshiping God in African and African-American contexts has opened doors of bodily communication that were closed during my German Mennonite Baptist upbringing. Worshiping God in alien contexts helps us know God in new ways.

> If we can understand and verbalize our appreciation for these positive aspects, I believe we can sharpen and deepen our efforts at persuading our colleagues of the primordial benefits of heart music.

> As we forge new ways to communicate the fundamental importance of heart music in a Christian's life, let's work to understand the bigger picture.[19]

---

19   Brian Schrag, personal correspondence, November 29, 2004.

BIBLICAL PRINCIPLES FOR CHRISTIAN RELATIONSHIPS

Besides offering an empathetic understanding of others' ministries, the bigger picture also includes the *one-another's* of Scripture. We are to serve, comfort, and edify one another—in honor preferring, forgiving, admonishing, exhorting, and forbearing with one another in love, fervently and with a pure heart.[20] In our kingdom endeavors, we cannot settle for loving only those who agree with us in our application of ethnodoxology principles. We must also show love to those who oppose us.

EXAMPLE: INDIRECT APPROACH

When dealing with opponents to ethnodoxology approaches, try the indirect approach. This is what we did when the indigenous church leaders—not the missionaries—were dead set against indigenous songs, in spite of the fact that there was a traditional singer singing about his faith. One time a small group of people who had been at one of our workshops got excited about using this traditional singer's songs in church. Unfortunately, their enthusiasm was met with a strong "NO!" After some discussion with us, they decided on an *indirect approach*. They made literacy materials out of the Christian traditional singer's songs and distributed them in books and on tape to literacy classes. Soon the songs were having such an impact on people from their language group that the church leaders started asking to have the songs sung in church. (Todd and Mary Beth Saurman, personal correspondence with Robin Harris, December 7, 2004)

EXAMPLE: "THE MUSICS OF ____"

I designed a four-hour seminar called "The Musics of ____" (my field) and opened it up to anyone who wanted to attend. This seminar also served as an orientation for new people being assigned to that field. I tried to make it as fun and nonthreatening as possible. We listened to several clips of music from around the continent and played a game, trying to match the song with its country of origin. The most effective session involved viewing the introduction to the film *The African Queen*. It shows the fictional congregation of the First Methodist Church of Kungdu trying to sing along to Katharine Hepburn leading a Western hymn from the organ. No one in the congregation seems to have any comprehension of how to sing it properly, but Hepburn and her preacher brother plow ahead. It's quite funny, and most people who see it laugh. Many of the translators respond with, "That's how it is in my village!" This film clip enables people to talk openly about the dangers of doing music work without an ethnoarts perspective. (Glenn Stallsmith, posted on ICE's Current Issues forum, November 24, 2004; Glenn notes that the idea for using this video clip originally came from Karen Boring in the early 1990s)

---

20   Rom 12:10; 15:14; Gal 5:13; Eph 4:2,32; Col 3:16; 1 Thess 4:18; 5:11; Heb 3:13; 1 Pet 1:22.

EXAMPLE: DEALING WITH RELUCTANCE

I went with an organization as their very first ethnomusicologist ever. Talk about a daunting situation. They were pretty hesitant, but I had talked them into letting me go short term to a people group who had mentioned the need for an ethnomusicologist. When I arrived overseas, I found that it was actually a mix-up, that the previous field director had asked for an ethnomusicologist a while back, but the current one did not see the need. So here I was, four thousand miles from home, being told that my services were not really needed.

I talked them into letting me feel out the situation anyway, since I was already there. It turned out that they actually did need an ethnomusicologist, but just didn't know it. They were ripe for worship teaching and songwriting efforts. We organized a seminar and at the end of the day had a tape of Scripture songs and other worship songs. We had a beautiful morning of worship the next day, and we even had the Abraham story recorded on tape by a secular musician. When the team saw the results of the seminar, they realized the worth of ethnomusicology and asked me to consider coming back full time. This filtered back to the organization in the US and they were really excited about it. Now they are open to sending ethnomusicologists worldwide.

When faced with reluctance, sometimes all of the ethnomusicology theory in the world will get us nowhere, and all we can say is, "Let's just try it and see what God does." I would encourage future interns not to worry about proving their own worth to the field or organization. Others may not be excited about you. They might not catch your vision right away. Just remember that it was God's vision first for all the earth to worship him. When we go prepared and open to God's Spirit, he will provide all the proof we need. (Katherine Morehouse, posted on the ICE Current Issues forum, December 16, 2004)

120. WHEN THEY WON'T LISTEN
By William N. Harris

You know that culturally relevant and biblically appropriate church planting is important. You see the potential surge forward in your team's effectiveness if only the Western cultural baggage can be trimmed away. But your team doesn't get it, and instead a few of them are enthusiastically getting their favorite Hillsong *Greatest Hits* choruses translated into the local language. Worse, you feel blocked, marginalized, shut out. Been there?

Dr. Sarah Sumner has a fantastic book called *Leadership above the Line* that I heartily recommend, especially because this short chapter can only begin to mine its riches.[21] Applied to ethnodoxologists, here are a few nuggets. Sumner sees each of us as a combination of three kinds of people, with one quality generally dominating the other two. When operating "above the line," we act on behalf of others. When "below the line," we act primarily for ourselves at the expense of others. Her three categories of people are *strategists*, *humanitarians*, and *diplomats*.

THE STRATEGISTS

Approaching life primarily as *strategists*, we think a lot about shining light on a situation and getting at the truth. Strategists want their ministry to *be* good. *Humanitarians* care most about compassionately nurturing healthy relationships. They want the ministry team to *feel* good. *Diplomats* are all about beauty, public perception, and joining forces with others to accomplish more together. They want the ministry to *look* good.

Okay, you're getting opposition from a *strategist* team member or supervisor. What do you do? Couch your arguments for strategist ears, starting with shared common ground: "We should be presenting the truth without compromise in bringing the light of the gospel here. These people will be right with God only when they worship him in both spirit and truth. That means we need to focus on both—grounding them in a right understanding of biblical truth *and* encouraging wholehearted worship. Our team is good at teaching the Bible and helping people understand how to apply scriptural principles to their lives. What about heart worship? Are we doing all we can to help believers open their spirits to God? It would be wrong to make somebody just copy

---

21   See Sarah Sumner, *Leadership above the Line* (Carol Stream, IL: Tyndale House Publishers, 2006).

us instead of being genuine with God; that's phoniness. We need to start with people where they truly are. Their hearts have a lifetime of preconditioning to love their own language, culture, music, and arts, just as we are preconditioned to prefer our own culture. Rather than try to retrain their taste, what can we learn about this context so that we support helping them redeem their own culture for the gospel, and through those forms, genuinely worship God?"

THE HUMANITARIANS

When talking to *humanitarians*: "We all agree that the best way to heal a community is to work toward restoring the people's relationships with each other and most importantly with God. Their relationships with each other and with God should be unhindered by conflict and artificiality. How can we help people to do better than just go through the motions of worship? I want to invite people into genuine worship that isn't forced, but rather spontaneous and natural. We need to let them help us understand their heart's music and arts. What an opportunity to build bridges of understanding by inviting them to share their hearts with us, starting with helping us know what they love about their own culture's music and arts. What would they like to see in this church that includes that kind of response to God? How can we encourage them to bring the best of their culture into how they relate to God and each other?"

THE DIPLOMATS

When talking to *diplomats*, try this: "We all agree that we want to see visible progress in our ministry—more people taking an interest in the gospel, an increasing respect in the community for this church, and growing coalitions of support both in the local government and in our donor base to help the work go forward. That means we need to be attracting the right people in our networking efforts here on the field and communicating the right message to people back home so that they are enthusiastic about what we are doing. The best way to make progress is to appeal to local people according to their tastes rather than ours, so that they feel comfortable in this church and naturally want to join with us. We'll grow the work faster by speaking the local language and reflecting their heart music and arts when we gather for worship and teaching. The less foreign we look, the less resistance we'll get from people who don't like foreigners. We can make what we're doing here an example other ministries look to with respect. I believe our culturally contextualized approach can influence lots of other ministries, increasing not only our influence here but in places far beyond our reach. We can be standard bearers that others look to, an inspiration to others as we reach this whole region together."

IN SUMMARY

Leadership above the Line has a lot more to say about shedding light, helping our relationships, and strengthening our ministries in ways I don't have space here to address. For now, let's think about how to present to team members and supervisors the value of our contribution, not according to how *we* think, but rather how *they* do.

- We do that by showing *strategists* how contextualization of music and arts in ministry is congruent with their desire to help people truly embrace Christ.
- We do it by showing *humanitarians* that we too value nurturing relationships with others and with God by encouraging genuine heart worship.
- We do it by encouraging *diplomats* to see that our approach can produce more visible fruitfulness in the community, rally support at home, and grow our ministry.

Far from being manipulative, speaking into the lives of others by showing loving attention to who *they* are shows we care enough to think in terms they naturally embrace, not for our sakes, but for theirs and our Lord.

TEACHING

HOW TO DESIGN AND CONDUCT AN ARTS WORKSHOP

121. DESIGNING ARTS WORKSHOPS FOR MOTHER-TONGUE SPEAKERS

By Kenneth R. Hollingsworth and Héber Negrão

GETTING ORGANIZED: WHAT TO DO BEFORE SENDING OUT THE INVITATIONS

Sometimes an outside organization will ask you to organize an arts workshop. In other instances, you will be the one who is the initiator. In either case, there are certain things to determine even before you send out the invitations. This may require starting a year or more in advance.

Audience

You must define for whom the workshop is aimed. Is the workshop for mission or church leaders in order to train others? Is it only for skilled musicians who are already actively "doing" art/music? Is it for mother-tongue speakers to compose in their own music and language? Once you decide your target audience, you can then better define your goals and participants to invite.

Goals

What is the ultimate goal of the workshop? Is it to produce hymns or other art? Or do you have more modest goals such as introducing the idea of using indigenous music and art in local worship, doing a survey of local arts, etc., perhaps as a first step towards inspiring the creation of local Christian art. Knowing your ultimate goal will help you determine the instruction and activities and give you an idea of whom you should invite to the workshop.

Participants

Who should come to this workshop? Is it for one language group or for a number of language groups from a certain area? Who from a language group should attend? Determine who you want as participants and their qualifications. Do they need to be able to read and write in their mother tongue? Will you invite only believers, or can non-Christian artists attend? Do participants need to be recommended by a pastor or their church elders? Will you require that at least two people from a language attend so they can work as a team/group? Do they need to have already composed or done drawings or created a drama?

Dates, times, and duration

When will the workshop be held and for how many days? The dates of the workshop should be determined by when the potential participants would be most free to come—dry season for people who are farmers, weekends or evenings for city people who work during the day, etc. The length of the workshop and the starting and ending days should take into consideration how far the participants would need to travel.

You will need to determine how long the workshop should run. Do you need to present several workshops, spaced out over a period of time? That is, should you teach some principles, send the people home to work on what has been taught, then after several months or a year, bring them back to build on what they have done? Most groups find either a four-day or a two-week workshop adequate, especially if there can be a follow-up workshop several months to a year later. If you are conducting 8:00–5:00 sessions, you will need to decide whether evening or weekend sessions are also necessary.

The location of the workshop must also be determined. Is the site located where it is convenient for the participants to get to, especially those coming by public transportation? Does the site have an adequate meeting room? Does it have adequate space for sleeping, eating, and washing? Are there places where groups can compose music or do other art without being disturbed?

Staff

Who should help staff this workshop? Who can serve as teacher or mentor? What language or languages will be used for instruction in the workshop? Are interpreters for one or more languages needed? Who will help with the practical needs such as workshop administration (to collect fees, pay bills, and otherwise see to people's needs), cooking, recording the songs produced, and duplicating cassettes or CDs for the participants to take home.

Funding

Where will the funding for the workshop come from? How much funding is available? How much should the participants pay? Should the participants pay in cash or provide food items? The funding available may be the major factor as to how long the workshop will run.

Pre-workshop information

Decide what information, if any, needs to be obtained from the participants before the workshop and how to obtain it. A good thing to know for a hymn-writing workshop is what Scripture, if any, exists in the language of the participants.

Decide what kinds of things the participants need to bring to the workshop—toilet items, towel, sheet, sleeping mat, Bible, pen, notebook, etc.—and also what other things participants might have available such as cassette recorders, cell phones with recorders, indigenous music instruments, etc.

Prayer team

It is very helpful—and necessary!—to have a team of people praying for you and the workshop, in addition to your own prayers.

Once you have established these things—goals, dates, places, participant information, etc.—you can write up your invitations and send them out. Make sure you have given directions to the center where the workshop will be held and specify any costs to be borne by the participant. Now you are ready to begin planning the workshop content and timetable.

DETERMINING THE WORKSHOP CONTENT

Both planning and flexibility are important

If the main goal of the workshop is to create Scripture hymns or some other artwork based on Scripture, some leaders are happy to simply have a minimum of a start time, prayer time, meal times, etc., and leave the rest to the leading of the Holy Spirit. While this seems to work well for some—especially for those who have considerable previous experience in leading arts workshops—other workshop planners feel the need for a precise timetable of events. This doesn't mean that lessons and times can't be changed as the workshop takes place. Flexibility is essential. But for leaders and workshop participants who like to know what is happening and when, a timetable can give confidence to everyone that the workshop is organized and heading in a good direction.

Establish a daily rhythm

We recommend structuring the content by charting a daily schedule. Much of the structure will depend upon the customs of the locale where you are holding the workshop. In hotter climates this may mean beginning with an early breakfast (7:00–7:30), followed by a devotional time of thirty minutes or more. Somewhere in midmorning there should be a break time for coffee or tea. Other time slots to fill are lunch at midday, a possible siesta and/or another break in the afternoon, followed by a meal at sundown or soon afterwards. The time periods in between the fixed time slots are times for teaching and creating.

Shaping the content

If this is the first time for many of the participants to attend an arts workshop, the participants need some biblical groundwork for using local arts in worship. Often it is helpful for them to see or hear examples of how others have created songs or drama or art for the Lord. This could also be done in evening sessions.

Participants may need guidance on to how to begin creating songs, dance, drama, etc., in their own style and language. Be careful not to do excessive lecturing at the beginning! Too much theory will dampen enthusiasm for creating and reduce the time needed to create. Remember that many adults come to workshops with considerable experience. The key is to draw out this experience and help participants use their expertise and knowledge in new ways. Many adults only need a few examples as models in order to move directly into the creation phase. Remember to leave plenty of time for creating new songs, dramas, etc. Creativity takes time!

For creating hymns, it is advisable to start small. Begin with a bit of teaching, followed by an effort to work with a short text of not more than two to four lines. If you are creating a drama, start with a simple idea and aim for a sketch of one or two minutes. With this simple beginning, you can expand with more extensive lectures, discovery times, and additional assignments to create more lengthy songs, dramatic productions, etc.

Discussion times and group sharing are important

In structuring the class sessions remember that people learn best when they can discuss among themselves the subject taught or otherwise apply what they have just learned. It is profitable therefore to take time to process what you are learning in small or large groups after each class presentation. If your audience consists of people of various ethnic groups, it is usually most advantageous to have members of the same group work together. It is also advantageous, however, to discuss as a whole group so that participants can share their experiences and learn from each other.

Preparing summaries of key principles makes for better learning

Many groups appreciate having written summaries of the principles taught and what they have learned. Sometimes it is helpful to ask one or two of the participants to prepare a five- to ten-minute summary of one or more topics covered in the previous day. In addition to serving as a group review, the summaries give the director an idea of what is important to students and also allow for catching any misconceptions of the material taught. Usually one of the teaching or mentoring staff will draft a written summary based on the teaching notes. These will be given to the participants. In this way students do not need to write down everything that happens in class and are free to listen and participate more fully in class discussions and activities. The notes they take home with them are also generally of a bit better quality as well.

Attention must be given to recording for future reference

It is helpful to the participants if they have a way to remember the tunes they are creating. During the song creation time they could use a cassette recorder, a cell phone with recorder, or some other digital recorder. Participants also find it helpful to be able to take home a copy of the final product. For a permanent copy of the final product they could have a cassette tape, CD, or DVD, depending on the media player they have at their disposal at home. The workshop staff should think of a way to provide a recording of the final product in either audio or video form.

Don't forget the closing ceremony!

An essential part of the workshop is the closing ceremony. This can be done only for the participants or for outsiders invited by the participants. At the ceremony different individuals or groups can perform the songs or dramas they've created. They can also do skits which teach some of the principles they have learned during the workshop. The workshop organizer generally gives a speech outlining the goals and hopes for the workshop and recognizes the contributions of the staff and others. In many instances it is customary to award "Certificates of Participation" to the participants.

INTRODUCTION

SECTION 1: FOUNDATIONS

SECTION 2: STORIES

SECTION 3: TOOLS

CLOSING

122. ENCOURAGING THE DEVELOPMENT OF RELEVANT ARTS IN THE LIVES OF BELIEVERS

By Todd and Mary Beth Saurman

THE PURPOSE OF ARTS WORKSHOPS

Arts workshops are opportunities for people to gather and interact, to gain common vision in the midst of diversity, and to strengthen their gifts and encourage each other through sharing them. An arts workshop should be a flexible time for training, learning, and problem solving, for using our strengths, and building unity as we work together. It should provide a venue where we can listen to the Lord and each other for direction.

A workshop is most effective if its purpose and design are based on the needs and interests of the participants. Then they soak up the subject matter and engage in the activities with energy and enthusiasm. To gain this result, it is advisable to plan the workshop activities in dialogue with those who know the participants well or understand their needs. An effective workshop has a solid plan for tools and focused activities, but leaves room for adaptation in order to better meet the participants' needs and deal with the issues that are relevant to them at that particular time.

The possibilities for workshop content and approaches are as wide as one's imagination and God's creativity. They are not limited to predetermined formats. Because of this, the facilitators should listen well to the Lord and to the participants as they plan a particular workshop. They should use their skills as facilitators to draw others into the discussion and the planning experience.

APPROACHING A WORKSHOP

Arts workshops are mainly facilitated by adults and with adults. Varied adult learning approaches offer formats for engaging adults in discussions that lead them toward self-discovery. Participatory methods techniques and adult learning approaches are helpful tools for designing activities that invite relevant discussion, both prior to and during the workshop.

WHO SHOULD ATTEND

After the goals and focus for the arts workshop are established, the workshop team can better assess who should be invited as participants. It is good to think through not only who will directly benefit from the overall goals of the workshop, but also who might be stakeholders, people of influence, and other people affected by the outcomes.

CHURCH CULTURE/COMMUNITY CULTURE ENGAGEMENT

Although a workshop may be held by the church, its results should stretch beyond the walls of the church, just as the results of Sunday morning worship should stretch beyond the church building and influence our whole lives (Rom 12:1). One common barrier to this stretch is the chasm that often exists between "church culture" and "community culture."

Like other cultures, church culture has its own set of standards, beliefs, language, and other features. This church culture should be a culture that stands out as distinct in the world, a culture based on the teachings of Christ and his word. The chasm we are discussing here as a barrier, however, occurs when the church culture is so separate from the surrounding secular culture that [Sometimes] those outside the church must go "cross cultural" to relate to and understand what is happening in the church. This type of chasm is the reverse of Christ's model of reaching the lost. It requires nonbelievers to change, learn, and adjust in order to fit in and understand what is communicated in the church experience.

It is true that there are many necessary adjustments that nonbelievers must make to move towards a relationship with Jesus. However, when nonbelievers become the ones who are striving to build a bridge in order to reach the church, their striving may show that we in the church have not yet understood how to reflect the way Christ has sought and reached us.

SELF-GENERATED RESEARCH ACTIVITIES

One way to build bridges is to help church members try to understand how community members think, how they approach life, and how they face struggles. This understanding will prepare them to relevantly present the gospel to the community.

In one workshop, participants from a Southeast Asian language group had a revelation. For years they had preached the gospel through dramas they created. These dramas were filled with church culture talk and condemnation for those who followed Buddhism. The drama groups were chased out of many communities, and the dramas created division and anger between the Christians and the nonbelievers in many communities in which they performed. "I finally understand," said one of the workshop participants, "why the community rejected us. We were speaking against them instead of finding ways to relate to them and allow them to relate to the truth of God's word. We need to learn what communicates effectively to the insiders in the community."

The believers were in a church culture that had a very Western church form. They no longer knew their community culture. So, with a few basic research tools, they began seeking to learn about the community values, beliefs, and communication methods including art forms. They wanted to learn how the insiders thought and how to communicate effectively to them. This research also propelled them into filling another chasm that had occurred in their context—an intergenerational divide. The young people who filled the church were mostly interested in contemporary art forms. But the experts in their own community culture were older individuals with years of experience and wisdom. Through self-generated research activity, the young people began understanding more about the meaningful traditional art forms and began building a bridge with the art experts in the community. In time the younger people studied with the experts and found effective ways to present meaningful art forms to the community.

Meaningful art forms are the central catalyst for any arts workshop. The relevant art forms that communicate effectively are vital worship mediums that help believers respond to the Lord and reach out to the community in which they live and minister.

BEFORE THE WORKSHOP

Facilitating arts workshops can be challenge in many ways, but it also presents exciting and rewarding opportunities. People share their culture and language, their dances and instruments, their drama and verbal arts, their visual arts and songs. The resulting interconnection often acts as a dynamic, energizing stimulus. The exploration and sharing encourages participants by validating their root identity. It can also motivate believers to use these various forms of community expression in worship.

A workshop can be limited to members of one language or community group, or it can combine members of several different language or community groups. In either case, dividing into smaller work groups, when appropriate, can be helpful in the sharing and creation processes and in facilitating discussion and development of ideas. It seems wise to have someone who is a cultural insider to assist in appropriately assigning the attendees to smaller work groups.

WORKSHOP MODEL

Flexibility and ability are key factors in leading any workshop. Each workshop, although uniquely sculpted, can draw from some core tools. The module tools included in this paper were developed during our years of experience as workshop facilitators. These are just a few of the possible tool sets that could be used for any arts workshop. They are, of course, most effective when adapted and changed for the specific context and established goals.

WORKSHOP OVERVIEW

In this section we give one example of a workshop overview to clarify what happens during the meeting times, and the goals and desired outcomes.

The main objective of our sample workshop is to *pass on a vision* to church leaders, community members, composers, musicians, storytellers, visual artists, and dancers. We want them to see the value of using language and arts that speak effectively to people within their own culture, so we facilitate as they explore culturally relevant ways to express their Christian faith in song, poetry, dance, drama, and other art forms from their cultural context.

The workshop has two main tracks:

1. For one track we focus on *what the Bible says and does not say about arts.* Scripture passages that deal with art in Hebrew culture are integrated into small group activities. Scriptures that relate to worship, creating new art forms, and other culturally relevant issues are also read and discussed.

2. The second track deals more with *community and church culture issues.* We encourage participants to gain deeper insight into language, arts, and culture, including music. Our areas of discussion include music terminology, arts genres and categories, poetic form analysis, arts analysis, performance practices and contexts, dance, drama, and storytelling, and methods for presenting new creations. There is also discussion of the creative process, worldview, and culture change.

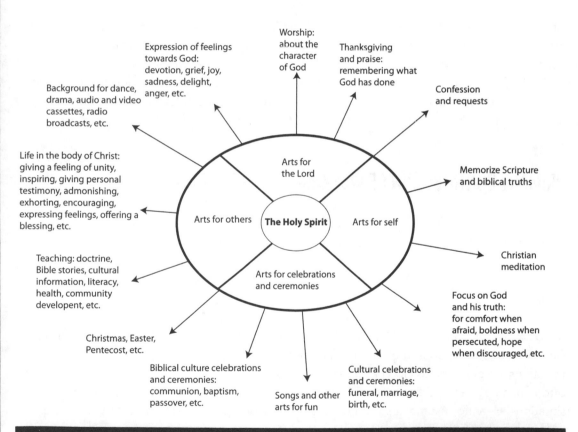

Worship Wheel [10]

22   Adapted from Todd Saurman and Mary Saurman, "The Worship Wheel: Developing Culturally Appropriate Music as Expressions of Worship in the Lives of Believers," in Schrag and Neeley, *All the World Will Worship,* 53–64.

As the workshop progresses, these two tracks are integrated in order to consider practical ways to apply the discovered information to culturally relevant Scripture use, worship, communicating the faith to others, community development, and literacy. Activities with discussion and participatory elements help participants understand ways that metaphors and redemptive analogies can be used as a bridge to help people understand scriptural truths and to target various subcultures within each people group (see "The Two Tracks" below).[23]

Ideally the goal is for new, relevant art forms to be created, but this may not happen in the brief time of the workshop. Whether or not new arts are created, we discuss ways to check existing or newly produced art forms for clarity, naturalness, and scriptural accuracy. The most important part of the workshop is spending time in prayer. The creation of new arts needs to happen in both a natural and a supernatural way.

CHOOSING AND DESIGNING MODULES FOR THE WORKSHOP

After the focus of the workshop is more clearly defined and the range of participants is decided, modules can be chosen and designed to meet the specific goals of your particular arts workshop. For more on module development, see our resource entitled "Ideas for Arts Workshop Modules," available on the *Handbook's* accompanying DVD, where we suggest examples of some types of modules that we have adapted over the years. The examples we offer are skeletal and need the honing of the facilitators for application to specific situations.

PRIMARY CONTRIBUTION OF WORKSHOP FACILITATORS

Since the workshop involves exploring and discovering, we as facilitators make it clear to the participants, translators, and other attendees that we are seeking to learn from and with them. In the workshop we will all participate in the process of discovering together. This focus helps us hold lightly what we have brought to teach but tightly to what is important to explore as a group. The result is that relevant and useful learning and application will be more likely to occur.

Two main contributions we can make to a workshop are: (1) facilitating discussions to keep things moving forward, and (2) sharing from stories and examples things we have learned from working with other groups throughout Asia. This second contribution follows the biblical model to tell others the great things God has done.[24] The stories and examples we share from other groups often encourage the participants and spark new, unique ideas that they can apply to their own situations. Hearing testimonies from other language groups can also motivate the participants to look for what God is doing in their own language group and to share them with others. The stories can also spark ideas about their own language group that contrast with what has happened in other groups.

---

23   For a better understanding of how the use of these "two tracks" fit more generally into a week-long arts workshop, see the sample "Workshop Schedule" at the end of this chapter.

24   See, for example, 1 Chr 16:8; Ps 9:11; 66:16; 78:4; 98:1; 105:1; 118:15–17; 126:2,3; Isa 12:4,5; 44:23; 63:7; Jer 51:10; and Luke 8:39.

KEY PRINCIPLES OF THE WORKSHOP PROCESS

Seven key principles keep us focused during the workshop process:

1. **Listen well. Listen for deeper understanding.** Learning requires us to really listen. We seek to listen to every idea, struggle, and thought that the participants desire to share. Sometimes, because time is limited, we must shorten a sharing period, but we usually try to use some other time—a meal or a break time—to talk with those who have not had the opportunity to share with us. These interactions give us valuable insights into the types of issues that are present in people's personal lives, in their communities, in their Christian experience, and in their church culture. They also help us to see more clearly some of the spiritual issues people are facing.

   - We design the activities so that the participants interact with the materials and the topics that are to be covered. During the process, we constantly look for ways to help them integrate the new things they are discovering into their lives as believers. We want them to not only interact with the materials, but then to come back and share what they've discovered, created, or designed with the other participants. Listening to each other is an opportunity for cross-fertilization and a catalyst for producing new ideas and approaches.

2. **Meet the participants where they are.** We seek to draw information from the participants in order to know more about their individual, cultural, and spiritual needs. Like therapists or doctors, we want to know what the participants' struggles are and what issues need to be addressed so that we will present relevant material. If we have not done this during a workshop, we have not achieved what we were hoping to accomplish.

   - It takes time to understand the participants' real needs. Workshops usually range in duration from several days to a month. This time limitation makes it crucial for us to quickly gain as much insight as possible so that we can decide which activities will be most appropriate for each language group. The participants are usually able to identify and share the felt needs and expectations they come with. For example, participants often say, "We have come to this workshop to learn how to play the guitar and sing better." Another frequent request is for us to assist participants in translating hymns and making a hymnbook. We meet them there—listening to their expectations, acknowledging them completely, affirming their desires, but encouraging them to think about their real needs in worship.
   - We cannot, of course, always meet the heartfelt needs of each participant, but as we listen and try to address some of the expressed needs during the workshop time, the Lord comes and ministers. As we dig deeper and pray together for God's Spirit to guide, we find that he himself brings revelation and healing to the participants. He meets them on deeper levels than we ever could.

INTRODUCTION

SECTION 1: FOUNDATIONS

SECTION 2: STORIES

SECTION 3: TOOLS

CLOSING

3. **Support the participants in moving to where they need or desire to be.** Participants usually come to the workshops with needs and desires in mind. We facilitators also come with an agenda. A doctor will often listen past a list of symptoms and realize that there are possibly deeper needs that should be addressed. We are always trying to diagnose possible practical and spiritual needs of the group. We do not want to assume that we know their needs, but we seek to remain open to deeper insights that the Lord may give.

- As we address the need for believers to find meaningful ways to worship, we try to help them overcome obstacles to fully realizing that worship. Meaningful worship is not just on Sunday morning, and it does not depend on a particular form or ritual. We aim to help participants receive the revelation of grace, find freedom from strongholds, and discover ways to express grace and freedom in ways that will reach others effectively.
- We usually find that it takes the first couple days of a workshop for the participants' needs to become apparent. As we listen to them during this time, we also present some activities as catalysts to help them understand that God wants them to feel free to worship through their language, art forms, and culture. We encourage them to consider how they can bring together the appropriate cultural art forms to glorify him and to express their faith more meaningfully within their communities. As they grapple with this, individuals will slowly begin to make a needed paradigm shift. They will accept that they as believers can use the various music styles, dances, and art forms that really speak to a variety of people.

4. **Flex and then flex some more.** Flexibility is a major component of a successful workshop. We hold our initial plans lightly, looking to the Lord for constant guidance as to what the next step should be. Listening well to the workshop participants opens opportunities for us to respond together to the Holy Spirit's guidance.

- When the workshop staff is flexible and adjusts to meet the needs of the participants, every workshop becomes a unique experience and creation. No two workshops look the same. Since each language group and participant is unique, there are endless possibilities for different workshops to evolve. With God at the helm, he in his creativity directs amazing experiences.
- The unknowns of each workshop can be a test of faith, of course, as we try to let go of our plans and allow God to direct what is happening moment by moment. As people wrestle with radically new ideas, they often experience feelings of elation or discouragement. Initially, they may feel anger, grief, loss, and disappointment. Experiencing emotional highs and lows can be exhausting, but it is worth it when people obtain the peaceful assurance that God wants them to use meaningful art forms that will speak effectively to people in their cultures. When they reach this place of rest, there is peace and joy for us leaders, as well.

5. **Affirm the participants as unique people whom God created in his image.** Art forms that are meaningful to each of us are connected in some way to our emotions, memo-

ries of life experiences, and our cultural interpretations of those art forms. These intangibles are in a place deep within each of us. Meaningful art forms reach that deeply personal place where mere words cannot always reach. It is a spiritual place, and it is vulnerable when exposed. Workshop facilitators need to guard the approaching of that place as each person presents it to others. We are cautious to remain unbiased and nonjudgmental with any art forms that are presented. We want each person's creation to be shown honor and respect.

- In the course of the workshop, we watch many participants increasingly express the true music of their hearts or of the communities that they identify with the most. To be willing to do this, they must feel safe. Then, as the Holy Spirit helps them understand God's word and the value he puts on their culture, people begin to openly admit their love for their traditional songs and their desire to reach others through the use of their traditional art forms.

6. **Study God's word and address spiritual strongholds.** A vital element of every workshop is the time we spend studying God's word. The participants work in small groups to grapple with what God says about worship, about following him, and about communication with others about him. We also talk about our roles, gifts, and responsibilities in our lives as believers.

- Evil spiritual forces are also active in these workshops. The enemy does not want us to lead people into songs of victory or into new freeing worship experiences. In every area of Asia where we have led a workshop, we have experienced certain resistant spirits or forces working against this freeing process. So we must seek the Lord to give us insight about barriers that come up in any given workshop. Then we must pray through the strongholds and roadblocks.

7. **Pray together and for each other.** Throughout each workshop, we pray for and with the participants many times. It is unifying and healing. For us, prayer is the most important principle in a successful workshop. It is through talking with and listening to God that we see him at work in the lives of the participants and in our own lives. This prayer is not a matter of just listing what we want from God, but rather of thanking him for what he is doing and asking that we will not miss anything he wants to do. We watch expectantly and are never disappointed, since he always fulfills his promise to bless all nations and ethnic groups. We then celebrate these blessings together.

- We want to commit everything we do during the workshop time to the Lord. We put all the participants' ideas, vision, hopes, and revelations before the Lord, asking him to be our guide. Since everything is from him and through him, we desire to give everything back to him for his glory (Rom 11:36). We spend time listening for what God is speaking to each of us. Then we share with each other what we are learning from him.
- Whenever we hit a barrier in a workshop, whether mental, emotional, or spiritual, we pray about it specifically. There are many barriers that can emerge. Often such

barriers involve some type of spiritual bondage. Since God desires for people to worship with freedom, as soon as he is approached we generally see him respond. His response is powerful and often even overwhelming for all of us.

CONCLUSION

A skilled workshop facilitator should be always seeking to understand the evolving dynamics unique to each workshop. Such a leader will listen well to the participants and to the Lord. As the leader responds to the participants' true needs, they will begin to use the art forms of their culture in relevant ways and to build a reservoir of such experiences. There will then be a medium for effectively communicating to their communities the scriptural truths that address their needs and issues. It may take time for a workshop facilitator to develop the necessary skills and sensitivity, but the basic principles, when applied to any workshop experience, can assist the facilitator in taking beginning steps towards success.[25]

CULTURE   TRUTH OF
                GOD's WORD

Defining Terms   Music & Meaning
Art Forms in Your Culture   Art Forms in Church
                                    New Artistic Creations

Building a BRIDGE

Look at Cultural Art Forms in Light of God's Truth
Redeeming Art Forms: Transformation and Application in Unity
God-honoring Choices

Developing New Songs, Dances, Dramas, Visual Arts, or Verbal Arts
Highlighting Specific Aspects of Culture through Scripture and Arts
The Worship Wheel: Context and Target Audience
Arts Checking: How to Check Art Forms
Goal Planning

Workshop Schedule

---

25   For additional resources in workshop leading, see Thomas N. Hart, *The Art of Christian Listening* (New York: Paulist Press, 1980); Somesh Kumar, *Methods for Community Participation: A Complete Guide for Practitioners* (New Delhi: Vistaar Publications, 2002); Sherwood G. Lingenfelter, *Leading Cross-culturally: Covenant Relationships for Effective Christian Leadership* (Grand Rapids: Baker Academic, 2008); Michael P. Nichols, *The Lost Art of Listening: How Learning to Listen Can Improve Relationships* (New York: Guilford Press, 1995); and James E. Pleuddeman, *Leading across Cultures: Effective Ministry and Mission in the Global Church* (Downers Grove, IL: InterVarsity Press, 2009).

HOW TO CREATE AN ARTS CURRICULUM

123. CREATIVE ARTS IN MISSION TRAINING AT ALL NATIONS CHRISTIAN COLLEGE

By Jill Ford

All Nations Christian College is an international cross-cultural mission training college in the UK which recognizes the importance of the creative arts in mission training.[26] Over the last ten years, I have served as the arts program leader and have designed, developed, and delivered the Arts Pathway specialization. Here are some helpful aspects of our journey in designing the arts curriculum.

ORIGINS OF OUR PROGRAM

There had been a previous course at All Nations, a diploma in Performing Arts with an emphasis on physical theatre and dance. This had run for approximately four years under the direction of John and Corrina Persson and was aimed at those with performance experience. There was a 50/50 split between the Performing Arts and Biblical and Intercultural Studies. This course paved the way for the next step which was to produce more arts subject areas into the curriculum and to make the modules accessible to all students. Those who wanted to exit with a certificate in the Arts and Intercultural Studies completed up to a third of their course in arts subjects and the rest in Biblical and Intercultural Studies. Other students had the benefit of selecting a particular arts module that interested them. Many did this to enhance their personal and creative development.

WHERE WE BEGAN

I was in the fortunate position of having just completed the diploma in Biblical and Intercultural Studies myself, so I was very familiar with the modules and subject areas across the All Nations curriculum. This really helped. The conversations around the new Arts Certificate had come out of the need for the college to provide training for those with musical skills as well as performance art skills and to broaden the range of creative experience. Practically, I had to play to my own

---

26   For more about All Nations Christian College, see http://www.allnations.ac.uk.

strengths which were in music and drama, recognizing that I would be delivering the majority of the modules except some specialist areas.

In the first year, from September 2003 to 2004, we had nine arts modules at level 1 entry that were half modules. The following subject areas were made available:

- biblical framework for the arts
- visual arts
- performing arts
- music, worship, and the art of song
- dance
- creative evangelism
- exploring moral and social issues in the performing arts
- postmodernism
- ethnomusicology

In the second year, from September 2004 to 2005, we launched two more modules—Film Studies and Creative Writing—and began to develop some arts modules to level 2 standard to provide the option for students to complete a two-year diploma majoring in the arts. We also revised our music and worship modules and created a World Worship module at level 1 and an Ethnomusicology module at level 2.

In the third year of development, from September 2005 to 2006, we had twelve complete modules available in the arts and we began planning and preparing for Open University accreditation towards an Arts Pathway. This meant that students would be able to complete a one-year (certificate), two-year (diploma), and/or three-year (BA honors degree) accredited qualification in Biblical and Intercultural Studies with Arts as a specialization.

Further development of arts modules took place by combining and organizing them into 3 levels. They were then extended to full modules. The following modules were offered at this stage as an Arts Pathway. Students specializing in the arts had to choose three from each level. Other students not on the Arts Pathway could choose up to two modules per year.

Level 1	Level 2	Level 3
Introduction to Performing Arts	Exploring Moral/Social Issues in the Performing Arts	Performing Arts in Practice
Dance	Creative Evangelism	Art, Culture, and Identity
Music and Worship	World Worship Music	Ethnomusicology
Biblical Framework for the Arts	Film Studies	Extended Arts Project

Having created the Arts Pathway, which we were pleased with, we had to restructure the whole of the BA program and rethink the number of modules we could offer. We streamlined the subject areas into music, performing arts, and visual arts. We currently have the following structure available:

Level 1 (integrated)	Level 2	Level 3
Introduction to Performing Arts	Exploring Moral/Social Issues in the Performing Arts	Performing Arts in Practice
Music and Worship	World Worship Music	Ethnomusicology
Creative Evangelism	Visual Culture	Art, Culture, and Identity
		Extended Arts Project

In designing this I initially went with what I already knew, and I was very much a learner along the way. God was helping me to connect my previous arts experiences into a whole new context which was for mission. My heart was to release the students' God-given creativity whether or not they had musical, dramatic, artistic gifting, etc., to help them not only appreciate their own creativity but also to make connections between the arts, God's word, and God's world. I was also very aware of how the arts helped integrate the student's whole learning experience and preparation for mission. This is why I actively encouraged all the students to take at least one module. I didn't want to produce an exclusive program, but one that was accessible for all students to benefit from.

Many students were transformed and gained more confidence through stepping out into new creative areas. Some were able to process difficult personal issues; many were ministered to through the act of creating. Students learned how to work with others in creative ways, and many transferable skills were being taught through the sessions. At the time it felt like a big experiment, but God really blessed it.

CENTRAL ELEMENTS FOR THE CURRICULUM

I expect most curriculum designers will be working with an existing structure within their institute and alongside their accrediting body, so these will serve as necessary guides. It is helpful to consider which arts subject areas can help aid the learning outcomes of those main areas so that you are working with others to implement and integrate the arts into the curriculum. For example, at All Nations our program is built around four key areas:

1. biblical
2. cross-cultural
3. personal development
4. relevant practical and ministry skills

What helps is to consider balance and how the arts subject areas are complementing these key areas by assisting in achieving the learning outcomes. At All Nations they are centred on the following four outcomes, around which each arts module/discipline can be constructed:

1. knowledge and understanding
2. cognitive skills (evaluating, assessing, and critiquing)
3. practical skills
4. transferable skills

We have streamlined subject areas contained in our Arts Pathway where you can build in progression. We have three arts areas—performing arts, music, and visual arts. Each level builds on knowledge, skills, and application.

- Level 1: *Appreciating* the art form and giving skills
- Level 2: *Applying* the skills to a range of contexts
- Level 3: *Transferring* the skills for a range of contexts

In the performing arts, for example, Level 1 is centred on learning skills—creating, performing, responding, and being introduced to a range of theatre skills. Level 2 is centred on using and applying those skills to devise theatre pieces that educate different audiences in moral and social issues such as HIV/AIDS, prejudice, and discrimination. Level 3 is about transferring the skills and teaching workshops that facilitate others in performance art and help them to explore moral, social, and biblical issues.

INCORPORATING THE ARTS INTO THE CORE OFFERINGS OF OUR INSTITUTION

Thankfully, we have successfully integrated the arts into All Nations' mission training. At the first entry level (certificate) all students are required to do performing arts as part of their personal development, music and worship as part of their biblical studies, and creative evangelism as part of their cross-cultural studies. We have found this to be a great way to both integrate and educate our students in a holistic manner. The students have also been able to learn in a variety of ways, and it has had a major impact in opening them up to creative and imaginative thinking, helping them think very practically for a variety of missions contexts, and giving them helpful tools.

Currently we are redesigning our curriculum, and as students progress on to the diploma and degree there will be an arts module within the core as well as the elective options. Again, this means every student will study an arts module in their second and third year, which allows for continuity throughout the program. Those who want to specialize further in the arts will have the opportunity to do so by choosing more arts modules to make up their program. This is an exciting time for us because the arts subject areas are being valued as integral to missions training. We are recognizing more and more that the arts cross-cut into many other areas of the curriculum and link subject areas together. They are also very practical in nature, which is helping us to achieve a balanced curriculum.

HIGHLIGHTS AND OBSTACLES OF OUR JOURNEY

Highlights:
- Working with others who have specialist arts skills and collaborating and teaching with them.
- Being able to experiment with new modules and also integrating some subject areas together, such as visual arts and film into a visual culture module.
- Introducing the "Artist in Residence" program to the college and seeing amazing benefits from it.
- Getting the accreditation of the Arts Pathway with the Open University.
- Observing the transformational impact of the arts on the students and seeing them released in arts-focused ministries.
- Growing the college community through arts-focused activities.
- Being part of the World Evangelical Alliance (WEA) Arts in Mission global taskforce team and hosting the 2011 conference at All Nations.[27]
- Integrating the arts into cross-cultural mission training!

Obstacles:
- Some lack of understanding within the team at certain times.
- Financial cutbacks when we went through a time of restructuring. My tutor hours in the arts were cut back to half time, and we had to rethink which arts subjects we could offer.
- Finding specialists in certain areas who were able to teach in the arts and missions context.

FUTURE HOPES FOR COURSE DEVELOPMENT

I would really like to develop the arts at postgraduate level. An MA degree in Ethnoarts would be an excellent addition to the program. This would help to train those who have already received training at the undergraduate level as well as those who have some experience in this area of missions. It would be preferable to do this in partnership with another arts/mission organization.

WORDS OF ENCOURAGEMENT FOR THOSE EMBARKING ON THE JOURNEY

- Be confident and expectant in the Lord.
- Play to your strengths if you are leading the initiative.
- Try to structure your ideas coherently, and articulate the vision plan clearly.
- Introduce an Artist in Residence (artist, musician, poet, dancer, etc.) into your organization. This allows you to have a cosupporter and the benefit of exhibitions, concerts, workshops days, etc., in which the whole organization gets involved.

---

27   For more information about the "Arts in Mission 2011" training event, see the ICE site under "networking" and "ICE events" at http://www.worldofworship.org.

- Encourage as many people as possible to take part in any arts activities you offer, whether in the formal or informal curriculum. The more they experience the better!
- Take time to help the rest of your team see and understand the value and importance of the arts for their teaching in other subject areas.
- If possible, work with people who have more experience than you. Otherwise get good counsel.
- Be involved yourself at every level.
- Enjoy it! The joy of the Lord is your strength!

124. DIPLOMA PROGRAM AT LUTHER W. NEW JR. THEOLOGICAL COLLEGE

By Jacob Joseph

DESIGN OF THE PROGRAM

The diploma in Worship and Music (DWM) is a one-year diploma program designed to train indigenous worship leaders for churches of diverse contexts in India. The program is conducted at Luther W. New Jr. Theological College in Dehradun, India.

The curriculum of the DWM program revolves around the goal of "developing theologically founded and musically skilled worship leaders for the Indian church." To attain this goal, we have structured our program to be a combination of biblical/theological courses and music courses. The music portion of the course includes training in both Indian and Western music.

Biblical subjects are heavily emphasized as a part of our diploma program. India is a multireligious society and Hinduism is a dominating force in all spheres of life. In the area of arts, the influence of religion is very strong. People who seek to incorporate diverse indigenous art forms in worship need to have a strong foundation in biblical doctrines. Failure to lay such a foundation can lead to religious syncretism and also the inclusion of nonbiblical elements in worship. Several past attempts at indigenization were abandoned due to syncretism and use of elements that could not be validated with biblical principles.

In the first semester of studies, therefore, the program incorporates basic biblical courses like New Testament Introduction, Old Testament Introduction, and Introduction to Worship. These provide a solid, biblical foundation for students, especially those who are new to the Christian faith. In the second semester we also offer Introduction to Theology, a course which deals with basic Christian doctrines.

COMBINING WESTERN AND INDIAN MUSIC

Our music courses include a combination of Western and Indian music. Western music theory is taught extensively, providing students a good platform to work on their music skills and a vocabulary with which to communicate. Teaching Western music also helps students to get jobs in schools. Because most village churches in India are not able to pay a music minister, Western music training allows the students to be self-supporting while working freely with churches or missions organizations. Music theory, recorder, and keyboard training provide them a means to earn their living in addition to serving in the church.

In the second semester of the program, we offer an introductory course in ethnomusicology. Rather than being a technical course, the purpose of the course is to create in the minds of the students an awareness of their own music. We have found that most people coming from village backgrounds have little appreciation for their music, and that their ethnic art forms are being overtaken by Bollywood and Western music. Through this course in ethnomusicology, we try to make students aware of the value of their ethnic art forms and their effectiveness in communicating the gospel.

We also offer year-long classes on Hindustani music. We understand that the Hindustani music is not the most popular music among the people groups in India. Although the diverse people groups in India have their own musical heritage, most of them have roots in Hindustani music. A strong background in Hindustani music gives students a foundation to work on their native musical traditions. We also emphasize semiclassical singing and learning various indigenous Indian musical genres, such as *bhajans* and *keertans*. For many students this is their first experience in worshiping God using traditional Indian classical music. In our Sunday worship time, we conduct *satsangs* to create in students an interest in developing indigenous worship forms.

OTHER FEATURES INCLUDE ELECTRONIC NOTATION, CONDUCTING, AND KEYBOARD

Another area of training is in the use of electronic notation software. We understand that the printing of music notation is the cheapest means of circulating songs, especially among village musicians who do not have access to the Internet and other communication forms. Most of them cannot afford to record their songs. By learning to notate their songs on free music notation software, they can write down songs from their region and circulate them among people who speak a similar language. Printed music notation may be the cheapest means for sharing songs among musicians who can read music.

We also offer a basic course on conducting. We train students to conduct Indian songs as well as Western songs. Systematic training in conducting helps the students to form choirs in their respective language groups and prepares them to lead congregational singing.

At present our primary applied instrument is keyboard. We are working on offering *sitar* and *tabla* as applied instruments in the coming year. Due to the varied backgrounds of our students, keyboard lessons are tailored to help meet each student's individual contextual needs. For example, we have students from a Nissi ethnic group in Arunachal Pradesh who need to learn to play their group's songs, and we also have students from cities like Bangalore and Mumbai who need instruction in contemporary Christian music. We work with students individually to meet the needs of each group represented.

KEEPING IT SIMPLE AND FOCUSED

We keep our program very simple, staying focused on the goal of developing biblically founded worship leaders for the Indian church. In the future we hope to develop a two-year program, allowing students more time to advance musical skills and enabling us to cater more personally to the needs of the students.

125. ARTS CURRICULUM AT FULLER THEOLOGICAL SEMINARY

By Roberta R. King

PERSONAL BEGINNINGS IN MUSIC AND MISSIONS

My journey in developing an arts curriculum began as the Lord called me into missions. Once I finally agreed with God that I was called to music in mission, I found myself confronted with a huge gap in understanding how music could be employed for the sake of the kingdom in cross-cultural ministry. While the history of the church, from Genesis to our own era, is replete with the theme of God communicating through music, music and the performing arts are either assumed or ignored in relevance to gospel communication and cross-cultural church ministry.

I believe much of this posture comes from a myopic focus on literacy and a lack of understanding of the importance of orality. Theologically, we know and affirm that the Word became flesh (John 1). But we seem to repeatedly forget this and condense the Word to paper only. Thankfully, when I began my journey there was at least one mission organization—the Summer Institute of Linguistics, now SIL International—which understood the significance of music's intimate link with language and Bible translation. Yet music and translation were not my own personal focus, as important as they are. And in addition, the mission focus at that time was on church planting, reaching the unreached, and limited mostly to men.

Eventually I discovered Daystar Communications,[28] a fledgling mission that recognized the critical importance of music for communicating Christ. I left for Nairobi, Kenya, asking God if he could use me, a woman and a musician, and if so, how? After coming to understand foundational concepts in Christian communication, I realized music's potential for powerfully communicating Christ cross-culturally.

---

28   Now Daystar University.

KEY PRINCIPLES IN THE FULLER PROGRAM

The key foundational grounding for the program at Fuller Theological Seminary today centers on music as communication in relation to making Christ known.[29]

The Psalmist exclaims, "All the nations you have made will come and worship before you, Lord; they will bring glory to your name" (Ps 86:9). Responding to this, central elements for the arts curriculum—"Global Christian Worship and Ethnomusicology"—at Fuller Seminary's School of Intercultural Studies focus on the question: what contribution do music and the performing arts make in bringing all nations to worship before God?

Based on the discipline of missiology—the study of mission—the curriculum integrates four main arenas of study (see the figure, "Four-arena Approach to Missiology"):

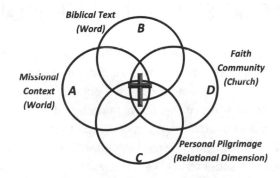

Four-arena Approach to Missiology[18]

- word
- world
- church
- spiritual pilgrimage

Specializing in studies in the world dimension, the main theoretical focus is on ethnomusicology as the study of music and culture. We offer courses such as "Exegeting a Music Culture," "Christian Communication through Music," and "Ethnomusicology—Theory and Analysis." These address learning local contexts and ethnic musics. Ethnomusicology, then, is applied in courses such as "Perspectives in Global Christian Worship" and "Communicating Christ through Storytelling and Song." A biblical theology of music and the arts is addressed in each course in addition to reflection on one's own song and spiritual pilgrimage. "Theology in Song" and "Gospel Music in a Global World" complement the courses offered.

EXPANDING TO INTEGRATE GLOBAL CHRISTIAN WORSHIP

With the founding of the Brehm Center for Worship, Theology, and the Arts at Fuller in 2001, a great step forward was taken in integrating the arts into the core seminary curricula. The Global Christian Worship program partners with the Brehm Center and was established in the School of Intercultural Studies. Another highlight of my journey includes the recognition of ethnomusicol-

---

29   Roberta R. King, *Pathways in Christian Music Communication: The Case of the Senufo of Côte d'Ivoire*, American Society of Missiology Monograph Series 3 (Eugene, OR: Pickwick Publications, 2009). Revised from material that first appeared in *Missiology: An International Review*.

30   Charles E. Van Engen, "Toward a Contextually Appropriate Methodology in Mission Theology," *in Appropriate Christianity*, ed. Charles H. Kraft (Pasadena: William Carey Library, 2006).

INTRODUCTION

SECTION 1: FOUNDATIONS

SECTION 2: STORIES

SECTION 3: TOOLS

CLOSING

ogy's role in effective ministry and mission in the twenty-first century. This recognition addresses the initial gap I faced as I began my journey in the late 1970s. Further, the establishment of a full-time faculty position in ethnomusicology in a major seminary is a milestone.

OBSTACLES AND OPPORTUNITIES IN LAUNCHING A PROGRAM

Yet, whenever one pioneers in a field, there are numerous obstacles to face. The greatest for me has been overcoming the lack of understanding of the significance of ethnomusicology for developing effective, culturally appropriate means to the work of the church in worship and witness. Moving cross-cultural music and the arts from a tangential discipline to a core foundation requires overcoming decades, indeed centuries, of worshiping and witnessing in predominantly Western ways. Constant, intentional philosophical and biblical foundations need to be put forward in order to keep ethnomusicology in the forefront of seminary curriculum and to surmount musical ethnocentrism. Areas we are seeking to further address include music and the arts for interfaith dialogue, especially among Muslims and Christians (see our new website, http://www.songsforpeaceproject.org); worship and world religions; and contemporary Christian worship in the twenty-first century's global context.

CRITICAL STEPS IN PROMOTING CULTURALLY APPROPRIATE ARTS FOR THE GLOBAL CHURCH

As we empower churches around the world to incorporate arts in worship and in witness, critical steps include

1. building a network of colleagues within your organization who are open to developing an arts curriculum and always keeping it in the conversation;
2. studying ethnomusicology in light of missional goals and pursuing the best training and education possible;
3. getting as much in-depth field experience as possible;
4. developing a biblical theology of employing ethnomusicology in worship and witness;
5. networking with other arts-in-mission participants and institutions; and
6. making your curricula and research findings known and published to help others on the same road.

Finally, it will be important to you in this initiative to allow God to lead you each step of the way as you develop a deep spirituality in your walk with the Lord Jesus Christ and seek to join him in his purposes. He is, after all, the One who is making mission happen.[31]

---

31   For additional reading, see King, *Pathways*; and Charles Van Engen, "Toward a Contextually Appropriate Methodology in Mission Theology," in *Appropriate Christianity*, ed. Charles H. Kraft (Pasadena: William Carey Library, 2006).

401

INTRODUCTION

SECTION 1: FOUNDATIONS

SECTION 2: STORIES

SECTION 3: TOOLS

CLOSING

126. ETHNOMUSICOLOGY DEVELOPMENTS AT LIBERTY UNIVERSITY

By John L. Benham

HISTORY

As a child I responded to the call of God to serve in the dual areas of music and missions. At that point I was only aware of one opportunity where I could pursue both—HCJB[32] in Quito, Ecuador—and this program became my goal well into my early college career. While my commitment and desire to fulfill that childhood call remained, it was not until my first trip to Indonesia in 1989 that I began to understand what this call would mean for me. After returning home with requests from several other islands and the invitation to work full time with that particular mission agency, it became obvious to me that my call was not only in the going, but in the preparation of others as well.

PROCESS

Recognizing that none of my education had been in ethnomusicology,[33] it became obvious that the first step in developing a curriculum to combine music and missions was to get some assistance. I found a local Christian college in which there were two individuals who caught the vision. With the financial assistance of Music in World Cultures (MIWC) and with the cooperation of the college, we began the process of developing a program. Among others who were contacted about curricular content, we brought in Roberta King, Brian Schrag, and Tom Avery as primary consultants.

The process of developing an arts curriculum includes the following steps:

- **Step 1**: Get help from those with education and experience in the field.

---

32   HCJB (Hoy Cristo Jesús Bendice) was founded in 1931 and was one of the first evangelical missionary radio stations in the world. In English it is known as "The Voice of the Andes."

33   UCLA (University of California, Los Angeles) had the only ethnomusicology program in existence during my collegiate years.

- **Step 2**: Don't start with courses and credits. Rather, determine the needs of the graduate. Specifically, develop statements of learner outcomes. These are developed by completing the sentence, "Upon completion of this program (or course), the student will know and be able to _____." Each of these statements must be specific, achievable, and measureable (SAM).
- **Step 3**: Once you have all of these statements completed, divide them into categories that are similar. Out of this you will develop your courses.
- **Step 4**: As you develop courses you will identify how each course and each assignment fulfills one or more of the learner outcomes. It sounds tedious. It is, but it is the only way that you will be able to assess the viability of what you have put together and whether or not your students are fully prepared to serve. Further, it is the only way you will be able to evaluate the ability of your faculty to provide adequate instruction.
- **Step 5**: Determine whether a course or two is sufficient for your needs, or whether your goal is a specific degree program. This will, of course, necessitate such things as meeting accreditation requirements and submitting all of the required documentation required by your academic institution.

ROLE OF THE ETHNOMUSICOLOGIST

At Liberty University we envision the role of the ethnomusicologist (EM) from four perspectives that certainly may be applied to the other arts:

- **Preevangelism/evangelism.** The EM serves as researcher. How do the arts reveal cultural identity and worldview? Are there, for example, redemptive analogies? How may the EM act as a means of breaking down cultural barriers and building bridges toward positive preevangelistic relationships, such as in the development of schools of music? How may the local arts be used as a means of sharing the gospel?
- **Worship.** How may the EM serve as a catalyst for the development of indigenous music forms for worship, using the concept of critical contextualization?[34] (See Eph 5:18–20.)
- **Discipleship.** How may the EM serve as a catalyst for the development of indigenous music forms for use in Christian education, teaching and admonishing "with psalms, hymns, and spiritual songs"? (See the Apostle Paul's whole mandate in Col 3:14–17.) This should include Scripture memory and principles of Christian doctrine and living.
- **Equipping.** EMs serve for the equipping of national leaders to assume responsibility for the music ministry in the local church once EMs have helped develop programs and moved on to their next project.

---

34   Paul Hiebert develops this concept at various places in his book *Anthropological Insights for Missionaries* (Grand Rapids: Baker Books, 1986).

CURRICULUM QUALITIES

Having adopted these principles in the development of the curriculum now housed at Liberty University, we determined that our curriculum would consist of four qualities within the context of the integration of Christian faith and practice:

- **Scholarship.** Our students will study the writings and theories of traditional practitioners in the field. They will be able to communicate on a scholarly level with both secular and Christian EMs.
- **Skill development.** Our students will have sufficient skills to meet the needs of the mission or other agencies that they serve, including cultural and music analysis.
- **Performance.** Our students will develop a beginning to intermediate level of proficiency in some vocal or instrumental genre, providing an additional means of accessing culture.
- **Application.** Our students will demonstrate acquisition of scholarship, skill development, and performance in extended field experience and the completion of a master's thesis or project.

Our program has been supported strongly at Liberty with the approval of the 45-credit master of arts in Ethnomusicology and an 18-credit graduate specialization in Ethnomusicology. We currently have 65–70 majors and 25–30 students in the specialization. An undergraduate course in World Music is offered as a general education elective and has been approved for integrative studies majors and as an honors course, offering six sections each year. A bachelor's of arts in Ethnomusicology has been submitted for approval.

A FEW ADDITIONAL THINGS WE'VE LEARNED

Of the 45-credit requirement for the master's degree, 39 credits are offered online.[35] The remaining six credits can be completed in two back-to-back, one-week intensive courses in the summer. There are two advantages to this arrangement: (1) those serving in the international setting are able to complete resident requirements in one furlough, and (2) all students are able to make practical application of their course work in the setting in which they currently serve.

Developing curriculum is the easy part. There is still marketing, recruiting, and dealing with all of the skeptics. Skeptics may be in administration or your own department, or perhaps the individuals or small groups that were initially supporting you have assumed positions in other institutions. Additionally, there are the financial issues. What is the basis upon which a Christian institution balances its vision for missions with financial viability? Though there are many areas to consider before you begin, creating an arts curriculum with clear learning outcomes and an understanding of the roles graduates will play when they enter the field are foundational considerations for your new program.

---

35   Katherine Morehouse describes in more detail Liberty's online program in her chapter in this *Handbook*. See chapter 127, entitled "Teaching an Arts Course Online."

127. TEACHING AN ARTS COURSE ONLINE

By Katherine Morehouse

"WHERE IS THE CLASS?"

One day my two-year-old asked me what I was doing, and I told her I was teaching a class. She looked up at me with her piercingly sweet eyes and asked, "Where is the *class*?" I tried to explain to her that the class was on the computer, but she looked at my screen and said, "No it's not." She asked again, "Where *is* the *class*?"

That question is key to understanding online classroom facilitation, because the classroom is not a physical environment in which relationships can develop and interactions happen almost effortlessly. What makes an online learning experience unique is that it requires all classroom interaction to move to a virtual field of play. The benefit of online learning is that location is not an issue. Worship training can take place between teachers in Africa and students in Kansas. Missionaries, researchers, and ethnoarts facilitators in the field can serve as mentors to those interested in these professions. The possibilities are almost endless for online topics and course material, but the format of online courses usually consists of three primary aspects:

1. reading/listening assignments
2. discussion forums
3. assessments in the form of writing assignments, papers, or projects

THE THREE ASPECTS OF ONLINE COURSE FACILITATION

Reading/listening assignments. Most assignments are taken from books that are purchased by students before the class begins or from journals accessible in online databases such as JSTOR and Project Muse. Typically, university libraries purchase access to these databases for their students. Each week students are asked to read a certain selection from their course reading materials. This will provide the basis for discussion boards and assessments.

Listening assignments may be based on the reading. Some books will come with accompanying CDs or links to online listening portals. If listening examples are not provided, certain websites such as Amazon, iTunes, and Smithsonian Folkways provide relatively stable access to world music online for a decent price at about a dollar per song.

It is not recommended to use YouTube or other similar sites for listening examples because the content is not guaranteed to remain accessible from day to day. Furthermore, there are also copyright considerations with these sites. It is possible to upload media content directly onto the website from which the class is being launched. If the school, however, does not own the material or rights to the material, this could become problematic.

Discussion board. The discussion board provides the student with space to "speak" with other students. It is typically set up to track conversations between students by date and time and may be filtered by topic or author as well. The instructor may set up forums ahead of time—usually one per week—and these forums may be preloaded with questions designed to instigate conversation or direct the discussion in some way.

An alternative is that the instructor does not guide the discussion by predetermined questions. In this approach, the students find their own topics derived from the reading assignments for that week. Within the forum, the student starts a thread to which other students, along with the instructor, may reply. Though this format is typical for learning platforms such as Blackboard, WebCT, or Vista, it could also be emulated via online chat rooms or email groups. A course blog could be a useful tool as well.

The discussion board may serve initially as a sounding board as you get started and may include introductions between class members, questions about the site, or problems with the course setup. Generally, the first week is used for this purpose. Another discussion forum could be set up for prayer requests and community-building that may be unrelated to course content. This forum remains active throughout the duration of the course. Subsequent discussion forums will focus on the reading and/or listening assignments.

During a typical week, the student will post a certain number of initial postings, due midway through the week, then post a certain number of response postings due by the end of the week. The instructor will determine the number of postings based on the number of students in the course or the desired level of interaction. In a class of fifteen students, one may find five postings per student to be a manageable amount of work for them if the instructor is expecting them to read the other posts. It is also useful for students to have a grading rubric for discussions, including requirements for posting length, depth, and other expectations. The instructor should make an intentional decision as to his or her role in forum discussions (i.e., a judge, a codiscussant, or a moderator) and remain consistent so that students will know what to expect from them.

Assessments. Assessments may take the form of tests, papers, or projects. One useful tool is a reading reflection paper in which the student is asked to use the following basic outline, developed for Liberty University's online classes:

1. **Introduction/synopsis.** Summarize what you have read, boiling the book down into 250 "tight" words (one page). Prove you comprehend the readings by writing a no-nonsense summary. The abstract is not a commentary or listing of topics, but rather an objective summary from the reader's viewpoint. This section should include specific references to the text you have read.

INTRODUCTION

SECTION 1: FOUNDATIONS

SECTION 2: STORIES

SECTION 3: TOOLS

CLOSING

2. **Critical analysis.** This is the critical thinking part of the review—not critical in the sense of negative, but in the sense of questioning. In five hundred words (two pages), describe what questions pop up for you in response to what you have read. Keep a rough note sheet on hand as you read. Outsmart the author by asking better questions than he or she has raised in the book. Tell how the author could have made the book better or more appealing to those in your field of service.

3. **Reflection (optional).** Get vulnerable! In 250 words (one page) relate a personal life episode that this book triggered for you. Relate your story in first person, describing action and quoting exact words you remember hearing or saying. In the teaching style of Jesus, this is a do-it-yourself parable, case study, and confession. You will remember almost nothing you have read unless you make this critical, personal connection. What video memory began to roll? This is your chance to tell your story and make new ideas your own.

4. **Action section.** What are you going to do about what you have learned? In 250 words (one page) describe what actions or changes you are going to make in your life, ministry, and/or work as a result of your reading. This "so what" section should tell the readers what future directions you see for research, either for you or for your readers.

Assignments like this one offer the possibility for instructors to make sure that the students are processing information from the readings and applying the ideas to their own lives. Once the student has written the assignment, they upload it to the grade book, if they are working within an online platform operated through a school. This could also be done through email.

Above all, the community remains central to the online class. The ability of the instructor to create and maintain a relaxed, respectful, and inspiring space for student interaction is key to the success of online teaching.

HOW TO MENTOR AND LEARN FROM ARTISTS

128. MENTORING ARTISTS
By Sue Hall-Heimbecker

> The Kingdom of God is not about one or two people "doing the stuff"—it's about going for it in ministry with all we have, all the while seeking to pass on as much as we can to those we see beginning to flourish around us. And in turn, urging them to do the same with others they see being raised up. This is the economy of the Kingdom.[36]

Mentoring sits at the heart of the values that belong to the kingdom of God. Jesus mentored his disciples over several years of life-sharing intimacy. Paul urged his protégé, Timothy, to teach reliable people who would be able to pass on what they knew to others. Investing in the lives and ministries of other believers is an expression of the love of God in our hearts, whether these are local believers or cross-cultural workers. Surely, as people concerned with the increase of the glory of God through worship brought by all the nations, we can't afford to ignore these patterns of training, encouraging, and envisioning which are suggested to us by the Scriptures.

> **A mentoring relationship is reciprocal, with both participants bringing experience and input to the relationship.**

This chapter draws on the experiences of many mentors and learners in the field of missionary arts to offer practical insights into the "whys" and "hows" of growing the next generation of ethnodoxologists. It comes at the questions from a Christian perspective, seeking to integrate our lives as whole people into our work in mission and ministry in the arts, and includes our concern for developing expatriate, cross-cultural, and own-culture worship catalysts.

Throughout these reflections, the term "mentor" will be used for the more experienced teacher, and "learner" for the one primarily learning, although it is clear that a mentoring relationship is reciprocal, with both participants bringing experience and input to the relationship. I am mostly assuming that both the mentor and the learner are Christians, though some ideas could be used to help a non-Christian artist grow in their gifts and depth of life with God.

---

36   Matt Redman, "The Kingdom Mind-set of a Mentor," in *Inside Out Worship: Insights for Passionate and Purposeful Worship*, ed. Matt Redman, et al. (Portland: Regal, 2005), 141.

WHAT IS MENTORING?

Mentoring happens when
one person makes himself/herself and her life experiences,
and attitudes, knowledge, skills, and resources
available to another for the purpose of maximizing
that person's growth in his/her life setting,
communicating not only task-information
but life skills, values and character. (Larrie Gardner)[37]

Although "mentoring" is a contemporary buzz word, the concept of a more experienced person walking alongside a learner is an established one. This may be in a formal relationship, such as one with a supervisor within an organization, or it may flow more informally through a network of connections and communication. However it is structured, the foundation of mentoring is character formation rather than just teaching knowledge or skills.

For missionary artists, skills and character development happen on a practical and everyday-life level. This is God-initiated, and we model, teach, and discover together what God is doing. Effective ministry flows out of our being right with God and others. Mentors encourage learners in different activities, and then teach based on an actual event or experience. The aim is to focus on the way God has already gifted the person and to discover how that gifting fits into the body of Christ rather than seeking to mold the learner to a predetermined form. Success is defined in terms of growth, learning, and character formation, rather than outward signs of success and productivity—though the latter are much easier to measure!

> However it is structured, the foundation of mentoring is character formation rather than just teaching knowledge or skills.

Mentoring may appear to slow things down: "It is so much easier and much less time-consuming to just do the job by myself." But this perspective is short term, and neglects the kingdom values of drawing alongside others for multiplication and discipleship. The mentoring relationship is essentially a mutual one—mentors benefit and grow in multiple ways as they invest in the life of learners, who in turn grow and mature to be ready to pass on what they have learned to the next "generation."

Besides communicating particular knowledge, skills, and attitudes, the role of a mentor includes guidance in planning future career paths and evaluating the strengths and weaknesses of the learner. Such evaluation may be one of the most challenging areas for the mentor, but it is one of the most helpful things to enable future and long-term growth.

---

37   Larrie Gardner, quoted in Frank Robbins, "Mentoring in SIL and WBT: A Sequel" (unpublished paper, 2001), 1.

WHAT ASPECTS SHOULD A MENTORING RELATIONSHIP INCLUDE?

The following are suggested as essential ingredients in a mentoring relationship:

- caring for and listening to the learner in all areas of concern, not just work
- sharing of self with learner—at appropriate times and drawing on own experiences
- encouraging the learner
- humility, including sharing of mistakes made
- modeling, including task and vision, and demonstrating a balanced lifestyle
- patience, for gaining a more complete understanding of the learner's concerns and for being able to make appropriate suggestions or comments
- ongoing interest and involvement with the learner after any formal relationship is ended[38]

The mentoring model is built on authentic relationships, which require an investment of energy and time. With an open and honest relationship base it is possible to notice teachable moments and reflect together about what God is doing. This in turn leads to learning how to respond to the learner. "An effective mentoring program is based on relationship, and relationship cannot be developed without personal interaction."[39]

WHAT ARE THE CHARACTERISTICS OF A MENTOR?

These are some of the characteristics of a good mentor. Even though none of us will meet these ideals completely, it is good to keep on moving towards them as we mature in our faith and ministry:[40]

- deep spiritual life flowing from a desire to please God and obey his word
- humility
- respect and kindness for other people
- integrity and trustworthiness
- moral purity
- good ego strength—secure enough to be free from self-preoccupation, give credit to others, take responsibility for failure and bounce back
- teachable, committed to perpetual learning and growth
- analytical and reflective
- visionary, honoring the past but not shackled to it or committed to copy it

---

38   Frank Robbins, "Mentoring in SIL and WBT" (paper presented at the SIL Africa Area Conference, Brackenhurst, Kenya, on May 20, 1998).

39   Larrie Gardner, "Mentoring: The Urgent Task" (unpublished paper, 2000), 2.

40   Principles drawn from Larrie Gardner, "Demystifying Mentoring" (unpublished paper, 2003).

WHO SHOULD WE BE MENTORING?

Along the way we are likely to be in mentoring relationships with both expatriate cross-cultural workers and local church members. Many of the things to think about are similar for both these groups. Here are some ideas of people who might benefit:

1. Someone with an interest and/or training in arts and mission who can come to you for a short-term visit (e.g., 1–6 weeks).
2. A student requiring an internship for part of a course with specific goals. (Remember the importance of helping the student grow in faith as well as working along with the course requirements.)
3. A long-term worker in arts and mission who needs some field experience first. (This would be the longest internship, typically at least six months of interactions and conversations; some of these relationships can happen long distance if need be.)
4. Someone interested in arts and worship, probably a local believer whom you can meet with regularly but informally over a long period of time.

Local believers who may benefit from mentoring include church leaders, indigenous missionaries serving their own ethnic group or cross-culturally, worship leaders and musicians, those involved in media recordings, and others whom God brings with a vision for indigenous worship and music.

Many mentoring relationships emerge out of groups of participants at workshops, where individuals approach the staff members for follow-up later on. There are also situations where workers have taken the initiative to invite an individual to a workshop/teaching opportunity or to join them for a research trip in order to pursue mentoring goals with that individual. Several experienced mentors aim to always include a local coworker as a learner or coleader in every workshop situation in order to maximize the number of people having input into and being exposed to God's work in developing indigenous arts, since this vision should ideally be owned by the local church.

Such training and mentoring can also happen in a more formalized setting, such as a seminary program in a country where the mentor works or with students sent from a college in another country for a learning experience. However, again it is often the practical aspects and skills that are most helpful to these educated people. The academic/practical balance has proven to be very important, as many local believers report, "Oh, this is how it looks when you *do* it!"

WHAT DO WE WANT TO SHARE WITH LEARNERS?

"We must recognize that mentoring, no matter how well motivated and skillful, will not always be successful. We cannot develop people; we can only facilitate development and offer help when they want it."[41] Prayer that they will accept the help of God and others is the starting place!

Although the lists below start with knowledge items, it is probably the attitudes list that is most important for a person desiring to serve God through the arts. A mentor will pray for God to help build these aspects into each learner, and find creative ways to help them grow in each area. Note: these lists are not complete, but they do provide some ideas to begin with.

---

41   Robbins, "A Sequel," 4.

Knowledge:

- *Field of ethnoarts*: scope of the field and specific areas of interest
- *Biblical studies*: including the place of arts and worship in the life of God's people and the character of a disciple
- *Applied ethnoarts*: for missiology/church work
- *Arts theory*
- *Analysis theory*
- *Regional studies*: of arts and culture from the secular and religious literature
- *Religious studies*: of non-Christian and nonevangelical faith traditions in the area of interest
- *Research tools*: including key textual and Internet resources
- *Appropriate technology*: for recording and media production
- *Language learning*: for clear communication in the local area and the region

Skills:

- *Planning and budgeting skills*: for planning use of time and resources for projects and workshops alongside other responsibilities
- *Relational skills*: e.g., working with local teachers and sources, or affirming the contributions of all participants in a workshop
- *Research skills*: how to do arts/social research through reading others' research and through conducting original research
- *Arts performance skills*: beginning to learn how to perform a local instrument, dance, drama, poetry, or song style
- *Facilitation skills*: for aiding group discussion of local people
- *Application and guidance skills*: how to present options and guide local people in making artistic applications of research according to biblical standards
- *Teaching skills*: being able to teach and interpret what the Bible says about arts and worship in the most appropriate form and style for the context and the group
- *Technology skills*: how to record art forms (audio and video), and often how to edit and duplicate recordings, in formal and nonstudio settings
- *Documentation skills*: how to write up a report and/or article; how to document work with photos and video for a range of different audiences; how to archive recorded resources
- *Life skills*: balancing life and ministry in a healthy way

Attitudes:

- *Appreciation*: valuing indigenous worship and Christian arts
- *Growth*: desire to continue to grow as a worshiper and a disciple
- *Humility*: in the face of other peoples' cultures and art forms
- *Partnership*: where the contributions of different specialists are valued (e.g., composers/writers, Bible students, technology masters, performers)
- *Flexibility*
- *Willingness to learn*: continually
- *Openness*: willing to work with a variety of Christian groups and churches, as well as non-Christian contacts
- *Understanding*: of own role and contribution to make to the field

MENTORING LOCAL COLLEAGUES

The mentoring of local colleagues must clearly be a serious focus for missionary artists in terms of both multiplying themselves as the church grows and discipling believers whom God brings their way. In a sense every interaction with a local believer informally or during a workshop is an opportunity to be intentional about mentoring them, envisioning them, and developing their knowledge, skills, and attitudes (see above).

However, there will be some who are more motivated, gifted, or available into whom we can invest more time and energy, in turn receiving from them insights into the practice of missionary arts in the local context that are hidden from outsiders. Such relationships will stretch workers in their abilities to relate well across cultures, since cultural distances between themselves and the environments in which they work are generally greater than those within missionary teams. Frank Robbins comments that "developing relationships for effective mentoring across such cultural differences involves a depth of cultural learning and being mentored on our part that is far beyond just training" in specific knowledge or skills.[42] Mentors need also to be acutely aware of the power imbalances that exist in intercultural relationships and to act appropriately.

CROSS-CULTURAL ASPECTS

Cross-cultural aspects of arts in mission are important to teach and model with local learners as well as expatriate ones. Many national church workers are assigned or called to work outside their own ethnolinguistic area and may be lacking in training and cross-cultural awareness. This can even be true for those working among their own people who have had Western models of church and ministry taught to them, or who have never had the opportunity to reflect in depth on their own culture and language.

It is vital for the learner to go more deeply into the language and the culture with which they work. There are ways to equip them to think through aspects that they *need* to understand and access for a more effective ministry; e.g., by asking strategic questions or offering research tools. Mentors have worked with many who began to dig deeper into the culture and the language and had dramatic revelations about more effective and meaningful ways to present the word of God to both those inside and outside the church, including through the arts.

MENTORING AND ENCOURAGING

> Mentoring is not just to help a person assess how they are doing in practical terms. The real foundational stuff is all about character. A good mentor helps you evaluate the state of your heart, and helps you move on to higher heart standards. They speak into areas that might otherwise go unchecked—not to condemn but to cultivate.[43]

---

42   Ibid., 5.

43   Matt Redman, "The Kingdom Mind-set of a Mentor," in *Inside Out Worship: Insights for Passionate and Purposeful Worship*, ed. Matt Redman, et al. (Portland: Regal, 2005), 141.

Prayer is a key feature of mentoring relationships. Encouraging a lonely believer in her passion for worship and raising up others to join her happens primarily through shared prayer. Often we start to see a group of learners develop. It is exciting when an expatriate church worker has the original vision, but several local church leaders, a poet, a composer, a musician, etc., then develop the vision together. In this type of situation, the mentor would work with the local team for follow-up. Other times mentors work with just one lone believer who has a passion and vision, and they pray together for ways to grow others towards this same passion. Artist mentors have seen a team of passionate worship-encouragers grow out of prayer.

Encouraging the learner in their walk with Christ is perhaps the most fundamental aspect of mentoring. Without this sense of being gifted as a worshiper first, and a minister or artist second, the learner could be headed for dangerous waters where performance takes priority over right living. This will mean spending significant time with the learner (see "Many Ways to Mentor" [below] for ideas on mentoring formats) and being very honest with them as you look at the Scriptures together.

HOW DO I MENTOR?

There are many ways to mentor another person. Admittedly, matters of *location* (physical distance from mentor), *chemistry* (not everyone likes their mentor/supervisor or will disclose more personal thoughts to them), and *trust* (some people trust no one and feel no need to change) affect how you will be able to mentor. You need to work through these issues as you connect with a potential learner in order for the mentoring to be profitable (see sidebar for more ideas on formats for mentoring).

Once you have someone to mentor, begin by spending time together.

- Dream together, pray together, and make some goals together for the learner's growth.
- Take the learner with you to meetings and workshops and give them a role—prepare them and debrief afterwards.
- Explain to them how you are making decisions.
- Pray together some more.
- Read the Bible together, for personal growth and to grow in vision for the arts and faith.
- Pass them readings that will be interesting to them.
- Encourage them in their strengths and in taking new risks of faith.
- Help them to grow closer to Jesus and become more heartfelt worshipers, using all their gifts for God.
- Look at the above lists of knowledge, skills, and attitudes with the learner, and design a plan to research the arts in the area that interests them, using the *Ethnodoxology Handbook* as a guide.
- Have dinner together if you can.
- Take a research trip together.
- Lend them some of your books and recordings.
- Invite a friend each and make music or poetry or drama together.
- Help them begin to mentor someone else.
- And keep on with this as long as it is helpful.

May you be blessed in your ministry as you bring others into the white-hot worship of the Living God!

THE ROLE OF WORKSHOPS IN TRAINING LEARNERS

Not every practicing arts missionary is actively involved in workshop settings. This is especially true of those working in a pre-evangelism or pre-church setting, or those focusing on one ethnic group with alternative strategies. However, many missionary artists do find themselves ministering in workshops of different kinds; e.g., "arts discovery" or "song composition." Many mentors express the benefits for sharing their workshop involvement with learners as a part of their learning experience, alongside other strategies.

One mentor comments:

> A village time for field research and a workshop is a good combination. Learners should be open to thinking about all aspects of ethnoarts. For instance, before the trip one learner didn't think that leading workshops was "real ethnomusicology." But instead of the [field research] being the highlight, the learner was most blessed by the workshop week. Reading helps, but cannot cement a new idea before it's been experienced.

Another underlines: "Actually 'doing' workshops is in my opinion the most important aspect of any mentoring . . . The only way to learn what works and what doesn't is to try it." The workshop can be an ideal training ground in which multiple layers of mentoring can take place—with short-termers, long-termers, local colleagues, etc. Experienced leaders can allow learners to observe and then take a turn in leading. Time set aside for planning together beforehand and for at least daily debriefing during the workshop is crucial to the success of the mentoring aspects of the workshop, as is clear delineation of each person's role in the workshop and effective communication. Giving people a real part to play, especially if it pushes them beyond their comfort zone while backup and encouragement is offered, allows real growth in a safe environment.

> Seeing a mentor react in a godly way under stress can teach lessons which weeks of "safe" interactions will never communicate.

Using modular, practical teaching in workshops can help learners and give a basis for more in-depth teaching for those who are especially interested. Materials may need to be translated into national or minority languages in order for this to be possible. Grappling with biblical and cultural information helps to integrate theory and practice for learners, and can give them a passion to share this with others.

Workshops can be a place of communicating vision to an intern/learner, where the reality of the joy of seeing people coming to worship from the heart is experienced. They are also a cauldron where the temperature is raised and the mentor's true character can show under the pressures of rapid changes, unexpected happenings, and fresh complications. Seeing a mentor react in a godly way under stress can teach lessons which weeks of "safe" interactions will never communicate.

MANY WAYS TO MENTOR

One mentor, many learners

Over two years, one trained ethnomusicologist in West Africa began to encourage several local believers as well as eight expatriate workers—including Shari—with an interest in the arts. He invited them to come along to workshops and gave them increasing responsibilities; he shared readings, discussions, and recordings with them to help them grow in their understanding of how God was at work through the arts. This took a lot of his energy and time, but at least seven of those mentored during this time are still active in missionary ethnomusicology and related ministries: long-term fruit.

Long-distance mentoring

Shari was beginning work in a new country where there were no other arts missionaries. She asked her organizational supervisor, Joe, to help her for the first few years by scheduling regular calls, emails, and suggested readings and activities. Joe had a lot of good experience in the arts, but lived on the other side of the continent. Modern communications made it possible for him to be in touch with Shari often and in an appropriate way despite their age and gender differences. Joe was grateful for Shari's enthusiasm and new perspectives, which in turn inspired him in his work.

Life sharing mentoring

Once Shari had been working for a while with Joe's support, she agreed to host Maimuna, a young woman finishing Bible school who wanted to experience arts ministry in the mission field. Maimuna was from another country and culture, so she and Shari talked a lot about how to help each other. Because they were both single, they decided to live together and share as much as possible of their life and work. This meant spending a lot of time together in prayer as well as Bible study, talking about arts readings, and challenging each other to love God and people more. They also took trips for research and held workshops together, planning and debriefing. They divided up the work to be done, with Shari giving Maimuna more support for her tasks, as needed. Maimuna invested a lot of energy in learning the trade language and in building great relationships with local musicians she met during the year she was with Shari. A few years later she got married and took up a new arts assignment in another location with her husband.

> With an open and honest relationship base, it is possible to notice teachable moments and reflect together about what God is doing.

Student:	Date:
Site Supervisor:	Position:
Organization:	Location:

Please evaluate the learner by marking the appropriate column.

	Superior - - - - - - - -Average - - - - - - - - - Deficient				
	5	4	3	2	1
Works well with peers					
Completes work as assigned					
Works independently					
Establishes appropriate goals					
Accepts / profits from criticism					
Exhibits cultural sensitivity					
Interacts appropriately with the culture					
Makes appropriate cultural adjustments					
Participates in cultural events					
Able to analyze local arts					
Able to perform an art form of the culture					
Exhibits discretion in issues of contextualization					
Demonstrates professional skill					
Demonstrates cross-cultural competence					
Demonstrates enthusiasm for the profession					
Potential for career service in the field					

Sample evaluation form for missionary arts learners

129. STARTING AN APPRENTICESHIP PROGRAM
By Ian Collinge

In 2008 my wife, Helen, and I launched Resonance, a music and arts training ministry within WEC International. Our aim is to promote a range of arts, starting with music, that incorporate both cross-cultural engagement with particular cultures (research and creative workshops) and multi-cultural worship for mixed ethnicity settings (leading worship and running workshops).

There are two types of Resonance apprenticeships. The first is a more formal cross-cultural musical internship program for short-term mission projects, focused on particular cultures. The future plan is to migrate this program into a broader cross-cultural arts internship as a team develops. The second apprenticeship scheme is participation in a UK-based multicultural worship band, including formal training elements. This chapter will focus on the cross-cultural internships.

TRIANGLE OF PARTNERS

Resonance has been able to start these apprenticeship schemes relatively easily through WEC (Worldwide Evangelization Crusade), as WEC has existing structures with which Resonance has partnered for short-term projects. This readily enabled a threefold relationship of interns, senders, and receiving partners.

Interns usually find out about opportunities through websites, personal contact, and leaflets. Next, application formalities are handled by a short-term missions department in the applicant's home country. The receiving partners are teams, colleges, or churches in the country being visited.

PURPOSE AND SCOPE

A fundamental question to ask in setting up an apprenticeship concerns the purpose and scope of the scheme for each party involved.

For interns the scope is a short-term missions experience in another country—from three weeks to twelve months—often in the context of a team. Its purpose is clearly summed up in the words of one gifted musician: "I got to see firsthand the mission field and realized the huge need and challenges [for missions] in Europe. I got a clear idea of what ethnomusicology looks like in missions and now feel confident it's what I want to do."

For senders the purpose is to train and discern which interns might have a future in this type of work. Receiving partners often see the internships as an opportunity to explore new possibilities and to help local believers envisage using their own culture more in Christian expression. The limited time frame means that all can get a taste of involving arts in ministry and then assess any ongoing response. In every case so far, new creativity has resulted. Another intern wrote, "Each group was passionately singing, writing, and discussing as they were released into new musical creativity and freedom!"

APPRENTICESHIP TRAINING

Training is a core part of Resonance apprenticeships. All cross-cultural internships include two weeks of practical prefield training in how to apply the principles of ethnodoxology using various tools, such as music and arts surveys, questionnaires, group songwriting, learning songs of other cultures, and playing non-Western instruments. Time each day is given to research the arts of the host culture. Training also includes short-term mission and spiritual training, group prayer, and some learning about the language and culture of the host ministry. On-field orientation often includes some days dedicated to music and arts research with specialists in the community and some start in learning an instrument. One intern took lessons on a Mongolian plucked zither and wrote, "I fell in love with the people and their music. In fact I am still in touch with many of them and I have a new release of creativity in me as well. Praise God!"

LONG-TERM FOLLOW-THROUGH: INTERNS

A vital part of the success of short-term experiences for long-term missions is what happens in the first year after a missions trip. Immediate group and personal debriefing sessions are vital. In addition, reunions focused around an agreed task can be most helpful; e.g., a studio recording, group debriefing sessions, a concert, or a global worship time.

Former interns have been involved in ongoing UK-based activities, such as workshops, teaching, leading worship, recording music, transcribing songs, working on copyright issues, and helping set up a multicultural band.

Three years into Resonance cross-cultural internships, we have trained twenty interns who have visited six countries. One has enrolled in an ethnomusicology master's program, and three are already residents in another culture—either that of their internship field or another country—engaging in language study for long-term ministry. Interns increasingly apply for further internship experiences. Many recent interns are still studying but seriously considering making missions, ethnomusicology, or ethnodoxology the focus of their future lives.

The Resonance internship program is still very young. We are constantly learning, developing, adjusting, and correcting what we do, but we are clear that the purpose is to give an introduction to ethnodoxology, rather than a longer, in-depth training, and to provide a sufficient taste for this type of ministry so that interns can make an informed judgment about whether this should be part of their future career.

LONG-TERM FOLLOW-THROUGH: RECEIVING PARTNERS

The internship would not be of any value if the needs of those receiving the interns were not being met. This consideration needs to shape all that we do, from recruitment to debriefing. Fortunately, in every project so far, interns have witnessed national believers creating new songs in mainly indigenous styles. Very often these were the first songs written by those believers, and sometimes these new songs are the very first Christian songs in their own language. In France a group of North African believers were so inspired by the workshop that they planned to get together again the very next month. With such results, a common request by the hosts is for "more"! Some enquire as to how an ethnoarts focus can become a more permanent feature of their overall ministry.

> I got a clear idea of what ethnomusicology looks like in missions and now feel confident it's what I want to do.

CONCLUDING THOUGHTS

The prerequisites of an ethnoarts apprenticeship are:

- a clarity of purpose,
- a suitable training approach,
- people to run each part of the program (from initial contact to post-trip follow-up), and
- ministry opportunities.

In the three-year experience of Resonance, we have found that each of these takes time to build up and that it is important to lay good foundations from the beginning. Then, as interns begin to make a positive impact in one or two ministry contexts, the news spreads. More interns apply, and more requests for such arts-focused visitors are made.

WORSHIP

HOW TO DEVELOP CULTURALLY APPROPRIATE WORSHIP

130. DEVELOPING CULTURALLY APPROPRIATE WORSHIP

By Julisa Rowe

As I travel around the world and participate in church services in many countries, it often seems that all worship services look the same! I hear the same music, experience the same format, enter the same type of worship hall—in other words, I see a "worship colonialism" that establishes churches without taking into consideration the culture they are in, or sometimes even a true view of worship. A "worship service" in these cases means a time of singing, a time of announcements, and a sermon.

Gerrit Gustafson points out that worship is, or should be, interactive, but many services reinforce passivity by their format of sitting and listening.[44] Isaiah 6 gives us the model of revelation and response—God reveals himself and we can do no other but respond. That is worship!

The purpose of this chapter is to help us think outside our box as to how worship services should look, find out what Scripture says, and discover ways that our worship can be informed by culture.

BIBLICAL WORSHIP

What is biblical worship? Let's look at what Scripture says.

1. *Worship is our Christian lives.* Worship is our response to God (Ps 89:15; Rom 12:1,2). Worship is lifestyle and daily activity.
2. *Worship is involvement.* The very act of worship demands involvement; without involvement, there is no worship, only spectators to a show. Worship is a verb—for it to happen means action on the part of the worshiper, not an observation of a performance. Involvement is seen in the very nature of the words used in describing worship: to bow down, to do homage, to kiss toward, to serve, to confess sin, to sing, to shout, to clap, to bring an offering (Gen 18:2; Ps 100:2; Isa 19:21; Matt 4:10; 18:26; John 4:21–24; Heb 9:9,14; Rev 4:11; 5:12; 13:4; 22:3).

---

44   Gerrit Gustafson, *The Adventure of Worship: Discovering Your Highest Calling* (Grand Rapids: Chosen Books, 2006), 31.

3. *Worship is wholehearted and totally focused* (Deut 6:5; Ps 27:4; Matt 22:37).
4. *Worship is communication, not transmission.* Transmission merely sends facts from giver to recipient. There is no feedback, no continual cycle of learning, no communication. In other words, there is no *response.* The ultimate communication is God revealing himself to us and us responding to the revelation (Neh 8:6; Ps 106:48; Isa 6).
5. *Worship is caring for one another.* Throughout the Bible we see God's concern for the poor and disadvantaged, as well as those around us (Amos 5:21–24; Jas 1:27). Worship is holistic. We fail miserably when we limit our Christianity to church services and prayer meetings. As we see in the Amos passage and others throughout Scripture, if we do not integrate our faith into all aspects of our lives and work for justice, social and otherwise, we are merely hypocrites and abhorrent to God.
6. *Worship is delight, not duty.* John Piper says, "God is glorified precisely when we are satisfied in him—when we delight in his presence, when we like to be around him, when we treasure his fellowship" (Eph 1:5,6, 11–14).[45]
7. *Worship witnesses* (Ps 57:9; Acts 2:42–47; 1 Pet 2:4,5).
8. *Worship sacrifices.* It is an action and a giving of something that costs (Rom 12:1). It is not easy to give our whole selves to God in service and servitude, putting him first rather than our desires or wants. Yet that is sacrifice, and it is pleasing to God.
9. *Worship remembers Jesus Christ.* Without Christ, our worship becomes no different from any other religion. We are told to meet together to fully realize the benefits of the new relationship with God made possible by Christ because we need to express our faith continually as an ongoing relationship and to fully understand what has been done (Acts 10; 13; 18:5–8; Eph 5:19,20).

With a solid understanding of what Scripture tells of us worship, we can then move into any culture and help to create services that allow a people group to worship God in a way that speaks to their hearts.

WORSHIP SERVICE

What is a worship service? It is

- a celebration of the personal worship that has gone on during the week,
- a "rehearsal for life,"[46]
- a time to declare what God has done and celebrate him, and
- a time to increase commitment to God.

In studying the Scriptures, we find the following essentials of worship:

- prayer (Acts 2:42)

---

45   John Piper, *Let the Nations Be Glad!:The Supremacy of God in Missions through Worship*, 3rd ed., (Grand Rapids: Baker Academic, 2010), 51.

46   Donald P. Hustad, *Jubilate! Church Music in the Evangelical Tradition* (Carol Stream, IL: Hope Publishing, 1980), 78.

- praise (Ps 29:2; 96:9; 99)
- teaching the word (Acts 2:42)
- confession and assurance (Isa 6)
- singing (2 Chr 29:28)
- Communion (Acts 2:42)
- giving (Gen 22)
- fellowship (Acts 2:42)
- response (Isa 6)

We are not given a template for how a worship service should be put together, which frees us to look at cultural elements of presentation. I suggest that you put aside your automatic assumption of service structure and start instead from an understanding of biblical worship and cultural expression.

Your services could look very different and reach much deeper into the heart of the people! For example, most Western-style church buildings are very off-putting and foreign to those in Middle Eastern and Asian countries. Look at the architecture of their places of worship and the reasons behind them to see what can be used. Muslims prostrate themselves to pray. It is a strong signal of submission to God; to pray while standing could trivialize the prayer or the deity in their eyes. In less urbanized parts of Africa, time is not an issue, so one hour and fifteen minute services are often too short! Hindus worship individually or in family groups, in temples and homes, using *bhajans*—Hindu-style songs that reflect and teach. They receive religious instruction from gurus or in *ashrams* (living/learning communities). Many cultures are story-oriented and pass on values and learning through stories or community engagement.

> Perhaps singing as a group is foreign, and it would be more appropriate to recite Scripture together.

Some of the areas to consider when developing the worship service include

- architecture,
- time,
- modes of learning (do they learn through story, poetry, songs, participation?),
- ways of worship (do they worship through academic learning, dance, singing, sacrifice, contemplation?),
- people involved, and
- opportunities in the community.

How can the scriptural essentials of worship be carried out in ways that are indigenous to the culture? When you consider these areas, you may see that a sermon-oriented service is inappropriate. It would be more effective, and culturally appropriate, to tell stories and have discussion, or spend time declaring Scripture and responding in song and prayer. Perhaps singing as a group is foreign, and it would be more appropriate to recite Scripture together.

As you explore culturally relevant worship, look at the following communication signals of that culture and see how they can be applied to worship:[47]

1. *Verbal*: speech or language.
2. *Written*: symbols representing speech. How is writing used or not used? A literate society will utilize notes and bulletins; an oral society prefers the spoken word. Muslims don't make pictures, but they create beautiful things with script.
3. *Numeric*: numbers and number systems.
4. *Pictorial*: two-dimensional representations. What role do pictures and images play? How can they be utilized (e.g., PowerPoint, videos, paintings that express worship)?
5. *Artifactual*: three-dimensional representations and objects. Sculptures are an artistic communication, but even the type of seating the congregation uses says something, as does the floor covering, instruments, pulpit, plants, clothes, etc.
6. *Audio*: use of nonverbal sounds, music, and silence. Using a people's heart music is a powerful expression of who they are as they relate to God. Silence is powerful, meditative, and convicting.
7. *Kinesic*: body motions, facial expressions, posture. Do people worship on their feet, on their knees, or prostrate?
8. *Optical*: light and color.
9. *Tactile*: touch, the sense of feel. Clapping is often used in song, in response, and in praise. What about greeting one another with a "holy kiss" (or the equivalent)?
10. *Spatial*: utilization of space. How is the space set for worship? Is one area given more space or meaning than another?
11. *Temporal*: utilization of time.
12. *Olfactory*: taste and smell. Hindu worship makes heavy use of incense, flowers, and fruit offerings. For Christians, a great use of the olfactory is at the Communion table. This is the ultimate symbol of identification with Christ.

May God guide your journey of worship in many lands.[48]

INTRODUCTION

SECTION 1: FOUNDATIONS

SECTION 2: STORIES

SECTION 3: TOOLS

CLOSING

---

47   Donald K. Smith, *Creating Understanding: A Handbook for Christian Communication across Cultural Landscapes* (Grand Rapids: Zondervan, 1992), 146.

48   For additional reading, see the following resources in the *Handbook* bibliography: Allen and Borror (1988); Hayford, Killinger, and Stevenson (1990); Piper (2003); D. K. Smith (1992); Webber (1997); and Wiersbe (1990).

131. DEVELOPING URBAN ARTS

By David M. Bailey

There is a connection between people and stories. No matter what culture or generation, from the earliest beginnings of humanity, people have passed on stories about what has happened, what is, what should be, and what could be. Historically, cities have often been a place where these stories were created and passed on. Because of the multitude of people in a city, stories spread easily. Cities tend to be the place where the marketplace of ideas are exchanged, innovation thrives, and where cultural development is the fertile ground in which new stories are created and told.

It is important for Christian communities to be active in the cultivation of culture. Whether it is the culture that is being developed in society at large or the culture that is being developed in the church, we should be people who are proclaiming the goodness in the world that God has created and sharing the good news God has given us. When Christians are engaged in creating, we are bearing witness to our God who chose to reveal himself as the Creator (Gen 1–2). Christian communities should be engaged in the storytelling of the cultures we participate in.

> When Christians are engaged in creating, we are bearing witness to our God who chose to reveal himself as the Creator (Gen 1–2).

CULTIVATING CULTURE AND TELLING STORIES FOR ALL

As Christians, in our pursuit of cultivating and developing new stories and cultures, we have a particular uniqueness we must consider when we do anything, especially when we endeavor to develop arts in urban contexts. Cities offer us many different types of people living together, especially those who are economically diverse. In most urban settings there are the rich and powerful, the poor and weak, and those in between, trying to move up or trying not to be pushed down the economic ladder. In many cities, culture making, storytelling, and the arts are created for the rich by the rich and the upwardly mobile, and the poor are isolated from this process. There are exceptions for the especially talented, but for the most part, the urban poor are considered a problem to be dealt with, therefore generally walked over or shuffled around.

God has given Christians the mandate to care for the poor (Matt 25:31–46; James 1:27; 2:2–6; 1 John 3:17,18). He has called us to be the kind of people who care for and develop "the least of these" in our cities. When we explore how to develop urban arts, we should not only think about how to develop arts for the upwardly mobile, but also consider the urban poor.

It is important to be aware of how economics affect the cultural dynamics of developing urban arts. Church planter and pastor Eric Russ makes this distinction:

> Although urban is sometimes used more generically to include the inner city, it typi-
> cally refers to that part of the city that acts as a hotbed of cultural formation. This is
> where ideas are formed, things are invented, entertainment is produced, and people
> are educated. In urban areas the pedigree of the people is upwardly mobile—they are
> educating others in some fashion or in the process of being educated. These people
> are, in some way, developing the culture or being trained to do so on some scale.
> These urban dwellers are not necessarily financially well off. *What makes them up-
> wardly mobile is that they have options* [italics in the original]. The city center is rich
> in resources and options to move upward socially, economically, and vocationally. If
> the city center is in formation, it will receive a great amount of resources toward the
> hopeful end of becoming an urban center.
>
> What, then, is the distinguishing mark between city center and inner city? The issue
> of opportunity is what separates urban from inner city. In the inner city, resources are
> taken out and it remains under resourced. Generally speaking, there is no agenda for
> resources investment in the inner city. It is a byproduct of city center growth. This is
> often how an impoverished area is formed (taking resources out of an already unre-
> sourced area) . . .
>
> But getting grace into these issues can't begin until we see the drastic difference be-
> tween the two contexts. Although they are close in proximity they are worlds apart in
> worldview.[49]

THE HARLEM RENAISSANCE: A MODEL FOR URBAN POTENTIAL

We can get some ideas of how to develop urban arts by learning from a great period in American history, the Harlem Renaissance.

The Harlem Renaissance happened between the 1920s and 1930s. This was a period in American history when African-Americans were a few generations beyond the emancipation of chattel slavery, but still under the yoke of the Jim Crow Segregation Laws which held African-Americans as second-class citizens. During this period a few key black leaders came to the conclusion that it was time for black people to tell a different story than that of the racist image many whites were projecting on them.

Gentleman like W. E. B. Du Bois, James Weldon Johnson, Charles Spurgeon Johnson, and others were prosperous black intellectuals that helped facilitate the new story about who blacks were and what black people could be. Prosperous black intellectuals connected with upwardly

---

49   Eric Russ, "Discipling African-Americans in an Urban Context," Gospel Centered Discipleship, http://www. gospelcentereddiscipleship.com/discipling-african-americans-in-an-urban-context/?format=pdf.

mobile and poor, talented artists and encouraged them to create art that told a different story about black people. The black intellectuals of the Harlem Renaissance served as a connecting bridge between wealthy patrons and poor or middle-class black artists. They created an economic engine that made the Harlem Renaissance culturally and economically prosperous for all people. This era was a prosperous time in which new stories were told and the culture was cultivated for the betterment of everyone in the community.

> The black intellectuals of the Harlem Renaissance served as a connecting bridge between wealthy patrons and poor or middle-class black artists.

FOUR GUIDELINES FOR DEVELOPING URBAN ARTS

From observing the Harlem Renaissance we find four guidelines for how to develop urban arts.

1. **Assess.** When starting an urban arts initiative, assess *who is in the community.* Take a look at all of the people who make up the community, whether they are active or not. Pay close attention to the marginalized in the community, because they have a lot to contribute and very few people will provide them with an opportunity to do so.

    Next, take an inventory of the *assets in the community.* No matter how poor or prosperous, God has given good gifts to these communities, and it is up to the people of God to discover them. Make sure that you cultivate this process with much prayer, because even though we don't always see the assets of the community, God does.

    Next, begin to assess the *needs of the community.* Make sure, however, not to start by looking at the needs. Start by assessing the people; they in turn can help you discover the assets and needs.

2. **Invest.** After assessment comes investment. Start by investing in a good vision. Invest in a vision of beauty and of a flourishing community—based on the people, their assets, and their needs. Cultivate a new story, one that will bless the whole community.

    Invest in arts education. Provide skills training so that the quality of arts being created will be excellent. During the education process make sure the teacher teaches in a way that cultivates what is already present in the community rather than imposing his or her culture on the student. Education and cultivation will unlock an abundance of art in urban communities.

    If you are creating Christian-based urban arts, invest in theological education for the artists. If you are from the West or have been heavily influenced by the West, don't assume theological training means that the artists need to go to seminary. Seminary training is designed for educated people. Do not limit the possibilities of those who can be theologically formed to those who have high literacy levels. Discover ways to teach good theology and theological practices to a wide range of educational levels, from the illiterate to the scholars.

Last but not least, invest financially. Many people don't have the time to create art because they spend most of their time trying to survive financially. Whether it is your money or someone else's money, try to invest in the flourishing of urban communities through arts. When you find the money, be wise and creative in how you invest it. One thousand dollars, for example, could potentially be used to commission a professional to create a work, or to commission a few up-and-coming, talented artists to create their art. There is a place for both uses of money, so the way to determine how to use the money would be determined by the people, assets, and needs of the community.

3. **Commission.** Commission arts based on what you have assessed. If you invest and cultivate, you will be surprised at what you receive from commissioned work. Commission artistic experts and up-and-coming artists. Commission community arts projects as well so that people who are not artists can participate in beautifying the community. If you choose a community arts project, make sure you choose a quality artist who is good at working with people as well as within their artistic discipline.

    Find patrons who will pay for commissioned urban arts projects. Be a bridge builder for the community between artists and patrons. When you and/or a patron commission an artistic piece, make sure that you commission art in the way God did in the Garden of Eden. God brought the animals to Adam to see what he would name them (Gen 2:19). God provided Adam with the materials, but he didn't micromanage Adam's creativity process. The Great Creator sat back and watched what kind of names Adam would come up with. We should do the same.

4. **Encourage entrepreneurship.** Finally, look for opportunities. Look for opportunities to tell good stories. Look for good stories in the community that you can share with others and back to the community about what is happening. Look for new stories that can make a better future for the community. Get other people to share those stories too. The better stories we tell, the better our cultures will be.

    Look for opportunities for entrepreneurship and economic development with urban arts. When a community is telling good stories creatively and through the arts, there is a lot of potential for economic activity that will help the community. Artists need to make a living in order to continue to create good art, and people need to experience good stories in order to live well. If you can help, therefore, to create a bridge that has a great economic flow, you create a winning situation for all parties involved.

INTRODUCTION

SECTION 1: FOUNDATIONS

SECTION 2: STORIES

SECTION 3: TOOLS

CLOSING

INTRODUCTION

SECTION 1: FOUNDATIONS

SECTION 2: STORIES

SECTION 3: TOOLS

CLOSING

REMEMBER THE STORY OF JESUS

As you pursue developing urban arts, remember the story that Jesus told about the judgment of nations:

> When the Son of Man comes in his glory, and all the angels with him, he will sit on his glorious throne. All the nations will be gathered before him, and he will separate the people one from another as a shepherd separates the sheep from the goats. He will put the sheep on his right and the goats on his left.
>
> Then the King will say to those on his right, "Come, you who are blessed by my Father; take your inheritance, the kingdom prepared for you since the creation of the world. For I was hungry and you gave me something to eat, I was thirsty and you gave me something to drink, I was a stranger and you invited me in, I needed clothes and you clothed me, I was sick and you looked after me, I was in prison and you came to visit me."
>
> Then the righteous will answer him, "Lord, when did we see you hungry and feed you, or thirsty and give you something to drink? When did we see you a stranger and invite you in, or needing clothes and clothe you? When did we see you sick or in prison and go to visit you?"
>
> The King will reply, "Truly I tell you, whatever you did for one of the least of these brothers and sisters of mine, you did for me."
>
> Then he will say to those on his left, "Depart from me, you who are cursed, into the eternal fire prepared for the devil and his angels. For I was hungry and you gave me nothing to eat, I was thirsty and you gave me nothing to drink, I was a stranger and you did not invite me in, I needed clothes and you did not clothe me, I was sick and in prison and you did not look after me."
>
> They also will answer, "Lord, when did we see you hungry or thirsty or a stranger or needing clothes or sick or in prison, and did not help you?"
>
> He will reply, "Truly I tell you, whatever you did not do for one of the least of these, you did not do for me."
>
> Then they will go away to eternal punishment, but the righteous to eternal life. (Matt 25:31–46)

HOW TO FOSTER MULTICULTUAL WORSHIP

132. WORSHIPING WITH THE GLOBAL CHURCH

By C. Michael Hawn

"A FORETASTE OF GLORY DIVINE"

Revelation 7:9,10 offers a vision of a multitude from every "nation, from all tribes and peoples and languages, standing before the throne and before the Lamb" singing, "Salvation belongs to our God who sits on the throne, and to the Lamb!" (ESV) This passage points the church today to the end of time as we know it and offers a vision of what will be—a time when our praise will be universal and our diversity will reveal the splendor of the Creator's imagination. Is this only a vision of the future, or might we have, in the words of the hymn writer Fanny Crosby, a "foretaste of glory divine" on earth?

As twenty-first-century Christians, the prophecy of this passage is more relevant and accessible to us now than at any time before. Embodying such a vision will require that the church, as the body of Christ, embrace a different understanding of culture than our forbearers. It will require that the body of Christ assume a counter-cultural posture toward society and its expectations. It also assumes that we re-vision our ecclesiology—what it means to be the church, and the church at worship.

THE CHURCH NEEDS TO SING ITSELF INTO A NEW REALITY

Rather than a place where our individual comfort is the highest priority; rather than a gathering that prefers similar ethnic, socioeconomic, or political profiles; rather than an institution that only looks backwards toward "the good old days" —we need to see the church as a place where we can be vulnerable, where diversity reflects a creative God, where our fascination with the past is balanced with our hope for an inclusive future. Among the many ways that the church can capture this vision is to sing itself into a new understanding of what it means to be the church.

European minister Albert van den Heuvel noted in 1966, "There is ample literature about the great formative influence of the hymns of a tradition on its members. Tell me what you sing, and

I'll tell you who you are!"[50] Perhaps we should reframe this assertion with the question, "What should we sing to become a faithful, visionary, inclusive church?" The church in the West tends to sing only songs that focus on our past (often under the label of "traditional") or songs that reflect the current culture (often under the label of "contemporary"). The songs of our heritage are important witnesses to the saints who have gone before us, and songs of today are records of the struggles and hopes of the current age. What songs might we sing to pull the hope of Revelation into the present? What songs might we sing that would give us glimpses of the gathering described in Revelation 7?

Exploring the songs of the world church is one place to begin. In an age where two-thirds of the Christian community lives in the Southern Hemisphere, the "flat earth" of Christianity indicates that songs of faith no longer flow only from the West to the rest, but also may flow from the South to the North. Where might we begin?

There is no guaranteed method for guiding the church toward the vision of Revelation 7. Whatever the approach, moving a congregation toward a renewed understanding of what it means to be the church is not easy.

- It requires a clear understanding of what could be rather than what is.
- It requires a willingness to listen to those different from us, rather than to share only what we think.
- It requires a spirit that is willing to leave the security of the known to explore the vulnerability of the unknown.

SEVEN STEPS TOWARD BECOMING A CHURCH WITH A VISION FOR GLOBAL WORSHIP

If no methodology exists, what strategies might we employ to become a church with a vision for global worship?

1. **Start with your neighborhood.** Who lives among you who may be invisible to your community? Most neighborhoods have ethnic diversity. A demographic analysis of your community may reveal minority persons. Praying and singing for your neighbors in their own language and with songs from their culture may be a way to establish a connection.

2. **Read the Bible together.** A cross-cultural Bible study opens up new understandings of the Scripture. The limitations of our culture of origin create myopia when sharing Scripture. Sharing a Bible study across cultures reveals a richness and depth that point to the God of all, whose Son redeemed all people.

3. **Observing the Christian year.** Specific seasons of the Christian liturgical year lend themselves naturally to incorporating songs from the world church. Christmas celebrates the Son of God born in a specific place and time for all places and times. Epiphany is the season when many Christian faith traditions celebrate world missions,

---

50   Albert van den Heuvel, preface to Risk: New Hymns for a New Day (Geneva: World Council of Churches, 1966).

drawing the inspiration from the Magi who returned home spreading the news of the Christ child. Easter is a season of cosmic dimensions, when Christ rose from the dead to redeem all humanity. Pentecost celebrates the miracle of Acts when the Holy Spirit fostered understanding among many peoples at the birth of the church. Sharing the songs of the world church throughout the Christian year expands our understanding of the reach of the gospel around the globe.

4. **Praying for the world.** While we often pray for those who are near and dear to us, praying for the needs of the world is one of the reasons that Christians have gathered throughout the centuries. World crises featured in the media should be the subject of our prayers as we gather for worship. Singing songs from a region where strife or oppression emanates is one way to empathize with the suffering persons whom God came to save.

5. **Church music education.** The world in which our children and young people are growing up is much different than the one of previous generations. Exposing them to cultures beyond their culture of origin encourages trust rather than building walls of hostility and fear. Singing songs from different Christian communities around the world may be one of the ways to build bridges between young people and other ethnic groups.

6. **Changing the soundscape of worship.** When we gather in our places of worship, we expect to encounter specific sounds that will guide our prayer and praise. These sounds nurture our faith. They are the common heartbeat of our gatherings. However, our worship is organic rather than frozen. Praying in the twenty-first century requires that we expand the ways that we pray together. Through the music of other cultures we can experience a sense of the presence of others among us and broaden the ways that we pray. This does not mean that we give up the songs and prayers of our culture of origin. We broaden our songs as a means of praying more fully and completely. In addition to new songs, the soundscape of worship is enlivened with instruments and languages. Hearing prayers, singing songs, and sharing Scripture in at least one language other than the one usually used in worship reminds us of a God that is much bigger than any one cultural perspective.

7. **Hospitality as a principle of worship.** From the earliest recorded Christian worship experiences, hospitality has been an integral part of these gatherings. Welcoming others is fundamental to Christian worship. Matthew 25:31–46 speaks of our hospitality to all peoples. This hospitality extends to our worship. In a cross-cultural world where the migration of people is a way of life, the church, through its worship, has many opportunities to extend hospitality to those beyond our cultural context, demonstrating that Christ is among us in the faces of the stranger and the alien.

INTRODUCTION

SECTION 1: FOUNDATIONS

SECTION 2: STORIES

SECTION 3: TOOLS

CLOSING

133. THREE OBSTACLES TO OVERCOME

By David M. Bailey

To be clear, multicultural worship in community is hard.

Now that you have been warned, it is also important to know that multicultural worship in community is very rewarding.

When communities learn to worship in a culturally different way, they learn more about who God is and more about the variety of people who have been made in the image of God. The benefits of knowing God more comprehensively make overcoming the obstacles to multicultural worship worth the undertaking.

In my work as a worship leader in various churches and cultural contexts, I have found that there are three major obstacles to multicultural worship that need to be overcome:[51]

1. awareness
2. finding qualified people
3. acquiring skills and resources

AWARENESS

The worshiping community must first be made aware of the theological and practical reasons for why it should practice multicultural worship. We humans tend to focus only on our own personal culture unless a person or a situation makes us aware of others. Multicultural worship is not even on most people's radar. For this reason it is very important to patiently and intentionally help people achieve this awareness.

All positional leaders, decision makers, and influential leaders must embrace the need for multicultural worship. This step is foundational. If the leadership of the community is not committed to this cause both theologically and practically, they will abort the mission when hard times come.

Next, the worship leaders, musicians, and artists need to embrace multicultural worship. These artists will bear the initial criticisms and complaints from the community. If the community has only experienced monocultural worship expressions, worship leaders will need to be taught

---

51   David M. Bailey, *Arrabon: Learning Reconciliation through Community and Worship Music* (Richmond, VA: Lulu, 2011), 47–48.

and coached on how to lead the community through the transitional process. As a community becomes accustomed to multicultural worship, the worship leaders will also need to be continually reminded of the importance of a multicultural focus.

Last, but definitely not least, the congregation needs to undergo a process to cultivate multicultural awareness. This process needs to be shepherded in a way that the congregation feels nudged, not pushed or runover, to embrace new ways of worship.

It is essential to understand that raising awareness of the importance for multicultural worship lays a solid foundation for its future practice, so the process must be intentional and patient. Listen to the Holy Spirit and the community. By listening to both God and the community, you will you know if you are moving too fast or too slow in bringing the community to an awareness of the fullness of God in worship.

FINDING QUALIFIED PEOPLE

The second obstacle to overcome is having qualified people to execute the vision of multicultural worship. There are two ways to meet this obstacle: find new people or cultivate the people you have.

This chapter focused first on cultivating the right atmosphere within the community that you presently have. Qualified worship leaders can be developed within the community you presently have as well—brought into the vision simultaneously with the process of raising awareness. If instead you recruit someone new to accomplish the vision of multicultural worship, it is important to note that the community must stay on its course; otherwise, those who have been recruited could potentially feel taken advantage of if the mission is later aborted.

> All positional leaders, decision makers, and influential leaders must embrace the need for multicultural worship.

There are a few options for recruiting outside qualified musicians. One of the obvious options is to hire someone. I always encourage communities to be willing to invest resources in developing multicultural worship because where the community puts their money speaks about where they are putting their heart (Matt 6:19–21). That said, hiring someone isn't always the answer to the problem of finding qualified people. The community might not be able to afford it, or the money might be used in a different way. Chapters 4 and 5 in my book cited earlier, *Arrabon: Learning Reconciliation through Community and Worship Music*, explore other ways money can be used for bringing in qualified worship leaders.

A nonmonetary way of cultivating multicultural worship is to barter through cultural exchanges. The musicians of your community can swap with musicians from other communities of a different culture. This can be a rich experience, available whether or not you have the money to hire someone.

Regardless of whether outside musicians are brought to the community, cultivating the musicians already in the community is essential to fostering a full multicultural worship environment. This leads us to our last area of concern.

ACQUIRING SKILLS AND RESOURCES

Education is an essential value and practice in cultivating multicultural worship. In multicultural worship, it is important to honor various cultures; however, it is difficult to honor a culture or musical style that one is ignorant of. No one person knows everything about all cultures, so having a system of musical and cultural education allows the worship leaders and musicians to grow in their musical and cultural competencies. Use this *Handbook* as a tool to find musical educational resources for various cultural styles. A list of music education resources and musical styles can also be found in my work, *Arrabon: Learning Reconciliation through Community and Worship Music.*

Creating an environment of safety, awareness, and education will eventually equip the community with the resources to overcome the three primary obstacles to implementing multicultural worship.

134. DRAWING YOUR COMMUNITY TOWARD A CULTURE OF MULTIETHNIC WORSHIP

By Kenneth L. Wallace, Jr.

"Thy kingdom come, Thy will be done in earth, as it is in heaven" (Matt 6:10 KJV). We pray this prayer in our churches every Sunday, but do we really understand what it is we pray? Fortunately, many churches today are starting to understand more and more. Revelation 7:9 tells us exactly what heaven looks like around God's throne. There are people from every tribe, tongue, and nation worshiping God together. Churches today are looking at their congregations and realizing that they are not reflecting this image on *earth* as it is in heaven. When asked what they should do, I often tell them to begin with multiethnic musical worship.

DEVELOPING MULTIETHNIC MUSICAL WORSHIP

It is well known that music can serve as a tool to carry a message. In the case of multiethnic musical worship, a dual purpose is served. First, worship is a response to God, the orientation of one's heart to the one that we love. Second, worship can teach us about how God has left his fingerprints on our brothers and sisters from around the world. Worshiping with another person is a very intimate activity and allows us to see the *namste*—that which is divine within each person.

How can we move toward a culture of multiethnic worship? First, start with Scripture and teach your community to look for those fingerprints. Teach them to seek out God's heart for the nations and to ask questions in humility. If you meet a Christian from a different culture, ask them, "How do you experience God's love?" "What aspect of God's character do you most identify with?" Of course, no one person can speak for the whole of a culture, yet you can apply what they have answered to help your community move closer to God in the particular area highlighted. For example:

- Hispanic cultures tend to celebrate the power of God.
- African-American cultures tend to connect with the God of the breakthrough.
- Euro-Americans herald the inerrancy of Scripture and theological accuracy.
- First Nations people rejoice in the unity that is seen in the Great Spirit in the Trinity.

INTRODUCTION

SECTION 1: FOUNDATIONS

SECTION 2: STORIES

SECTION 3: TOOLS

CLOSING

Second, gather resources and build relationships. Many people are blessed to be able to travel often and to many places. But not all of us are so fortunate. All of us, however, know someone who has been enriched by travel. While meeting an actual person from a given culture is always best, asking a traveler to bring back a song from a trip instead of a souvenir could be just as much of a blessing. Ask this person to write down the song and record it. Most cell phones and cameras have recording functions that can be used to remember the melody of the song. Find help to learn pronunciation. One should be cautious, however, that just as most people in our own culture don't like to be put on the spot, neither do many people from other cultures either. This is why building relationships across cultures is so important. Affirmation of people's culture by showing interest in their form of worship will bless them and encourage them to share a part of themselves with you.

DIFFERENT STYLES OF MUSIC BRING DIFFERENT CHALLENGES

Once you have determined that your community should sing a particular song from a different culture—based preferably on the need to connect with the theme of that song—you should then begin to share the song with your church body. Typically, songs with a call-and-response form are easier to learn. Many African-based songs—such as the Swahili chorus, *Yesu Ni Wangu*, for example—tend to repeat simple phrases in a call-and-response fashion. Another option is to have the church choir or the entire congregation sing the chorus, which is generally repeated multiple times throughout the song while the leader sings the verses. For instance, a Hindi *bhajan*, *Bhajo Naam*, works well when the worshiping body sings the repetitive chorus while the leader offers the more complex verses. Short choruses or songs tend also to work well when introducing multiethnic worship. Spanish *coritos*—like *"Santo, santo, santo"*—are short and repetitive, allowing singers to sing them over again until the words feel comfortable. Always have the translation of the lyrics available for the singers. Although God understands every language, for the people in the congregation to connect with the song, they should have some idea what it is they are singing.

> Affirmation of people's culture by showing interest in their form of worship will bless them and encourage them to share a part of themselves with you.

TEACHING SONGS WILL TAKE TIME

When teaching a song, be sure to introduce it well. Tell the story, describe the setting, and present the theme. You can teach the song line by line—this usually works well with longer songs—or sing through the song slowly before singing it again *a tempo*. Don't be afraid to sing the song multiple times in succession. It may take several times for people to feel comfortable enough with a song to connect with it. Also consider the complexity of the language in which the song is written. Swahili, for example, is an easier language to pronounce than some because each letter is pronounced, whereas Chinese is more challenging because of tonalities which change the meaning of a word. If it is a more difficult language, you will need to spend more time teaching the song.

A WORD OF ENCOURAGEMENT TO KEEP GOING

As you lead your communities toward multiethnic worship, you will see people beginning to talk about God differently. They will ask questions they have never asked before. They will begin to connect to the Church with a capital C—the *universal* Church. As they catch the vision that was laid out for us in Scripture of what eternal worship will look like, they will truly become more of a reflection of "Thy will be done in earth, as it is in heaven."

135. MOVING FROM MONOCULTURAL TO MULTICULTURAL WORSHIP

By Ian Collinge

INTRODUCTION

At a conference in 2003, instruments, languages, and music from around the world blended together in a great offering of praise. I saw that we do not have to worship segregated by music styles. There is a better way—a way that is also profoundly enriching and unifying! In multicultural worship we honor the heritage of others, and our worship horizons are expanded.

AIM: TO MOVE FROM MONOCULTURAL TO MULTICULTURAL WORSHIP

Many urban churches around the world draw ethnically mixed congregations and musicians with diverse stylistic backgrounds. Frequently, however, one culture's music dominates. The purpose of this chapter is to point to ways in which churches can move from monocultural to multicultural worship in their music.[52]

I define multicultural worship music as a body of Christian worship music that reflects several cultures.[53] Various motivations for this may be that a church

- already includes a mix of ethnicities,
- aims to attract a more multicultural membership,
- desires to identify with the global church, or
- seeks to reach out to specific cultures in their community.

---

[52] The same principles can also apply to other worshiping bodies such as youth groups, home groups, and mission teams.

[53] Many of the same issues apply to generational and subcultural differences within a church, but our focus here is primarily on ethnic identities.

Multiculturalism is a journey. There are two initiating phases: first, an honest assessment, and then steps to embark on the process. After these, fresh evaluation can lead to further steps.

PHASE 1:
ASSESSING OUR CURRENT APPROACH TO UNITY AND DIVERSITY IN WORSHIP

One major reason church and music leaders do not move into greater musical diversity is a lack of clarity about the role that culture plays in worship. Therefore, the first step is to ask two stark questions:
1. Whose musical culture currently prevails in our church's worship?
2. Does our lack of diversity expose an underlying lack of acceptance of other cultures?

The following "Multicultural Worship Assessment Tool" may help in identifying your "Worship and Culture Profile." Five common approaches to unity and diversity in worship are presented (see diagram below). Which most fits your situation? These approaches are as follows:

1. **Inherited patterns: Unity without diversity**
    *   In this most common approach, there is no change to the existing formulas of music—ancient or contemporary—when other ethnicities join the church. The message to other cultures is, "Sing our songs."

2. **Independent groups: Diversity without unity**
    *   Leaders acknowledge cultural diversity by separating the church into distinct ethnolinguistic congregations. The message is, "Sing your songs in your groups."

3. **Inclusive involvement: Unity with invited diversity**
    *   Members of different ethnic groups are invited to offer contributions for the whole congregation, whether as special items or as a full worship time. The message is, "Sing your songs to us."

4. **Integrated music: Unity with blended diversity**
    *   Church musicians, often ethnically mixed, include and/or adapt music from various cultures. The message is, "Let's sing one another's songs together."

5. **Innovative fusion: Unity with creative diversity**
    *   Church musicians from diverse ethnic backgrounds create new music together. The message is, "Let's make new songs together."

PHASE 2:
ENCOURAGING MUSICAL DIVERSITY IN WORSHIP

It may be that a church using approach 1 or 2 wants to move to approach 3, 4, or 5. It would be unwise to attempt this too quickly. Solid foundations need to be laid. A workshop may help to address several of these over a weekend. These foundations include:

1. **Providing biblical teaching**
   - Regular biblical teaching on the subject will help church members understand that
     - worship is a living sacrifice,
     - God loves every people group equally and wants them to glorify him with their own voice,
     - corporate worship is not just about "me and God" but about "us and God," and
     - "accepting one another" means giving space to the voice of others.

2. **Conducting a heart-music survey**
   - One way to discover the most meaningful music for the church or the wider community is to conduct a "heart-music" questionnaire,[54] with questions such as, "What music would you most prefer when you . . ."
     - feel sad or sick?
     - are falling asleep or waking up?
     - feel energetic (e.g., exercising)?
     - are doing practical jobs or traveling?
     - want to express yourself in private?
     - want to pray?

3. **Learning appropriate songs**
   - Once the people's heart-music styles are understood, musicians can look for suitable songs—often from other church members—that they can learn. They may translate the words and arrange the song to fit the multicultural context.

4. **Planning inspiring experiences**
   - Many worshipers need to overcome a sense of inadequacy when faced with different languages and musical styles. The best way is through positive, meaningful, and inspiring experiences in which they conclude, "This is good and I really can do this!"

5. **Using accessible songs**
   - For such a conclusion to be reached, songs should be chosen which are accessible by a large number of the congregation. People should feel that they can pronounce the words, sing the melody, and enjoy the song. As they gain confidence, they may embrace more challenging songs.

---

54   Music that is learned in a person's childhood and youth/teenage years and that most deeply expresses his or her emotions.

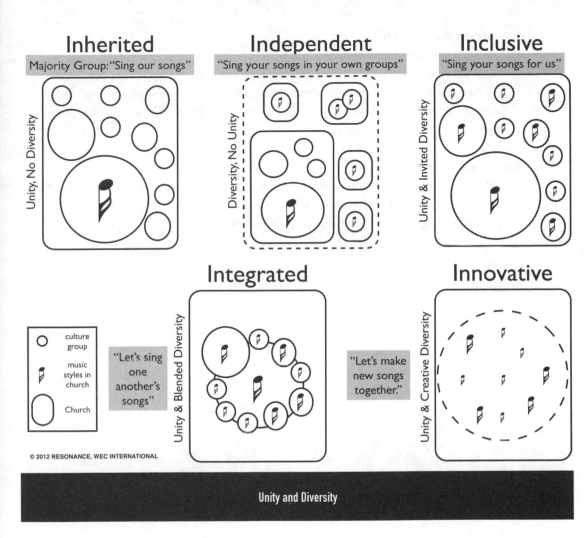

Inherited
Majority Group: "Sing our songs"

Unity, No Diversity

Independent
"Sing your songs in your own groups"

Diversity, No Unity

Inclusive
"Sing your songs for us"

Unity & Invited Diversity

○ culture group

♪ music styles in church

⬭ Church

Integrated

"Let's sing one another's songs"

Unity & Blended Diversity

Innovative

"Let's make new songs together."

Unity & Creative Diversity

© 2012 RESONANCE, WEC INTERNATIONAL

Unity and Diversity

6. **Introducing songs gradually**
   - It is important that transitions are gradual. Everything should be carefully explained and songs introduced in ways appropriate to the church. Sometimes a prayer meeting or social gathering may be the place to start. Alternatively, presenting a song as a special item may help others to warm to this new style. Then the song should be repeated fairly soon to be learned and accepted.

7. **Making worship meaningful**
   - Understanding is most important. Paul said, "I will sing with my spirit, but I will also sing with my understanding" (1 Cor 14:15). Clear translations of words into a common language are vital, whether these are sung, explained, printed, or displayed. Songs which use different languages enable different language groups to be involved, as do songs written in call-and-response form that alternate languages in each phrase.

8. **Integrating the repertoire**
    - For a church to become musically multicultural, music from a range of cultures should be integrated into the church's regular worship life. Musicians are the main key to success in this by mixing songs in ways that work well together and, as they gain confidence, using appropriate musical features from different cultures; e.g., rhythms, instruments, sounds, etc.

9. **Reevaluating the experience**
    - With positive and negative feedback, leaders and musicians can assess how their approach is working, which songs work best, what teaching to give, how to integrate material, and what new music would be helpful.

443

INTRODUCTION

SECTION 1: FOUNDATIONS

SECTION 2: STORIES

SECTION 3: TOOLS

CLOSING

136. HONORING DIVERSE HEART LANGUAGES IN A CHRISTIAN COMMUNITY

By David M. Bailey

One of the hardest things in the world to do is to take something from someone when they believe that they have the right of ownership to it. A fight will ensue. Generally, the only time that a person does not put up a fight when confronted with this kind of loss is when they feel that the other party has more power. A few will fight when they feel powerless, but the majority will throw in the towel of defeat when they feel helpless.

One of the biggest struggles I've experienced in any Christian community is the struggle for culture. I'm not talking about the cultural struggles between biblical Christianity and secular society, but the struggle within Christian communities about which social, ethnic, or age group's behaviors and beliefs will be expressed in the context of the community.[55]

The challenge of a culture war within a Christian community is that every person believes they have the "right" to their own culture. When another person or people group's cultural choices appear to take that right away, the fight for personal cultural identity begins. This is a core issue because our culture is part of how God has made us. Our cultural heart languages are a gift from God to us and a gift that we should share with each other. The process of learning to honor and understand the various heart languages of our brothers and sisters with whom we are in Christian community is a key element of spiritual formation that can't be easily substituted.

UNITY IN DIVERSITY

The first practical step you should take when learning how to honor diverse heart languages in a Christian community is to conduct a survey of what cultures are in your Christian community, what cultures are in your surrounding neighborhood or community, and what cultures are not represented in your Christian community but that you hope become a part of it. When you take a survey of cultures, include race and ethnic groups, but don't limit culture to those types of de-

---

55   I follow the definition of the word "culture" as "the behaviors and beliefs characteristic of a particular social, ethnic, or age group" (Dictionary.com, s.v. "culture," http://dictionary.reference.com/browse/culture).

mographics. Observe the culture and heart languages of people of various ages, socioeconomic groups, gender, Christian traditions, etc.

Christian communities have wrestled with cultural issues ever since the book of Acts. In Acts 15, a group of Jewish believers endeavored to get Gentile believers to assimilate to the Jewish culture in order for the Gentiles to be more faithful to God. Paul and Barnabas saw that this issue was a big deal, so they traveled back to Jerusalem in order to discern the will of God on this matter. After a lot of discussion and prayer, it seemed right with the apostles and elders, through the guidance of the Holy Spirit, to

> The type of unity that glorifies the redemptive work of God is not the type of unity that is accomplished through assimilation, but is unity with diversity.

allow the Gentiles to express their culture as long as their activities were not idolatrous or immoral (Acts 15:1–35). This scriptural account set a precedent for the church to learn how to live in unity through diversity instead of unity through assimilation. When we read Acts and the Epistles, we see that the church becomes more diverse in its culture the further it gets away from Jerusalem. The church in Antioch is different from the church in Jerusalem, and the church in Ephesus is different from the church in Corinth. When we look through the New Testament and see the various types of cultural diversity, we can open ourselves up to reimagine the various possibilities of what our local church culture can be like.

When cultural expression is only limited by things that are either idolatrous or immoral, there is an increased possibility of expression, but sometimes the various cultural possibilities can conflict within the community. For example, if one culture's preferred heart language of expression is to be loud and demonstrative, and another cultural group's expression is quiet and meditative, there will inevitably be a conflict, so how can the Christian community live in unity with heart language expressions that are so different from one another?

GUIDANCE FROM PHILIPPIANS

Many years of ministry after the Jerusalem Council of Acts 15, the Apostle Paul gives us guidance in Philippians on how to reconcile a dilemma of this nature:

> If you have any encouragement from being united with Christ, if any comfort from his love, if any fellowship with the Spirit, if any tenderness and compassion, then make my joy complete by being like-minded, having the same love, being one in spirit and purpose. (Phil 2:1,2)

In essence Paul is saying if Christ and the Holy Spirit are at work in your community, there should be unity. Unity in a Christian community is significant evidence of the redemptive work of God (John 17:20,21). The type of unity that glorifies the redemptive work of God is not the type of unity that is accomplished through assimilation, but is unity with diversity that can only be accomplished by being united in Christ and through the power of the Holy Spirit. When Paul encourages us to be of like mind, having the same love, and having one spirit and purpose, this is not a mandate to have one dominant culture make other cultures assimilate.

> Do nothing out of selfish ambition or vain conceit, but in humility consider others better than yourselves. Each of you should look not only to your own interests, but also to the interests of others. (Phil 2:3,4)

Verses 3 and 4 are the key verses for how to honor diverse heart languages in a Christian community. In humility we are to honor and consider one another more than we consider and honor ourselves. Whoever is a part of the decision-making process needs to take an inventory of their own cultural biases and consider these verses. When leading the community through this process, it is important that the leaders demonstrate and articulate the importance of Philippians 2:3,4. In my worshiping community we have a 70 percent rule—if you find yourself comfortable more than 70 percent of the time, then something is wrong, because that means your culture is dominating the community!

> Your attitude should be the same as that of Christ Jesus: Who, being in very nature God, did not consider equality with God something to be grasped, but made himself nothing, taking the very nature of a servant, being made in human likeness. And being found in appearance as a man, he humbled himself and became obedient to death—even death on a cross! (Phil 2:5–8)

My mentor, Don Coleman, has a saying: "Everybody wants to be like Jesus, but nobody wants to die on the cross." This is true. Jesus himself didn't want to die on the cross (Matt 26:42; Mark 14:36; Luke 22:42)! But thank God that Jesus moved beyond what he wanted to do and what he was comfortable with and decided to do the will of his Father. In this text, Scripture is calling us to have the same attitude of Christ. Our first attitude is an attitude of intentionally putting ourselves in a lower social and power position so that we can use our influence to serve and empower others in our community. We see in verses 7–8 that Jesus took off the fullness of his power as God and lowered himself to become a man. It is important to note that when Jesus

> **We have a 70 percent rule—if you find yourself comfortable more than 70 percent of the time, then something is wrong, because that means your culture is dominating the community!**

became a man, he didn't choose to be a socially powerful man (Lev 12:2–8; Zech 9:9; Luke 2:22–24; 2 Cor 8:9). Nor did he choose to be an ethnically powerful man; he was born to a minority group that was weak, small, and even oppressed (Deut 7:7–9; Matt 2; 5:41,42; 22:15–22; 27:11–66; Mark 14:43–15:47; Luke 2; 7:1–10; 23; John 18:1–20:10). Throughout Scripture we see that God tends to pursue and even give preference to the "least of these" (Matt 25:31–46). If God gives preference to the least of these, then we should do the same in our community when given a neutral choice.

The way of Jesus is a glorious way, but it is not an easy way. The idea of diversity is a great and glorious idea, but it is a costly practice. The way of Jesus and the way of unity in diversity is the way of the cross. There has to be death to the preferences of everyone, but especially to the culturally powerful of the Christian community. There *is* hope however:

> Therefore God exalted him to the highest place and gave him the name that is above every name, that at the name of Jesus every knee should bow, in heaven and on earth and under the earth, and every tongue confess that Jesus Christ is Lord. (Phil 2:9–11)

INTRODUCTION

SECTION 1: FOUNDATIONS

SECTION 2: STORIES

SECTION 3: TOOLS

CLOSING

God has called Christians to live a life of the cross so that God's resurrection power can be manifested on the earth. When we have Christian communities that pursue unity in diversity in Christ, through the means of the cross and in the power of the Holy Spirit, we will see God glorified through his Son Jesus.

CONCLUSION

In summary, when pursuing the vision of a Christian community honoring diverse heart languages, do so within these six guidelines:

1. Take an inventory of the various types of cultures and heart languages in your community.
2. The only limitations in cultural expressions should be the limits of sin and idolatry.
3. Pursue unity through diversity, instead of unity through assimilation.
4. The leaders and the powerful in your community should position themselves in a place of humble servanthood.
5. Honor and defer to the "least of these" in your community.
6. Pursue the way of the cross.

HOW TO DISCIPLE WORSHIP LEADERSHIP

137. G-A-T-H-E-R:
SIX PRINCIPLES FOR DISCIPLING WORSHIP LEADERS
By Byron Spradlin

Worship is central because God is supreme. Most believers acknowledge this. But if worship is central to all of life because God is supreme, then it clearly follows that discipling worship leaders should be both strategic and a high priority.

Tragically, few pastors or church leaders provide any intentional and specialized effort toward discipling worship leaders. Yet something good seems to be bubbling up.

This chapter assumes the Lord is doing something new in the hearts of church leaders, giving some a new desire to gather artistic kingdom servants into their congregations and disciple them for his service, especially for the service of facilitating innovative gathered worship. So the following reflections attempt to offer church leaders six principles that, if followed, will GATHER artistic worship leaders into their congregations and accelerate their release into God's service of worship.

GATHER—A SIMPLE ACRONYM FOR REMEMBERING SIX KEY PRINCIPLES

Here is a simple acronym to remember these six principles: the pastor or mission leader must GATHER artists—intentionally, regularly, and repeatedly. Let us unpack what we mean by GATHER.

1. GROW YOUR OWN GROUP

First, ministry leaders need to intentionally GROW their own GROUP of artistic worship leaders. To start, spread the word throughout your network, congregation, or ministry that you intend to focus on artists and creatives. Gather them specifically and often. For example, plan a dinner party or desert meeting; artists like parties just like everyone else.

You might ask, "If I call a meeting for creatives, what will we do when they come?" The answer is simple: affirm them. Affirm them in three ways. One, ask them to bring an example of their art with them. Let them know there may be a few minutes to let the others at the gathering see their work.

Two, give each fifteen minutes to tell their story. Listen to them. Ask them questions, such as, "How has God wired you artistically?" "What artistic dreams has God put in your heart?" "What artistic things has God put in your heart to do?"

Three, after you have let them share their story a bit, gather around them and pray for them. Prayer has a very special impact on artists, regardless of denominational background. They will feel appreciated and very thankful. *Gathering* musicians, artists, and creatives in your sphere of relationship will jump-start the growth of your own group of these God-designed specialists.

2. ADVOCATE FOR ARTISTS

Second, ADVOCATE for the creatives in your ministry context. Unfortunately there exist several typical but incorrect attitudes toward artists within the body of Christ. Often leadership simply does not think to involve them. Some leaders presume artists are counterculture critics, standing outside the general flow of the community and their church.[56] Some hold a secular humanist notion that "the arts" are abstract activities and objects of creative expression, and that those artistic objects and activities are only for contemplation or entertainment. All these notions cut against the biblical understanding of artistic creativity and the biblical role of the craftsmen who specialize in creating the environments wherein God actually comes and meets with his believing community.

Therefore artistic Christians need nonartistic advocates who both *admire* what they do and *affirm* the importance of their contributions to Christ's body. These arts advocates are helpful, especially if well received in the artist's congregation, in guiding congregational leaders to discover the artists' strategic, powerful, and beautiful contribution. Also, arts advocates can help the artistic Christian understand themselves, their important role in leading the congregation into touching the transcendent connection with God himself, and their specialty of dealing with the mysterious realities of the human community's God-designed transcendence.

> Spread the word throughout your network, congregation, or ministry that you intend to focus on artists and creatives.

Many a church leader is more a modernist than a biblicist. The wonderful printing press of the Reformation to get the word of God into the hands of everyday people, and the press to understand the objective truth about God that it reveals, has a negative side—the drift towards modernism and rationalism, where church leaders put an emphasis on information rather than encounter, an emphasis on biblical reasoning *about* God over the biblical priority of relating *to* God.[57]

One key challenge for Protestants is to regain an appreciation of the ways God reveals his reality and his truth within the contexts of beauty and through our participation in *transcendence-touching* activities—any activities that would include the use of metaphors and symbols, especially

---

56   In fact, that notion is not historically the case. Most often throughout history the creatives have been the voice, the heart-expressions of the community or culture. God made artistic people. The Bible labels them as *craftsmen*—people unusually wise at imaginative design and expression—for the purpose of leading people and human communities into touching the transcendent realities of life and God. Throughout the history of human communities, artistic specialists have expressed and reflected the core values, perspectives, rituals, celebrations, and liturgies of those communities.

57   This negative side of the Reformation/Protestant movement also includes a pressing against interacting with the mysteries of our relationship with God—in awe, reverence, humility, silence, etc.—experienced in contexts that rely on the imaginal and emotional dynamics of intelligence. Many problems within the Protestant movement have developed out of these emphases—which this chapter is far too short to address.

the *human* activities of worship which we so often call *liturgies*. Nonartistic arts advocates can play strategic roles for both the artist and general church leadership in experiencing and fostering artistic expressions in the life of the church.[58]

3. TOUCH THE ARTIST OVER TIME

Church leaders must TOUCH the artist over extended periods of TIME. Worship practitioners are, at heart, artists—those God has designed as human-emotion-and-imagination specialists. Church leaders must not only understand this reality, they must see the value of emotional and imaginal intelligence and how those dynamics sync with intellectual intelligence. Then they must appreciate the artist-specialists whom God has provided to lead the church, in line with Scripture, into the realm of things beautiful, mysterious, and transcendent.[59]

Artists and creatives need stable, virtuous, caring, and safe relationships; they need a community of believers wherein they are appreciated, but wherein they also can have normal, healthy, and regular involvement.[60]

Therefore, especially in these days when mainstream culture has left the Age of the Orator and entered the Age of the Artist,[61] it is strategically important for Christian leaders to develop relationships with artists, intentionally and consistently, in their network of relationships. This sort of regular, appreciative, and encouraging touch by Christian leaders will result in many artists growing in Christ and moving more directly into ministry—simply because you have been one of the few Christian leaders who extended real relationship to them.

---

58 Advocates see the importance of the artistic dimension of life and of the artistic specialists who lead the community into touching and entering into these transcendent environments, where the mysterious transactions occur. In fact, in today's mainstream culture, if Christian leaders do not make it clear that the church is concerned about things beautiful, mysterious, and transcendent—and demonstrate how the Christian Scriptures speak to these realities and our daily walk with God—the gospel will have great difficulty in seeming relevant to daily life and living.

59 When church leaders grasp the interplay of the intellect, the emotions, and the imagination, perhaps they will recognize how much they need these human-emotion-and-imagination specialists. Perhaps they will then see the value, for themselves as well as for their congregations, of spending time touching these creative types. If creatives feel the appreciation that goes with time and touch from these leaders, they will respond with over-and-above investment of their God-designed strengths into congregational ministry.

60 Unfortunately artists have often not felt safe in our churches, nor have they felt encouraged to be who God made them to be—artistic and innovative. Protestant church leaders over the last 150 or 200 years have actually considered involvement in the arts "worldly" and have spent a good deal of effort discouraging artistically gifted Christians from developing their gifts, let alone applying those skills and aptitudes to the life and ministries of our churches. Some would say that the artistic specialist has been faced with much suspicion and mistrust in the Protestant church for its entire five-hundred-year history. There are some good historical reasons why Protestant leadership has inadvertently developed these feelings towards the artists in its midst—with the possible exception of musicians. For an overview of some these issues, see texts like James F. White, *Protestant Worship* (Louisville: Westminster, 1989), and Friedrich Blume, *Protestant Church Music: A History* (New York: Norton, 1974). For more on the biblical role of the arts, see Nicholas Wolterstorff, *Art in Action: Toward a Christian Aesthetic* (Grand Rapids: Eerdmans, 1980).

61 This observation that mainstream culture has left the Age of the Orator and has entered the Age of the Artist could not possibly be original to me. But I have been seeing this reality for some time, and do not recall reading that particular phrase in the writings of others.

4. HONOR THE ARTIST

HONORING the art maker is much different than flattering or pandering them—catering to them in order to exploit their talents for the sake of your ministry. Honoring them must be done in truth. Insincerity will be picked up immediately. Artists will feel used and ultimately will be put off. Most will leave. To legitimately honor the artistic dimension of your congregation or ministry, you must go public.

The honoring dynamic submitted here is very similar to the biblical definition of *praise*—to publicly acknowledge the value and virtues of the person and their work. Anything else will encourage some sort of vain conceit or selfish ambition in the artist or the discipler (see Phil 2:3; Jas 3:14,16). Encourage true and honest appreciation of the person's creative capacities and honed skills. If potential disciplers hold honest appreciation for the artist's capacities and skills, they will find public places and times where honoring them is natural, balanced, and appropriate.[62]

5. ENCOURAGE ARTISTS

To ENCOURAGE the artists around you is the fifth principle. Tragically, most artists are not encouraged by the churches they attend.[63] When one realizes, however, the biblical purpose for artistic expression specialists (like Bezalel and Oholiab; Ex 35:30–36:3)—to create the environments of worship wherein believers actually touch the transcendent, mysterious reality of interaction with God—church leaders *will* find ways to encourage artists.

Artistic Christians must be encouraged to carry out artistic stewardship in their congregations. They must be loved into applying their artistic skills creatively to the life of their local parish. This will not happen, however, unless and until leadership invites them. Church and mission leaders must therefore become proactive at encouraging artist-believers to get involved.[64]

---

62   In my own congregation the pastor frequently brings a writer, a painter, an actor, a songwriter, or some other creative person to the platform and praises them for their project. Often this happens spontaneously and with no motive to get something from artists except to praise and honor them for what God has done in and through them. This action not only honors artists, but also honors, but also honors the entire artistic dimension in humanity, and more specifically in the body of Christ.

63   Dianne B. Collard, "The Role of Visual Art in the (Free) Evangelical Churches in Germany and Spain" (DMiss diss., Biola University, 2004). This thesis, as indicated, specifically focuses on the role of visual artists in the churches of Germany and Spain. Dr. Collard discovered that church and mission leaders rarely think there is any way artistic Christians can make a strategic contribution to ministry strategy or programming. In fact the study pointed out that after some time, the artists in one region of Europe actually left the church. Artists in another region simply resigned themselves to applying none of their artistic capacities to the contexts of their local congregations.

64   Leaders must encourage the artistic specialists to imagine how the congregation could worship better, learn God's word better, disciple better, and engage the nonbelieving community better—and then actually follow their lead. Encouragement of artists is absolutely critical to effective living, not to mention effective ministry. But how can you encourage artists and creatives? Four suggestions: (1) Request to *experience* some of *their art making*. See it, read it, receive it. Experience some of their art making. Receive what they want you to receive, see, or experience. (2) *Listen to them*. Listen to their story, their situation, their history—and in the process don't try to immediately fix them. Just listen. (3) *Invite them* to keep you posted on their situation. (4) Directly and publicly *affirm them*.

My pastor brings artists to the platform who have achieved some sort of milestone—an article published, a CD released, a book published, a commercial finished. He honors them publicly, prays for them, and asks the congregation to affirm them, whether or not their particular milestone is religious or mainstream in nature. The pastor's practice seems to be tremendously affirming, both for the particular artist and for other artists in general.

Prayerfully ask the Lord to give you meaningful, legitimate ways to encourage these creatives, and you will gather artists to you and your ministry context.

6. RESOURCE ARTISTS

Finally, the sixth principle for Christian leaders concerning artists is to RESOURCE them. In order to see artistic Christians become more productive as general believers and as specialized kingdom servants in our churches and missions work, Christian leadership must resource them in at least five ways: ministry vision, pastoral permission, direct discipleship, ministry structures, and in many cases, finances. These resource areas are key to enabling artistic ministry initiators to actually venture out in ministry—especially into the community at large.

CONCLUSION

Regretfully, very few artistic Christians become the recipients of such a GATHERing embrace. But if you do repeatedly and prayerfully practice efforts to GROW your group of artists, ADVOCATE for artistic Christians, TOUCH artists regularly and legitimately, HONOR artists for the beauty of their role in leading others into touching the transcendent things of God and life, ENCOURAGE artists to move forward in their biblical assignment to work out their God-designed artistic assignments (Phil 2:12,13), and RE-SOURCE them with ministry vision, pastoral permission, direct

> Encourage true and honest appreciation of the person's creative capacities and honed skills.

discipleship, ministry structures, and finances, then you will disciple scores of worship leaders who will in turn dynamically release God's truth, beauty, goodness, and forgiveness in ways most congregations and ministries dream about, but only few seem to accomplish.

May the Lord give you increased grace to grow in your own heart the need and importance of discipling worship leadership. If so, you will see God honor your ministry efforts, while at the same time glorifying himself as you move to more intentionally acknowledge his supremacy and make his worship central to all your life and ministry.

138. SEVEN RECOMMENDATIONS FOR MENTORING WORSHIP LEADERS

By Jaewoo and Joy Kim

MULTIPLYING WORSHIP LEADERS

For the last fifty years, worship—what A. W. Tozer called the missing jewel of the church—has received global attention from churches around the world.[65] Worship recordings, books, and other resources have poured out, and worship-related events have flourished.[66]

Some confusion and debate exist over the definition of the term "worship leader." We intend to use this term to describe a person who is appointed by the church leadership to help a local congregation engage their hearts and minds in honoring God through the musical portion of worship. Here is an elaborated definition of a worship leader:

> A faithful worship leader
> magnifies the greatness of God in Jesus Christ
> through the power of the Holy Spirit
> by skillfully combining God's word with music,
> thereby motivating the gathered church
> to proclaim the gospel,
> to cherish God's presence,
> and to live for God's glory.[67]

Though there are a few well-known worship leaders who travel around the world leading big worship events using their original songs, most worship leaders in global churches are nameless and faceless. Most are unlikely to impact anyone outside their own congregation. According to

---

65   A. W. Tozer, *Worship: The Missing Jewel* (Camp Hill, PA: Christian Publications, 1992).

66   Ron Man, "Lessons from Global Worship" (paper presentation, Biblical Worship Section of the Evangelical Theological Society, San Francisco, CA, Nov. 17, 2011).

67   Bob Kauflin, *Worship Matters: Leading Others to Encounter the Greatness of God* (Wheaton: Crossway, 2008), 55.

a survey by Christian Copyright Licensing International (CCLI), conducted among its member churches in North America, 75 percent of churches are under two hundred people in size. Seventy-five percent of churches have worship leaders, but almost half of them are nonpaid volunteers.[68]

The context of this survey is in North America. How about the other parts of the world? In most places, worship leaders would not expect any financial compensation or public recognition. In some places, leading worship publicly means putting yourself and your family at risk for persecution and threats.

NEEDED: JOYFUL, FAITHFUL, AND SKILLFUL GLOBAL WORSHIP LEADERS

When a church gathers, it sings. Christianity is a singing faith. The church has been singing throughout history, and it will continue to express her love toward God by singing. When God-glorifying words are combined with singable melodies, they become a powerful tool for personal and corporate worship in churches around the world. In some parts of the world, there may be no electricity or no instruments.

Yet believers still express their faith through singing. Nothing can stop the church from singing for eternity. We need to multiply worship leaders for global churches—leaders who will joyfully, faithfully, skillfully, and boldly lead God's church to sing in every season.

> Speak to one another with psalms, hymns and spiritual songs. Sing and make music in your heart to the Lord. (Eph 5:19 NIV)

> Come before his presence with singing. (Ps 100:2 KJV)

SEVEN RECOMMENDATIONS FOR MENTORING WORSHIP LEADERS

1. **Look for lead worshipers**

    When a church needs worship leaders, hiring professionals may in some cases be the fastest and easiest solution. But raising worship leaders from within the congregation is always ideal because a homegrown worship leader understands and cherishes the local church. Growing a worship leader may take much longer, but it will be worth the effort. Worship leaders should be lead worshipers before receiving training to lead others. Lead worshipers are passionate and noticeable, are not afraid of expressing their faith in public, and inspire others to worship. Look for lead worshipers in your church; they are contagious, and they are potential worship leaders.

2. **Teach a biblical theology of worship**

    Worship leaders must possess a biblical theology of worship. Some worship leaders build their entire theology of worship on a few selected verses from Scripture or on their personal experiences. It is critical that worship leaders understand worship as a

---

68   Quoted in a presentation by Howard Rachinski, CCLI president, "Orlando Gathering," Jan. 19, 2012.

grand narrative of Scripture.[69] Theology of worship directly influences song selection and everything else the leader does. When there is no biblical theology of worship, personal preferences become the primary agenda in planning and practicing worship.

3. **Help develop musical skills**

    The following verses imply the importance of musical skills for worship leaders:

    Sing to him a new song; play skillfully on the strings, with loud shouts. (Ps 33:3 ESV)

    Now these, the singers, the heads of fathers' houses of the Levites, were in the chambers of the temple free from other service, for they were on duty day and night. (1 Chr 9:33 ESV)

    Musically unskilled and unprepared worship leaders will distract and hinder worship rather than helping people worship. The level of musical skills required for worship leaders may differ depending on the style and size of a church, but worship leaders are responsible for the musical preparation and presentation of corporate worship. Worship leaders must be skillful in choosing songs that are appropriate. This is not a simple job. There is no biblical way to select songs; nonetheless it requires skill, intuition, and experience. After carefully selecting songs and arranging the set, the worship leader must have the musical skills to capture and carry the song's emotion.

4. **Help foster communication skills**

    The primary job of a worship leader is to lead worship through songs. But they also teach worship to team members and the congregation by what they say and through other means of communication. Leaders may make short comments at the beginning of a song or during song transitions. Some are required to speak, others are not. However, these comments can be a great opportunity to encourage the congregation to engage their hearts and minds in worship. Therefore worship leaders must develop good communication skills by preparing what they will say and how they will say it in a concise manner. Encourage leaders to memorize various Bible verses and short but powerful prayers that can be used during appropriate times and settings.

5. **Help develop pastoral hearts**

    Worship leaders may feel inadequate when they realize that leading worship falls into a category of pastoral ministry. Indeed leading worship is pastoral ministry. It is a long-term process of painting the portrait of God in the minds of people and transforming hearts to desire God more. In the spiritual life of a church, worship is inseparable from healing, spiritual formation, and missions. Worship leaders must therefore see the bigger goal of building a worshiping community. Ultimately worship is not a musical event but a spiritual event. Leading worship should be an extension of the long-term process of building a worshiping community. Worship leaders who see the big picture know that worship is continuous, multigenerational, and multicultural.

---

69   Robert E. Webber, *Ancient-future Worship: Proclaiming and Enacting God's Narrative* (Grand Rapids: Baker, 2008).

6. **Learn from mistakes**

There must be room for worship leaders to make mistakes. When appropriate evaluation and mentoring are provided, mistakes can be the best teachers. Plan worship together based on selected criteria and then continue to evaluate why specific songs are selected and why certain words between songs are necessary. Find the strengths and weaknesses in each person, then mentor and help each to be who they are. Do not try to duplicate yourself or any famous worship leaders. When God uses people, he works through the unique personality of each person.

7. **Emphasize private worship**

Though Christ has made us righteous and forgiven us all of our sins once for all—past, present, and future—guilt and shame, habitual sins, and relational conflicts can be real barriers and hindrances to leading worship. Private worship is the key to worship leaders keeping their hearts pure. Jesus is the real worship leader, and the Holy Spirit makes worship happen. Worship leaders are mere instruments and channels of blessing. But being a visible spiritual leader makes leaders vulnerable to discouragements and temptations. Building a habit of private worship will protect leaders from their shortcomings.

INTRODUCTION

SECTION 1: FOUNDATIONS

SECTION 2: STORIES

SECTION 3: TOOLS

CLOSING

HOW TO INTEGRATE ARTS AND PREACHING

139. ILLUMINATING THE WORD: ARTS IN PREACHING

By Kenneth L. Wallace, Jr.

"And the word . . . became . . . flesh." As the dramatic reading of John 1 was played out on the stage at Urbana 2009—InterVarsity Christian Fellowship's global missions conference—I sat enthralled by a passage of Scripture that I had probably heard a thousand times. This time, however, it was different. Perhaps it was the tap dancers portraying Jesus, or maybe it was the lights changing in the background along with the phrasing of the passage. Whatever the reasons, the word of God reached my heart in a different way. It was brought alive for me by the artistic expression that was presented by the actors on the stage. The job of a preacher is much the same. No, not to act or to dance in the pulpit—though if the Spirit leads, so be it—but rather to illuminate the word for those listening to the sermon.

Various art forms have been used to stir the soul since humans first picked up a piece of coal and drew an image on a cave wall. Why would one not incorporate art in a practice whose very purpose is to exhort people to respond with their souls? I feel that the use of artistic expression in worship through preaching is often ignored because of a limited understanding of "art." The first image of art that may come to mind is visual art, such as painting. While having an artist paint their interpretation of the sermon while you preach may be moving, it might not have the stirring effect that you are looking for. Art, however, extends far beyond the bounds of the visual. In this chapter we will examine three ways that art can be incorporated into the preaching ministry, through *storytelling*, *movement*, and *song*.

STORYTELLING

Storytelling is about as ancient an art as those cave paintings mentioned earlier. Stories stir the soul because they cause the hearer to use his or her imagination. Jesus understood this principle and used it repeatedly when teaching his followers. The parables themselves were stories. We read them today in print, but Jesus' disciples were most likely simply walking along with him as he told stories. These stories had the power to draw crowds, or make people angry, or shock the hearers. The parable of the Good Samaritan (Luke 10:25–37) was one of these latter types. Jesus knew that the lawyer was less interested in his actual question—"What must I do to inherit eternal life?"—than in justifying himself before the other hearers. Rather than getting ensnared by the lawyer's trick question, Jesus told a story he knew would have a significant punch.

The characters in the story had particular relevance to the crowd, but to modern listeners that relevance could be lost. What if the parable were retold from the pulpit (with apologies to Dr. Luke) replacing the priest, the Levite, and the Samaritan with modern equivalents, like a pastor, a deacon, and a Muslim—or any other person who seems to be at odds with Christians at a given moment. A parishioner would be appalled that a pastor would pass by, but would understand that it happens all the time. He or she would "tsk" at the deacon, but could probably name such a person in the congregation. But that *other person*, how could it be that he or she would be the one to have compassion on the beat-up Christian? The characters could be changed to fit any context, but the main idea is to connect the old story to the modern era.

Another means of using stories could be to borrow from other cultures. Many cultures have been blessed with the gift of handing down oral histories and stories in rich ways. Most First Nations people, for example, have stories that parallel the morals taught in the Bible, especially around themes of unity and caring for each other. When you meet people of other cultures, ask them to teach you a story. You might be surprised at how you can see God's fingerprint on their culture and how their stories can be applied to kingdom purposes, even if they are not overtly Christian.

> There are over fifty-eight Hebrew words for worship, and many of them have an emphasis on some sort of movement.

Finally, read the Bible itself out loud as if it were written to your congregation—after all, it was! If the portion of Scripture is an epistle, read it as if you were reading a letter to a friend. I often insert an actual person's name to make it personal. Where second-person pronouns are used (i.e., "you"), indicate people who are in the listening audience. If the passage is poetic, like the Psalms, add corresponding emotion to your voice. Don't just say, "I will bless the Lord at all times"; instead create emphasis—"I will bless the Lord at *all* times." Imagine that you are the author of the Scripture passage and that you are trying to get *your* point across. The African-American worship culture does this well. You might be surprised at how people will sit up in their seats or lean forward to catch the next phrase you present.

MOVEMENT

When movement is mentioned in conjunction with performance art, it is most often connected to dance. However, there are over fifty-eight Hebrew words for worship, and many of them have an emphasis on some sort of movement. When preaching, the message might make more of an impression on the hearer if movement were added to complement your points. On one occasion, for instance, while preaching on the passage about the two believers walking on the road to Emmaus (Luke 24:14–35), I casually but purposefully walked down the center aisle of the church, reading the passage as I went. After the service several people mentioned to me that they felt as if they were walking with Jesus along that road as well.

I believe that God has given us a holy imagination to serve him and to connect with his written word. What effect would it have on a hearer if the preacher would reach out his hand and pluck the fruit from the tree of the garden, or take the hand of the little girl raised from the dead? If you

INTRODUCTION

SECTION 1: FOUNDATIONS

SECTION 2: STORIES

SECTION 3: TOOLS

CLOSING

are preaching about Paul on the road to Damascus, how much more of an impression would it make if you actually were imaginarily knocked off your donkey?

I do not intend to imply by suggesting these things that we should attempt to entertain those listening to sermons, but rather that we use movement as a tool to transmit the message we are trying to impart. Scripture is full of movement, from the Spirit hovering over the waters in Genesis, to the word being alive and *active* in Hebrews. It may be that by the use of our bodies in worshiping God through preaching, those who hear our messages may be freer to respond physically to God as well.

SONG

"I say yes, Lord, yes to your will and to your way . . ." Brenda Salter-McNeil often starts a sermon with this popular African-American chorus. The result is that people are instantly drawn into the message that she is presenting because they connect with the song. Music has a very strong influence on the brain. People can remember a melody much easier than anything from a didactic monologue. The addition, therefore, of a well-placed song within the structure of a sermon can emphasize and underscore the point of the message. If you are teaching, for example, on the character of God, it could be helpful to sing the chorus of Martha Munizzi's "Because of Who You Are." Or if you if you are teaching on what it means to worship, you could emphasize your point using Matt Redmond's "Heart of Worship." Once you have found a song that can help drive home a point, think about where best to use it. The song does not necessarily need to be at the beginning or the end of the message. It could be more powerful to sing a chorus, or even just a line of a song, within the message itself.

Now I can already hear the opposition: "But I can't sing!" This is no excuse for avoiding the use of art in preaching. We *could* run a PowerPoint by ourselves for our sermons, but we often have a PowerPoint person who does that for us. We *could* run the sound system or the lights by ourselves, flicking a switch here or turning a knob there, but we have audiovisual teams to perform these functions for us. In the same way, we *could* have an artistic-expression coordinator who is ready and willing to sing on cue at a particular moment previously indicated or to close a sermon with an appropriately chosen song.

> The addition of a well-placed song within the structure of a sermon can emphasize and underscore the point of the message.

And as with storytelling, it is good to borrow music from other cultures. God has uniquely revealed himself to each culture and left a piece of his character with them. Many peoples express this character through song. If your sermon connects to a theme that could be better emphasized by a song from a culture that presents this theme well, then use the gift that God has given us in a diverse family. One such example is the *bhajans* performed and recorded by an Indian-style music group called Aradhna. These songs express devotion and love, and I have often led my congregation during the sermon in the chorus of one of these love poems set to music. Another example along these lines was the use of First Nations songs at the Urbana 2009 global missions conference to punctuate the themes of unity or creation. Those striking rhythms and melodies helped me to remember the message presented there long after I had left the venue.

MOVING BEYOND WORDS TO ARTISTIC EXPRESSION

Traditional homiletics has generally not included much room for artistic expression. Today's post-modern society, however, seeks experience and authentic connection as much as truth and the message itself, so the use of art is practically necessary to bridge the message and the hearer's soul. Incorporate a melody here or a dramatic reading there and begin to see the message you are delivering illuminate those in your congregation. As people are stirred deep within by the attachment formed by artistic expression, the Holy Spirit will continue to write his words on the tablets of their hearts. And as God has gifted each of us with creativity to deliver his message, we declare to him in the words of the African-American chorus, "Yes, Lord, yes to your will and to your way. We say yes, Lord, yes we will trust you and obey. When your Spirit speaks to me, with my whole heart I'll agree. And my answer will be yes, Lord, yes."

INTRODUCTION

SECTION 1: FOUNDATIONS

SECTION 2: STORIES

SECTION 3: TOOLS

CLOSING

140. INTEGRATING ARTS AND PREACHING

By Rochelle L. Cathcart

I've never been good at making up stories on the spot, but when my nephew looks at me with his big, blue eyes and says, "Aunt Rochelle, will you tell me a story?" it is hard to resist. He picks the key character (usually a T-Rex), but the rest is up to me. The best stories are simple, filled with concrete descriptions from everyday life, and full of suspense. When I tell a good story, you can see the goosebumps on his skin, hear his breathing slow, and watch his eyes widen with emotion and anticipation. Although I rarely remember the plots, my nephew has begged me to tell the same story weeks and months later. He remembers because I excited his emotions and engaged his imagination.

The arts do many things for us. They allow us to express ourselves, be creative, and enter new worlds; they can awaken emotions and imaginations and connect with us in deep and profound ways. What we feel, we remember more vividly. What we experience—through action, imagination, and identification—we more readily recall. Advertisers, educators, and rhetoricians recognize that visual and aural messages are understood faster and remembered longer than words alone. Research by the 3M Corporation suggests that visual items are taken in sixty thousand times *faster* than text.[70] Why not harness the power of arts in sermons?

Some people fear bringing arts into the preaching event—concerned that the sacredness of the event will become slave to empty entertainment—but this does not have to be the case. Through wise use of a variety of mediums, the preacher can use the God-given gifts of the arts to herald the good news in ways that have maximum effect. Below are some suggestions on how the preacher can incorporate the arts into the preaching event. This list certainly isn't exhaustive; it is intended, instead, to get creative juices flowing.

STORYTELLING

As Kenneth L. Wallace mentions in the previous chapter of the *Handbook*,[71] storytelling is a powerful way in which to connect with the audience. Done well, a story can engage emotions and imagination

---

70   Michael Parkinson, "Visual Marketing Matters," 24 Hour Company, http://www.24hrco.com/images/articles/VisualMarketingMatters.pdf, 2.

71   See Kenneth L. Wallace, "Illuminating the Word: Arts in Preaching," *Handbook*, chpt. 139.

and, according to Robert Priest, it can (1) allow hearers to "vicariously experience what the story's actor experiences," and (2) provide people "sufficient distance" from their own experiences to safely examine situations that directly speak into their lives.[72] The prophet Nathan understood this when he confronted King David about Bathsheba and Uriah. Had Nathan directly accused David of adultery and murder, the prophet would likely have joined Uriah in the grave. Instead Nathan tells a story. And not just any story, but one filled with sheep and shepherds—something David understood and identified with emotionally and experientially. Upon hearing the story, David's sense of justice is enflamed and he pronounces judgment on the situation before realizing he is pronouncing judgment on himself. Through story, Nathan *indirectly* addresses the issue at hand and gets "David's conscience to work collaboratively with [Nathan's] external pronouncement of sin and judgment."[73]

A few tips for storytelling:

- Remember to *tell* the story, not tell *about* a story.[74] There is a big difference. People aren't as interested when you summarize a story or explain it. The power of a good story, told well, is that it explains itself.
- Tell the story without interrupting the narrative.[75] It is harder to understand a movie and experience the full impact of the plot if you keep hitting the pause button. In the same way, if you constantly interrupt the story, people will have a hard time tracking with you.
- View the entire sermon as a story. This does not mean you ignore propositional truth or explanations of deep theological issues, but as one noted communicator says, every sermon should have an "arc," an underlying story line that is going somewhere and leading to a key moment.[76] The sermon should not be a newscast, it should be a story. "A newscast," this same preacher says, "is a series of linear fragments that are lined up with no relation to each other, and you can turn it off at any point because of that." A story, however, is connected—you can "be sucked in completely in three minutes."[77] Where "newscast" sermons can be turned off at any point, a sermon with an arc will keep the audience engaged.
- Remember that word choice matters. The best stories are told in concrete language the audience understands. Words can inspire worlds of meaning. One preacher phrases Scripture in the urban, earthy, inner-city language of the "street" with which his audience best identifies. Where Psalm 102:2 says, "Do not hide your face from me when I am in distress," this pastor cries out, "God, this ain't the time to play hide-and-seek. This ain't the time, God, that I need you to be distant from me."
- Use traditional storytelling methods. How does your own culture transmit stories? Does it include sound effects, chants, repetition, etc.? Are there proverbs or other traditional

---

72   Robert J. Priest, "Tell Me about a Time You Were Bad," *CIU Quarterly* (Winter 1994), personal reprint, 2.

73   Robert J. Priest, "Missionary Elenctics: Conscience and Culture," *Missiology* 22, no. 3 (July 1994), 292.

74   Jean Johnson and Diane Campbell, *Worldview Strategic Church Planting among Oral Cultures: A Field Guide for Contemporary Grass-roots Cross-cultural Church Planters and Trainers of National Church Planters* (Springfield, MO: Life Publishers International, 2007), 148.

75   Ibid.

76   Rob Bell quoted in Dave Stone, *Refining Your Style: Learning from Respected Communicators* (Loveland, CO: Group Publishing, 2004), 215.

77   Ibid., 215–16.

stories from your culture that parallel the message? Use the stories and the storytelling methods that best speak to your audience.

SONGS

Few of us remember long passages of text; e.g., memorizing whole chapters or books of the Bible. The issue, however, is not one of *inability*, but rather *medium*. Think about how many songs you know by heart—hundreds, thousands? Even when there aren't words or we don't understand the words, music creates feelings and moods. We might not cry just because the main character in a movie dies, but if we hear a lamenting song when the character dies, we are moved to tears.

- Have the congregation sing a song that matches the message. Recently my pastor had the congregation sing a song of meditation in the middle of his sermon that brought the words of his first point to life.
- Play music in the background. African-American churches often accent the preacher's message with music. The music ebbs and flows in response, in echo, or in unison with the preacher's words, increasing the listener's participation with the sermon.
- Play a song as part of the message. I was in a service once where the preacher critiqued the fast-paced, "busy, busy, busy, get and grasp as much as you can" kind of life that typifies many Americans. There are three kinds of hands that describe us, he says (using Eccl 4:5,6), and modern American life is often like "two handfuls with toil and chasing after the wind" (v. 6). To demonstrate this, he plays the opening words of a popular rap song over the sound system. When the clip is done, he asks the audience if they understand the two grasping hands. "Yes," the audience replies. He later circles the topic and the song is again used to make and explain his point. When I heard that song on TV a few weeks later, my mind instantly thought, "Grasping after the world," and the message of the sermon was renewed in me.

PAINTING AND SCULPTING

It is harder to use painting and sculpting within the sermon itself, but there are ways that preachers have used these effectively.

- Focus on a painting or sculpture in the sermon. One Easter I sat in a service where chairs were lined up to face an artist's depiction of the seven stations of the cross. As each picture was contemplated, a man and woman in the back of the room dramatically read the matching Scriptures. Likewise, Rick Blackwood describes a six-part sermon series he preached on the attributes of God, in which he used one painting for each sermon. During the last sermon, the six paintings were hung together to form a cross. Visually, people were able to see how the attributes of God came into play at the cross. The final sermon was on God's holiness and, as Blackwood talked of our inability to be holy without God's sacrifice, he put red paint on the picture of God's feet.[78]

- Pictures and videos. Not every church has a projection system to play video clips or show photographs. For those that do—or those that find creative ways in which to do this—the use of pictorial images, as the old adage says, often "speak louder than words." Let people that are gifted in photography visually "capture" what you want to say, and let the picture say it. Recently a city close to where I was born was destroyed by a tornado. I thought I understood the destruction when I heard word descriptions, and I was sad to hear about it. However, when I saw my first photograph of a neighborhood that was literally wiped off the earth, I felt like someone had punched me, and I cried.

DRAMA

One of the benefits of drama is that it brings words and events to life, makes them believable, and makes them real. The key to drama is in the action; however, the action does not have to be complicated.

- Get into character. If you have a flare for the dramatic, dress up and tell the biblical story from a first-person point of view. Even without a costume, act out what you are telling. "The resurrection is like a boxer," one preacher announced while jumping around the stage like a boxer in a boxing ring. He acts out a fight in which the opponent could not defeat him, though the opponent gave him his hardest punch. At the end, Jesus is said to have remained standing after Satan's hardest punch, and the preacher summarizes, "O death, where is your victory? O grave, where is your right hook?"
- Read the text with passion and feeling and get into character through your tone, volume, and speed.
- Present a dramatic reading of the text. When preaching on Acts 2, one church acted it out with simple drama. Five people stood on the stage with scripts, one narrated the scene. The sound of wind was played, flames were shown on the video screen, a chorus of people shouted praise to God from the back of the auditorium, and the people onstage responded as if they were the Jews from various cities. Finally, a man stepped forward and dramatically proclaimed Peter's words. This simple "drama" helped the audience remember that Acts 2 is not just words—it is real story.
- Use smell to enhance the story. Are you talking about worship in the Old Testament? Have people walk up and down the aisle with incense. If you don't want to bring a particular smell into the church, talk about it vividly (e.g., the smell of fresh baked bread, meat on the grill, smoke from a campfire, or rotting trash).
- Let others participate. Pull in volunteers to participate for a point. One sermon I heard was set up as a dialogue between God and a Christian struggling with lust. The preacher played the Christian, and the audience was "God." When "God" spoke, his lines appeared on the screen and the audience read them aloud together. The audience, in

---

78   Rick Blackwood, *The Power of Multi-sensory Preaching and Teaching* (Grand Rapids: Zondervan, 2008), 199–200.

INTRODUCTION

SECTION 1: FOUNDATIONS

SECTION 2: STORIES

SECTION 3: TOOLS

CLOSING

a sense, preached the message, proclaiming God's good news on a topic with which many of them also struggled. How powerful!

OTHER VISUALS

- Nature is God's palette. The world in which we live everyday is filled with props, pictures, and examples from which to draw. Talking about rocks crying out in praise? Hand everyone a stone before the sermon. Talking about what new birth means? Ask a couple in the audience to let you hold their baby while you talk about the possibilities that birth presents us. People understand the natural world around them, and using it in the sermon provides common, everyday ways by which they can continue to experience the sermon.
- Props, as one writer suggests, "serve as visuals that listeners deposit into their memory banks."[79] These don't have to be elaborate. One preacher had seven lighted candles on the stage while he preached a series on the seven churches in Revelation. When God warns that he will blow out one church's candle unless they repent, the preacher blows out a candle and waits in silence while the audience looks at the smoke hanging in the air.

It should be mentioned that not everything works just because it can be classified under the arts. Chip and Dan Heath discovered that the key is to communicate in ways that stick. People take in and readily connect with information when it is simple, unexpected, concrete, credible, emotional, and framed in story.[80]

Thinking of the sermon in terms of the arts, we might embrace one preacher's idea that in the sermon you "want to work off of many different surfaces." "I'll try any method," he says, "to get you thinking, feeling, touching, and smelling. I want to assault as many senses as possible. I want as many contact points as possible."[81] Preachers who use the arts—"drama, dance, movie clips, sculpture, humor, mime, painting, smells, sounds, video, and more"—provide a place where a variety of people can be reached. And by using the arts, they help to "make memories that last a lifetime for church members."[82]

---

79   Stone, *Refining Your Style*, 219.

80   Chip Heath and Dan Heath, *Made to Stick: Why Some Ideas Survive and Others Die* (New York: Random House, 2007).

81   Stone, *Refining Your Style*, 214.

82   Ibid., 209.

465

INTRODUCTION

SECTION 1: FOUNDATIONS

SECTION 2. STORIES

SECTION 3. TOOLS

CLOSING

HOW TO INTEGRATE ARTS WITH SCRIPTURE PROCLAMATION

141. BRINGING SCRIPTURE TO LIFE WITH ARTISTIC CREATIVITY

By Julisa Rowe

As the preacher walked toward the pulpit following the morning Scripture reading, he turned to the drama team: "I don't need to preach now—it's all been said!" After the service, congregants said, "It was all so clear! I understood everything in that passage! You really made me pay attention." All we did was read the Scripture—but read it with feeling, showing the action and picturing it for the congregation. Those few techniques helped people to experience the word in a new, fresh way.

Over the years, I have worked with churches and drama teams to bring readings alive, most recently working with churches in Kenya to put these techniques into regular practice.[83] Here are some ways we have used to help bring creativity and new life to proclaiming Scripture.

THE BASICS OF DRAMATIZING SCRIPTURE STORIES

One challenge in reading Scripture is the problem of one voice being monotonous, or a poor reader laboring through the text. How can this be overcome? The first step in bringing the Scripture to life is reading it aloud to yourself. You, as the leader dividing the Scripture passage, have the privilege of steeping yourself in God's word. It will change you. It is the best Bible study you can ask for! Take time to read the passage thoroughly, several times. Pray through it and about it. Begin to conceptualize ways that you can bring it to life, including the emotions and attitudes behind it. Do a background study of the Scripture passage—what is its historical context? Where was it written and why? Who wrote it, and who or what were they writing about?

Next, divide the Scripture passage according to the voices speaking in the passage—the different characters and the narrator. Passages of Scripture that are stories (i.e., with characters and a narrator inherent in the text) are the easiest to dramatize.

---

83   A full description of these techniques can be found in Julisa Rowe, *Dramatising Scripture: A Step by Step Guide to Bringing the Word Alive* (Nairobi: Daystar Research Centre, 2010), available at http://www.ethnodrama.com.

1. Look at the passage and list all the characters that speak.
2. Rewrite the passage in script form; i.e., write each character name on the left, followed by their lines. This makes it easier for the readers to find their place and follow the division of voices. It also makes it easier to write notes about line delivery, blocking, or other relevant information.
3. Everything that is not spoken by a character is given to a narrator. In the narrative form of the written Scripture, there are often many "said Jesus" and "he/she/they said" phrases. When scripting the passage, these short lines could be given to the narrator. Assign readers to the different parts, and practice the reading together several times for fluency, meaning, and expression.

CREATIVE PRESENTATION OF SCRIPTURE

Lining the readers up onstage with their scripts is an easy way to begin when dramatizing Scripture. Just the simple act of dividing out the different voices of characters and narrator will help the congregation focus more readily on the content. Once you are comfortable with this technique, however, you can begin to bring in additional elements to bring even more life to the passage.

1. Have the readers memorize their lines.
2. Costume the piece, either according to the period (e.g., biblical era), in coordinated outfits or a uniform (e.g., black pants and solid color shirts), in contemporary clothes that would help people relate the scriptural event to a modern-day equivalent (e.g., priests in modern clerical collars, or the crowd in sportswear), or in representational clothing.
3. Use blocking—creating stage pictures and movement with the actors—to bring movement and action to the piece. This can be done in several ways:
   • Place the narrator to one side of the stage, or have him/her interact with the action as it unfolds. Use a voice-over for the narration so that the narrator is not seen.
   • Have the characters interact with one another naturally in the course of their lines.
   • In the case of the crowd, place them in a group onstage, or scatter them throughout the audience. (I love this option because it serves to draw the audience more into the feel and sounds of the passage—such as the Acts 19 riot—engaging their imagination even more!)
   • Be creative with where you have the action take place—on the stage, throughout the sanctuary, in the balcony, or any combination thereof.
   • Use tableaux—still pictures or sculptures created by the actors' bodies—to illustrate some of the scenes.
   • Include the congregation in some way, vocally or physically.
   • As you read a passage, you will develop a set of pictures or images in your mind that arise from what is being described or evoked. You can bring those images to the stage through the incorporation of sound effects, visual effects, props, or anything else you can think of.

What about those passages that just have one voice? While a good reader can keep the audience's interest throughout, it is also possible to divide it among several voices so that there is variety for the listener. The division of lines among different readers is called "voicing."

When voicing the passage, pay attention to the inherent rhythms, pacing, and meaning. This will help you effectively assign the voices. Each voice, or combination of voices, has a unique quality which communicates a distinctive mood. Lines may remain as they appear in the original text, or they may be repeated, echoed, spoken in unison, given to a chorus, and so on.

There are different types of line voicing that can be used:

- *Antiphonal*: two groups exchanging passages back and forth
- *Cumulative*: begins with a lone voice, then gradually adds on another, and another, and another, until all voices are speaking together
- *Unison*: which gives a sense of community
- *Line-around*: one person at a time speaks in sequence
- *Solo and chorus*: a leader guides the audience in appropriate response to the information that unfolds, giving new information in each line while the chorus/audience responds with the same phrase again and again

These ideas are by no means exhaustive; many other creative ideas can be added. Creativity comes as we try things and learn in the process. The more you do, the more you realize the possibilities that exist for bringing Scripture to life dramatically, artistically, creatively, and with power!

142. SCRIPTURE AND THE ARTS OF STORY, MOVEMENT, AND MUSIC

By Jeff Barker

A young woman came up to me at a conference a couple of years ago. It was just before the final worship gathering of that event. She said, "This is the first time in my life I've ever looked forward to the Scripture-reading part of a worship service." I immediately knew she was speaking for many of us, maybe even most of us throughout the world's churches. Anticipating effective Scripture presentation has not been our usual experience.

What had changed for this young woman? During each of the conference's six worship services, a group of college students had presented an Old Testament story. They presented the text verbatim from memory, using simple actions—sometimes in movement, sometimes frozen—along with a hint of music. Suddenly an ancient power was in the room. It was a reunion with an old friend who had been hidden by cold readings. We were once again remembering the beauty of the story of God.

STORIES ARE FOR TELLING

The story of God is a family story, and the whole family should get involved in its retelling. Bible scholars are now reminding us that the entire Bible was birthed out of oral cultures, originally intended to be heard, seen, and felt in community as opposed to being read silently and alone. (A good place to start exploring what these scholars are saying is the Biblical Performance Criticism website: http://www.biblicalperformancecriticism.org.) It is fine to read the Bible quietly. But there is much to be discovered through the process of artful performance.

My goal here is to focus specifically on reclaiming the power of the ancient Hebrew dramas. In his fine essay "Drama and the Sacred," Dr. Tom Boogaart reminds us that the historical narratives of the Old Testament are, in reality, plays.[84] Notice their dialogue, dramatic structure, and metaphoric gestures. These stories, like all dramas, need actors, designers, directors, open playing spaces, and audiences to provide their full impact.

---

84   Thomas A. Boogaart, "Drama and the Sacred: Recovering the Dramatic Tradition in Scripture and Worship," in *Touching the Altar: The Old Testament for Christian Worship*, ed. Carol M. Bechtel (Grand Rapids: Eerdmans, 2008), 41.

To start exploring the presentation of a Bible reading, use a group of presenters. Each Bible character who speaks or acts in the passage gets an actor assigned. The narrator takes the remainder of the text. For example, here is the verbatim beginning of the text in 2 Kings 6:8–23 (KJV), the story of the bands of Syria:

STORYTELLER

Then the king of Syria warred against Israel.

(SYRIAN SWORDSMAN and SYRIAN ARCHER move into *tableau* to
receive their king's plan. KING OF SYRIA kneels, pointing to the place where
the secret attack will occur.)

STORYTELLER (continued)

And took counsel with his servants, saying.

KING OF SYRIA

(breaking the frozen image)
In such and such a place shall be my camp.

Or you can eliminate the narrator, assigning the narrative lines to the character for whom that narration is most significant:

KING OF SYRIA

(entering)
Then the king of Syria
(looking across at KING OF ISRAEL)
warred against Israel.

(SYRIAN SWORDSMAN and SYRIAN ARCHER move into position to receive the
plan.)

SYRIAN SWORDSMAN

And took counsel with his servants, saying.

KING OF SYRIA

(kneeling, pointing)
In such and such a place shall be my camp.

Obviously, the casting will be shaped by the way the director divides up the text. But this ancient art form is part of the folk-storytelling tradition rather than a modern professional theater. Persons male and female, old and young, may be assigned parts without much concern for realistic appropriateness. Everyone may join in.

PLAYS ARE FOR SEEING

If you will approach the Old Testament historical narratives as plays, you will readily discover what is true of almost every play: it is a visual art form. There are things to see that you do not notice until you perform these stories. There is a difference between the page and the stage. Here is an example from Exodus 2:

> And Pharaoh's daughter said unto her, Take this child away, and nurse it for me, and I will give thee thy wages. And the woman took the child, and nursed it. And the child grew, and she brought him unto Pharaoh's daughter, and he became her son. And she called his name Moses: and she said, Because I drew him out of the water. (vv. 9,10 KJV)

Now look at the same text with descriptions of what might happen if you simply perform the actions suggested by the story:

NARRATOR

And Pharaoh's daughter said unto her.

PHARAOH'S DAUGHTER

Take this child away, and nurse it for me, and I will give thee thy wages.

(PHARAOH'S DAUGHTER and MAID exit as MOTHER and SISTER take baby Moses and cross to FATHER. There is a reunion of great joy and wonder. Then MOTHER takes the baby aside to nurse as the child's FATHER and SISTER exit.)

NARRATOR

And the woman took the child, and nursed it.

(MOTHER croons a wordless lullaby to the child while miming breastfeeding it under her shawl. Near the end of the lullaby she exits and reenters with a five-year-old MOSES.)

NARRATOR (continued)

And the child grew, and she brought him unto Pharaoh's daughter.

(PHAROAH'S DAUGHTER enters. MOTHER and MOSES kneel.)

NARRATOR (continued)

And he became her son. And she called his name

PHAROAH'S DAUGHTER

(bending to look him in the face)
Moses.

NARRATOR

And she said,

PHARAOH'S DAUGHTER
(to MOTHER)

Because I drew him out of the water.

(MOTHER encourages MOSES to stand. PHAROAH'S DAUGHTER and MOSES leave together. MOTHER is left on the stage in tears.)

The action reveals the meaning and emotion of the events. Faithfulness to clear communication of the text will usually reveal simple, appropriate, memorable, and often profound images. I have seen this happen again and again. Be patient and wait for these discoveries during the rehearsal process.

A WORD ABOUT TRANSLATION AND MEMORIZATION

All artistry requires some degree of craft, which is simply technical discipline. Two of the disciplines needing attention at this point in the process are selecting a translation and committing that translation to memory. I urge you to choose a translation that keeps the narrations—especially the "he said / she said" parts—before the dialogue rather than during or after. When such narrations occur before the dialogue, they can provide focus and foreshadowing. When they occur after the dialogue has begun, they seem absurd.

A commitment to memorization is a beneficial part of the artistic process for many reasons, not the least of which is clarity of understanding that the performer receives. And, of course, it is difficult to explore the movement and emotion of a text unless the Scripture presenters have the text memorized.

MUSIC

The Hebrew people were musical, and it is likely they would have supported their storytelling with music. I suggest that you always ask how music can undergird your storytelling. It is appropriate and relatively simple to provide a bed of sound from a percussive instrument—drum, shaker, clave, strummed guitar, keyboard. Perhaps someone at rehearsal can add singing—a spontaneous, unknown melody. But do not simply add a wash of sound which has no changes. The value of music is that it provides shape to the story's journey. The musical sounds should support the tension and release of the story. Are there one or two key moments in the plot that can be supported by a significant change in the music? When our team performed "The Bands of Syria," we used drum and voice throughout. At one moment in the action, Elisha confronts the king of Israel, suggesting that he should feed his enemies rather than killing them. Here is how we supported this decisive turning point with music:

(The KING OF ISRAEL attempts to get ELISHA to back down by threatening him, pointing the bow directly at him! The percussion builds to a furious climax and stops. There is frozen silence as we wait for one of the two powerful leaders to back down. Suddenly there is a single, sharp whack with a percussive instrument. Then one more. The KING OF ISRAEL backs down. He sets his bow aside and moves to get some food for the enemy soldiers. The singing resumes.)

LEADERSHIP

This project calls leaders to assist participants in the rediscovery of the truth and beauty lying beneath the surface of these ancient dramas. Much of this truth remains hidden until artists reveal it. One important question we each must ask is, "Who will help reclaim the Scripture presentation part of worship at my church?" It will take someone in respectful relationship to the congregation's leadership team. It will take someone who loves God and therefore loves God's word. It will take someone who understands the congregation and its traditions. It will take someone who seeks beauty. It will take someone who can help others pursue a worthy project even when it is difficult. Do these qualities describe you? If so, the needed leader in your church may very likely be you.

I dream of the time when each week, along about Wednesday, the people of our churches will begin to say to one another, "I wonder what the Scripture-reading part of worship will be like this coming Sunday." But they won't mean just reading. And they'll also expect that someday soon they will be among those memorizing and rehearsing for Sunday's artful remembering of God's great story.

143. SCRIPTURE RELEVANCE DRAMAS
By Michelle Petersen

In one rural West African community, 276 people prayed to ask Jesus to be their Lord after watching open-air Scripture drama in their local language, and a church began. In another language group, a radio station began airing *Scripture Relevance Dramas*—plays that relate Scripture to local life. This station told us that those plays are their most popular program, and that people from other language groups were calling the station to ask if radio theater programs could be created in their languages as well. That series spread to fifty-seven radio stations in three countries.

I have been blessed to work with drama groups in several cultures and languages, including the two just mentioned, creating live or recorded Scripture Relevance Dramas. Rather than translating foreign scripts that were created with a different culture in mind, we create dramas addressing local questions, worldview, interests, and background knowledge. We either develop locally authored scripts, or we agree on a story line to follow and improvise from a *scenario*—an oral or written outline of scenes, helpful for low-literacy situations. Scripture Relevance Dramas increase people's engagement with Scripture by bringing God near to people's everyday lives.

WHY SHOW THE RELEVANCE OF SCRIPTURE TO LIFE?

In *The Bible Translation Strategy*, Wayne Dye identified factors which influence how people respond to Scripture. He studied how well Scripture was received by fifteen language communities and concluded that one factor was more important to the reception of Scripture than any other: "People respond to the Gospel in proportion to their conviction that God and His Word are relevant to the concerns of daily life." Dye writes that we can help bring this conviction to someone by applying the good news to everyday encounters to maximize personal relevance.[85] Scripture Relevance Dramas apply this principle by relating Scripture to local cultures with the aim of increasing people's perception of the usefulness of Scripture.

---

85   T. Wayne Dye, *The Bible Translation Strategy: An Analysis of Its Spiritual Impact* (Dallas: Wycliffe Bible Translators, 1980), 61.

TYPES OF SCRIPTURE RELEVANCE DRAMAS

Scripture Relevance Dramas show a parallel between local life and Scripture. The following are ways to make Scripture relevant:

- **Jesus' parables (teaching stories)** lend themselves easily to dramatization. They can be portrayed in today's cultural context or in their own historical context with parallels drawn to current life situations. Jesus often taught a parable in response to a question. Actors in Burkina Faso set the Parable of the Good Samaritan in its context by first dramatizing Jesus answering the questions in Luke 10:25–29. They introduced their parable drama of Luke 10:30–35 by Jesus saying, "Let me tell you a parable." The actors all wore costumes that were local representations of their character types. They closed their parable drama with the dialogue in Luke 10:36,37.

- **Some historical events from Scripture** may be contextualized when introduced with a clear explanation. In Burkina Faso, local actors portrayed the story of Tabitha from Acts 9:36–43. Their Tabitha interacted with the audience. She showed audience members her generosity in typical local ways, acting like some audience members were needy and Tabitha giving them local clothes. When Tabitha died, her friends mourned in the local way. During rehearsal a neighbor came running to ask who had died because the way actors were grieving sounded authentic. When Peter prayed for Tabitha and she came back to life, the actors playing her friends rejoiced with a local song and dance. During the performance, the church erupted into cheers and jubilation at this point.

- **Local stories, folktales, and cultural parables or proverbs** may show biblical parallels. Not all local stories emphasize biblical points, but many serve as memorable illustrations of Scripture. One acting group in Senegal dramatized a man being invited to one marriage and subsequently being invited to a second marriage to be held at exactly the same time in a different town. The man wonders to himself how he can attend both weddings. On the appointed day he walks one leg down one road and the other leg down the other road until he falls over, to great audience applause and laughter. A narrator adds, "In the same way, Jesus says, 'No one can serve two masters. Either he will hate the one and love the other, or he will be devoted to the one and despise the other. You cannot serve both God and money'" (see Matt 6:24).

- **Problem stories** from life today show family or friends in the midst of a difficulty. A character empathetically shares a Bible story to help others work through the difficulty, saying something like, "You aren't the first person to experience this. Something similar happened to me. God's word helped me. May I tell you a story from God's word about someone who had a similar experience to yours?" Or "May I tell you a true story that helped me?" Alternatively, the character with the problem may remember a verse of Scripture that helps him or her work through the difficulty. In the *Scripture Relevance Dramas* program airing in West Africa, for example, actors paralleled the problems of a family with sibling rivalry to the story of Joseph from Genesis.

THREE ESSENTIALS TO CREATING A MEANINGFUL PLAY

To create live or recorded theater, the work you bring to life together needs three important elements:

1. **Interesting ideas.** People come to a play not only to have fun, but also to learn through vicarious experiences. Direct your audience's attention to your main point through the characters' words and actions. People's comedies often make fun of behavior that is opposite to behavior they value. Their dramas often show the results of following or not following a value they care about. In some cultures, people prefer to infer the meaning of the story. In other cultures, acting teams prefer to have a narrator or master of ceremonies (MC) state the moral of each play overtly at its end, or even at the beginning to introduce it. Ask and follow your culture's ways of emphasizing your main idea.

2. **Interesting characters.** The team needs to decide what each character is like, what each character wants, and how each character is going about trying to achieve what he or she wants. As professional storyteller Doug Lipman likes to say, a great actress playing a grandmother is not a great actress because she performs a fantastic imitation of a grandmother; rather, she is a great actress because she makes her grandmother character contribute greatly to the story's main idea. If you are a director or team leader, you can encourage actors to play their parts well by asking each one to find and play their character's objective with their whole heart and show what their character is like with their whole person.

3. **Interesting actions.** Stories tell; plays show. Stories happen in the past, but plays pull the action of the past or the future into the present. Decide what actions happen in each scene. Actors should move frequently to show the story as well as tell the story through their words. Create actionable goals for each character. Break down the logical order of scenes and decide how people enter and exit. Set the pace. The play needs to move quickly enough to keep people's interest, but slowly enough for the audience to follow the action without becoming lost. When a character is not central to telling the story during a particular moment, the actor should pay attention to the other characters without unnecessarily drawing the audience's attention by shifting position or speaking. When it is an actor's turn to show a certain central part of the story, it is often helpful for that actor not only to speak but also to move, because audience attention tends to follow movement.

I call the last two elements, character and action, the play's "feet." A play with interesting characters, but where little happens, is like a play hopping on one foot—*the character foot*. A play with interesting actions, but where we don't get to know the characters well, is also a play hopping on just one foot—*the action foot*. A strong play runs on two feet, interesting characters and interesting actions, rather than hopping. Both feet take a journey toward an interesting idea. Ideas are remembered well when they involve performers' and audiences' hearts. People remember what makes them laugh or what touches them. If the team cares about their characters and their story, then their audience will go on their journey with them.

Through action and character the audience grasps interesting ideas. Audiences come to the theater or listen to a play to deal with life vicariously through other people's experiences in an enjoyable way, or as one of my Burkinabé director friends said, "People watch plays to learn without pain." A play may allow people to hypothesize how needed change could happen in their world, or it may reaffirm endangered parts of a society that should be strengthened.

CREATING SCRIPTURE RELEVANCE DRAMAS

Scripture is full of interesting ideas, characters, and actions. Our lives are full of these three things too. Scripture Relevance Dramas show applications of Scripture to people's lives. Here are some pointers for how to create a successful Scripture Relevance Drama:

Research the characteristics of different kinds of local plays to meet audience expectations well. If you are working cross-culturally, you cannot assume that all your criteria for good acting are universal.

- **Ask to what extent actors interact with audiences.** Some acting traditions involve audience members as impromptu actors, while others maintain a strict imaginary wall between performers and actors.
- **Ask how to introduce and close a play in ways that let the audience know what kind of story you are portraying**, such as fiction or news. In the West we may start a children's fictional story with "Once upon a time," but people who believe Scripture is true would not start a story from Scripture that way.
- **Research how to begin your play in a way that meets audience expectations for a good story of this type.** Meet genre norms for setting up a good story so your audience wants to know what happens next.
- **Research how "the moral of the story" is communicated.** As previously mentioned, in some cultures a narrator or MC tells audiences at the beginning what the story will be about and what it teaches. In other cultures the narrator or MC states at the end what has been seen and learned. In still other cultures, audiences infer the meaning for themselves without being overtly told.
- **Ask how actors introduce themselves.** Some traditions introduce all the actors at the beginning; in other cultures, actors introduce themselves at the end; in others, actors never introduce themselves, but audiences have a printed program. Give your actors respect in the appropriate ways.
- **Ask how long play events typically are and whether they consist of one story or a series of stories.** Some traditions perform a series of short plays on different topics; other traditions deal with one story at length.
- **Research how to end your chosen type of story well.** Show the story's problem being resolved in a satisfying way that meets audience expectations for how a good story of this type ends. Find responses that are empathetic, culturally appropriate, and scriptural. Consultation with experts such as leaders, elders, or health practitioners may be needed to provide the most accurate information possible to resolve certain problems well, rather than relying only on the team's limited understanding of an issue.
- **Find out about your audience's interests.** Discuss topics, themes, or issues your drama team cares about exploring, and ones you believe your audiences will care about. In West Africa, for example, actors initially wanted to create stories about subjects like

tithing, which they then realized would be of little interest to a wider audience. They learned to engage whole communities with Scripture, not just the church audience. They created live drama and radio drama about topics like being reliable with money, leadership, and relationships.

When you have finished your research, you are ready to create. Do this by paying close attention to the following guidelines:

- **Work with your *gatekeepers*—**people who have influence and need to give you their blessing for the performances to happen. Ask your gatekeepers to announce your performances, recommend you for other possible venues, and critique your rehearsals.
- **Listen together to your chosen Scripture, read it aloud, and discuss it** to make sure all members of the team know the story well with all its details. Agree together about the meaning and implications of the passage before rehearsals begin. In oral societies, actors may like to hear the Scripture read aloud in their local language more than once before they talk about it together.
- **Decide the scenes that are needed to build the story.** The team can either write a full script or agree on a scenario of events. In the latter type of theater, every performance is slightly different. Determine who needs to be part of each scene, and the main action of each scene. Decide how to show a difficulty or conflict building and what its resolution or ending will be. Decide how Scripture can be shown, paralleled, or integrated.
- **Show your story through movement and placement.** Make sure during rehearsal that everyone in the audience will be able to see every part of the performance well. Make sure actors do not obscure one another from the audience's line of vision. Actors should keep their faces or profiles to the audience as much as possible. Actors should generally turn their backs to the audience as infrequently as possible because emotion is expressed mainly through the face. If the audience is seated on many sides of the actors, then actors may need to change position frequently so no part of the audience sees a given actor's back for very long. Even if you are creating audio-only drama, such as radio theater, actors' gestures and hypothetical movements can be heard through their voices.
- **Through their words, actors show their characters and work toward attaining their goals.** Ask actors to speak loudly enough that everyone in the audience will be able to hear clearly. Remind actors during rehearsal that when audiences laugh during a performance, the actors should wait to continue the story until the audience has stopped laughing, otherwise the audience will not hear what the actor says next.
- **Empathize with your characters and with your audience.** There is an old saying that people don't care how much you know until they know how much you care. A danger of Scripture Relevance Dramas can be giving shallow answers to deep pains, but the audience leaves satisfied when they know they are valued and respected because the characters they identified with were valued and respected.
- **Add details your audience may not know that they need to know to grasp your story.** Weave needed background information in. Think of how people could misunderstand what you're trying to say, and try to make it hard for them to understand you wrongly. Characters can ask other characters questions that allow the audience's questions to be answered as the characters' questions are answered.

- **Rehearse well.** Actors are less nervous the better they know their parts. Rehearse for a small group before performing for a large one. You may be most familiar with acting traditions in which you need to rehearse for weeks or months before a performance and create realistic costumes and props. In improvisational traditions, actors use objects they find on hand to represent whatever they need them to be as they improvise from scenarios or from Scripture. For such traditions, rehearsing over the course of a few days is rehearsing well, because they rely heavily on their improvisational versatility. Improvisational actors often put a two-hour performance together in a few days, usually consisting of a series of shorter plays.
- **Establish a time and place for a performance and invite people to attend.** Ask your gatekeepers to invite people to the event.
- **Perform and keep performing.** Encourage and inspire one another's creativity. Evaluate and refine the work, as laid out in the section "Improving New Works" below.

COACHING ACTORS DURING REHEARSALS

Some cultures like to establish a director to make choices. Other cultures like to advise one another and make choices by consensus. *Synergogy* means teaching one another and learning from one another, including deciding together how to tell the story through movement. When leadership is by consensus, every member of a drama team has something to learn from every other team member. New teams learn not to be defensive when improvements are suggested. Sometimes an idea may be helpful, other times less so. Share ideas respectfully and sensitively, and listen to one another. It is a good idea to have a pastor or Christian leader be part of your group to help shape your work. Be sensitive to cultural ways to lead and to provide critique.

To develop acting skills at rehearsals, we use Philip Bernardi's book *Improvisation Starters: A Collection of 900 Improvisation Situations for the Theater* (Cincinnati: Betterway Books, 1992). Bernardi's situations are American, but with a little thought we adapt improvisational situations. One of Bernardi's situations asks two actors to play two students working together on a research paper; one wants to make up footnotes so the paper appears more impressive, and the other is afraid of getting caught. West Africans generally have little interest in research papers, but a local actor helped me adapt it:

> Two seamstresses are working in the tailor's shop. Their boss isn't there. A client pays an apprentice for a dress. One apprentice tailor wants to keep the money without telling her boss that the client paid. The other apprentice tailor would never dream of doing that, and wants to convince the other not to do this.

Every actor in the group has a chance to improvise a two- to five-minute scene with another actor. The other actors watch, applaud, and make suggestions for improvement. Sometimes an improvisational exercise gives the team an idea for making a performance piece. Actors make use of their improvisational skills while performing to help a character sound more natural, interesting, and believable. When using scripts, writing that sounds natural in print may need revising as it comes to life in oral form. Actors become progressively more natural by learning from one another, repetition, and practice.

IMPROVING NEW WORKS

There are three ways a new work can improve *before* it is publicly presented, and a fourth way a work can improve for future performances *after* it is publicly presented.

1. **Self-check.** During story creation and rehearsals, each member of the team may consider how to improve their own performance and how to strengthen their clear presentation of the play's ideas, characters, and actions. The director or actors who are not part of a given scene may watch the other actors and advise them. Help one another play each objective wholeheartedly. Decide together how to make the acting more touching, powerful, or believable. Remind actors not to turn their backs to the audience for long, and not to stand in a place that cuts off the audience's view of some of the other actors.

2. **Consultant check.** Ask people who have a strong grasp of the word of God and local culture, such as pastors or consultants knowledgeable about the issues involved, to tell you how accurately and empathetically you are applying Scripture to local life. You may want to ask a few people who have experienced similar circumstances to tell you how well you are drawing them into your story.

3. **Pre-performance community check.** Rehearse for a small audience before performing for a large one. Initial audience members need to be people who trust the team enough not to be excessively polite. Instead you need people who will tell you how to improve, rather than tell you only what you would like to hear. Ask them what they liked, what they did not like, what they did not understand, what they learned, what parts needed to be louder, and what parts were difficult to see. You probably want audience members to empathize with some characters more than others. Verify that people liked the characters you wanted them to like and did not like the characters you did not want them to like—they may like the talents of an actor playing a negative role, of course. If needed, ask actors to speak more loudly, change their arrangement in the performance space, or emphasize different elements.

4. **Post-performance audience check.** After a performance, ask a few audience members for feedback to help improve the next performance. Ask them the same kinds of questions that you asked during the pre-performance community check.

During all four kinds of checking, evaluate the following:

Clarity of the story. Ask what people remember happening in the play. If their attention was captivated by less important aspects, diminish those aspects and place more emphasis through action and words on more crucial aspects. When people are unclear on an important story point, add necessary background. Verify that the main point people understand is the main point your team intends; if not, bring the main point to the forefront again.

Biblical and cultural accuracy. How balanced is the way the issue is handled, according to the full picture of the word of God? Does the presentation come across as local or foreign? Is it really "us"? The resolution in particular needs to be believable. At one rehearsal in West Africa, the play's theme was a troubled husband-wife relationship. In the original script, the couple heard from a friend how the Bible says they should love and respect each other. The narrator said something

INTRODUCTION

SECTION 1: FOUNDATIONS

SECTION 2: STORIES

SECTION 3: TOOLS

CLOSING

like, "and they lived happily ever after." Another team member said, "Wait! I don't believe the narrator. Show me how their relationship works out." The story was revised to show, not just tell, how they worked out their marriage.

Audience engagement. Character and action should both be equally well developed so the story is moving forward on both feet toward the main idea. Some team members should watch your audience watch the performance and suggest parts that need to move more rapidly or parts that need to be cut. How engaging is the Scripture? Making Scripture audible is not the same thing as making Scripture engaging in its style of presentation. You may want to have a character read God's word aloud formally, but consider having a character give God's word in a less formal style, or act out a portion of Scripture or its application. When you need to deal with hard issues, verify that characters are respected and issues are dealt with sensitively.

RESPONSE TO SCRIPTURE RELEVANCE DRAMAS

As illustrated by the two examples at the beginning of this description, Scripture Relevance Dramas have been well received in many cultures. In rural villages in Burkina Faso, evenings of live play performances drew crowds of around 150 in a church setting, and around 350 in an open air performance. Actors trained to perform Scripture Relevance Dramas during three-day workshops say they intend to continue presenting dramas to their communities on a regular basis. In a West African regional language, listeners to Scripture Relevance Radio Dramas commented to actors: "Where do you get all this wisdom from?" "Your teaching is good. We like your stories." "No one can interrupt our friend when she is listening to your program. She doesn't want to miss a word." "I made peace with my rival wife (co-wife in a polygamous marriage) after I listened to the story about the unforgiving servant." "Can you make me a cassette copy? I need to give it to a friend."

> Making Scripture audible is not the same thing as making Scripture engaging in its style of presentation.

Actors sometimes have lively discussions at rehearsals, trying to find the most appropriate ways to show the Bible's applicability to local life. Applying the Bible to life situations has become so natural to them that sometimes they may be overheard saying to their real-life friends and neighbors, "Your situation reminds me of a story in the word of God. May I tell you a story?"

CONCLUSION

Scripture Relevance Dramas hone the presentation of Scripture to each audience's background knowledge, artistic styles, cultural wisdom, and values. Drama teams work with local talent to tailor local plays to each audience, rather than relying on mass-media approaches that supply as many cultural audiences as possible with the same media product. Locally created plays can make people feel at home with Scripture, so God is not seen as a foreigner.[86]

---

86   For additional resources, see the following items in the *Handbook* bibliography: Bernardi (1992); Dye (1980); Frakes (2005); M. Hill and H. Hill (2010); Lipman; McLaughlin (1997); and Pederson (1999).

RESEARCH AND COCREATION

HOW TO PLAN FOR MORE LOCAL ARTS EFFECTIVENESS

144. PLANNING AN ARTS SHOWCASE EVENT
By Brian Schrag

DETERMINING WHAT KIND OF AN EVENT OR ACTIVITY

Communities can promote positive cultural identity through local arts in at least three ways, by

- organizing cultural celebrations—e.g., concerts, festivals, contests, etc.;
- documenting—e.g., through written descriptions, audio recordings, photography, and video; and
- publishing—on locally distributable media, websites, etc.

These activities should always be done with the leading and input of key community members and artists, and always in a way that will be appreciated by the community itself.

REASONS FOR A SHOWCASE EVENT

You may help a community plan or run a festival or competition that highlights creativity in local artistic genres. Festivals are events designed to showcase a community's cultural identity and creative output. Many ethnic or religious groups already have celebratory gatherings that may be open to including new works of art produced by Christians. It may also be possible to start a new festival tradition fueled by Christians' celebration of their God-given artistic gifts. Prizes for the best new works add the energy and excitement that events like these produce. Festivals also provide great opportunities for cooperation between different Christian, cultural, religious, and other groups within a community.

> Start a new festival tradition fueled by Christians' celebration of their God-given artistic gifts.

PLANNING PROCESSES FOR AN EVENT

Showcase events normally emerge from a five-phase process:

1. **Imagining and planning.** How will we get from here to there? The larger the event, the more planning it requires. Some communities excel in creating detailed schedules and goals. Other communities excel in pulling together fabulous celebrations through organic social dynamics. Contribute ideas, but don't impose a system.
2. **Promotion and networking.** How can we ensure the participation of key artists and a wide public? Festivals sometimes incorporate contests or prizes to motivate artists. Make sure to clearly communicate the kinds of arts that will be rewarded and how they will be evaluated.
3. **Composition and preparation.** Will artists have time and resources to create and practice their performance?
4. **Running the event.**
5. **Evaluation and planning.** A big event requires a dedicated time afterward to graciously evaluate with key people how it went. It is also a great moment to discuss the possibility of similar future events.

KEY ELEMENTS IN HELPING TO ORGANIZE A FESTIVAL CELEBRATING COMMUNITY ART FORMS

The purpose of a showcase arts event is to encourage and invigorate the use of local arts in a community. A festival can raise the status of the local arts, aid in their preservation, encourage innovation, and bring about positive changes.

Participants

Invite individuals from as many different social, age, and economic groups as possible, including community leaders, church leaders, skilled artists, members of older generations, and younger people with a passion for their culture. By including all of these groups, the festival will be more likely to bring about lasting artistic change, particularly if younger people are engaged. Note that a church's involvement in the organization and implementation of the festival could result in deepened relationships and witness.

> A festival can raise the status of the local arts, aid in their preservation, encourage innovation, and bring about positive changes.

Kinds of things you will need to research

1. A list of artistic genres in the community and those you intend to feature in the showcase event (see the accompanying *Manual*, "Take a First Glance at a Community's Arts," Step 1).
2. Event descriptions ("Take a First Glance at an Event," Step 4, Part A) that include as many genres as possible.

Tasks to accomplish

1. **Initial community meeting.** Meet with community representatives to discuss the list of artistic genres. Ask and offer reasons why local arts are valuable and explain the benefits a festival celebrating these arts could provide.

2. **Logistics.** After initial commitment to a festival, discuss goals and plans through questions like these:
    *   Who will organize the festival?
    *   Can we achieve broad inclusion and unity?
    *   What items need to be in the budget? How much will the budget be, and who will underwrite it?
    *   Which arts will be promoted?
    *   Who are the influential and respected artists that should be included? Who is in charge of inviting them?
    *   Shall the festival include competitions for new works in traditional forms?
    *   When should the festival take place? Should it be included as part of another regular cultural event, ritual, or festival?
    *   What use will be made of audio and video recordings? The organizing group should plan to obtain any necessary government or local permissions from authorities and permissions from artists for the future use of recordings.

3. **Implement the plans agreed upon.**

4. **Evaluate.** After the festival, meet with the organizers or a larger community forum and reflect on the event:
    *   Evaluate such things as community involvement, the quality of the artistic works, and the overall successful and unsuccessful aspects of the event. What parts of the festival were members of the community most excited about? Did anything catch their attention?
    *   Explore how the community can draw on the excitement and encourage new works for other purposes. Did new purposes for traditional arts emerge? For example, it might be more possible after the festival to promote local arts for use in Christians' spiritual lives or in health education. Plan for more activities that feed into signs of the kingdom.
    *   Plan to create products from recordings of aspects of the festival and distribute them, such as DVDs, a website, storybook, collection of poetry, or song books. There might also be interest in developing a Community Arts Archive, housed locally or in a government or educational organization.
    *   Decide whether the festival should become a regular event.

THE ROLE OF THE ARTS ADVOCATE

Your role (or roles) as an arts advocate will vary according to the skills and needs of the community. You may be able to contribute through making and organizing audio and video recordings, obtaining authorizations for use, and in providing international perspective on the value of their arts. You could also publish an article about the festival, an artist, or a particular tradition. If you are an outsider to an artistic tradition, you might lend prestige by learning to perform one of the showcased genres. Approach this humbly, however, to ensure that your efforts to learn and perform are viewed positively.

INTRODUCTION

SECTION 1: FOUNDATIONS

SECTION 2: STORIES

SECTION 3: TOOLS

CLOSING

485

INTRODUCTION

SECTION 1: FOUNDATIONS

SECTION 2: STORIES

SECTION 3: TOOLS

CLOSING

145. EVALUATING AND IMPROVING LOCAL ARTS
By Brian Schrag

We want communities to integrate creativity into their lives in such a way that their spiritual, social, and physical goals are not only met but truly exceeded. Evaluating according to agreed-upon criteria helps them to make their imperfect artistic communication more effective. Remember that the goal of evaluating is construction, not destruction; building up, not tearing down (Eph 4:29). Note, too, that the community can greatly reduce the need for critique by including the right people from the beginning of the cocreative process: social and religious leaders, expert creators, and expert performers.

The more we understand and can talk about the arts and their various forms, the more we can identify negative elements that keep positive effects from happening. In this chapter we will look at four procedures which should assist in the process of evaluating and improving local arts. These procedures encourage us to

1.   follow comforting guidelines for deciding what is good and bad,
2.   design an evaluative process using a conceptual approach,
3.   design a recurring cycle of evaluation, and
4.   evaluate Scripture-infused arts.

FOLLOW COMFORTING GUIDELINES FOR DECIDING WHAT IS GOOD AND BAD

How do you decide what is good or bad? When, for example, someone says, "I never liked the Beatles' music," do they mean they didn't like their tunes, they didn't like their lyrics, or they didn't like their long hair? People are seldom able to articulate what exactly they like or don't like about an artwork. This is not surprising, because artistic communication works through the production and reception of a staggering number of possible signs and their associated meanings. People could be evaluating arts according to any of these kinds of signs: line; syntax; enjambment; rhyme; assonance; alliteration; metaphor; simile; verses; stanzas; refrains; pulse; tempo; meter; accents; figures; motifs; phrases; tonal center; keys; intervals; modes; scales; range; tessitura; themes; contours; cadences; parallel, chordal, or polyphonic relationships between concurrent pitches; formulas; progressions; tonality; strophes; iterations; through-composition; theme variation; solo; duo; trio;

choir; unison; vibrato; accompaniment; use of space; characterization; number and location of participants; blocking; plot structure; idea; dramatic premise; frames; improvisation; movements; gestures; movement phrasing; dynamics; efforts; spatial relationships; visual unity; balance; rhythm; proportion; shape; value; color; hue; shade; tint; texture. And so on. And so on.

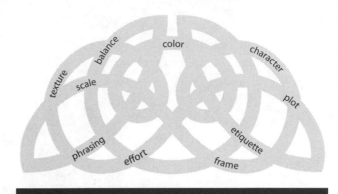

Sample Intertwined Artistic Features in an Event

But there is more. Not only are the kinds of signs seemingly endless, but each group and individual may have diverse associations with any given sign. One person may smile whenever he hears Latin percussion because he met the woman who would become his wife at a party where they danced the *samba*. Another man may detest *samba* because his fiancée broke up with him at a similar event. There could be zillions of signs multiplied by zillions of associations at an artistic event, any one of which could make it fail.

But, unbelievably, our predicament is even more dire. For not only does productive evaluation require us to perceive an infinite number of signs, their combinations, and their meanings, but we need to be aware of personal relationships and social dynamics. An epic poet might perform brilliantly, but if an influential audience member is holding a grudge against him, the community might ultimately dismiss the artist's skill.

Take a deep breath. The complexity of artistic communication should keep us humble, but there are several factors that make identifying criteria for improvement possible. We present these factors here as guidelines for designing evaluation and improvement exercises:

1. **Trust the local system**. Groups usually share a sense of when an artwork is good or not and have ways of communicating what needs to be fixed. Find out how correction normally works in the community.[87] In some situations communities may get rid of inferior products by blocking them from future presentation and letting them die.

2. **Evaluate according to effects.** What are the effects that new artistry should have on people in order to move them toward kingdom goals?[88] Observe and ask about experiencers' responses to the new bits of artistry. Did they have the effect that you wanted? If an orator's performance is meant to motivate people to join a parade celebrating their ethnic identity, but participants watch distractedly and then disperse to their homes, the oration failed.

3. **Relax, but keep learning.** You can't study all of the possible signs, so do this: watch people's reactions and listen to what they say, then perform more research.[89] For example, if you are getting to know people who carve fruit, schedule several research

---

87   See "Aesthetics and Evaluation" in Step 4, Part C, of the accompanying *Manual*.
88   See Step 3 in the *Manual*.
89   For examples of activities, see the *Manual*, Step 4.

activities suggested in the *Manual*,[90] and then start learning to carve the fruit yourself. This education will sensitize you to factors that may prove important in the improvement of new artistry.

4. **Identify what kinds of evaluation should happen when.** Artistic activity can benefit from evaluation at two points in the cocreative process. First, when you are helping people during the act of creation, everyone can evaluate intermediate versions of the works. Second, you may help people reflect on a work after it has been completed and presented.

DESIGN AN EVALUATIVE PROCESS USING A CONCEPTUAL APPROACH

Here is a process you can follow that will increase the likelihood of useful evaluation results:

1. Identify and work through **local social structures** and help everyone involved provide correction in locally appropriate ways—using standards of politeness, respect, indirection, roles within a social hierarchy, etc.
2. Define together the **criteria** for deciding how good a work is and how it could be improved. We have found this standard helpful: a created work is good insofar as its features work together to affect the purposes demanded by the context of its performance and experience. These purposes could include the work's theological correctness, accuracy of information communicated, ability to communicate, ability to touch people through its aesthetic quality, ability to motivate to action, etc.
3. Identify the **elements** of an artistic communication event.[91] These should include how the work utilizes space, materials, participants, shape through time, performance features, feeling, content, themes, and community values.
4. Identify the **purpose(s)** of the artistic communication event. These could include to educate, to motivate to action, etc.
5. Identify **people** to include in the process of evaluation. These people need to have the knowledge, skills, and respect necessary to critique various elements.
6. Identify **objects** that can provide a focal point and reference for discussion, so that you don't need to rely exclusively on memory for critique. These could include song texts, drama scripts, musical notation, masks, dance moves, and video and audio recordings.
7. Together **affirm** the aspects of the creation that work well, and encourage the creators to **do something even better** based on the evaluation.

The following table lists examples of evaluation in several creative contexts:

---

90   See Step 4, Part B5, in the *Manual*, where you will find these activities: "Describe Spatial Relationships between an Object's Visual Features," "Document the Creation of an Object," and "Identify the Role(s) in Visual Art Creation."

91   For help, see the *Manual*, "Take a First Glance at an Event," Step 4, Part A.

INTRODUCTION

SECTION 1: FOUNDATIONS

SECTION 2: STORIES

SECTION 3: TOOLS

CLOSING

Kinds of Elements to Evaluate	Examples of Such Elements	Qualified to Evaluate	Example Methods of Evaluation
Space/location, time, participants, etc.	Storytelling around a fire at night, with all ages	Genre experts, traditional leaders	With written summary of the event description: • Discuss relationship to genre.
Performance features (music, dance, verbal arts, drama, visual, etc.)	Proverb choice, movement characteristics, melody shape	Expert performers	With audio and video recordings: • Review for aesthetic/technical successses, weaknesses of performance. • Transcribe melody, lyrics, movements, poetic features, colors, etc., for analysis.
Message(s)	Theological content	Church leaders	With transcriptions of texts: • Analyze texts of songs, dramas, stories (with back-translation if critiquer doesn't know language) according to clarity, truth. • Comprehension testing: ask experiencers what they understood.
	Medical content	Health worker	
Purpose(s)	• church use: education, worship, evangelism • AIDS education	Agenda setters for the communication event	With a summary of all aspects of the event, discuss degrees that the event fulfilled its intended purposes and other purposes, and how the event could be improved; may use a focus group or exit interviews.

Examples of Evaluation Components and Processes

DESIGN A RECURRING CYCLE OF EVALUATION[92]

It is important to check art forms in order to know if the created product is meaningful to the target audience. So, for example, if we draw a picture for children, we need to know if

- the symbols and colors in the picture are meaningful;
- the overall message of the picture is clear;
- the image(s) are natural for them to both understand and imitate, as best they can;
- the children can easily absorb and restate the meaning of the visual image;
- the image clearly comes from their cultural context;
- the art forms relate meaningfully to the community as a whole; etc.

Here are some ideas for checking an art form, though the approach should be designed appropriately for each cultural context:

1. **Determine carefully who should help with the checking.** Two starter ideas might include: (a) four or five target audience members, and (b) at least two older experts in the community.
2. **Use all of the following tests with each of the above people.** It is important to write down anything you learn about the art form so that improvements can be made. Checking with each person can take anywhere from five minutes to about twenty minutes. It is important to take time and learn as much as you can about what needs to be improved. To acquire the kind of information you will need, three kinds of tests will be necessary.
   a. **Test for meaning:**
      - Show or demonstrate the artwork.
      - Ask respondents to tell you what the artwork communicates to them.
      - Listen to them and see if they seem to understand the meaning. If the work includes biblical texts, make sure that people understand it accurately.
      - If not, show them the artwork again and ask them for the meaning once again.
      - Write down their response, and write down what parts of the artwork are clear and what parts are unclear. This could be words, phrases, themes, colors, patterns, actions, etc.

   b. **Test for naturalness:**
      - Show or demonstrate the artwork.
      - Ask respondents if they can reproduce some portion of the artwork back to you.
      - Let them do this on their own and see what they can remember.
      - If they are having some difficulty remembering, show or demonstrate the artwork again.
      - Ask them again to reproduce some portion of the artwork.

---

92   See also: Mary Beth Saurman and Todd Saurman, "Song Checking," in Schrag and Neeley, *All the World Will Worship*, 179–85.

- If they are having some difficulty, you can prompt them a little, but it is wise to not prompt much.
- Write down parts that are difficult to replicate.

c. **Test for ownership and accuracy:**
   - Ask respondents how they feel about the artwork.
   - Would they use it? How would they use it?
   - Would they enjoy hearing, seeing, or experiencing the artwork? When?
   - What do they not like? What would they change?
   - What would make the art better or more meaningful for them?
   - Does it feel to them as though it's their own?
   - Does it feel as though it belongs to their community?
   - Is this form consistent with
     o the listener's learning or education level?
     o local teaching methods?
     o the appropriate language and symbol or sound?

3. **When you have finished the testing, correct the artwork.** Take the results from the arts checking to the artwork creator or meet with the creation committee and change or adjust its unclear portions.
4. **Test for effectiveness.** Test again to see if you hit the target audience.

DESIGN AN EVALUATIVE PROCESS THAT FOCUSES ON SCRIPTURAL FIDELITY

There are three kinds of checks to help make Scripture-infused arts better. For all three, ask open-ended questions that lend themselves to exploratory answers, not "yes or no" short answers.

1. **Self-check.** Ask the artist to think of ways to make the work communicate more clearly to the desired audience. Encourage the artist to think about the work from the audience's point of view, taking into consideration the prevalent background knowledge and worldview assumptions of the local area. What could be changed that would make the work clearer? To what extent is the most important thing the artist wants to communicate the most important thing the audience is likely to grasp from this performance?
2. **Consultant check.** When the text of an artistic work is based closely on Scripture, the need for evaluation and improvement is especially important. In these cases, experts in Scripture and the arts should be consulted. When consultants don't speak the local language, they need a translation into a language they know well.
   - Two types of translation are important for evaluation. First, a word-for-word translation reveals poetic and discourse features of the text. Although slight adjustments of word order may be made, it follows the original text almost exactly. Second, a free translation attempts to convey the original meaning naturally in the target language. This helps the consultant understand the overall importance of the text.
   - Translations will be better if they result from following these guidelines: the translator should be a mother-tongue speaker of the source language; the translator

should not already be familiar with the text; the translation could be oral and audio recorded, or written; if the translator doesn't understand what the artist meant, they should discuss it together; if there are unintended misunderstandings, the artist should strongly consider changing the text.

- With these translations in hand, check whether the material has these characteristics:
  - relates Scripture meaningfully to the local worldview
  - the rate of information flow is neither too fast nor too slow
  - meaning, form, style, and emotion go together
  - not insulting to any particular group
  - nonoffensive portrayal of sensitive issues, like violence
  - believable portrayal of interesting characters
  - balance of character development and actions
  - biblical background knowledge is either already generally known or provided
  - follows the discourse rules of similar materials in the genre
  - the way the material opens and closes—greetings and leave-takings, for example—is culturally appropriate
  - time frame is clear

3. **Community check.** The third check tests the material with a small audience of the target group before the material is presented to a larger audience. In general, the same person who made a translation and the artist should not check the work with the community. Record the work, play it back for the focus group, and ask questions like these:
    - What was it about?
    - What else was it about?
    - *For an illustration or visual artwork*: What do you see? What else do you see?
    - *After a dance*: What did you see? What else did you see?
    - *After a drama*: What happened? And then what happened? And then what happened? Do not tell people the answers. What do you think the author/artist/storyteller/actors/dancers wanted to communicate?
    - *After a song*: What did you hear? What else did you hear?
    - What did you learn? Do not explain the intended meaning to them; if you do, you will not get a valid impression of their comprehension.
    - What did you like? What did you appreciate?
    - What did you not like? Did anything offend you?

Following these questions, testers should talk with the creator(s) and work together to revise the work accordingly.

146. MAKING EFFECTIVE VIDEO AND AUDIO RECORDINGS

By Cory Cummins, William N. Harris, and Mary Hendershott

This chapter introduces workers to the use of video and audio equipment and to recording techniques in the field.

RECORDING VIDEO

Think like a storyteller. When you pick up a video camera, what is the story you want to tell? Who will you be telling it to? How do you want to change your audience's thoughts, feelings, and future actions by the end of the piece?

Composition. The term "composition" refers to how you arrange elements in the camera frame. Some basics of composition are:

- **Rule of thirds**—Imagine a tic-tac-toe board on your screen dividing it into thirds horizontally and vertically. The eyes of the subject(s) in your shot should be placed on the upper intersecting points of the horizontal and vertical lines. Usually, avoid centering the subject in the middle tic-tac-toe square.
- **Headroom**—The "headroom" is the space between the top of your subject's head and the top of the frame. If you are shooting a **medium shot** (head and chest) or **close-up** (head and shoulders), follow the "rule of thirds" and place the subject's eyes on the upper third horizontal line. When you frame tightly, as long as the eyes remain on the upper third horizontal line, it's okay for the top or side of the head to be out of the frame.
- **Looking room**—The space in front of the subjects in the direction they are looking, talking, or moving is the "looking room." For example, if the subjects are moving from left to right, place them on the left third of the frame, leaving the right third empty.

Types of video framing. There are several types of shots involved in video framing:

- Often the **establishing shot** is the first scene. It may be an aerial shot of the desert, a cityscape, or some other context-setting view. Alternately, the establishing shot can be a montage of visuals that establish context in the broadest terms. It shows the relationship between the environment and the main subject(s) and draws viewers into the story. For example, an establishing shot might show a lush forest. A complex rhythm is heard coming from somewhere in the green foliage. The camera searches for the source of the sound, catching a hint of color.

- In a **wide shot**, we see all of the subject(s) to be recorded—several women, almost hidden by the foliage. The camera position changes to show four women standing around a mortar with four pestles. The bits of color seen in an earlier shot are their African wraparound skirts, and the complex rhythm is created by their pestles striking the mortar in turn.

- Cut to a **medium shot** (showing only portions of the women) as each pounds with an evenly spaced cadence, but at different tempos, duples against triples, creating an interlocking rhythm pattern and never missing a beat.

- Cut to a **close-up shot** at a low angle—of pestles punching the sky like the pistons in a well-oiled precision engine. The rhythm continues, but the timbre changes; pounding segues into clapping, work morphs into song. Sound precedes a cross-fade into the next image: Christian women sing newly composed Scripture songs, accompanied by duple juxtaposed against triple, the same patterns made by mortar and pestle at the beginning of the sequence.

Other elements in video recording. The following practical instructions should be helpful:

- **Camera moves** while recording are meant to reveal new information. They should be used sparingly. It is usually much better to shoot well-composed still shots and angles and then move the camera to new positions rather than change the framing while recording. When shooting, stay on the same shot for a minimum of ten seconds before moving to another shot or angle. Don't "fire hose" the scene.

- Use a **tripod** whenever possible. When a tripod is impractical, find other ways to stabilize the camera. Hold the camera with both hands, brace your elbows against your body, or find something to lean against.

- Whenever possible, **light from the side** rather than directly from the camera.

- Find a **focal point** that catches your eye and frame accordingly, using the rule of thirds. If you don't know what your focal point is as you film, then the viewer will also not know what to focus on.

- **Think as you record.** While you are filming one shot, use your peripheral vision to find your next shot or angle and plan how you will get there. At minimum, have a clear idea of how you want to begin and end your presentation. Your video should not just peter out; it should have a **clear beginning, main body, and ending**.

- When filming a performance event, take in as much of the establishing scene as possible, **including both the performers and the audience**. Ruth Stone reminds us that "participants in music events include both the individuals producing the music and the people experiencing the music performance as listeners or audience, and the auditors' meanings and interpretations are just as significant as those of the performers."[93]

- Getting **cutaway shots** (showing others' reaction to the subject) will give a more complete perspective of the event, which can subsequently be used for review and feedback.

Recording location. Here are some factors in choosing a location for recording:

- The decision on where to record (inside or outside) depends on factors such as instrumentation, climate, and acoustics. Generally, try to record in **the most natural setting**. If instruments are normally played outdoors, move the recording outside. When possible, find a location isolated from unwanted noise.
- Find a good recording location **ahead of time**, noticing the shade, acoustics, and isolation. Use fabric on interior walls to reduce reverberation when possible. You may be able to create nice acoustics by placing the musicians and singers in a circle formation around the microphone under some trees for shade.

RECORDING AUDIO

For starters. Consider the following factors when making an audio recording:

- Getting the right balance "live" is tricky, even with isolating headphones, so do a practice take.
- Stop, listen, and make small adjustments until you are happy with the balance.
- Involve some of the participating musicians in balancing the levels between instruments and vocals. Remember, sound balance is also a cultural preference. Listen to the advice of the local musical specialists, even if it does not match your own sense of aesthetics.
- For better sound, keep your microphone close to the subject.
- Decide on a few simple hand signals (e.g., silence, begin, stop) and practice these with the group before starting to record.
- Learn the musical terminology used in your region to communicate with performers. For example, in certain contexts in West Africa to "sing higher," translated literally, means "sing louder."
- Find out the preferred ending to each song. This might be a clear cadence (rhythmic or melodic), a change in volume, or even linking several songs together. Some groups may prefer fading out gradually through editing, but do not assume that this is the case. If you notice a few performers tend to begin chattering as a song is almost ended, caution the group to wait for your signal that recording has stopped before they are free to talk. It is very hard to remove this problem later when editing!

---

93   Ruth M. Stone, *Let the Inside Be Sweet: The Interpretation of Music Event among the Kpelle of Liberia* (Bloomington: Indiana University Press, 1982), 4.

Keep it natural. Here are some suggestions for a making a natural recording:

- If a song style involves dancing or movement, let them dance. Normally, only the lead singer's head needs to remain stationary. The more natural the performance, the better the recording will be.
- If a song style involves moving in a large circle dance, place the microphone(s) in the center of the circle. The acoustic mix is often surprisingly good in the heart of the circle.
- If instrumentalists move their bodies while playing, place the microphones at an appropriate distance to capture the sound globally or use lapel microphones. Minimize the rustle of clothing against microphones.

Basic equipment. As soon as you can, purchase a video camera and audio recorder with external microphone and earphone plug-in capability. Add to them a full-spectrum (20–20,000 Hz) condenser microphone and headphones that fully cover the ears or, at minimum, ear buds.

Until you can buy new equipment, start recording with the equipment that you have. Experiment with microphone placement to create a decent balance between vocal and instrumental sounds. Use proximity to get the mix you want.

Consider battery-operated equipment (mixer, digital recorder). This allows you to record anywhere and also avoids line interference due to unstable electricity.

Integral and analytical performance contexts. An *integral performance* is one that is familiar to the performers and that has a high number of normal social and artistic components.

1. Choose video recording
   - to discover overall flow of a performance through time, including subdivisions;
   - to see how sounds are produced, and by whom;
   - to see how movements, dynamics, phrases, and relationships are produced;
   - to see how artists create visual objects;
   - to show rather than only tell; and
   - to create a record of cultural practices that can be shared with the world.

2. Choose audio recording
   - to learn language and culture through repetition of recordings, and through joint observation with an "insider";
   - where only sound has significance (visual support of the sound is irrelevant); and
   - to transcribe melodies, rhythms, and texts.

An *analytical performance*, on the other hand, is designed by the researcher to isolate features of artistic production. One important purpose for such recordings is to collect components of different artistic genres for analysis and comparison. These may include songs, proverbs, dances, or stories.

Design recording events in analytical settings

- to enable subsequent feedback—by using video, performers and others can watch and verbally annotate the video recording of a performance with the researcher;

- to describe playing or movement or acting techniques; and
- to document movement in a clear manner for future viewing.

For example, in her research with the Kpelle of Liberia, Ruth Stone was able to use video recordings and feedback to identify specific dance movements that three months of research and interviews had failed to make possible.[94]

HOW TO COLLECT AND RECORD SONGS

1. Ask people you know, "Who are the best singers of this kind of song? Who (often older people) knows the most songs? Please introduce me to them."
2. Create an analytical recording context: meet the person, describe what you'll do, and get permission to record.
3. Slate the recording: Say, "This is [recorder's name], recording with [type of equipment], recording [name of subject], at [time and place], on [date]. Do I have your permission to record you?" Then, "This is song #1."
4. Record a native speaker of the language translating the main elements of the lyrics into a language of wider communication—like a trade, national, or international language—after each song.

HOW TO COLLECT AND RECORD PROVERBS

The vast majority of languages include condensed, specially formed bits of wisdom that we call proverbs. To truly understand a proverb, you need to learn not only what its words mean, but also other cultural information it refers to. You also need to know how it is performed in a social context: who can use it and for what purpose(s)? Try to gather integral video or audio recordings of the proverbs in natural use.

1. Gather people together, turn on a recording device, have everyone speak in the vernacular (if possible), and ask people to think of as many proverbs as they can.
2. Suggest situations in which proverbs might be used. These could include what a mother might say to a daughter who is angry with a friend, or a father to a son who is misbehaving. You can also suggest topics that proverbs might address, like laziness, animals, children, or food.
3. Suggest kinds of people that proverbs might mention, like debtors, merchants, old people, midwives, children, hunters, or ancestors.
4. Listen to the recording with someone who knows local proverbs well and can help you translate them in a language of wider communication. When a proverb occurs in the recording, stop recording, and have your friend(s) help you write and translate the proverb.

---

94   Ibid., 54.

CONCLUDING COUNSEL

Become a student of others' work, watching documentaries and other field recordings to hone your skill set. It is well worth it to strive for excellence!

147. COMMISSIONING ARTISTIC WORKS
By Paul Neeley

New works can substantially affect attitudes towards using indigenous art forms with Christian content, encouraging others to use them as well. This can be especially true if more than one artistic work is commissioned and created—for example, a corpus of ten new songs or dramas. Commissioned works can also generate interest in written media, and oral and written media can potentially work in tandem—such as Scripture booklets, songs, and radio dramas.

I use the phrase "commissioning artistic works" to refer to a facilitator who provides the impetus for an indigenous or local artist to create a particular artistic work. The facilitator, who may be either a cultural insider or outsider, asks for a song, drama, painting, or other work to be created and suggests potential themes to be communicated, scriptural or otherwise. The artistic work may be geared towards use in or out of the church setting.

DECISION MAKERS

The original facilitator may make some or all of the choices involved in commissioning a work.[95] Or the facilitator may realize the need for artistic works made with culturally appropriate forms, then give most of the detail work to someone else who has shown some interest and skill. This situation worked well in examples from the Yoruba in Nigeria and Sabaot in Kenya.[96] A team approach can also be used where cultural insiders and outsiders share their knowledge and creative ideas.

The decisions may be made in any order according to the situation. For example, if a biblical text—the *message*—is chosen first, that decision will influence which genre of music, poetry, or other art form is chosen, and the genre in turn will influence the choice of creator. Alternatively, the *creator* may be chosen first, and that creator may have a preferred genre in a certain artistic domain, which will then influence the choice of message to be communicated.

---

95   For case studies where the outsider facilitator, after considerable study, made most or all of the choices, see Paul Neeley, "A Case Study: Commissioning Scripture Songs among the Akyode of Ghana," *Research Review* (Legon, Ghana: University of Ghana), *supplementary issue*, no. 10 (1997): 118–29; and Brian Schrag, "Commissioning Songs among the Mono of Zaire," *Research Review* (Legon, Ghana: University of Ghana), *supplementary issue*, no. 10 (1997): 130–39.

96   See Neeley, "Commissioning Scripture Songs."

COMMISSIONING AN ARTISTIC WORK: FOUR KEY CONSIDERATIONS

There are four basic considerations in commissioning an artistic work: the artistic genre, the creator, the message to be communicated, and how the completed work will be made public.

Choosing the artistic genre. To choose an appropriate genre for an artistic work, research local artistic resources, including the typical method used for creating a new work within each genre being considered.

Choosing the creator. When choosing someone to create a work, look for someone who has experience in creating new works and is recognized as experienced by others in the culture. The society in which you work may have many such qualified people to choose from, or perhaps only one or two old people. Note that in some cases the choice of certain artistic genres may automatically determine the gender of the creator. Local people will be able to make a list of potential experienced creators. Be aware that many creators specialize in a specific area within their artistic domain; for example, two out of twelve dance forms in the society.

> The facilitator asks for a song, drama, painting, or other work to be created and suggests potential themes to be communicated, scriptural or otherwise.

In some cultures the number of Christians may be very small, and it may be difficult to find someone who is both a Christian and has experience creating artistic works. In this case you can consider commissioning a work from a non-Christian. Questions to ask in this case include:

- Are they interested?
- Are they respected by the community? By the church?
- If their name is made known, will that be a help or a hindrance to acceptance of the work?
- What do local Christians think of the idea?
- How might non-Christians react?
- What will local Christians think of the recompense of money or materials to a non-Christian artist? How will this affect relationships?
- If there are local Christian artists, will they feel snubbed?

There have been situations where commissioning a Scripture song from a non-Christian composer was an acceptable plan. For example, among the Akyode of Ghana, the culture's most respected and popular musician was not a Christian. However, he had a good reputation within the society, his name would actually help the song's acceptance, he was interested in the idea, and the local church saw nothing wrong in approaching him.[97] In the Nkonya culture of Ghana, however, the most famous composer was viewed as a drunkard, and the local church decided not to approach him.

In some cultures there is already an established role for composers who create songs for other people. In West Africa, especially in areas influenced by Islam, there may be a local form of *griot* (praise singer). There are examples from Nigeria, Benin, and Ghana where such a Muslim praise singer agreed to work with a biblical text to compose and record a Scripture song.[98] Investigate the

---

97   Ibid.

98   Ibid.; Klaus Wedekind, "The Praise Singers," *Bible Translator* 26, no. 2 (1975): 245–47.

musical culture in your area to see if an institutionalized form of composing for patrons is already in place. Such professional composers are used to working for a cash payment. "Composers-for-hire" also appear in some Asian cultures, including parts of Nepal and the Philippines.

The composer of a commissioned song or art piece usually gets some sort of recompense, such as public recognition, a free recording, a gift, medical care, or cash. In some places the facilitator agrees to pay a fixed price for the composing and recording of each commissioned song or artwork.[99] In other cases there may be a looser agreement concerning recompense.

Choosing the message. The choice of message for the artwork will be made hand in hand with the choice of genre, for reasons of both emotional fit and message fit. One would probably not try to fit joyful lyrics with the musical genre of a funeral dirge.

> One would probably not try to fit joyful lyrics with the musical genre of a funeral dirge.

Research is necessary to match message and art forms together. For example, examine sample lyrics in the musical or poetic genres you are considering. Some genres may accommodate lyrics of literally epic proportions, while the lyrics of other genres may typically be one sentence long. Potential messages can be paired with the most appropriate genre(s). Genres that require short lyrics work well with a message from a stand-alone Bible verse. A different genre may be used for a lengthy passage or an entire story. Similar research applies for other artistic domains.

Composers of songs will find it extremely helpful if the facilitator writes out the message line by line and does not give it to the composer in paragraph form. If the composer is not literate, have someone recite the passage to them line by line until it is memorized. In some cases the facilitator may want to be involved with arranging the text into lyrical form, such as verse and chorus, or call and response.[100] In other cases, the composer may do all such arranging of lyrical lines.

Some changes will probably be made in the scriptural text when adapting it for song lyrics, drama, painting, or other possible domains. The completed artistic work should be checked by a local pastor to ensure that the message has been communicated correctly and that it sounds or looks natural in the local idioms.

Local church leaders may be invited to be involved in choosing the message. For example, church leaders in Ghana were asked by letter to choose their own favorite verses from a Gospel and ask someone in their congregation to set these verses to music within a month. In another group, church leaders were assembled and assigned specific passages. They were asked to work with composers in their congregations to compose a song within a few days. In both cases initial discussions had previously been held.

> Find a way to get the dance, drama, painting, or other artwork into public use fairly quickly, and this will motivate the creator.

Choosing how to make the new artistic work public. In many parts of the world, giving a composer or artist some printed words and saying, "Please communicate these in a song or sculpture," is not a typical method of creation. However, if the motivation of the creator is strong enough, it may work. The artistic works can be composed "on request," or "commissioned," if the artist understands that there is a good reason to do so.

---

99   See the Sabaot example in Neeley, "Commissioning Scripture Songs," *Handbook* chpt 147.

100   See Paul Neeley, "Basic Guidelines for Adapting Written Scriptural Texts into Song Lyrics," *Notes on Translation* 10, no. 2 (1996): 41–51.

One such motivating factor can be a coming event that will provide a quick public use for the work. Songs have been commissioned for dedications of houses, offices, literature publication, and for recordings and/or concerts. Commissioning Scripture songs or dramas for other public gatherings is also possible, such as a special church service; e.g., Christmas or Easter. Find a way to get the dance, drama, painting, or other artwork into public use fairly quickly, and this will motivate the creator.

However the details come together, commissioning artistic works can be a valuable way to help people catch a vision of the benefits of using local artistic works to impact their society for good.

INTRODUCTION

SECTION 1: FOUNDATIONS

SECTION 2: STORIES

SECTION 3: TOOLS

CLOSING

HOW TO CREATE LOCAL ARTS TOGETHER

148. CREATING LOCAL ARTS TOGETHER: THE MANUAL SUMMARY

By Julisa Rowe

The accompanying volume to this publication—*Creating Local Arts Together: A Manual to Help Communities Reach Their Kingdom Goals* by Brian Schrag—is a marvelous tool that will greatly benefit the arts missions community. Having an in-depth manual that shows how to discover local arts and then work with the local community and artists to create new art to further the kingdom of God is long overdue. However, not everyone will be able to dedicate the amount of time needed to absorb everything in the *Manual*, regardless of how valuable and necessary that information is. You may be constrained by time factors—such as a short-term trip—or want to get an overview so that you can see how to create your artistic work more effectively, or encourage the artists working with you through presenting a quick overview to inspire them to further study.

The following pages give a summary of the process detailed in the main manual; namely, how to create local arts together with local artists and communities to bring about God's kingdom goals in that community. For examples and greater explanation, please read the corresponding sections in the *Manual*.

A SUMMARY

There are seven basic steps to creating local arts together. Research underpins it all, emphasizing the need to be a learner at all times. The steps are:

- <u>Meet</u> a Community and Its Arts. Explore artistic and social resources that exist in the community.
- <u>Specify</u> Kingdom Goals. Discover the kingdom goals that the community wants to work toward.
- <u>Select </u>Effects, Content, Genre, and Events. Choose an artistic genre that can help the community meet its goals, and activities that can result in purposeful creativity in this genre.
- <u>Analyze</u> an Event Containing the Chosen Genre. Describe the event as a whole, and its artistic forms as arts and in relationship to broader cultural context. Detailed knowledge of the art forms is crucial to sparking creativity, improving what is produced, and integrating it into the community.
- <u>Spark</u> Creativity. Implement activities the community has chosen to spark creativity within the genre they have chosen.
- <u>Improve</u> New Works. Evaluate results of the sparking activities and make them better.
- <u>Integrate and Celebrate</u> Old and New Works. Plan and implement ways that this new kind of creativity can continue into the future. Identify more contexts where the new and old arts can be displayed and performed.

STEP 1: MEET A COMMUNITY AND ITS ARTS

Step 1 is about initial discovery and description of a community and its arts. When entering a community, or beginning work with them, it is important to engage in observation (research) to find out as much about them as you can. This applies to both the community at large and its arts, since art rises out of its context.

What community are you targeting? There are many ways to define a community (see the *Manual*, Step 1), but here are some shared characteristics. A community shares a story; i.e., they have events, characters, and ideas that have occurred in their past that they all know and can refer to. These things give them a reason to keep gathering together. A community also shares an identity. These "identity markers" distinguish them from other communities and may be such things as language, food, dress, religion, or shared struggles. Communities will also have shared patterns of interaction, such as rituals, festivals, family living quarters, visual and tactile symbols and patterns, and many more. It is important to remember that communities are always changing, because they are made up of individuals who come and go, make their own decisions, and respond differently to the many situations they encounter.

As you begin your exploration of your community, it is important to have a place to write down all your discoveries. We call this a **Community Arts Profile** (CAP). This is some form of database or document where you keep all the information you have gained on the community and its arts.

Take a first glance at a community

This is important because it will help you understand the context in which the arts are developed and performed. After all, art does not exist in a vacuum. Get initial information about the community's geographical location, language, identity markers, and modes of communication. Decide the scope of your activities—e.g., one clan in a village, or everyone in a region who speaks the same language. Start describing things from as many angles as possible. The chart below gives you a starting place for questions to ask. There are also many places to get the information:

- From friends, leaders, and other contacts from the community. Ask them to point you to other people and resources.
- Read and observe how community members have presented themselves in books, articles, videos, recordings, and other media.
- Read academic research, encyclopedias, and other presentations to see what others have said about the community.

Start exploring the community's social and conceptual life

It is important to have a broad understanding of the community. This is accomplished through anthropological study, which is outside the scope of the *Manual*. However, the following chart shows several important anthropological concepts and a few related questions to stimulate your thoughts.

STUDYING THE COMMUNITY: QUESTIONS TO ASK

- Where is the community and how many people comprise it? This includes basic information like village or town, province, and nation.
- What ties the community together? Answers could include factors like language, geography, ethnic identity, and social structure.
- How do they communicate with each other and how often? This question involves languages and modes of communication, such as face-to-face, telephone, and electronic social media.
- How did they get there? Identify important historical events and patterns that have brought the community to its geographical location and affected its identity.

Take a first glance at a community's arts

A core feature of our approach is that we help communities create from artistic resources that they already possess. So one of the very first things we have to do is list these resources, and that means that you will have to do some more research! Here are ideas for your initial exploration:

Language in its sociocultural context

1. In what contexts do people use different languages or types of language?
2. How do people use silence in their communication?
3. What value do people place on different types of speech?

Material culture and economics

1. How do people use and value objects?
2. How do people produce, distribute, and use goods and services?
3. How is labor distributed among genders, classes, and ages?

Kinship

1. How do people describe their relationships to other people in their community? What are the named categories for blood relatives?
2. How do people describe their relationships to their ancestors?
3. What social obligations are associated with each kind of relationship?

Marriage and family

1. How do people define the social union between men and women that results in children? How many men and women are involved, and what behaviors define the relationships between each? Who can marry whom in the community? Where do married partners live?
2. What constitutes a household?
3. How do households relate to extended family?

Social organization

1. What roles do gender, age, kinship, locality, and shared interests play in organizing social groups?
2. How are social groups ranked by status?
3. How do people enter or exit groups?

Power relationships

1. How does a community organize itself politically? How does it relate to government structures?
2. How much power does each smaller group hold?
3. How do individuals and groups exert, gain, or lose power?

Religion

1. What sorts of supernatural beings do people talk about or relate to? Do these include ancestral, nature, human, or supreme spirits?
2. What rituals do the community perform regularly, and for what reasons?
3. How do people use and control supernatural power?

Worldview and values

1. How do people categorize reality, and what attributes does it have?
2. How can people know what is true about reality?
3. What do people say they think is important? How does people's allocation of time and resources show what they think is important?

1. Attend artistic events and describe them briefly in a notebook. Give them their local names and terms.
2. Make lists of artistic genres, such as types of song, dance, drama, visual, storytelling, or proverbs. When are they performed and for what purpose? Who performs them?
3. Collect instruments.
4. Transcribe song texts or play texts.
5. Study language and culture with artists. Spend relaxed social time with them.
6. Make systematic audio or video recordings of an art form.
7. Learn to play an instrument, sing, dance, act, weave, or tell a story in a local genre.

UNDERSTANDING ARTISTIC GENRES: QUESTIONS TO ASK

- How did the kinds of arts in the community come about? Who created the items people use or perform with?
- What are people's general attitudes toward people involved in different local art forms? Positive? Negative?
- Are there parts of a performance that have special symbolic significance? For example, colors, shapes, instruments, or clothes?
- How does the way people do local art forms now differ from how they did them in the past? Are young people learning how to do them? How does someone get good at it?
- Are there certain art forms that only men or only women can do?
- How do people feel when they're involved in different local art forms? Do they ever enter into ecstatic states?
- How are local art forms connected to religious beliefs?
- What artistic expressions in the culture are not currently being used in the worship of God? Why? How might God want to redeem one for a purpose in his kingdom?

Cultures often mark important events and transitions with artistically rendered communication. Identify rituals and special events that exist in a community and explore what arts might be associated with each. See the *Manual* for a good outline[101] for identifying key events. Events to look at include life cycle and historical events, activities, ceremonies, and nature.

Keep in mind that art may look different than you're used to, but it is still art; for example, drama in a community may not necessarily be actors on a stage in front of an audience. It may be a community participatory event.

---

101   See Schrag, *Manual*, Step 1, "Take a First Glance at a Community's Arts" section, adapted from Vida Chenoweth, *Melodic Perception and Analysis* (Ukarumpa, Papua New Guinea: Summer Institute of Linguistics, 1972), 24–25.

HOW TO RECOGNIZE ARTISTIC "COMMUNICATION ACTS"

- **Arts may have a distinctive performance context.** The art occasion is set off from everyday occurrence by such things as time of day, place, language, participants, and so on.
- **Arts may expand or contract the density of information.** Poetry, for example, conveys a great deal in just a few words. Other forms of artistic expression expand the information through space, music, and repetition.
- **Arts may assume more or special knowledge.** Sometimes terminology or alternative meanings of words are specific to a particular artistic genre.
- **Arts exhibit special formal structure.** Artistic expressions are often limited by constraints of form which do not pertain in everyday communication.
- **Arts may elicit unusual responses.** Artistic expressions often produce a strong emotional or physical response from people who experience them.
- **Arts may require unusual expertise.** Artistic expressions often seem to take specialized training to perform; not everyone can do them.

Many of the activities in the *Manual* require basic research skills. For an in-depth discussion of what research methods to use, see the *Manual*.[102] There are many methods available—learning by watching, while doing, by asking, by writing, by capturing and viewing audio and video, and by taking photographs.

We want all of our interactions with people to be guided and marked by love. In all your research be loving, humble, generous, and want the best for your community.

STEP 2: SPECIFY KINGDOM GOALS

Our goal as followers of Christ is to see God's kingdom revealed and lived as fully as possible on earth, knowing that only in heaven will we experience God's kingdom fully. All communities want a better life in some way. They are often unknowingly striving toward the kingdom of God. You can help them on this journey. The gospel is holistic, so the term "kingdom goals" helps us see the myriad ways in which God can be revealed on earth. What follows is a brief summary of some of these ways. You will notice that we don't specifically mention evangelism, but that mandate is at the root of every kingdom goal (see the *Manual*, Step 2, for fuller descriptions).

Identify kingdom goals

A. *Identity and sustainability*
Valuing identity. Where the kingdom of God thrives, communities value their culture. In many places, minority groups think more highly of other people and so denigrate the usefulness, beauty, or intrinsic value of their own culture. Yet "God created human beings in his own image"

---

102   See Schrag, *Manual*, Step 1, "Prepare to Use Research Methods to Learn More" section.

(Gen 1:27 NLT). It is a right, healthy, and holy thing for people to value the good aspects of their societies. We have seen that the more a community appropriately values its own culture, the more the kingdom of God is likely to thrive. Further, a community's artistic genres constitute some of the most identifiable and valuable parts of their culture. If they see no good in their own arts, they will not use them to worship God or communicate truth to each other. We want to explore ways that a community can affirm its artistic resources and create new works that foster strong, godly cultural identity.

Teaching children. One telling sign of the identity health of a community is how much they pass on good parts of their culture to their children and grandchildren. Identifying patterns of what and how each generation is passing on artistic knowledge to the next will reveal a community's health in this area.

Media. Where the kingdom of God thrives, communities contribute to local, regional, and global recording industries. People around the world are constantly figuring out new ways to communicate with each other. A community with an appropriately strong sense of its value will not only receive and learn artistic communication from others, but will also contribute recordings of their own arts through local, regional, and global media.

B. *Shalom*

Jesus entered human society so that his followers would be able to live life to the fullest (John 10:10) and to have peace (John 14:27). The Hebrew word *shalom* captures much of what he promised: a state of peace, completeness, social harmony, justice, and health. Bryant Myers suggests that while "shalom and abundant life are ideals that we will not see this side of the second coming, the vision of a shalom that leads to life in its fullness is a powerful image that must inform and shape our understanding of any better human future."[103]

Healing: The forces arrayed against shalom are formidable: war, natural disasters, sexual exploitation, disease, slavery, hunger, and thirst. A community marked by the kingdom of God responds to these groanings of creation with healing and restoration. Artistic activity plays crucial roles in increasing shalom because it can point suffering people to hope, instill solidarity within a community, and aid emotional and physical healing.

Reconciliation. Where the kingdom of God thrives, communities reconcile with each other and outside communities. Artistic communication can help us open our arms to each other and feel unity that draws on something deeper than our histories. Singing and dancing together require us to mold our individuality into coordinated sound and movement. The joy, pleasure, and solidarity that arts evoke pull us out of patterns of distrust, lift our eyes from our hurt to transcendent truths. Artistic forms of communication can lead to powerful moments of repentance, forgiveness, solidarity, love, and lasting reconciliation.

C. *Justice*

Social justice. Where the kingdom of God thrives, communities love and strengthen the poor and others in their margins. God has communicated clearly and repeatedly throughout Scripture that he cares for people without power. He highlights orphans, widows, and foreigners (Deut 10:18; Jas 1:27), people without enough money (Deut 15:7,8; Ps 9:18; Luke 4:18; 6:20), the politically and socially oppressed (Neh 9:15; Luke 1:46–55), prisoners (Ps 146:7), and hungry and

---

103   Bryant L. Myers, *Walking with the Poor: Principles and Practices of Transformational Development* (Maryknoll, NY: Orbis Books, 1999), 51.

homeless people (Isa 58:6–11; Matt 25:34–40). Jesus made a special point of telling the poor that they could have the kingdom of God (Luke 6:20–26). And God shows how the lack of justice for marginalized people often—though not always—results from the callousness and sin of people in power (Ps 12:5; 35:10; 72:12–14; Prov 22:22,23; Isa 10:1–3).

In response to these realities, God told people with resources to be generous (Deut 15:7,8; Prov 11:24,25; Rom 12:13; 2 Cor 9:6–13; Jas 2:15–17) and kind to the marginalized (Prov 14:31), to defend them (Prov 31:8,9) and break the systems that keep them down (Isa 58:6–11). Communities can work toward kingdom justice by drawing on their arts' abilities to instill hope, speak unwelcome truth to those in power, and encourage solidarity.

Education. Communities not marked by the kingdom signs of health and the valuing of their identity often have weak educational systems. Rapid social change—when new economic and political realities devalue previous knowledge—can also leave people without the knowledge or training to thrive. Because the arts are such penetrating and memorable systems of communication, communities can integrate them into all educational subjects and teaching contexts.

Literacy. Members of a community marked by the kingdom of God will be able to access Scripture and other literature through written and aural means. This means that there needs to be people who can read, write, and listen. Literacy goals relate to both technical (e.g., understanding language structure) and social issues (e.g., wanting to read and write in a language and feeling capable of acquiring these skills). This makes it likely that artistic forms with both heavy language components (e.g., songs, drama, storytelling, proverbs, and riddles) and those without (e.g., dance, visual arts) will feed into these goals.

Economic opportunity. Where the kingdom of God thrives, all community members can work to contribute to their material well-being. From God's own crafting of the universe (Gen 1) to putting Adam in charge of the garden of Eden (Gen 2:15), and admonitions to be productive (Prov 18:9; Col 3:23; 2 Thess 3:10; 1 Tim 5:18) and to reward labor (1 Tim 5:18), Scripture shows that humans are meant to work. The members of a community marked by the kingdom of God have opportunities to engage in meaningful, materially rewarding endeavors. Artists benefit from their activities when people pay for performances or objects. Artistic communication can also grease the wheels of commerce in advertising, and can motivate and coordinate people who are laboring. A thriving community values and rewards the contributions of its artists to its material health.

D. *Scripture*

Translating Scripture. A community marked by the kingdom of God will know what he has communicated through Scripture. To do this, they must first have access to a translation of the Bible that is faithful to the original documents, communicates in ways that are clear to the vast majority of its members, renders texts in the most appropriate and penetrating forms of the local language, is interpretable by various Christian traditions, and can be transformed into oral communication forms with ease. Since the Bible is riddled with artistic forms of communication—parables, proverbs, stories, song lyrics, poetry—insights into local artistic genres will likely help a community translate Scripture in ways that feed into these goals.

Oral Scripture/storytelling. Where the kingdom of God thrives, communities access Scripture through familiar forms. A community marked by the kingdom of God will have access to Scripture in many forms. Local art forms—especially those that people use to tell stories—can play key roles in integrating Scripture into communities' lives.

E.   *Church life*

Corporate worship. Where the kingdom of God thrives, Christ-followers gather to worship in ways that promote deep communication with God and each other. In its deepest sense, biblical worship is a life completely sacrificed and given to God (Rom 12:1,2). It is the moment by moment choice to live for God's glory and not one's own. But this whole life of worship includes particular times of gathering with other believers for heartfelt adoration of God and communication with him (Ps 95:6; 96:9; Acts 2:42; Heb 10:24,25; Rev 19:10). Local arts provide languages for these moments of worshiping God and listening to him that increase the use of our whole heart, soul, strength, and mind (Ps 100:2; Mark 12:29,30). Jesus taught that it doesn't matter where you worship, as long as it's done in spirit and in truth (John 4:21–24). This opens the door to people from every nation and language using their own forms of communication to honor God.

Spiritual formation. Where the kingdom of God is strong, Christ-followers grow in their knowledge and experience of God, their obedience to God, and in godly character traits and habits. Artistic forms of communication can energize and provide structure for formal and informal spiritual training, coaching, and mentoring.

Studying and remembering Scripture. A community that is coming more and more under the rule of the kingdom of God will study, remember, and understand Scripture. The more ways we learn Scripture—including through local arts—the more likely we are to remember it. Studies have shown that memorizing words through song and/or motions involves more areas of the brain.

Christian rites. Where the kingdom of God is strong, people mark important moments with intense spiritual events. These could include weddings, Communion or the Eucharist, funerals, rites of passage, and/or agricultural feasts. Artistic forms of communication mark these events as special, provide historical continuity through unique repertoire and forms, and open up holistic channels of communication with God.

Witness. A community marked by the kingdom of God will learn that he is their Creator and Savior. Local arts provide penetrating means for communicating truth about God because they are often intertwined with both special and daily activities of life: important life events, social interaction, entertainment, teaching, and the like.

F.   *Personal spiritual life*

Prayer and meditation. A community marked by the kingdom of God will have followers of Christ who communicate with God frequently and wholeheartedly. Artistic forms of communication can help this happen because they are enjoyable and connect deeply to people's emotions and wills.

Personal Bible study. Community members examine Scripture accurately and faithfully. When community members integrate artistic forms of communication into their personal Bible study, they remember, understand, and are changed more.

Applying Scripture. A community becoming more and more like the kingdom of God will apply the teachings of Scripture to their daily life experiences. Yet the Bible was written to people in different cultures and at different times. How can we accurately apply it to our lives today, in all our various cultures? Local artistic communication can help people connect scriptural truths to their lives in memorable, motivating ways.

Be aware that, unless you are working with Christians, the community you're with will not be motivated to work toward goals stated in terms of the kingdom of God. But because all humans are created in God's image, we all yearn for many of these signs: peace, health, joy, significance, and justice; you may simply call them "Signs of a Better Future." So when a community wants these things, we can join wholeheartedly in helping according to our skills and calling. If we are working with a local church, then their goals will also naturally include deepening their relationship to God. The ultimate King of the kingdom of God is Jesus. As we journey alongside individuals and communities who don't know Jesus, our love and words can point them to him.

Steps to specifying kingdom goals

It is one thing to have a list of kingdom goals and another to know which ones to pursue. Work with the community to determine which goal is important to them or which they would like to work toward. Creating together will include a continual process of specifying and refining community goals. Here are some steps to begin the process:

1. Talk with and listen to people. Social structures (such as government organizations, churches, mosques, savings and credit associations, or conferences) are a good place to have such conversations.
2. Explore and identify the strengths and aspirations of the community. Ask the community what they have been doing well and what their hopes are for their children, themselves, and their community.
3. Relate each strength or aspiration to a kingdom goal. Put it in a chart for easy reference, such as the chart below.

Strengths and Aspirations	Goals for the Kingdom / a Better Future
Respect between generations	Identity and sustainability
Celebration	Identity and sustainability
Hospitality	Shalom

4. Explore the problems of the community. Ask about issues that are difficult, things that cause significant worry, and what is worse in the community now compared to five, ten, or twenty years ago. Chart these in a similar fashion (see below) so that you can more easily see how they relate to kingdom goals.

Problems	Goals for the Kingdom / a Better Future
Disease: HIV/AIDS, malaria	Shalom
War, crime, violence	Shalom
Intergenerational conflict, loss of traditions	Identity and sustainability
Fear of death	Personal spiritual life

Exploitation: slavery, prostitution	Justice
Inability to read or write	Justice
Lack of access to the Bible	Scripture
Lack of spiritual growth	Personal spiritual life
Lack of unity in Christian community	Church life
Some groups left out of worship	Church life
Inadequate communion with God	Personal spiritual life
Poor education	Justice
Hunger	Justice

5. Choose a goal. Discuss which problem the community would most like to address or the strength they would most like to build on.
6. Write down and develop your plan for cocreating art that helps to reach this goal. (A sample of such a document can be found in the *Manual* "Cocreation Plan.")

STEP 3: SELECT EFFECTS, CONTENT, GENRE, AND EVENTS

Once a community has identified a goal or goals that they want to work toward, it's time to figure out how their arts can help them get there. Each genre is particularly apt for communicating certain kinds of content and producing certain kinds of effects. This section contains steps to take you through this process.

Choose the desired effects of the new artistry

What effect do you want the arts to produce in the community? Some examples might be that

- they understand an important message;
- they act differently;
- they change an unhelpful or dangerous behavior;
- they do something new;
- they think differently;
- they feel solidarity with others; and
- they experience hope, joy, anger, remorse, elation, peace, satisfaction, relief, empathy, surprise, or other emotions.

Explore together how you want people to change in ways that move them toward kingdom goals, and write down the results of your discussion.

Choose the content of the new artistry

If the desired effects depend on people learning ideas through arts, then it's crucial to make sure that those ideas are trustworthy. Study the truth content to be taught so that an accurate message is conveyed. If the message is about how malaria may be prevented, make sure you know the facts about how malaria is actually prevented: talk to your health care professional. For Scripture, study the passage before creating a message based upon the passage: talk to Bible scholars and translators. Talk about the content with God, other artists, and leaders. Together, discuss and write down the answer to these questions:

- What content do we want to communicate?
- How can we make sure that the content is reliable?

Choose a genre to communicate the content and produce the desired effects

Every artistic genre has characteristics that affect the messages it conveys and the effects it has. Together, review the list of artistic genres you produced in Step 1. For each genre, ask:

- Would a new artistic work in this genre have the effects we've chosen? If not, why not?
- Would a new artistic work in this genre communicate the content we've chosen well? If not, why not?

Narrow the list to one or two genres that would be the best for effecting these changes and communicating this content now.

Remember that all artistic genres have characteristics that can be redeemed for God's purposes but that not all are appropriate at a given moment in a community's life. Encourage all involved to pray and listen for the wisdom of the Holy Spirit. Do not force a genre into new uses in a community unless leaders involved see it as wise and you are certain that God wants it to happen now.

Brainstorm about events that could include a performance of the new work

Before we start planning how to create new works in a genre, it's important to start imagining the contexts for their presentation and how they work as communication. Some examples of such communication contexts can be seen in the chart below.

COMMUNICATION CONTEXTS FOR NEW WORKS

- Mass, worship service, Bible study, Sunday school, home group, outreach, weddings, funerals, baptisms
- harvest celebrations, courting rituals, birth rites, rites of passage, teaching contexts
- listening to an audio recording, watching a video recording, transmitting live audio or video to other locations, viewing a sculpture in a museum, looking at a skyscraper in a city
- concert, rehearsal, gig, awards ceremony, sporting event
- intimate family discussion, smoking a peace pipe, court, war

Together, do the following:

- Make a list of kinds of events that new works in the artistic genre could be part of.
- Remind yourselves of your choices thus far: effects, content (messages), and genre.
- Choose a few of the event types you came up with, and briefly describe them in terms of their communication components:
  - Who are the communicators?
  - When and where might such an event happen?
  - What senses will participants use in experiencing the content?
  - How will the genre affect the messages that people experience?
  - When people experience the artistry, will it have the effects you'd like?
  - How will people respond to the original communicators?
- Choose an event in which you might want to perform or present the new work.

STEP 4: ANALYZE AN EVENT CONTAINING THE CHOSEN GENRE

Containing the chosen genre

In order to effectively create a new piece, it is important to understand existing genres. This section gives ideas on how to analyze and explore in detail. Like culture, events and genres are always changing, creating fusion forms. Just be aware of that!

In order to be effective in the creation, evaluation, integration, and celebration of a new work, it is essential to pay attention to the details of the form. Any small element may have significant symbolic or emotive meaning which, in turn, has importance for perceived meaning. To help you do this, we have created categories called "lenses" from which to view the art.

Look at an event through lenses

In physical terms, a lens is a piece of glass that has been polished or otherwise changed in a way that alters any light coming through it. Depending on its maker's goal, someone who looks through a lens at an object may see that object as closer, farther, or perhaps with one color intensified. A lens, then, is a way of looking at bringing one of its aspects into focus. We are using this same idea metaphorically to guide our research in the arts. In particular, we present a method that will guide your eyes, ears, and bodies to reveal seven categories of detail: space, materials, participant organization, shape of the event through time, performance features, content, and underlying symbolic systems.

Note that each of these lenses may interact very closely with others, describing the same thing from a different perspective; don't be surprised if you come up with recurring patterns. Also, each lens may not reveal insights equally well in any given event, so if a lens does not seem to help much, choose another to view the art through.

We've designed these lenses to help you understand more about a particular event that has artistic content. If it is the first event you have seen of its type, you won't know yet if it is a normal example or if it differs in significant ways from what usually happens. As you use the lenses to describe more events of this same type, you'll see patterns and points of divergence.

LENS #1: SPACE

- Space is the location, demarcation, and physical characteristics of the area used for artistic communication. It affects the movement of participants and their relationships to one another, lengthening or shortening the time it takes for participants to move around it and other elements of a performance.
- Space is a big feature in forms such as drama and dance. Creators of art objects manipulate space to create formal structure through features like proportion, rhythm, balance, and the like.
- What is the meaning behind the use of space? Is there symbolism involved? How does the use of space relate to broader cultural themes?

SAMPLE QUESTIONS AND ACTIVITIES

- Did it occur inside, outside, or both? If inside, give type and size of building.
- What are some characteristics of the place where it happened? Shape and size, for example.
- What parts was the space separated into? Were there physical and/or conceptual markers to separate these parts?
- Draw a floor diagram, including boundaries and demarcations.
- Take photographs of the place and its surroundings.

(See the *Manual* for further questions and activities.)

LENS #2: MATERIALS

- Materials are all of the tangible things associated with an event, like clothing, regalia, instruments, props, and lighting. Some objects are more important to the execution and experience of the event than others. They may be made by humans (as in a mask) or appropriated to fill a function (as an eagle feather marking regalia as royal). Objects may serve multiple purposes, conveying meaning at many levels. For example, the Atumpan drum (Ghana) both serves as a functional member of the musical ensemble while also indicating royalty by its shape, colors, and construction; it plays both a functional and symbolic role. Note also that some objects may not be a part of the event's activity.

- Drama uses costumes and props to show characterization and provide dramatic settings. The most common objects used to produce musical features are instruments. In dance, costumes and props may highlight motion. A storyteller might use a prop to symbolize an event in her story, and visual artists use all sorts of materials to create objects.

SAMPLE QUESTIONS AND ACTIVITIES

- What is the meaning behind the materials? Is there symbolism involved? How does the use of materials relate to broader cultural themes? Make a list of objects associated with the event.
- What objects were present, including structures (like buildings)?
    - What objects did people bring expressly for the event?
    - What did people wear?
    - What did people hold? Kick? Otherwise manipulate with their bodies?
    - Were there objects on surfaces, like walls, floors, or ceilings?
- Describe each object (e.g., weight, materials, design) and its function and placement.
- What meaning(s) do people attach to these objects?
- Were some objects treated in unusual or special ways?
- From what you know of the genre of this event, did people use objects in normal ways within the genre? Uncommon ways?
- Were there technologies that produced atmospheric effects and performance enhancements, such as lighting, sound amplification, smoke, or incense?
    - Were there live objects, like animals, in the event?
    - Were there foods or drinks involved in the event?
    - Were there humanly crafted or natural objects that were repurposed for this event?
- Photograph, draw, list, or obtain samples.

(See the *Manual* for further questions and activities.)

LENS #3: PARTICIPANT ORGANIZATION

- At an artistic event, virtually everyone present participates in some way (and sometimes people who aren't even there). Each participant in an event plays a role that affects the form of the performance. Roles can include creators, performers (e.g., singers, instrument players, actors, dancers, storytellers), audience (e.g., aficionados, spect-actors, hecklers), helpers (e.g., set builders, stage managers, gaffers, ticket takers, bouncers, ushers), producers, directors, and so on. Also relevant to the formal characteristics of an event are participants' histories; skills; kin and other relationships to each other; status and role in everyday life; and ethnic, religious, and social identities. For example, a priest may be the only one who can play certain roles in a religious ceremony.
- As usual, look for meaning, symbolism, and broader cultural themes.

SAMPLE QUESTIONS AND ACTIVITIES

- How many participants were there (be sure to include ancestors or gods that are not physically present)? What were each of their roles?
- How did the participants use performance features to interact with each other? Were there obvious patterns (etiquette)?
- How did participants interact with different sections of the event space? Were any roles associated with particular places?
- Which participants exerted creative control and to what degrees?
- Did any participants receive payment in goods, services, or money for performing their role?
- Ask a friend involved in the event what role(s) you might be able to fill. Note what background and competencies you would have to have or acquire to fill different roles.
- Draw a floor diagram, showing where participants were at different times, or what roles were associated with certain places.

(See the *Manual* for further questions and activities.)

LENS #4: SHAPE OF THE EVENT THROUGH TIME

- One way to describe the shape of an event is by splitting it into sequential segments. You can identify the time at which one segment ends and the next begins by noting significant changes in elements of the event as viewed through each of the other lenses. These changes are called *markers*. For example, mark-

INTRODUCTION

SECTION 1: FOUNDATIONS

SECTION 2: STORIES

SECTION 3: TOOLS

CLOSING

ers could include pauses, sudden contrasts in features of participants, beginning and ending of participants' activities, beginning and ending of songs, and the like.

- An example from drama would be a play, broken into acts, scenes, and eventually into gestures and movements. An example of music's highest hierarchical level could be a concert or song, split into movements, phrases, and notes. Dances may consist of pieces, motifs, and gestures. An oral verbal art like a poem may contain stanzas, lines, and beats.
- As usual, look for meanings, symbolism, and broader cultural themes.

SAMPLE QUESTIONS AND ACTIVITIES

- What were the segments of the event?
- How did you know when one segment ended and another began? What marked these transitions?
- From what you know of its genre, was this event longer or shorter than normal? Did it have the same number and size of segments as normal?
- Make audio and video recordings of the event.
- Create a time line. Highlight major segments, then subsegments and the transition markers.
- Create a time line by listing the smallest segments, their beginning and ending times, and how they're assembled to create larger segments.

(See the *Manual* for further questions and activities.)

LENS #5: PERFORMANCE FEATURES

- Performance features are the skills, processes, and conventions that the performers in an event must master to make the event successful. It is possible to write them down (transcribe) using various notation systems. (For examples of notation systems, see the *Manual*)
- Performance features can be grouped into these categories: vocal, body movement, object manipulation, visual, rhythm, narrating, and poetic.
- Participants manipulate *vocal features* in drama to help them act, in music to help them sing, in dance to coordinate breath with movement patterns, and in oral verbal arts to create effects by changing the pitch or timbre of their voices.
- Participants *move their bodies* in ways that contribute to dramatic aspects of performance though acting, characterization, and space organization; in music through instrument playing; in dance through movement dynamics, phrasing, and body and space organization; and in oral verbal arts through gesturing.

- People *manipulate objects* in drama to help them act and produce spectacle, in music to help them play instruments and modify their voice, in dance to support or facilitate movement, in oral verbal arts to emphasize oratorical elements, and in visual arts to make or present a communicative object.
- *Visual features* play important roles in dramatic events, including costuming, makeup, puppets, and spectacle; in dance, including costuming and makeup; and in visual arts, including design and composition.
- *Rhythm features* contribute to musical characteristics like polyrhythm, proportional rhythm, or free rhythm. How does external rhythm (e.g., music experienced through auditory channels) affect movement in dance? What about meter used in oral verbal arts?
- *Narrating features* play significant roles in presenting or recounting events in drama and oral verbal arts.
- Finally, participants may use *poetic devices* for acting in drama, song lyrics in music, and throughout oral verbal arts.

Other kinds of socially meaningful actions and their performance features

- Participants may produce features not associated with a particular artistic domain in order to express opinions and emotions. These opinions and emotions could be to affirm or reject, encourage or discourage, express pleasure or displeasure, attract or repel, assist or impede, unify or divide, goad or hinder aspects of the performance. Examples of such features include hand clapping, stomping, cheering, ululating, heckling, "the wave," throwing rotten fruit, throwing candy, holding up lighters and cell phones.
- Participants may express basic emotions by crying, laughing, screaming, or wailing. These expressions often take on artistic form.
- People may produce other bits of communication with their bodies that contribute to an event that you may not have categories for. These could include actions like snapping fingers, belching, whistling, or producing vocal overtones. Keep all of your senses open to bodily communication.

SAMPLE QUESTIONS AND ACTIVITIES

- Make audio, video, and photographic recordings of the event.
- What patterns emerge from the performance features?
- What meaning(s) do people attach to each performance feature?
- What are the stock motifs or clichés that emerge?
- What sounds did you hear?
- What movements, colors, lights, and shapes did you see?
- What aromas did you smell?
- What sensations did you feel?
- What flavors did you taste?
- What did participants do with their voices? Common vocal actions include singing, acting, orating, narrating, or producing sound effects.
- What did participants do with their bodies? Common bodily actions include acting, instrument playing, and dancing.
- What did participants do with their words? Common word-related activities include poetry, singing, acting, orating, and narrating.
- What did participants do with objects? Common actions with objects include instrument playing, acting, spectacle, dancing, oratory, narrating, and presenting a communicative object.
- How did people express intensity, weight, flow?
- How did people organize time?

(See the *Manual* for further questions and activities.)

LENS #6: CONTENT

- Content is the subject matter or topic of an artistic event. It is most closely tied to symbols like words and movements in signed languages or dances. There may be multiple layers of meanings, which may be implied or explicit.

SAMPLE QUESTIONS AND ACTIVITIES

- How did participants communicate the subject matter at different points in the event?
- What was the event about? What else was it about? What was its most important point? Second most important point?
- What assumed background knowledge does someone who experiences the event need to understand the subject matter?
- Ask participants what they intended to communicate during the event.
- Ask participants what emotions or actions they hoped to elicit in other people because of the event.
- Ask participants what topics were angering, humorous, boring, or rousing?

(See the *Manual* for further questions and activities.)

LENS #7: UNDERLYING SYMBOLIC SYSTEMS

- Participants draw on all sorts of rules, expectations, grammatical structures, motivations, and experiences to decide what to do at any given moment of a performance. This is their cognitive and emotive environment, the hidden set of knowledge that participants share which allows composition and interpretation.
- Some underlying systems are simple and easily discoverable. For example, the cyclic pattern of an Indonesian *gamelan* piece is quickly discernible by noting the regular interval at which the big gong in the ensemble sounds. Similarly, the metric division of a Strauss waltz into groups of three beats, with an accented first beat, does not require extensive analysis. As another example, stock characters in Thai *likay* drama are easily recognizable after a brief description of their behavior and costume conventions.
- However, deriving some systems may take intensive, methodologically rigorous analysis, interview, and participation. For example, grammatical rules governing melodic or rhythmic structure of a song, the allowable movements in a dance, or the use of space in a painting are often not immediately evident. The *Manual* can give you further guidelines to begin analyzing the complexities.
- One underlying system that's common to each artistic event is the *degree of variability* its genre allows. You can research this by asking a wide variety of people questions like these:
  - Which characteristics do people state must exist in order for an event to be a good example of this genre?
  - What is acceptable but not necessary?
  - What is not permitted?
  - Is any of this contested?

- Look at the *Manual,* Step 4B, for specific examples of these questions in different artistic genres.
- Be aware that there are things you won't be able to understand about analyzing artistic production using just this written manual. For you to make the most of some of these activities—especially those related to performance features and underlying symbolic systems—you will need to study their specialized vocabulary with an expert.

Relate the event's genre(s) to its broader cultural context

Keep in mind that artistic characteristics are always intertwined with other realities in communities; you won't be able to fully understand the music, drama, dance, oral verbal arts, visual arts, or food without a more complete picture. In particular, locate the event in its broader physical context (nationally, regionally, and locally), and its broader temporal context (month, day, hour, season, and occurrence in the overall event).

Listed in this section are some very useful areas to investigate that will help gain more insight into how the art form you are studying fits into its culture and what you can learn about it as a result.

A. Artists

Get to know the artists involved in the art form you are studying. You may decide to study formally or informally with a skilled artist; join artists in their personal and artistic worlds; sit with a composer and see how he or she creates; ask to watch an artist teach someone else; or share your own life and artistic gifts with him or her.

- How do artists in this genre relate to their community?

What status does an artist hold in the community? Is there a difference in the status based on the type of art they do (such as drumming for royalty, creating songs for important events in a person's life, lewd drama for a brothel, etc.)?

- How do people become artists in this genre?

Is it based on societal patterns (artist caste), achieved by individual effort and skill, or a combination?

B. Creativity

Understanding creativity is a dynamic process and needs to be done through observations, questions, participation, and commissioning of new works. During this process you can discover who creates the new works and how they come into being. Are new works created deliberately and consciously, or received through visions? Are they created by an individual or a group? What techniques are used to create (improvisation, community creation, individual crafting)? Does the community value work that departs from tradition or enhances it? (The *Manual*, Step 4C, has a useful table for laying out the components of creativity.)

C. Language

The language, or languages, and types of language used in an artistic event can reveal much about its relationship to its broader cultural context. Song lyrics in a regional or national language support regional or national identity. A woven tapestry with words in a minority language, using that language's unique alphabet, accentuates identity with a minority community. It is also common in artistic communication to use archaic or special registers, forms not used in everyday speech. This may reflect a sense of mystery or fear associated with the genre, or it may simply have been frozen in that form for other reasons.

D. Transmission and change

How do people learn the skills of the art form? Is there a social structure or do they learn by watching? What changes in the process? Has it always been this way?

E. Cultural dynamism

Healthy communities maintain a mix of continuity and change. Artistic genres can feed into this vitality through interactions between their stable and malleable elements. *Stable elements* occur regularly in time and place and are tightly organized. *More malleable elements* are less predictable (perhaps marked by improvisation) and more loosely organized. Cultural dynamism happens when artists masterfully use the most malleable elements of their arts to invigorate the most stable.

F. Identity and power

How is authority affirmed or opposed in the artistic expression? Who is participating in the art and why? Are there hidden messages? Are the overt messages affirming or opposing a person, institution, or other entity?

G. Aesthetics and evaluation

Humans are quick to judge others' arts by their own aesthetic, but we must help ourselves and others not fall into this trap. Here are a few activities you can perform to find out how the community you're working with approaches correction and evaluation in general:

- Ask a friend how (or if) he or she would correct someone older, younger, and in roles of higher and lower status. The community might value direct correction in some contexts or require indirection.
- Ask the same friend how the kinds of people he or she just described would correct him or her.

Here are ways to explore evaluation, specifically on the form of artistic objects:

- Ask people what makes a component of an art form good or bad.
- Observe experts teaching an art form to someone else—perhaps you—and write down what advice they give or mistakes they correct. These may point to an ideal.
- Notice items that are put in a place of prominence, spoken of with reverence, or that take special expertise and time to create. These are likely to have ideal characteristics. Ask people what makes them good or pleasing.

H. Time

Time may flow more quickly, more slowly, or in unpredictably complex ways to someone experiencing a performance. Secondly, the structure, flow, and timing of a performance may intersect with broader cultural temporal patterns. In many communities certain events only occur at particular points in agricultural, religious, or other calendrical cycles.

I. Emotions

One of the most celebrated characteristics of artistic communication is its capacity to express and evoke emotion. Through observation and questions, find out what emotions are expressed and to what the audience is responding.

J. Subject matter

The verbal content of songs, proverbs, plays, tapestries, and other arts flows from the minds, experiences, and histories of the participating individuals and communities. Sometimes artistic communication reveals information about subjects available almost nowhere else, such as spiritual actors or historical events. Other times it communicates the values of the community in memorable form; proverbs are a strong example of this. The references of textual content may be metaphorical or cryptic, so your first understanding may not be the only one, or the deepest.

K. Community values shown

Artistic communication often provides a place to challenge community authorities. However, how it is organized and performed may also reflect a community's values and social structures in important ways. Reflecting on the physical and social organization of participants may provide clues to broader community values.

L. Communal investment

The amount of energy a community invests in different kinds of artistic activity varies widely. A grandfather speaking a proverb to his granddaughter involves only two people, requires no preparation, costs no money, and lasts for only a few seconds. A funeral for a king in western Cameroon, on the other hand, may last a month, include hundreds of people, and require significant finances to pay for food, transportation, and gifts. An assessment of the social, material, financial, and spiritual resources a community invests in an event provides important clues to its importance and influence.

STEP 5: SPARK CREATIVITY

A sparking activity is anything anybody does that results in the creation of new artistry. It will require different amounts of community investment, from low to high. For example, the act could be as casual as suggesting to a friend that she respond with painting during an oration at a meeting that afternoon, or entail the enormous complexity of planning a festival involving scores of artists and government officials.

A sparking activity may lead to immediate fruit or provide a structure where future creativity can happen. For example, artists may learn how to make, tune, and play a traditional instrument through a sparking activity, but this lays the foundation for composing new songs in the future. Finally, such an activity may fold in many or all of the seven Creating Local Arts Together (CLAT) steps or focus on just one. Workshops often include times to identify kingdom goals, perform initial analysis of a genre, and create and improve works. Other kinds of activities may focus solely on the act of creating. In any case, the community needs to see the sparking activity in the context of the whole cocreation process.

INTRODUCTION

SECTION 1: FOUNDATIONS

SECTION 2: STORIES

SECTION 3: TOOLS

CLOSING

THINGS TO WRITE DOWN WHEN DESIGNING A SPARKING ACTIVITY

- **Title and summary**: A brief overview of the activity and its main purposes. Include its overall type: commissioning, workshop, showcase event, mentoring, apprenticeship, publication, creators' club, or other. Overview should not be more than a paragraph long.
- **Participants**: All of the types of people who need to be involved for the activity to succeed. This may include creators and gatekeepers of various kinds. Identify actual people when possible.
- **Kinds of things you'll need from the Community Arts Profile**: Information someone needs to learn about the community or genre for the activity to succeed. Note which information is already in the Community Arts Profile and which still needs exploration.
- **Resources needed**: Financial, technical, logistical, formal, and other requirements needed to make the activity happen.
- **Tasks**: The items that someone needs to perform to carry out the activity. You may make these as detailed or broad as you like, depending on your context.
- **Big picture analysis**: Make three lists.
  1. CLAT steps included in the activity.
  2. CLAT steps done outside the activity, such as analysis of an event that someone else already completed.
  3. Plans to address any missing steps in the future.

How to organize a sparking activity

A. Prepare to draw on familiar methods of composition.

Each community and especially each creative individual has patterns they follow to create art, and you want to draw on those as much as possible. In a Mono example, a musician was asked to compose a new example of *gbaguru* based on one of Jesus' parables. He asked questions, thought awhile, started playing a repeated pattern on his *kundi*, then said he needed to be by himself to compose the song. Others may compose in a pair or group, with pencil and paper, in dreams or visions, on paid commission, with spontaneous improvisation, or use any number of methods. The activity you and the community design will likely include both familiar and new kinds of invention.

B. Think carefully about the key composer.[104]

This is the one person we cannot do without because of their artistic abilities, skill, and influence on others. It is important to look for this person, or people, who will create the best works and have the social credentials to help the project spread in the community.

---

104 The word "composer" here is meant to include anyone who creates something, including painters, weavers, dramatists, and the like.

There may be many such qualified people to choose from or only a few. Sometimes, for example, the choice of certain music genres will automatically determine the gender of the composer and performer. Local people will be able to make a list of potential experienced composers.

In some cultures there is already an established role for composers who create songs for other people. In West Africa, especially in areas influenced by Islam, there may be a local form of *griot* (praise singer). There are examples from Nigeria, Benin, and Ghana where such a Muslim praise singer agreed to work with a biblical text to compose and record a Scripture song.[105] Investigate the musical culture in your area to see if an institutionalized form of composing for patrons is already in place. Such professional composers are used to working for a cash payment. "Composers-for-hire" also appear in some Asian cultures, including parts of Nepal and the Philippines.

If you are working in a Christian community, it may be difficult to find someone who is both a Christian and an experienced composer in certain artistic genres. In this case, you can consider commissioning the work from a non-Christian composer. Questions to ask in this case: Are they interested? Are they respected by their community? If their name is made known, will that be a help or hindrance to acceptance of the work? What do local Christians think of the idea? Find out if an institutionalized form of composing for patrons is already in place. Note that such professional composers are used to working for some form of compensation.[106]

C.   Identify opportunities to maximize and barriers to overcome.

Identify barriers and opportunities in the community associated with creativity in the genre. Here are a few common examples of each:

Opportunities
- talented artists eager to use their gifts in new contexts
- government interest in promoting local art forms
- growing recognition of the value of local arts and fear for their loss in the wider community
- a respected champion of local arts and the community who could lead innovation

Barriers
- negative attitudes toward use of local language and art forms in some domains
- lack of knowledge and skills associated with a genre
- apathy toward change in the community
- weakening of interest in local cultural forms due to urbanization and globalization

After discussing these examples with members of the community, ask:

- What might help us spark a rich flowering of new works in this genre? How could we draw on these opportunities when designing a sparking activity?
- What might stop us from achieving this flowering? How could we overcome these barriers when designing a sparking activity?

---

105   Ibid.; Klaus Wedekind, "The Praise Singers," *Bible Translator* 26, no. 2 (1975): 245–47.

106   For examples of how this issue works out in some specific cultures, see Paul Neeley's chapter in this *Handbook*, "Commissioning Artistic Works," chpt. 147.

D. Organize an activity. Below are several types of activities that you could choose, depending on the need.

Decide on the type of activity

There are many types of activities that spark creativity. Choose one of the following options.

A. Commissioning

This is to charge an artist or group of artists with the task of creating a new instance of an artistic genre for an agreed-upon purpose. Commissioning commonly consists of these steps:

1. With the community, identify
   - *the event* for which the item will be created,
   - *the purpose(s)* for the created item (e.g., literacy, church worship, or community development),
   - *the genre* of creation (e.g., *haiku*, *olonkho*, or Broadway musical),
   - *the content*, and
   - *the creator(s)*.

2. Then
   - work with the maker(s) in the creative process, including evaluation and revision of the work(s);
   - prepare the rest of the community and the event organizers for a public presentation;
   - explore other distribution means, including recordings; and
   - explore ways that this work, and others like it, can enter into other domains of the community's life.

Find out what sort of compensation is appropriate for the artist, genre, and event. Compensation may be in the form of money, services, goods, social capital, or goodwill borne of friendship. Develop respect and trust with the artist(s).

It is also important to think through the commissioner's roles during the composition process. Who will decide what is good and what needs to be changed? How much freedom will the artist have to innovate? As much as possible, the commissioner and artist should agree on these things before the composition process begins.

It is possible to commission yourself to create a new work, but always do so in relationship with the community.

B. Workshops

Workshops are short events—typically one or two weeks—that gather people to make progress together on a particular task. A lot can be accomplished and produced when participants interact with each other in a concentrated way.

It is helpful to have an organization take care of logistics for the workshop. It is also important to set goals for the workshop, such as composing songs for church worship or creating and recording works with dramatic content to be distributed through radio or other media. See the *Manual*, Step 4D, for a sample workshop outline and the *Handbook* DVD for "Ideas for Arts Workshop Modules" by Todd and Mary Beth Saurman.

C. Showcase events

You may help a community plan or run a festival or competition that highlights creativity in local artistic genres. Festivals are events designed to showcase a community's cultural identity and creative output. Many ethnic or religious groups already have celebratory gatherings that may be open to including new works of art produced by Christians. It may also be possible to start a new festival tradition fueled by Christians' celebration of their God-given artistic gifts. Prizes for the best new works add energy and excitement. Festivals also provide great opportunities for cooperation between different Christian, cultural, religious, and other groups within a community.

Showcase events normally have five stages:

1. Imagining and planning
    How will we get from here to there? The larger the event, the more planning it requires. Some communities excel in creating detailed schedules and goals. Other communities excel in pulling together fabulous celebrations through organic social dynamics. Contribute ideas, but don't impose a system.

2. Promotion and networking
    How can we ensure the participation of key artists and a wide public? Festivals sometimes incorporate contests or prizes to motivate artists. Make sure to clearly communicate the kinds of arts that will be rewarded and how they will be evaluated.

3. Composition of and preparation for performance
    Will artists have time and resources to create and practice?

4. Running the event itself

5. Evaluation and planning
    A big event requires a dedicated time afterward to graciously evaluate how it went with key people. It's also a great moment to see how the event relates to all of the seven CLAT steps, and discuss the possibility of similar future events.

D. Mentoring

Sometimes because of your age, education, or social position, you may enter a long-term relationship that benefits an individual artist or group of artists. This relationship usually develops over time from personal rapport and common goals. Mentors may help influence a mentee's professional, spiritual, and character growth, opening doors to new opportunities and sharing instructive stories from their own lives. Mentorship includes reciprocal learning as well, especially if the relationship crosses cultures because the mentee will teach the mentor skills and cultural insights. Over time this bond often grows increasingly deep and satisfying.

E.   Structured apprenticeship

Apprenticeship consists of providing a structure consistent with existing cultural forms where artistic experts can transfer their skills and knowledge to other members of their community. Structured apprenticeship makes sense when experts in the genre exist, contexts for transfer of competencies in the genre are declining, but community members value it.

A community may institute such a program in this way:

1.   Choose the genre to be taught.
2.   Choose a master of the genre.
3.   Choose the apprentices.
4.   Design a training context that
    a.   draws on familiar educational forms;
    b.   includes a place, time, and frequency that the master and apprentices can commit to;
    c.   covers the knowledge, skills, and attitudes crucial to the genre; and
    d.   lasts long enough for apprentices to reach a sustainable level of competency.
5.   Implement the program.
6.   During the program, explore how participants can continue to develop their skills and perform in various contexts.

F.   Publications

Almost any activity will have more long-term success if it turns thoughts and artistic production into media other than live performance. Paper, recordings, and electronic data of all kinds allow ideas and artistry to live beyond a single moment and reach people beyond a single place. Periodicals and websites make it possible to disseminate information and inspire discussion on a wide range of topics. Audio and video products can be used to provide content for training programs and entertainment. And publications become repositories of history and biography when people begin to forget what came before them.

General aspects to planning a publication include the following:

1.   Determine the target audience.
2.   Identify editors, advisors, and contributors.
3.   Solicit, select, and prepare the materials to be published.
4.   Determine a scheme for the distribution of the publication.
5.   Determine a schedule for ongoing publication.
6.   Carry out the publication and distribution.
7.   Develop and use feedback tools (e.g., electronic comments, letters to the editor, surveys, etc.) to help determine past effectiveness and plan for future developments.

G. Creators' clubs

Artists form associations, clubs, and fellowships to encourage each other, critique each others' work, share resources and ideas, perform, and collaborate on products. Groups like these meet regularly in certain places and times, have expectations—however modest—of each other, and often center on a particular art form and purpose.

Each group will look different, but you should consider the following subjects when starting or modifying a group:

- A meeting place and time that accommodates the members and allows for artistic activity.
- A discussion of the goals for the group and expectations of its members. This could vary from very fluid and informal to strict and explicit, depending on the group's wishes.
- If the group forms part of a church or wants to create things for Christian communities, then it's essential to integrate spiritual formation into its activities. Artists act like God in their creativity (except that he creates out of nothing), and sometimes get drawn into unhealthy applications of the power they yield. Prayer, Bible study, accountability, and other disciplines need to provide a spiritual anchor for all artists' creative directions and performance.

For information on how to design a new (or modify an existing) activity, see the *Manual* for examples, especially those in the section on Kingdom Goals (Step 2).

STEP 6: IMPROVE NEW WORKS

> Do not let any unwholesome talk come out of your mouths, but only what is helpful
> for building others up according to their needs, that it may benefit those who listen.
> (Eph 4:29)

Evaluate the new work according to criteria agreed upon with the community. Remember that the goal of evaluating is construction, not destruction; building up, not tearing down. Note, too, that the community can greatly reduce the need for critique by including the right people from the beginning of the cocreative process: social and religious leaders, expert creators, and expert performers.

How do you decide what art is good or bad? Evaluation is complex, but there are tools that can guide the whole process.

Trust the system

Groups usually share a sense of when a work of art is good or not and have ways of communicating what needs to be fixed. Research how correction normally works in the community. In some situations they may get rid of inferior products by blocking them from future presentation and letting them die.

Evaluate according to effects

In Step 3 you identified the effects that new artistry should have on people in order to move them toward kingdom goals. Observe and ask about people's responses to the new bits of artistry. Did it have the effects you wanted? If an orator's performance is meant to motivate people to join a parade celebrating their ethnic identity, but participants watch distractedly and then disperse to their homes, then the oration failed.

Relax but keep learning

You can't study all of the possible signs, so do this: watch people's reactions and listen to what they say and dip into research activities related to the genres you're working with regularly (see the *Manual*, Step 4, for examples)—maybe one activity a week or month.

Identify what kinds of evaluation should happen when

Evaluation can take place during the initial creation of the work, and/or after it has been presented, as you help people reflect on the work.

AN APPROACH TO EFFECTIVE EVALUATION

Identify and work through **local social structures**, and together define the criteria for evaluating the work. Identify the following aspects of the artistic event:

- The **elements**. These should include how the work utilizes space, materials, participants, shape through time, performance features, feeling, content, themes, and community values.
- The **purpose(s)**. These could include to educate, motivate to action, etc.
- **People** to include in the process of evaluation. These people need to have the knowledge, skills, and respect necessary to critique various elements.
- **Objects** that can provide a focal point and reference for discussion, so that you don't have to rely exclusively on memory for critique. These could include song texts, drama scripts, musical notation, masks, dance moves, and video and audio recordings.

Together **affirm** the aspects of the creation that work well, and encourage the creators to **do something even better** based on the evaluation.

There are several tests that are important to do when you are working long term with a community. Even short-term work should be subjected to evaluation. A full description of these tests can be found in the *Manual*, and they includes tests for meaning, naturalness, ownership, and accuracy.

STEP 7: INTEGRATE AND CELEBRATE FOR CONTINUITY

We don't just want to see new arts created for the kingdom once, but again and again and again. So it is also essential to plan for the future. A good place to start is to reflect with the community on the ways that they teach each other things like new songs, dances, and carving skills. If possible, their plans should include these means of transmission. In order to keep creativity going, the community may decide to repeat sparking activities like workshops or commissioning. Existing social groups like dance associations or literacy clubs may also have motivation to keep creating. Or communities might decide to form new groups that meet regularly to help members create for kingdom purposes.

CONCLUSION

If you have been following the CLAT process, there is not much more to say about integrating and celebrating. This is because the most important way to keep something good going is to start it in the right way. This process encourages you to make relationships, encourage others to create, get to know and value artists, plan, include all of the important artists and decision makers in sparking activities, and help make artistic products and their presentation better.

This overview will get you started and hopefully will inspire you to dig more deeply into the detailed and broader steps found in the *Manual* itself.

INTRODUCTION

SECTION 1: FOUNDATIONS

SECTION 2: STORIES

SECTION 3: TOOLS

CLOSING

535

INTRODUCTION

SECTION 1: FOUNDATIONS

SECTION 2: STORIES

SECTION 3: TOOLS

CLOSING

BIBLIOGRAPHY

Allen, Ronald, and Gordon Borror. *Worship: Rediscovering the Missing Jewel.* Portland, OR: Multnomah Press, 1988.

Allender, Dan B. "The Hidden Hope in Lament." *Mars Hill Review* 1 (Winter-Spring 1995): 25-37.

Allmen, J. J. von. *Worship: Its Theology and Practice.* New York: Oxford University Press, 1965.

ArtWay. "ArtWay Visual Meditation March 18, 2012." http://www.artway.eu/content.asp?id=1142&action=show&lang=en.

Ausland, Aaron. "Facipulation." *Staying for Tea.* June 5, 2011. http://stayingfortea.org/2011/06/05/ (accessed October 22, 2011).

Bailey, David M. *Arrabon: Learning Reconciliation through Community and Worship Music.* Richmond, VA: Lulu, 2011.

Bailey, John M., ed. *Pursuing the Mission of God in Church Planting.* Alpharetta, GA: North American Mission Board, 2006.

Balisky, Lila W. "Theology in Song: Ethiopia's Tesfaye Gabbiso." *Missiology: An International Review* 25, no. 4 (1997): 447-56.

Balonek, Michael. "'You Can Use That in the Church?' Musical Contextualization and the Sinhala Church." Master's thesis, Bethel University, 2009.

Barker, Jeff. *The Storytelling Church: Adventures in Reclaiming the Role of Story in Worship.* Cleveland, TN: Webber Institute Books, 2011.

Bartholomew, Craig G., and Michael W. Goheen. *The Drama of Scripture: Finding Our Place in the Biblical Story.* Grand Rapids: Baker Academic, 2004.

Barz, Gregory F. *Performing Religion: Negotiating Past and Present in Kwaya Music of Tanzania.* New York: Editions Rodopi B. V., 2003.

Bateman, Herbert W. *Authentic Worship: Hearing Scripture's Voice, Applying Its Truths.* Grand Rapids: Kregel Academic & Professional, 2002.

Beck, Guy L., ed. *Sacred Sound: Experiencing Music in World Religions.* Waterloo, Canada: Wilfrid Laurier University Press, 2006.

Bediako, Kwame. *Jesus and the Gospel in Africa: History and Experience.* Maryknoll, NY: Orbis Books, 2004.

Begbie, Jeremy S. *Beholding the Glory: Incarnation through the Arts.* Grand Rapids: Baker Books, 2000.

Berhane, Helen, with Emma Newrick. *Song of the Nightingale.* Tyrone, GA: Authentic Media, 2009.

Bernardi, Philip. *Improvisation Starters: A Collection of 900 Improvisation Situations for the Theater.* Cincinnati: Betterway Books, 1992.

Best, Harold M. *Unceasing Worship: Biblical Perspectives on Worship and the Arts.* Downers Grove: InterVarsity Press, 2003.

Black, Cathy. *Culturally-conscious Worship.* St. Louis: Chalice Press. 2000.

Blacking, John. "Music, Culture, and Experience." In *Music, Culture and Experience*, edited by Reginald Byron, 223–42. Chicago: Chicago University Press, 1995.

Blume, Friedrich. *Protestant Church Music: A History.* New York: Norton, 1974.

Bohlman, Philip V., Edith W. Blumhofer, and Maria M. Chow. *Music in American Religious Experience.* New York: Oxford University Press, 2006.

Boogaart, Thomas A. "Drama and the Sacred: Recovering the Dramatic Tradition in Scripture and Worship." In *Touching the Altar: The Old Testament for Christian Worship*, edited by Carol M. Bechtel, 35–61. Grand Rapids: Eerdmans, 2008.

Borchert, Gerard L. *Worship in the New Testament: Divine Mystery and Human Response*. St. Louis: Chalice Press, 2008.

Borrup, Tom. *The Creative Community Builder's Handbook: How to Transform Communities Using Local Assets, Art, and Culture*. St. Paul, MN: Fieldstone Alliance, 2006.

Bowden, Sandra, and Dianne B. Collard, eds. *Helps in Planning and Developing Church-related Galleries*. Wenham, MA: CIVA, 2009.

Brand, Hilary, and Adrienne Chaplin. *Art and Soul: Signposts for Christians in the Arts*. Downers Grove: InterVarsity Press, 2001.

Braun, Joachim. *Music in Ancient Israel/Palestine: Archaeological, Written, and Comparative Sources*. Grand Rapids: Eerdmans, 2002.

Brink, Emily R., and Bert Polman, eds. *Psalter Hymnal Handbook*. Grand Rapids: Faith Alive Christian Resources, 1998.

———, and Walter Brueggemann. *The Message of the Psalms: A Theological Commentary*. Minneapolis: Augsburg Publishing House, 1995.

Brueggemann, Walter. *Israel's Praise: Doxology against Idolatory and Ideology*. Philadelphia: Fortress Press, 1988.

———. *Psalms and the Life of Faith*. Edited by Patrick D. Miller. Minneapolis: Fortress Press, 1995.

Byam, L. Dale. *Community in Motion: Theatre for Development in Africa*. Edited by Henry A. Giroux. Westport, CT: Bergen & Garvey, 1999.

Campbell, Robert. "Believing Is Singing." *EM News* 3, no. 1 (1994).

Center for Worship. "Master of Arts in Ethnomusicology." Liberty University. http://www.liberty.edu/academics/religion/centerforworship/index.cfm?PID=17234.

Chambers, Robert. *Ideas for Development*. Sterling, VA: Earthscan, 2005.

Chan, Simon. *Liturgical Theology: The Church as Worshiping Community*. Downers Grove: InterVarsity Press, 2006.

Chapell, Bryan. *Christ-centered Worship: Letting the Gospel Shape Our Practice*. Grand Rapids: Baker Academic, 2009.

Chenoweth, Vida, and Darlene Bee. "On Ethnic Music." *Practical Anthropology* 15 (September–October 1968): 212.

Cherry, Constance M. *The Worship Architect*. Grand Rapids: Baker Academic, 2010.

Collard, Dianne B. "The Role of Visual Art in the (Free) Evangelical Churches in Germany and Spain." DMiss diss., Biola University, 2004.

Collinge, Ian. "A Kaleidoscope of Doxology: Exploring Ethnodoxology and Theology." *Doon Theological Journal* 8, no. 1 (March 2011).

Corbett, Steve, and Brian Fikkert. "Doing Short-term Missions without Doing Long-term Harm." In *When Helping Hurts: How to Alleviate Poverty without Hurting the Poor—and Yourself*, 161–80. Chicago: Moody Publishers, 2009.

Corbitt, J. Nathan. *The Sound of the Harvest: Music's Mission in Church and Culture*. Grand Rapids: Baker Books, 1998.

———, and Vivian Nix-Early. *Taking It to the Streets: Using the Arts to Transform Your Community*. Grand Rapids: Baker Books, 2003.

Crouch, Andy. *Culture Making: Recovering our Creative Calling*. Downers Grove, IL: InterVarsity, 2008.

Darkwa, Asante. "New Horizons in Music and Worship in Ghana." *African Urban Studies* 8, African Studies Center, Michigan State University (Fall 1980): 69.

Davis, John Jefferson. *Worship and the Reality of God: An Evangelical Theology of Real Presence.* Downers Grove: InterVarsity Press, 2010.

Dawn, Marva J. *How Shall We Worship?* Wheaton: Tyndale House, 2003.

———. *Reaching Out without Dumbing Down: A Theology of Worship for This Urgent Time.* Grand Rapids: Eerdmans, 1995.

DeNeui, Paul H. "What Happened when Grandma Danced." *Mission Frontiers* 23, no. 2 (June 2001): 18–19.

———, ed. *Communicating Christ through Story and Song.* Pasadena: William Carey Library, 2008.

Dicran, C. H. "Hindi Christian Bhajans: A Survey of Their Use by Christians and a Critique by Hindu Professionals in the Music World." Master's thesis, Briercrest Biblical Seminary, 2000.

Dillenberger, John. *Images and Relics: Theological Perceptions and Visual Images in Sixteenth Century Europe.* New York: Oxford University Press, 1999.

Dix, Gregory. *The Shape of the Liturgy.* London: Dacre Press, 1949.

Dolbeer, M. L. "The Caste Mass Movements in the Telugu Area." *National Christian Council Review* 52, no. 8 (August 1933): 425.

Dowley, Tim. *Christian Music: A Global History.* Minneapolis: Fortress Press, 2011.

Duncan, Stephen Frederick. "Christian Bhajans: A Study of the Uses of Indigenous Music in the Rites of the Catholic Church on the Sub-continent of India since the Second Vatican Council with Particular Attention to Bhajan and Kirtan." PhD diss., Memphis State University, 1992.

Duerksen, Darren. "Ecclesial Identities in a Multi-faith Context: Jesus Truth-gatherings (*Yeshu Satsangs*) among Hindus and Sikhs in Northwest India." PhD diss., Fuller Theological Seminary, 2011.

Dye, T. Wayne. *The Bible Translation Strategy: An Analysis of Its Spiritual Impact.* Dallas: Wycliffe Bible Translators, 1980.

Dyrness, William A. *Learning about Theology from the Third World.* Grand Rapids: Zondervan, 1990.

———. *A Primer on Christian Worship.* Grand Rapids: Eerdmans, 2009.

———. *Visual Faith: Art, Theology, and Worship in Dialogue.* Grand Rapids: Baker Academic, 2001.

Eck, Diana L. *A New Religious America: How a "Christian Country" Has Become the World's Most Religiously Diverse Nation.* New York: HarperCollins, 2001.

EthnoDoxology. Paul Neeley, ed. Duncanville, TX: Artists in Christian Testimony.

The Ethnomusicology and Arts Group. "Arts Consultant: Understanding." SIL International, 2007; 4 min., 58 sec.; video. Applied Linguistics Department, "Master of Arts in World Arts," Graduate Institute of Applied Linguistics. http://www.gial.edu/academics/world-arts.

Evans, Mark. *Open Up the Doors: Music in the Modern Church.* London: Equinox, 2006.

Eubank, L. Allan. *Dance-drama before the Throne: A Thai Experience.* Chiang Mai: TCF Press, 2004.

Farhadian, Charles E. *Christian Worship Worldwide: Expanding Horizons, Deepening Practices.* Grand Rapids: Eerdmans, 2007.

Feintuch, Burt, ed. *Eight Words for the Study of Expressive Culture.* Chicago: University of Illinois Press, 2003.

Fortunato, Frank, ed., with Paul Neeley and Carol Brinneman. *All the World Is Singing: Glorifying God through the Worship Music of the Nations.* Tyrone, GA: Authentic, 2006.

Frakes, Jack. *Acting for Life: A Textbook on Acting.* Colorado Springs: Meriwether, 2005.

Fujino, Gary. "'Glocal' Japanese Self-identity: A Missiological Perspective on Paradigmatic Shifts in Urban Tokyo." *International Journal of Frontier Missiology* 27, no. 4 (Winter 2010): 171–82.

———. "O Happy Day! Using Gospel Choirs to Multiply Congregations." *Japan Harvest* 62, no. 2 (Fall 2010): 14.

Gardner, Larrie. "Demystifying Mentoring." Unpublished paper, 2003.

———. "Mentoring: The Urgent Task." Unpublished paper, 2000.

Global Consultation on Music and Missions: The Proceedings. CD-ROM of GCoMM consultation held at Bethel University, St. Paul, MN, July 11-15, 2006; edited by Paul Neeley, Linda Neeley, Paul McAndrew, and Cathy McAndrew. Duncanville, TX: EthnoDoxology/ACT, 2006.

Gustafson, Gerrit. *The Adventure of Worship: Discovering Your Highest Calling.* Grand Rapids: Chosen Books, 2006.

Hale, Chris. "Aradhna: From Comfort to Discomfort, Church to Temple." *International Journal of Frontier Missiology* 24, no. 3 (Fall 2007): 147–50.

Harris, Robin P., and Frank Fortunato. "The Crescendo of Local Arts in Orality." In *Orality Breakouts: Using Heart Language to Transform Hearts,* edited by Samuel E. Chiang et al., 113-18. Hong Kong: International Orality Network / LCWE.

Hastings, Adrian. *African Christianity.* New York: Seabury Press, 1976.

Hatcher, Mark J. "Poetry, Singing, and Contextualization." *Missiology: An International Review* 29, no. 4 (2001): 475-88.

Hayford, Jack, John Killinger, and Howard Stevenson. *Mastering Worship.* Portland, OR: Multnomah Press, 1990.

Heath, Chip, and Dan Heath. *Made to Stick: Why Some Ideas Survive and Others Die.* New York: Random House, 2007.

Henri, Robert. *The Art Spirit.* Cambridge, MA: Basic Books, 2007.

Hiebert, Paul. *Anthropological Insights for Missionaries.* Grand Rapids: Baker Books, 1986.

———. *Mission et Culture.* Translated by Gérard Chaillon. St-Legier, Switzerland: Editions Emmaüs, 2002. Originally published as *Anthropological Insights for Missionaries* (Grand Rapids: Baker Books, 1986).

Hill, Andrew E. *Enter His Courts with Praise!* Grand Rapids: Baker Books, 1993.

Hill, Margaret. *Using Your Bible: A Manual in Scripture Use.* UK: Wycliffe Bible Translators, 1993.

———, and Harriet Hill. "Engaging People with Scripture through Drama." Ch. 23 in *Translating the Bible into Action.* Carlisle, UK: Piquant Editions, 2010.

———, et al. *Healing the Wounds of Trauma: How the Church Can Help.* Nairobi: Paulines Publications Africa, 2004.

Hipps, Shane. *Flickering Pixels: How Technology Shapes Your Faith.* Grand Rapids: Zondervan, 2009.

———. *The Hidden Power of Electronic Culture: How Media Shapes Faith, the Gospel, and Church.* Grand Rapids: Zondervan, 2005.

Hollingsworth, Ken. "Hymnbooks as a Stimulus to Reading—and More." *EM News* 8, no. 4 (1999): 5.

Hope DVD. Mars Hill Productions, 2002. http://www.mars-hill.org.

Hope DVD (Central Tibetan Adaptation). Kathmandu, Nepal: Mars Hill Productions and Promise Productions Private Lmt. of Kathmandu, 2007. http://www.rewahope.com/tibetanthangka.

Hunter, George. *The Celtic Way of Evangelism: How Christianity Can Reach the West . . . Again.* Nashville: Abingdon Press, 2000.

Hustad, Donald P. *Jubilate! Church Music in the Evangelical Tradition.* Carol Stream, IL: Hope Publishing, 1980.

International Arts Movement Conference, "Redemptive Culture: Creating the World that Ought to Be," February 23, 2007, New York City.

Issue Group on Redeeming the Arts. "Redeeming the Arts: The Restoration of the Arts to God's Creational Intention." Lausanne Occasional Paper No. 46. Forum for World Evangelization, Pattaya, Thailand, September 29 to October 5, 2004. http://www.lausanne.org/docs/2004forum/LOP46_IG17.pdf.

Jenkins, Philip. *The New Faces of Christianity: Believing the Bible in the Global South.* New York: Oxford University Press, 2006.

———. *The Next Christendom: The Coming of Global Christianity.* New York: Oxford University Press, 2002.

Johnson, Jean, and Diane Campbell. *Worldview Strategic Church Planting among Oral Cultures: A Field Guide for Contemporary Grass-roots Cross-cultural Church Planters and Trainers of National Church Planters.* Springfield, MO: Life Publishers International, 2007.

Johnson, Todd M., and Kenneth R. Ross, eds. *Atlas of Global Christianity 1910–2010.* Edinburgh: Edinburgh University Press, 2009.

Josephus, Flavius. "Antiquities of the Jews." Bk. 14, ch. 7.2 in *The Complete Works.* Translated by W. Whiston. Reprint, Grand Rapids: Kregel, 1960.

Kauflin, Bob. *Worship Matters: Leading Others to Encounter the Greatness of God.* Wheaton: Crossway, 2008.

Kaushal, Molly, ed. *Chanted Narratives: The Living "Katha-Vachana" Tradition.* New Delhi: Indira Gandhi National Centre for the Arts, 2001.

Key, Mary. "Hymn Writing with Indigenous Tunes." *Practical Anthropology* 9 (November–December 1962): 258–59.

Kidd, Reggie M. *With One Voice: Discovering Christ's Song in Our Worship.* Grand Rapids: Baker Books, 2005.

King, Roberta R. "The Impact of Global Christian Music in Worship." In *Theology, News, and Notes.* Pasadena: Fuller Theological Seminary, Spring 2006. http://www.worldofworship.org/cd/Site/global/TheImpactofGlobalChristianMusicinWorship.pdf (accessed June 14, 2012).

———. *Pathways in Christian Music Communication: The Case of the Senufo of Côte d'Ivoire.* American Society of Missiology Monograph Series 3. Eugene, OR: Pickwick Publications, 2009.

———. *A Time to Sing: A Manual for the African Church.* Nairobi: Evangel Publishing House, 1999.

———, Jean Ngoya Kidula, James R. Krabill, and Thomas Oduro. *Music in the Life of the African Church.* Waco: Baylor University Press, 2008.

Kinney, Kedra Larsen. "Your Ways Are Straight: A Scripture Song Workshop in Sierra Leone." *EthnoDoxology* 4, no. 2 (2010): 20–21.

Koehler, Paul E. *Telling God's Stories With Power—Biblical Storytelling In Oral Cultures.* Pasadena: William Carey Library, 2010.

Kolb, David. *Experiential Learning: Experience as the Source of Learning and Development.* Upper Saddle River, NJ: Pearson Education, 1983.

Krabill, James R. "Gospel Meets Culture." Ch. 7 in *Is It Insensitive to Share Your Faith?* Intercourse, PA: Good Books, 2005.

———. "The Hymnody of the Harrist Church among the Dida of South-central Ivory Coast (1913–1949): An Historico-religious Study." *Studies in the Intercultural History of Christianity*, vol. 74. Frankfurt: Peter Lang, 1995.

Kraft, Charles H. *Anthropology for Christian Witness*. Maryknoll, NY: Orbis Books, 1996.

———. *Christianity in Culture*. Maryknoll, NY: Orbis Books, 1979.

———. *Communication Theory for Christian Witness*. Revised ed. Maryknoll, NY: Orbis Books, 1991.

———. "What Kind of Encounters Do We Need?" *Evangelical Missions Quarterly* 27, no. 3 (1991): 258–65.

Krauss, M. "The World's Languages in Crisis." *Language* 68, no. 1 (1992): 4–10.

Lapiz, Ed. *Pagpapahiyang: Redeeming Culture and Indigenizing Christianity*. Paranaque City, Philippines: CSM Publishing, 2010.

Lenski, R. C. H. *Interpretation of the Acts of the Apostles*. Minneapolis: Augsburg, 1961.

Leonard, Richard C. "Singing the Psalms: A Brief History of Psalmody." Laudemont Ministries. http://www.laudemont.org/a-stp.htm (accessed October 2, 2010).

Lilley, Ian. "Archaeology, Diaspora and Decolonization." *Journal of Social Archaeology* 6, no. 1 (2006): 28–47.

Lillo, Kember. "Dééba's Story." *EthnoDoxology* 2, no. 4 (2010): 22–23.

Lim, Swee Hong. *Giving Voice to Asian Christians: An Appraisal of the Pioneering Work of I-to Loh in the Area of Congregational Song*. Dudweiler, Germany: VDM Verlag Dr. Muller Aktiengesellschaft & Co. KG., 2008.

Lipman, Doug. *Storytelling Workshop in a Box*. Story Dynamics. http://www.storydynamics.com/publications/Memberships/swb.html.

Loh, I-to. *Hymnal Companion to "Sound the Bamboo": Asian Hymns in Their Cultural and Liturgical Contexts*. Chicago: GIA Publishers, 2011.

———. *In Search for Asian Sounds and Symbols in Worship*. Edited by Michael Nai-Chiu Poon. Singapore: Trinity Theological College, 2012.

———. "Revisiting Ways of Contextualization of Church Music in Asia." *Theology and the Church* 30, no. 2 (2005): 450–74.

———. "Sound a Mystic Bamboo Song: Sounds and Images of Christ in Asian Hymns." Plenary address, annual conference of the Hymn Society in the United States and Canada, Colorado Springs, July 17–21, 2011.

———. "Toward Contextualization of Church Music in Asia." In *Hymnology Annual*, edited by Vernon Wicker. Vol. 1, 89–114. Berrien Springs, MI: Vande Vere Publishing, 1991.

———, Francisco Feliciano, and James Minchin, eds. *Sound the Bamboo: CCA Hymnal 2000*. Tainan: CCA / Taiwan Church Press, 2000.

Magowan, Fiona. *Melodies of Mourning: Music and Emotion in Northern Australia*. World Anthropology. Oxford: James Currey, 2007.

Maire, Charles-Daniel. *Parole de Dieu & Cultures des Hommes*. Valence, France: Editions LLB, 2006.

Man, Ron. "Global Worship: What in the World Can I Do about It?" *Worship Leader* (November–December 2009): 82.

———. "Lessons from Global Worship." Paper presented to the Biblical Worship Section of the Evangelical Theological Society, San Francisco, CA, November 2011.

———.."Worship Bridges." *Worship Leader* (September 2005): 18–21.

Mayer-Thurman, Christa C. *Raiment for the Lord's Service: A Thousand Years of Western Vestments*. Chicago: Art Institute, 1975.

McLaughlin, Buzz. *The Playwright's Process: Learning the Craft from Today's Leading Dramatists*. New York: Back Stage Books, 1997.

Merriam, Alan. *The Anthropology of Music.* Evanston, IL: Northwestern University Press, 1964.

Mission Frontiers. July 2, 1996. http://www.missionfrontiers.org/issue/archive/worship-and-missions.

Mitman, F. Russell. *Worship in the Shape of Scripture.* Cleveland, OH: The Pilgrim Press, 2001.

Montagu, Jeremy. *Musical Instruments of the Bible.* Oxford: Scarecrow Press, 2002.

Moon, Steve S. C. "NamSeoul Grace Church: Glorifying God through the Arts." In William D. Taylor, ed., "Arts in Mission," special issue, *Connections: The Journal of the WEA Mission Commission* 9, nos. 2 and 3 (September 2010): 40.

Moon, W. Jay. *African Proverbs Reveal Christianity in Culture: A Narrative Portrayal of Builsa Proverbs Contextualizing Christianity in Ghana.* American Society of Missiology Monograph Series 5. Eugene, OR: Pickwick Publications, 2009.

———. "Sweet Talk in Africa: Using Proverbs in Ministry." *Evangelical Missions Quarterly* 40, no. 2 (2004): 162–69.

Muljadi, Gandhi, and Angeline Muljadi. "Wayang." Batik 'n Craft. http://www.batikncraft.com/art-in-indonesia/wayang.

Morse, Laverne R. "Ethnomusicology: A New Frontier." *Evangelical Missions Quarterly* 11 (January 1975): 35.

Myers, Bryant L. *Walking with the Poor: Principles and Practices of Transformational Development.* Maryknoll, NY: Orbis Books, 1

Nairobi Statement on Worship and Culture: Contemporary Challenges and Opportunities. Lutheran World Federation, Department for Theology and Studies, 1996. http://www.worship.ca/docs/lwf_ns.html (accessed June 15, 2012). For Spanish and Korean translations of the Nairobi Statement visit the Calvin Institute of Christian Worship website, Resource Library: http://www.calvin.edu/worship.

Neeley, Paul. "A Case Study: Commissioning Scripture Songs among the Akyode of Ghana." *Research Review* (Legon, Ghana: University of Ghana), *supplementary issue*, no. 10 (1997): 118–29.

———. "Reflections of a Gatekeeper." *EM News* 6, no. 1 (1997).

Nethercott, Paul. "Japanese Flock to Join Black Gospel Choirs: Churches Harness New Outreach Strategy." *World Pulse*, June 4, 2004. http://www.jbfjapan.com/creative/images/WordPulseInterview.pdf.

Nicholls, Kathleen. *Asian Arts and Christian Hope.* New Delhi: Select Books, 1983.

Nketia, J. H. Kwabena. "The Contribution of African Culture to Christian Worship." *International Review of Missions* 47 (1958): 274.

O'Connor, Kathleen M. *Lamentations and the Tears of the World.* Maryknoll, NY: Orbis Books, 2002.

Old, Hughes Oliphant. *Leading in Prayer—A Workbook for Worship.* Grand Rapids: William B. Eerdmans Publishing Company, 1995.

———. *Worship—Reformed According to Scripture, Revised and Expanded Edition.* Louisville: Westminster John Knox Press, 2002.

Ong, Walter J. *Orality and Literacy: The Technologizing of the Word.* London: Methuen, 1982.

Opstal, Sandra van. *The Mission of Worship.* Downers Grove: InterVarsity Press, 2012.

Oswald, John. "Gospel Communication in Tibetan Song." In *Communicating Christ through Story and Song: Orality in Buddhist Contexts*, edited by Paul H. DeNeui, 237–72. Pasadena: William Carey Library, 2008.

———. *A New Song Rising in Tibetan Hearts: Tibetan Christian Worship in the Early 21st Century.* Thailand: Central Asian Publishing, 2001.

INTRODUCTION

SECTION 1: FOUNDATIONS

SECTION 2: STORIES

SECTION 3: TOOLS

CLOSING

Parkinson, Michael. "Visual Marketing Matters." 24 Hour Company. http://www.24hrco.com/images/articles/VisualMarketingMatters.pdf.

Pederson, Steve. *Drama Ministry*, CD. Grand Rapids: Zondervan, 1999.

Peterson, David. *Engaging with God: A Biblical Theology of Worship*. Reprint. Downers Grove: InterVarsity Press, 2002.

Peterson, Eugene H. *Eat This Book: A Conversation in the Art of Spiritual Reading*. Grand

Rapids: William B. Eerdmans Publishing Company, 2006.

———. "The Pastor: How Artists Shape Pastoral Identity." In *For the Beauty of the Church*, edited by W. David O. Taylor, 83–101. Grand Rapids: Baker Books, 2010.

Pierce, John. "Faith and the Arts: Baileys Share in Bali's Diverse, Creative Culture." *Baptists Today News Journal* 29, no. 8 (August 2011): 4–5. http://issuu.com/baptiststoday/docs/btaugust11_071611final?mode=a_p&wmode=0.

Piper, John. *Gravity and Gladness on Sunday Morning: The Pursuit of God in Corporate Worship*, 3rd ed. Minneapolis: Desiring God Ministries, 2010.

———. *Let the Nations Be Glad: The Supremacy of God in Missions*. Grand Rapids: Baker Book House, 2003.

Ponraj, S. Devasagayam. *Tribal Challenge and the Church's Response: A Study of the Problems of the Tribals in India and the Possible Response from the Church in Terms of Holistic Mission*. Madhupur, India: Mission Educational Books, 1996.

Poplawska, Marzanna. "Wayang Wahyu as an Example of Christian Forms of Shadow Theatre." *Asian Theatre Journal* 21, no. 2 (Autumn 2004): 2–6.

Priest, Robert J. "Tell Me about a Time You Were Bad." *CIU Quarterly* (Winter 1994): 4–6.

———. "Missionary Elenctics: Conscience and Culture." *Missiology* 22, no. 3 (July 1994): 291–315.

Ramshaw, Gail. *Christian Worship: 100,000 Sundays of Symbols and Rituals*. Minneapolis: Fortress Press, 2009.

Rayl, Scott. "Tibetan Christian Thangka Ministry." *Indigenous Jesus*. November 22, 2011. http://indigenousjesus.blogspot.com/2011/11/tibetan-christian-thangka-ministry.html.

Redman, Matt. "The Kingdom Mind-set of a Mentor." In *Inside Out Worship: Insights for Passionate and Purposeful Worship*, edited by Matt Redman et al., 139–44. Portland: Regal, 2005.

Richard, H. L. *Christ-Bhakti: Narayan Vaman Tilak and Christian Work among Hindus*. Delhi: ISPCK, 1991.

Ripken, Nik. "Victorious Faith in the Midst of Persecution." Manuscript, n.d.

Roberts, Bob, Jr. *Glocalization: How Followers of Jesus Engage a Flat World*. Grand Rapids: Zondervan, 2007.

Robbins, Frank. "Mentoring in SIL and WBT." Paper presented at the SIL Africa Area Conference, May 1998.

———. "Mentoring in SIL and WBT: A Sequel." Unpublished paper, 2001.

Ross, Allen P. *Recalling the Hope of Glory: Biblical Worship from the Garden to the New Creation*. Grand Rapids: Kregel, 2006.

Routley, Erik, and Paul A. Richardson. *Panorama of Christian Hymnody*. Chicago: GIA Publications, 2005.

Rowe, Julisa. *Dramatising Scripture: A Step by Step Guide to Bringing the Word Alive*. Nairobi: Daystar Research Centre, 2010.

Russ, Eric. "Discipling African-Americans in an Urban Context." Gospel Centered Discipleship. http://www.gospelcentereddiscipleship.com/discipling-african-americans-in-an-urban-context/?format=pdf.

Ryken, Philip Graham. *Give Praise to God—A Vision for Reforming Worship, Celebrating the Legacy of James Montgomery Boice.* Phillipsburg, NJ: P&R Publishing, 2003.

Sacred Congregation of Rites. *Instruction on Music in the Liturgy.* Second Vatican Council, 1967. http://www.ewtn.com/library/curia/cdwmusic.htm.

Sacred Dance Guild. http://www.sacreddanceguild.org (accessed October 11, 2011).

Saint Augustine. *St. Augustine Confessions.* Translated by Henry Chadwick. New York: Oxford University Press, 1992.

Schrag, Brian. *Creating Local Arts Together: A Manual to Help Communities Reach Their Kingdom Goals.* Edited by James Krabill. Pasadena: William Carey Library, 2013.

———, and Paul Neeley, eds. *All the World Will Worship: Helps for Developing Indigenous Hymns.* 3rd ed. Duncanville, TX: EthnoDoxology Publications, 2005.

Scott, Graham R., and Eleonora L. Scott. "Heart-Language Worship in Multilingual Contexts." *Crucible and Theology and Ministry* 4, no 1 (April 2012): 1–17. http://www.ea.org.au/Crucible/Issues/Heart-Language-Worship-in-Multilingual Contexts.aspx.

Scott, Joyce. *Tuning into a Different Song: Using Music to Bridge Cross Cultural Differences.* Pietermaritzburg, South Africa: Cluster Publications, 2007.

Seever, Janet. "Singing from the Hills." *Prayer Alive* (Wycliffe Canada newsletter, Fall 2007): 11.

Segler, Franklin M. *Christian Worship—It's Theology and Practice.* 3rd ed. Nashville: B&H Publishing Group, 2006.

Sendrey, Alfred. *Music in Ancient Israel.* New York: Philosophical Library, 1969.

Smith, Donald K. *Creating Understanding: A Handbook for Christian Communication across Cultural Landscapes.* Grand Rapids: Zondervan, 1992.

Stapert, Calvin R. *A New Song for an Old World: Musical Thought in the Early Church.* Grand Rapids: Eerdmans, 2007.

———. "Singing Psalms from Bible Times." In *Psalter Hymnal Handbook,* edited by Emily R. Brink and Bert Polman, 14–27. Grand Rapids: Faith Alive Christian Resources, 1998.

Stone, Dave. *Refining Your Style: Learning from Respected Communicators.* Loveland, CO: Group Publishing, 2004.

Stone, Ruth M. *Let the Inside Be Sweet: The Interpretation of Music Event among the Kpelle of Liberia.* Bloomington: Indiana University Press, 1982.

Sullivan, Lawrence E., ed. *Enchanting Powers: Music in the World's Religions.* Cambridge, MA: Harvard University Press, 1997.

Sun, Irene Ai-Ling. "Songs of Canaan: Hymnody of the House-church Christians in China." *Studia Liturgica* 37 (2007) and *EthnoDoxology* 4, no. 3 (2010): 1–10.

Tan, Sooi Ling. "Transformative Worship among the Salako of Sarawak, Malaysia." PhD diss., Fuller Theological Seminary, 2008.

Taylor, Julie. "Beyond Song: Transforming the Reality of God's Kingdom through All the Arts." *Evangelical Missions Quarterly,* 48, no. 1, http://www.emisdirect.com/emq/issue-318.

———. "Coexistence of Causal and Cultural Expressions of Musical Values among the Sabaot of Kenya." In *The Oxford Handbook of Music and World Christianities,* edited by Suzel Reily and Jonathan Dueck. New York: Oxford University Press, 2012.

Taylor, W. David O., ed. *For the Beauty of the Church*. Grand Rapids: Baker Books, 2010.

Taylor, William D., ed. "Arts in Mission." Special issue, *Connections: The Journal of the WEA Mission Commission*, vol. 9, nos. 2 and 3 (September 2010). http://www.weaconnections.com/Back-issues/Arts-in-Mission.aspx.

Tickle, Phyllis. *The Great Emergence: How Christianity Is Changing and Why*. Grand Rapids: Baker Books, 2008.

Tillich, Paul. *The Courage to Be*. New Haven, CT: Yale University Press, 1952.

Titon, Jeff Todd, ed. *Worlds of Music: An Introduction to the Music of the World's Peoples*. 5th ed. Belmont, CA: Schirmer Cengage Learning, 2009.

Torrance, James B. *Worship, Community, and the Triune God of Grace*. Downers Grove: InterVarsity Press, 1997.

Tozer, A. W. *Worship: The Missing Jewel*. Camp Hill, PA: Christian Publications, 1992.

Van den Heuvel, Albert. Preface to *Risk: New Hymns for a New Day*. Geneva: World Council of Churches, 1966.

Wallace, W. J. "Hymns in Ethiopia." *Practical Anthropology* 9 (November–December 1962): 271.

Webber, Robert E. *Ancient-future Worship: Proclaiming and Enacting God's Narrative*. Grand Rapids: Baker Books, 2008.

———. "The Crisis of Evangelical Worship." In *Worship at the Next Level: Insight from Contemporary Voices*, edited by Tim A. Dearborn and Scott Coil. Grand Rapids: Baker Books, 2004.

———. *The Divine Embrace: Recovering the Passionate Spiritual Life*. Grand Rapids: Baker Books, 2006.

———. *Renew Your Worship: A Study in the Blending of Traditional and Contemporary Worship*. Peabody, MA: Hendrickson, 1997.

———. *Worship Is a Verb*. Waco: Word, 1985.

———. *Worship Old and New: A Biblical, Historical, and Practical Introduction*. 2nd ed. Grand Rapids: Zondervan, 1994.

———, ed. *The Complete Library of Christian Worship*. Nashville: StarSong Publishing Group, 1993.

Westermann, Claus. *Praise and Lament in the Psalms*. Atlanta: John Knox Press, 1981.

Westermeyer, Paul. *Te Deum: The Church and Music*. Minneapolis: Fortress Press, 1998.

White, James F. *A Brief History of Christian Worship*. Nashville: Abingdon Press, 1993.

———. "A Protestant Worship Manifesto." Religion-online. http://www.religion-online.org/showarticle.asp?title=1278 (accessed October 4, 2010).

———. *Protestant Worship: Traditions in Transition*. Louisville: Westminster / John Knox Press, 1989.

Weman, Henry. *African Music and the Church in Africa*. Vol. 3 of *Studia Missionalia Upsaliensia*. Translated by Eric J. Sharpe. Uppsala, Sweden: Svenska Institutet för Missionsforkning, 1960.

Wiersbe, Warren W. *Real Worship: It Will Transform Your Life*. Nashville: Nelson, 1990.

Williams, Laurie. "Haiti's Unending Song." In William D. Taylor, ed., "Arts in Mission," special issue, *Connections: The Journal of the WEA Mission Commission* 9, nos. 2 and 3 (September 2010): 175.

Wilson-Dickson, Andrew. *The Story of Christian Music: From Gregorian Chant to Black Gospel*. Oxford: Lion Publishing, 1992.

Witvliet, John. "Worship in a Beatitude-shaped World. Learning from Psalm 73." *Reformed Worship* 100 (June 2011). http://www.reformedworship.org/article/june-2011/worship-beatitude-shaped-world (accessed June 15, 2012).

————. "Worship Worldwide." Session given at the Conference on World Christianity, Calvin College, Grand Rapids, MI, 2003.

Wolterstorff, Nicholas. *Art in Action: Toward a Christian Aesthetic.* Grand Rapids: Eerdmans, 1980.

Wooding, Dan. "How Sister Act Has Inspired the Formation of 30 Japanese Gospel Choirs Run by a Filipino Former Night Club Entertainer Who Found Christ." ASSIST News Service, July 8, 2009. http://www.assistnews.net/Stories/2009/s09070045.htm.

Worshiping the Triune God: Receiving and Sharing Christian Wisdom across Continents and Centuries. World Communion of Reformed Churches, 205–29. http://wcrc.ch/sites/default/files/Worshiping_the_Triune_God.pdf (accessed June 15, 2012).

Zschech, Darlene. "Shout to the Lord." Shout to the Lord, CD. Sydney: Hillsong Music Australia, 1993.

INTRODUCTION

SECTION 1: FOUNDATIONS

SECTION 2: STORIES

SECTION 3: TOOLS

CLOSING

INTRODUCTION

SECTION 1: FOUNDATIONS

SECTION 2: STORIES

SECTION 3: TOOLS

CLOSING

INDEX

INTRODUCTION

SECTION 1: FOUNDATIONS

SECTION 2: STORIES

SECTION 3: TOOLS

CLOSING

INTRODUCTION

SECTION 1: FOUNDATIONS

SECTION 2: STORIES

SECTION 3: TOOLS

CLOSING

INTRODUCTION

SECTION 1: FOUNDATIONS

SECTION 2: STORIES

SECTION 3: TOOLS

CLOSING

PRIMARY EDITORS

JAMES R. KRABILL (GENERAL EDITOR) » is senior executive for Global Ministries at Mennonite Mission Network in Elkhart, Indiana. For fourteen years he served in West Africa, primarily the Ivory Coast, as a Bible and church history teacher among African Initiated Churches (AICs) in various village settings, Bible institutes and theological faculties. For eight of those years he lived and worked with members of the Harrist Church among Ivory Coast's Dida people— collecting, recording, transcribing, and publishing over 500 original Harrist hymns for use in literacy and music training. Many of these hymns appeared in his published PhD thesis, *The Hymnody of the Harrist Church* (Frankfurt: Peter Lang, 1995). James is a frequent speaker in various church and academic settings across the United States and has lectured or taught courses in over a dozen countries. He holds memberships in the African Studies Association, the Association of Anabaptist Missiologists, the International Council of Ethnodoxologists (board of trustees), the Association of Mission Professors (president, 2009–10), and the American Society of Missiology (current chair of Scholarly Monograph Series). Krabill is the editor of *Missio Dei* (a quarterly missiological journal) and has authored or edited numerous other books and articles, including, "Scripture Use in AIC Hymnody," in *Afro-Christian Religion at the Grassroots in Southern Africa* (1991), 293-331; *Nos racines racontées* (1996); *Anabaptism and Mission: A Bibliography, 1859-2000*, with Chad Mullet Bauman (2002); "Eine Theologie der Mission für heute," in *Mission im Zeichen des Friedens* (2003), 183–95; *Anabaptists Meeting Muslims*, with David Shenk and Linford Stutzman (2005); *Is It Insensitive to Share Your Faith?* (2005); *Evangelical, Ecumenical and Anabaptist Missiologies in Conversation*, with Walter Sawatsky and Charles van Engen (2006); *Even the Demons Submit: Continuing Jesus' Ministry of Deliverance*, with Loren Johns (2006); *Music in the Life of the African Church* with Roberta King (lead author), *Jean Kidula and Thomas Oduro* (2008); *Jesus Matters: Good News for the 21st Century*, with David W. Shenk (2009); *Mission from the Margins* (2010); and *Forming Christian Habits in Post-Christendom*, with Stuart Murray Williams (2011). Krabill is a member of Prairie Street Mennonite Church in Elkhart, IN. He and his wife, Jeanette, have three adult children and two grandchildren.

FRANK FORTUNATO » has served in music ministry his entire life. After several years of teaching music courses in colleges in the Midwest, he began his ministry with Operation Mobilization, where he served as a music missionary for many years with OM's mission ships. Following his time on board, Frank completed his master's studies in ethnomusicology, to which he has more recently added a doctorate in biblical worship. Currently, Frank serves as OM's International Music Consultant and the vice president for the International Council of Ethnodoxologists (ICE). He is the co-founder of OM's Heart Sounds International (HSI), a ministry which sends out teams to promote indigenous worship and the arts through seminars, songwriting events, and audio and video recordings of non-Western worship, mostly in restricted parts of the world. HSI teams have released more than fifty audio and video recordings from five continents. Over the years Frank has helped international ministries and networks begin task forces focused on using music and the arts in evangelism and church planting, and has served as a music leader at various global missions gatherings. Based at OM's USA headquarters in Atlanta, Frank has also done adjunct college teaching on global music, piano, and improvisation. He leads worship at a local church and conducts worship seminars annually with OM India. His publications include *All the World is Singing—Glorifying God through the Worship Music of the Nations.* He has compiled and edited multilingual songbooks for OM international gatherings. His articles have been published in Christian magazines, missions journals, and electronic music periodicals. Frank's wife Berit is from Sweden and teaches elementary grades. They have two grown children, one granddaughter, and have adopted two children from India.

ROBIN P. HARRIS » is the president of the International Council of Ethnodoxologists (ICE). In addition, she enjoys serving as assistant professor and coordinator for the MA in World Arts at the Graduate Institute of Applied Linguistics (GIAL) in Dallas, Texas. She has been on loan since 2010 from Operation Mobilization for her roles in Dallas.

Robin grew up in Alaska, daughter of missionaries who served among Native Americans there for twenty years. After graduation as a music major from Biola University in 1983, she began cross-cultural service with her husband, Bill, first in Alaska, then Canada, and eventually for a decade in the Russian North. Their years in Siberia included focused work among the Sakha, a minority group whose epic narrative song-story genre *olonkho* eventually became the focus of Robin's PhD dissertation from the University of Georgia Athens. Prior to her doctoral studies, she earned MAs in Intercultural Studies (Columbia International University) and Ethnomusicology (Bethel University). In addition to her leadership role in ICE, she has actively participated for a number of years in the Applied Ethnomusicology sections of the Society for Ethnomusicology (SEM) and the International Council for Traditional Music (ICTM).

Robin's mission in life is to celebrate and reflect God's glory through the arts, spoken and written communication, and in leading, mentoring, and learning from others—all with the goal of bringing more worshipers into his Kingdom. To that end, she seeks to find and/or create beauty every day, and enjoys the opportunities God gives her for speaking, teaching, writing, and investing in the lives of students and other ethnodoxologists around the world. The Harrises' two grown children, James and Katherine, are also involved in the arts and kingdom service.

BRIAN SCHRAG » is SIL International's ethnomusicology and arts coordinator, and developed the World Arts program at the Graduate Institute of Applied Linguistics (GIAL, Dallas); he serves as adjunct professor in the program at GIAL. Brian has worked as a linguist, Bible translator, and ethnomusicologist in the Democratic Republic of Congo and Cameroon, and holds a PhD in Ethnomusicology (University of California, Los Angeles), an MA in Intercultural Studies (Wheaton College), and a BS in Cognitive Science (Brown University). Brian fills the role of vice president of Training and Education on the board of the International Council of Ethnodoxologists (ICE), and has been an active member of the Society for Ethnomusicology (SEM) and the International Council of Traditional Music (ICTM) for many years. He writes and presents on such topics as ethnoarts endangerment and revitalization, music criticism, applied ethnomusicology, Central African music, intersections of faith and scholarship, communication theory, and research as love. Brian has performed and recorded albums with Malian artist Cheick Tidiane Seck, Malawian musician Donald Kachamba, and Christian world music band *Izibongo*.

Brian's life purpose is to enact truth through music, words, and human organization in ways that open profound conversations with God, and to help others do the same. He encourages more people to create more things for more purposes in their communities, and tries to model this in his own life. He thus composes and performs songs for his family, weddings, funerals, anniversaries, and romantic and bluesy occasions. He is active in the Huntington's Disease Society of America, planning to draw on the arts' power to spark hope and healing by connecting artists and sufferers of this illness. Brian also integrates off-kilter wit into many of his activities. He loves his wife, Barb, and children Mindy, Austin, and Lydia.

From left to right: Frank Fortunato, James R. Krabill, Robin P. Harris, and Brian Schrag

INTRODUCTION

SECTION 1: FOUNDATIONS

SECTION 2: STORIES

SECTION 3: TOOLS

CLOSING

INTERNATIONAL COUNCIL OF ETHNODOXOLOGISTS (ICE) COPYEDITORS

 CAROL BRINNEMAN » is a career member of Wycliffe Bible Translators. She spent about twenty years in Côte d'Ivoire and Togo, with her husband and two sons, in translation and literacy work. Since 2002 she has served as a writer and editor for JAARS, Inc., in Waxhaw, N.C.

 KOE PAHLKA » is a freelance copyeditor and desktop publisher. She lives in Ferndale, Washington with her husband and eight children. When not working on a publication, Koe helps her family raise goats, chickens, rabbits, and vegetables. She has a BA from Stanford University.

 LINDA NEELEY » worked in Ghana for twenty years with Wycliffe Bible Translators, where she was part of a team who translated the Gikyode New Testament. She and her husband Paul now live in Dallas and are members of Artists in Christian Testimony. They have two grown sons. Linda is also employed by SIL, where she works on the Translator's Notes project.

CONTRIBUTORS

 TOM AVERY » (PhD) served as the international coordinator for ethnomusicology for Wycliffe International, working in various parts of Latin America and holding workshops, leading seminars, and training interns. He promoted the concept of "heart music" in worship. Despite an untimely death in 2008, his materials on music and missions continue to be used throughout the world.

 DAVID M. BAILEY » is an American music director, producer, and speaker who is passionate about worship music that reflects sound theology in a cultural context that represents all people. He's the founder of Making A Melody, a ministry that connects people, cultures, and communities through music.

 ROB BAKER » (MPhil) is an ethnomusicology consultant with SIL. He lived in West Africa for eight years, where he researched the music and ran numerous songwriting workshops. He has also taught ethnoarts courses in Togo, Benin, Mali, and England. He is author of the book *Adventures in Music and Culture* (forthcoming from Ambassador International). He is now resident in the UK. Read more on his blog: www.robbaker.org.

 LILA BALISKY » and her husband, Paul, served the SIM and Ethiopian Kale Heywet Church from 1967 to 2005. She has published "Theology in Song: Ethiopia's Tesfaye Gabbiso" (*Missiology*, October 1997) and an Amharic/English diglot of 105 hymns in *The Songs of Tesfaye Gabbiso* (SIM Press, Addis Ababa, 2011). In 2008 she taught an ethnomusicology course at the Ethiopian Graduate School of Theology.

 MICHAEL T. BALONEK » originally from Brockport, NY, holds a master's degree in Ethnomusicology from Bethel University. He has focused his musical studies in South Asia, specializing in indigenous drumming. In 2011, Balonek published the first ever lesson book for one of Sri Lanka's drums (*Sri Lankan Drumming: The Thammattama*). A western vocalist, Michael received his Bachelor of Music in Music Education from the Crane School of Music at SUNY Potsdam.

 JEFF BARKER'S » latest book is *The Storytelling Church*. His greatest passion these days is reclaiming the presentation of the Bible within worship, including what he calls "the ancient dramas of the Hebrew people." He teaches in the theatre program at Northwestern College and also in the doctoral program at the Robert E. Webber Institute for Worship Studies. His work can be found at: http://home.nwciowa.edu/barkerplays.

INTRODUCTION

SECTION 1: FOUNDATIONS

SECTION 2: STORIES

SECTION 3: TOOLS

CLOSING

INTRODUCTION

SECTION 1: FOUNDATIONS

SECTION 2: STORIES

SECTION 3: TOOLS

CLOSING

JOHN BENHAM » is founder of Music in World Cultures, Inc., an organization he established to assist missionaries with work as an ethnomusicologist. Since its initial formation MIWC has expanded its ministry to include the use of indigenous music in worship, discipleship, and evangelism in a variety of international settings. He developed the curriculum in ethnomusicology at Liberty University and serves as coordinator of that program.

HAROLD M. BEST » is emeritus dean/professor of music of the Wheaton College Conservatory of Music. He is also a past president of the National Association of Schools of Music. His books include *Music Through the Eyes of Faith* (Harper San Francisco, 1993), *Unceasing Worship: Biblical Perspectives on Worship and the Arts* (InterVarsity Press, 2003), *and Dumbfounded Praying* (Wipf & Stock, 2011).

RON BINDER » first met the Wounaan while doing language survey in Colombia and Panama in 1969. He and Kathy worked with them from 1970 to 1992. In 2000 the Wounaan churches requested their help in developing media and other resources that would equip them for outreach and discipleship ministries. Since then the Binders have coordinated Wounaan projects by traveling to Panama twice a year and maintain contact via Skype with Wounaan colleagues in Panama City.

JIM AND CARLA BOWMAN » founded Scriptures in Use (www.siutraining.org) in 1987. The curriculum they authored, Communication Bridges to Oral Cultures, has been taught around the world. In 2006, Carla developed Bridges for Women, a course to empower non-reading women with the memorized Word of God in story. SIU holds over two hundred training events each year in over fifty countries. The Bowmans served as missionaries in Latin America and subsequently extended their training courses worldwide.

EMILY R. BRINK » is a senior research fellow of the Calvin Institute of Christian Worship, Grand Rapids, Michigan, with a focus on conference planning and global resources. She was founding editor of *Reformed Worship*, editor of four hymnals, and in 2004 was named a Fellow of the Hymn Society in the United States and Canada in recognition of distinguished services to hymnody and hymnology.

CAROL BRINNEMAN » is a career member of Wycliffe Bible Translators. She spent about twenty years in Côte d'Ivoire and Togo, with her husband and two sons, in translation and literacy work. Since 2002 she has served as a writer and editor for JAARS, Inc., in Waxhaw, NC.

ROBERT CAMPBELL » and his wife, Barbara, with Wycliffe Bible Translators, have lived and worked with the Jamamadi people of Brazil since 1963 and have translated the New Testament into their language.

GEINENE CARSON » has a BFA in Painting and Sculpture. She has been with Operation Mobilization (OM) since 1999 serving in Europe, North Africa, and the Middle East. She now resides in Atlanta, GA, serving as a consultant for ArtsLink, the visual arts ministry she founded within OM. She is a wife, mother, practicing artist, and well-traveled advocate and mentor for using the arts as a bridge between peoples and cultures.

ROCHELLE L. CATHCART » is director and assistant professor of intercultural studies at Lincoln Christian University. She completed her MDiv at the Assemblies of God Theological Seminary and a PhD in Intercultural Studies at Trinity Evangelical Divinity School. Her dissertation focused on preaching and culture. She has ministered in Southeast Asia, served as associate pastor at a church plant in Salt Lake City, Utah, and co-authored the textbook, *Preaching in the Contemporary World.*

MARK CHARLES » a Navajo, is a speaker, writer, and consultant. Mark seeks to understand the complexities of American history regarding race, culture, and faith in order to help forge a path of healing and reconciliation for the nation. Links to his writings can be found at http://worship.calvin.edu/charles.

VIDA CHENOWETH » is known not only as the first professional solo classical marimbist, but as a pioneer ethnomusicologist and a linguist. Her thirteen years with Wycliffe Bible Translators resulted in a translation of the New Testament in the Usarufa language (with Darlene Bee) and a new method of ethnic music analysis. Before her retirement, she authored eleven books and developed a program in ethnomusicology for the Wheaton College Conservatory of Music.

SAMUEL CHIANG » is the executive director of the International Orality Network. Samuel serves the church through writing, discipling, and exploring implementable orality strategies. A graduate of Dallas Seminary, he is passionate about "faith and work." Samuel and Roberta and their three children have lived in Hong Kong for twenty-two years.

DIANNE COLLARD » has been a missionary and intercultural trainer for twenty-six years. She is the Europe ministries director for Artists in Christian Testimony International and is the director of Montage International which includes an international publication and speaking ministry. She holds a BA in Speech/Communications from San Francisco State University, an MA in Intercultural Studies, and a DMiss from Biola University. Dianne lives in North Carolina.

INTRODUCTION

SECTION 1: FOUNDATIONS

SECTION 2: STORIES

SECTION 3: TOOLS

CLOSING

INTRODUCTION

SECTION 1: FOUNDATIONS

SECTION 2: STORIES

SECTION 3: TOOLS

CLOSING

IAN COLLINGE » is an ethnomusicologist and ethnodoxology practitioner and trainer. He spent several years in Asia, researching indigenous music and developing music and arts resources for churches. Since returning to England, he has been teaching ethnomusicology, world worship music, and multicultural worship in Christian training institutes. In 2008 he and his wife, Helen, launched Resonance (www.wec-int.org.uk/resonance), the music and arts training ministry of WEC International.

ALICE COMPAIN » a veteran OMF International missionary to Cambodia and Laos, died in 2008 at the age of 74. She went to Laos in 1959. It is due mainly to Alice that the Lao and Cambodian churches can sing the praises of God not only in their own languages but also in their own cultural music forms.

J. NATHAN CORBITT » (DMA) is president of BuildaBridge International (www.buildabridge.org) an arts-education and intervention organization that engages the transforming power of the arts in developing hope and healing and resilience for those living in the contexts of poverty and crisis. He is professor of cross-cultural studies in the MA in Urban Studies Program of Eastern University where he coordinates the arts in transformation concentration.

CORY CUMMINS » has been the office manager for the SIL ethnomusicology and arts group for nearly ten years. He performed and directed the Wycliffe World Music Band and co-directs the ethnic music performance group, *Izibongo*. He also helped to coordinate the compilation of the *Handbook* DVD. Married and father of seven children, Cory spends much of his time singing and running with his family (although not often at the same time).

JOSH DAVIS » a former missionary kid, Josh is a multi-ethnic worship leader and a prolific songwriter. He founded Proskuneo Ministries in 2001, and currently serves as the director. Proskuneo exists to bring nations together in worship. Josh's heart's desire is to see the Kingdom of God come on earth as it is in heaven. Josh and his wife, Jennifer, live in Georgia with their four children.

LETICIA DZOKOTOE » and her husband Dan worked as non-print media specialists and recording engineers with the Ghana Institute of Linguistics, Literacy, and Bible Translation, an affiliate of SIL. Leticia died in 2005, and is sorely missed by many.

TOM FERGUSON » has served as an ethnoarts and orality specialist with the IMB since 1994. He and his wife Tina have worked in Africa and Asia, equipping local believers and missionaries in the use of creative arts and oral communication in church planting strategies. Tom holds music degrees from the University of Southern Mississippi and Southwestern Baptist Theological Seminary. He is a charter member of the International Council of Ethnodoxologists.

JILL FORD » is the arts tutor at All Nations Christian College. She holds a first class degree in music and related arts and an MA in Education (culture, language and identity) from Goldsmiths College London. Jill has a wide range of experience in the arts. For the last ten years she has been developing and integrating the arts in to the training curriculum at All Nations.

 FRANK FORTUNATO » has served in music ministry his entire lifetime. He taught college music courses, followed by music ministry with Operation Mobilization's mission ships. Following his time on board, Frank completed graduate studies in ethnomusicology and biblical studies. Based at the OM USA headquarters, currently he serves as OM's international music coordinator, and most recently founded Heart Sounds International, a ministry promoting indigenous worship and arts mostly in restricted countries and oral cultures.

 CHRISTOPHER DICRAN HALE » was raised in Nepal and India where he began studies in sitar. He studied jazz guitar and classical composition at Berklee College of Music after which he formed a band in India that included Indian devotional music in worship of Christ in its repertoire. In 1999 Christopher formed Aradhna with Pete Hicks (aradhnamusic.com). He is based in Toronto and travels extensively, teaching and performing sitar and Indian vocal music (christopherhalesitar.com).

 SUE HALL-HEIMBECKER » with Wycliffe Bible Translators and Pioneers International, lived and worked in rural and urban West Africa (Ghana, Senegal, and The Gambia) from 1996 to 2006. She loved the people, the music, and the big dresses. Now based in multi-cultural Calgary, Canada, Sue is a stay-at-home mum and supports arts in mission through writing and seminars.

 ROBIN P. HARRIS » (PhD) is president of the International Council of Ethnodoxologists and coordinator of the MA in World Arts at the Graduate Institute of Applied Linguistics in Dallas, Texas. She has served for decades in cross-cultural ministry, including ten years in northern Russia.

 WILLIAM N. HARRIS » holds MAs in Communication, Intercultural studies, and Organizational Leadership. He has served as a missionary since 1984, including ten years as a church planter in Siberia. Currently, he serves as an administrator and video producer with Operation Mobilization and as chief financial officer for the International Council of Ethnodoxologists. He also chairs the USA board of Expatriate Education International. His passion is to prepare missionaries to live cross-culturally.

 C. MICHAEL HAWN » is the University Distinguished Professor of Church Music, Perkins School of Theology, Southern Methodist University, Dallas, Texas. A student of global music, he has published numerous articles in church music journals and several books including *Gather into One: Praying and Singing Globally (2003)*. He has studied church music and worship and taught in seminaries in Africa, Asia, Australia, and Latin America.

INTRODUCTION

SECTION 1: FOUNDATIONS

SECTION 2: STORIES

SECTION 3: TOOLS

CLOSING

STEVEN C. HAWTHORNE » co-edited the course and textbook called *Perspectives on the World Christian Movement*. He co-authored, with Graham Kendrick, the book *Prayerwalking: Praying On-Site With Insight*. He has been involved with the leadership and theology of global worship and prayer movements, among them, March for Jesus and the Global Day of Prayer. He says of his ministry, "I like to commit arson of the heart."

MARY HENDERSHOTT » works with SIL International in West Africa as an arts consultant. She has an MA in Flute Performance from Wichita State University and an MA in ethnomusicology from Bethel University, St. Paul, Minnesota. Mary is involved in leading songwriting workshops, seminars, and training courses that encourage the use of local art forms as expressions of worship and proclamation. She resides in Burkina Faso.

MICHAEL T. HENEISE » is a PhD student in South Asian Studies at the University of Edinburgh, conducting research on dreams, memory, and agency in the eastern Himalayas. Co-editor of *The South Asianist*, he studied music at Berklee College and Florida State University (BME, 2000); sociology at Eastern University; and theology at the International Baptist Theological Seminary in Prague (MTh, 2005). He resides with his wife and son in Edinburgh, Scotland.

ANDREW E. HILL » (PhD, University of Michigan) is professor of Old Testament at Wheaton College (Wheaton, IL). He is the author of biblical commentaries in the *Anchor Bible* (Malachi), *NIV Application Commentary* series (1 and 2 Chronicles), and the *Tyndale Old Testament Commentary* series (Haggai, Zechariah, and Malachi). Other writing includes *Enter His Courts with Praise!* and he serves as an adjunct professor for the Robert E. Webber Institute for Worship Studies.

HARRIET HILL » serves as the program director for the Trauma Healing Institute, a ministry of the American Bible Society. She became involved in Bible translation as a means to Scripture Engagement in 1980, serving with SIL first in Côte d'Ivoire, then across Africa, and finally internationally. She completed her PhD at Fuller in 2003. Trauma Healing came into her life in 2001 as a means of helping communities devastated by war find restoration.

KEN HOLLINGSWORTH » a graduate of Elon University with a double major in vocal music and English, studied ethnomusicology under Dr. Vida Chenoweth as part of an MA in Linguistics at University of Texas–Arlington. He and his wife, Judy, oversaw the translation of the Mofu-Gudur New Testament in Cameroon. Ken has led numerous music workshops in Cameroon and Chad. He served as an adjunct professor of ethnomusicology at Southwestern Baptist Theological Seminary 1997–2000.

JACOB JOSEPH » is the dean of the School of Worship and Music at New Theological College, Dehradun, India. He holds a master's in church music from Southern Baptist Theological Seminary (Kentucky), a certificate in applied ethnomusicology from Payap University (Chiang Mai), and is currently pursuing DMin studies at Gordon Cornwell Theological Seminary (Massachusetts). His ministerial passion is training indigenous worship leaders, giving them a solid biblical foundation and musical skills.

 GREG KERNAGHAN » has served with Operation Mobilization since 1978 in various capacities. Since 1995, Greg has been part of an international communications team for OM whose purpose is to help truly great stories tell themselves.

 JEAN NGOYA KIDULA » (PhD) is an associate professor of Ethnomusicology at the University of Georgia–Athens; co-author of *Music in the Life of the African Church,* and author of the forthcoming *Music in Kenyan Christianity: Logooli Religious Song.* She serves on the ICE Board and as a church music director in both her native Kenya and in the United States.

 JAEWOO AND JOY KIM » are worship-arts missionaries with Artists in Christian Testimonies International, based in Dallas, TX, where they lead King's Region Worship Community to mobilize and equip Korean diaspora worship leaders and artists for worship renewal and global missions.

 ROBERTA R. KING » (PhD) is associate professor of Communication and Ethnomusicology at Fuller Seminary. She directs the Global Christian Worship (ethnomusicology) program where master's and doctoral students grapple with issues in music, culture, and the church in cross-cultural worship, witness, spiritual formation, and peacebuilding. She taught at Daystar University in Nairobi, Kenya (twenty-two years) and has done fieldwork and ministry across Africa and beyond.

 KEDRA LARSEN KINNEY » an ethnomusicology specialist, served with Lutheran Bible Translators from 2001 to 2011, based in Illinois and taking extended trips to southern and western Africa.

 JAMES AND JEANETTE KRABILL » served from 1978–96 as Mennonite mission workers with African-initiated churches in West Africa. They currently live in Indiana where James is senior executive for the Mennonite Mission Network and Jeanette teaches third grade. The Krabills' adult children—Matthew, Elisabeth Anne, and Mary-Laura—were all born in Côte d'Ivoire, but now live in the US.

INTRODUCTION

SECTION 1: FOUNDATIONS

SECTION 2: STORIES

SECTION 3: TOOLS

CLOSING

 ELEANOR KREIDER » a Mennonite liturgical scholar and missionary, is now retired and lives in Elkhart, Indiana with her husband Alan Kreider. They are joint-authors of *Worship and Mission after Christendom* (Herald Press, 2011).

 CHIEKO LARRIMORE » a native of Japan, attended World Arts courses at the Graduate Institute of Applied Linguistics in fall 2010. She and her husband, Ian, hope to serve in the fields of ethnoarts and community development.

 WIL LAVEIST » is the managing editor for multimedia for Mennonite Mission Network. Based in Virginia, he attends Calvary Community Church in Hampton with his wife and family.

 JAMES LHOMI » is a songwriter, poet, author, and music teacher. He serves as an elder and worship leader in the Ghangri (Himalayas) Lhomi church, Kathmandu, Nepal, and is the founder and director of Lareso Tibetan Music Institute of Ministry. In addition, he is the president of the Nepal Lhomi society (NELHOS) www.nelhos.org.np and the editor of the *Morning Star,* a newspaper in Lhomi and Nepali languages.

 KEMBER LILLO » served as an arts specialist intern in Burkina Faso from 2008 to 2009. She has finished her master's in ethnomusicology at the University of Montreal, Quebec, and is now mobilizing young Canadians for ethnoarts ministry with Wycliffe Bible Translators.

 SWEE HONG LIM » is the Deer Park assistant professor of Sacred Music and director of the Master of Sacred Music Program at Emmanuel College of Victoria University in the University of Toronto, Canada. Presently he co-chairs the Worship Committee for the 10th General Assembly of the World Council of Churches.

 I-TO LOH » (MDiv, SMM, PhD–UCLA), taught Asian and Global Church Music, as well as Ethnomusicology and Worship, at Asian Institute for Liturgy and Music, Manila, and Tainan Theological College and Seminary, Taiwan. His publications include over 100 hymns and anthems and more than twenty hymn compilations. Retired from the presidency at Tainan Seminary in 2002, he has been an itinerant professor in Taiwan, Hong Kong, Malaysia, Singapore, and the US.

 ROGER LOWTHER » is a professional musician working with Grace City Church in central Tokyo. He has been serving with Mission to the World in Japan with his wife, Abi, and three young sons since 2005 (www. missionart.org). He graduated from The Juilliard School with a master's in Organ Performance. Both Roger and Abi have a passion to see artists use their talents to spread the message of the gospel in ways that engage and challenge the culture of Japan and the world.

GEORGE LUKE » used to host and produce United Christian Broadcasters' *World Beat* radio show, which ran for seven years on British radio. As a result, George has written several articles about gospel music from various countries around the world. George was born in London, raised in Sierra Leone, and now lives in London. He currently works for the Methodist Church in Britain as a writer and editor.

 RON MAN » (MM, ThM, DMin) studied music and later theology. During 1983–88, he served at the International Chapel in Vienna, Austria; 1988–2000 at First Evangelical Church in Memphis, Tennessee, USA; 2000–2008 with Greater Europe Mission. Since 2009 he is again at First Evangelical as pastor of Worship/Missionary in Residence, continuing to teach overseas with Worship Resources International (www.worr.org). He wrote *Proclamation and Praise: Hebrews 2:12 and the Christology of Worship* (Wipf & Stock, 2007).

 RICHARD MAUNEY » with Greater Europe Mission, has served in Romania since 1996. Previously he served for two years in the Philippines, and also as minister of music and worship in numerous churches in the United States. He has studied at Furman University (BME), Florida State University (MME), and Southwestern Baptist Theological Seminary (DMA). His colleagues with the Jubilate Foundation are Susan Strohschein, Kenneth Tucker, Ruben Muresan, and Mariana Gherasim.

 W. JAY MOON » (PhD) is a professor of Intercultural Studies at Sioux Falls Seminary in South Dakota. Prior to that, he and his family served as SIM missionaries from 1992 to 2005, working among the Builsa people of Ghana, West Africa. Moon's research focuses on oral art, particularly African proverbs.

 STEVE S. C. MOON » (PhD) is the executive director of Korea Research Institute for Mission and pastor of mission education at NamSeoul Grace Church.

 KATHERINE MOREHOUSE » has carried out field research in West Africa, working with hereditary musicians and Christian churches, and in Kerala, India, where she studied the socio-musical interactions of Christian, Muslim, and Hindu drummers in religious festival contexts. She holds an MA in ethnomusicology from Bethel University and a PhD in ethnomusicology from the University of Maryland. She currently teaches for Liberty University and Kennesaw State University.

 PAUL NEELEY » lived in Africa for years working with SIL, leading music workshops with nearly forty ethnic groups. He is also involved with music ministries in Asia. He is part of Artists in Christian Testimony, International Orality Network, and Heart Sounds International. He's published two books, over fifty articles, and edited the journal *EthnoDoxology*. He teaches ethnomusicology and global worship at several schools and consults for multiple mission agencies. Paul co-founded global worship ensembles and produces CDs.

INTRODUCTION

SECTION 1: FOUNDATIONS

SECTION 2: STORIES

SECTION 3: TOOLS

CLOSING

INTRODUCTION

SECTION 1: FOUNDATIONS

SECTION 2: STORIES

SECTION 3: TOOLS

CLOSING

HÉBER NEGRÃO » has a master's degree in ethnomusicology. He is a member of the Mission Commission of the World Evangelical Alliance, International Council of Ethnodoxologists, and Associoación Latino Americana de Etno Artes. He and his wife, Sophia, are missionaries with Evangelical Mission to Brazilian Indians in north Brazil.

ROCH NTANKEH » holds a diploma in musical studies as well as an MA in Theology (minor in missiology/ethnomusicology). Besides being the secretary general of the *Chantres Unis du Cameroun* (Cameroon Worshippers Fellowship), he is a pastor, worship leader, lecturer, and music instructor. He is also the founding president of a ministry which aims at restoring and developing traditional music in the church according to ethnodoxology principles.

B. E. BHARATHI NUTHALAPATI » earned a PhD in Church History from Fuller Theological Seminary. She is a freelance writer and a visiting teacher and serves as editor of the socio-spiritual magazine *Neighbour.*

JOHN OSWALD » is author and compiler of several books and articles on Tibetan Christian music. These include *A New Song Rising in Tibetan Hearts: Tibetan Christian Worship in the Early 21st Century* (CAF 2001), "Gospel Communication in Tibetan Song" in *Communicating Christ through Story and Song: Orality in Buddhist Contexts* (ed. Paul De Neui, 2008, William Carey Library), and a Tibetan Songbook *Offer Up a Praise Song* (compiled 2011, Central Asia Publishing, contact@CentralAsiaPublishing.com).

MARY K. OYER » combined studies of music and art for her BA, MM, and DMA degrees, culminating in the development of a college course integrating music with the visual arts which she taught during her career and into retirement. For thirty years she worked with research in hymnody and compiling hymnals and supplements for the Mennonite Church. Cross-cultural teaching took place in Kenya, 1980–82, Taiwan, 1999–2003, and various venues in the US.

MICHELLE PETERSEN » is an arts consultant working with actors in West Africa to create Scripture-infused dramas in local languages. She holds an MA in Language Development with a Specialization in Scripture Use from the Graduate Institute of Applied Linguistics in Dallas, where she is an associate instructor. She teaches Scripture Use at the Canada Institute of Linguistics in Langley, BC. She has been serving with Wycliffe Bible Translators since 1993.

JOHN D. PIERCE » has served as executive editor of *Baptists Today* since 2000. A native of Ringgold, GA, he is a graduate of Berry College (BA), Southeastern Baptist Theological Seminary (MDiv), and Columbia Theological Seminary (DMin). He speaks frequently in churches, consults with congregations concerning communications, and holds interim pastorates.

INTRODUCTION

SECTION 1: FOUNDATIONS

SECTION 2: STORIES

SECTION 3: TOOLS

CLOSING

JOHN PIPER » is founder and teacher of desiringGod.org, and chancellor of Bethlehem College & Seminary, Minneapolis, Minnesota. He served over thirty years as senior pastor of Bethlehem Baptist Church, Minneapolis. His books include *Desiring God* (Colorado Spring: Multnomah, revised and expanded 2011); *What Jesus Demands from the World* (Wheaton: Crossway, 2006); *God Is the Gospel* (Wheaton: Crossway, 2004); and *Don't Waste Your Life* (Wheaton: Crossway, 2003).

JACK POPJES » and his wife, Jo, served as linguist-translators with the Canela people of Brazil from 1968 to 1990. They left the Canelas with a partial Bible, including some Old Testament and nearly all the New Testament, as well as a set of hymns composed in the Canela musical system. Popjes was the president of Wycliffe Canada for six years and for Wycliffe Caribbean for three years. He has spoken in four hundred cities in twenty countries and has written three books.

SCOTT RAYL » is a graduate of Tulane University with a degree in anthropology and studio art. He has taught both informally and at the graduate level on indigenous art and Christianity, and seeks to better understand the role of indigenous visual art in missions and in the life of the global church. Rayl blogs at http://indigenousjesus.blogspot.com.

MAE ALICE REGGY » (PhD) served as literacy consultant with United Bible Societies in Africa for twenty-seven years. She presently serves on the faculty at Beulah Heights University in Atlanta, GA and as guest lecturer at the Monrovia Bible College in Liberia, West Africa.

JO-ANN RICHARDS » is a Jamaican teacher, author, singer/songwriter and global messenger. She is a member of the International Council of Ethnodoxologists and Founding Director of CREW 40:4, a non-profit organization established to promote love and unity in Christ through culturally relevant expressions of worship. Jo-Ann holds a MA in Ethnomusicology from Bethel University in Minnesota and a BA in Theology from the Jamaica Theological Seminary where she currently serves as adjunct lecturer.

TANYA RICHES » is pursuing a PhD at Fuller Theological Seminary, investigating the identity narratives found within urban Indigenous Australian Pentecostal congregational song. She is also a congregational songwriter, with her first solo album, entitled *Grace*, released in 2012. Her songs published by Hillsong include "Jesus What a Beautiful Name" (1996), "Hear our Prayer" (1998), and "King of Love" (2003).

NIK RIPKEN » (DMin) is a missionary veteran of twenty-eight years, having served in Malawi, South Africa, Kenya, Somalia, Ethiopia, and Germany. He and his wife currently serve as mission strategists in sensitive countries. He is the author of numerous articles on missions and, along with his wife, has done extensive interviews and research in regard to bold witness and church planting among followers of Christ who live in environments framed by persecution.

SARAH ROHRER » has received the International Baccalaureate and Torrey Honors Institute diplomas. She graduated Summa Cum Laude with a BA in Intercultural Studies from Biola University, after studying in Uganda. Sarah worked with BuildaBridge International throughout 2011, exploring the arts' role in transforming children's lives in the face of trauma. She now works as a teacher and full-time coordinator at Molly's Music.

JULISA ROWE » is with Artists in Christian Testimony and is based in Kenya where she trains leaders in using drama as a powerful tool for communicating God's truth and touching hearts for transformation. She has a BA in Theatre and an MA in Intercultural Ministries. She received a Doctor of Missiology in Ethnodramatology from Fuller Theological Seminary.

DAVID RUIZ » has served as international president of COMIBAM International (The Ibero-American Missionary Cooperation) since 2000, and before that as pastor at Centro Biblico El Camino in Guatemala City. During those years, he played an active role in the development of the Guatemalan National Missionary Movement and became the National Coordinator. He is one of the founders of the Missions Education Centre for Central America (CEMCA), the first centre for cross cultural studies in Guatemala.

ERIC SARWAR » is an ethnodoxologist, composer, writer, and teacher. He also is an ordained minister of the Presbyterian Church of Pakistan and founder of the Tehillim School of Church Music and Worship in Pakistan.

MARY SAURMAN » has a BS in Music Therapy, an MA in Intercultural Studies/ethnomusicology, and is starting doctoral studies with a focus on ethnoarts combined with multilingual education. She has worked in Asia with SIL International for the last eighteen years as an advocate for the music and arts of ethnic minority groups. In Thailand she trains others as catalysts for the creation of culturally relevant arts throughout Asia.

TODD SAURMAN » has a BS in Music Therapy, an MA in Intercultural Studies/Ethnomusicology, and is completing a PhD in Social Science. He has worked in Asia with SIL International for the last eighteen years as an advocate for the music and arts of ethnic minority groups. In Thailand he trains others as catalysts for the creation of culturally relevant arts throughout Asia.

BRIAN SCHRAG » (PhD) serves as head of SIL International's Ethnomusicology and Arts Group. He worked as an arts consultant in Central Africa and founded the World Arts program at the Graduate Institute of Applied Linguistics.

JOYCE SCOTT » spent twenty-eight years in cross-cultural missionary work in East Africa under the African Inland Church, learning music from grassroots interaction with African friends and mentors in eleven language groups in Kenya. Her experience also included being a consultant on indigenous music for ministry in Namibia, Sudan, Lesotho, Algeria, and the Comoro Islands. She has taught courses in Music for Inter-Cultural Ministry in six Bible colleges and at Daystar University in Nairobi, Kenya.

JANET SEEVER » a member of Wycliffe Bible Translators since 1975, has served in Papua New Guinea, the Philippines, Australia, and Dallas, Texas. Since 1993, she has been a writer in the Wycliffe Canada office in Calgary and edits *Prayer Alive*, a quarterly prayer bulletin.

RICHARD SHAWYER » (MB, BS, MTH) and his family served with WEC International in a church planting ministry among an unreached Muslim people group in West Africa from 1993 to 2009, seeking to see a community of faith incarnate Christ within the context of their local culture. He is a medical practitioner with training in anthropology and music and an interest in ministry to oral communicators.

BYRON SPRADLIN » (DMin in Worship Studies) is the founder and president of *Artists in Christian Testimony Intl*, an organization with over 250 artists doing creative Kingdom ministry touching over twenty nations. He chairs the School of Worship, Imagination and the Arts at Williamson Christian College in Franklin, TN and serves the Board of Jews for Jesus as the Vice-Chair. He is Lausanne's senior Associate for The Arts since June 2012.

CHUCK STEDDOM » (DMA in Choral Conducting) served at Prairie Bible College as Fine Arts faculty and the associate dean of academics before joining the pastoral staff of Bethlehem Baptist Church in Minneapolis, MN, in 1997. He now serves concurrently as the pastor for Worship and Music at Bethlehem's downtown campus, associate professor of Worship Studies at Bethlehem College & Seminary and Worship, and as a consultant for the Kachin Baptist Convention in northern Myanmar.

IRENE AI-LING SUN » is a mother of three boys—Emeth, Yohanan, and a baby due in January 2012. This is, for the moment, her life of worship and service. She studied liturgical theology and biblical theology at Yale University and Trinity Evangelical Divinity School. Nowadays, she thinks the most invigorating liturgy comes out of lives lived for the sake of others—lovingly demonstrated by her husband Hans.

INTRODUCTION

SECTION 1: FOUNDATIONS

SECTION 2: STORIES

SECTION 3: TOOLS

CLOSING

SOOI-LING TAN » (PhD) is an adjunct lecturer of Worship Studies at Malaysian Baptist Theological Seminary. She was a Brehm postdoctoral fellow at Fuller Theological Seminary working on the project, "Songs of Peace and Reconciliation among Muslims and Christians" and is an adjunct assistant professor there. Her passion lies in establishing theological foundations and exploring local expressions of worship.

JULIE TAYLOR » serves with SIL International as the coordinator of anthropology and ethnomusicology/arts training in Africa. She is also a senior arts consultant, with a PhD in Ethnomusicology from the University of Edinburgh.

KENNETH L. WALLACE, JR. » has led worship seminars for students in InterVarsity Christian Fellowship and has spoken on related topics at international conferences and consultations. He led global worship at his former church, Mosaic Church of North Carolina. He currently leads worship in various contexts and is pursuing his dream of opening a multi-ethnic worship school.

LAURIE WILLIAMS » is a writer in the Washington, DC, area. She served as research assistant for the *Taking It to the Streets* book project, and earned her master's degrees in urban economic development and multicultural education from Eastern University. A second-generation Haitian, she currently teaches English as a Second Language to adults.

PAM WILSON » lives in Istanbul where she serves with TACO (www.tacoteam. org), a ministry that creatively proclaims the gospel of Jesus Christ to Muslim peoples.

JOHN D. WITVLIET » is director of the Calvin Institute of Christian Worship and professor of worship, theology, and music at Calvin College and Calvin Theological Seminary. He is the author of *The Biblical Psalms in Christian Worship* (Eerdmans, 2007), *Worship Seeking Understanding* (Baker Academic, 2003), and co-editor of *Worship in Medieval and Early Modern Europe* (University of Notre Dame Press, 2004) and *Psalms for All Seasons* (Baker Books/Faith Alive, 2012).

ANNE ZAKI » resource development specialist for global and multi-cultural resources at the Calvin Institute of Christian Worship, is based in Cairo, Egypt. She also teaches worship at the Evangelical Theological Seminary in Cairo. She grew up in Egypt in a pastor's home and received a Master's of Divinity from Calvin Theological Seminary in 2009. She and her husband, Naji Umran, are parents of four sons: Jonathan, Sebastian, Emmanuel, and Alexander.

In addition to the article authors listed above, the editors would like to express their gratefulness to the following people and organizations for their contributions of articles and media for the *Handbook* DVD: Artists in Christian Testimony, Wendy Atkins, Belhaven College, Karen Campbell, Mat Carson, Isaiah Dau, Graduate Institute of Applied Linguistics, Colin Harbinson, Susan Hargrave, Heart Sounds International, International Orality Network, IziBongo, Maria Kononova, Aidyn Kurmanov, Lausanne Committee for World Evangelism, April Longenecker, Jim Mills, Von Newcomb, Stan Nussbaum, Sabeel Media, Pioneers, SIL International, Glenn Stallsmith, Richard Twiss, Pete Unseth, Viña Studios, WEC Resonance, and Heather Wright.

INTRODUCTION

SECTION 1: FOUNDATIONS

SECTION 2: STORIES

SECTION 3: TOOLS

CLOSING

DISCUSSION QUESTIONS

ENCOUNTERING GOD: WORSHIP AND BODY LIFE

Biblical

1. Biblical Foundations of Christian Worship (Andrew E. Hill)
2. The Significance of Beauty and Excellence in Biblical Worship (Emily R. Brink)
3. God's Creation and Human Creativity: Seven Affirmations (Harold M. Best)

- Discuss the implications of Andrew Hill's definition of worship and how it intersects with the themes of beauty and excellence in worship emphasized by Emily Brink's chapter. In what practical ways can we work toward infusing our life of worship—in addition to our gathered worship—with beauty and excellence?
- In Harold Best's "Affirmation 6" he proposes that there may be *affective* power in the nontexted arts, but not *causal* power. What does he mean by this? Why doesn't he agree with "Christian" vs. "pagan" labels for artistic creations?
- How does Best's view of the connections between the arts and a life of worship apply to you personally? To your missional activities? How does it help our understanding of the importance of creativity and the arts for each Christian?

Cultural

4. "The Bridge": Worship between Bible and Culture (Ron Man)
5. Artistic Expression in Early Christianity (Eleanor Kreider)
6. Ways of Contextualizing Church Music: Some Asian Examples (I-to Loh)

- Ron Man's "Bridge" model emphasizes how the stable pillars of "Biblical Constants" and "Biblical Principles" provide a framework for malleable forms of worship which are culturally meaningful and appropriate. Choose two or three stories from section 2 of this volume which have stretched your understanding of biblically appropriate worship, relating them to at least one of the two pillars in the "Bridge" model.
- In Eleanor Kreider's article she raises the question, "How can Christians engage in practices and create artifacts through which Christian truths become comprehensible yet challenge aspects of wider culture in the name of the gospel?" Discuss a "practice or artifact" which would make Christian truth comprehensible yet challenge the ungodly cultural norms of your own context.
- As you reflect on Kreider's examples from early Christian communities and on I-to Loh's challenge to contextualize both *texts* and *styles* of music, discuss how the creativity of your own worshiping community might more effectively be both *contextual* and *countercultural*. For more resources in this discussion, see also Anne Zaki's chapter 13 on the Nairobi statement.

Historical

7. How Song Sustained the Church (Frank Fortunato)
8. Global Shift from North to South: Implication for Latin American Worship (David D. Ruiz)
9. The Whole World Has Gone "Glocal" (Jaewoo Kim)

- Frank Fortunato's overview of the historical and geographical sweep of God's people expressing their worship in song sets the stage for David Ruiz's exploration of the recent global forces behind Latin American worship renewal. What does Ruiz see as the key components of this renewal, and what are the threats to its connection to Latin American understandings of identity?
- Jaewoo Kim also addresses the globalization of worship practices but notes that another powerful force—*glocalization*—allows Christian worship to become more diverse than it has ever been. Discuss how your worshiping community might engage Kim's ideas for implementing *glocal* worship practices.
- Fortunato ends his chapter by "peering into the future" and focusing on a vision of every nation, tribe, and tongue declaring the praises of God. As you reflect on Ruiz's words regarding the global shift from North to South, and Kim's assertion that "wholehearted worship by the whole world is the goal of missions," discuss how your mission committee, training institution, church, or organization might take concrete action to support what God is doing around the world through the ethnodoxology movement. See http://ethnodoxologyhandbook.com for ideas and collaborators.

Missiological

10. Ethnoartistic Cocreation in the Kingdom of God (Brian Schrag)
11. Designing Multicultural Worship with the *Missio Dei* in Mind (Josh Davis)
12. Ethnodramatology for Community Engagement (Julisa Rowe)

- Brian Schrag explores a key theme—the kingdom of God—that links the companion volumes of the *Ethnodoxology Handbook* and the manual *Creating Local Arts Together*. How do the "now and not yet" aspects of the kingdom give impetus to the *missio Dei* that Josh Davis engages in his article? In what practical ways can we reflect these themes in how we design worship services and interact with artists? What are some concrete ways that we can celebrate the artistic voices of those creating in marginalized and at-risk artistic traditions?
- Julisa Rowe outlines the ways in which the practice of ethnodramatology engages the dramatic traditions indigenous to each context, including contemporary fusions grounded in local styles. How might Rowe's reflections inform the planning of multicultural worship services such as those discussed by Davis in the preceding chapter?
- How does ethnodramatology intersect with Schrag's outline of the three common approaches to arts in mission engagement (*Bring It—Teach It*, *Build New Bridges*, and *Find It—Encourage It*)? What can you do to learn more about local drama styles before going on a short-term mission trip or engaging in a long-term assignment?

INTRODUCTION

SECTION 1: FOUNDATIONS

SECTION 2: STORIES

SECTION 3: TOOLS

CLOSING

Liturgical

13. Shall We Dance? Reflections on the *Nairobi Statement on Worship and Culture* (Anne Zaki)
14. Worship Challenges in Multicultural Churches: The Bethlehem Baptist Experience (Chuck Steddom)
15. "The Canaan Hymns": Songs of the House-church Christians in China (Irene Ai-Ling Sun)

- Anne Zaki's reflections on the *Nairobi Statement* provide some powerful artistic metaphors for understanding the intersection of worship and culture. Discuss which of the four areas creates the biggest challenge for your worshiping community: worship as transcultural, contextual, countercultural, or cross-cultural.
- In what ways does the *Nairobi Statement* speak to and exemplify the journey of worship leader Chuck Steddom as he worked toward creating a welcoming space for a variety of cultures at Bethlehem Baptist?
- How might the four lenses of the *Nairobi Statement* clarify some reasons for the effectiveness of the Canaan Hymns in China?

Personal

16. The Great Misconception: Why Music Is Not a Universal Language (Robin P. Harris)
17. Mentoring Artists (Mary Elizabeth Saurman)
18. Culturally Appropriate Worship: My Story as a Cameroonian Pastor (Roch Ntankeh)

- Robin Harris asserts that one of the reasons for judgmental attitudes in the worship wars is that we don't understand the parallels between language and music. We are often blind, she asserts, to the fact that our negative assumptions on the meaning and value of other "musical languages" reflect our own ignorance of those systems. What musical and artistic traditions in the worship life of your church do you find most difficult to understand and appreciate? How might you seek to learn more about those traditions with the goal of understanding and appreciating their value for those who speak that "musical language" in your community?
- Mary Saurman's extensive experience in mentoring leads her to underscore the importance of encouraging individual gifting and integrating those gifts into a wider team of people. Discuss why encouraging people to work from their gifts might help to strengthen them for work outside their areas of comfort. Do a self-check on how well you are doing in the list of mentoring skills outlined in Saurman's chapter.
- Cameroonian pastor Roch Ntankeh demonstrates, through both missiological and theological reflection, that using culturally appropriate music and methods to worship is pleasing to God. Reflect on his questions directed to Western partners at the end of the article: "Are you ready to trust us in the decision-making process? Are you ready to allow us to have our autonomy?" Discuss what you can do in your circles to encourage ethnodoxology—culturally appropriate worship—in mission, both locally and globally.

ENGAGING GOD'S WORLD: WITNESS AND COMMUNITY-BASED MINISTRY

Biblical

19. The Missional Impulse toward Incarnational Worship in the New Testament (John Piper)
20. Bible Storying with the Creative Arts for Church Planting (Tom Ferguson)
21. Art and Gospel: The Necessity of Artistic Fullness (Steven C. Hawthorne)

- John Piper's writings on the dynamic intersections of mission and worship have motivated and inspired many in the current generation of ethnodoxologists. What statements in this chapter particularly expand or refocus your paradigm of worship, arts, and mission?
- Bible storying with the creative arts is a practical application of ethnodoxology to mission and demonstrates the importance of arts in church planting movements. How do Tom Ferguson's real-life examples demonstrate the importance of an approach to arts in mission that is more than music-focused? How might the engagement of these kinds of arts intersect with Piper's vision for incarnational worship?
- Paralleling the worship focus of Piper, Steven Hawthorne delivers a powerful challenge for expanding our view of arts in mission beyond such simple utilitarian purposes as sparking attention or evoking responses. As you ponder Hawthorne's "greater vision" for art and the gospel, discuss situations in which artistic expressions help to form a community and mediate its conversation with God.

Cultural

22. Musical Bridges in Christian Communication: Lessons for the Church (Roberta R. King)
23. Spare Them Western Music! (Vida Chenoweth)
24. Making a Difference in a Week: Eight Principles for Art Making in Short-term Engagement (J. Nathan Corbitt, with Sarah Rohrer)

- At the end of her chapter, Roberta King proposes four ways that we can engage music and the arts in a discerning way for the purposes of the Great Commission. Discuss how you might practically get involved, working toward implementing one or more of these suggestions in your own faith community. In addition, how might you communicate Christ in culturally appropriate ways to other communities, either nearby or through the mission connections of your church or organization?
- Vida Chenoweth, a pioneer in the field of ethnomusicology and missions, asserts in her seminal article from 1984 that there are significant dangers in rejecting people's music and importing foreign music in our cross-cultural service. Utilizing the recommended roles proposed by Corbitt and Rohrer of *catalyst*, *consultant*, and *connector*, brainstorm how you might participate in reversing the unfortunate trend which Chenoweth describes as "capturing all the birds of the forest, painting them grey, and giving them all the same song."
- Short-term mission trips provide specific challenges, but Nathan Corbitt and Sarah Rohrer propose an effective goal for short-term arts engagement in mission: "to assist local communities to meet their own needs." The eight principles they suggest for seeing this goal achieved are practical and achievable. Discuss how your church or organi-

zation might implement these principles for spiritual, societal, and artistic transformation in communities.

Historical

25. Cross-cultural Communication through Symbol (C. Michael Hawn and Swee Hong Lim)
26. The Challenge of Indigenizing Christian Worship: An Example from India (Jacob Joseph)
27. Contextualizing Visual Arts for Faith Sharing (Scott Rayl)

- Proposing that symbols contribute powerfully to the spread of the gospel, Michael Hawn and Swee Hong Lim explore visual, aural, movement, and olfactory symbols which the church through the ages has employed in its worship and witness. Discuss the ways this chapter helped you to better understand symbols unfamiliar to your experience.
- Avoiding syncretism while achieving biblical contextualization is one of the primary challenges for ethnodoxology workers in missions. Jacob Joseph writes about meeting these challenges in the context of India, and Scott Rayl offers some successful examples in storying and the visual arts. Discuss how you might find out more about these and other contextualized resources for recommending to mission workers and national church leaders around the world.
- Arts missionaries often struggle with maintaining adequate financial support levels due to an underappreciation of their connection to the important work of church planting and evangelism. How do the chapters in this section—and the reflections in the rest of the *Handbook*—speak to this issue?

Missiological

28. What Happens to Music When Cultures Meet? Six Stages of Music Development in African Churches (James R. Krabill)
29. A Framework for Incorporating Arts in Short-term Missions (Ian Collinge)
30. Visual Arts as a Bridge to Engaging People of Other Cultures (Geinene Carson)

- Discuss James Krabill's "Six Stages of Music Development" in relation to the mission contexts with which you are familiar. How might you engage a few of the principles proposed in this *Handbook* and partner with others, working toward the goal of enabling local churches to see stages 5 and 6 become reality for them? How might this process apply to your home church as well?
- Short-term missions can be a great place for effective arts engagement if the crucial considerations, like those outlined by Ian Collinge and Geinene Carson, can be implemented. Discuss the ways in which these two chapters compare with or contrast to perspectives shared in chapter 24.
- Collinge notes in his chapter that specialized training is essential for short-term teams to effectively engage the arts in mission. Discuss ways that your church or mission agency can integrate the *Ethnodoxology Handbook* and accompanying *Manual* into your short-

term training programs. Check the website (http://www.ethnodoxologyhandbook.com) for national and international training events based on these volumes.

Liturgical

31. Transformative Worship in a Malaysian Context (Sooi Ling Tan)
32. The Worship Wheel (Todd Saurman)
33. Local Arts and Worship Development in Church Planting (William N. Harris)

- Lament is described as part of a transformational dynamic of worship in Sooi Ling Tan's chapter (see also chapter 35), but many worshiping communities have not experienced the value of creating laments. Discuss the ways your faith community might use the Saurmans' "Worship Wheel" to round out your expressions of worship, creating laments to address the difficult situations you face.
- The Worship Wheel is a flexible and powerful tool for creating a wide range of new arts creations for the Lord, for ourselves, for celebrations/ceremonies, and for others. As you examine the Worship Wheel diagram in chapter 32, identify the occasions for which music and arts resources are sparse in your worshiping community. Make plans for a workshop in your context which will help you to develop these important ways of responding to God.
- William Harris asserts that the "hard hearts" and "stony ground" encountered in church planting can often be softened dramatically through the engagement of culturally appropriate music and arts. Note the practical steps offered by Julisa Rowe in the *Manual* summary (chapter 148) at the end of this "Foundations" section which can be used by church planters to do research and cocreation with local people. Discuss one or more activities that you might be able to do in support of the church planting efforts close to your heart, whether in your own community or in a cross-cultural context.

Personal

34. Each Person's Part Nourishes the Whole: My Story (Jean Ngoya Kidula)
35. The Arts and Trauma Healing in Situations of Violence and Conflict (Harriet Hill)
36. Three Worlds Converged: Living in an Oral, Literate, and Digital Culture (Samuel E. Chiang)

- The editors of this volume asked Jean Kidula, an ethnomusicology educator and ICE board member, to share her personal story of involvement in music throughout her lifetime. She notes that already early on in Kenya her parents nurtured the individuality of each of their nine children and that she was given opportunities at a young age to minister to people through music. Think about the children in your worshiping community. How might you encourage them to use their musical and artistic gifts? How might you respond to Kidula's challenge to be available for God to use your artistic gifts, even if you feel they are minimal?
- Many churches around the world unintentionally send the message that lament is not appropriate for Christian artistic expression. Harriet Hill's chapter points out, however, that the Bible honors voices of pain, that there are more lament songs than any other category in the Old Testament book of Psalms. Discuss ways that your worshiping community or missions outreach might use the arts to help people who are suffering from

traumatic experiences. For more ideas, see Margaret Hill et al., *Healing the Wounds of Trauma: How the Church Can Help* in the *Handbook* bibliography.

- Samuel Chiang asserts that the communal experience of social networking in the new digital reality is creating a hunger for meaningful stories—inspiring belief, renewing hope, and recounting a life in action. Engage with Chiang's closing questions, pondering how your stories—recounted in print, online, and face to face—can impact others for the kingdom.

- Note: Discussion questions for sections 2 and 3 and other pedagogical helps are available on the website—http://www.ethnodoxologyhandbook.com—as well as instruction regarding how to submit your own teaching ideas for others to use.

INTRODUCTION

SECTION 1: FOUNDATIONS

SECTION 2: STORIES

SECTION 3: TOOLS